The Victorians at War

The Victorians at War 1815–1914

An Encyclopedia of British Military History

HAROLD E. RAUGH, JR.

ABC☙CLIO

Santa Barbara, California • Denver, Colorado • Oxford, England

Copyright © 2004 by Harold E. Raugh, Jr.

All rights reserved. No part of this publication may be reproduced, stored in a retrieval system, or transmitted, in any form or by any means, electronic, mechanical, photocopying, recording, or otherwise, except for the inclusion of brief quotations in a review, without prior permission in writing from the publishers.

Library of Congress Cataloging-in-Publication Data

Raugh, Harold E.
 The Victorians at war, 1815–1914 : an encyclopedia of British military history /
   Harold E. Raugh, Jr.
     p. cm.
   Includes bibliographical references and index.
   ISBN 1-57607-925-2 (hardcover : alk. paper) e-ISBN 1-57607-926-0 (e-book)
   1. Great Britain—History, Military—19th century—Encyclopedias. 2. Great Britain—History, Military—20th century—Encyclopedias. 3. Great Britain—History— Victoria, 1837–1901—Encyclopedias. 4. Great Britain—History—Edward VII, 1901–1910—Encyclopedias. I. Title.
 DA68.R38 2004
 355'.00941'09034—dc22

2004005845

07 06 05 04   10 9 8 7 6 5 4 3 2 1

This book is also available on the World Wide Web as an e-book. Visit http://www.abc-clio.com for details.

ABC-CLIO, Inc.
130 Cremona Drive, P.O. Box 1911
Santa Barbara, California 93116-1911

This book is printed on acid-free paper.
Manufactured in the United States of America

Contents

Preface, xi

Introduction, xiii

Abu Klea, Battle of (17 January 1885), **1**
Abyssinia, **2**
Abyssinian War (1867–1868), **3**
Addiscombe, Military Seminary, **5**
Adjutant-General, British Army, **5**
Adye, General Sir John M. (1819–1900), **6**
Afghan War, First (1839–1842), **7**
Afghan War, Second (1878–1880), **9**
Afghanistan, **10**
Aldershot, **11**
Alexandria, Bombardment of (11 July 1882), **12**
Alison, General Sir Archibald (1826–1907), **13**
Aliwal, Battle of (28 January 1846), **13**
Alma, Battle of the (20 September 1854), **14**
Amoaful, Battle of (31 January 1874), **15**
Animals, Transport, **16**
Arabi Pasha, Ahmed (c. 1840–1911), **17**
Arabi Rebellion (1882), **18**
Army and Society, **21**
Army Estimates, **22**
Army Service Corps, **23**
Artillery, British Army—Organization, **24**
Artillery, British Army—Tactics, **25**
Artillery, British Army—Training, **26**
Artillery, British Army—Weapons and Equipment, **27**
Artists, War, **28**
Ashanti, **28**
Ashanti Expedition (1895–1896), **30**
Ashanti Ring, **31**
Ashanti War (1900), **32**
Ashanti War, First (1823–1826), **33**
Ashanti War, Second (1873–1874), **34**

Atbara, Battle of (8 April 1898), **37**
Awards and Decorations, **38**

Baden-Powell, Lieutenant General Sir Robert S. S., First Baron Baden-Powell of Gilwell (1857–1941), **41**
Baker Pasha, Lieutenant General Valentine (1827–1887), **42**
Balaklava, Battle of (25 October 1854), **42**
Balloons, **44**
Baltic Sea Operations, Crimean War, **44**
Bengal Army, **45**
Bitter-Ender, **46**
Blockhouses, **47**
Blood, General Sir Bindon (1842–1940), **48**
Boer War, First (1880–1881), **49**
Boer War, Second (1899–1902), **51**
Boers, **53**
Bombay Army, **55**
Boomplaats, Battle of (29 August 1848), **56**
Botha, Commandant-General Louis (1862–1919), **56**
Boxer Rebellion (1900–1901), **57**
Brackenbury, General Sir Henry (1837–1914), **59**
Bromhead, Major Gonville, V.C. (1845–1892), **60**
Bronkhorstspruit, Battle of (20 December 1880), **60**
Brown, General Sir George (1790–1865), **61**
Browne, General Sir Samuel J., V.C. (1824–1901), **61**
Buller, General Sir Redvers H., V.C. (1839–1908), **63**
Bullets, **64**
Buner Field Force (1898), **65**
Burma, **66**
Burma War, First (1824–1826), **67**
Burma War, Second (1852–1853), **69**
Burma War, Third (1885), **70**

Contents

Burnaby, Lieutenant Colonel Frederick G. (1842–1885), **71**
Butler, Lieutenant General Sir William F. (1838–1910), **72**

Camberley, Staff College, **75**
Cambridge, Field Marshal H.R.H. Prince George F., Second Duke of (1819–1904), **76**
Campaign Medals, **76**
Campbell, Field Marshal Colin, First Baron Clyde of Clydesdale (1792–1863), **77**
Canada, **78**
Cape Frontier Wars, Southern Africa, **79**
Cardigan, Lieutenant General James T. Brudenell, Seventh Earl of (1797–1868), **80**
Cardwell, Edward T., First Viscount Cardwell of Ellerbeck (1813–1886), **81**
Cardwell Reforms, **82**
Cathcart, Lieutenant General Sir George (1794–1854), **84**
Cavagnari, Major Sir Pierre L. N. (1841–1879), **84**
Cavalry, British Army—Organization, **85**
Cavalry, British Army—Tactics, **86**
Cavalry, British Army—Training, **87**
Cavalry, British Army—Weapons and Equipment, **87**
Cawnpore, Siege and Relief of (1857), **88**
Cetshwayo kaMpande (c. 1832–1884), **89**
Chamberlain, Field Marshal Sir Neville B. (1820–1902), **90**
Chaplains, **90**
Charasia, Battle of (6 October 1879), **91**
Chard, Colonel John R. M., V.C. (1847–1897), **92**
Charge of the Light Brigade, **92**
Charge of the 21st Lancers, **93**
Chelmsford, General Frederick A. Thesiger, Second Baron (1827–1905), **94**
Chernaya, Battle of (16 August 1855), **95**
Chesney, Lieutenant Colonel Charles C. (1826–1876), **95**
Chillianwalla, Battle of (13 January 1849), **96**
China, **97**
China War, First (1839–1842), **98**
China War, Second (1856–1860), **100**
Churchill, Sir Winston L. S. (1874–1965), **101**
Civil-Military Relations, **102**
Coastal Fortifications, **103**
Colenso, Battle of (15 December 1899), **104**
Commander in Chief, British Army, **105**
Commando System, **106**
Communications, **107**
Concentration Camps, **108**

Correspondents, War, **109**
Crimean War (1854–1856), **110**
Cronje, Assistant Commandant-General Piet A. (1835–1911), **113**
Curragh Camp, **114**
Curragh Incident (March 1914), **115**

De la Rey, Assistant Commandant-General Jacobus (1847–1914), **117**
De Wet, Chief Commandant Christiaan R. (1854–1922), **118**
Delhi, Siege and Storming of (1857), **118**
Dervishes, **119**
Discipline and Justice, British Army, **120**
Disraeli, Benjamin, First Earl of Beaconsfield (1804–1881), **122**
Dongola, Capture of (23 September 1896), **122**
Dost Mohammed (1793–1863), **123**
Dundas, Admiral Sir James W. D. (1785–1862), **124**
Durand, Sir Henry Mortimer (1850–1924), **124**

Earle, Major General William (1833–1885), **127**
East India Company, **127**
East India Company, Military Forces, **128**
Egypt, **130**
Egyptian Army, **131**
El Teb, Battle of (4 February 1884), **132**
Engineers, British Army—Employment, **132**
Engineers, British Army—Organization, **133**
Engineers, British Army—Training, **134**
Engineers, British Army—Weapons and Equipment, **134**
Esher, Reginald B. B., Second Viscount (1852–1930), **135**
Esher Committee (1904), **135**
Eupatoria, Battle of (17 February 1855), **136**
Evans, General Sir George de Lacy (1787–1870), **137**

Fashoda Incident (1898), **139**
Ferozeshah, Battle of (21–22 December 1845), **140**
French, Field Marshal John D. P., First Earl of Ypres (1852–1925), **141**
French Forces, Crimean War, **142**

Gatacre, Lieutenant General Sir William F. (1843–1906), **143**
Ginnis, Battle of (30 December 1885), **144**
Gladstone, William E. (1809–1898), **145**

Gordon, Major General Charles G. (1833–1885), **145**
Gordon Relief Expedition (1884–1885), **146**
Gough, General Sir Hubert de la P. (1870–1963), **149**
Gough, Field Marshal Hugh, First Viscount Gough of Chinkiangfoo in China and of Maharajpore and the Sutlej in the East Indies (1779–1869), **149**
Graham, Lieutenant General Sir Gerald, V.C. (1831–1899), **150**
Grant, General Sir James Hope (1808–1875), **151**
Great Game, **151**
Greaves, General Sir George R. (1831–1922), **153**
Grenfell, Field Marshal Francis W., First Baron Grenfell of Kilvey (1841–1925), **153**
Gujerat, Battle of (21 February 1849), **154**
Gurkha War (1814–1816), **155**
Gurkhas, **156**
Gwalior, Battle of (19 June 1858), **156**
Gwalior Campaign (1843), **157**

Haldane, Richard B., Viscount Haldane of Cloan (1856–1928), **159**
Hamilton, General Sir Ian S. M. (1853–1947), **160**
Hamley, Lieutenant General Sir Edward B. (1824–1893), **161**
Hardinge, Field Marshal Henry, First Viscount Hardinge of Lahore and of King's Newton (1785–1856), **162**
Havelock, Major General Sir Henry (1795–1857), **163**
Hazara Field Force (1888), **163**
Henderson, Colonel G. F. R. (1854–1903), **164**
Hicks Pasha, Major General William (1830–1883), **165**
Hobhouse, Emily (1860–1926), **166**
Home Defense, **167**
Horse Guards, **167**
Hunter, General Sir Archibald (1856–1936), **168**

Imperial Service Troops, **171**
Imperialism, **171**
India, **173**
India, British Army in, **175**
Indian Army Operations, **176**
Indian Army Organization, **177**
Indian Mutiny (1857–1859), **179**
Infantry, British Army—Organization, **181**
Infantry, British Army—Small Arms, **182**
Infantry, British Army—Tactics, **183**
Infantry, British Army—Training, **184**

Ingogo, Battle of (8 February 1881), **185**
Inkerman, Battle of (5 November 1854), **186**
Intellectuals, British Army, **187**
Intelligence, **189**
Isandlwana, Battle of (22 January 1879), **190**

Jameson, Dr. Leander Starr (1853–1917), **193**
Jameson Raid (29 December 1895–2 January 1896), **193**
Japan, **194**
Japan, Operations against (1863–1866), **194**
Joubert, Commandant-General Petrus J. (1831–1900), **195**

Kabul to Kandahar March (August 1880), **197**
Kandahar, Battle of (1 September 1880), **198**
Kars, Siege of (June–26 November 1855), **199**
Kashgil, Battle of (3–5 November 1883), **199**
Khalifa (?–1899), **200**
Kitchener, Field Marshal Horatio H., First Earl Kitchener of Khartoum and of Broome (1850–1916), **201**
Kofi Karikari (1837–1884), **203**
Kruger, S. J. Paulus (1825–1904), **204**

Ladysmith, Siege of (2 November 1899–28 February 1900), **205**
Laing's Nek, Battle of (28 January 1881), **206**
Land Transport Corps, **206**
Lawrence, Brigadier General Sir Henry M. (1806–1857), **207**
Lines of Communication, **208**
Lockhart, General Sir William S. A. (1841–1900), **208**
Long Service, **209**
Lucan, Field Marshal George C. Bingham, Third Earl of (1800–1888), **209**
Lucknow, Siege and Relief of (1857–1858), **210**
Lyons, Admiral Sir Edmund, First Baron (1790–1858), **211**

Macdonald, Major General Sir Hector A. (1853–1903), **213**
MacDougall, Major General Sir Patrick L. (1819–1894), **214**
Machine Guns, **215**
Madras Army, **216**
Mafeking, Siege of (13 October 1899–17 May 1900), **216**
Magdala, Capture of (13 April 1868), **217**
Magersfontein, Battle of (11 December 1899), **218**
Mahdi (1844–1885), **219**
Maiwand, Battle of (27 July 1880), **220**
Majuba Hill, Battle of (27 February 1881), **221**

Contents

Malakand Field Force (1897), **222**
Maneuvers, British Army, **223**
Maori War, First (1843–1848), **225**
Maori War, Second (1863–1869), **226**
Maoris, **227**
Maps, **227**
Master-General of the Ordnance, British Army, **228**
Maurice, Major General Sir (John) Frederick (1841–1912), **229**
McNeill, General Sir John C., V.C. (1831–1904), **230**
Methuen, Field Marshal Paul S., Third Baron (1845–1932), **230**
Military and Popular Culture, **231**
Military Medicine, British Army—Enlistment Physical Standards, **232**
Military Medicine, British Army—Hospitals and Soldier Treatment, **233**
Military Medicine, British Army—Medical Personnel, **234**
Military Medicine, British Army—Sanitation, **235**
Military Medicine, British Army—Venereal Disease, **235**
Military Music, **236**
Militia, **237**
Miranzai Field Force (1891), **237**
Mobilization Planning, **238**
Modder River, Battle of (28 November 1899), **239**
Mohmand Field Force (1897), **240**

Nana Sahib (c. 1821–?), **241**
Napier, Admiral Sir Charles (1786–1860), **241**
Napier, Field Marshal Robert C., First Baron Napier of Magdala and Carynton (1810–1890), **242**
Napier, General Sir Charles J. (1782–1853), **243**
Nicholson, Brigadier General John (1822–1857), **244**
Nightingale, Florence (1820–1910), **244**
North-West Frontier, **245**

Officers, British Army—Pay, **249**
Officers, British Army—Retirement, **250**
Officers, British Army—Social Background, **250**
Officers, British Army—Sources of Commissioning, **251**
Officers, British Army—Training and Education, **252**
Officers, British Army—Uniforms and Equipment, **252**
Officers, Indian Army—Pay, **253**
Officers, Indian Army—Retirement, **253**
Officers, Indian Army—Social Background, **254**
Officers, Indian Army—Sources of Commissioning, **254**
Officers, Indian Army—Training and Education, **255**
Officers, Indian Army—Uniforms and Equipment, **255**
Omdurman, Battle of (2 September 1898), **256**
Outram, Lieutenant General Sir James (1803–1863), **258**

Paardeberg, Battle of (18–27 February 1900), **259**
Pacific Ocean Operations, Crimean War, **260**
Peiwar Kotal, Battle of (2 December 1878), **260**
Penjdeh Incident (30 March 1885), **261**
Perak, Punitive Expedition to (1875–1876), **262**
Persia, **263**
Persian War (1856–1857), **264**
Photographers, War, **265**
Pistols, **266**
Pomeroy-Colley, Major General Sir George (1835–1881), **266**
Punjab Frontier Force, **268**
Purchase System, **268**

Quartermaster-General, British Army, **271**

Raglan, Field Marshal Fitzroy J. H. Somerset, First Baron (1788–1855), **273**
Railways, **274**
Rank and File, British Army—Enlistment, **275**
Rank and File, British Army—Pay, **276**
Rank and File, British Army—Retirement, **276**
Rank and File, British Army—Social Background, **277**
Rank and File, British Army—Training and Education, **277**
Rank and File, British Army—Uniforms and Equipment, **278**
Reconquest of the Sudan (1896–1898), **279**
Recruiting, **281**
Red River Expedition (1870), **282**
Religion, **283**
Rhani of Jhansi (c. 1828–1858), **284**
Rhodes, Cecil J. (1853–1902), **284**
Roberts, Field Marshal Frederick S., V.C., First Earl Roberts of Kandahar, Pretoria, and Waterford (1832–1914), **285**
Rockets, **287**
Rorke's Drift, Defense of (22–23 January 1879), **288**
Rose, Field Marshal Hugh H., First Baron Strathnairn of Strathnairn and Jhansi (1801–1885), **289**
Royal Army Medical Corps, **289**
Russian Forces, Crimean War, **290**

Sale, Major General Sir Robert (1782–1845), **293**

Sandhurst, Royal Military College, **293**
Sardinian Forces, Crimean War, **294**
Sevastopol, Siege of (8 October 1854–9 September 1855), **295**
Sher Ali Khan (1825–1879), **296**
Sherpur, Battle of (23 December 1879), **297**
Short Service, **297**
Sikh War, First (1845–1846), **298**
Sikh War, Second (1848–1849), **300**
Sikhs, **301**
Simpson, General Sir James M. (1792–1868), **302**
Sind, Operations in (1843), **303**
Sirdar, **303**
Sittana Field Force (1858), **304**
Slavery, **305**
Smith, Lieutenant General Sir Harry G. W. (1787–1860), **306**
Smuts, Assistant Commandant-General Jan Christian (1870–1950), **306**
Sobraon, Battle of (10 February 1846), **307**
Soldier's Pocket Book for Field Service, **308**
Spion Kop, Battle of (23–24 January 1900), **308**
Sports and Recreation, **309**
Stanhope, Edward (1840–1893), **310**
Stanhope Memorandum, **311**
Stephenson, General Sir Frederick C. A. (1821–1911), **311**
Stewart, Field Marshal Sir Donald M. (1824–1900), **312**
Stewart, Major General Sir Herbert (1843–1885), **313**
Steyn, Marthinus T. (1857–1916), **314**
Stormberg, Battle of (10 December 1899), **314**
Sudan, **315**
Suez Canal, **315**

Tamai, Battle of (13 March 1884), **317**
Tantia Topi (c. 1819–1859), **318**
Taranaki War (1860–1861), **318**
Tel el-Kebir, Battle of (13 September 1882), **319**

Theodore, Emperor (c. 1818–1868), **320**
Tibet, Expedition to (1903–1904), **321**
Tirah Field Force (1897–1898), **322**
Tochi Field Force (1897–1898), **324**
Tofrek, Battle of (22 March 1885), **324**
Toski, Battle of (3 August 1889), **325**
Transvaal, **326**
Turkish Forces, Crimean War, **327**

Ulundi, Battle of (4 July 1879), **329**

Vaal Krantz, Battle of (5–7 February 1900), **331**
Victoria Cross, **332**
Volunteers, **333**

War Office, **335**
Warren, General Sir Charles (1840–1927), **337**
Wauchope, Major General Andrew G. (1846–1899), **338**
Wellington, Field Marshal Arthur Wellesley, First Duke of (1769–1852), **339**
White, Field Marshal Sir George S., V.C. (1835–1912), **340**
White Sea Operations, Crimean War, **340**
Wilson, Major General Sir Charles W. (1836–1905), **341**
Wingate, General Sir (Francis) Reginald (1861–1953), **341**
Wolseley, Field Marshal Garnet J., First Viscount Wolseley of Cairo and Wolseley in the County of Stafford (1833–1913), **342**
Women and the Army, **345**
Wood, Field Marshal Sir (Henry) Evelyn M., V.C. (1838–1919), **346**
Woolwich, Royal Military Academy, **347**

Yeomanry, **349**
Younghusband, Colonel Sir Francis E. (1863–1942), **349**

Zulu War (1879), **351**
Zululand, **354**

Appendix One: Chronology, **355**
Appendix Two: British Army Commanders in Chief, **365**
Appendix Three: Indian Army Commanders in Chief, **367**
Appendix Four: A Note on Currency, **369**
Bibliography, **371**
Index, **391**
About the Author, **405**

Preface

Capturing the strength and might of the British Army from 1815 to 1914, this groundbreaking reference volume incorporates the most recent research on the most significant wars, campaigns, battles, and leaders of the Victorian era.

Covering approximately one-quarter of the earth's landmass, Britain's empire required an enormously powerful army, and *The Victorians at War, 1815–1914: An Encyclopedia of British Military History* explores all aspects of the history of this imperial British Army, including its many wars, campaigns, military leaders, weaponry, training, and education.

Containing numerous maps depicting various theaters of war, this all-encompassing volume explains why the numerous military operations took place and what the results were. Biographies reveal fascinating facts about British and Indian Army officers and other ranks, while other entries cover recruitment, training, education and literacy, uniforms, equipment, pay and conditions, social backgrounds of the officers and soldiers, diseases and wounds they fell victim to, and much more. This volume is indispensable to those wanting to gain information about the British Army during this remarkable imperial era.

The goal of this volume, *The Victorians at War, 1815–1914: An Encyclopedia of British Military History*, is to convey the exciting, dynamic story of the British Army and its soldiers during the British imperial century. It presents a concise summary of current knowledge and historical background for each of the more than 350 entries. This encyclopedia is scholastically and academically uncompromising and comprehensive, but not exhaustive. All entries are presented in a conventional A-to-Z format for ease in locating topics. Each entry contains cross-references to related entries ("See also"), as well as bibliographic references ("References"). "Blind" entries include the headwords only, but no detailed explanation or entry, and references to related topics with full entries. The presence of a certain degree of overlap is intentional, frequently providing additional contextual information to linked entries.

The Victorians at War, 1815–1914: An Encyclopedia of British Military History provides accurate, comprehensive information of interest to professional historians, students, and the general public. I hope that military history enthusiasts will find this volume inspiring as a definitive single-volume, higher-level encyclopedic work on the British Army during Great Britain's imperial century.

I am grateful to a number of people who have contributed to this book's success. The first is Colonel Spencer C. Tucker, the John Biggs Professor of Military History at the Virginia Military Institute, who recommended that I receive the commission to write this book. At ABC-CLIO's Oxford office, first Dr. Robert Neville, then Mr. Simon Mason provided me with guidance and encouragement to complete the project. Last but not least, after my frequent bouts of burning the midnight oil to complete additional drafts, Naida P. Esquero patiently and professionally used her superb English grammar and language skills to promptly polish up my entries.

Harold E. Raugh, Jr., Ph.D., F.R.Hist.S.,
Lieutenant Colonel, U.S. Army (Ret.)

Introduction

"Whilst the armies of other European powers can only gain annually some insight into war with the blank ammunition fired during autumn manoeuvres," observed British Army General (later Field Marshal) Viscount Garnet J. Wolseley in 1890, "Queen Victoria's soldiers learn their lesson with ball-cartridge fired in real warfare, and with almost annually recurring regularity. It is the varied experience, and frequent practice in war, provided for our officers by the nature of our wide-extending empire, which makes them what I believe them to be—the best in the world."

Wolseley wrote this at the height of the Pax Britannica, or British peace, the century-long period that began with the end of the Napoleonic Wars in 1815 and continued until World War I broke out in 1914. This era, as Wolseley alluded, was anything but peaceful, with the British Army participating in "real warfare" almost every year.

The term "Pax Britannica," as a result, is a misnomer. Between 1815 and 1914, perhaps only six years—1820, 1829, 1830, 1833, 1907, and 1909—witnessed no major wars, campaigns, punitive expeditions, or other recorded military operations, although British soldiers were probably killed in hostile action nonetheless. All six of these years occurred outside the long, progressive reign of Queen Victoria, who served as sovereign from 1837 to 1901. As a result of wars and other military operations conducted and officially recognized during the Pax Britannica, the British Government between 1815 and 1914 awarded to soldiers at least 43 campaign medals with a total of 202 clasps.

The British Army fought in two major conflicts during the Pax Britannica. The first was the Crimean War, in which Britain, allied with France, Turkey, and later Sardinia, fought against Russian forces in the Crimea and other far-flung theaters from 1854 to 1856. The Crimean War was noted for British military and administrative incompetence. Out of a British force numbering 111,313 officers and men, 4,774 all ranks (officers and enlisted men) were killed in action or died of wounds, while another 16,323 died of disease. The second major conflict was the Second Boer War (1899–1902). Frequently dismissed as only one of "Queen Victoria's little wars," the Second Boer War was much more significant. It was Britain's longest (lasting over 32 months), most expensive (costing over £200 million), and bloodiest war (with over 22,000 British, 25,000 Boers, and 12,000 Africans losing their lives) fought from the end of the Napoleonic Wars in 1815 until the beginning of the Great War in 1914.

The British Army that fought in these numerous "savage wars of peace" evolved tremendously in the process and throughout the Pax Britannica. After the allied victory at the Battle of Waterloo on 18 June 1815, the British Army was considered the unrivaled military force in Europe. This perception had myriad repercussions. Since it was thought invincible, nothing could be done, especially in terms of reform, to make the British Army more effective or efficient. After more than two decades of expensive and enervating warfare, the British Government and public were concerned more with fiscal retrenchment, inflation, unemployment, and democratization than with the army. In addition, Field Marshal Arthur Wellesley, the First Duke of Wellington, victor of Waterloo, was exalted to such a high degree of reverence and infallibility that no one would dare question his opinions and conservative outlook on military matters. The British Army was also frequently used to quell domestic unrest. These multiple factors combined to cause apathy and complacency, and the British Army atrophied and stagnated for decades. As a result, significant military reform did not begin until Wellington died in 1852, initially at a glacial pace.

The British Army, in terms of its leadership, tactics, and logistical support systems, was inadequate to fight effectively and efficiently in the Crimean War (1854–1856). These basic deficiencies and the tremendous privations suffered by the British soldiers were most glaringly revealed during the harsh winter of 1854–1855. The invention of the electric telegraph in the 1830s, and the extension of its cable to the allied positions near Sevastopol during the Crimean War, permitted war correspondents to send instant reports directly to their newspapers, bypassing military authorities.

Introduction

Coming from the battlefield, these reports were considered factual and honest. The newspapers were carried overnight by railroads to the breakfast tables of the increasingly literate and conscientious middle class, who for the very first time in history knew and cared about what their soldiers were doing and going through. Pressure on the government, plus the realization that the British Army needed to be modernized and reformed in order to retain its perceived hegemony and fighting prowess, shocked the army out of its lethargy and delusional contentment. The pace of reform was accelerated in the British Army. Various types of organizational and systemic reform, to include improvements in training, education, sanitation, terms of service, and living conditions, then continued until the beginning of the First World War.

The strength of the British Army in 1815, at the height of the Napoleonic Wars, was 233,952 men. This number fell to 102,539 in 1828 and to 87,993 ten years later. Additional overseas and domestic military commitments resulted in an increase in the British Army strength, from 91,338 in 1839 to 116,434 in 1846. In 1853, immediately prior to the Crimean War, the British Army consisted of about 102,000 men, of whom about 26,000 were stationed in India and another 20,000 in other colonial postings. In 1888, when the British Army was heavily engaged in territorial expansion, its strength was 210,174, with 108,288 soldiers stationed in England and 101,886 posted abroad.

The indispensable infantry composed the overwhelming majority of British Army troops, and the infantry was the basic combat arm. In 1850, the British Army contained 102 infantry regiments (battalions), 26 cavalry regiments, the Rifle Brigade, the Royal Regiment of Artillery, and the Corps of Royal Engineers. There were 144 infantry battalions as against only 31 cavalry regiments in the British Army in 1870. Of the 210,174 soldiers in the British Army in 1888, 140,278 were infantrymen.

The infantry battalion was the primary independent tactical element of the British Army throughout this period. The force structure and size of the infantry battalion fluctuated, usually numbering 700–800 officers and men. The infantry battalion was a very cohesive unit, veritably a "tribe," with its members generally sharing common traditions, standards, and cultural and geographical identities. Officers, and especially enlisted soldiers, would frequently serve their entire career in the same unit. While battalion unity and solidarity enhanced discipline and combat effectiveness, they could also discourage reform and change.

The commissioned officers provided the leadership and generally established the tone and values of the battalion. This was a strength as well as a weakness of the British Army. In the rigidly hierarchical British class structure, officers generally came from the classes that provided the "natural" leaders of society, and the officers were the natural leaders of the British Army. A key requirement to be a commissioned officer was wealth, since officers were generally required to purchase their initial commissions and promotions to the rank of lieutenant colonel. Financial exclusivity did not ensure competence, character, diligence, or professionalism, and many officers, while honorable and courageous in action, were deficient in these attributes. Competent officers could not compete with those having money and influence. The purchase system, in which officers purchased their commissions, was abolished in 1871. This crucial reform did not significantly alter the social composition of the British Army officer corps, and many, if not a majority, of the officers continued to come from the aristocracy and landed gentry. The abolition of purchase was, however, a step in the right direction of encouraging professionalism and enhancing the military training and education of the British officer corps. The tremendous expansion of the British Army in World War I and simultaneous demand for additional officers irrevocably altered the social composition of the British Army officer corps.

The rank and file of the British Army generally came from the lowest segment of British society, frequently forced into the army by starvation, unemployment, and poverty, and occasionally as an alternative to prison. The public perception of the enlisted soldiers was only slightly tainted by Wellington's view that the troops were the "scum of the earth." The pay, quality, training, education, and living conditions of the other ranks steadily improved during the latter half of Queen Victoria's long reign.

The Pax Britannica was also the British imperial century, with Great Britain dominating the world and the British Empire expanding at an unprecedented rate. Alfred, Lord Tennyson wrote enthusiastically about this phenomena and the mid-Victorian perception of imperialism: "We sailed wherever ship could sail, / We founded many a mighty state; / Pray God our greatness many not fail / Through craven fears of being great."

There were many reasons for this imperialist imperative. First, the British had a lead on potential competitors because of their productivity and because of the Industrial Revolution.

Introduction

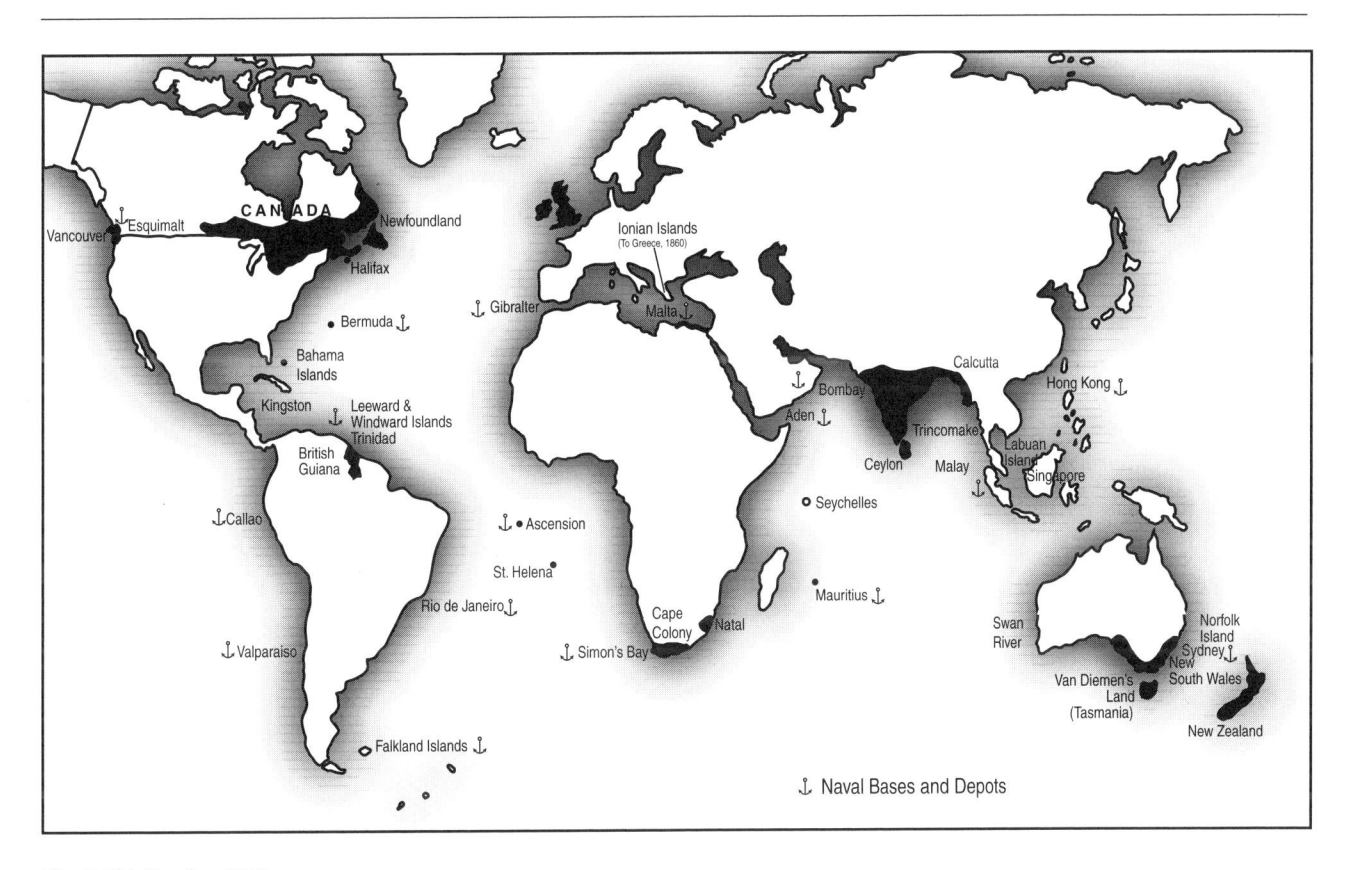

The British Empire, 1850

Additional factors included the search for raw materials and markets for Great Britain's manufactured goods, and especially free trade; Social Darwinism, in which the British felt superior to other races and thought it was their duty to civilize other people by spreading their superior culture, religion, influence, and government; to retain the balance of power of European nations; rivalry among industrialized great powers; and the need to create allies and deter hostile aggression.

Until the middle of the nineteenth century, British imperialism focused on India and the Far East. Sea power was essential to conduct imperialism and maintain overseas colonies and markets. It is generally agreed that the period of mercantilism ended with the repeal of the Corn Laws in 1846, which ushered in a period of free trade.

The Indian Mutiny (1857–1859) transformed British Army units stationed in India into an army of occupation that assisted the civil power in maintaining British rule. Russian encroachment in Central Asia, dangerously close to British India, provided the British Army with a definite mission.

The 1860s saw tremendous turmoil, as the British textile industry was destroyed by the lack of cotton caused by the American Civil War. Numerous domestic and foreign pressures bore on Great Britain. France and Prussia—the latter soon to be a major component of a united Germany—began to challenge British hegemony. In 1867, Prime Minister Benjamin Disraeli launched an expedition to Abyssinia. During the first half of the nineteenth century, Great Britain and other European nations generally neglected Africa, due to a lack of raw materials, the abolition of slavery, and perceptions of primitive cultures. Disraeli timed this operation to distract attention from domestic woes, demonstrate the popular appeal of imperialism, and secure Abyssinia, to the south of Egypt, where the French would be completing the Suez Canal the following year. Disraeli wanted to forestall French influence in Africa while securing Britain's new lifeline via the Suez Canal to India and the Far East.

Imperialism became popular in the 1870s, as did the British Army. War and conflict, in the context of Social Darwinism, was seen as a natural occurrence in evolution and

Introduction

suggested British superiority in all areas. This ideology provided a rationale for war and conquest against "inferior peoples." The popular press, available to an increasingly literate public, encouraged these patriotic and militaristic sentiments as the British Army engaged in frequently romanticized colonial wars and campaigns.

A new wave of European rivalry and imperialism, the "scramble for Africa," began in 1876, when King Leopold II of Belgium established a private company to exploit the wealth of the Congo basin. France, which had lost the provinces of Alsace and Lorraine to the Germans in the Franco-Prussian War (1870–1871), was eager to regain lost prestige by gaining overseas colonies and supported a rival of the Belgians. In 1877, the British annexed the Transvaal in order to protect South Africa. The French occupied Tunisia in 1881, and two years later the British divided up the Niger with France. In 1884, accelerating European imperialism in Africa, the Germans seized Cameroon, Togoland, and South-West Africa, and Great Britain reacted by claiming more colonies. The rapid pace and relative ease of colonial conquest was aided by technological innovations, including machine guns.

Imperialistic rivalry between Great Britain and France culminated at Fashoda, in the south Sudan, in September 1898. France withdrew from Fashoda in December 1898 and tension decreased.

The British conducted imperialism in Africa and around the globe, until the eve of World War I, to maintain their empire, taking South Africa and Egypt in order to protect India. Other areas were annexed to be able to compete economically with France and Germany, and to establish allies in the event of war with either country.

In 1860, the British Empire contained about 9.5 million square miles, out of the earth's total land surface of about 52.5 million square miles. By 1909, this total had risen to about 12.7 million square miles, around 25 percent of the earth's land surface. This made the British Empire about three times the size of the French Empire and 10 times the size of the German Empire. Moreover, about 4.5 million people, or about a quarter of the total earth's population, lived under some form of British rule. It was said proudly and accurately that "the sun never set on the British Empire."

The British Army was the instrument frequently used to further the British Government's foreign, and occasionally domestic, policies. After regaining its global maritime supremacy with the defeat of France in 1815, Great Britain's Royal Navy secured the sea lanes and trade routes, while the British Army was used to conquer, generally by force of arms, and administer a growing colonial empire and market. The British Army was seen by the public as a civilizing and moderating influence in its military ventures.

As the instrument of British imperialism, the British Army fought its nation's small wars and colonial campaigns and then administered these conquered territories. In disease-ridden jungles to snow-capped mountains, and through dismal defeats at places such as Isandlwana, Maiwand, and Majuba Hill, to inspiring victories at Aliwal, Rorke's Drift, and Tel el-Kebir, the indomitable British soldier, through well-aimed rifle and artillery fire and the fearless and indefatigable use of cold steel, was instrumental in expanding and governing the British Empire and ensuring its success.

Thomas Augustine Barrett (better known as Leslie Stuart) recognized the importance of the British soldier and his indispensable contribution toward building and governing the British Empire in his popular 1895 song, "The Soldiers of the Queen." In response to, "So when we say that England's master, / Remember who has made her so," the refrain appropriately was:

It's the Soldiers of the Queen, my lads,
Who've been my lads, who've seen my lads,
In the fight for England's glory, lads,
When we've had to show them what we mean.
And when we say we've always won,
And when they ask us how it's done,
We'll proudly point to ev'ry one
Of England's Soldiers of the Queen!

A

Abdullahi bin Mohammed
See Khalifa

Abolition of Purchase
See Cardwell, Edward T.; Cardwell Reforms; Purchase System

Abu Klea, Battle of (17 January 1885)

The fierce Battle of Abu Klea was fought between British soldiers of the Gordon Relief Expedition and dervishes in the Sudan. The dervish onslaught, aided by British command and control problems, broke the British units deployed in the square formation in a battle characterized by courage on both sides.

A British expeditionary force was formed in the fall of 1884 under the command of General (later Field Marshal Viscount) Lord Garnet J. Wolseley to rescue Major General Charles G. Gordon, who was besieged in Khartoum. Gordon had been sent on a mission to assess the feasibility of evacuating Egyptians from the Sudan after the spread of Islamic fundamentalism. In December 1884, to hasten the relief, Wolseley divided his force into two elements. The first was the River Column, which was to follow the Nile River, and the second was the Desert Column, under the command of Brigadier General (later Major General) Sir Herbert Stewart, with Lieutenant Colonel Frederick G. Burnaby as second in command. The camel-mounted Desert Column was to cross the Bayuda Desert from Korti and reach Metemmeh on the Nile by 7 January 1885.

The Desert Column was delayed due to water and supply shortages, and Stewart planned to reach the wells at Abu Klea on 16 January 1885. Dervish forces contested his advance, and Stewart's force halted and built a zareba (a stone redoubt enclosed by a thorny mimosa bush hedge) that night.

Stewart left soldiers wounded by dervish harassing fire, as well as baggage, in the zareba and formed his 1,450-man force into a hollow square formation to advance. The front face of the square contained two Mounted Infantry Regiment companies, guns, and Coldstream and Scots Guards companies. Guards and Grenadier troops, Royal Marines, and soldiers of the Royal Sussex Regiment formed the right face of the square. On the opposite side were two companies of the Mounted Infantry and one of the Heavy Regiment, with the rear consisting of four companies of the Heavy Regiment and the naval brigade with its rapid-firing Gardner gun in the center. The soldiers were formed in double ranks on each side of the square and numbered 235 rifles on the left face and 300 or more on the other three faces. Staff and supply elements, with about 150 camels, were in the center of the square.

The square advanced slowly over the undulating ground and soon halted to re-form because the camels in the center were delaying the rear side of the square. As this was taking place, about 5,000 dervishes in two columns attacked the left front corner of the square. British fire forced the dervishes to veer off course and join other dervishes who attacked the left rear corner of the formation.

The ensuing action was chaotic. It seems Burnaby decided on his own and ordered companies on the left face of the square to open up a gap to permit the Gardner gun to move outside the square and open fire. As the dervishes assaulted, the Gardner gun jammed and was overrun. The dervishes poured through the gap in the square, killing Burnaby by a spear thrust to the neck, and forced Heavy Regiment soldiers back against the camels in the center of the square. This stopped the momentum of the dervish onslaught. Fierce hand-to-hand fighting took place, and the rear ranks of the soldiers on the square's right face turned about and began firing rapidly into the densely packed groups of dervishes inside the square. As the dervishes in the rear saw the piles of their dead comrades to their front, they wavered and finally broke off their attack. Dervish cavalry made a last attempt on the right rear corner of the square, but withering rifle fire drove them off.

After this sharp, fifteen-minute engagement, about 1,100 dead dervishes were found in and near the British square. The Desert Column lost 74 all ranks (officers and enlisted ranks) killed and 94 wounded, two of whom later died. These significant losses did not prevent the Desert Column from continuing to advance the next day, and had little overall impact on the outcome of the campaign.

   See also Burnaby, Lieutenant Colonel Frederick G.; Dervishes; Gordon, Major General Charles G.; Gordon Relief Expedition; Mahdi; Stewart, Major General Sir Herbert; Sudan; Wilson, Major General Sir Charles W.; Wolseley, Field Marshal Garnet J.
   References: Barthorp (1984); Keown-Boyd (1986); Neillands (1996); Robson (1993b)

Abyssinia

Abyssinia (now known as Ethiopia) was an ancient and generally isolated and inaccessible kingdom located in east central Africa. The Abyssinian kingdom, according to tradition, was founded in the tenth century B.C. by Menelik I, the first son born to King Solomon of Israel and the Queen of Sheba. It was a Christian state surrounded by Muslim countries.

The geography of Abyssinia was unique to the African continent: a basaltic mass forming the Abyssinian mountain chain towers above the surrounding plains. The main ridge on the eastern side of the country averages 8,000 feet in elevation. Plateaus of varying heights dominate the western part of the country and are broken up by mountains reaching from 6,600 to 13,000 feet. Deep ravines and sheer precipices are found throughout the country.

The rugged terrain and natural divisions of Abyssinia helped perpetuate a state of patriarchal feudalism. The three main provinces of Abyssinia included Tigre in the north, Amhara in the center, and Shoa in the south. The leader of a tribe was called the *ras*, or prince, and the ruler of a province was known as the *negus*, or king. Amhara was generally considered the paramount province, and its ruler, called the *negus-se-neghest*, or "king of kings," received tribute from the other provinces.

Lij Kassa, an ambitious warlord in mid-nineteenth-century Abyssinia, was crowned Emperor Theodore II in 1855. Theodore began to consolidate his power and modernize the legal, administrative, and tax systems of Abyssinia, which reduced the autonomy of local rulers and antagonized them. Consequently they revolted against him.

Theodore's isolation and paranoia, caused by Abyssinia's geography and internal turmoil, hindered communications with Great Britain, and a number of misperceptions and misunderstandings resulted. He imprisoned Captain Charles D. Cameron, who had arrived in Abyssinia in 1862 to serve as his adviser, as well as other Europeans. Eventually, on 13 August 1867, Great Britain authorized military intervention to free the prisoners. Commanded by Lieutenant General (later Field Marshal Lord) Sir Robert C. Napier, the British expeditionary force stormed Theodore's mountain fortress at Magdala on 13 April 1868 and released the hostages. Theodore, realizing the hopelessness of his situation, killed himself.

The Abyssinian military forces that met Napier were ill disciplined and ill trained, although they were considered brave and were generally willing to engage in hand-to-hand combat. While there was no Abyssinian "standing army," efforts had been made to form 50-, 100-, 500-, and 1,000-man military units capable of executing such simple tactics as charging and defending stationery positions.

Military clothing, equipment, and weapons varied among the Abyssinian soldiers and forces. Abyssinian military leaders wore elaborate costumes, while the ordinary soldiers were dressed in white shirt, trousers, and cloak. The latter were generally armed with spears, swords, and small round shields, although soldiers called "musketeers" were armed with primitive matchlocks or more modern double-barreled percussion guns. Most of the Abyssinian troops were infantrymen and only the more affluent were cavalrymen. Theodore seems to have employed these mounted troops more as scouts and skirmishers than as shock troops. The Abyssinian emperor also possessed a number of artillery pieces, which were symbols of power, including a 70-ton mortar named "Theodorus"—which blew up after firing its first round.

On 1 March 1896, an invading Italian force commanded by General Oreste Baratieri was soundly defeated by the Abyssinians at the Battle of Adowa. The Italians suffered about 6,500 casualties, with about 2,500 soldiers captured in this humiliating debacle.

See also Abyssinian War; Magdala, Capture of; Napier, Field Marshal Robert C.; Theodore, Emperor
References: Bates (1979); Chandler (1967); Featherstone (1989); Haythornthwaite (1995); Myatt (1970)

Abyssinian War (1867–1868)

The Abyssinian Emperor Theodore II, after a perceived insult from Queen Victoria, imprisoned the British consul and a number of other Europeans in 1864. Diplomats made numerous attempts to assuage Theodore's hurt feelings and help facilitate the release of the hostages, but the emperor kept asking for additional material assistance. The British eventually realized that they were being blackmailed by the cunning Theodore, and on 13 August 1867, the British Cabinet authorized military intervention to free the prisoners.

Anticipating the need to send a force to Abyssinia, the British had begun preliminary planning in June 1867. It was decided to send troops from the presidency of Bombay in India, because of their proximity to east Africa, availability of shipping, acclimatization to the heat, and recent combat experience. Moreover, their experienced commander in chief, Lieutenant General (later Field Marshal Lord) Sir Robert C. Napier, was considered an outstanding commander.

The British Government naively believed Napier could take a small flying column of about 1,000 soldiers and make a quick dash to Abyssinia to rescue the European hostages from Theodore. This concept failed to consider the topography of the region and associated logistical difficulties. Napier initially estimated that he would need a force of at least 12,000 men, 20,000 baggage animals, and three to four months to accomplish the mission, which had to be concluded before the torrential rains began in June.

The British issued a final ultimatum to Theodore on 9 September 1867 to release his hostages. No response was received, and administrative and logistical preparations for the force continued. The detailed organization of the force was determined: four British and ten Indian infantry battalions, a squadron of British and four Indian regiments of cavalry, five batteries of artillery, a rocket brigade, and eight companies of sappers and miners. The troops eventually numbered 14,214 British and Indian soldiers.

This expedition, perhaps utilizing logistical lessons learned from the Crimean War, was armed with some of the most advanced equipment and weapons then available. Two batteries of 7-pounder mountain guns, with 1,000 rounds each, had been adopted for mule carriage; the latest breach-loading, rifled Armstrong guns and four "rocket machines" (with 340 6-pounder "Hale's war rockets") were part of the expeditionary force. The European soldiers carried for the first time Snider-Enfield breech-loading rifles. Fresh water condensers were taken, as were the latest types of tubes and pumps for water wells. An electric telegraph unit and photographers also accompanied the force.

Organizing sufficient supply and maintenance assets for a

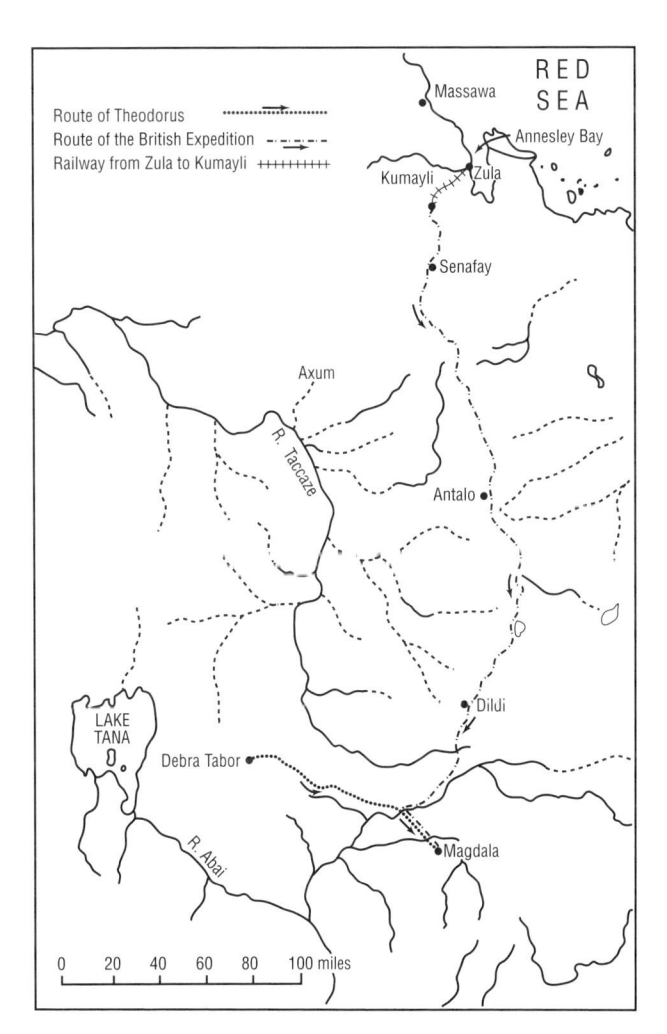

Abyssinian War, 1867–1868: Area of Operations

large force was an equal challenge. The force eventually required 26,254 "followers" (laborers, etc.), 2,538 horses for cavalry and staff, 19,580 transport horses or mules, 6,045 camels, 7,086 bullocks, 1,850 donkeys, and 44 elephants. The transport and provision of this large force necessitated hiring 205 sailing vessels and 75 steamers, as well as purchasing 11 small craft. This expedition was a tremendous logistical undertaking.

The advance party of the expedition arrived at Zula on Annesley Bay, south of Massawa, on 21 October 1867. Logistical preparations, including the construction of a 900-yard jetty, began. By mid-December 1867, about 2,000 British and 5,500 Indian troops were ashore, and Napier and his staff arrived on 2 January 1868. Reconnaissance elements were sent inland to seek out routes and befriend local chiefs. The stockpiling of supplies continued at Zula, and a forward operating base was established at Senafay, about 40 miles from the coast at an altitude of 8,000 feet. An attempt was made to build a railway.

Napier had learned that Theodore was moving with a large force to the mountain fortress of Magdala, about 400 miles from Zula. The British force deployed from Zula toward that objective on 25 January 1868, with a 7-mile logistical "tail" of support elements snaking its way through the mountain paths. Movement was difficult and slower than anticipated, although relatively uneventful. The lead brigade reached Antalo, 200 miles from the coast, on 14 February 1868, with the force headquarters arriving there on 2 March 1868. After a reduction in baggage, the force was organized into two divisions. The 1st Division, commanded by Major General Sir Charles Staveley, totaled about 5,000 soldiers of the "strike force" divided into two brigades, an advance guard, and all the artillery. Commanded by Major General G. Malcolm, the 2nd Division included the lines of communication and all garrisons from Zula to Antalo.

After a 10-day halt, the force continued marching toward Magdala on 12 March 1868. Tension mounted as the British force marched deeper into enemy territory. On 24 March, the force entered Dildi, from which they could see Magdala, but the rugged terrain required a meandering 60-mile march before the objective was reached. In early April 1868, Napier sent a formal demand for surrender to Theodore, who ignored the ultimatum. Two days later, the British advanced to reconnoiter the route to the Arogi Plateau, the probable assault position for the attack on the Islamgee Plateau. The terrain and heat caused elements of the column to fall behind the others. The British, first believing the pass to the Arogi Plateau was undefended and then believing it secured, sent their baggage animals and guns to the pass.

After the supply trains began to move forward, Napier noticed that the pass was unsecured and ordered an engineer unit to secure the defile. Theodore also observed the situation and ordered an attack on the seemingly unprotected, vulnerable baggage train. The result was a fierce battle in which Theodore's defeated army lost about 700 killed and 1,500 wounded, while the British had 20 soldiers wounded (of whom 2 died later).

Napier sent messages to the demoralized Theodore in an attempt to end the impasse. The emperor freed the hostages the next day, 12 April 1868, but refused to surrender. The British commander realized he needed to attack and decisively defeat Theodore and his ardent followers before they melted away into the rugged countryside. The British attacked and captured Magdala on 13 April 1868, and Theodore committed suicide by shooting himself in the mouth. Two days later, the sappers and miners destroyed Theodore's artillery and the fortress itself. British casualties in the Battle of Magdala were surprisingly light: 2 officers killed and 15 all ranks wounded.

After Napier accomplished his mission, the troops marched back to Zula, all arriving there by 2 June 1868. The majority of the force returned to India, and Napier and many of the British troops landed at Portsmouth around 20 June. A tremendous crowd greeted the returning soldiers, and the expedition was considered a resounding success. Through the nine-month campaign, the British had suffered only 35 deaths from all causes, and 333 seriously wounded or ill. The only criticism leveled at Napier was the expense of the campaign: the original cost estimate of the expedition was £2 million while the actual cost was £8.6 million. The prime minister, however, rightly declared, "Money is not to be considered in such matters: success alone is to be thought of" (Chandler 1967, p. 152). As a result of his success in Abyssinia, Napier was deservedly ennobled and received two knighthoods. England's honor was vindicated, as were the martial qualities of the post–Crimean War and post–Indian Mutiny British Army.

See also Abyssinia; Animals, Transport; Lines of Communication; Magdala, Capture of; Napier, Field Marshal Robert C.; Rockets; Theodore, Emperor

References: Bates (1979); Chandler (1967); Farwell (1972); Myatt (1970); Rodgers (1984)

Act for the Better Government of India (1858)
See East India Company; East India Company, Military Forces; India; Indian Mutiny

Addiscombe, Military Seminary

The East India Company's army underwent a considerable expansion at the end of the eighteenth century, which continued into the early nineteenth century. Royal Military Academy, Woolwich, and Royal Military College, Sandhurst, could not assist in training officers for the company's military forces due to increased officer demand during the Napoleonic Wars. Consequently the East India Company established its own military college in 1809 to meet the increased demand for trained British officers in its expanding military forces, especially technical branches such as the artillery and engineers.

The Addiscombe Military Seminary, the company's military college, was opened at the former mansion of the Earl of Liverpool, near Croydon, Surrey. (The company also opened a college to educate its civilian administrators, Haileybury, in 1806.) The nomination of a company director was normally required for admission, and the average age of a cadet on admission was fifteen. Tuition fees for the first student were £30 per year.

The course of instruction lasted two years and closely followed that of the Royal Military Academy, Woolwich. There were both military and civilian instructors. Academic subjects included fortification, mathematics, military and landscape drawing, chemistry, geology, French, and Hindustani. Military instruction was provided in individual, musketry, and gun drill.

Cadets who passed their final examinations were commissioned into the company's engineers, artillery, and infantry on the basis of merit. From 1809 to 1821, 62 Addiscombe graduates were commissioned into the company engineers, 215 into the artillery, and 113 into the infantry. Newly commissioned company engineer and artillery officers received additional training at the British Army schools at Chatham and Woolwich, respectively. Those who wished to join the company infantry as cadets could do so by going directly to India. Company cavalry lieutenants received direct appointments and did not attend Addiscombe.

As a result of the India Act of 1833, patronage for entry to Addiscombe was ended and vacancies were thereafter filled by open competition.

With the virtual abolition of the East India Company and the transfer of its authority to the British Crown in 1858, it was decided that Woolwich and Sandhurst would be sufficient to train new officers for both the British Army and the Indian Army, and Addiscombe was closed in 1861. During Addiscombe's fifty-two-year existence, about 2,000 infantry, 1,100 artillery, and 500 engineer officers were commissioned into the East India Company military forces.

See also East India Company; East India Company, Military Forces; India, British Army in; Indian Army Organization; Officers, British Army—Sources of Commissioning; Officers, Indian Army—Sources of Commissioning; Sandhurst, Royal Military College; Woolwich, Royal Military Academy
References: Farwell (1989); Gardner (1971); Heathcote (1974); Hervey (1988); Masefield (1995); Mason (1974); Mason (1985)

Adjutant-General, British Army

The adjutant-general was one of the three original British Army staff positions (including military secretary and quartermaster-general) created by Field Marshal H.R.H. Frederick, Duke of York, commander in chief, in 1795. This staff, originally located in Whitehall, became known as the Horse Guards.

The duties and responsibilities of the adjutant-general evolved slightly between 1815 and 1914. While he remained responsible for discipline, personnel, and administration, his responsibilities for training and doctrine were transferred to the General Staff when it was established in 1904. The authority of the adjutant-general increased through much of the nineteenth century, but decreased with the establishment of the War Office Council in 1888 and the Army Council and the General Staff in 1904.

In 1850, it was proposed to merge the offices of adjutant-general and quartermaster-general to create a chief of staff for the Horse Guards. Field Marshal Arthur Wellesley, First Duke of Wellington, then commander in chief, opposed this recommendation because he felt the two departments would have to continue under the chief of staff. Wellington probably saw the establishment of the new office as a prelude to the eventual abolition of the commander in chief post.

By 1853, the duties and responsibilities of the adjutant-general focused on military discipline. In this area, he advised the commander in chief on courts-martial and arranged for the passage of troops going overseas, coordinated interregimental transfers, and was concerned with the establishment of regimental schools. The adjutant-general also supervised the selection and inspection of general issue clothing. He was responsible for issues pertaining to the reserve forces (militia, yeomanry, and enrolled pensioners). The adjutant-general had three officers with subordinates to assist him at the Horse Guards. All military commandants in the United Kingdom and abroad, the deputy adjutant-general in Edinburgh, and the adjutant-generals of all stations in Ireland and overseas were required to send periodic reports to the adjutant-general at the Horse Guards. The assistant adjutant-generals of military districts in the United Kingdom, appointed on the recommendation of the adjutant-general, were also responsible to the Horse Guards. In sum, the adjutant-general was directly responsible to the commander in chief for the efficiency of the army. Service as adjutant-general at this time was very arduous and demanding. As one adjutant-general observed, "I by no means relish the thought of imprisonment with hard labour which is a condition inseparable from the appointment of Adjutant-General" (Sweetman 1984, p. 81).

A number of organizational changes took place when Field Marshal H.R.H. Prince George F., Second Duke of Cambridge, retired in 1895 and was replaced as commander in chief by Field Marshal Viscount Garnet J. Wolseley. The adjutant-general, quartermaster-general, inspector-general of fortifications, and inspector-general of the ordnance were made directly responsible to the secretary of state for war. Together with the commander in chief, serving as president, these four senior officers would compose the Army Board.

In November 1901, during the Second Boer War (1899–1902), a number of additional reforms were enacted, including the subordination of the adjutant-general and other principal staff officers to the commander in chief.

The Army Council, in addition to a general staff, was established in 1904 as a result of recommendations of the War Office Reconstitution, or Esher, Committee. The Army Council was to consist of seven members. The second military member was the adjutant-general, responsible for the provision of personnel, organization, mobilization of units, discipline and military law, medical services, army schools, and the administration of votes (in the Army Estimates) for these services. The adjutant-general's key subordinates were the director of recruiting and organization, the director of personal services, the director-general of medical services, the director of auxiliary services, and the judge-advocate.

See also Army Estimates; Cambridge, Field Marshal H.R.H. Prince George F., Second Duke of; Commander in Chief, British Army; Esher Committee; Horse Guards; Master-General of the Ordnance, British Army; Militia; Quartermaster-General, British Army; War Office; Wellington, Field Marshal Arthur Wellesley, First Duke of; Wolseley, Field Marshal Garnet J.; Yeomanry

References: Barnett (1970); Bond (1972); Hamer (1970); Moyse-Bartlett (1974); Spiers (1992); Sweetman (1984)

Adye, General Sir John M. (1819–1900)

General Sir John M. Adye was a competent Royal Artillery officer who served gallantly in many Victorian military campaigns. As a senior officer, especially at the War Office, he was generally known as an able, conscientious administrator.

Born on 1 November 1819, Adye was commissioned a second lieutenant in the Royal Artillery in 1836 after graduation from Woolwich. He distinguished himself while serving in artillery appointments during the Crimean War (1854–1856), Indian Mutiny (1857–1859), and the 1863 Ambela campaign on the North-West Frontier of India. Adye later wrote three candid accounts of his experiences in these campaigns.

As a colonel, Adye was assigned as director of artillery and stores at the War Office in 1870. Some sources suggest that during Adye's tenure British artillery development failed to keep pace with technological advances and rival nations. The Armstrong gun, a rifled-barrel breech-loading gun, was first employed in China in 1860. Even though effective, the Armstrong gun was considered complicated and expensive, and after trials in the late 1860s, the artillery reverted to muzzle loaders, albeit with a rifled barrel. After additional improvements in gunpowder were made, rifled breechloaders were adopted permanently in 1885.

In 1875, Adye became governor of the Royal Military Academy, Woolwich. Five years later, after William Gladstone and the Liberals returned to power, Adye was appointed as surveyor-general of the ordnance, a position for which he was considered ideally suited.

In August 1882, when the Arabi Rebellion broke out, Adye accompanied the commander of the British expedition, General (later Field Marshal Viscount) Sir Garnet J. Wolseley, to Egypt as chief of staff. While Adye was somewhat chagrined at being subordinate to an officer fourteen years younger than he was, he proved to be a very loyal and generally capable chief of staff. When Wolseley explained his plan for a night approach march and attack on Egyptian positions at Tel el-Kebir, Adye was supposedly concerned about potential navigation problems and inexperienced young soldiers. Adye seemingly failed to properly organize an efficient supply train as directed and was unable to procure mules from the Ottomans. Adye's overall efforts, however, as Wolseley's chief of staff contributed significantly to the expedition's success.

Adye became governor of Gibraltar at the end of 1882, was promoted to general in 1884, and retired two years later. In retirement, he kept up with regimental affairs, participated in discussions on Indian frontier policy, and wrote his autobiography, *Recollections of a Military Life*. General Sir John M. Adye died on 26 August 1900.

See also Arabi Rebellion; Artillery, British Army—Weapons and Equipment; Crimean War; Gladstone, William E.; Indian Mutiny; Tel el-Kebir, Battle of; Wolseley, Field Marshal Garnet J.
References: Adye (1860); Adye (1867); Adye (1895); Adye (1925); Kochanski (1999); Lehmann (1964); Maurice and Arthur (1924); Spiers (1992); Stephen and Lee (1964–1965); Williams (1967)

Afghan War, First (1839–1842)

The First Afghan War (1839–1842) was the first large conflict in Afghanistan, the frontier area between Czarist Russia and British India during the "Great Game," the quest of each imperial nation to expand and increase its influence. The entire war was characterized by British military miscalculations, complacency, and incompetence.

Dynastic struggles and internal strife typified Afghanistan early in the nineteenth century. Dost Mohammed seized power in Kabul, Afghanistan, in 1826 and became the virtual king of Afghanistan. At the time, Afghanistan faced two major external threats, the Sikhs in the east and the Persians in the west. The Sikhs captured the city of Peshawar in the Punjab in 1834, and the Persians threatened Herat in 1836.

The British refused to assist Dost Mohammed in recovering Peshawar from the Sikhs and were concerned that the Russians would increase their influence in Afghanistan. The British decided to invade and occupy Afghanistan, depose Dost Mohammed, and replace him with the pliant pro-British Shah Shujah, a former ruler living in exile in India.

The British "Army of the Indus," commanded by General Sir John Keane and consisting of about 15,000 East India Company soldiers, Shah Shujah's 6,000-man force, as well as 38,000 camp followers with 30,000 camels, departed India in December 1838. The British force finally reached Kandahar in April 1839.

In June 1839, the British force began its march to Kabul. The formidable fortress of Ghazni, on the route to Kabul, was captured on 23 July 1839 after the British received information that the fortress's Kabul Gate was weaker than the others. After the gate was blown, assault troops led by Brigadier General (later Major General Sir) Robert Sale captured the fortress in a confusing action. The British forces lost 17 killed and 165 wounded, while the Afghans reportedly suffered over 1,200 killed, thousands wounded, and about 1,500 taken prisoner.

The capture of Ghazni cleared the route to Kabul, and Dost Mohammed fled before the British arrived in Kabul on 7 August 1839. The British, who had crowned Shah Shujah amir of Afghanistan on 3 May 1839, propped up his unpopular regime with their continued presence in Kabul. The British had seemingly accomplished their mission. Major General Sir Willoughby Cotton replaced Keane, and the Bombay contingent of the Army of the Indus returned to India.

The British constructed a large cantonment, or fortified military encampment, north of Kabul and about 2 miles from the Bala Hissar fortress, in which Shah Shujah and his court resided. This site was on a plain dominated by high ground, none of it occupied by the British, and filled with orchards, irrigation ditches, streams, and other terrain obstacles. When completed, the cantonment, with a 2-mile perimeter, was virtually indefensible. Moreover, the garrison's commissariat stores were a quarter mile outside the cantonment, and the security of the lines of communication depended on "friendly" Afghan tribesmen. The situation seemed so stable that many British officers sent for their families to join them.

Cotton retired in 1841 and was replaced by the elderly, ailing Major General William G. K. Elphinstone. Later in the year, the East India Company took measures to reduce its expenses in Afghanistan, which included collecting taxes and withdrawing the subsidy to the tribesmen guarding the lines of communications between Kabul and India. As a result, the first British caravan to travel in the area was plun-

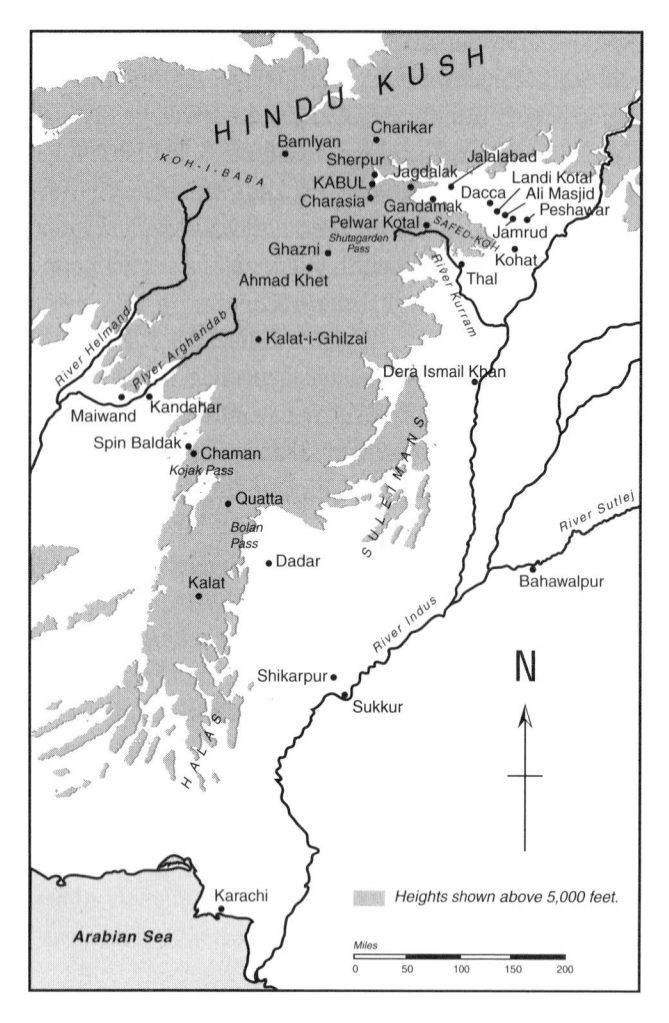

First Afghan War, 1839–1842: Area of Operations

dered in October 1841. To demonstrate continued British control, Sale's brigade was ordered to march back to India via the Khyber Pass and scatter the impertinent tribesmen. Sale's brigade entered Jalalabad on 13 November 1841.

In Kabul, the situation had deteriorated. An angry Afghan mob surrounded and sacked the British residency on 2 November 1841, while Elphinstone in the nearby cantonment failed to take any action. The Afghans surrounded the cantonment and captured the commissariat. On 13 November, the Afghans placed guns on the Beymaroo hills and began pouring accurate artillery fire into the cantonment. A seventeen-company British force, with attached cavalry and engineers and one artillery piece, marched on 23 November to dislodge the Afghan artillery but was soundly defeated.

Surrounded and facing starvation, the British attempted to negotiate a capitulation with the Afghans. During final negotiations on 23 December 1841, the Afghans treacherously attacked the British and hacked to death Sir William H. Macnaghten, the British envoy. His head and limbs were paraded around the city and his trunk was hung in the bazaar.

The British force, consisting of about 4,500 soldiers (including 700 Europeans) and 12,000 camp followers, was permitted to retreat from Kabul on 6 January 1842. Through deep snow, biting cold, and deep mountain passes, with little food and no shelter, the group was expected to travel 90 miles to Jalalabad. During the following week, tribesmen repeatedly attacked the British, whose route was marked by bloodstained snow and frozen corpses. Finally, on 13 January, about 120 soldiers of the 44th Regiment of Foot and 25 artillerymen—all that remained of the British force, except for about 93 taken hostage—struggled through the Jagdalak Pass and were massacred at Gandamak. While there were reportedly a few survivors, only one European from the Army of the Indus, Dr. William Brydon, reached Jalalabad.

The retreat from Kabul was one of the most humiliating catastrophes suffered by the British Army in the nineteenth century. The British, in an attempt to regain some prestige, organized the so-called Army of Retribution and sent it to Afghanistan, where they retained garrisons at Jalalabad, Ghazni, and Kandahar. Commanded by Major General Sir George Pollock, this force assembled at Peshawar, forced the Khyber Pass on 5 April 1842, and reached Jalalabad on 16 April, where the siege had been lifted only nine days earlier.

Pollock's army later advanced on Kabul and reached it on 15 September 1842. Two days later, it was joined by Major General Sir William Nott's force, which had held Kandahar. The combined 14,000-man British Army retrieved their hostages, blew up the city bazaar in revenge, and departed Kabul on 12 October 1842. The army reached Ferozepore on 23 December 1842, which ended the First Afghan War.

The British, as a result of the actions of the Army of Retribution, disingenuously claimed success in the First Afghan War. In addition to the debacle of the retreat from Kabul, the British had lost their aura of invincibility, a key factor in the subsequent Sikh Wars and Indian Mutiny.

See also Afghanistan; Bombay Army; Dost Mohammed; East India Company; East India Company, Military Forces; Great Game; India; Indian Mutiny; Lines of Communication; Sale, Major General Sir Robert; Sher Ali Khan; Sikhs

References: Buttery (2001); Cunningham (2001); Forbes (1892); Fredericks (1971); James (1998); Judd (1973); Lunt (1969); Macrory (1966); Pottinger (1983); Tanner (2002); Waller (1990)

Afghan War, Second (1878–1880)

Afghanistan served as the battleground for a second time in 1878–1880 during the imperial rivalry between Great Britain and Russia known as the Great Game. Advocates of the so-called forward policy of Indian and imperial defense argued that the British needed to extend their influence in Afghanistan, by occupation if necessary, to forestall Russian encroachment in the region. The British, as they had attempted to do in the First Afghan War, wanted to transform Afghanistan from a neutral buffer state into a British client.

The Afghan ruler, Amir Sher Ali Khan, was attempting to consolidate his rule in the late 1870s and wanted to avoid involvement in the Anglo-Russian rivalry. The Russians, victorious in the 1877–1878 Russo-Turkish War, sent an uninvited mission to Afghanistan. As Sher Ali was struggling with his relative Abdur Rahman Khan for the throne, he began to distance himself from the British and sought Russian assistance. The British, in turn, demanded to send a similar mission to Afghanistan and, rebuffed, issued an ultimatum to Sher Ali. This demand went unanswered, and on 21 November 1878, the British invaded Afghanistan and started the Second Afghan War.

Three British columns advanced into Afghanistan simultaneously. The largest was the 16,000-man, 48-gun Peshawar Valley Field Force, commanded by Lieutenant General (later General) Sir Samuel Browne, V.C. Its mission was to advance on a northerly route through the Khyber Pass to Jalalabad and to clear the way of all opposition. The 6,500-man, 18-gun Kurram Valley Force, commanded by Major General (later Field Marshal Earl) Frederick S. Roberts, V.C., was tasked to occupy the Kurram Valley and then march to the Shutagardan Pass dominating Kabul. Lieutenant General (later Field Marshal) Sir Donald M. Stewart's 13,000-man, 78-gun Kandahar Field Force was to march via the Bolan Pass, reinforce the Quetta garrison, then occupy Kandahar.

Browne's force entered the Khyber Pass, but its progress was obstructed by the Afghan-held fort of Ali Masjid, situated 500 feet above the gorge and flanked by other fortifications. Browne attempted to coordinate the actions of his three brigades in an attack in the difficult terrain on 21 November 1878 that ultimately failed. Fearful of being outflanked, the Afghans evacuated Ali Masjid that night and stumbled into the first brigade blocking their escape. Most of the Afghans were taken prisoner. The way was then clear for Browne to advance on Jalalabad, which was occupied on 20 December 1878.

After marching through the Kurram Valley, Roberts's force found its advance blocked by Afghans with artillery at the Peiwar Kotal (Pass). Late on 1 December 1878, Roberts led a large column on a flanking movement that reached the left of the Afghan position. At dawn on the following morning, his troops assaulted and eventually defeated the Afghans, thus clearing the route to Kabul. The victory at the Battle of Peiwar Kotal established Roberts's reputation as a commander.

Stewart's force faced little opposition but suffered from logistical problems. It captured Kandahar in early January 1879. At this stage, with three British columns operating in his country, Sher Ali's grip on Afghanistan became tenuous and he fled north and died on 21 February 1879. He was succeeded by his son, Yakub Khan. After a British victory at Fatehabad on 2 April 1879, Browne's force occupied Gandamak, and Yakub Khan decided to negotiate with the British. The main British negotiator was Major (later Sir) Pierre L. N. Cavagnari, Browne's political officer. On 26 May 1879, the Treaty of Gandamak, in which Yakub Khan was recognized as amir in exchange for transferring the Kurram Valley and the Khyber Pass to the British, was signed. In addition, the British received control of Afghanistan's foreign affairs while guaranteeing the protection of Afghanistan and paying an annual subsidy. The Second Afghan War seemed to be over.

Cavagnari was appointed British envoy to Kabul. His mission, which arrived in Kabul on 24 July 1879, included political assistants and a Corps of Guides military escort totaling eighty people. In late August 1879, six undefeated and resentful Afghan regiments were transferred from Herat to Kabul. On 3 September 1879, these Herati soldiers received only a fraction of the pay owed them. Enraged, they briefly attacked the British residency, then retreated. Some 2,000 armed Afghan soldiers later returned, ferociously attacked the residency, and massacred Cavagnari and his mission. This atrocity sparked the renewal of hostilities.

Both the Peshawar Valley Field Force and Kurram Valley Force had been withdrawn earlier, and Stewart's Kandahar Field Force had begun redeploying to India on 1 September 1879. After news of the Cavagnari massacre reached India on 5 September, the order to withdraw was immediately canceled. Stewart's force remained in Kandahar and the surrounding area and engaged in pacification operations.

Roberts was ordered to advance on Kabul with the newly formed Kabul Field Force. He began his advance on 27 September 1879, but the force found its way blocked when it reached a defile near Charasia, about 10 miles from Kabul, on 5 October 1879. The following day, without his full force assembled, Roberts attacked the Afghans with a 4,000-man, 18-gun force. The British, again employing a flanking movement, defeated the Afghans and entered Kabul on 8 October. British martial law was ruthlessly applied. Buildings were demolished and drumhead courts-martial were held. Eighty-seven Afghans reportedly involved in the attack on the residency were hanged. Yakub Khan, who had joined Roberts before his force began its march, was not restored to his throne and abdicated on 12 October. The united 7,000-man Kabul Field Force then occupied the large, fortified Sherpur Cantonment near Kabul.

As the months wore on, Afghans increasingly resented the British occupation of Kabul. On 11 December 1879, the British sent troops to disperse assembling Afghans, and after 14 December, Roberts's force in Sherpur was besieged. Before dawn on 23 December, the assembled Afghan tribal levies, inspired by a call for holy war against the infidels, attacked the forewarned British in the Sherpur Cantonment. They charged determinedly with their scaling ladders and suffered heavy casualties from the disciplined British rifle and artillery fire. By early afternoon, the Afghans lost heart and started to melt away, and the British sent cavalry to pursue the fleeing tribesmen.

In early April 1880, Stewart left the defense of Kandahar to Major General J. M. Primrose and his Bombay Army force and marched to Kabul. Stewart's force found its way blocked by a strong tribal force at Ahmad Khel on 19 April 1880. The British fought a desperate battle that day and eventually routed the enemy, who lost about 1,000 killed and more than 2,000 wounded. The British force, which lost 17 killed and 115 wounded, then continued to Kabul.

Stewart's force arrived at Kabul on 2 May 1880, and he, as the senior officer, assumed command of the combined force. The fall of the Conservative Government in England on 28 April 1880 signaled the end of the "forward policy" and direct British involvement in Afghanistan. With withdrawal imminent, the British looked for a capable Afghan to rule the country. They selected Abdur Rahman, a nephew of Sher Ali who appeared sensible, and on 22 July 1880, he was proclaimed amir.

Ayub Khan, a brother of Yakub Khan, believed himself to be the rightful ruler of Afghanistan, and had, since the beginning of July 1880, been marching with a large force toward Kandahar. Primrose sent a 2,500-strong brigade under Brigadier General G. R. S. Burrows to support allied Afghan troops, who deserted in the field. On 27 July, Burrows's brigade was caught in the open and overwhelmed as it attempted to attack Ayub Khan's large force at Maiwand, the sole British battalion being veritably annihilated. About half of Burrows's unit was able to retreat to Kandahar, which was immediately besieged.

Roberts was then directed to lead a relief force from Kabul to Kandahar, about 318 miles away. Roberts's 10,000-man combined arms force, containing a logistical element purposely tailored for the mission, began its precarious march on 9 August 1880. Over difficult terrain, through waterless desert, suffering great extremes of temperature, the force reached the outskirts of Kandahar on 31 August. The following morning, Roberts attacked Ayub Khan's force, turned the Afghan left flank, and soundly defeated the Afghan force.

The Battle of Kandahar basically ended the Second Afghan War and propelled Roberts into the limelight, overshadowing the success of the 1879 Zulu War and other operations in South Africa. Abdur Rahman extended his rule over all of Afghanistan, and British troops returned to India shortly thereafter. While the final battle may have restored some British prestige, overall the Second Afghan War was a Pyrrhic victory for the British.

See also Afghan War, First (1839–1842); Afghanistan; Bombay Army; Browne, General Sir Samuel J., V.C.; Cavagnari, Major Sir Pierre L. N.; Chamberlain, Field Marshal Sir Neville B.; Charasia, Battle of; Great Game; India; Indian Army Operations; Kabul to Kandahar March; Kandahar, Battle of; Maiwand, Battle of; Peiwar Kotal, Battle of; Roberts, Field Marshal Frederick S., V.C.; Sher Ali Khan; Sherpur, Battle of; Stewart, Field Marshal Sir Donald M.

References: Barthorp (1982); Featherstone (1989); Forbes (1892); Fredericks (1971); James (1998); Mason (1974); Owen (1985); Roberts (1897); Tanner (2002)

Afghanistan

Afghanistan has been accurately described as "a land of mountains, ferocious warriors, uncompromising Islam, vicious tribal rivalries and a political complexity that entwines bloodlines, religion, history, opportunism and treachery into a mix as incomprehensible to the outsider today as it has ever been" (First Afghan War n.d., pp. 3–4).

Since the time of Alexander the Great, Afghanistan has been a crossroads of civilizations. This was especially true in the nineteenth century, as Persia tried to increase its influence and, more importantly, British India and Czarist Russia competed with each other to influence and control the vast, uncharted mountainous regions of Central Asia. The British played the Great Game to protect India, the "jewel in the imperial crown," while the Russians wanted to keep the British from interfering with their eastern destiny, a strong belief in the inevitability of their eastern expansion. As the buffer area between these two competing empires, Afghanistan was frequently the scene of conflict.

Mountainous and landlocked, Afghanistan was shaped like an egg, tilting slightly to the right. Persia was located to the west of Afghanistan, with central Asia to the north, and a small section of China to the northeast. In the first half of the nineteenth century, the Sikh-dominated Punjab was situated to the east, and Baluchistan to the east and south of Afghanistan. The Punjab was annexed by the British East India Company after the Second Sikh War in 1849, and Baluchistan (Sind) was conquered by the British in 1843. After 1849, therefore, British India bordered the entire southern and eastern half of Afghanistan. In 1893, the disputed and ambiguous border between Afghanistan and India was delineated and called the Durand Line after the British diplomat responsible for its negotiation.

Three strategically important cities lie north and south of the central mountain range, the Hindu Kush: Herat, in a fertile valley not far from Persia; Kandahar in the south; and Kabul in the northeast, accessible through mountain passes from India. A number of passes in the Hindu Kush permit travel from north and south in Afghanistan.

Afghanistan experienced considerable dynastic and internal strife in the early nineteenth century. In 1823, the Afghans invaded the Punjab attempting to restore lost territories, but were soundly defeated by Sikhs led by Ranjit Singh. Dost Mohammed, the brother of an earlier Afghan chief minister, seized power in Kabul in 1826. After this time, Afghanistan became fully embroiled in the Great Game between Russia and British India, resulting in the First Afghan War (1839–1842), and the Second Afghan War (1878–1880).

Afghanistan was organized on a tribal basis, and by the time of the First Afghan War, there was no "national" Afghan army. A feudal system of land tenure required large landowners to provide troops to the central government when directed. The Afghans, armed with long *jezails* (muskets), swords, long-bladed knives, and round shields, were courageous and cunning guerrilla warriors.

Shah Shujah, the Afghan ruler just before the First Afghan War, established a 6,000-man force commanded by and consisting mainly of Europeans. It originally had two regiments of cavalry and five of infantry, plus a horse artillery troop. This force fought with distinction as British allies during the First Afghan War.

See also Afghan War, First (1839–1842); Afghan War, Second (1878–1880); Dost Mohammed; Durand, Sir Henry Mortimer; East India Company; Great Game; India; North-West Frontier; Penjdeh Incident; Persia; Sikh War, Second (1848–1849); Sikhs
References: Featherstone (1989); First Afghan War (n.d.); Fredericks (1971); James (1998); Judd (1973); Lunt (1969); Macrory (1966); Pottinger (1983); Tanner (2002); Waller (1990)

Aldershot

Aldershot (meaning a wood or copse of alder trees) was the British Army's first and largest permanent camp for large-scale training exercises and military maneuvers. Lying about 40 miles southwest of central London near Farnborough, Aldershot was founded during the Victorian era and remains the "home" of the British Army.

The unprecedented British Army maneuvers at Chobham in 1853 were a tremendous success. They not only pointed out shortcomings in Army organization, tactics, and equipment, but also stimulated in some progressive circles the quest for greater military readiness and proficiency.

General (later Field Marshal) Viscount Henry Hardinge, the British Army commander in chief, wanted to ensure that the following year's maneuvers were even more successful. He also wanted to establish a permanent "camp of instruction" that would function year-round and not depend entirely on annual Parliamentary funding. Land in the vicinity of Aldershot was surveyed, and the government purchased parcels of land (for £12 per acre) totaling about 10,000 acres in 1853–1854. Additional purchases through 1861 increased the size of the Aldershot training area to about 25,000 acres. Prior to the establishment of Aldershot, the British Army did not have a training area in England large enough to exercise even one brigade.

Initially, only a summer tented encampment was envisioned. It was soon realized that a longer period of training would be needed, especially as militia units were called out during the Crimean War (1854–1856). All-weather barracks would also be needed for troops defending the southern coast of England. Accordingly, construction of hutted camps, each for a division, one north and the other south of the Basingstoke Canal, was begun in February 1855. North Camp was occupied in May 1855. Plans were subsequently approved for permanent brick barracks to house another two brigades of cavalry, infantry, and artillery near the village of Aldershot.

In 1854, Aldershot consisted of a church, a manor house, a few farms, and 163 houses. By 1864, it had been transformed into a small town, assisted by the establishment of the permanent military garrison. The population of Aldershot in 1851 was 875; ten years later the population was over 16,000, which included about 9,000 soldiers.

Large-scale maneuvers were held at Aldershot in 1871 and 1872. British Army training above the battalion level stagnated until the 1890s, and two divisions participated in autumn maneuvers at Aldershot in 1891. Training exercises and maneuvers were held at Aldershot throughout the 1890s and until the eve of World War I.

The first Mounted Infantry training school was established at Aldershot in 1888. Veterinary and signaling schools were also established there.

Large tracts of land totaling 41,000 acres at Salisbury Plain were purchased in 1898. These were to be used mainly for cavalry and artillery maneuvers and range firing and supplemented the training area at Aldershot. A new barracks complex to accommodate training and other units was built at Tidworth in 1902.

After the Second Boer War, the 1st Corps—the only one of six corps actually organized and manned—was stationed at Aldershot. The 1st Corps was to serve as the nucleus of any planned expeditionary force.

See also Hardinge, Field Marshal Henry; Infantry, British Army—Training; Maneuvers, British Army

References: Edelman (2001); Farwell (1981); Partridge (1989); Spiers (1992)

Alexandria, Bombardment of (11 July 1882)

The British naval bombardment of Alexandria, Egypt, on 11 July 1882, the first and the last time a British ironclad squadron went into action, marked an escalation of hostilities in the Arabi Rebellion. This engagement paved the way for the decisive defeat of the Egyptian Army two months later and the British occupation of Egypt and control of the Suez Canal.

On 20 May 1882, British and French warships entered Alexandria Harbor to Egypt to support the faltering Egyptian khedive (viceroy) and to protect British and French citizens and interests.

As tensions increased and the political situation became more volatile in Egypt, the Egyptians began strengthening the seaward fortifications at Alexandria Harbor. The Egyptian defensive line, containing about 180 to 200 guns, stretched about 4.5 miles from the Pharos in the north, around the harbor, and along the shore to Fort Marabout in the southwest. The strong point of Fort Meks with its 31 guns was at the center of the Egyptian line of fortifications.

British Admiral Sir Beauchamp Seymour, concerned about the safety of his squadron, demanded that the Egyptians cease reinforcing their fortifications and dismantle their gun batteries. Although the Egyptians appeared to comply with Seymour's order, British searchlights revealed the Egyptians working frantically on their positions at night. Infuriated by this duplicity, Seymour (with the permission of the British Government) issued an ultimatum to the Egyptians on 10 July 1882 to surrender selected threatening forts within twelve hours or face a possible bombardment within twenty-four hours. The French ships, unwilling to become embroiled in hostilities, sailed away that night.

But there was no response from the Egyptians, and at 7:00 A.M. on 11 July 1882, Seymour's eight battleships and eleven gunboats opened fire on the shore fortifications. Two of his battleships, H.M.S. *Invincible* (Seymour's flagship) and H.M.S. *Inflexible,* each had four 80-ton (16-inch) main guns mounted in pairs in two turrets, designed to fire ahead and astern, as well as broadside. Shells from these guns "wobbled in the air with a noise like that of a distant train" (Padfield 1981, p. 173). The five-year-old H.M.S. *Alexandra,* another of Seymour's ships, mounted two 11-inch and ten 10-inch muzzle-loading, rifled-barreled guns. While many of Seymour's vessels were older and not as heavily armed, and the British had some difficulties in aiming, adjusting, and controlling naval gunfire, the outcome of the bombardment was never in doubt. The Egyptians, although generally manning their guns bravely (albeit somewhat ineffectively) could not withstand the thunderous barrage indefinitely. After about 900 men were killed and wounded out of the 8,000 who had manned the forts, the Egyptians abandoned their positions. The Egyptian guns were silent that afternoon. The British fleet suffered 10 men killed and 27 wounded, with no ships receiving substantive damage.

See also Arabi Rebellion; Egypt; Egyptian Army; Suez Canal
References: Barthorp (1984); Featherstone (1989); James (1985); Maurice (1887); Padfield (1981); Stokesbury (1983); Williams (1967)

Alison, General Sir Archibald (1826–1907)

General Sir Archibald Alison was a courageous and charismatic yet self-effacing senior British Army officer. He is probably best known as a brigade commander during both the Second Ashanti War (1873–1874) and the Arabi Rebellion (1882) in Egypt.

Alison, the eldest son of the eminent historian of the same name, was born on 21 January 1826. Commissioned an ensign in the 72nd Foot (later Seaforth Highlanders) in 1846, Alison served in Scotland, Barbados, and Nova Scotia before returning to England. When the Crimean War broke out, Alison was serving with his regiment on Malta and participated in the expedition to Kertch. Alison repeatedly demonstrated coolness under fire in the trenches before Sevastopol and during an assault on the Redan, and he gained the attention of the Highland Brigade commander, Major General Sir Colin Campbell (later Field Marshal Colin Campbell, First Baron Clyde of Clydesdale).

When Campbell was sent to India as commander in chief in July 1857 to quell the Indian Mutiny, he took Alison with him as military secretary and Alison's younger brother Frederick as aide-de-camp. During the second relief of Lucknow, both Alison brothers were wounded; Archibald lost his left arm. While recuperating, Alison was on half pay from 1858 to 1862.

From 1862 to 1873, Alison served in staff positions of increasing responsibility. He was selected to command the European Brigade, with the local rank of brigadier-general, in the 1873–1874 expedition to Ashantiland on the Gold Coast of Africa. The goal of the Ashanti expedition, under the overall command of Major General (later Field Marshal Viscount) Sir Garnet J. Wolseley, was to capture Kumasi, the Ashanti capital. Alison was in tactical command during the difficult march through dense rainforest. The British were ambushed near Amoaful on 31 January 1874, where Alison distinguished himself by his cool leadership. The British force, however, pushed on, fighting the Ashanti near Ordahsu before entering the empty Kumasi on 4 February. After the Second Ashanti War, Alison was knighted for his services upon his return to England.

After service at Aldershot and in Ireland, and a short stint as commandant of the Staff College, Camberley, Alison was assigned as deputy quartermaster-general for intelligence at the War Office (1878–1882). He played a key role in the Arabi Rebellion (1882). On 14 July 1882, he arrived in Cyprus and assumed command of a force that occupied Alexandria after the 11 July 1882 naval bombardment. Alison's task was to keep insurgent leader Ahmed Arabi Pasha distracted and thinking that the main British attack would come from Alexandria, when in fact Wolseley's force was occupying the Suez Canal and Ismailia and moving overland to engage the Egyptians at Tel el-Kebir. At the Battle of Tel el-Kebir, 13 September 1882, Alison gallantly led the Highland Brigade in storming the Egyptian fortifications. When Wolseley returned to England in October, Alison remained in command of the 12,000 British troops in Egypt.

Alison commanded the division at Aldershot from 1883 to 1888, with the exception of 1885, when he acted as adjutant-general during Wolseley's absence in the Sudan. In 1889, he was appointed a member of the Indian Council, retiring in 1893. Alison, considered "the beau ideal of a soldier and a gentleman" (Alison 1907, p. 442), died in London on 5 February 1907.

See also Adjutant-General, British Army; Amoaful, Battle of; Arabi Rebellion; Ashanti War, Second (1873–1874); Campbell, Field Marshal Colin; Crimean War; Indian Mutiny; Intelligence; Lucknow, Siege and Relief of; Tel el-Kebir, Battle of; Wolseley, Field Marshal Garnet J.
References: Alison (1907); Edgerton (1995); Keegan (1967); Kochanski (1999); Lee (1912); Lehmann (1964); Maurice (1887); Maxwell (1985)

Aliwal, Battle of (28 January 1846)

After the fortuitous British victory at the Battle of Ferozeshah, 21–22 December 1845, during the First Sikh War, Lieutenant General (later Field Marshal Viscount) Sir Hugh Gough, commander in chief, India, decided to rest his troops and wait for additional reinforcements from Sind.

To protect his lines of communication and the British garrison at Ludhiana, Gough detached a force under the command of Major General (later Lieutenant General) Sir Harry G. W. Smith. Smith's force, which eventually totaled about 10,000 men with 32 guns, had short clashes with the Sikhs on 21 and 25 January 1846.

Runjoor Singh's 20,000-soldier, 67-gun army was entrenched with its left flank near the village of Aliwal and right flank near Bhundri, with the Sutlej River a mile to its rear. Smith's force, with cavalry and horse artillery leading, swiftly attacked the surprised Sikhs, who were actually starting to march away, on 28 January 1846.

As the British cavalry reached the open plain, they wheeled to each flank, and the rest of the British force deployed into attack formation. Brigadier General Stedman's cavalry was on the right flank, and to his left was Brigadier General Godby's brigade, then Brigadier General Hicks's brigade, with 18 guns plus two 8-inch howitzers to their left. Continuing from right to left were Brigadier General Wheeler's brigade, two horse artillery batteries, and finally Brigadier General Wilson's brigade. The 16th Lancers and 3rd Light Cavalry covered the left flank.

The battle began in typical fashion with the British guns being pushed forward to engage the enemy. Hicks's brigade easily captured Aliwal, and troops of Wheeler's brigade fired one volley and charged the Sikh positions. The 53rd Foot, in Wilson's brigade, moved innovatively in short rushes and captured Bhundri with few casualties. The British cavalry, notably the 16th Lancers, repeatedly charged the Sikh squares until they broke and were routed. Many Sikhs crossed the ford over the Sutlej, while very few of those who failed to escape survived.

Smith's victory at Aliwal was complete; Sir John Fortescue called it "a battle without a mistake" (Featherstone 1973, p. 59). British casualties were 151 all ranks killed, 413 wounded, and 25 missing, and the Sikhs lost about 3,000 men and all 67 guns. The Battle of Aliwal was, unlike Gough's typical bludgeoning frontal assaults, a masterful example of the coordination and control of infantry, cavalry, and artillery units. "I never read an account of any affair," Field Marshal Arthur Wellesley, First Duke of Wellington, reported to the House of Lords, "in which an officer has shown himself more capable than this officer [Smith] did of commanding troops in the field" (Young 1977, p. 56).

See also East India Company, Military Forces; Ferozeshah, Battle of; Gough, Field Marshal Hugh; India; Indian Army Operations; Lines of Communication; Sikh War, First (1845–1846); Sikhs; Smith, Lieutenant General Sir Harry G. W.; Sobraon, Battle of; Wellington, Field Marshal Arthur Wellesley, First Duke of

References: Cook (1975); Crawford (1967); Featherstone (1968); Featherstone (1973); Featherstone (1992), Fraser (1994); Young (1977)

Alma, Battle of the (20 September 1854)

The Battle of the Alma was the first large-scale battle between opposing land forces during the Crimean War (1854–1856).

A joint British-French-Turkish force of over 50,000 soldiers, many weakened by disease, landed at Calamita Bay on the Crimean Peninsula about 35 miles north of Sevastopol between 13 September and 18 September 1854. After assembling, the allied force, with the French (commanded by Marshal Jacques Leroy de Saint-Arnaud) on the right with the coast protecting their flank and the British (under the command of General [later Field Marshal] Fitzroy J. H. Somerset, First Baron Raglan) on the left, began its southward advance toward Sevastopol.

The Russians, commanded by Prince Alexander Sergeevich Menshikov, had established defensive positions on the southern cliffs of the Alma River that crossed the allied axis of advance. Telegraph Hill was situated about 2 miles east of the Alma's mouth, and Kourgane Hill, key terrain that dominated the area, was slightly to the east of Telegraph Hill. The road to Sevastopol ran between Telegraph and Kourgane Hills, close to the village of Bourliouk, and was covered by Russian artillery. The 36,000-man Russian force was centered on the road, with its right flank on Kourgane Hill and its left flank out of range of the allied fleet.

The allied plan was for the French force (totaling about 37,000 men, with attached Turks) to assault the cliffs on their right (the western end, near the sea) and turn the Russian left flank, with the British attacking the Russian center and left. The 26,000-man British force, arrayed in two lines, advanced at 1:00 P.M., with Lieutenant General Sir George Brown's Light Division on the left and Lieutenant General (later General) Sir George de Lacy Evans's 2nd Division on the right. The second line consisted of the 1st Division, commanded by Lieutenant General (later Field Marshal) H.R.H. Prince George F., Second Duke of Cambridge, on the left, and Lieutenant General Sir Richard England's 3rd Division to its right. Lieutenant General Sir George Cathcart's 4th Division and the Cavalry Division, commanded by Lieutenant General (later Field Marshal) George C. Bingham, Third Earl of Lucan, were in reserve. Units became entangled with others and disorganized, and rather than face withering Russian fire in a frontal assault, Raglan ordered his soldiers to lie down and wait for the French advance on their right. The initial French attack made good progress but stalled after turning the Russian left flank.

To restore the momentum to the attack, Raglan ordered the British to again advance. The 2nd Division came under heavy Russian fire while passing Bourliouk, and the Light Division, after crossing the Alma, became congested at the high bank on the river's far side. A Light Division brigade commander exhorted his men to "Fix bayonets! Get up the bank and advance to the attack" (Judd 1975, p. 62) and captured the Russian Great Redoubt, northwest of Kourgane Hill. The 1st Division was rushed forward in support, but confusion reigned amid the noise and smoke in the Great Redoubt. Retreating Light Division soldiers fell back into the 1st Division, leaving about 900 dead or wounded behind them. By this time, the allied center was pinned down by Russian artillery and the French were unable to advance.

Commanding his troops, Raglan rode across the Alma to a position 800 yards behind the Russian lines. The arrival of two British guns held the Russians back from attacking the retreating Light Division, and the British were able to continue the attack. The 2nd and 3rd Divisions advanced to the relief of the Light Division. The Guards Brigade (1st Division) pressed forward to the Great Redoubt, while the Highland Brigade (1st Division) to its left advanced up the slopes of Kourgane Hill. Russians massed at the Great Redoubt charged the Guards, who were ordered to retreat (leaving 171 officers and men killed or wounded). The Guards took up defensive positions at the river line and used their new Minié rifles with deadly accuracy to stop the Russians. The Russians retreated, closely followed by the Guards, who then captured the Great Redoubt. The Highland Brigade, fighting against eleven Russian battalions, swept around the Great Redoubt and calmly advanced against the Russians. In the face of such stalwart opposition, the Russians began a general withdrawal.

The Battle of the Alma was clearly an allied victory, even though the cost was high and there was no pursuit. The British suffered 362 all ranks killed, and at least 1,621 wounded, many of whom would die from poor medical care. The French lost about 63 soldiers killed and 500 wounded, and the Russians sustained over 5,500 total casualties. While British generalship was criticized, "All that we have to be proud of," wrote one participant, "was the dash and valour of the regiments engaged" (Pemberton 1965, p. 67).

See also Cambridge, Field Marshal H.R.H. Prince George F., Second Duke of; Cathcart, Lieutenant General Sir George; Crimean War; Evans, General Sir George de Lacy; French Forces, Crimean War; Lucan, Field Marshal George C. Bingham, Third Earl of; Nightingale, Florence; Raglan, Field Marshal Fitzroy J. H. Somerset, First Baron; Russian Forces, Crimean War
References: Baumgart (1999); Judd (1975); Pemberton (1962); Royle (2000); Smith (1987); Warner (1972)

Amoaful, Battle of (31 January 1874)

Amoaful (also spelled Amoafo) was a village in Ashantiland where Major General (later Field Marshal Viscount) Sir Garnet J. Wolseley's British expeditionary force decisively defeated the Ashanti on 31 January 1874 during the Second Ashanti War.

Wolseley's force had been sent to the Gold Coast to drive the invading Ashanti north across the Pra River to Ashantiland, and to capture and destroy Kumasi, the Ashanti capital. Wolseley's entire force was assembled in January 1874 and consisted of the European Brigade (1st Battalion, Black Watch; 2nd Battalion, Rifle Brigade; and 2nd Battalion, Royal Welch Fusiliers), commanded by Brigadier General (later General) Sir Archibald Alison; the 1st and 2nd West Indian Regiments (although the former remained in support at Cape Coast); a 250-man naval brigade; and native regiments commanded by Lieutenant Colonel (later Field Marshal Sir) (Henry) Evelyn M. Wood and Major (later General Sir) Baker Russell. There were also Royal Artillery, Royal Engineer, and Royal Marine detachments.

The British force assembled at Prasu, a village on the Pra River about 70 miles south of Kumasi. Alison's brigade crossed into Ashantiland on 20 January 1874. Wolseley's force continued to follow the jungle track to Kumasi, pausing at Fomena four days later to establish a supply depot and treat soldiers ill with malaria. At the same time Wolseley sent an ultimatum to the *asantehene*, Kofi Karikari, stating that he would march on and destroy Kumasi if the Ashanti did not agree to end the war. The Ashanti built up their force during the delay. The British skirmished with the Ashanti on 26 and 29 January, unaware of being lured farther into the jungle.

On 30 January 1874, Wolseley's force entered the village of Egginassie. His intelligence had revealed that the Ashanti would make a stand at Amoaful, the next village on the path to Kumasi. This information was confirmed when patrolling British scouts heard war drums and other signs of Ashanti activity, and observed a large Ashanti encampment between Egginassie and Amoaful. These signs convinced Wolseley that a battle was imminent.

From Egginassie, the road to Amoaful generally followed the course of a stream that meandered through a defile for about 500 yards, then through a swampy area before rising to an escarpment. The terrain, coupled with nearly impenetrable jungle vegetation, made this a very difficult area in which to fight, maneuver, and communicate.

Early on 31 January 1874, the British force marched in column along the path to Amoaful. Wolseley's plan was that once contact was made with the Ashanti, his force would deploy into a large hollow square. After British scouts in the vanguard were ambushed at about 8:15 A.M., the British formed their large hollow square. The Black Watch, with two 7-pounder artillery pieces in the center and two rockets at each end, formed the front, which was commanded by Alison and extended about 300 yards on each side of the jungle road. The engineers and laborers helped clear the way for the lateral movement of the extending front. Each flank column was to cut a diagonal path outward, then march parallel to the main track while maintaining contact with the Black Watch. The left flank consisted of half the naval brigade and Baker Russell's native regiment, with the right flank composed of the other half of the naval brigade and Wood's unit. Wolseley and his staff, with a company of Fusiliers, were in the center of the square, which was closed in the rear by the Rifle Brigade.

Alison immediately passed two Black Watch companies through the scouts, who engaged the Ashanti. In the dense jungle Ashanti fire began to take its toll, although the disciplined rifle fire of the Black Watch, coupled with the withering artillery fire, began to push back the Ashanti. Alison, with five Black Watch companies in skirmishing order, directed the pipers to play "The Campbells Are Coming" and the regiment to charge. The stunned Ashanti retreated in the face of the British onslaught, and by 11:30 A.M., the village of Amoaful was in British hands.

In the dense undergrowth and under direct attack, however, the British flank elements had problems keeping up with the Black Watch. The situation was difficult, but Wolseley calmly received his subordinates' reports and skillfully and decisively sent five of the Rifle Brigade's eight reserve companies to fill gaps in the square. While the British attack was progressing, Ashanti were able to pass around the British flanks and attack Quarman, about 2 miles in the rear. Royal Engineers steadfastly defended their position there until relieved by the Rifle Brigade.

Alison's soldiers, supported by the artillery, were able to seize the high ground to their front. At about 1:30 P.M., Wolseley ordered Wood's regiment to clear and occupy the ridge to the right of the Black Watch. At about the same time, the left flank column eliminated all Ashanti resistance in its area before rejoining the main jungle track. Even though there was desultory firing later that night and the next day, as well as another engagement at Ordahsu on 3 February 1874, the Battle of Amoaful was decisive and paved the way for the British capture of Kumasi and clear-cut victory in the campaign shortly thereafter.

British casualties were surprisingly low, probably because the Ashanti were firing muskets, not rifles, and using slugs as ammunition. The British sustained 1 officer killed and 21 wounded; 2 British soldiers were killed and 144 wounded; and among the African soldiers, 1 was killed and 29 wounded. At least 150, and perhaps as many as 2,000, of the estimated 15,000 to 20,000 Ashanti fighting in the battle were killed.

Wolseley later described the Battle of Amoaful as "a brilliant affair" (Kochanski 1999, p. 70).

See also Alison, General Sir Archibald; Ashanti; Ashanti War, Second (1873–1874); Kofi Karikari; Rockets; Wolseley, Field Marshal Garnet J.; Wood, Field Marshal Sir (Henry) Evelyn M., V.C.

References: Brackenbury (1874); Callwell (1896); Keegan (1967); Kochanski (1999); Lehmann (1964); Lloyd (1964); Maxwell (1985)

Animals, Transport

The British Army used hundreds of thousands of transport animals during this period, including horses, mules, oxen, elephants, and camels, for hauling artillery and supplies and providing mounts for the cavalry.

The advent of the railroad in 1830 only partially eliminated the need for transport animals in the British Army, and then only in Great Britain and a few industrialized nations.

In 1815, the Royal Artillery had 14,000 horses, and in 1831, only 600. By 1850, British artillery horse teams had become standardized so that twelve horses pulled the 18-

pounder gun; eight horses pulled the 9-pounder, 24-pounder, and 32-pounder howitzer; and six the 7-pounder gun and 12-pounder howitzer.

In India, the bullock was harnessed in pairs and used to pull artillery and other transport. In 1859, as many as twenty pairs of bullocks were used to pull a 24-pounder siege gun. Elephants, considered very intelligent and capable, were also used to draw artillery pieces. Since they were easily frightened, their loads were transferred to bullocks near the noisy battle areas. Pack mules, beginning in about 1850, carried the guns and equipment of mountain batteries. Occasionally, mules and camels were used to pull other artillery and supply carts in India.

During the Crimean War (1854–1856), for example, it was alleged that 90 percent of all supply difficulties resulted from transport shortages. Plans were made to relieve the besieged Turkish garrison at Silistria but only 5,000 of the needed 14,000 packhorses and mules could be collected. After the allied forces landed in the Crimea in September 1854, transport officers were able to purchase only 67 camels, 253 horses, and 350 wagons to provide supplies to about 27,000 British soldiers and the Light Brigade's horses.

By the late 1870s, each infantry battalion required 18 wagons to carry its equipment, tents, ammunition, and other supplies. Transport was a key factor in the British invasion of Zululand in 1879, before which about 10,000 oxen and 400 mules were collected to pull 56 carts and 977 wagons.

The greatest single example of the use of camels was during the 1884–1885 Gordon Relief Expedition in the Sudan. A Camel Corps of about 1,500 officers and other ranks, 90 horses, and 2,200 camels was formed. The average weight each camel carried, including rider, was about 340 pounds. The camels consumed little food and water and were the only transport animals able to traverse the hot desert.

The lines of communication in South Africa, for troop movement and resupply, were especially long. The British Army Remount Department supplied about 520,000 horses and 150,000 mules to its forces during the Second Boer War, of which about 400,346 (including donkeys) died.

Institutional changes in the British Army assisted in the care of transport and other animals. The Army Veterinary Department was formed, and in 1880 the Army Veterinary School was established, which had a tremendous impact on the care and management of army horses. Prior to the establishment of the Army Remount Department in 1887, the commanders of artillery and cavalry units purchased their own horses. After 1887, uniform standards and prices were established by the Army Remount Department, which then purchased all horses (approximately 2,200 per year) for the home army.

See also Army Service Corps; Artillery, British Army—Organization; Boer War, Second (1899–1902); Crimean War; Gordon Relief Expedition; Indian Army Operations; Land Transport Corps; Lines of Communication; Tirah Field Force; Zulu War

References: Belfield (1975); Duxbury (1968); Featherstone (1978); Gleichen (1888); Pakenham (1979); Royle (2000); Sweetman (1984); Tylden (1968)

Arabi Pasha, Ahmed (c. 1840–1911)

Ahmed Arabi Pasha was a charismatic Egyptian Army officer and an ardent nationalist leader who repeatedly challenged the authority of the khedive (viceroy) of Egypt by threatening a military coup. Eventually Arabi became the war minister but was dismissed; with the army in open defiance, he was reinstated by an increasingly impotent khedive. Arabi's actions eventually resulted in confrontation with the British and the defeat of the Egyptian Army.

Sayed Ahmed Bey Arabi—Arabi Pasha—born around 1840, claimed to be descended from Hussein, the grandson of the Prophet Mohammed. The son of a small village sheikh, Arabi was conscripted into the Egyptian Army at age fourteen. Tall, intelligent, and hardworking, he caught the attention of his superiors. Three years later, Arabi was commissioned a lieutenant. Soon he became an aide-de-camp to the progressive ruler Mohammed Ali and was promoted to lieutenant colonel within three years.

After Ismail became khedive in 1863, Arabi fell out of favor and his once-promising military career stagnated. His personal discontent increased, especially during the debacle of the Egyptian Army's invasion of Abyssinia (1875–1876). The British persuaded the Ottoman sultan to depose Ismail and replace him with Tewfik, Ismail's son.

Loss of sovereignty, indebtedness, and related issues were keenly felt by many Egyptians. Arabi became a leader of the nationalists who were trying to overthrow foreign domination. On 1 February 1881, and again on 9 September, Arabi and other colonels used the threat of a coup by their troops to issue ultimatums to Tewfik for government and military reforms. On both occasions, the khedive gave in to Arabi's demands.

In February 1882, Arabi became the war minister. The British and French sent a joint naval squadron that arrived at Alexandria late in May 1882, and demanded the dismissal of Arabi. The khedive consented and his entire government resigned in protest. The Egyptian Army was in open defiance and the country was in chaos. Arabi was reinstated as war minister. Riots erupted in the afternoon of 11 June 1882 in Alexandria; over fifty Europeans were killed and many more injured, including the British consul.

British ships bombarded the Egyptian fortifications at Alexandria on 11 July 1882, the same day Arabi was appointed commander in chief. Later in July, the British sent an expeditionary force to Egypt, under the command of General (later Field Marshal Viscount) Sir Garnet J. Wolseley. The force began to disembark at Alexandria on 12 August 1882, but after a ruse, the British troops reembarked. After the British secured the Suez Canal, the troops landed at Ismailia.

Arabi seems to have eventually ascertained Wolseley's actual plan. After moving to the main Egyptian Army camp at Tel el-Kebir, Arabi attacked the British at Kassassin on 9 September 1882 and was strongly repulsed. Arabi commanded the Egyptian forces at Tel el-Kebir and was decisively defeated by the British on 13 September. After the British crushed the Egyptian Army, they hurriedly advanced to Cairo, hoping to prevent a rumored burning of the city.

When the British arrived in Cairo on 14 September 1882, they learned that Arabi was in his house there. Later that evening, Arabi and other senior Egyptian Army officers surrendered their swords, and with the arrival of Wolseley in Cairo the following day, Arabi's rebellion came to an end.

In December 1882, Arabi was brought and charged with rebellion before an Egyptian military court. He pleaded guilty and was sentenced to death. The British Government, concerned about further unrest if Arabi was executed and made a martyr, recommended leniency. The khedive commuted Arabi's sentence to "perpetual exile." Arabi was transported to Ceylon, and in 1901 he was permitted to return to Egypt, where he died in 1911.

See also Alexandria, Bombardment of; Arabi Rebellion; Egypt; Egyptian Army; Imperialism; Tel el-Kebir, Battle of; Wolseley, Field Marshal Garnet J.

References: Barthorp (1984); Farwell (1972); Featherstone (1989); Haythornthwaite (1995); Lehmann (1964); Maurice (1887); Raugh (2001b)

Arabi Rebellion (1882)

The Arabi Rebellion of 1882 was a nationalistic and military revolt, led by Egyptian Army Colonel Ahmed Arabi Pasha, against British and French domination of the internal and financial affairs of Egypt. To bolster the Egyptian khedive's (viceroy's) authority, protect Europeans living in Egypt, and ensure the control of the Suez Canal, the British sent an expeditionary force to Egypt that soundly defeated the nationalists in a short, decisive campaign. This victory paved the way for the British occupation of Egypt.

British strategic interest focused on Egypt with the opening of the Suez Canal in 1869, which dramatically reduced the sailing distances and times from England to India and elsewhere. The British were initially concerned that the Suez Canal was controlled by the Khedive Ismail and the French, the latter influencing the Suez Canal Company. By 1875, the profligate khedive was in serious financial difficulties and was forced to sell his shares in the Suez Canal Company to pay his creditors. Realizing the strategic importance of the canal, and with four-fifths of all shipping through it sailing under the British flag, British Prime Minister Benjamin Disraeli raised the money and purchased the khedive's outstanding shares. For £4 million, the British acquired a controlling interest in the Suez Canal.

Ismail's indebtedness continued to grow, a situation made worse by the Egyptian Army's debacle during its invasion of Abyssinia in 1875–1876. Egypt could not even pay the interest on its foreign debt. The British were concerned about their financial stake in Egypt and the Suez Canal, the strategic importance of the latter increasing with the Russian victory in the 1877–1878 Russo-Turkish War and Russian expansion in Central Asia. The British and French imposed a system of "dual control" over Egyptian finances, an arrangement that expanded into the other Egyptian ministries by 1878. In addition, this indebtedness forced an 80 percent reduction in the strength of the Egyptian Army. The British and French persuaded the Ottoman sultan to depose the obstructionist Ismail in favor of his more pliable son, Tewfik, in 1879. Egyptians' distress over loss of sovereignty was exacerbated by heavy taxation, religious fundamentalism, and ethnic friction in the military.

Arabi, personally disgruntled about his stagnated career and concerned about the perceived emasculation of Egypt, became a leader of nationalists who were trying to overthrow foreign domination. On 1 February 1881, Arabi and two other colonels used the strength of and threat of insur-

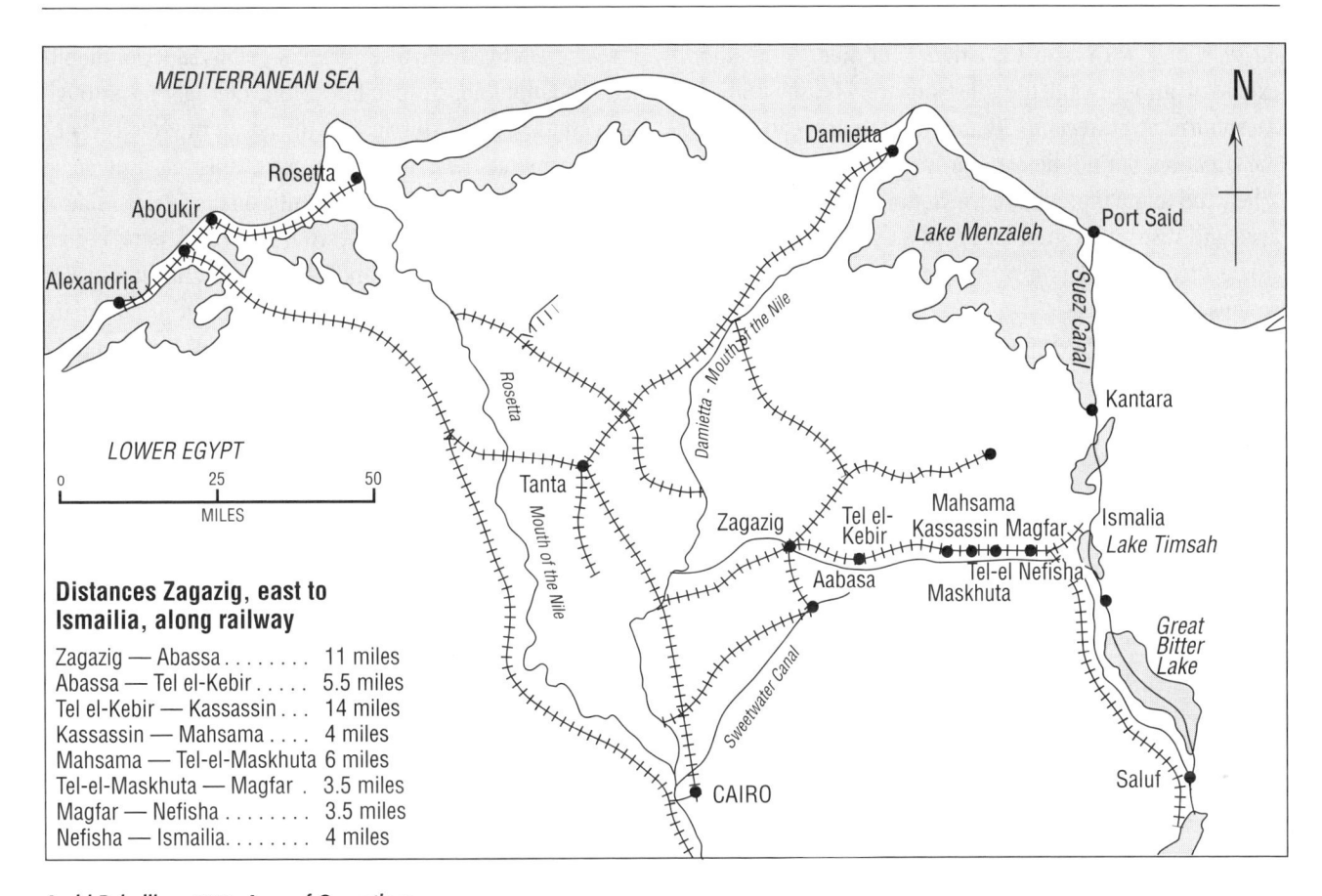

Arabi Rebellion, 1882: Area of Operations

Distances Zagazig, east to Ismailia, along railway

Zagazig — Abassa	11 miles
Abassa — Tel el-Kebir	5.5 miles
Tel el-Kebir — Kassassin	14 miles
Kassassin — Mahsama	4 miles
Mahsama — Tel-el-Maskhuta	6 miles
Tel-el-Maskhuta — Magfar	3.5 miles
Magfar — Nefisha	3.5 miles
Nefisha — Ismailia	4 miles

rection by their troops to demand the ouster of the war minister from Tewfik. The khedive acquiesced to Arabi's demands. This incident demonstrated the weakness of the khedive, and when it became known that the French agent may have been in collusion with the colonels, the khedive pressured the French government to recall its representative.

On 9 September 1881, Arabi again used the threat of military interference to confront the khedive and demand the dismissal of his entire ministry, government reform, and an increase in military strength and expenditures. The khedive, intimidated by the military's bayonets, yielded to Arabi's demands. Arabi's reputation and prestige as a fearless nationalist leader rose and spread throughout the country.

To alleviate Egyptian concerns, the British, who were not averse to the gradual development of a democratic system of government, declared they had "no other aim than the prosperity of the country and its full enjoyment of that liberty which it has obtained from the Sultan" (Barthorp 1984, p. 29). To further reinforce the khedive's authority, the British and French signed an agreement, the Joint Anglo-French Note, published in Egypt on 8 January 1882.

Instead of placating the Egyptians, the note enraged the nationalists. The following month, a new government took power with Arabi as war minister. Internecine tension and intrigue spread in the Egyptian Army to such an extent that the public safety of the country, as well as the 90,000 Europeans living there, was threatened. To support the khedive and protect the Europeans living in Egypt, the British and French dispatched a joint naval squadron that arrived at Alexandria on 20 May 1882.

Five days later, British and French agents demanded the dismissal of Arabi. The khedive consented and his entire government resigned in protest. With the army in open defiance, Arabi threatened the khedive with being deposed (or worse), unless he was reinstated as war minister. The khedive consented, and the nationalists saw in Arabi's victory the imminent expulsion of all foreigners and their influence from Egypt. Egyptian nationalism grew in popularity, along with anti-Christian sentiment, and soon exploded in a riot on the afternoon of 11 June 1882 in Alexandria. Arabi eventually ordered the army to restore the situation, but not before over fifty Europeans had been killed and many more injured, including the British consul. Fear and discontent grew in Egypt as soldiers, fearing an Anglo-French attack or invasion, reinforced seaward fortifications at Alexandria.

The Gladstone government considered the possibility of intervention and began to draw up contingency plans to send an expeditionary force to Egypt, initially hoping it would only have to protect the Suez Canal. Secret orders were issued to send two infantry battalions and an engineer company, under the command of Major General (later General) Sir Archibald Alison, from Malta to Cyprus to be prepared to assist the Royal Navy.

The Egyptians continued to work feverishly on their fortifications at Alexandria. The British naval commander, Admiral Sir Beauchamp Seymour, issued an ultimatum to the Egyptians on 10 July 1882 to surrender the forts or face bombardment within twenty-four hours. That night, the French ships, unwilling to become involved in hostilities, sailed away. The following morning Seymour's eight battleships and eleven gunboats began their bombardment, and by nightfall, the Egyptian forts had been silenced. Arabi, who had been named Egyptian commander in chief on 11 July 1882, withdrew his troops inland the following day. The British sent landing parties, reinforced later by Alison's troops, into Alexandria to restore order and prepare to defend the city.

The British began to assemble a powerful force of about 16,400 soldiers from Britain, 7,600 from Mediterranean garrisons, and almost 7,000 from India under the command of General (later Field Marshal Viscount) Sir Garnet J. Wolseley, who had been serving as adjutant-general at the War Office. His chief of staff was Lieutenant General (later General) Sir John M. Adye. On 27 July 1882, the House of Commons approved funding for the expedition, and three days later, the force began to sail from England to Egypt. The force began to disembark at Alexandria on 12 August 1882, and Wolseley arrived on 15 August.

Wolseley's objectives were to seize the Suez Canal to ensure free passage, destroy Arabi's army, and capture Cairo, the Egyptian capital. In order to seize the Suez Canal, before Arabi could shift his troops from Alexandria to defend the canal or block it, and then swiftly capture Cairo, Wolseley knew he would have to take advantage of his superior mobility and amphibious capabilities. To avoid fighting through the countless flooded irrigation ditches of the Nile Delta or the treacherous desert west of Cairo, Wolseley decided to shift his base of operations to Ismailia on the western side of the Suez Canal and attack westward to Cairo, parallel to a railway and the all-important Sweetwater Canal. It was also the shortest overland route to Cairo as well as the main Egyptian camp at Tel el-Kebir. On his first day in Alexandria, Wolseley coordinated the campaign plan with Seymour.

In order to deceive Arabi about British intentions, Wolseley devised a cover plan for the British to conduct a coordinated ground and naval attack on the Egyptian forts at Aboukir Bay, about 30 miles east of Alexandria. Wolseley issued guidance to Lieutenant General Sir Edward Hamley, commanding the 2nd Division, to develop a plan for his division to move overland from Alexandria and attack in conjunction with troops reportedly scheduled to disembark and attack at Aboukir Bay.

Wolseley planned and implemented a ruse to reinforce the idea that he was going to attack at Aboukir Bay. On 18 August 1882, British troops reembarked on transport ships, apparently bound for the assault on the Aboukir forts. At noon the following day, the powerful British fleet sailed east to Aboukir Bay. The British fleet anchored in Aboukir Bay, its purported destination, four hours later. The British warships appeared to prepare for action, and the Egyptian gunners stood by in anticipation of a heavy naval bombardment. At nightfall on 19 August 1882, the two small craft from the British fleet approached the shore and opened fire, giving the impression of a major bombardment. The naval firing was in fact a subterfuge, as the fleet, under cover of darkness and while seemingly engaged in a naval bombardment, weighed anchor and sailed further to the east. The stunned Egyptians at Aboukir woke up the following day to see that the British armada had disappeared. The British ships arrived at Port Said, at the northern entrance to the Suez Canal, after sunrise on 20 August. By that time, British naval forces had secured the entire length and key points of the Suez Canal.

As soon as Wolseley arrived at Ismailia the following day, he began preparations for the final advance on Cairo. Pushing out from Ismailia, Wolseley's units had a number of skirmishes (at Magfar on 24 August 1882, and at Kassassin two days later, where an Egyptian counterattack was repulsed on 9 September) before Hamley and his division rejoined the main force at Ismailia on 1 September 1882. It took the British forces over a week to inch their way to the outskirts of the heavily fortified Egyptian camp at Tel el-Kebir. Wolseley determined that the best course of action was to assault the Egyptian position at dawn after an almost unprecedented large-scale night march. After sunset on 12 September 1882, the British marched silently to assembly areas. At 1:00 A.M. on 13 September, the British troops began their stealthy march across the trackless desert. Shortly before dawn, the British force assaulted Arabi's fortifications. After fierce, often hand-to-hand fighting, the British soundly defeated the Egyptians in thirty-five minutes. This led to the collapse of the Arabi Rebellion.

A rapid pursuit of the vanquished enemy followed. Arabi surrendered on the night of 14 September 1882, and Wolseley entered Cairo the following day. The war was over on 15 September 1882.

See also Adye, General Sir John M.; Alison, General Sir Archibald; Arabi Pasha, Ahmed; Disraeli, Benjamin; Egypt; Egyptian Army; Gladstone, William E.; Great Game; Hamley, Lieutenant General Sir Edward B.; Imperialism; Suez Canal; Tel el-Kebir, Battle of; Wolseley, Field Marshal Garnet J.

References: Adye (1895); Adye (1925); Barthorp (1984); Bond (1960); Farwell (1972); Haythornthwaite (1995); Lehmann (1964); Low (1883); Maurice (1887); Raugh (2001b); Smith (1987)

Armstrong Rifled Breechloader
See Artillery, British Army—Weapons and Equipment

Army Act (1881)
See Discipline and Justice, British Army

Army and Society

The British Army existed on the fringes of British society, especially early in the period 1815–1914. Although it gained greater public attention and appreciation as social reforms were conducted and literacy was enhanced, the army was perceived more as the instrument of an increasingly successful imperialistic policy. Many Britons were ignorant of the army way of life and took little interest in it.

The social composition of the British Army remained relatively constant throughout this period, and the British Army remained a microcosm of the larger British society and reflected its class structure.

The financially exclusive aristocracy and landed gentry provided the backbone of the British Army officer corps. They were generally motivated by the ideal of service, honor, and prestige. As members of the "leisured class," the aristocrats and landed gentry were society's natural leaders and considered themselves duty-bound to protect the lower strata of the population. Moreover, since officers were generally required to purchase their initial commissions and subsequent promotions up to the rank of lieutenant colonel, only the wealthy were able to become officers.

The socioeconomic background of British Army officers during this period can be stated in general terms. Of the officers, 21 percent came from the aristocracy, 32 percent from the landed gentry, and 47 percent from the middle class in 1830. The percentage of aristocratic officers decreased slightly to 18 percent of the total by 1875, at which time 32 percent again came from the landed gentry and 50 percent from the middle class. In 1912, 9 percent of the officers came from the aristocracy, 32 percent from the landed gentry, and 59 percent from the middle class. The middle-class officers frequently came from the yeomen, who owned 100 to 3,000 acres of land, or the small proprietors, who owned between 1 and 100 acres. These two groups formed a considerable part of the landed interests.

The rank and file of the British Army were frequently called the "scum of the earth" (Blanco 1965, p. 126) by Field Marshal Arthur Wellesley, First Duke of Wellington. The enlisted men of the British Army came from the lowest segment of British society, generally forced into the army by starvation, unemployment, poverty, boredom, and problems with the law. Potential recruits were frequently plied with alcohol and given a small cash bounty, in addition to promises of high pay, bonuses, excellent living conditions, promotion possibilities, and adventure. British soldiers, misfits from society, were generally treated in a degrading and humiliating manner, with strict discipline, low pay, inadequate food, and unhealthy barracks. The living and service conditions of the rank and file improved steadily after the mid-nineteenth century.

The occupations of soldiers prior to enlistment help show their social status and the overall composition of the army. On 1 January 1860, there were 202,508 enlisted men serving in the British Army. Of this number, 36.7 percent had been industrial workers, 15.5 percent rural workers,

14.8 percent semiskilled tradesmen, 13.1 percent artisans, 6.3 percent domestic workers, 2.4 percent professional/semiprofessional, and 10.1 percent "other." Agricultural workers were often considered better recruits, due to physical superiority and better health. As Victorian society became more industrialized and urbanized, fewer recruits came from the rural areas.

The nationalities of the enlisted and noncommissioned ranks also fluctuated due to unemployment, urbanization, and other factors. In 1830 and 1840, more than half of the other ranks of the British Army came from Ireland and Scotland. Ireland provided 42.2 percent of the British Army's 42,897 soldiers in 1830. The potato famine of 1846 caused a significant decrease in Irish enlistments, a problem made worse by Irish emigration. In 1870, the percentage of Irishmen in the British Army had dropped to 27.9 percent and fell further to 15.6 percent in 1888 and 9.1 percent in 1912. Scotland provided 13,800 soldiers, or 13.6 percent of the total British Army, in 1830, a proportion that fell to 7.7 percent in 1879 and stabilized at 7.8 percent in 1912.

Numerous other changes took place in Great Britain, especially during the waning decades of the nineteenth century. Liberal movements, with increased democratization of government and enfranchisement of a larger portion of the populace, were having an effect on the composition of the British Army and its officer corps. Industrialization resulted in the creation of a new middle (and, to a degree, a new upper) class, based on monetary wealth and not the traditional symbol of wealth—land ownership. Unprecedented technological changes also sounded the death knell of the diminished landed class as the warrior class. War, instead of being the natural extension of country and agrarian pursuits, had become a sophisticated, scientific, intellectual affair demanding training, education, and marked proficiency. Competition and promotion by merit became preferred to a system based on property and patronage. These factors resulted in the abolition of purchase in 1871, when officers were no longer required to purchase their initial commissions and subsequent promotions to the rank of lieutenant colonel.

The abolition of purchase did not have an immediate impact on the composition of the British Army officer corps. For a few more decades, those who could afford to purchase their commissions were the ones who became the commissioned officers. Reform, however, accelerated at the beginning of the twentieth century. The public school middle class came to supersede the country house patricians as the dominant social group, especially as large estates were broken up. World War I—or the Great War from the British perspective—in which 42.3 percent of all British Army officers became casualties during the first year of the war, with 15.2 percent of all officers killed in action during the course of the war, marked a true watershed in the composition of the British Army officer corps.

The British Army was not an independent organization that operated in isolation, but a part of the larger parent society. The British Army's "professionalism, its administration and its political attitudes reflected the ethos of a part, if not the whole, of the society within which it operated" (Harries-Jenkins 1977, p. 280).

See also Cardwell Reforms; Officers, British Army—Social Background; Officers, British Army—Sources of Commissioning; Officers, Indian Army—Social Background; Purchase System; Rank and File, British Army—Enlistment; Rank and File, British Army—Social Background; Recruiting; Wellington, Field Marshal Arthur Wellesley, First Duke of
References: Harries-Jenkins (1977); Karsten (1983); Moyse-Bartlett (1974); Otley (1970); Razzell (1963); Skelley (1977); Spiers (1980a); Sweetman (1988a); Woodham-Smith (1953)

Army Enlistment Act (1870)
See Cardwell, Edward T.; Cardwell Reforms; Long Service; Short Service

Army Estimates

The Army Estimates, the proposed expenditures for the British Army, were prepared annually for Parliament's approval.

Until 1855, the British Army was administered under a system of "dual control." Even though the sovereign was the titular head of the army, the sovereign could no longer personally hold this position, so an army officer was appointed as commander in chief. As an integral component of a system of checks and balances, a civilian "financial officer," initially the secretary at war, was appointed and given responsibility for the Army Estimates. (The commander in chief had no authority to make policy that involved the expenditure of public funds.) This also helped divide the army's loyalties between the Crown and Parliament.

As a result of Crimean War–era military reforms, the secretary of state for war was separated from the position of secretary of state for the colonies in June 1854. The functions of the secretary at war were then performed by the secretary of state for war. The post of secretary at war was not filled after 1855 and was formally abolished in 1863. Moreover, the commander in chief became officially subordinate to the secretary of state for war in 1855. The War Office Act of 1870 created the post of financial secretary, subordinate to the secretary of state for war and responsible for the Army Estimates.

The financial secretary normally began the process of preparing the Army Estimates in November of each year. The draft budget was based on the establishment (number of soldiers) and expenditures of the previous year, and information, projections, and funding requests collected from the various departments. When the draft was completed, the secretary of state for war would negotiate with the chancellor of the exchequer. The sum granted to the War Office was usually much lower than the amount requested. The secretary of state would reduce the estimates. The estimates were divided into separate "votes," such as "stores," "supplies," and other areas that were generally fixed by Act of Parliament. Only on an exceptional basis could money be transferred from one vote to another. Only two votes, Vote 1 (number of soldiers) and Vote 12 (stores), could be readily manipulated, and the latter generally bore the brunt of any required reductions. Once reduced to the approved amount, the estimates were taken to the Treasury for approval before being submitted to Parliament in mid-March.

Military reform was conducted to streamline the organization, enhance the effectiveness and efficiency of the British Army, and save money. Secretary of State for War Edward T. Cardwell, for example, phased cost reductions over the 1869–1870 and 1870–1871 Army Estimates. Cardwell withdrew 25,709 men from colonial service, thus saving £2,330,800; slashed £641,370 from the stores vote; and reduced the size of infantry battalions to 560, later reduced to 520, other ranks. Cardwell's reductions were very popular.

By the mid-1880s, the Army Estimates totaled £16 million to £18 million annually. During the Second Boer War (1899–1902), the 1901 Army Estimates totaled £30,030,000.

See also Cardwell, Edward T.; Cardwell Reforms; Commander in Chief, British Army; Haldane, Richard B.; Horse Guards; Infantry, British Army—Organization; War Office
References: Hamer (1970); Moyse-Bartlett (1974); Partridge (1989); Spiers (1992); Sweetman (1984)

Army Ordnance Corps
See Artillery, British Army—Organization; Master-General of the Ordnance, British Army

Army Pay Corps
See Army Service Corps

Army Temperance Association
See Sports and Recreation

Army Service Corps
The horrible suffering of the troops during the Crimean War (1854–1856), especially during the harsh winter of 1854–1855, exposed tremendous shortcomings in the British Army transport and supply systems.

During the Crimean War, transport and supply responsibilities belonged to the civilian commissariat. The transport section was reorganized as the Land Transport Corps and placed under military control. This change was made permanent with the establishment of the Military Train in 1856. Supply responsibilities were partially taken out of civilian hands by an October 1858 Royal Warrant which ruled that supply was an ancillary responsibility of the army.

Further modifications were made to the supply and transport system. The officers of the Commissariat Staff Corps became the Control Department, and in 1869 the other ranks were formed into the first Army Service Corps. The officers were mainly responsible for supply and pay functions and the other ranks were organized into transport companies. By 1871, twelve transport companies, seven supply companies, and three ordnance store companies had been formed.

The Control Department was redesignated as the Commissariat and Transport Department in 1875, and after the Zulu War in 1880 it was called the Commissariat and Transport Staff. In 1881, the Army Service Corps was replaced by the Commissariat and Transport Corps. Hundreds of officers and men of the Commissariat and Transport Staff and the Commissariat and Transport Corps made significant contributions to the operations of the British expeditionary forces deployed to Egypt in 1882 and the Sudan in 1884–1885.

In the late 1880s, staff officers at the War Office were developing mobilization plans for home-based forces if required for overseas deployment. It was determined that sufficient troops could be provided to form two army corps, one cavalry division, and the lines of communication. It was obvious that the Commissariat and Transport Staff and Commissariat and Transport Corps were inadequate to support the two corps upon mobilization.

Major General (later General) Sir Redvers H. Buller, V.C., who became quartermaster-general at the War Office in October 1887, recognized these deficiencies. At the same time he deplored the continued existence of the Office of Civilian Commissary-General, and the Commissariat and Transport Staff was not fully integrated into the army. Buller saw the opportunity to fully link the responsibilities for supply and transport under military control and put officers and others ranks together in one corps. Accordingly, Buller proposed this merger, and the Army Service Corps was constituted by Royal Warrant on 11 December 1888. The Army Service Corps then offered specialized training and full career opportunities for incoming officers, whether they were newly commissioned or transferred from the combat arms. Pay, promotions, and retirement pensions were established on a scale equal to that of the Royal Engineers. Most officers initially transferred from the former Commissariat to the Army Service Corps. The new branch, however, successfully established a regimental identity and attracted members, so that the Army Service Corps numbered 4,098 officers and men by 1 October 1899.

The supply and transport system initially worked very well during the Second Boer War (1899–1902), fought on the South African veldt. Each unit and formation drew its supplies from the next higher headquarters and had its own transport. Field Marshal Lord (later Earl) Frederick S. Roberts, V.C., commander in chief, South Africa, and his chief of staff, Lieutenant General (later Field Marshal Earl) Lord Horatio H. Kitchener—both with extensive experience in colonial wars involving native troops—tried in February 1900 to "reorganize" the supply and transport system. The plan was to consolidate all supply and transport operations (except for those of the Cavalry Division and the frontline regimental transport) under centralized control. The result was a disaster. Within weeks a Boer force ambushed a 200-wagon convoy and stampeded about 3,000 grazing oxen. These wagons, with four days' rations and medicine, represented a large portion of the total transport available. Fortunately, the transport of the Cavalry Division made up for the lost wagons. The "old" supply and transport system, under the control of the Army Service Corps, was largely restored within weeks.

The Army Service Corps, as a result of its performance in and contributions to victory in World War I, was given the "Royal" appellation in 1918.

See also Animals, Transport; Boer War, Second (1899–1902); Buller, General Sir Redvers H., V.C.; Kitchener, Field Marshal Horatio H.; Land Transport Corps; Lines of Communication; Quartermaster-General, British Army; Roberts, Field Marshal Frederick S., V.C.

References: Barthorp (1987); Bennett (1997); Pakenham (1979); Powell (1994); Spiers (1992); Sweetman (1984)

"Arrow" War
See China War, Second (1856–1860)

Artillery, British Army—Organization

The Royal Regiment of Artillery was divided into two battalions, each with its own colonel-commandant and staff, in 1757. The first battalion consisted of twenty-one companies (later called batteries), and the second had twenty-two companies. The battalions, however, were basically administrative and not tactical units. Four troops of Royal Horse Artillery, designed to keep pace with and fight with the cavalry, were formed in 1793.

The main artillery unit of organization was the Royal Artillery (RA) battery and the Royal Horse Artillery (RHA) troop. Each of these normally contained six guns, four light and two heavier. RA batteries generally contained four 9-pounders and two 24-pounder howitzers. The RHA troops were normally equipped with four 6-pounders and two 12-pounder howitzers.

Each gun was drawn by a limber with three or more pairs of horses. A pair of guns and their limbers was designated a division, with three divisions—right, left, and center—to a battery or troop. A single gun and limber was called a subdivision.

The establishment of the battery or troop varied slightly, depending on the caliber of its guns. In 1854 an average battery consisted of 1 captain (commander), 1 second captain, 3 lieutenants, 1 assistant surgeon, 6 bombardiers, 2 staff sergeants, 4 corporals, 1 farrier, 6 shoeing smiths, 3 collar makers, 2 wheelwrights, 97 gunners, and 123 drivers. There were also 92 riding horses and 180 draft horses.

In 1855, during the Crimean War, the RA consisted of 12 battalions, totaling 96 batteries, and a brigade of RHA, with 7 troops and 1 rocket battery.

The master general of the ordnance commanded the Royal Artillery and the Royal Engineers until 1855, when this responsibility was transferred to the commander in chief.

Artillery organization was standardized in about 1860, and the term "troop" was replaced by "battery" for both RA and RHA units. Majors became battery commanders, and slight changes were made in unit establishments. In 1889, the terms "section" and "subsection" replaced the older terms "division" and "subdivision." At the same time, horse batteries were designated by a letter and field batteries by a number.

In 1898, shortly before the Second Boer War (1899–1902), there were 21 horse batteries, 103 planned field batteries (10 had yet to be formed), and 10 mountain batteries. During the Second Boer War, brigades of artillery, consisting of 3 batteries, were formed and supported the infantry division. Each of the 3 batteries had 6 guns (generally 15-pounders) and an ammunition column.

Field and garrison batteries were divided into the Royal Field Artillery and Royal Garrison Artillery in 1899. By 1906, there were 28 horse batteries and 150 field batteries in the British Army.

See also Animals, Transport; Artillery, British Army—Tactics; Artillery, British Army—Training; Artillery, British Army—Weapons and Equipment; Boer War, Second (1899–1902); Crimean War; Master-General of the Ordnance, British Army; Rockets

References: British Army (1855); Gordon (1971); Haythornthwaite (1995); Knight (1996); Stone and Schmidl (1988)

Artillery, British Army—Tactics

Experienced commanders frequently misunderstood the capabilities and uses of artillery and consequently limited its tactical role on the battlefield. In addition, artillery tactics during the nineteenth century failed to keep pace with technological advances in weaponry.

The primary role of artillery until the middle of the nineteenth century was to support the infantry. In the attack, artillery batteries could be positioned on the wings of the infantry where they would not disrupt the cohesion of the infantry line and at the same time protect the flanks. The split or multiple batteries forced the enemy to fire at multiple targets, while the British artillery firing could still converge on a single point. The oblique angle of firing would expose the largest portion of the enemy line to concentrated fire.

An alternate method was to mass the artillery behind the infantry and fire over their heads during the assault. One argument against this tactic was that a double target (i.e., infantry and artillery) was then vulnerable to enemy fire. In addition, some commanders were concerned that overhead fire intimidated their own troops. The allocation of two howitzers per each six-gun battery, however, encouraged such overhead firing.

In an offensive operation, massed artillery could concentrate its fire on one decisive point to breach the enemy's line and make an opening for the infantry attack. Artillery preparations in themselves were controversial in the post-Waterloo years, with some commanders believing such tactics revealed their plans to the enemy.

The field artillery, generally 6-pounders, was manned by crews generally on foot, moving at 2 miles per hour—too slow to react to sudden changes in the tactical situation. Horse artillery was considered a reserve force that moved rapidly around the battlefield as needed.

In defensive operations, it was initially not considered part of the artillery's mission to engage in counterbattery fire against the enemy's guns.

In operations in India in the 1840s, a heavy preparatory artillery bombardment was shown to minimize friendly casualties. The large-scale employment of artillery also made the battle shorter and more decisive, and limited casualties. To maximize the effects of the guns, proponents argued that they should be massed and should fire at the enemy at a range of 700–800 yards. Counterbattery fire then became an acceptable tactic. Moreover, the ratio of guns per 1,000 men in the force increased from 2 to 6.

By 1868 the Royal Artillery had adopted rifled guns. Battery commanders were authorized independent action in an 1875 artillery manual. Shortly thereafter seats were added to guns so all crew members would ride, which increased the speed of movement of the guns.

In 1883, the 12-pounder was introduced for both the Horse and Royal (Field) Artillery. By 1895 the 15-pounder, using smokeless powder, was the standard gun of the Field Artillery.

The first artillery tactical manual was issued in 1892. Four years later, *Field Artillery Drill* was published, which stated the role of the artillery was to "support other arms by fire establishing such a fire supremacy in the battle area that the enemy can neither interfere with operations nor develop his own effectively" (Marix Evans 2000, p. 10). To help in the concentration of fire during the Second Boer War, artillery divisions of three batteries each were organized. Distant to medium artillery ranges were set at 2,500 to 3,500 yards, and infantry fire at ranges over 1,000 yards was discounted. Guns were supposed to be on firm ground with a clear view of the target. When coming into action, they were to be positioned 200 yards in front of the limbers and ammunition wagons, with 20-yard intervals between guns—and well behind the attacking infantry. Indirect fire—which could exploit the potential of smokeless powder, minimize gunner exposure to rifle fire, and sustain effective concentrated fire—was not explicitly authorized. The artillery tactics employed during the Second Boer War were basically the same as those used at Waterloo: unprotected gunners fired their guns, using open sights, against a visible enemy. If the artillery failed to be positioned far enough to the rear of the friendly infantry and outside the range of enemy small arms and artillery fire, the result was frequently disaster, as happened at the Battle of Colenso, 15 December 1899.

Inadequate artillery pieces and tactics were replaced after the Second Boer War. A new quick-firing 18-pounder, with gun shields, sights, and hydraulic/spring buffer was introduced. It was originally employed in two-gun sections until battery firing was again shown to be more effective and efficient.

>   **See also** Artillery, British Army—Organization; Artillery, British Army—Training; Artillery, British Army—Weapons and Equipment; Boer War, Second (1899–1902); Colenso, Battle of; Indian Army Operations; Infantry, British Army—Tactics
>   **References:** Callwell (1896); Hall (1971); Hall (1973); Marix Evans (2000); Ramsay (2002); Spiers (1992); Strachan (1985)

Artillery, British Army–Training

Training individual artillery gunners, both officers and men, crews, and batteries, was very difficult and time-consuming and frequently limited by inadequate resources.

The artillery other ranks were generally trained at the Royal Artillery Depot at Woolwich and later in their batteries, and officers at the Royal Military Academy, Woolwich. The officers of the Royal Artillery (and Royal Engineers) were considered members of the "scientific corps," and relatively comprehensive training and proficiency were required prior to commissioning. A mid-nineteenth-century source, however, highlighted British artillery officer training shortcomings: "There is hardly an artillery in Europe officered by men of so deficient professional education as the British. Their information very seldom goes beyond the mere elements of the science of artillery, and, in practice, the handling of field-guns is as much as they understand, and that but imperfectly" (British Army 1855, p. 5).

For artillery recruits in 1834, it was calculated that a minimum of eighteen months was required to properly train a new gunner, yet the actual amount of time allotted was eight (and frequently only three) months. During the last decades of the nineteenth century, new soldiers were assigned to artillery batteries after eight weeks' basic training in drill and physical readiness. Battery officers lectured the new soldiers on the theory of artillery firing, drill at a single gun, then battery drill. Instruction was also given in methods of aiming, handling ammunition, and mounting and dismounting guns. Other training topics included loading materials, constructing gun pits, and carbine marksmanship. New soldiers were also trained to become proficient in stable work, and drivers received extensive training in riding and driving. During the winter months, drivers received additional training and gunners trained in sections. Batteries and sections generally marched to and established gun positions in the field one day a week.

During the later decades of this period, noncommissioned officers and officers frequently went to specialist courses, including those on gunnery at Shoeburyness and others.

In the 1840s and 1850s batteries were rotated through Woolwich for field training, although the demands of the Arsenal frequently required soldier labor. A shortage of horses also limited battery training. In 1848, the number of training rounds to be fired per gun per year was increased from thirty-two to eighty, although there was a shortage of suitable firing ranges at Woolwich.

Later in this period, the artillery devised and conducted an annual training plan. Training for batteries began on 1 March. To ensure all soldiers were available for training, they were exempted from all other duties for at least twelve consecutive days in 1893, which was increased to at least fourteen days in 1899. After batteries completed their drill, the three batteries of each artillery division assembled and trained in establishing firing positions, conducting ammunition resupply, and other collective tasks.

Live firing began in May at ranges at Morecombe, Glenbeigh, Hay, and Shoeburyness. Five divisions conducted their live fire training at the principal range at Okehampton, each firing about 400–500 rounds over a three-week period.

After the Second Boer War, artillery training included various target acquisition techniques to more effectively bracket and hit targets. In addition, the British artillery began to train in the use of concealment, dispersal, precision, and more complex control methods.

See also Artillery, British Army—Organization; Artillery, British Army—Tactics; Artillery, British Army—Weapons and Equipment; Infantry, British Army—Training; Woolwich, Royal Military Academy

References: British Army (1855); Spiers (1992); Stone and Schmidl (1988); Strachan (1985)

Artillery, British Army–Weapons and Equipment

As a result of technological and scientific advances, British field artillery underwent a tremendous transformation, as did small arms and other weapons, during the mid-nineteenth century.

Until the late 1850s, guns were smoothbore muzzle-loading cannons. The heavy barrel was supported on a carriage consisting of a pair of wheels and an axle, with the front end of the trail affixed to the gun, with the rear of the trail generally resting on the ground.

These cannons fired three types of ammunition: roundshot, case or canister, and common shell. The most useful and versatile projectile was roundshot, which could destroy walls and gates and was frequently deadly to close order formations in the open. Case shot or canister was especially effective against infantry or cavalry in the assault. These rounds consisted of a tin filled with cast bullets, which burst as it left the muzzle and the bullets shot out in an arc from the gun. It was most effective at close range up to about 300 yards. Common shell was fired from smaller howitzers and mortars, and contained a fuse timed to explode the shell over the target.

Royal Artillery (RA) batteries generally contained four 9-pounders and two 24-pounder howitzers. The 9-pounder gun (with a 3-pound charge) had a range of 1,400 yards. At a 4-degree barrel elevation, the 24-pounder howitzer had a range of 1,025 yards.

Royal Horse Artillery (RHA) troops were normally equipped with four 6-pounders and two 12-pounder howitzers. The 6-pounder (with a 1.5-pound charge) had a muzzle velocity of between 1,500 and 1,700 feet per second, and could fire roundshot up to 1,200 yards. The 12-pounder howitzer, at a 5-degree barrel elevation, had a range of 1,100 yards.

The Indian Mutiny (1857–1859) was the last major conflict in which smoothbore cannons were used. The Armstrong gun (developed by W. G. Armstrong), a rifled breech-loader (RBL), was developed in 1859 and first used in China in 1860. Its barrel was reinforced by shrinking wrought iron layers onto the tube. A hollow vent piece was also developed that permitted loading from the rear, or the breech. The projectile was coated with soft lead, making it slightly larger than the bore of the gun. Upon firing, the soft lead coating was compressed into the grooves of the rifled barrel. The rotating motion of the fired projectile gave it much better ballistics and a greater range. The 12-pounder RBL Armstrong was lighter than its predecessors, requiring only a six-horse team to pull it, instead of eight required of an old 9-pounder. It was reported that the 12-pounder RBL Armstrong could fire more accurately at 2 miles than a smoothbore cannon could at 0.5 miles.

Armstrong RBLs and the similar Whitworth RBLs were both used in the American Civil War (1861–1865), where many battles were fought at close range not requiring the advantages offered by these artillery pieces. For a number of reasons, including cost, simplicity, and conservatism, the British reverted to muzzle-loaders with rifled barrels. In 1871, the standard artillery pieces for RHA batteries were the 9-pounder rifled muzzle-loader (RMLs), sighted between 2,000 and 3,000 yards, and for RA batteries, the 16-pounder, sighted between 1,800 and 4,000 yards.

The British finally realized that muzzle-loading guns were outdated, and in 1885 issued the 12-pounder RBL to both field and horse artillery batteries. A lighter version was issued to RHA units in 1892, and the 12-pounder was converted to accept a 15-pounder shell for the RA. Firing case shot and the similar shrapnel with cordite (smokeless powder, replaced by lyddite in 1898), the 12-pounder (range 5,200 yards) and 15-pounder (range 5,500 yards) were the two most commonly used British guns of the Second Boer War.

After the Second Boer War, a composite gun containing the best features of all proposals submitted was developed. Containing an Armstrong wire-wound gun, a Vickers recoil system, ordnance factories, sighting and elevating equipment and ammunition-carrying system, 13-pounder and 18-pounder quick-firing guns were developed. The 18-

pounder was one of the most reliable and heavily used guns of World War I, with nearly 100 million rounds fired from the model during the war.

See also Adye, General Sir John M.; Animals, Transport; Artillery, British Army—Organization; Artillery, British Army—Tactics; Artillery, British Army—Training; Boer War, Second (1899–1902); Indian Mutiny

References: Adye (1895); Belfield (1975); Featherstone (1978); Hall (1972); Haythornthwaite (1995); Knight (1996); Spiers (1979)

Artists, War

War artists depicted colonial military campaigns and provided prints, paintings, and periodical illustrations to the British public. While plates showing military uniforms and equipment details were popular after the 1830s, painters seemingly tried to preserve the historical record (or their perception of it), and illustrators generally provided engravings and sketches to accompany newspaper and periodical articles.

Lady Elizabeth Butler (1846–1933), the wife of Lieutenant General Sir William F. Butler, specialized in oil paintings of military and equestrian subjects. She is best known for her famous quartet of paintings exhibited between 1874 and 1877: *Calling the Roll after an Engagement in the Crimea*, bought by Queen Victoria; *Quatre Bras; Balaklava;* and *The Return from Inkerman*. This was probably the high point of her career even though she was commissioned by Queen Victoria to paint *The Defence of Rorke's Drift* in 1880. To paint this depiction, Lady Butler traveled to the 24th Regiment's garrison to make sketches of the actual soldiers who had fought at Rorke's Drift reenacting the battle. Richard Caton Woodville (1856–1927) established his reputation as a war artist in the late 1870s and early 1880s. In his London studio, Woodville "drew imaginative reconstructions based in varying degrees on imagination, special artists' and others' sketches and photographs, his own observations, and information available to him in London" (Stearn 1999, p. 15). Woodville's *Maiwand: Saving the Guns* was exhibited in 1882 and impressed Queen Victoria, who commissioned him to depict additional battle scenes, including one of her son in *The Guards at Tel-el-Kebir*. A prolific painter, he also drew *The Absent-Minded Beggar* and many other romanticized military episodes that appealed to the Victorian sense of patriotism and martial superiority.

A leading artist-correspondent was Melton Prior (1845–1910), who covered numerous campaigns, including the Zulu War, campaigns in Egypt (1882) and the Sudan (1884–1885), and the Second Boer War for the *Illustrated London News*. Known for his lavish lifestyle, Prior provided firsthand, generally accurate drawings of battle scenes he had personally observed and on many occasions engaged in, rather than the sanitized and embellished "battle paintings."

Another noted war artist was Charles E. Fripp, who worked for the *Graphic* and later the *Daily Graphic*. He spent many years in South Africa and covered the Ninth Kaffir War, Zulu War, and both Boer Wars, as well as serving as "special artist" during the 1884–1885 Gordon Relief Expedition. Fripp is probably best remembered for his painting *The Last Stand at Isandhlula* [Isandlwana], which he painted on the spot, and *The Attack on General Sir John McNeil's Force Near Suakim* [Suakin] (1886).

War artists provided a valuable service for the British Army during the Victorian era. Drawers and others, especially those who actually witnessed battles, provided realistic illustrations for newspapers, indispensable until technology was developed in 1880 that permitted the mass reproduction of photographs and more accurate means of preserving history. Battle painters frequently depicted romanticized battle scenes that portrayed military courage and devotion and raised the prestige and appeal of soldiering.

See also Butler, Lieutenant General Sir William F.; Correspondents, War; Military and Popular Culture; Photographers, War

References: Droogleever (1992); Hart (1999); Haythornthwaite (1995); Stearn (1999)

Ashanti

Ashanti (or Asante) was the dominant kingdom on the Gold Coast of West Africa. It also refers to individual members of these tribes. The word "Ashanti" is derived from the phrase *osa nti*, meaning "for the sake of war." It was reportedly first used by a king of the Dankyera tribe in referring to an alliance of other tribes that was resisting his aggression. The Dankyera were defeated by a tribal alliance known as the Asante Aman Nnunu, or the Five Ashanti States, that subsequently established the Ashanti state in 1701. The dominant Ashanti tribe was Kumasi, which increased its power and size at the expense of the surrounding provinces, extending its frontier southward.

The most important symbol of the Ashanti kingdom was the "Golden Stool" *(Sika Dwa)*. At a gathering of Ashanti chiefs, Okomfo Anokye reportedly conjured the Golden Stool from the sky. He declared that the Golden Stool embodied the soul of the Ashanti nation, and that only the king of Kumasi could rule the Ashanti kingdom. In addition, if the Golden Stool was ever captured, the Ashanti kingdom would lose all its power and disintegrate into chaos.

By the beginning of the nineteenth century, the Ashanti controlled an area as large as modern-day Ghana and were challenging the Fante states for control of the coast, where Europeans had already established posts and forts for trading gold, ivory, and slaves. There was increasing friction between the Ashanti and the Fante, and the aggressive Ashanti launched successful military campaigns against the Fante in 1807, 1811, and 1816. By 1820, the Ashanti had become the strongest power in West Africa.

The Ashanti Army, at the beginning of the nineteenth century, was reputed to number 200,000 disciplined and brave warriors when fully mobilized. While the Ashanti officers were generally "aristocrats," the majority of the common soldiers were slaves. The organization and tactics of the Ashanti, reportedly modeled on ants, were highly standardized. The army, led by scouts, marched in several columns. After initial contact with an enemy was made, the scouts would withdraw. If the terrain and vegetation were open enough, the advance guard would then move forward in two or three long lines. The soldiers in the first line would reload after firing their muskets, while the next line moved forward, took their place, then fired their own muskets. The rear line would then move forward, fire, and this tactic was continually repeated until the advance was halted. Any soldier attempting to flee was whipped or slashed with a heavy sword by the "sword bearers." (Ashanti soldiers were told to memorize and repeat this saying: "If I go forward, I die; if I flee, I die; better to go forward and die in the mouth of battle" [Edgerton 1995, p. 55].) The main body of the Ashanti Army, numbering 20,000 men or more, followed the sword bearers. Equally large elements marched on the flanks of the main body, with the mission of surrounding the enemy.

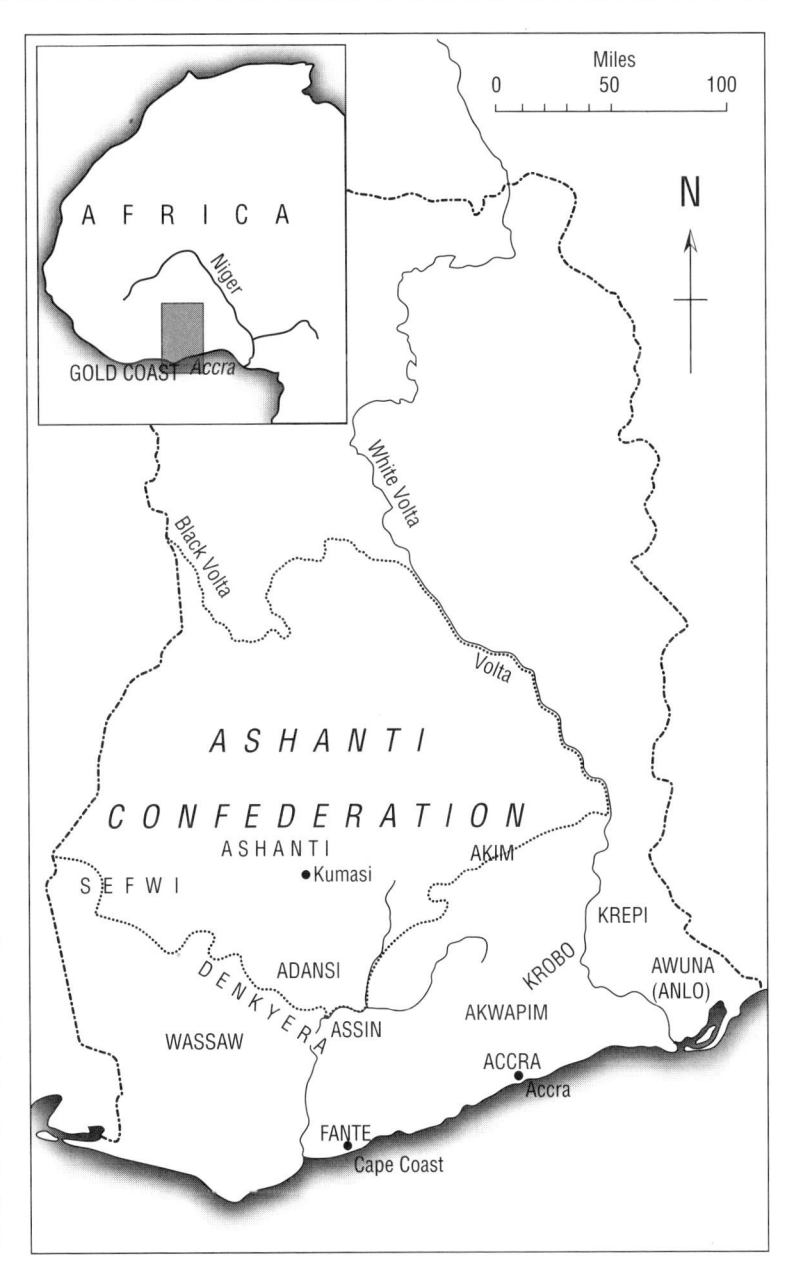

Ashantiland

The Ashanti possessed gold and were able to acquire muskets before other tribes could. These rudimentary muskets, which fired an assortment of nails and other shards, gave the Ashanti an advantage over other tribes. Prior to 1807, some soldiers carried poison arrows and javelins, and some officers carried heavy swords. The weapons and equipment of the Ashanti improved as the nineteenth century progressed.

The British Crown assumed control of the Gold Coast in 1821. The Ashanti resented British domination of the Gold Coast area because it interfered with their expansionist plans, and more significantly because the British abolition of the slave trade ruined the market for the most profitable Ashanti export. Economic and cultural friction between the Ashanti and the British ignited into open conflict in 1823–1826 (First Ashanti War), 1873–1874 (Second Ashanti War), 1895–1896 (Ashanti Expedition), and finally in 1900. The British formally annexed the Gold Coast in 1901.

See also Ashanti Expedition; Ashanti War; Ashanti War, First (1823–1826); Ashanti War, Second (1873–1874)
References: Edgerton (1995); Farwell (1972); Featherstone (1989); Haythornthwaite (1995); James (1985); Keegan (1967); Lloyd (1964)

Ashanti Expedition (1895–1896)

In the early 1890s, as European powers scrambled for imperial possessions in Africa and elsewhere, Great Britain attempted to reinforce its control and authority over the Gold Coast in West Africa. In 1894, the British requested that the Ashanti king, Prempeh (Kwaka Dua III), accept the imposition of a British protectorate and the establishment of a British resident at Kumasi, the Ashanti capital. Prempeh refused to surrender his sovereignty.

The British—fearing possible German encroachment from Togo or French expansion from the Ivory Coast—sought to justify potential military intervention and coercion by stating that the Ashanti had failed to comply with the terms of the 1874 Treaty of Fomena requiring the cessation of human sacrifice and the payment of a large indemnity. The Ashanti sent a delegation to London, which offered the British a large concession in the flourishing gold, cocoa, and rubber trade, as well as submission to the Crown. The British agreed to consider the matter, and the Ashanti returned to Kumasi believing that they had averted war. It seemed, however, that the British had already made up their mind to send a military force to the Gold Coast.

The British force, called the Ashantee Expeditionary Force, was commanded by Colonel Sir Francis Scott, a veteran of the Second Ashanti War (1873-1874). Scott's force consisted of 420 officers and men of the 2nd Battalion, West Yorkshire Regiment; a so-called Special Service Corps of 12 volunteer officers and 254 handpicked men from prestigious British Army regiments; about 1,000 Hausas (from northern Niger) and about 500 African levies led by 30 British officers; the 2nd Battalion, West India Regiment (of about 20 British officers and 380 African troops for lines of communication duties); plus support troops and over 10,000 equipment carriers. The force was armed mainly with Martini-Henry rifles, in addition to Maxim guns and newly issued 75-mm artillery pieces.

The majority of the British troops arrived at Cape Coast Castle in December 1895 and began their march inland to Kumasi shortly thereafter. Despite stockpiles of food and the use of quinine, soldiers' health was a significant concern throughout the operation. Scott's force followed the remnants of the road built to Kumasi by Major General (later Field Marshal Viscount) Sir Garnet J. Wolseley's engineers in 1874. The British soldiers did not encounter any opposition—only a group of Ashanti envoys who wanted to discuss peace—along the way.

By marching directly into Kumasi, Scott may have been trying to provoke Prempeh into resisting. The Ashanti king did not take the bait, however, and the British force marched unopposed into the Ashanti capital on 17 January 1896. The British tried to humiliate Prempeh and force him to pay an indemnity of 50,000 ounces of gold, which had been required under the Treaty of Fomena. Prempeh stated he had only 680 ounces of gold, and that he would give it all to the British. Scott and the governor, William E. Maxwell, were both infuriated. To convince the Ashanti that British authority had to be respected, the British imprisoned (and later deported) Prempeh and a large entourage to the Seychelles. Prempeh's exile also ensured that he could not, as he was entitled under international law, sign treaties with Germany or France. In 1897, Ashanti was declared a British Protectorate.

The British expeditionary force marched out of Kumasi on 22 January 1896 and arrived back at Cape Coast two weeks later. No shots had been fired, but over three-quarters of the officers and half the soldiers suffered from dysentery and malaria, despite taking quinine. Two officers, eight non-commissioned officers, and eight white soldiers died, including Prince Henry of Battenberg, Queen Victoria's son-in-law, who died during the voyage back to England.

See also Ashanti; Ashanti War, Second (1873–1874); Imperialism; Infantry, British Army—Small Arms; Lines of Communication; Machine Guns; Wolseley, Field Marshal Garnet J.

References: Edgerton (1995); Featherstone (1989); Featherstone (1992); Haythornthwaite (1995); James (1985); Jeal (1989)

Ashanti Ring

The "Ashanti Ring," which later evolved into the "Wolseley Ring," was the collective name—used either admiringly or derisively, depending on one's perspective—for a group of talented, reform-minded British Army officers originally handpicked by Major General (later Field Marshal Viscount) Sir Garnet J. Wolseley to accompany him as staff and special service officers on the 1873–1874 Ashanti campaign. Wolseley generally employed this same "Ring" of professional and battle-proven officers in his proconsular assignments and active service expeditionary force commands.

Wolseley became assistant adjutant-general at the War Office in May 1871, a period of rapid and fundamental reform of the British Army under the Liberal Secretary of State for War Edward T. Cardwell. Wolseley staunchly supported both army reform and Cardwell. In 1873, when plans were being considered to send a British expeditionary force to the Gold Coast to drive the invading Ashanti back across the Pra River to their homeland, Cardwell ensured his protégé Wolseley received the command.

On 13 August 1873, Wolseley was appointed commander of the force, over the heads of many senior, older, and more experienced officers. He departed for the Gold Coast aboard the *Ambriz* on 12 September 1873, taking 36 staff and special service officers handpicked from a list of Army volunteers. Wolseley selected these officers, the group that came to be known as the "Ashanti Ring," based on their proven qualifications, their reputations, and even their military writings.

The nucleus of the Ashanti Ring consisted of officers who had served under Wolseley and "proven" themselves during the 1870 Red River Expedition in Canada. The first was Lieutenant Colonel (later General Sir) John McNeill, V.C., as chief of staff, the same position he had held under Wolseley in 1870. Captain (later General Sir) Redvers H. Buller and Captain G. L. Huyshe, both Red River veterans who were given special permission to depart the Staff College course prior to completion, served as deputy assistant adjutant and quartermaster-generals in the Ashanti expedition. (Huyshe died of fever near Fomena in late January 1874.) Two other Red River participants, Captain (later Lieutenant General Sir) William F. Butler and Captain (later General Sir) Hugh McCalmont, served in Ashantiland as, respectively, a native force commander and aide-de-camp.

There were a number of other members of the Ashanti Ring. Lieutenant Colonel (later Field Marshal Sir) (Henry) Evelyn M. Wood, Major (later General Sir) Baker Russell, and Lieutenant Lord Gifford all appealed to Wolseley because of their reputations for bravery. During the Second Ashanti War, Wood and Russell raised and led irregular regiments, and Gifford won the Victoria Cross during the fighting for Amoaful. Other officers had already distinguished themselves by their insightful military writing. Captain (later General Sir) Henry Brackenbury, who was serving as professor of military science at Woolwich, served as Wolseley's military secretary. An instructor of tactics at Sandhurst who had defeated Wolseley in the 1872 Wellington Prize Essay competition was Lieutenant (later Major General Sir) (John) Frederick Maurice, who served as Wolseley's private secretary.

Joining the campaign in progress was Colonel (later General Sir) George R. Greaves, who took over as chief of staff after McNeill was severely wounded in a skirmish on 14 October 1873, and Lieutenant Colonel (later Major General Sir) George (Pomeroy-) Colley. The latter, who had served with Wolseley at the War Office on the Cardwell Reforms, was considered the most "brilliant" of the Ring. He voluntarily left his professorship at the Staff College to serve in Ashantiland, assuming all force transportation responsibilities on 22 December 1873.

The creation of the Ashanti Ring was a controversial result of the highly successful Second Ashanti War. Wolseley conscientiously tried to employ Staff College graduates, such as Colley, Wood, Buller, and Maurice, whenever possible. Wolseley observed later, "I do not believe that any general ever left England with an abler or more daring body of assistants" (Bond 1972, p. 128).

After the Second Ashanti War, the Wolseley Ring continued. Wolseley employed a large number of its members on his staff in Natal in 1875 and on Cyprus in 1878–1879. Many members of the Ring returned to active service when Wolseley became the commander during the closing stages of the Zulu War in 1879 and during the Sekukuni campaign later that year. Wolseley served as commander of the British expeditionary force sent to quell the Arabi Rebellion in Egypt in 1882, and attempted to muster his circle of loyal acolytes. By that time, however, Pomeroy-Colley was dead (killed in action against the Boers at Majuba Hill in 1881), and Wolseley's senior subordinates—Buller, Brackenbury, Wood, and Butler—had achieved relatively high rank that would make them difficult to employ in a small expeditionary force. Moreover, in such a select group of talented and ambitious officers, jealousy, rivalry, hubris, and other factors resulted in friction and an occasional lack of cooperation. The problems Wolseley encountered with his Ring in 1882 were even worse during the unsuccessful 1884–1885 Gordon Relief Expedition in the Sudan, Wolseley's last command in the field.

In the early 1870s, the British failure to create a General Staff, coupled with the abolition of the purchase system, made the establishment of the Ashanti Ring (and its continuation thereafter as the Wolseley Ring), as well as the creation of rival "rings," arguably inevitable. Factionalism, intrigue, and unhealthy competition frequently resulted, to the detriment of efficiency and esprit de corps within the British Army officer corps. Conservative and traditionalist officers tended to gather around Field Marshal H.R.H. Prince George F., Second Duke of Cambridge, commander in chief of the British Army. While members of the Wolseley Ring were also occasionally called the "Africans," because of their campaigns in Ashantiland, Zululand, Egypt, and the Sudan, another competing ring became known as the "Indians," or the "Roberts Ring," generally represented by General (later Field Marshal Earl) Sir Frederick S. Roberts, V.C. A significant difference between the Africans and the Indians was the strategic priorities of the British Empire. In any event, beginning with the Second Ashanti War, the Wolseley Ring was the dominant clique in the British Army, in the field and at the War Office, for the remainder of the nineteenth century.

These officers—McNeill, Buller, Huyshe, Butler, McCalmont, Wood, Baker Russell, Gifford, Brackenbury, Maurice, Greaves, and Colley—were the primary members of the Ashanti Ring and the beneficiaries of Wolseley's patronage. Wolseley knew that surrounding himself with the most professional, dedicated, loyal, and courageous officers available would increase the chance of success for his force, and for himself. Such a small circle of subordinates generated considerable resentment and criticism; one contemporary critic complained that Wolseley was "using the finest steel of our army to cut brushwood" (Lehmann 1964, p. 166). Wolseley was convinced that "he could not have done the work with the very ordinary humdrum men usually told off from a Horse Guards register, and that the claims of seniors should never be allowed to interfere with selection of the best officers in the army for all the little campaigns we so often have to carry out" (Maxwell 1985, p. 15).

See also Arabi Rebellion; Ashanti War, Second (1873–1874); Brackenbury, General Sir Henry; Buller, General Sir Redvers H., V.C.; Butler, Lieutenant General Sir William F.; Camberley, Staff College; Cambridge, Field Marshal H.R.H. Prince George F., Second Duke of; Commander in Chief, British Army; Gordon Relief Expedition; Greaves, General Sir George R.; Maurice, Major General Sir (John) Frederick; McNeill, General Sir John C., V.C.; Pomeroy-Colley, Major General Sir George; Purchase System; Red River Expedition; Roberts, Field Marshal Frederick S., V.C.; Wolseley, Field Marshal Garnet J.; Wood, Field Marshal Sir (Henry) Evelyn M., V.C.

References: Adye (1925); Beckett (1992); Bond (1972); Keegan (1967); Kochanski (1999); Lehmann (1964); Lloyd (1964); Maurice and Arthur (1924); Maxwell (1985)

Ashanti War (1900)

The Ashanti King Prempeh (Kwaka Dua III) was deposed and exiled by the British in 1896, and a British resident was established in the Ashanti capital, Kumasi, to administer Ashantiland. The Ashanti resented the fact that no king had been selected to replace Prempeh, that the sovereignty of the Ashanti nation had been lost, and that they were being pressed by the British into road building and other construction projects.

In 1899, the governor of the Gold Coast, Sir Frederick Hodgson, sought to locate the Ashanti's Golden Stool. Hodgson thought the Golden Stool was little more than a symbol of Ashanti sovereignty, like a throne, crown, or flag, and he thought its seizure would be similar to forcing Ashanti submission to British rule. The governor failed to comprehend that the Golden Stool was the Ashantis' most powerful religious, spiritual, and mystical symbol, embodying their souls and linking them to their ancestors.

Hodgson traveled to Kumasi to meet with the Ashanti chiefs on 28 March 1900. After arrogantly confirming British control of Ashantiland, he demanded to know not only the location of the Golden Stool but also why he was not sitting on it. Hodgson's confrontational and sacrilegious speech angered the Ashanti headmen, who met that night. Inspired by the compassionate goading of the queen mother of the Edweso, Yaa Asantewaa, the Ashanti leaders decided to rebel against the British.

The dissident Ashanti besieged Hodgson and others in

the British fort at Kumasi. In April and May 1900, Hodgson received about 600 reinforcements from the Gold Coast and Lagos. Shortly thereafter, with supplies low and disease rife, Hodgson and about 600 men broke out from the fort. They escaped south, reaching Cape Coast Castle on 10 July 1900, having lost 2 officers and 39 Hausa dead, and many wounded and missing, during their escape.

The demands of both the ongoing Second Boer War in South Africa and the Boxer Rebellion in China precluded reinforcements from being sent to the Gold Coast. A force of local units (the West African Regiment; the Nigeria and Gold Coast Regiments of the West African Field Force; the 1st Central African Battalion, King's African Rifles; Sierra Leone Frontier Police; and elements of the 1st and 2nd West India Regiments), totaling about 1,000 men with six artillery pieces and six Maxim machine guns, was organized by Colonel James Willcocks. This force fought its way to Kumasi, finally charging with fixed bayonets, and relieved the beleaguered garrison on 15 July 1900.

Willcocks established a supply base at nearby Bekwai. His next objective was to find and destroy dissident Ashanti forces and punish those tribes that had cooperated with them. After recruiting local levies and increasing his force to 3,500 men, Willcocks's columns attacked and defeated Ashanti at Kokofu and Dompoase. The force then returned to Kumasi to destroy the numerous stockades encircling the city and blocking the roads entering it. By early September 1900, Kumasi had been pacified, although much of the surrounding countryside remained rebellious.

Willcocks sent out flying columns to conduct a scorched-earth policy of burning villages, destroying crops, and seizing weapons to persuade the Ashanti that further resistance was futile. On 30 September 1900, the British attacked a large Ashanti force at Obassa. These Ashanti soldiers were more resolute than usual, remaining steadfast after two British bayonet assaults and in the face of withering machine-gun fire. After ferocious hand-to-hand fighting, the Ashanti were finally outflanked and fled the battlefield, leaving behind hundreds of dead. So much blood was shed in the grass that officers' legs were said to be stained red to the knees.

Throughout November 1900, British elements patrolled the jungle trying to eliminate any remaining pockets of Ashanti resistance. On 24 November, British troops returned to Kumasi with 31 captured kings and chiefs as prisoners, and considerable captured equipment. The war was basically over, with Willcocks and the majority of troops departing Kumasi on 5 December 1900. The remaining major renegade leaders (including Yaa Asantewaa, who was exiled to the Seychelles) surrendered or were captured in December.

British casualties, considering the savage fighting and the area pestilence, were relatively light: 16 officers were killed, 52 wounded, and another 54 sent to England as invalids; of the other ranks, 113 were killed in action, 102 died from disease, 41 were missing, and almost 700 were wounded, with almost 5,000 hospitalized at various times. Ashanti casualties cannot be ascertained, but they numbered in the thousands. The British formally annexed the territory on 26 September 1901—and the Golden Stool remained hidden.

See also Ashanti; Ashanti Expedition; Imperialism; Machine Guns
References: Edgerton (1995); Featherstone (1992); Haythornthwaite (1995); James (1985); Lloyd (1964)

Ashanti War, First (1823–1826)

The first significant conflict between the Ashanti and the British on the Gold Coast of Africa has become known as the First Ashanti War (1823–1826).

The British assumed control of the Gold Coast in 1821 on the dissolution of the African Company of Merchants. By this time the Ashanti, after inflicting defeats on the coastal Fante, had become the strongest power in West Africa. The first British governor, Sir Charles McCarthy, arrived at Cape Coast Castle in March 1822. Shortly after his arrival, the Ashanti captured an African sergeant and executed him. When McCarthy learned of this execution, he led a force of British and militia soldiers to attack the Ashanti near the execution site. The African guide, however, led McCarthy's small force into a well-prepared Ashanti ambush. The British had 10 soldiers killed and 39 wounded, and were forced to retreat ignominiously. In retaliation, McCarthy ordered a weapons embargo against the Ashanti and organized a Fante militia.

The Ashanti made attempts to negotiate all differences with the British, but the British rejected their overtures. After being rebuffed, the Ashanti advanced threateningly on Cape Coast Castle. McCarthy mustered his troops, dividing them into two columns, each inexplicably out of supporting distance from the other, and marched inland toward the Ashanti. Through torrential rains the governor personally led a small force of about 500 soldiers detached from the larger column of about 2,500 men directly toward the main Ashanti force of 10,000 to 20,000 men.

On the morning of 21 January 1824, near the village of Bonsaso on the fringe of Ashanti territory, the Ashanti approached the small British force. As McCarthy heard the Ashanti moving through the jungle, he ordered his band to play "God Save the King," under the misapprehension this would inspire disaffected Ashanti to desert their forces and join the British. Instead, the Ashanti attacked. The outnumbered British soon began to run out of ammunition. The Fante porters carrying the ammunition had deserted at the sound of gunfire, and only a few cases of ammunition reached McCarthy. As the ammunition from the first case was being distributed, the other boxes were opened and found to contain not bullets but macaroni.

The British fought desperately but the Ashanti overwhelmed them. McCarthy was wounded and, rather than face capture and torture by the Ashanti, shot himself. The Ashanti beheaded McCarthy's body and then, out of respect for his bravery, cut out his heart and ate it. The battle was soon over, with 9 British officers and 178 men killed, and 3 officers and 89 men wounded. McCarthy's skull was used for years afterward at Ashanti ceremonies.

The British, under the leadership of the new governor of the Gold Coast, Hope Smith, slowly assembled and trained a force to avenge the annihilation of McCarthy and his soldiers. This new British-led force, commanded by Lieutenant Colonel Purdon and numbering over 11,000 men, contained many Fante and other traditional enemies of the Ashanti. Purdon learned from Ashanti deserters that the Ashanti intended to capture the seaport of Accra. In August 1826, he deployed his force in defensive positions about 8 miles south of the village of Dodowa and about 10 miles north of Accra. Purdon's defensive positions stretched for about 4 miles on an open plain, with a small contingent of Royal Marines and his best-trained militia at the center, supported by Congreve rockets. This would force the Ashanti to charge across flat and open grasslands, exposing themselves to British fire before reaching their objective.

On 7 August 1826, the overconfident Ashanti attacked. The Ashanti chief decided that honor demanded he attack the center, the strongest part, of the British position. Attacking in disciplined lines, many Ashanti were shot and fell in the open before they were close enough to fire on the British. After firing a few volleys, which the British returned, the Ashanti charged and entered the British line, where a savage hand-to-hand fight ensued for hours. While the British native militia was pushing back the Ashanti flanks, the Ashanti fighting in the center appeared to be on the verge of victory. At the decisive moment, Purdon ordered the Congreve rockets to open fire. The overpowering sight and sounds of these new weapons, coupled with their tremendous explosions on the ground and the grievous wounds caused by flying shards of hot metal, convinced the Ashanti that the British had summoned the forces of thunder and lightning against them. The Ashanti fell back through the burning grass, leaving thousands dead and wounded on the battlefield. The First Ashanti War was for all practical purposes over, although a negotiated settlement was not concluded until 1831.

See also Ashanti; Imperialism; Rockets
References: Edgerton (1995); Farwell (1972); Featherstone (1989); Haythornthwaite (1995); Keegan (1967)

Ashanti War, Second (1873–1874)

The Second Ashanti War (1873–1874) was the culmination of a clash of cultures between the Ashanti and the British. Its immediate cause was the Ashanti invasion of the British Protectorate of the Gold Coast.

The Dutch ceded their fort and trading post at Elmina and other possessions on the Gold Coast to the British in 1872 due to continuous native warfare and turmoil. Because the British refused to pay the Ashanti an annual tribute (as the Dutch had done for many years), the Ashanti were incensed and eager for retribution. In December 1872, under the command of Amanquatia, the Ashanti crossed the Pra River (the southern boundary of Ashantiland) and invaded the British Protectorate of the Gold Coast. The jungle-fighting Ashanti seemed invincible as they defeated many tribes on their march to the sea. The Ashanti were within a day's march of Elmina on 13 June 1873. H.M.S. *Barracuda*'s Royal Marine detachment, commanded by Lieutenant Colonel Festing, was rushed to Elmina, defeated the attacking Ashanti, and occupied the town. Amanquatia decided to withdraw inland, where he intended to stay for the remainder of the rainy season, which usually ended in December.

In London, the British drew up contingency plans for sending an expeditionary force to the Gold Coast to drive the invading Ashanti back across the Pra River to their homeland. The British, however, were very concerned about oper-

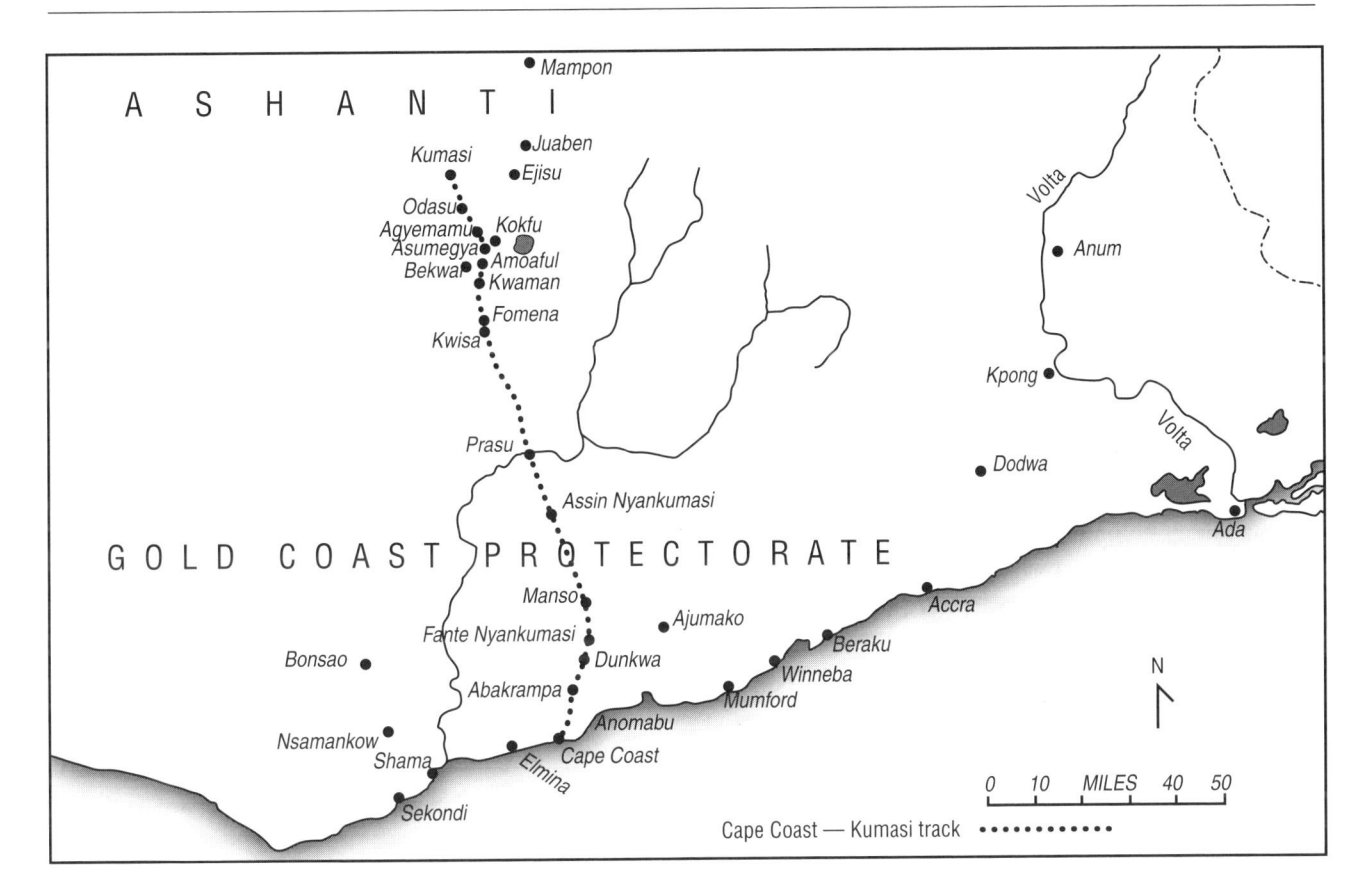

Second Ashanti War, 1873–1874: Area of Operations

ating in the Gold Coast, called the "white man's grave" because of the extreme heat, humidity, and pestilence. While considering their options, the British government accepted on 2 August 1873 the offer of Royal Navy Captain John Glover, the administrator of Lagos, to raise a native force, lead it up the unexplored Volta River, cause a diversion in the rear of the Ashanti, and threaten Kumasi.

Secretary of State for War Edward T. Cardwell had arranged for his loyal supporter and young protégé, Colonel (later Field Marshal Viscount) Sir Garnet J. Wolseley, the leader of the highly successful 1870 Red River Expedition in Canada and then assistant adjutant-general at the War Office, to prepare plans for sending a force to the Gold Coast that conformed to the government's constraints and desires. On 13 August 1873, Wolseley was appointed commander of the force, over the heads of many senior and more experienced officers, with the local rank of major general.

Wolseley's plan was to take a number of selected officers with him, raise and train local African units, and lead them to force the Ashanti to withdraw to their own territory. At the same time, an intelligence network would be developed, and a road, with overnight rest camps and supply depots, would be built from Cape Coast to Prasu, a town on the Pra River. These preliminary tasks were to be completed in December 1873, the first month of the annual December-March dry season, when European troops would be less susceptible to the inhospitable climate. If the British-led native forces were unable to drive the Ashanti from the Gold Coast, three British infantry battalions would advance from Prasu to capture and destroy Kumasi, the Ashanti capital. This final offensive would begin in January 1874 and be completed by the end of March.

Wolseley departed for the Gold Coast aboard H.M.S. *Ambriz* on 12 September 1873. He took with him thirty-six staff and special service officers handpicked from an army-wide list of volunteers. This group of officers came to be known as Wolseley's "Ashanti Ring." The nucleus of the Ashanti Ring consisted of officers who had served under Wolseley and "proven" themselves during the 1870 Red River Expedition in Canada.

Wolseley arrived at Cape Coast Castle on the Gold Coast on 2 October 1873. Immediately after landing, Wolseley and his staff began recruiting local levies; enlisting local "spies," other sources of information, and interpreters; and making logistical arrangements for the expected January 1874 arrival of the main body of British troops and the actual conduct of the campaign. His plan was to keep his troops in the country for as short a time as possible, thereby reducing the chances of disease and casualties.

During this time, Wolseley also summoned the local protectorate chiefs to attend a meeting to discuss cooperation and local strategy against the Ashanti. British prestige, however, was low at this time, as the Ashanti and their confederates had never encountered British military determination and might. Lieutenant Colonel (later Field Marshal Sir) (Henry) Evelyn M. Wood, one of Wolseley's subordinates, requested the chief of the village of Esamen, an Ashanti ally, to meet him in nearby Elmina. The Esamen leader brazenly replied, "Come and get me; white men dare not go into the bush" (Lehmann 1964, p. 173). Many of the chiefs were Ashanti sympathizers and were confident the British would never risk marching through the dense jungle to the villages.

Such blatant insolence by the indigenous populations was unacceptable to Wolseley, and he was determined to destroy Esamen and several nearby towns. This would chastise local tribes loyal to the Ashanti and demonstrate British decisiveness and power. An assault on this inland village would also cut off the Ashanti from their supplies, which came from the coast, and force them to withdraw to their own territory further in the interior. Moreover, British-controlled native intelligence had pinpointed Esamen as a center of enemy communications.

Wolseley knew it would be difficult to conceal troop concentrations and movements in such an environment. On 13 October 1873, in the presence of war correspondents, Wolseley mentioned that Glover's detachment near Accra—far to the east of Cape Coast Castle—was in grave danger of possible encirclement by the Ashanti and that he would soon sail there to assist. The war correspondents, eager to get a scoop on the situation and each other, ensured their home newspapers were informed and that the word was spread in the area that Wolseley and a number of soldiers would soon be departing for Accra.

On the same day, Wolseley sent an ultimatum to the *asantehene*, Kofi Karikari, giving him thirty days to withdraw his army from the protectorate, release all hostages, and guarantee indemnification. Wolseley warned him to expect "full punishment" if these conditions were not met. This helped lull the Ashanti into complacency, believing the British would not attack for at least a month, if at all.

That evening, Wolseley boarded a gunboat with his staff, a large infantry force, and two war correspondents. Ostensibly sailing to Accra in the east, the ship instead sailed west to Elmina, which was only a short march from Esamen. Wolseley landed at Elmina at 3:00 A.M., and after he linked up with Wood and his African soldiers, the entire force marched to Esamen. A short skirmish ensued, with the demoralized and defeated Ashanti warriors fleeing and abandoning their town. Esamen was razed, and Wolseley's column returned to the coast and destroyed a number of other villages. Only a few select officers and others had been privy to Wolseley's actual destination and plans.

While the battle at Esamen was a relatively small affair, it was significant in many ways. The skirmish at Esamen destroyed the myth of Ashanti invincibility. It also showed foes and African friends alike that the British had the ability and audacity to march through and fight in the densest jungles and swamps.

Desultory fighting took place between the British and their native forces and the Ashanti during the remainder of October and November 1873, while the British continued logistical preparations for the arrival of the British battalions and their attack on Kumasi. By 22 December 1873, the corduroy road to the forward base at Prasu, 70 miles from the coast and 60 from Kumasi, was completed. At 10-mile intervals along this route, overnight rest stations were built, each with huts for 400 soldiers, a hospital, supply point, fresh water, and personal hygiene facilities. The forward base at Prasu was even larger, with an encampment for 2,000 British soldiers, a hospital, ammunition magazine (to hold 1.1 million rounds of Snider ammunition), resupply point (with 30 days rations for 6,500 men, totaling 400 tons of food), canteen, post office, and headquarters. About 8,500 African porters were required to carry these supplies. Moreover, at Prasu a 200-foot bridge was constructed across the Pra River, the largest of 237 bridges constructed along the route.

On New Year's Day (1874) the European Brigade (1st Battalion, Black Watch; 2nd Battalion, Rifle Brigade; and 2nd Battalion, Royal Welch Fusiliers), under the command of Brigadier General (later General) Sir Archibald Alison, disembarked at Cape Coast Castle. Wolseley's force was then complete. In addition to Alison's brigade, Wolseley had the

1st and 2nd West India Regiments (although the former remained in support at Cape Coast); a 250-man naval brigade; native regiments commanded by Wood and by Major Baker Russell; and artillery and engineer detachments. Wolseley's strategy was to lead this main force from Prasu to Kumasi, where Glover's men and two smaller British-led columns would converge to defeat the Ashanti.

Wolseley's force assembled at Prasu, and Alison's brigade crossed into Ashantiland on 20 January 1874. The force initially encountered little Ashanti resistance and reached Fomena four days later, where Wolseley decided to halt temporarily to establish a supply depot and treat the scores of soldiers ill with malaria. At the same time, Wolseley informed Kofi Karikari that he would march on Kumasi and issued an ultimatum to end the conflict. The Ashanti took advantage of the delay to build up their force. The British skirmished with the Ashanti on 26 and 29 January, seemingly unaware that the Ashanti were luring them into a trap.

Wolseley believed a large battle to be imminent and knew that the Ashanti attacked in a horseshoe-type formation, with forces making frontal assaults while other men remained hidden to attack the enemy's flanks and rear. On 31 January 1874, Wolseley attempted to counter the Ashanti tactics by deploying his 2,200-man force in a large hollow square that extended about 300 yards on either side of the main road. After leaving the village of Egginassie and approaching Amoaful, the British scouts were ambushed. Alison immediately sent two Black Watch companies to their assistance. Fighting was fierce in the dense jungle, and the Ashanti muskets were seemingly taking their toll at close range. By adroitly reinforcing his weak areas and shifting troops to repulse Ashanti attacks—coupled with the discipline and marksmanship of individual soldiers and the slaughtering rapid fire from 7-pounder artillery pieces—Wolseley was able to defeat the Ashanti by early afternoon. British casualties in the Battle of Amoaful were surprisingly light: 1 officer killed and 21 wounded; 2 British soldiers killed and 144 wounded, and out of the African troops, 1 was killed and 29 wounded. At least 150 Ashanti were killed.

Another firefight took place on 1 February 1874, and two days later the British force deployed for speed in column to cover the final 15 miles to Kumasi. The expedition's advance was contested by Ashanti pickets, but the British forced their way through all opposition and torrential rainfall, entering a veritably empty Kumasi late on 4 February. Kofi had fled north.

Wolseley knew that short supplies and the returning rains would not permit him to stay in Kumasi for long. On 5 February 1874, his troops explored the city, fascinated with the Death Grove (reported to have held the remains of 120,000 sacrificial victims) and other sites. The next morning, after the royal palace was prepared for demolition, the entire force assembled and marched out of Kumasi. The fuses on the explosives were lit, and shortly thereafter all that remained of Kumasi was a heap of smoldering ruins.

After Wolseley threatened to hunt down Kofi, the latter's messengers finally caught up with Wolseley at Fomena on 13 February 1874. The *asantehene* stated he was anxious for peace and would agree to all the British demands in what became known as the Treaty of Fomena: payment of an indemnity of 50,000 ounces of gold, renunciation of suzerainty over a number of other tribes, cessation of rent payments on forts, free passage on all roads, and suppression of human sacrifice. The Second Ashanti War was over.

The Second Ashanti War was a model of planning, leadership, administration, and logistical preparations. The British victory cost less than £800,000, and total British casualties were 18 killed or dead from wounds, 55 dead from disease, and 185 wounded. As a result of his relatively quick and inexpensive success in the Ashanti War, Wolseley was promoted and showered with honors and became a popular hero in England. Wolseley considered the campaign "the most horrible war [he] ever took part in" (Lloyd 1964, p. 151), and Cardwell believed it was "a complete success" (Lloyd 1964, p. 152).

See also Alison, General Sir Archibald; Amoaful, Battle of; Ashanti; Ashanti Ring; Correspondents, War; Kofi Karikari; Lines of Communication; Wolseley, Field Marshal Garnet J.; Wood, Field Marshal Sir (Henry) Evelyn M., V.C.

References: Brackenbury (1874); Edgerton (1995); Keegan (1967); Kochanski (1999); Lehmann (1964); Lloyd (1964); Low (1883); Maxwell (1985); Raugh (2001b)

Atbara, Battle of (8 April 1898)

The Anglo-Egyptian Army victory over the dervishes at the hard-fought Battle of Atbara (8 April 1898) paved the way for the 200-mile southward advance to Khartoum and the completion of the reconquest of the Sudan.

Major General (later Field Marshal Earl) Sir Horatio H. Kitchener, commanding the Anglo-Egyptian Army in the Sudan, assembled his forces in early 1898. He sent one Egyptian Army brigade forward to the Atbara fort, located on the northeastern side of the confluence of the Atbara and Nile Rivers about 200 miles north of Khartoum, then assembled his entire force at the same location. The dervish forces were located on 30 March 1898, and after a period of irresolution, Kitchener decided to attack and his army advanced closer to the enemy on 4 April 1898. After cavalry skirmishes, the Anglo-Egyptian force was ready to attack the Khalifa's army. Before sunset on 7 April, Kitchener's four-brigade force advanced in large brigade squares on line, with the British brigade leading. The force halted at about 4:00 A.M. less than a thousand yards before the dervish positions.

At dawn on 8 April—Good Friday—the Anglo-Egyptian force attacked south to the heavily defended dervish camp. Kitchener's force was deployed with three infantry brigades on line and one brigade in reserve. From left to right, the Anglo-Egyptian units were: eight Egyptian cavalry squadrons on the left flank; the British Brigade (1st Battalions of the Cameron Highlander, Royal Warwickshire, Seaforth Highlander, and Lincolnshire Regiments), commanded by Major General (later Lieutenant General Sir) William F. Gatacre; the 2nd Egyptian Brigade (9th, 10th, and 11th Sudanese and 2nd Egyptian Battalions), under Colonel (later Major General Sir) Hector A. Macdonald; and the 1st Egyptian Brigade (12th, 13th, and 14th Sudanese and 8th Egyptian Battalions), under Colonel (later General Sir) John G. Maxwell. The 3rd Egyptian Brigade (3rd, 4th, and 7th Egyptian Battalions), commanded by Colonel D. F. Lewis, was in reserve. Major General (later General Sir) Archibald Hunter was in overall command of the Egyptian forces, organized into the Egyptian Division. Artillery and Maxim guns were positioned along the line. Kitchener's force totaled about 14,000 men, with 24 artillery pieces, 4 Maxim guns, and a rocket detachment.

The artillery and rockets began firing at 6:15 A.M., and their bombardment continued until 7:40 A.M. The Anglo-Egyptian force, led by their commanders on horseback and accompanied by shouts of "Remember Gordon" (Hunter 1996, p. 85), then advanced as if on the parade field. The enemy began a heavy fire on Kitchener's troops when they were 300 yards from the dervish zareba. On the second command of "advance," the Anglo-Egyptian units assaulted the dervish fortifications and fought their way with bullet and bayonet through the dense vegetation and maze of trenches. The Sudanese fought especially well, with Kitchener's brother writing that "the Blacks went through the zariba like paper" (Keown-Boyd 1986, p. 199). They finally pushed through the entire enemy position and soon reached the Atbara River bank.

At 8:25 A.M., the cease-fire was sounded and the battle was over. In spite of the unimaginative tactics used in the engagement, Anglo-Egyptian casualties were 81 killed and 478 wounded, while the dervishes suffered over 3,000 killed. The British Brigade fired over 56,000 rounds of rifle ammunition and the Egyptian Division shot over 193,000 rounds. One war correspondent, however, called the Battle of Atbara "this clean-jointed, well-oiled, smooth-running, clockwork-perfect masterpiece of a battle" (Steevens 1898, p. 151). At the Battle of Atbara, Kitchener's army destroyed the last major dervish force outside Omdurman.

See also Dervishes; Egyptian Army; Gatacre, Lieutenant General Sir William F.; Gordon, Major General Charles G.; Hunter, General Sir Archibald; Khalifa; Kitchener, Field Marshal Horatio H.; Macdonald, Major General Sir Hector A.; Reconquest of the Sudan; Sudan

References: Barthorp (1984); Hunter (1996); Keown-Boyd (1986); Magnus (1959); Meredith (1998); Nalson (1998); Neillands (1996); Steevens (1898)

Awards and Decorations

Many British military awards and decorations were instituted from the end of the Napoleonic Wars to the eve of World War I to recognize the long service, good conduct, and the demonstrated gallantry of soldiers.

In 1829 a long service and good conduct medal was established, followed in 1845 by a medal for "meritorious service," and later good conduct pay and gratuities. There was, however, no tangible means of recognizing gallantry in the field, other than the occasional brevet promotion for the deserving officer or mention in dispatches.

The unimaginable bravery and tremendous suffering of soldiers during the Crimean War reinforced the need for a medal recognizing combat gallantry. In December 1854, the Distinguished Conduct Medal (D.C.M.) was established (replacing the earlier Meritorious Service Medal) to recognize sergeants and lower ranks for "distinguished, gallant and good conduct" (Gooding 1994, p. 20). It was initially intended to issue the D.C.M. to each regiment on a quota basis, since there was a fixed amount of money available for the accompanying annuities. Until the abolition of the monetary reward in 1862, noncommissioned officers and men who had been awarded the D.C.M. received either a gratuity of £20 on discharge or an increase of pension of 6d per day. The Distinguished Conduct Medal (Colonial and Dominion) was instituted in 1894 to recognize colonial troops (in Canada, Natal, the King's African Rifles, and the West African Frontier Force) in the same manner as the D.C.M. had been awarded to British soldiers.

The Victoria Cross (V.C.), Great Britain's foremost decoration for gallantry, was established by Queen Victoria on 29 January 1856. Its provisions were made retroactive to acts of heroism performed since the beginning of the Crimean War in March 1854. The V.C. could be awarded to deserving recipients, regardless of rank, for "serving in the presence of the enemy, [who] should have performed some signal act of valor or devotion to their country" (This England 1981, p. 6).

The Conspicuous Gallantry Medal (C.G.M.) was established in 1855 as the Royal Navy and Royal Marine counterpart to the army's D.C.M. This decoration was awarded eleven times to ten recipients (one received it twice) for gallant service in the Baltic and the Crimea during the Crimean War. After the introduction of the Victoria Cross in 1856, no further awards of the C.G.M. were made and it fell into disuse. After the British success in the Second Ashanti War (1873–1874), the C.G.M. was reinstituted and awarded sparingly to deserving participants in that and subsequent campaigns.

The Victoria Cross could not be awarded to colonial soldiers until 1867, and then only to those serving with imperial troops. To fill in the vacuum, the New Zealand Cross was instituted on 10 March 1869. Only twenty-three officers and men of the New Zealand Forces "who had particularly distinguished themselves by bravery in action, or devotion to duty while on service during the war against the Maoris" (Dorling 1974, p. 100) from 1860 to 1872 received the New Zealand Cross. Due to the unusual nature of this award and its complicated eligibility rules, awards were sometimes made years after the action for which they were recommended. The last New Zealand Cross was awarded in 1910.

The Royal Red Cross (R.R.C.) was instituted by Queen Victoria on 27 April 1883 to reward cases of "special devotion in nursing the sick and wounded of the army and the navy" (Gooding 1994, p. 16). Thirty-one awards of the R.R.C. were initially made. It was the first example of a British military order solely for women.

After the Crimean War, the Indian Mutiny, and other mid-nineteenth-century campaigns, it was recognized that other than the Victoria Cross there was no means of recognizing the bravery on active service of a company grade officer. Similarly, other than the Companion of the Most Honorable Order of the Bath (C.B.), no suitable award existed to recognize the gallantry of majors and above. Consequently, the Distinguished Service Order (D.S.O.) was instituted in 1886 for officers of both the army and the Royal Navy. In fact, no officer was eligible for the D.S.O. who had not received a special mention in dispatches for "distinguished service under fire, or under conditions equivalent to service in actual combat with the enemy" (Dorling 1974, p. 68). The D.S.O. was issued in gold until 1890, after which the award was issued in silver gilt. Some 1,150 awards of the Distinguished Service Order were made during the Second Boer War.

In 1902, when the British Order of Merit (O.M.) was introduced, the award hitherto known as the Order of Merit (as originally created by the Honorable East India Company in 1837; it became an official British award in 1857) was renamed the Indian Order of Merit (I.O.M.). Instituted to reward acts of individual gallantry, the I.O.M. originally had three classes. The highest class was abolished in 1912 when Indian officers, noncommissioned officers, and men of the Indian Army became eligible for the Victoria Cross.

The Conspicuous Service Cross (C.S.C.) was instituted in 1901 by King Edward VII to recognize "meritorious or distinguished services before the enemy" (Dorling 1974, p. 71) performed by warrant officers and subordinate officers who were not eligible for the D.S.O. Only eight C.S.C.s were awarded for service in the Second Boer War and the Boxer Rebellion, three to warrant-rank gunners and five to midshipmen. This decoration's name was changed to the Distinguished Service Cross in 1914.

In 1907, as a means of recognizing the distinguished service of Indian officers, noncommissioned officers, and men of the Indian Army, the Indian Distinguished Service Medal (I.D.S.M.) was introduced.

See also Campaign Medals; Crimean War; India, British Army in; Victoria Cross

References: Brereton (1986); Dorling (1974); Gooding (1994); Joslin (1974); Strachan (1984); This England (1981)

Baden-Powell, Lieutenant General Sir Robert S. S., First Baron Baden-Powell of Gilwell (1857–1941)

Lieutenant General Sir Robert S. S. Baden-Powell was a highly respected British Army officer and an expert at irregular warfare and scouting who gained fame as the "hero of Mafeking" during the Second Boer War (1899–1902). He later founded the Boy Scout movement and devoted the last three decades of his life to it.

Baden-Powell was born in London on 22 February 1857 and was educated at Charterhouse School. The Royal Military College, Sandhurst, was closed when the purchase system, in which officers generally purchased their initial officer's commission and subsequent ranks through lieutenant colonel, was abolished in 1871 and entrance to the British Army as an officer was by open examination. Not known as a diligent student, Baden-Powell earned second place on the cavalry list and fifth on the infantry list in the 1876 examination. He was commissioned directly into the 13th Hussars and joined it in Lucknow, India, in late 1876. Baden-Powell missed the Second Afghan War but served in Afghanistan in 1880–1881. He became regimental adjutant in 1882.

Baden-Powell returned with his regiment to England in 1888. He then served as aide-de-camp to his uncle, Lieutenant General Sir Henry Smyth, in South Africa, where he participated in the suppression of the 1888 Zulu uprising, and on Malta from 1890 to 1893. After regimental service in Ireland, Baden-Powell commanded a native levy, or group of indigenous people raised into a unit, in the 1895–1896 Ashanti Expedition and served as chief staff officer during 1896–1897 operations in Matabeleland. In 1897, he was selected to command the 5th Dragoon Guards.

In 1899, Baden-Powell was assigned to raise a force of mounted rifles to be based at Mafeking, just inside the Cape Colony frontier and outside the Transvaal. During the Second Boer War, Boers laid siege to the town from 13 October 1899 to 17 May 1900. Baden-Powell's leadership, vigilance, creativity, and frequent use of ruses prevented the town from falling into enemy hands. When Mafeking was relieved, tremendous celebrations broke out throughout the empire, especially in London, where the enthusiastic scenes were described as "mafficking." Baden-Powell was propelled into the limelight and promoted to major general at age forty-three, reportedly the youngest general in the British Army. Some recent historians have noted that Baden-Powell could have avoided the siege of Mafeking, suggesting he was a publicity seeker who welcomed the situation. He has also been criticized for his treatment of blacks during the siege.

Baden-Powell subsequently served as inspector-general of the South African Constabulary from 1901 to 1903 and inspector-general of cavalry from 1903 to 1907; he commanded the Northumbrian Division of Territorials from 1908 to 1910. Promoted to lieutenant general in 1907 and knighted in 1909, he retired in 1910 to devote himself full-time to the Boy Scouts, a character-building youth organization he was instrumental in founding two years earlier. Ennobled in 1929 as Baron Baden-Powell of Gilwell, the defender of Mafeking died in Kenya on 8 January 1941.

See also Ashanti Expedition; Boer War, Second (1899–1902); Mafeking, Siege of; Officers, British Army—Sources of Commissioning; Purchase System; Sandhurst, Royal Military College
References: De Beaumont (1944); Jeal (1989); Pakenham (1979); Reynolds (1942); Sykes (1897)

Baker Pasha, Lieutenant General Valentine (1827–1887)

Valentine Baker was a talented British Army officer who, in 1875, was tried and found guilty of an alleged indiscretion, imprisoned, and dismissed from the service. The case stunned British society at the time.

Baker, a younger brother of famed African explorer Sir Samuel Baker, was born on 1 April 1827 at Enfield. He became an ensign in the Ceylon Rifles in 1848, but transferred to the 12th Lancers in 1852 and fought in the Eighth Cape Frontier War in South Africa. Baker served in the Crimean War, and upon obtaining his rank of major under the purchase system in 1859, exchanged into the 10th Hussars.

Baker assumed command (again by purchase) of the 10th Hussars in 1860 and commanded the regiment for thirteen years. During this period, he developed a new system of squadron drill and, unlike most cavalry commanders, trained his men in scouting and skirmishing tactics. Baker was also the first commander to practice cavalry movement by train. Interested in his profession, Baker also served as an observer during the 1866 Austro-Prussian War and 1870 Franco-Prussian War.

Relinquishing command in 1873, Baker went on half pay. He traveled to Persia to see for himself the extent of Russian imperialism in Central Asia, and on his return wrote *Clouds in the East* (1876), an account of his journey that warned of Russian encroachment in that area. Baker was assigned as assistant quartermaster-general at Aldershot in 1874.

The following summer Baker was accused of indecently assaulting a young woman on a train and was subsequently tried and convicted in a civilian court on the uncorroborated testimony of the woman. Baker was found guilty, sentenced to twelve months imprisonment, and fined. Subsequently he was dismissed from the army.

Baker joined and was commissioned a major general with the title "Pasha" in the Turkish gendarmerie during the 1877–1878 Russo-Turkish War. He later commanded a Turkish division in the Balkans and fought at Tashkessan in "one of the most brilliant and successful rearguard actions on record" (Stephen and Lee 1964–1965, p. 109) on 31 December 1877. Baker was promoted to lieutenant general in recognition of his services.

In 1882, after the British occupation of Egypt, he was offered and accepted the post of commander in chief of the Egyptian Army. This appointment was not confirmed, however, because of his earlier disgrace, and he was then designated commander of the ill-trained paramilitary Egyptian Gendarmerie. He attempted to relieve the besieged town of Tokar with this force but was soundly defeated at El Teb on 4 February 1884. After the arrival of reinforcements, Baker was designated intelligence officer of the British force and guided its advance to the successful battle of El Teb, 29 February 1884, where he was wounded.

Baker remained in command of the Egyptian Gendarmerie and died of heart disease in Egypt on 17 November 1887. In announcing his death, the *Times* observed that Baker's "career might have been among the most brilliant in our military services" (Barthorp 1984a, p. 35).

See also Burnaby, Lieutenant Colonel Frederick G.; Cape Frontier Wars, Southern Africa; Cavalry, British Army—Training; Crimean War; Egyptian Army; El Teb, Battle of; Great Game; Purchase System

References: Baker (1996); Barthorp (1984a); Barthorp (1984b); Furneaux (1958); Stephen and Lee (1964–65)

Balaklava, Battle of (25 October 1854)

The Battle of Balaklava is probably the best known of the four major battles of the Crimean War (1854–1856). It was, in essence, a Russian attempt to drive through the British lines and seize Balaklava, the British base of operations and supply port. The battle was characterized by gallant small unit actions, culminating in the memorable Charge of the Light Brigade.

The Battle of the Alma (20 September 1854) had resulted in an allied victory. General (later Field Marshal) Fitzroy J. H. Somerset, First Baron Raglan, the British commander in chief, wanted to immediately continue the advance southward to the Russian citadel of Sevastopol, but his French counterpart, Marshal Jacques Leroy de Saint-Arnaud, seemed less willing. Advisers recommended an attack on Sevastopol from the south, where the defenses were not completed and the element of surprise would be in their favor.

The allies marched around the eastern flank of Sevastopol—possibly missing an opportunity to capture the city—and began digging trenches on the semicircular heights to the south of Sevastopol and the suburb of Korabelnaya. The allies formed a "corps of siege" to invest and a "corps of observation" oriented to the east and northeast to guard against a possible attack by Prince Alexander Sergeevich Menshikov's Russian field army (that had departed Sevastopol on 25 September 1854).

An allied war council was held on 7 October 1854, and the siege of Sevastopol began on 8 October 1854. The first allied sea and land artillery bombardment of Sevastopol took place on 17 October, with the allies' wooden ships suffering considerably from effective Russian fire from the Sevastopol forts. This bombardment ended in relative failure.

Balaklava Harbor, about 8 miles south of the British siege positions, was the British supply port. It was defended by two lines of defenses. The outer line of defense consisted of four redoubts (manned by Turkish soldiers) situated on the Woronzov Road that ran generally from east to west along the Causeway Heights, connecting Balaklava with Sevastopol and separating the North and South Valleys. These hastily built defenses faced the Fedukhine Heights across the North Valley. The inner line of defenses consisted of a number of artillery and Royal Marine positions, forming a semicircle less than a mile from the entrance of the gorge to Balaklava. The British Cavalry Division, commanded by Major General (later Field Marshal) George C. Bingham, Third Earl of Lucan, and the 93rd Highland Regiment, were positioned in the South Valley.

On 24 October 1854, the British observed a Russian force under the command of Lieutenant General Pavel Liprandi consisting of about 25,000 infantrymen, 34 cavalry squadrons, and 78 guns assembling near the village of Chorgun, northeast of Balaklava. The Russian plan was to cut the Woronzov Road and capture Balaklava.

The Russians began their attack early on 25 October 1854 and were initially successful. They occupied the Fedukhine Heights and overran the redoubts on the Causeway Heights. Continuing their advance, the Russian cavalry was met by the 93rd Highlanders, under the command of Major General (later Field Marshal Lord) Sir Colin Campbell. Campbell exhorted his men, "Remember, there is no retreat. You must die where you stand" (Warner 1972, p. 63). The Highlanders, armed with Minié rifles, fired their first volley at long range, then a second volley. As the Russian cavalry turned to wheel around the British, the Highlanders, in a supreme test of discipline, stood fast and poured accurate fire into the exposed flank of the Russian cavalry. The Russian cavalry turned in the thick smoke and retreated. *Times* correspondent William Howard Russell observed this engagement and characterized the stalwart 93rd Highlanders as "that thin red streak topped with a line of steel" (Grey 1971, p. 114), a phrase shortened to the "thin red line."

The Heavy Brigade, commanded by Brigadier General (later Lieutenant General Sir) James Y. Scarlett, was located to the west of the 93rd Highlanders. The Heavy Brigade was organized in two parallel columns of three squadrons each. Scarlett observed about 3,000 Russian cavalry pouring over the Causeway Heights and responded quickly. As if on parade, Scarlett—who had never before seen action—wheeled the left column into line and led the charge himself. The Russian cavalry, surprised by the British audacity, gave ground and retreated.

As the Russian cavalry withdrew, the Light Brigade, under the command of Brigadier General (later Lieutenant General) James T. Brudenell, Seventh Earl of Cardigan and despised brother-in-law of Lucan, remained inactive. The Russians sent horses to drag away the guns in the British redoubts they had overrun earlier. In the following confusion, Raglan ordered Lucan to advance his cavalry, and Lucan believed the Light Brigade was to attack eastward through the North Valley, which was subject to enfilading fire from Russian positions on the Fedukhine Heights and on the Causeway Heights. An angry Lucan delivered the order personally to Cardigan, who led the charge of the Light Brigade through withering fire into the North Valley. Although shot to pieces by Russian artillery and musket fire from the elevated flanks, the British cavalry troopers were exhausted but reached and hacked their way through the Russian guns to their front. When the British horsemen realized they were hopelessly outnumbered, they wheeled around and retreated. Of the 673 men who participated in the Charge of the Light Brigade, 113 were killed and 134 wounded, and over 500 horses were killed or later destroyed. The charge was an example of misplaced British courage, determination, and discipline and basically accomplished nothing.

The disastrous attack of the Light Brigade was the last action of the Battle of Balaklava. The results of the battle were mixed. The Russians, who suffered about 550 total casualties, could claim a tactical success. They occupied the Fedukhine Heights and two of the four redoubts on the Causeway Heights but were unable to occupy or destroy the British supply port. The British, who suffered about the same number of casualties, reveled in the heroic failure of the Charge of the Light Brigade.

See also Alma, Battle of the; Campbell, Field Marshal Colin; Cardigan, Lieutenant General James T. Brudenell, Seventh Earl of; Charge of the Light Brigade; Crimean War; Lucan, Field Marshal George C. Bingham, Third Earl of; Raglan, Field

Marshal Fitzroy J. H. Somerset, First Baron; Sevastopol, Siege of
References: Grey (1971); Judd (1975); Palmer (1987); Pemberton (1962); Royle (2000); Selby (1970); Warner (1972); Warner (1977)

Balloons

The British Army used balloons on a limited basis, mainly for observation, and primarily during the Second Boer War (1899–1902).

The first manned balloon flight took place over Paris on 21 November 1783. Less than a year later, on 15 September 1784, the first balloon voyage occurred from British soil, from London to Ware. The French first experimented with balloons for military purposes when they used tethered balloons for reconnaissance at the Battle of Fleurus in 1794 and at the Siege of Mantua in 1797. The French also proposed invading England in balloons.

The use of balloons increased during the nineteenth century. The Austrians first used explosive balloons in 1849 against insurgents in Venice. At the Battle of Solferino in 1859, balloons were used for observation purposes. The first use of balloons for systematic intelligence gathering was during the American Civil War (1861–1865). Balloons were also used for directing fire, with a forward observer in the balloon using a telegraph to report the impact and adjustment of artillery rounds. During the Franco-Prussian War (1870–1871) balloons were used to carry messages and transport people out of the besieged city of Paris.

In Britain, military experiments with balloons began at Woolwich Arsenal in 1878. A small military balloon unit was established at Chatham in 1882 to supply balloons used in military expeditions, and this was formalized as the Balloon Section, Royal Engineers, in May 1890. The Balloon Section was moved to Farnborough in 1892, where the Balloon Factory—the lineal parent of the Royal Aircraft Establishment—was later created.

While balloons were reportedly employed during small military maneuvers at Aldershot in June 1880, the first operational use of balloons was during the 1884 expedition to Bechuanaland.

Four balloon sections of the Royal Engineers took part in the Second Boer War (1899–1902). The helium-filled balloons were designed to ascend to a height of 4,000 feet and were tethered to the ground by ropes. To the Boers, these balloons caused some excitement and even fear, thinking the British might use them to bomb Boer towns. On 24 October 1899, only two weeks after the war broke out, an official telegram was received at the Boer headquarters that read: "Balloons—Yesterday evening two balloons were seen at Irene, proceeding in the direction of Springs. Official telegraphists instructed to inform the Commander in Chief about any objects seen in the sky" (Lee 1985, p. 36). This alarmist telegram caused the Boers to frequently scan the night sky with powerful searchlights for the British balloons.

During the Second Boer War the British used balloons at the Modder River and at Magersfontein in December 1899, at Ladysmith, prior to the Battle of Spion Kop in January 1900, and on the march to Pretoria in May 1900. While the British did occasionally use balloons as observation platforms, their full potential was never realized.

See also Aldershot; Boer War, Second (1899–1902); Engineers, British Army—Employment; Engineers, British Army—Organization; Intelligence
References: Dean (1979); Fergusson (1984); Gordon (1971); Lee (1985); Pakenham (1979)

Baltic Sea Operations, Crimean War

The British and French operations in the Baltic Sea are a frequently overlooked but indispensable component of the overall allied strategy of the Crimean War.

After being invaded by Russia, Turkey declared war on the aggressor on 5 October 1853. To help maintain the Ottoman Empire and preserve the balance of power in Europe, the British and later the French fleets entered the Black Sea to bolster Turkey. A larger war became imminent. In February 1854, British troops sailed for Turkey, with the French deploying forces a few weeks later.

British Vice Admiral Sir Charles Napier was appointed commander of the hastily assembled Baltic Fleet and sailed for the Baltic on 10 March 1854. With British and French expeditionary forces en route to Turkey, Napier's mission was to seal the Baltic, destroy the Russian fleet, protect Danish and Swedish shipping and territory from Russian attack, and report on the possibilities of attacking fortified Russian ports.

War was declared on 28 March 1854. Napier's fifteen-ship fleet arrived at the entrance to the Gulf of Finland on 17 April 1854. When the weather improved in May 1854, Napier reconnoitered Russian defenses at Hango and Sveaborg but found them to be too strong for his guns. Leaving ships at Sveaborg, Napier sailed for Kronstadt, arriving on 26 June 1854. Thirty Russian ships were anchored nearby. After a careful reconnaissance, it was determined that only shallow-draught ships could approach the Russian fortress.

Napier sailed back to Sveaborg and received word that about 10,000 French soldiers with ten guns would be sent on British ships to attack either Sveaborg or Bomarsund, the latter guarding the best entrance to the large harbor on Aland. On 8 August 1854, a contingent of Royal Marines and engineers and a French brigade landed north of Bomarsund, and the main French force landed south of it. The forts guarding the harbor entrance were surrounded by the allied force and artillery positioned near it. The allied force began bombarding Bomarsund on 13 August 1854, and it surrendered shortly thereafter. This success, however, achieved very little.

Napier wanted to continue operations, but the French fleet began to withdraw from the Baltic on 4 September 1854. The Royal Navy maintained the blockade on the Russians until the end of October 1854 and then returned to port at Spithead. Napier was abruptly relieved of command, although later vindicated.

In March 1855, Baltic Sea operations recommenced. The British fleet, under the command of Admiral Sir James W. D. Dundas, with a French contingent, detached squadrons to again blockade Russian Baltic ports. Revel, Aland, Hango, Sveaborg, and Kronstadt were reconnoitered by Dundas, who found the defenses of Kronstadt greatly reinforced over the preceding winter months. Dundas believed his naval strength inadequate for attack.

The Royal Navy also operated in the Gulf of Bothnia and at the mouth of the Gulf of Finland to prevent Russian ships from breaking through the blockade. Dundas's ships also bombarded and destroyed the Russian forts at Svastholm and Frederiksham. Anglo-French vessels began a thunderous bombardment of Sveaborg on 9 August 1855. Two days later Dundas reported that the allies had fired over 1,100 tons of iron shells into Sveaborg, and that the Russian fleet's naval base had been destroyed. While a British success, the destruction of Sveaborg did little except raise morale at home and expectations that perhaps Sevastopol was equally vulnerable to a continuous allied bombardment.

In November 1855, the fleet withdrew for the winter. The opening of the Paris Peace Conference on 24 February 1856 meant that the Baltic Sea operations were not renewed.

Crimean War, 1854–1856: Baltic Sea Operations

See also Crimean War; Dundas, Admiral Sir James W. D.; Napier, Admiral Sir Charles; Pacific Ocean Operations, Crimean War; White Sea Operations, Crimean War
References: Judd (1975); Padfield (1981); Palmer (1987); Royle (2000); Warner (1972)

Barnard, Lieutenant General Sir Henry W.
See Delhi, Siege and Storming of

Bayonets
See Infantry, British Army–Small Arms

Bengal Army
The Bengal Army was the military force of the Bengal Presidency in India from the middle of the eighteenth century until the three presidency armies (Bengal, Bombay, and Madras) were abolished in 1895 and replaced by one unified Indian Army under a single commander in chief. The Bengal Presidency was the largest of the three presidencies. As a result, its governor was designated the governor-general, India, in 1853, and the commander in chief of the Bengal Army was styled the commander in chief, India.

The most reliable Bengal units consisted of European troops. The Bengal European Regiment was organized in 1756 and expanded to two regiments in 1822; the two were amalgamated in 1829. A second European regiment was formed in 1839 and a third in 1854. The first native battalion was raised in 1757, and by 1815 there were 30 native infantry regiments. The number of Bengal Native Infantry regiments was increased to 69 by 1857. Ten cavalry regiments existed in 1826, and by 1847 there were 17 cavalry regiments, a number that later rose to 29. Bengal artillery increased in strength early in this period, and by 1845 there were 3 artillery battalions of 6 companies each. The Bengal Sappers and Miners were organized in 1819, and in 1833 the Bengal Pioneers were merged into them.

One key difference between the Bengal Army and the Bombay and Madras Armies was that caste was recognized and practiced as much as possible in Bengal. In the Bombay and Madras Armies, soldiering came first, and caste was a secondary concern. One Madras Army officer noted in the 1830s that "the prejudices of the Bengal troops on many points are often difficult to overcome, partly in consequence of the great numbers of Brahmins among them; and partly because they consider themselves collectively of a higher caste than the Madras sepoy, whose prejudices in comparison are trivial" (Beaumont 1977, p. 8). The Bengal Army had a widespread reputation for lack of discipline, and it was not unusual for a lower-caste officer to defer to a higher-caste sepoy. Of the seven Bengal Native Infantry regiments for which data exists from 1858, 60 percent of the other ranks were high-caste Hindus (Brahmins and Rajputs), as compared to about 25 percent of the Bombay Native Infantry in 1858.

The sensitive issue of caste, and potential defilement, especially in light of the "greased cartridge" controversy, can be seen as a factor in igniting the Indian Mutiny at Meerut, Oudh, within the Bengal Army's area. Sixty-four Bengal Army battalions mutinied or were preemptively disarmed during the mutiny, compared to only two Bombay Army battalions and no Madras Army units.

The effects of the Indian Mutiny were far-reaching and resulted in the transfer of power in India from the East India Company to the British Crown. The company's European regiments became British Army line regiments, although there were numerous difficulties over conditions of service and pay, with the resultant protests called the White Mutiny. (The 5th Bengal European Regiment, for example, mutinied and was disarmed and disbanded in 1860, with one of its soldiers being executed by firing squad on the day of unit dissolution.) Five Bengal European cavalry regiments were disbanded in 1861 and its soldiers encouraged to join one of three new British cavalry regiments. European artillery units became batteries of the Royal Artillery.

Only 15 Bengal Native Infantry regiments survived the mutiny, and with new regiments added, the total of Bengal Native Infantry regiments that existed in 1864 was 45. The number of Bengal irregular cavalry regiments was reduced to 17. Recruitment emphasized class and caste more than previously, and preference was given to recruiting members of the "martial classes." Single-caste battalions, which had been receptive and vulnerable to insurrection, were generally replaced by mixed battalions containing a number of single-caste companies. Moreover, the percent of Hindus in the mixed battalions was reduced from 60 percent (of the high-caste Hindus) to about 50 percent (of all caste Hindus), "balanced by Muslims 19%, Sikhs 20%, and Gurkhas 12%" (Robson 1995a, p. 22).

By the end of the reorganization in 1861, the strength of the Bengal Army was 135,000 Indian troops and 62,000 British troops. This was close to the 2:1 post-Mutiny recommended ratio of native to British soldiers, as compared to the pre-Mutiny ratio of about 5.5:1. In 1876, there were 63,151 Indian Army officers and men and 41,517 British Army officers and men, a total of 104,668 officers and men in the Bengal Presidency.

See also Bombay Army; East India Company; East India Company, Military Forces; India, British Army in; Indian Army Operations; Indian Army Organization; Indian Mutiny; Madras Army
References: Beaumont (1977); Haythornthwaite (1995); Kaul (2002); Roberts (1995); Robson (1995a); Robson (1995b); Stanley (1999); Wolseley (1878)

Bitter-Ender

A "bitter-ender" (*bittereinder*) was a Boer who refused to surrender to the British during the Second Boer War and doggedly fought to the "bitter end" of the conflict, the signing of the Treaty of Vereeniging on 31 May 1902.

The turn of the tide in the Second Boer War arguably coincided with the British capture of Johannesburg on 30 May 1900 and of Pretoria on 5 June 1900, coupled with the British Proclamation No. 5 on 16 June to start burning Boer farms to retaliate against the combatant Boers and deprive them of support. Fatalism and war weariness seemed to grip many Boer leaders and soldiers. In fact, on 1 June 1900, the Boer leadership held a conference to consider surrendering to the British. More aggressive Boer leaders, including Christiaan R. De Wet and Marthinus T. Steyn, advocated guerrilla warfare and vowed to fight to the "bitter end." These two men became the leaders and symbols of Boer resistance and the bitter-enders.

During the following months, many Boers voluntarily surrendered to the British, earning the epithet "hands-uppers." After fighting at the Brandwater Basin in late July 1900, for example, Boer General Marthinus Prinsloo surprised the British by surrendering his entire force of about 4,314 Boers. These Boers were required only to swear an oath that they would not fight against the British, aid or provide information to the Boers, and "further promise and swear to remain quietly at my home until the war is over" (Solomon 1974, p. 6). Some Boers surrendered because they were physically or psychologically unequal to the demands of modern warfare, while others, convinced the war was lost and further resistance would destroy the country, became hands-uppers.

One group of hands-uppers in September 1901 approached the British and volunteered to fight on the British side against their former Boer compatriots. They were then derisively labeled "joiners" ("yoiners"). These men, the "National Scouts," seemed motivated by loot, money, and the suggestion of a privileged position in society after the British won the war. Their traitorous actions caused a great schism in South Africa after the war.

At the end of the war, about 21,000 defiant Boer bitter-enders—more than twice the number estimated by British intelligence—surrendered to the British.

See also Boer War, Second (1899–1902); Boers; De Wet, Chief Commandant Christiaan R.; Steyn, Marthinus T.
References: Lee (1985); Marix Evans (2000); Pakenham (1979); Solomon (1974); Wulfsohn (1991)

Blockhouses

The British constructed thousands of blockhouses in South Africa during the Second Boer War (1899–1902). The blockhouses were built initially to protect the railway, the main British supply route and lines of communication. Blockhouses were later built in a series of lines, as obstacles against which pursuing British columns could literally fence in the Boers and trap them.

The first blockhouses appear to have been constructed shortly after the fall of Pretoria on 5 June 1900, during the early months of the guerrilla phase of the war. The early structures were masonry built of mortared stonework or concrete, one to three stories in height, with a roof of timber and corrugated iron or concrete. There was usually a platform in one corner on the roof for mounting a machine gun. Entrance was by a ladder through a door on the first floor, about seven or eight feet off the ground. Rifle ports, windows, and doors were protected by loop-holed steel plates. While these blockhouses were virtually indestructible, they were very expensive (about £800 to £1,000 each) and took about three months to build. The British constructed a total of about 441 masonry blockhouses.

The strategy of General (later Field Marshal Earl) Lord Horatio H. Kitchener, who became commander in chief, South Africa, in December 1900, was to integrate the function of fortified blockhouses with that of mobile attacking units on "drives." The country could be divided into smaller areas by fortified lines, and the Boers would be restricted to operating in shrinking areas that had been cleared previously of all inhabitants and shelter. Mobile British troops could then sweep through an area and drive the Boers into a fortified line of blockhouses.

The high cost and long construction period made further construction of masonry blockhouses impractical. As a result, Major S. R. Rice, 23rd Field Company, Royal Engineers, designed a relatively inexpensive, easily constructed octagonal corrugated iron blockhouse in early 1901. By this time the Boers had lost most of their artillery and a double-thickness corrugated iron wall with a shingle-and-rubble filling provided sufficient protection against small arms fire.

Rice developed the circular corrugated blockhouse shortly thereafter. The circular design enhanced all-around observation. In addition, the absence of corners reduced the need for wood, which was subject to rot and splintered when hit by bullets or shrapnel. The circular corrugated blockhouse had an interior diameter of 13 feet with a standing height of 6 feet. The first blockhouse of this type cost £44, and when mass-produced, the price dropped to £16. Reportedly six men could construct the circular corrugated blockhouse in six hours.

Low walls of stones or sandbags and trenches were frequently placed or dug around, and later between, blockhouses. Soldiers could use this cover and concealment to defend their blockhouse. Barbed wire entanglements were constructed around the blockhouses by twisting rolls and strands together, elevating them to various heights, and staking them into the ground to prevent the passage of Boers or their animals. Frequently bells and empty tin cans were hung on the wire to serve as alarms. As more blockhouses were built, the distances between them decreased, allowing interlocking fields of fire to be designated between blockhouses. This effect was increased by the blockhouses being built in an intricate wave pattern and not in a straight line, to prevent soldiers in one blockhouse from firing on an adjacent blockhouse.

One noncommissioned officer and six men normally manned one blockhouse. A lieutenant was in charge of three or four blockhouses and a captain ten to twelve. A battalion would normally occupy about sixty blockhouses.

The first line of blockhouses was built in January 1901 between Kapmurden and Komatipoort in the Eastern Transvaal. After their success was proven, additional blockhouse lines were built in July and August 1901. Gradually thirty-four lines of blockhouses were constructed, the longest running for 175 miles along the railway line from Komatipoort to Wonderfontein and garrisoned by 3,200 soldiers. From January 1901 to May 1902, an average of forty blockhouses per month were built.

By the end of the war, over 8,000 blockhouses had been built over 3,700 miles, an average of one blockhouse every half mile. These interconnected blockhouses were manned by 50,000 troops, augmented by about 16,000 Africans who patrolled mainly at night. Blockhouses were an important component in the success of the war.

See also Boer War, Second (1899–1902); Commando System; Kitchener, Field Marshal Horatio H.; Lines of Communication; Transvaal

References: Baden-Powell (1903); Barthorp (1987); Jones (1996); Lee (1985); Pakenham (1979); Raugh (1994); Sixsmith (1974); Tomlinson (1997); Trew (1999)

Blood, General Sir Bindon (1842–1940)

General Sir Bindon Blood was a British Army officer best known for his long service in India and skillful command of the Malakand Field Force and the Buner Field Force during the 1897–1898 Pathan uprising on the North-West Frontier.

Blood was born on 7 November 1842 and was said to take pride in his distant ancestor, Colonel James Blood, who attempted to seize the Crown Jewels in 1671. After attending the Indian Military Seminary at Addiscombe, Blood was commissioned a temporary lieutenant in the Royal Engineers. He specialized in signaling and pontoon boat construction. In 1870, he became the first commander of the newly raised Royal Engineer Telegraph Troop. Blood was sent to India in 1871 where he served until 1907, with exceptions of participation in the Zulu War (1879), Arabi Rebellion (1882), and Second Boer War (1901), as well as periods of home leave.

Blood's first experience of active service on the North-West Frontier came in 1877–1878 in the punitive expedition against the Jowacki Afridis. After active service with the Zulu Field Force in 1879, he returned to India and proceeded to Kabul and limited participation in the Second Afghan War. Reassigned from India to England in 1882, Blood took command of a field company. He was ordered to active service in Egypt, fought with his sappers in the Battle of Tel el-Kebir, and returned to India via England in 1883.

Blood served in staff positions in India and honed the skills that helped him ensure his future success. In 1895, as a brigadier general, he became chief of staff to Major General Sir R. C. Low, commander of the 15,000-man Chitral Relief Force. The six-week operation to relieve the beleaguered fort at Chitral involved tremendous hardships and detailed logistical coordination as the Chitral Relief Force marched over difficult, frequently snowbound terrain and through hostile tribal areas. Blood was knighted for this service.

In 1897, Blood was appointed to command the Malakand Field Force organized to punish revolting tribes in the Swat Valley. Before he was able to complete his mission, he attached one of his brigades to the Mohmand Field Force. After destroying a number of enemy villages and prevailing in a heated engagement at Gat, the Malakand Field Force met its objectives and was disbanded in October 1897.

At the end of 1897, the only rebellious tribes that had not been properly chastised were the Bunerwals and the tribes living between Buner and the Indus River. The Buner Field Force, under Blood's command, was organized for that purpose in late 1897. Blood's expedition operated aggressively in attacking and entering Buner Province, then traversed the entire area in a show of force receiving the submission of all tribes encountered, including the Bunerwals. The operation was completed quickly, in large measure due to Blood's leadership, and the Buner Field Force was inactivated on 20 January 1898.

Blood then commanded the Meerut Division for over two years before being ordered in 1901 to South Africa, where he commanded, as a lieutenant general, operations in the Eastern Transvaal. Returning to India later in 1901, he commanded the important Punjab area, was promoted to full general in 1906, and retired the following year. In retirement, Blood remained active in regimental affairs and recruiting efforts during World War I.

Blood is best remembered as the commander of the Malakand Field Force, the subject of Winston L. S. Churchill's first book, *The Story of the Malakand Field Force* (1898). Churchill dedicated his maiden literary effort to Blood, "under whose command the operations therein recorded were carried out; by whose generalship they were brought to a successful conclusion; and to whose kindness the author is indebted for the most valuable and fascinating experience of his life" (Churchill 1898, p. v). Blood, a very popular commander, wrote his autobiography, *Four Score Years and Ten*, in 1933. He died in London on 16 May 1940, age ninety-seven. Blood's name had appeared in the *Army List* for eighty years.

See also Addiscombe, Military Seminary; Arabi Rebellion; Boer War, Second (1899–1902); Buner Field Force; Churchill, Sir Winston L. S.; India; Malakand Field Force; North-West Frontier; Tel el-Kebir, Battle of; Zulu War

References: Barthorp (1982); Churchill (1898); Farwell (1972); Fincastle and Eliott-Lockhart (1898); Miller (1977); Nevill (1912); Wickham Legg (1949)

Boer War, First (1880–1881)

The First Boer War (1880–1881), or from the Boer perspective, the First War of Independence, was caused mainly by the collision of British imperial aspirations and the South African desire for independence. This was a relatively short campaign best known for the humiliating defeat suffered by the British at the Battle of Majuba Hill and for setting the stage for another and much more significant war two decades later.

The British, concerned for a number of reasons in the 1870s that anarchy in the Transvaal could weaken their entire position in the region, and interested in retaining the diamond and gold deposits there, annexed the Transvaal in January 1877. British colonial officials believed the Transvaal would welcome British annexation, but this was a tremendous miscalculation: the Boers bitterly resented it. The Boer nationalists were becoming increasingly militant, especially after the 1880 election in Great Britain when the prime minister stated that the Transvaal could only be independent as a member of a South African confederation. Finally, the insurgent Boers proclaimed the Transvaal a republic on 16 December 1880. Hostilities began immediately with the Boers investing the two British Army companies at Potchefstroom. Other Boers rode to besiege British garrisons at locations in the Transvaal including Pretoria, Wakkerstroom, Standerton, Marabastadt, Rustenburg, and Lydenburg.

This led directly to the First Boer War (1880–1881). This was a short, sharp conflict in which the British, under the command of Major General Sir George Pomeroy-Colley (who had been promoted to major general and became the governor and commander in chief of Natal and the Transvaal and high commissioner for South-East Africa in April 1880), were defeated and humiliated by the Boers in four engagements.

The first action of the war took place on 20 December 1880, when a British column was intercepted by Boers at Bronkhorstspruit, about 30 miles east of Pretoria. In the short battle, characterized by accurate and rapid Boer rifle firing, the British lost about 57 soldiers killed and more than 100 wounded (including 20 fatally) out of a total force of 263. The survivors surrendered. This was the first devastating defeat for the British in the conflict.

Pomeroy-Colley learned on Christmas Day (1880) that a debacle had occurred at Bronkhorstspruit and that the British garrisons in the Transvaal were in various stages of being surrounded. At the time the British had 1,759 troops in the Transvaal and 1,772 in Natal. Headquartered in Pietermaritzburg, Natal, he knew he would have to lead a force to quell the Boer unrest and relieve the British garrisons in the Transvaal. The only pass in the Drakensberg Mountain range through which an army could enter the Transvaal from Natal was at Laing's Nek, which the Boers were expected to defend. The 1,400-man composite Natal Field Force departed Pietermaritzburg on 10 January 1881.

On 28 January 1881, Pomeroy-Colley's force was at a farm named Mount Prospect, 3 miles south of Laing's Nek. There were an estimated 2,000 Boers in defensive positions on Laing's Nek. Pomeroy-Colley intended to turn the Boer position by a frontal attack, but the British were stopped by a

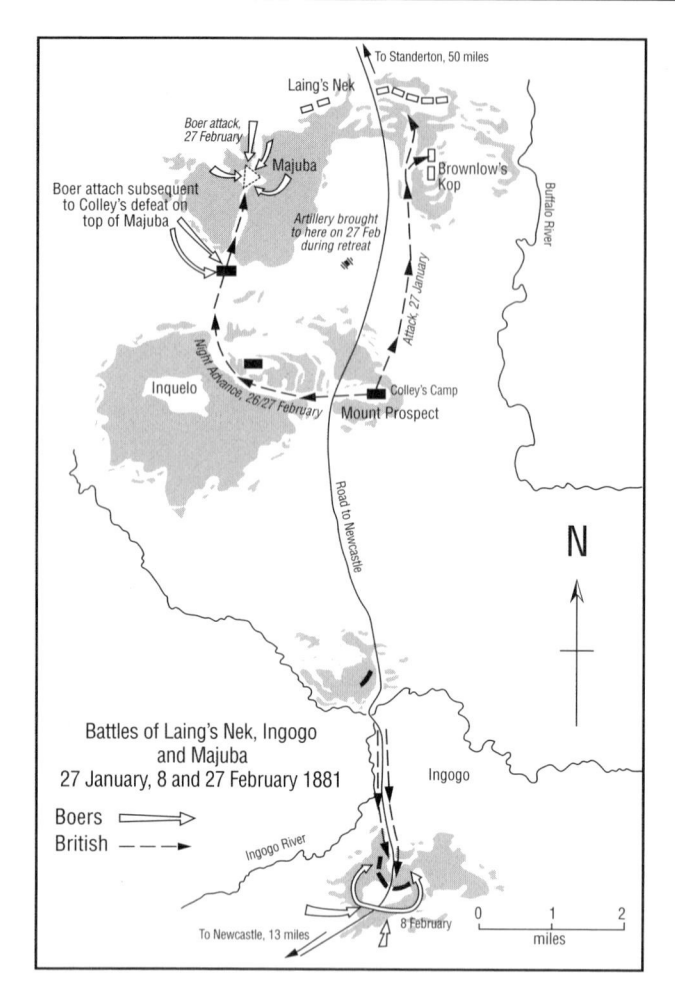

Battles of Laing's Nek, Ingogo, and Majuba Hill, 28 January and 8 and 27 February 1881.

Source: Michael Barthorp. *The Anglo-Boer Wars: The British and the Afrikaners, 1815–1902.* Dorset, UK: Blandford Press, 1987.

fierce Boer fusillade. The attack was a dismal failure and the British casualties were 83 killed and 111 wounded.

The British withdrew to Mount Prospect to await reinforcements. On 7 February 1881, the Boers started a flanking movement to isolate the British force. The Colonial Office was also pressuring Pomeroy-Colley to defeat the Boers quickly or end hostilities before they spread further. The next day he personally led a five-company force on the road to Newcastle to ensure the route was still open and apparently to frighten the Boers known to be in the area. Some 8 miles south of Mount Prospect, near the Ingogo River, the British encountered and fought a large Boer force. In this fiasco, the Battle of Ingogo, the British lost 76 men killed and another 67 wounded.

Pomeroy-Colley learned that the Boer positions at Laing's Nek had been strengthened considerably. He thought he would be able to outflank the Boers by seizing the undefended mountain of Majuba, to the west of and dominating Laing's Nek, and from that vantage point force the Boers to abandon their positions. After conducting a night march on 26–27 February 1881, Pomeroy-Colley's soldiers reached Majuba's unoccupied summit by 5:00 A.M. on 27 February. The British soldiers, uninformed about the situation and plans, did not dig defensive fighting positions. Pomeroy-Colley then became inactive and possibly fatalistic, perhaps through complacency or fatigue.

The Boers, after seeing British soldiers on Majuba Hill, were surprised at not receiving a British artillery barrage on their positions. A number of Boers, while covered by supporting fire from comrades, ascended toward the British positions. It took about five hours, during which heavy rifle fire was exchanged, before about 400 Boers had reached positions within striking distance of the summit. In the early afternoon, the Boers fired at close range at Gordon's Knoll and occupied it in a few minutes, then began pouring fire into the main body of soldiers. The Boers continued to advance, increased their accurate rifle fire, and confusion reigned. Soon many of the demoralized British soldiers panicked, threw down their rifles, and stampeded to the rear. The Boers were close behind, shooting the fleeing soldiers. Only a half hour had gone by since the Boers had seized Gordon's Knoll. In the ensuing melee, Pomeroy-Colley was shot and died instantly. There were 285 British soldiers, out of a force of about 365 on the summit, killed or wounded at the Battle of Majuba Hill.

The Boer victory at the Battle of Majuba Hill effectively ended the war. Major General (later Field Marshal) Sir (Henry) Evelyn M. Wood, V.C., who had brought reinforcements and had become the British second in command, signed a truce with the Boers on 6 March 1881 that was ratified by the Convention of Pretoria six months later. This largely restored independence to the Transvaal, subject to British "suzerainty." This convention was replaced by the London Convention of 1884, in which all mention of suzerainty was removed but to which Britain retained the right to veto external treaties.

See also Boers; Bronkhorstspruit, Battle of; Commando System; Imperialism; Ingogo, Battle of; Laing's Nek, Battle of; Majuba Hill, Battle of; Pomeroy-Colley, Major General Sir George; Transvaal; Wood, Field Marshal Sir (Henry) Evelyn M., V.C.

References: Barthorp (1987); Bennett (2001); Bond (1967); Bond (1972); Conan Doyle (1901); Farwell (1972); Ransford (1967)

Boer War, Second (1899–1902)

The Second Boer War (1899–1902), known commonly as the Boer War, has frequently been dismissed as one of "Queen Victoria's little wars." In reality it was Britain's longest (lasting over thirty-two months), most expensive (costing over UK £200 million), and bloodiest war (with about 22,000 British, 25,000 Boers, and 12,000 Africans losing their lives) fought from the end of the Napoleonic Wars in 1815 to the outbreak of World War I in 1914.

The primary issue that sparked the outbreak of the Boer War on 11 October 1899 was the political rights of the *uitlanders* (foreigners) in the Transvaal South African Republic. Gold was discovered in 1886 on the Witwatersrand west of Johannesburg, and this attracted large numbers of *uitlanders* to the area. This in turn upset the stability of the area, and the Transvaal Government was unwilling to give full political rights to these immigrants, concerned that they (the Boers) would become the minority and be outvoted by the mainly British foreigners.

The Cape Colony prime minister, Cecil Rhodes, was the driving force behind an unsuccessful raid conducted by Dr. Leander Starr Jameson in 1895–1896 to support a planned uprising of *uitlanders* and overthrow the Transvaal Government. This episode led directly to confrontation between the Transvaal and Great Britain. In light of increasing pressure and after an ultimatum issued by the Transvaal, war broke out on 11 October 1899.

Upon the outbreak of the Boer War, the strength of the entire British Army (not including the Indian Army and colonial forces) was about 235,500. Of that number, only 22,104 of these soldiers were in or en route to South Africa. A total of 14,704 British soldiers were in or on their way to Natal, and 7,400 were in or in transit to Cape Colony. Including local colonial units, the British initially had about 27,000 men present for duty in South Africa.

Boer forces, organized into commandos of various sizes, included a 17,500-man force deployed on the Natal border at the beginning of the war. There were another 6,000 burghers in the Western Transvaal, 1,700 men on the Northern Transvaal border, and 4,800 Boers in the Western Orange Free State. Other mobilized Boer elements totaled about 3,500 men.

The Boer War, based upon the nature of the operations, can be divided into four main phases. The first phase of the war (11–30 October 1899) consisted of limited Boer offensives in Cape Colony and Natal after the outbreak of hostilities. Boers under the command of Assistant Commandant-General Jacobus De la Rey won the first skirmish at Kraaipan on 12–13 October, and the Boer siege of Mafeking began on 13 October and of Kimberley the following day. The ill-prepared British forces were defeated at a number of engagements and retreated from other positions. On "Mournful Monday," 30 October, the British were beaten at Nicholson's Nek and Lombard's Kop.

General Sir Redvers H. Buller, V.C., commanding the British 1st Army Corps at Aldershot since 1898, was designated the commander in chief of the South African Field Force in October 1899. He arrived in South Africa on 31 October 1899, which begins the second phase of the Boer War. This phase, also known as the Buller phase, consisted of the first unsuccessful British counteroffensives. Buller was under tremendous political pressure to relieve the besieged British garrisons at Mafeking, Kimberley, and Ladysmith (which was surrounded by Boer forces on 2 November 1899).

Buller divided the British forces in South Africa into three main elements in November 1899, commanding one himself, to accomplish three different missions. The westernmost force, the 10,000-man 1st Division commanded by Lieutenant General (later Field Marshal) Lord Paul S. Methuen, was given the task of relieving Kimberley. On 21 November, his force began to advance north from Orange River Station, winning engagements at Belmont (23 November) and Graspan (25 November). His force was pinned down by Boers at the Modder River south of Kimberley on 28 November. This battle was characterized by poor command and control on Methuen's part, and a lack of British appreciation of Boer marksmanship, firepower, and ability to fight from camouflage defensive positions. The Boers abandoned their positions that night, giving the British an expensive victory.

Lieutenant General Sir William F. Gatacre, who had arrived in South Africa in November 1899, was in nominal command of the 3rd Division. He was tasked, with a small ad hoc force, to control as much of the northeastern section of Cape Colony as he could and prevent any Boer advances from Stormberg. Gatacre, even though instructed to remain on the defensive until reinforced, was determined to seize Stormberg in a dawn attack after a night march. Gatacre failed to conduct a reconnaissance, changed the route and direction of attack (or got lost en route) at the last minute, and then led tired troops in rugged terrain in an attempt to surprise the Boers. At daylight on 10 December 1899, Gat-

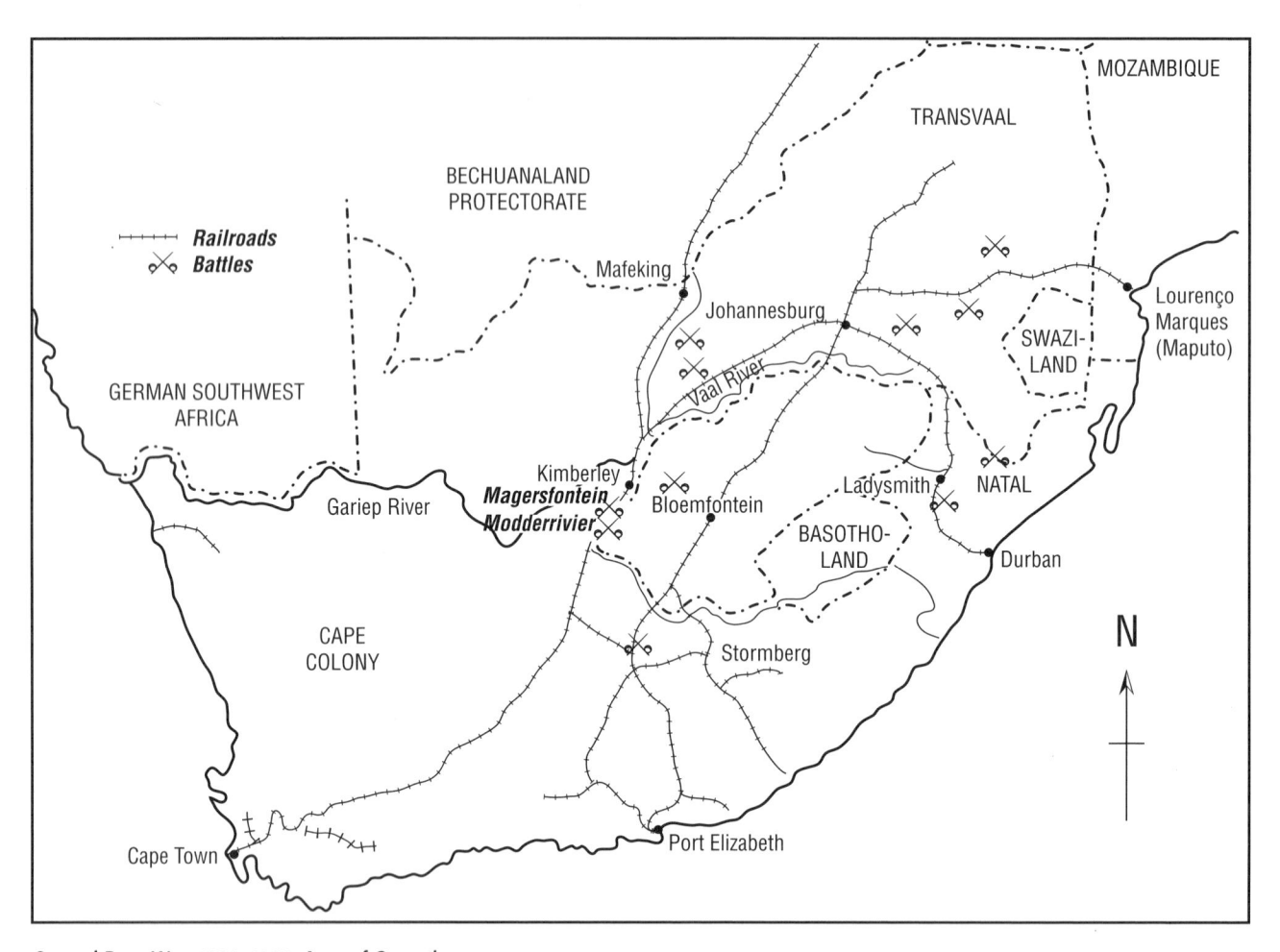

Second Boer War, 1899–1902: Area of Operations

acre's exhausted column was caught in a pass with Boers on the high ground. The Boers opened fire on the British, some of whom were able to occupy nearby high ground, but most were worn out and withdrew hastily. The Battle of Stormberg, the first of three significant British defeats constituting Black Week, resulted in British casualties of 28 killed, 51 wounded, and 634 captured.

Methuen continued to advance to relieve Kimberley. He attempted a night attack on 11 December 1899 to defeat Boers entrenched at Magersfontein, south of Kimberley. This assault turned into a horrible defeat with British casualties numbering 210 killed and 728 wounded, and was the second major defeat of Black Week.

Buller's force continued to march to the relief of Ladysmith. His units were repulsed while trying to cross the Tugela River at Colenso on 15 December 1899, at a cost of 1,138 total British casualties. The Battle of Colenso was the third British defeat in Black Week. The British public was shocked by these British failures, which, together with Buller's suggestion that the Ladysmith garrison consider surrendering, resulted in his relief by Field Marshal Lord (later Earl) Frederick S. Roberts, V.C., on 18 December 1899. Buller did not return to England then, but he remained in South Africa and commanded British troops in Natal until October 1900. He was in overall command at the Spion Kop disaster, 23–24 January 1900, at which at least 322 men were killed, 585 wounded, and 300 captured. Moreover, the Boers continued to besiege Ladysmith.

Roberts and his new chief of staff, Lieutenant General (later Field Marshal Earl) Lord Horatio H. Kitchener, arrived at Cape Town on 10 January 1900. Revising Buller's strategy, Roberts implemented a more indirect strategy concerned with seizing the enemy's capitals, believing enemy resistance would then crumble. The third phase of the Second Boer

War, also called the Roberts phase, began on 11 February 1900 and consisted of generally successful British counteroffensives. Kimberley was relieved on 15 February 1900, Ladysmith on 28 February, and after a 217-day encirclement, Mafeking was relieved on 17 May 1900.

Roberts and Kitchener tried to "reorganize" the supply and transport system in February 1900, but the result was a failure. Within weeks, the "old" supply and transport system, under the control of the Army Service Corps, was largely restored.

Kitchener, in Roberts's absence, commanded British troops at Paardeberg on 18 February 1900. Kitchener committed his troops in numerous futile frontal assaults against the entrenched Boers, failing to understand the lethality of an enemy armed with magazine-fed rifles using smokeless powder. Kitchener's dogmatic use of outdated tactics resulted in the most British casualties—1,270—suffered in a single day during the entire war.

Roberts's offensive, after the capture of Bloemfontein (13 March 1900), Johannesburg (31 May 1900), and Pretoria (5 June 1900), seemed to lose its momentum. Roberts failed to secure areas behind the British advances, thus making them vulnerable to guerrilla warfare—an unconventional type of fighting he only belatedly recognized and had difficulties understanding. Although he initiated the policy of farm burning in June 1900, Roberts had convinced himself for many months that the war was basically over. He relinquished command on 29 November 1900 to Kitchener, returned to England, and superseded Field Marshal Viscount Garnet J. Wolseley as British Army commander in chief. This concluded the third phase of the Second Boer War.

The fourth phase of the Second Boer War began on 31 March 1900 with the Battle of Sannaspos. Thus the third and fourth phases of the Second Boer War overlapped (from 31 March to 29 November 1900) and marked the transition from semiconventional operations to guerrilla warfare.

Kitchener resorted to drastic methods, frequently criticized, to defeat the continued Boer insurgency. In order to deprive the Boer guerrillas of food, shelter, information, and other support, he increased farm burning, removed Boer families from their homesteads and resettled them in concentration camps, and constructed an increasingly large network of blockhouses. Mobile columns attempted to hunt down and isolate Boer forces. Kitchener's draconian measures ravaged the countryside and finally wore down Boer resistance. The conflict ended in a British "victory" with the signing of the Treaty of Vereeniging on 31 May 1902.

A total of 365,695 imperial and 82,742 colonial soldiers fought for the British during the Boer War. Of this number, 21,942 were killed in action or died of wounds or disease. Boer combatants totaled 87,365, of whom about 7,000 died. The number of Boer civilians who died in the concentration camps has been estimated at between 18,000 and 25,000. The British rationalized or forgot the reasons for their early defeats by the Boers and failed to appreciate the major tactical lesson of the Boer War: "It was that the smokeless, long-range, high-velocity, small-bore magazine bullet from rifle or machine-gun—plus the trench—had decisively tilted the balance against attack and in favour of defence" (Pakenham 1979, p. 610).

The Second Boer War was the last great British imperial war. It would take the hecatombs of casualties a generation later in the static and putrid trench warfare of the Western Front and the Dardanelles before the British and other armies learned that the era of colonial warfare was over.

See also Baden-Powell, Lieutenant General Sir Robert S. S.; Bitter-Ender; Blockhouses; Boer War, First (1880–1881); Boers; Botha, Commandant-General Louis; Buller, General Sir Redvers H., V.C.; Colenso, Battle of; Commando System; Concentration Camps; Cronje, Assistant Commandant-General Piet A.; De la Rey, Assistant Commandant-General Jacobus; De Wet, Chief Commandant Christiaan R.; Gatacre, Lieutenant General Sir William F.; Gough, General Sir Hubert de la P.; Imperialism; Jameson Raid; Joubert, Commandant-General Petrus J.; Kitchener, Field Marshal Horatio H.; Kruger, S. J. Paulus; Ladysmith, Siege of; Mafeking, Siege of; Magersfontein, Battle of; Methuen, Field Marshal Paul S.; Modder River, Battle of; Paardeberg, Battle of; Rhodes, Cecil J.; Roberts, Field Marshal Frederick S., V.C.; Spion Kop, Battle of; Steyn, Marthinus T.; Stormberg, Battle of; Transvaal; Vaal Krantz, Battle of; Warren, General Sir Charles; Wauchope, Major General Andrew G.; White, Field Marshal Sir George S., V.C.; Wolseley, Field Marshal Garnet J.

References: Belfield (1975); Carver (1999); Hamilton (1966); Jackson (1999); Lee (1985); Melville (1923); Nasson (1999); Pakenham (1979); Pollock (2001); Powell (1994); Stone and Schmidl (1988); Symons (1963); Trew (1999); Wessels (2000)

Boers

"Boer" (from the German *bauer*, or farmer) was the general name for the people of Dutch descent who left Cape Colony in southern Africa and traveled inland during the "Great

Trek" of 1836–1846 to establish their own republics. In the twentieth century, "Afrikaner" replaced "Boer."

The Dutch first landed at the Cape of Good Hope in 1652. Dutch settlement increased, with German Protestants and French Huguenots (and other displaced Europeans) also migrating to South Africa, resulting in expansion onto the lands of the indigenous Khoikhoi (called Hottentots by whites), San (Bushmen, to whites), and Xhosa on the Fish River to the east. The Dutch and other immigrants developed the commando system and sent expeditions against the tribes, virtually exterminating many of them. The whites (Afrikaners) had servants drawn from the local black population and imported slaves from East Africa, Mozambique, and other Dutch colonies.

In 1795, the British replaced the bankrupt Dutch East India Company as custodians of the Cape, and twenty years later, at the end of the Napoleonic Wars, the Cape became British permanently. The British abolished slavery without compensation in 1834, bringing Boer discontent to a head. Frustrated with British administration and a land shortage, and believing in their own racial superiority, a number of Boers—numbering about 14,000 between 1836 and 1846—embarked on the "Great Trek" inland to establish their own independent nations. Called the Voortrekkers, they crossed the Orange River, which formed the southern boundary of what became the Orange Free State; farther north, they crossed the Vaal River, the boundary between the Orange Free State and what became the Transvaal. During their exodus, the Boers encountered opposition from the Matabele and the Zulus. Some 500 Boers fought and defeated about 11,000 Zulus, killing about 3,000 of them, at the Battle of Blood River on 16 December 1838. The Boers considered this victory a blessing of the Lord and justification for their encroachment on the lands of and dominance over the indigenous black people. It further underscored their attitudes later to British imperialism.

The Boers, by allying themselves with a Zulu chief, declared their own "Republic of Port Natal and adjacent countries." They sought British recognition, but the British were prepared to permit self-government only under overall British control and with a British military presence. In 1842, a 260-man British force encamped near Durban, a British settlement established many years earlier, and skirmishes took place between them and the Boers. The following year the British Government declared Natal to be a British colony, and in 1844 Natal became a dependency of the Cape Colony.

Further conflict took place in 1845 in Griqualand, the area west of Natal. British soldiers were deployed to the area to support the Griquas in a skirmish against aggressive Boer settlers. The Seventh Frontier War between the British and Gaika people (another clan of the Xhosa) took place in 1846–1847. In early 1848, to try to ease tension between the British and Boers on the Orange River frontier, British Lieutenant General Sir Harry G. W. Smith, the governor and commander in chief of Cape Colony, annexed the territory between the Orange and Vaal Rivers, to be called the Orange River Sovereignty. The Boers resented this action, and another clash, the Battle of Boomplaats, took place on 29 August 1848. At Boomplaats, Smith defeated the Boers, who were unable to withstand the speed of his attack and skillful infantry-artillery coordination.

The Sand River Convention of 1852 and the Bloemfontein Convention of 1854 recognized, with limitations, the independence of the Transvaal (renamed the South African Republic) and the Orange Free State, respectively. In 1867, diamonds were discovered in land contiguous to and claimed by both the Orange Free State and the Transvaal. The diamond fields were annexed to the Cape, and the British annexed nearby Basutoland. The diamonds brought in an influx of immigrants and reawakened British strategic interest in the area.

Friction between the expansionist Boers and indigenous peoples continued. In 1876, a strong Boer commando failed to capture a Basuto mountain stronghold. It became obvious that the Boers were unable to manage their own finances as the Transvaal neared bankruptcy. The British, concerned that potential insolvency and anarchy in the Transvaal could weaken their entire position in the region, annexed the Transvaal in January 1877. British colonial officials believed the Transvaal would welcome British annexation, protection, and efficient governance, especially as a prelude to confederation with the Cape Colony. This was a tremendous miscalculation, and the Boers bitterly resented this action.

The British fought and defeated the Zulus in 1879, and by the end of the year had also vanquished the rebellious Bapedi chief Sekukuni. The Boer nationalists were becoming more militant, especially after the 1880 election in Great Britain when the prime minister stated that the Transvaal could be independent only as a member of a South African confederation. Finally, the insurgent Boers proclaimed the Transvaal a republic on 16 December 1880.

This led directly to the First Boer War (1880–1881). This

was a short, sharp conflict in which the British, under the command of Major General Sir George Pomeroy-Colley (who became the governor and commander in chief of Natal and the Transvaal and high commissioner for South-East Africa in April 1880), were defeated and humiliated by the Boers at Bronkhorstspruit (20 December 1880), Laing's Nek (28 January 1881), and Ingogo (8 February 1881). The decisive engagement of the war was the Battle of Majuba Hill (27 February 1881) in which Pomeroy-Colley was mortally wounded and the British soundly defeated. This effectively ended the war, and a truce was signed on 6 March 1881 and ratified by the Convention of Pretoria six months later. This largely restored independence to the Transvaal, subject to British "suzerainty," or control of the Transvaal's external and internal affairs. This convention was replaced by the London Convention of 1884, in which all mention of suzerainty was removed, with Britain retaining the right to veto external treaties. Gold was discovered in 1886 on the Witwatersrand, a range of hills west of Johannesburg. This upset the stability of the area as large numbers of *uitlanders* (foreigners) migrated to the area. The Transvaal Government was averse to giving full political rights to these immigrants, concerned that they (the Boers) would become the minority and could be outvoted by the mainly British foreigners.

The Cape Colony prime minister, Cecil J. Rhodes, was the driving force behind an unsuccessful raid conducted by Dr. Leander Starr Jameson in 1895–1896 to support a planned uprising of *uitlanders* and overthrow the Transvaal Government. This episode led directly to confrontation between the Transvaal and Great Britain. In light of increasing pressure and after an ultimatum issued by the Transvaal, war broke out on 11 October 1899. The Second Boer War (1899–1902) was the result, a conflict prolonged by guerrilla warfare that ravaged South Africa. The British achieved victory in the Second Boer War, which ended with the Treaty of Vereeniging on 31 May 1902.

In 1910, the four former colonies—Cape Colony, Natal, the Orange Free State, and the Transvaal—were granted full independence within the British Empire as the Union of South Africa.

See also Boer War, First (1880–1881); Boer War, Second (1899–1902); Boomplaats, Battle of; Cape Frontier Wars, Southern Africa; Commando System; Jameson Raid; Pomeroy-Colley, Major General Sir George; Rhodes, Cecil J.; Smith, Lieutenant General Sir Harry G. W.; Transvaal; Zulu War

References: Barthorp (1987); Bond (1967); Conan Doyle (1901); Marix Evans (2000); Ransford (1967)

Bombay Army

The Bombay Army was one of three presidential armies in India established by the East India Company. It was transferred to Crown control after the 1857–1859 Indian Mutiny, and was operational until abolished and replaced by one single Indian Army in 1895. The other two presidential armies were the Bengal Army and the Madras Army.

The Bombay Army had a long history. Its European Regiment was formed in 1662 from independent companies. The Bombay European Regiment consisted of 2 battalions in the mid-1820s, when the Bombay Native Infantry consisted of about 26 battalions. Three light cavalry regiments and a company of sappers and miners had been formed by 1820. In 1824, Bombay Foot Artillery consisted of 2 battalions of 4 companies each, and there were 4 horse artillery troops.

In 1857, on the eve of the Indian Mutiny, the major units of the Bombay Army included 29 regular native infantry regiments (battalions), several irregular native infantry battalions, 3 light cavalry regiments, and 3 European artillery battalions, each consisting of 4 companies of 6 guns each.

The Bombay Army, like the Madras Army, contained soldiers from a wide variety of religious and social backgrounds. Its recruits were mainly Hindustanis from the Ganges River plains areas. Caste and class in the Bombay Army, unlike the Bengal Army, were secondary to soldiering. Consequently, although 64 Bengal Army battalions mutinied or were disarmed during the Indian Mutiny, portions of only 2 Bombay Army battalions were disaffected during the Mutiny.

After the Indian Mutiny, the Bombay European infantry units became British Army line regiments. The number of regular Bombay native infantry battalions was increased to thirty-one. The native artillery, except for two mountain batteries, was disbanded. Other relatively minor changes were also made.

In 1876, there were 31,753 Indian Army officers and men and 12,027 British Army officers and solders in the Bombay Army, totaling 43,780 officers and men in the Bombay Army. The Bombay Army was the smallest of the three presidency armies at this time, as the Bengal Army consisted of 104,668 officers and men, and the Madras Army contained 47,144 officers and soldiers.

See also Bengal Army; East India Company; East India Company, Military Forces; India, British Army in; Indian Army Operations; Indian Army Organization; Indian Mutiny; Madras Army

References: Beaumont (1977); Haythornthwaite (1995); Heathcote (1974); Mason (1974); Mason (1985); Wolseley (1878); Yong (2002)

Boomplaats, Battle of (29 August 1848)

British Lieutenant General Sir Harry G. W. Smith, the governor and commander in chief of Cape Colony, annexed the territory between the Orange and Vaal Rivers on 3 February 1848, to be called the Orange River Sovereignty, to try to ease tension between the British and Boers on the Orange River frontier. The Orange Free State Boers acquiesced to this annexation, until a number of Boers from the Transvaal, led by Andries Pretorius, incited them to rebel. The Boers then forced Major Henry Warden, the British resident in Bloemfontein, out of the city. They then took up defensive positions south of Bloemfontein at Boomplaats to await the expected British retaliation.

Smith led his force across the Orange River on 26 August 1848 to confront the insurgent Boers. The force consisted of about 800 British soldiers (detachments of the 45th Foot, the 91st Foot, and the Rifle Brigade) and the Cape Mounted Rifles, some loyal Boers, and about 250 Griquas. The approximately 750 Boers were hiding in positions in a stony, brush-covered, horseshoe-shaped ridge astride the road Smith would have to traverse. There were higher hills behind these positions, and Pretorius put an artillery piece there to give the British the impression this was the Boer main defense. The Boers, if necessary, could also withdraw to these secondary positions.

As the British advance guard of Cape Mounted Rifles approached the Boer positions on 29 August 1848, it came under heavy fire from the Boer left, then the Boer center. Smith, who had fought in the Peninsula, at Waterloo, and elsewhere, stated, "A more rapid, fierce, and well-directed fire I have never seen maintained" (Berkeley 1899, p. 3). Smith reacted quickly, bringing his three artillery pieces into action against the Boers while withdrawing his wagons to the rear to be laagered. The Cape Mounted Rifles regrouped and the 45th Foot and Rifle Brigade, covered by artillery, attacked to outflank the Boer left.

At about the same time Boers on the British left rode out to capture the British wagons, but were repulsed by the Cape Mounted Rifles and heavy British artillery fire. The British infantry on the right advanced so rapidly that the Boers were unable to regain their horses and ran to the center of their position. All the Boers tried to withdraw and consolidate in their secondary positions. Withering British artillery fire and assaulting infantry dispersed the Boers, some of whom tried to make a brief "last stand" in a saddle between two hills before retreating over the plain beyond. The battle ended the Boer uprising.

The Battle of Boomplaats was over in about an hour. Smith's decisive leadership and adroit coordination of his disciplined infantry and well-trained artillery contributed to the British victory. Casualty figures differ, with the British probably losing 16 killed and 40 wounded, with the Boers sustaining 49 killed. Smith considered the Battle of Boomplaats "one of the most severe skirmishes I believe I ever witnessed" (Berkeley 1899, p. 4).

The British had earlier defeated the Boers in an engagement at Zwartkopjes in 1845, and the relative ease in which the British won the Battle of Bloomplaats reinforced British contempt for the Boers' fighting abilities.

See also Boers; Smith, Lieutenant General Sir Harry G. W.; Transvaal

References: Barthorp (1987); Berkeley (1899); Featherstone (1973); Haythornthwaite (1995); Ransford (1967)

Botha, Commandant-General Louis (1862–1919)

Louis Botha was a leading Boer general of the Second Boer War. He played a prominent role in the fighting at Ladysmith, Colenso, and Spion Kop and became commander of the Transvaal forces in 1900. Botha was known as a resolute, skillful, and charismatic commander, fighting until the end of the war.

Botha was born near Greytown, Natal, on 27 September 1862. In 1884, Botha joined a Boer expedition led by Louis Meyer that supported Dinizulu against other Zulu rivals and gained military experience. He became active in politics and was elected to the Transvaal *Volksraad* (parliament) in 1897.

At the outbreak of war in October 1899, Meyer was the general in command of Boer commandos from the Southeastern Transvaal. Botha was appointed his second in command. At the Battle of Modderspruit, 30 October 1899, Meyer collapsed from ill health and Botha assumed command, becoming the youngest Boer general. He participated in a number of battles before the Boers decided to withdraw to Colenso.

Botha understood the importance of key terrain and organized the Boer defenses on the Tugela River. He commanded about 4,500 Boers at the Battle of Colenso, 15 December 1899. The attacking British deployed their artillery in front of the infantry. When the British barrage commenced, the Boer forces responded with well-aimed rifle and artillery fire, silencing the 12 British guns in a half hour. After vain attempts to recover their guns, the disheartened British called off the attack. Botha, with 3,000 men and 5 guns, defeated a British army of 20,000 soldiers with 44 guns at Colenso. He emerged from this battle a veritable national hero.

The Boers continued to defend against the British attempt to relieve besieged Ladysmith. In an attempted breakthrough at Spion Kop, 23–24 January 1900, the British captured the undermanned position. Many Boers deserted, but Botha grasped the situation and implored his men to return to their positions and restore the situation.

The Boers could not stop the eventual British relief of Ladysmith that occurred on 28 February 1900. On 27 March 1900, Commandant-General Petrus J. Joubert died and Botha succeeded him in command of the Transvaal forces. After Pretoria fell to the British on 5 June 1900, defiant Boers rallied to Botha, who was able to hold off the British for two days (11–12 June 1900) at Diamond Hill but was beaten by the British on 27 August 1900 at Bergendal. The British thought the war was over, but Botha and other Boer leaders initiated large-scale guerrilla warfare.

Botha quickly realized that Boer defeat in the war was inevitable and wanted to save South Africa from destruction. He negotiated unsuccessfully with the British commander in chief in Middelburg on 7 March 1901. Botha, however, continued to fight and elude the British, and was able to defeat them at Blood River Poort (17 September 1901) and Bakenlaagte (30 October 1901). He took part in the negotiations leading up to and signed the Treaty of Vereeniging on 31 May 1902.

Botha became the first prime minister of the Transvaal in 1907 and the first premier of the Union of South Africa in 1910. During World War I, he suppressed a rebellion and then led the successful attack on German South-West Africa. Botha attended the Versailles Peace Conference in 1919 and died later that year in Pretoria.

See also Boer War, Second (1899–1902); Boers; Colenso, Battle of; Commando System; Joubert, Commandant-General Petrus J.; Ladysmith, Siege of; Spion Kop, Battle of; Transvaal

References: Barnard (1970); Barnard (1971); Marix Evans (2000); Pakenham (1979); Trew (1999)

Boxer Rebellion (1900–1901)

Chinese resentment over the further encroachment into their kingdom of Western "barbarians" and Christian missionaries, plus the increased importation of manufactured goods after the end of the Second China War in 1860, festered in the following decades. Great Britain, Austria, France, Germany, Italy, Japan, and Russia all claimed exclusive trading rights at various Chinese ports and were dividing a weak China into national spheres of influence. The United States, a newcomer to overseas imperialism, advocated an open door policy that would end discrimination against nations and give it access to China.

A Chinese nationalist uprising by the secret *I Ho Chuan*, or Society of the Righteous and Harmonious Fists (the Boxers), grew in strength. Its goal was to resist westernization and Christianity to preserve the purity of China by killing all "foreign devils" and their allies. The Empress Dowager Tsu Hsi officially denounced the Boxers, but the Chinese government covertly supported them.

In 1899, the Boxers began attacking Catholics in Shantung Province, and their violence spread to the southern part of China and included Christian converts. By early 1900, thousands of Boxers roamed the countryside, attacking symbols of Western influence, including missions, and killed Chinese Christians. "Men and women were hacked to death with swords," noted one source, "burned alive in their compounds, and sometimes dragged and tortured through howling mobs before their execution, after which their severed heads were displayed in cages on village gates" (Dobrahner 1998, p. 1).

The Boxers marched on Peking, where the foreign legations and many Christian churches were located. Late in May 1900, amid a tense and deteriorating situation, foreign ministers telegraphed to Tientsin for soldiers to protect the legations. Several nations sent military detachments, totaling about 500 men, to Peking. By 7 June 1900, the legations were surrounded by Boxers and Chinese soldiers. The British Minister, Sir Claude MacDonald, wired British Admiral Sir Edward H. Seymour, commander in chief of the British China Station, on 9 June and requested a relief force advance on Peking.

Boxer Rebellion

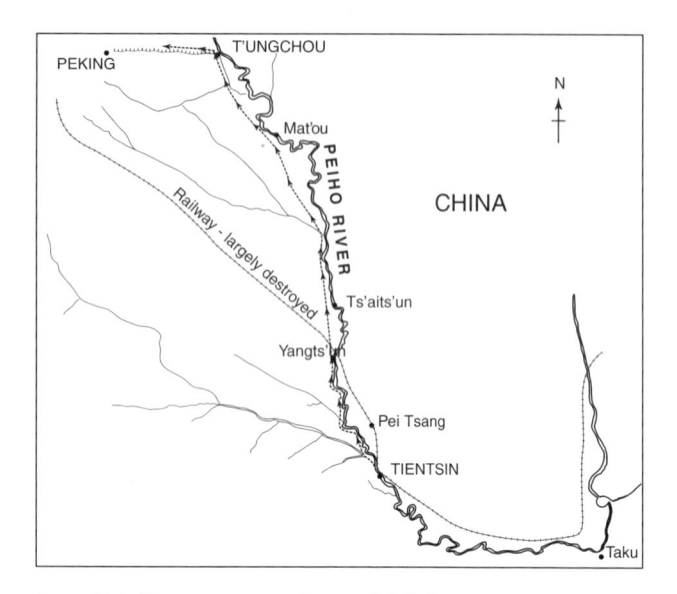

Boxer Rebellion, 1900–1901: Route of Relief Force

Seymour formed a relief column consisting of 915 British, 111 American, 26 Austrian, 157 French, 512 German, 42 Italian, 54 Japanese, and 312 Russian soldiers, with artillery and machine-gun support. This was the first time the major powers ever subordinated their own goals and united against a common foe. This force, loaded into five trains, departed Taku on 10 June 1900. Seymour expected it to be in Peking that night. The force encountered destroyed railways, damaged bridges, and frequently fierce Chinese resistance. Seymour's force advanced to Langfang but was unable to break through to Peking and retreated to Tsiku, near Tientsin, the latter about 80 miles southeast of Peking.

In Seymour's absence another international force had been organized. Allied admirals cooperated and captured the key Taku Forts on 17 June 1900, with ground forces conducting an amphibious assault under a supporting naval bombardment. The Chinese government then openly supported the Boxers, and on 20 June, the German minister was assassinated and the siege of Peking officially began.

Advance elements of the second relief force departed for Tientsin on 21 June 1900 and were joined by other elements. On 25 June, these troops "rescued" Seymour's beleaguered force at Tsiku, and the united force returned to Tientsin to await reinforcements. Seymour's failed attempt to reach Peking had cost his force 62 dead and 232 wounded; the British casualties were 29 killed and 89 wounded.

The undermanned garrison continued to hold out in Peking, defending against strong Chinese infantry attacks and artillery bombardments and making aggressive sorties to attack the Chinese. The growing allied relief force, as a preliminary to advancing to Peking, assaulted and captured the Walled City of Tientsin on 13–14 July 1900. Believing the besieged Peking garrison had been massacred, the allied powers decided to assemble a large force prior to an advance. German General Albrecht, Graf von Waldersee was appointed to command the international relief force.

Before von Waldersee arrived in China, it was learned the Peking garrison was still holding out, and a force, under the command of British General Sir Alfred Gaselee, was organized on 3 August 1900. It consisted of about 2,900 soldiers and 12 guns from Great Britain (300 men in the Naval Brigade; 12th Battery, Royal Field Artillery, and Hong Kong and Singapore Artillery; 300 men, 2nd Battalion, Royal Welsh Fusiliers; 400 men, 1st Bengal Lancers; and about 1,500 soldiers of the 1st Indian Brigade, plus support troops); 2,200 Americans with 6 guns; 9,000 Japanese and 24 guns; 2,900 Russians with 16 guns; and 1,230 French with 12 guns. There were also smaller German, Italian, and Austrian contingents.

The British Naval Brigade, advancing along the Peiho River, departed for Peking on 3 August 1900 with the main body following the next day. The allies fought battles with both the Boxers and Chinese troops at Pei Tsang (5 August), Yang Tsun (6 August), and Tungchow (12 August). The international force made a general advance on Peking early on 14 August. Many soldiers entered the city through the sluice gate, and by that afternoon the Peking legations were relieved after their fifty-five-day siege. The Imperial and Forbidden Cities of Peking were occupied the next day.

Von Waldersee and his German East Asia Brigade arrived in September 1900 as peace negotiations were in progress. The Germans conducted punitive operations in China until 1901. After long negotiations, the Peace Protocol of Peking, also known as the Boxer Protocol, was signed on 7 September 1901. China was ordered to pay a huge indemnity of £67.5 million over thirty-nine years; numerous Chinese officials were executed or banished; an embargo on arms imports was directed; foreign legations were expanded and areas designated for allied military occupation; and the Taku Forts were ordered to be destroyed. The Boxer Rebellion crushed China's resistance to Western occupation and accelerated its imperial decay. The Republic of China was proclaimed on 1 January 1912.

See also China; China War, First (1839–1842); China War; Second (1856–1860); Imperialism

References: Dobrahner (1998); Fleming (1959); Hibbert (1970); Keown-Boyd (1991); Preston (1999); Selby (1968)

Brackenbury, General Sir Henry (1837–1914)

General Sir Henry Brackenbury was a competent military intellectual, historian, and administrator; an excellent director of the Intelligence Branch at the War Office; and was considered by some the most brilliant member of the Ashanti Ring.

Brackenbury was born in England in 1837. He was educated at Eton, and after spending a few years in Canada, he entered the Royal Military Academy, Woolwich, in 1854. Commissioned in the Royal Artillery in April 1856, Brackenbury saw no action in the Crimean War. He sailed to India in 1857 and participated in the closing phases of the Indian Mutiny. Poor health forced his return to England in 1858.

Serving in routine assignments, Brackenbury developed an interest in military history and began writing articles. In 1868, he was appointed professor of military history at Woolwich, serving in that position for five years, and wrote *The Tactics of the Three Arms* (1873). In 1873, largely on the basis of his military reform-advocating writings, Major General (later Field Marshal Viscount) Sir Garnet J. Wolseley selected him as military secretary on the force he was leading to Ashantiland. After the Second Ashanti War, Brackenbury wrote and produced a 795-page two-volume history of the campaign in six weeks. He became an initial member of the Ashanti Ring and owed much of his later success to Wolseley's patronage, even though Wolseley at times did not like his condescending, arrogant, and self-serving attitudes.

"The indispensable Major Brackenbury" (Lehmann 1964, p. 209) served as Wolseley's military secretary in Natal (1875), on his staff on Cyprus (1878–1879), and again as Wolseley's military secretary during the Zulu War (1879). He also served as Wolseley's chief of staff during the Sekukuni campaign (1879–1880).

In 1880, Brackenbury served as private secretary to the viceroy of India, then as military attaché in Paris (1881–1882). He was not able to participate in Wolseley's 1882 Egyptian expedition, but Wolseley took him as a staff officer to the Sudan in 1884. Wolseley decided in December 1884 to divide his force into the Desert Column and the River Column in an attempt to hasten the relief of Major General Charles G. Gordon in Khartoum. The River Column was commanded by Major General William Earle, with Brigadier General Brackenbury as his second in command. After Earle was killed at Kirbekan on 10 February 1885, Brackenbury assumed command of the column. He directed the force's continuing advance until ordered to withdraw later that month. Brackenbury performed his duties well—even though he was said to hate "live soldiers" (real flesh-and-blood enlisted soldiers)—and was promoted to major general for distinguished service. Upon his return to England, he wrote *The River Column: A Narrative of the Advance of the River Column of the Nile Expeditionary Force, and Its Return down the Rapids*.

Wolseley returned to his position of adjutant-general in 1885 and secured Brackenbury's appointment as deputy quartermaster-general for intelligence, shortly thereafter redesignated as director of military intelligence. Brackenbury bemoaned the lack of a General Staff and was instrumental in collecting information and initially in developing home defense and mobilization plans. He was promoted to lieutenant general in 1888 and served as the only military member of the Hartington Commission (1888–1890). In 1891, Brackenbury was posted to India as military member of the Viceroy's Council, and apparently began to favor Indian defense policies and strategy.

Brackenbury returned to England in 1896 and served as president of the ordnance committee before becoming director-general of ordnance in 1899. He held the latter demanding position through the Second Boer War until 1904, when he retired as a full general.

Brackenbury, a keen intellectual whom Wolseley believed "was not one of the cleverest, but *the* cleverest man in the British Army" (Maurice and Arthur 1924, p. 224), had a positive and enduring impact upon British military reform, education, and intelligence. One of the foremost military administrators of his time, Brackenbury died on 20 April 1914.

See also Ashanti Ring; Ashanti War, Second (1873–1874); Earle, Major General William; Gordon Relief Expedition; India; Intellectuals, British Army; Intelligence; Mobilization Planning; War Office; Wolseley, Field Marshal Sir Garnet J.; Woolwich, Royal Military Academy; Zulu War

References: Beckett (1992); Brackenbury (1874); Brackenbury (1885); Fergusson (1984); Hamilton (1944); Harvie (1999); Lehmann (1964); Maxwell (1984); Preston (1967); Preston (1973); Spiers (1992)

Bromhead, Major Gonville, V.C. (1845–1892)

Major Gonville Bromhead served as a lieutenant in the 24th Regiment during the 1879 Zulu War. During the Zulu onslaught on Rorke's Drift, 22–23 January 1879, Bromhead served as second in command of the post and later received the Victoria Cross for his intrepid leadership during its defense.

Bromhead was born into a well-known British military family in Versailles, France, on 29 August 1845. He purchased an ensign's commission in April 1867 and was promoted to lieutenant in October 1871. He became commander of B Company, 2nd Battalion, 24th Regiment. Bromhead was almost entirely deaf, and his superiors, generally taking pity on him, gave his company less demanding tasks, such as guarding supply points.

The senior officer at Rorke's Drift was Lieutenant (later Colonel) John R. M. Chard. Bromhead's B Company was on detached duty guarding the station, which served as a hospital and supply point for one of the columns invading Zululand. Bromhead served as second in command to Chard and commanded his eighty-one B Company soldiers. Bromhead helped plan and prepare the hasty defenses, and throughout the numerous overnight Zulu attacks helped Chard command the operation and frequently filled gaps in the firing line himself.

Bromhead, along with Chard and nine other Rorke's Drift defenders, were awarded the Victoria Cross. He was also awarded a brevet majority. He seemed to have overcome his deafness through his gallant actions at Rorke's Drift and subsequent fame, and he was allowed to soldier on. Bromhead was not promoted again and died of typhoid fever at Allahabad, India, on 9 February 1892.

See also Chard, Colonel John R. M., V.C.; Purchase System; Rorke's Drift, Defense of; Victoria Cross; Zulu War
References: Glover (1975); Knight (1990); Morris (1965)

Bronkhorstspruit, Battle of (20 December 1880)

On 16 December 1880, the insurgent Boers proclaimed the Transvaal a republic, thus igniting the First Boer War (1880–1881). They immediately invested Potchefstroom and rode to besiege a number of isolated British garrisons.

The first action of the war took place on 20 December 1880, when Boers intercepted a thirty-four-wagon column of the 94th Foot (Connaught Rangers), commanded by Lieutenant Colonel Philip Anstruther, at Bronkhorstspruit, 38 miles east of Pretoria. This British force consisted of the regimental headquarters and A and F Companies, with 6 officers and 230 other ranks; the Commissariat and Transport Company, with 1 officer, 1 warrant officer, and 5 other ranks; the medical section, with 1 officer, 3 other ranks, and 3 women and 3 children (the wives and children of soldiers), for a total of 8 officers, 1 warrant officer, and 238 other ranks (excluding the wives and children).

Around midday on 20 December 1880, Anstruther was riding behind his scouts but ahead of the regimental band (playing "Kiss Me, Mother, Kiss Your Darling") and column main body. A party of about 150 Boers, commanded by Franz Joubert, was sighted to the column's left. This should not have surprised Anstruther, since he had been warned on 17 December 1880 that fighting could break out at any moment and he could be ambushed on the road. Anstruther galloped back to the column to give the order to halt, when a Boer messenger, under a flag of truce, handed a message to Anstruther. The message requested Anstruther to halt the column and return to Lydenburg, and two minutes were reportedly allowed for an answer. Anstruther purportedly replied, "I have my order to proceed with all possible dispatch to Pretoria, and to Pretoria I am going, but tell the Commandant I have no wish to meet him in a hostile spirit" (Duxbury 1980a, p. 8).

After the Boer messenger relayed Anstruther's response to Joubert, the Boers closed in on the British column as the soldiers extended in skirmishing order and distributed ammunition. The Boers opened up a murderous fire on the British, hitting all the officers, and dominated the battlefield. After about fifteen minutes of fighting, the mortally wounded Anstruther, shot five times in the legs, ordered his bugler to sound the cease-fire and surrendered his force.

In this short engagement, the British lost about 57 soldiers killed and more than 100 wounded (including 20 fatally) out of a total force of 247, with the Boers losing 2 men killed and 5 wounded. The Boer marksmanship was especially devastating, with each of the wounded British soldiers receiving an average of five wounds. The Boers also treated the British kindly, treating the wounded and paroling prisoners.

The British decried this skirmish as a "massacre," although before he died Anstruther instructed a Boer to go tell his commander that "all he did against me was honest" (Ransford 1967, p. 28). After the British surrender, Joubert joined Anstruther in a champagne toast to Queen Victoria.

As the unwounded British prisoners were marched away, the surviving British bandsmen played "Rule Britannia."

The Battle of Bronkhorstspruit was the first devastating and humiliating British defeat in the First Boer War.

See also Boer War, First (1880–1881); Boers; Transvaal
References: Barthorp (1987); Bennett (2001); Duxbury (1980a); Haythornthwaite (1995); Ransford (1967)

Brown Bess
See Infantry, British Army—Small Arms

Brown, General Sir George (1790–1865)

General Sir George Brown served as a British Army officer for almost six decades, and the highlight of his service was probably as commander of the 5th (Light) Division during the Crimean War. While he was a brave officer, in the Crimea he was considered a bullying martinet and an "old wretch [who was] more hated than any man ever was" (Hibbert 1961, p. 14).

Brown was born on 3 July 1790, and in 1806 was commissioned an ensign in the 43rd Foot. He participated in the 1807 Copenhagen expedition and served at various times on the Iberian Peninsula from 1807 to 1813. After being promoted to major in 1814, Brown was sent to the United States during the War of 1812 and was wounded seriously at the Battle of Bladensburg (24 August 1814).

Brown was promoted to lieutenant colonel in September 1814 and then held a number of staff appointments at home and abroad, including Malta, before being assigned to the Horse Guards in 1828. He served in various staff appointments at the Horse Guards until 1853, and was promoted to colonel in 1831 and major general in 1841. He became adjutant-general in 1850 and was promoted to lieutenant general the next year, but resigned in December 1853 in a disagreement with the commander in chief, Field Marshal Viscount Henry Hardinge.

Perhaps surprisingly, Brown was appointed to command the 5th (Light) Division for operations in the Crimea. Field Marshal Fitzroy J. H. Somerset, First Baron Raglan, commanding the British forces in the Crimea, frequently confided in Brown and asked his advice, probably because the two were almost the same age (Raglan was born in 1788; Brown in 1790) and had served together for many years in the Horse Guards. Brown's performance as commander of the Light Division and impact on the Battle of the Alma (20 September 1854) was basically "nil, but he was reputed to have been the only man in the army to have shaved that morning" (Pemberton 1962, p. 56). He was wounded slightly at the Battle of Inkerman (5 November 1854).

In 1855, Brown commanded the British troops during the aborted raid on Kertch on 2 May, and later that month when the raid was actually conducted. Brown also directed the unsuccessful assault on the Redan on 18 June 1855 before being invalided home on 28 June 1855.

Brown was promoted to general in 1855 and five years later was appointed commander in chief in Ireland. He held that position until April 1865 and died on 27 August 1865.

See also Alma, Battle of the; Crimean War; Hardinge, Field Marshal Henry; Horse Guards; Inkerman, Battle of; Raglan, Field Marshal Fitzroy J. H. Somerset, First Baron; Sevastopol, Siege of
References: Hibbert (1961); Judd (1975); Palmer (1987); Pemberton (1962); Raugh (1987a); Royle (2000); Sweetman (1993)

Browne, General Sir Samuel J., V.C. (1824–1901)

Samuel J. Browne was a senior army officer whose heroism—he earned the Victoria Cross during an engagement in the Indian Mutiny in which his left arm was severed—and service in many Indian campaigns and in the Second Afghan War was near legendary. He is best remembered, however, as the inventor of the "Sam Browne" sword belt that allowed a one-armed man to draw his sword and return it to the scabbard with ease.

Browne was born on 3 October 1824 in India, where his father served in the East India Company's medical service. After being educated in England, Browne returned to India and was commissioned an ensign in the 46th Bengal Native Infantry in 1840. Browne served in the Second Sikh War, participating in many skirmishes and engagements, including the Battles of Chillianwalla (13 January 1849) and Gujerat (21 February 1849).

During the 1850s, Browne served extensively on the North-West Frontier. He served under Major (later Brigadier General) John Nicholson in the 1852 punitive expedition against the Waziris, in the March 1857 campaign against the Bozdars, and in the fighting against the Hindustani Fanatics later that year.

As commander of the 2nd Punjab Cavalry, Browne saw action throughout the 1857–1859 Indian Mutiny, notably at Lucknow, Kursi, Ruyah, Aligunge, and Mohunpour. On 31 August 1858, Browne's combined cavalry-infantry force conducted a surprise attack against rebels at Sirpura. He forced his way to the enemy's rear and charged the gunners almost singlehandedly to prevent them from firing on his advancing infantry. In the ensuing vicious hand-to-hand fight, Browne was wounded twice in the knee and had his left arm cut off. For his gallantry in action, Browne was awarded the Victoria Cross in 1861.

Promoted to lieutenant colonel in 1859 and full colonel in 1865, Browne was then appointed to command the Corps of Guides. He was promoted to major general in 1870 and five years later represented the Indian Army during the Indian portion of the tour of the Prince of Wales (later King Edward VII). At the completion of the successful tour in 1876, Browne was knighted and advanced to lieutenant general in 1877.

In 1878, Browne served as military member of the Governor-General's Council, and was keenly aware of the events leading up to the Second Afghan War. Afghanistan was a pawn in the Great Game, and Great Britain wanted to use it as a buffer state to prevent further Russian encroachment toward India.

Afghanistan was, however, in the throes of internal dynastic struggles in the late 1870s, and the amir, Sher Ali Khan, tried to avoid involvement in the Anglo-Russian rivalry. After their victory over the Turks, in 1878 the Russians sent an uninvited mission to Afghanistan. As Sher Ali was struggling with his cousin Abdur Rahman Khan for the throne, he began to distance himself from the British and sought Russian assistance. The British, in sum, demanded to send a similar mission to Afghanistan and, rebuffed, issued an ultimatum to Sher Ali. This demand went unanswered, and on 21 November 1878, the British invaded Afghanistan and started the Second Afghan War.

The British invaded Afghanistan with three forces on three separate axes of advance. Browne commanded the 16,000-man Peshawar Valley Field Force designated to follow the northern—from Peshawar through the Khyber Pass to Jellalabad—line of advance. Browne's Force entered the Khyber Pass, but its progress was obstructed by the Afghan-held fort of Ali Masjid, situated 500 feet above the gorge with other fortifications on either side. Browne sent the first of his three brigades on a wide turning movement north of the Khyber Pass to block the enemy's rear and to be prepared to intercept the enemy's retreat. The second brigade climbed the hills to attack the left flank of Ali Masjid while the third brigade would conduct a coordinated and simultaneous frontal assault. The frontal assault failed on 21 November 1878, partly because the second brigade had failed to reach its objective and did not attack at the same time as the third brigade. The Afghans, fearful of being outflanked, evacuated Ali Masjid that night and stumbled into the first brigade blocking their escape. Most of the Afghans were taken prisoner. The way was then clear for Browne to advance on Jellalabad, which was occupied on 20 December 1878.

Sher Ali, with three British columns operating in his country, fled north and died in February 1879. A British victory at Fatehabad on 2 April 1879 permitted Browne to occupy Gandamak. Yakub Khan, Sher Ali's son and successor, decided to negotiate with the British. On 26 May 1879 a treaty was concluded at Gandamak in which Yakub Khan was recognized as amir in exchange for the Khurram Valley and the Khyber Pass being transferred to the British. The British, in addition, received control of Afghanistan's foreign affairs while guaranteeing the protection of Afghanistan and the payment of an annual subsidy. The Second Afghan War was over—or so it was thought at the time.

Browne and his Peshawar Valley Field Force returned to India. The viceroy seemingly blamed Browne for shortcomings in the transport and logistical systems of his force during the Afghan operations, and Browne was relegated to command the Lahore District. Shortly thereafter he retired, and when the Second Afghan War again broke out in September 1879, Browne was not eligible for a command.

Browne returned to England and lived in retirement on the Isle of Wight. He was promoted to general in 1888 and died on 14 March 1901. At his daughter's request, *The Journal of the Late General Sir Sam Browne, VC, GCB, KCSI (1849–1898)* was published in 1937.

See also Afghan War, Second (1878–1880); Chillianwalla, Battle of; East India Company, Military Forces; Great Game; Gujerat, Battle of; India; Indian Mutiny; Nicholson, Brigadier General John; North-West Frontier; Sher Ali Khan; Sikh War, Second (1848–1849); Victoria Cross

References: Barthorp (1982); Callwell (1896); Featherstone (1973); Lee (1912); Maxwell (1979); Roberts (1897)

Brunswick Rifle
See Infantry, British Army—Small Arms

Buller, General Sir Redvers H., V.C. (1839–1908)

General Sir Redvers H. Buller was a very gallant and experienced British Army general who served in many campaigns and never lost the "common touch" with his soldiers. His long career culminated in controversy as he served as the commander in chief of British forces during the initial stages of the Second Boer War (1899–1902).

Buller, the son of James W. Buller, a longtime Member of Parliament, was born on 7 December 1839 in Devonshire. After attending Eton, he purchased his commission as an ensign in the 60th Rifles in 1858. Buller was posted to India in 1859, participated in the Second China War in 1860, and was sent to Canada in 1862. He returned to England in 1869 and was again sent to Canada in 1870. Buller served in his regiment's 1st Battalion, then assembling as part of the Red River Expedition, under the command of Colonel (later Field Marshal Viscount) Garnet J. Wolseley. Buller's energy and professionalism made a lasting impression on Wolseley. Buller returned to England and entered the Staff College in 1872.

In 1873, Wolseley was designated to lead the British expedition to Ashantiland in West Africa. For his staff he selected a number of officers who had proven themselves on the Red River Expedition, including Buller, who initially served as intelligence officer, then raised a native unit. Buller became a member of Wolseley's Ashanti Ring.

Buller served at the War Office from 1874 to 1878, and then he was posted to South Africa, where he saw active service in the Ninth Cape Frontier War. This was fortunate for Buller, as he was in the area when the Zulu War broke out in January 1879. He commanded the Frontier Light Horse, an element of Colonel (later Field Marshal Sir Henry) Evelyn M. Wood's column, with great distinction, and earned the Victoria Cross for intrepidity at Hlobane on 28 March 1879. The Zulus reportedly called Buller "'the Steam Engine,' because he was always rushing out of unexpected places, and 'the Brother of the Devil,' because he led to so much bereavement in their families" (Gosse 1900, p. 111).

After a short period of staff service, Buller sailed to South Africa, arriving at the end of the First Boer War. He interrupted his honeymoon in 1882 to serve on Wolseley's staff in Egypt. His performance as intelligence officer was recognized by a knighthood. After home leave and staff duties, Buller was appointed to command the 1st Brigade of the force under Major General (later Lieutenant General) Sir Gerald Graham, V.C., being sent to Suakin on the Red Sea. Buller commanded his brigade effectively against dervishes at the Battles of El Teb (29 February 1884) and Tamai (13 March 1884). Graham wrote in his official dispatch of Buller's "coolness in action, his knowledge of soldiers and experience in the field, combined with his great personal ascendancy over both officers and men" (Powell 1994, p. 68), which was recognized by permanent promotion to major general.

Buller next served as chief of staff to Wolseley in the Gordon Relief Expedition (1884–1885). This was a difficult operation that ultimately failed and revealed friction between Wolseley and some members of his ring, including Buller, who had achieved relatively senior rank and were ambitious and jealous of each other. After the fall of Khartoum in January 1885, Buller was sent to take command of the Desert Column, which was ordered to return to its base camp. Wolseley also designated him to supervise the withdrawal of the entire force from the Upper Nile.

After another short stint at the War Office, Buller was posted to Ireland in 1886 to help quell disturbances there; then he returned to the War Office in 1887 as quartermaster-general. Buller reorganized service support branches of the British Army and formed the Army Service Corps.

From 1890 to 1897, Butler served as adjutant-general at the War Office and became a rival to Wolseley himself. In 1895, when it was known that Field Marshal H.R.H. Prince George F., Second Duke of Cambridge, was going to retire from the position of commander in chief, the government of the Earl of Rosebery made it known that it intended to appoint Buller, and not Wolseley, to succeed him. Before Buller's appointment was made public, Rosebery's government fell in the 1895 general election. The new Unionist government selected Wolseley and Buller remained adjutant-general. Buller was promoted to full general in 1896.

In 1898, Buller was appointed to command the 1st Army Corps at Aldershot, and at the start of the Second Boer War the following October, he was designated the commander in chief of the South African Field Force. He arrived in South Africa on 31 October 1899. He was under political pressure to relieve the besieged garrisons at Kimberley, Ladysmith, and Mafeking. Buller divided his force into three elements, leading one himself, but he was repulsed while trying to cross the Tugela River at Colenso on 15 December 1899. This was the third British defeat in a week, after Stormberg (10 December) and Magersfontein (11 December), which shocked the British public and was dubbed "Black Week."

These defeats, coupled with his suggestion that the Ladysmith garrison consider surrendering, resulted in his supersession by Field Marshal Lord (later Earl) Frederick S. Roberts, V.C., on 18 December 1899.

Buller remained in South Africa and commanded British troops in Natal. He was in overall command at the disaster at Spion Kop (23–24 January 1900), and was responsible for the capture of Vaal Krantz in early February 1900, and the relief of Ladysmith on 28 February. He later directed troops that outmaneuvered the Boers at Biggarsberg (14 May 1900), occupied Volksrust (12 June 1900), and fought and won the last set-piece battle of the war at Bergendal (27 August 1900). He departed South Africa on 24 October 1900 and received a hero's welcome on his arrival in England. He returned to his prewar command at Aldershot.

In October 1901, Buller was provocatively and intentionally taunted over the wording of the infamous telegram he sent in December 1899 suggesting Ladysmith surrender, which he had been ordered not to reveal. Buller paraphrased the telegram at a luncheon, and he was vindictively relieved of command and placed on half pay for indiscipline. It was an undeserved end to an outstanding military career. He lived the life of a country gentleman, did not complain about the unfair treatment he received, and remained highly popular with the soldiers. In 1905, a superb 13-foot-high equestrian statue of Buller, bearing the legend "He Saved Natal," was unveiled in Exeter. Buller died on 2 June 1908.

Recent studies have shown that the treatment Buller received at the time of the Second Boer War was politically motivated and relatively harsh. His performance, especially in Natal, was noteworthy, and he developed an effective "creeping barrage" for artillery support of advancing infantry and other tactical innovations. Shortly after the Second Boer War, one peer noted that Buller "appeared what he is, a brave and capable soldier, admirably adapted to hold a high secondary command, but unfitted, by his temperament, to be placed in supreme command of an Army in the field" (Powell 1994, p. 201).

See also Army Service Corps; Ashanti Ring; Ashanti War, Second (1873–1874); Boer War, First (1880–1881); Boer War, Second (1899–1902); Cambridge, Field Marshal H.R.H. Prince George F., Second Duke of; Canada; Cape Frontier Wars, Southern Africa; China War, Second (1856–1860); Colenso, Battle of; Commander in Chief, British Army; Dervishes; El Teb, Battle of; Gordon Relief Expedition; Ladysmith, Siege of; Quartermaster-General, British Army; Red River Expedition; Roberts, Field Marshal Frederick S., V.C.; Spion Kop, Battle of; Sudan; Tamai, Battle of; Vaal Krantz, Battle of; Victoria Cross; War Office; Wolseley, Field Marshal Garnet J.; Wood, Field Marshal Sir (Henry) Evelyn M., V.C.; Zulu War

References: Gosse (1900); Kochanski (1999); Lehmann (1964); Maxwell (1985); Melville (1923); Pakenham (1979); Powell (1994); Raugh (2001b); Robson (1993a); Symons (1963); Trew (1999); Wheeler (1914)

Bullets

An important component of weapons advancement and technology that increased the effectiveness and lethality of individual firearms, especially muskets and rifles, was the development and further refinement of the bullet.

The Brown Bess muzzle-loading, black powder–firing smoothbore flintlock musket and its variations was most commonly used by the infantry from 1815 until the mid-1840s. It was a superb weapon firing a .75-caliber ball. The Brown Bess cartridge was made of a cartridge paper tube containing six to eight drams of powder and a lead bullet. The bullet was loose fitting in the barrel and relatively accurate at ranges up to 50 yards. The soldier could fire this weapon two to three times per minute.

The Brunswick rifle, using the more reliable percussion instead of the flintlock firing system, was adopted in 1836. It had a caliber of .704 inches. It was considered unreliable because the bore was too tight and there was not enough powder in the cartridge to keep the bullet spinning fast enough to be accurate.

The Minié rifle officially replaced the smoothbore musket in 1851 and revolutionized warfare. To rectify the problems associated with loading a bullet into a rifle barrel, Captain Claude Minié of the Belgian Army developed a .702-caliber cylindrical-conoidal bullet. The bullet's base was flat, exposing a maximum surface to the charge, and it was hollow, expanding from the explosion to fit the four grooves of the rifle. Most of the British Army infantrymen carried the Minié rifle, which had an effective range of 800 yards, in the Crimean War (1854–1856).

The Enfield rifle, with a .577-inch bore, replaced the Minié rifle in 1853. The rifling in the Enfield rifle was three-grooved, unlike the four-grooved Minié rifle, which permitted the round to expand more easily and made it more stable. The Enfield, generally sighted up to 1,200 yards, was an accurate and effective rifle, although it remained a muzzle-loading rifle. The bullet and powder were sealed in a paper cartridge, with a thin coat of grease to make it waterproof and to lubricate the bullet.

The development of the Snider cartridge extractor in the early 1860s marked the advent of the breech-loading rifle for the British. Its efficiency was increased greatly by Colonel Boxer's development in 1866–1867 of a brass cartridge that held the bullet and powder together. The Snider-Enfield rifle developed in 1867 was an innovative weapon with tremendous accuracy and range.

The Martini-Henry rifle was selected in 1871 after numerous tests to be the British Army service rifle. It fired a black-powder, .45-caliber, center-fire brass cartridge with a lead slug, and was accurate to 1,000 yards or more. The Martini-Henry proved its effectiveness during the many colonial campaigns of the 1870s and 1880s.

The bolt-action, .303-caliber Lee-Metford rifle was adopted in 1888. It had an eight black powder–round magazine that was increased, with the advent of cordite ammunition (completed in 1893), to ten rounds, and it fit beneath the breech. Normally sighted to 1,800 yards, the Lee-Metford also had a special sight that permitted relatively accurate collective fire to 2,900 yards.

With an improved barrel-rifling system, the Lee-Enfield rifle replaced the Lee-Metford in 1895. These two rifles were carried by soldiers who fought later in the Sudan and in South Africa. The British learned during the 1895 Chitral Expedition on the North-West Frontier that the Mark II bullet, used in both the Lee-Metford and Lee-Enfield, was too light. The problem was that "savage tribes, with whom we were always conducting wars, refused to be sufficiently impressed by the Mark II bullet; in fact, they often ignored it altogether, and, having been hit in four or five places, came on to unpleasantly close quarters" (Headrick 1979, p. 256). The solution was a new bullet patented by Captain Bertie-Clay of the Indian ammunition works at Dum Dum, called the "dum dum" bullet.

The dum dum bullet was a mushrooming or expanding bullet that maximized the shock of injury, frequently requiring the amputation of limbs.

The dum dum bullet put the British in an ethical dilemma because they attempted to adhere to the St. Petersburg Declaration of 1868 by refraining to issue bullets that would "uselessly aggravate the sufferings of disabled men, or render their death inevitable" (Spiers 1975, p. 3).

In 1897, the British Army produced a Mark III bullet in which the conical end was hollowed and lined with nickel. Because expansion was minimal, the Mark III bullet was replaced by the Mark IV, which had a three-eighths inch cylindrical hole punched in its tip. The Mark IV bullet had a higher velocity and lower trajectory than the Indian-manufactured dum dum bullet, and was used with great effect in the Sudan in 1898.

Even though over 66 million Mark IV bullets were produced by March 1899, they were generally not used against white adversaries in the Second Boer War (1899–1902), ostensibly for humanitarian reasons. They were, however, used against Asians and Africans.

A Mark V bullet, which was similar to the Mark IV design except containing a harder lead/antimony core, began production in late 1899.

See also Boer War, Second (1899–1902); Crimean War; Infantry, British Army—Small Arms; Reconquest of the Sudan
References: Featherstone (1978); Headrick (1979); Miller (1996); Spiers (1975); Strachan (1985)

Buner Field Force (1898)

The general uprising on the North-West Frontier of India in 1897 involved many Pathan tribes. The hostilities instigated by the Madda Khel of the Isazais tribe with the "Maizar outrage" on 10 July 1897 were suppressed by the Tochi Field Force, which completed its mission and was disbanded. The Malakand Field Force punished the rebellious activities of many of the Swatis, Utman Khel, Mamunds, Salarzais, and others before being dissolved in October 1897.

After the final submission of the Utman Khel in November and December 1897, the only tribes remaining in revolt in the area that had not been punished were the Bunerwals and the tribes living between Buner and the Indus River. To properly castigate these tribes, the Buner Field Force was organized in late 1897 under the command of Major General (later General) Sir Bindon Blood, who had shortly before commanded successfully the Malakand Field Force. The Buner Field Force consisted of two infantry brigades and divisional troops. The 1st Brigade, under the command of Brigadier General W. H. Meiklejohn, consisted of the 1st Battalion, Royal West Kents; 16th Rajputs; and 20th and 31st Punjabis. Commanded by Brigadier General P. D. Jeffrey, the 2nd Brigade was composed of the 1st Battalion, East Kents; 21st Punjabis; and the Guides Infantry. Cavalry elements, three artillery batteries, two engineer companies, plus two additional infantry battalions (2nd Battalion, Highland Light Infantry, and 103rd Mahratta Light Infantry) and field hospitals rounded out the divisional troops.

Warned of the imminent operations of the Buner Field Force, all tribes between Buner and the Indus River—with the exception of the Bunerwals—submitted to the British rather than face the destruction of their villages. The Buner Field Force marched east from Kunda on 2 January 1898. Four days later, the force concentrated at Sanghao on the Buner border. Blood deployed two infantry battalions at Pirsai and five cavalry squadrons at Rustam. Reconnaissance revealed that the passes into Buner were held by the enemy, estimated at 3,000 to 4,000 tribesmen.

Blood's plan of operations, after assessing the situation, was that "the troops at Sanghao should force the Tanga Pass, the mouth of which is one mile north of Sanghao, while the Pirsai detachment was to force the pass of that name early the same day; and the cavalry from Rustam were then to cross the Pirsai Pass, working thence onwards toward the enemy's line of retreat from the Tanga Pass" (Nevill 1912, p. 244). This plan was executed audaciously on 7 January 1898. The 20th Punjabis conducted a turning movement against the enemy's right flank, and as this movement developed, a frontal assault by the 1st Brigade (minus the 20th Punjabis), supported by artillery (opening fire at 2,200 yards) and infantry, advanced uphill toward the tribesmen. The advancing infantry began volley firing at 1,500 yards. The steady, accurate British fire quickly demoralized the tribesmen, who fled from their positions, and the British seized the high ground. In this attack, the British lost only one man killed, and the tribesmen about fifty. The British also secured the Tanga Pass, then halted at Kingargali to replenish their supplies.

The British advance continued on 17 January 1898, with Blood dividing his force into two columns, commanding one himself with Meiklejohn in charge of the second. The force traversed and surveyed the entire Buner Province, meeting no opposition, receiving the submission of all tribesmen encountered, and in the process, humiliating the Bunerwals. By the end of the day the Bunerwals, who had established a martial reputation during the 1863 Ambela campaign, and the Chamlawals submitted to the British.

The mission of the Buner Field Force had been accomplished. The entire force withdrew over the Ambela Pass back into British India, where it was disbanded on 20 January 1898.

See also Blood, General Sir Bindon; India; Indian Army Operations; Malakand Field Force; North-West Frontier; Tochi Field Force
References: Barthorp (1982); Featherstone (1973); Fincastle and Eliott-Lockhart (1898); Nevill (1912)

Burleigh, Bennet
See Correspondents, War

Burma

In the nineteenth century Burma (now Myanmar) was located to the immediate east of British India, bordering eastern Bengal and Assam. This location brought it into conflict with the expanding East India Company in its quest for new markets. The Burmese had also been engaged in territorial conquest, having seized Tenasserim from Siam in 1766, subjugated the Kingdom of Arakan in 1784, and conquered Manipur, near the Surma Valley, in 1813.

As a result, the border area between British India and Burma provided a constant source of friction. In addition, the British would occasionally enter Burmese territory in pursuit of robbers, and the Burmese made a number of forays into British-protected areas in search of Arakanese rebels.

The First Burma War (1824–1826) was caused by the Burmese attacking a British detachment on the Chittagong frontier in 1823. In 1824, two Burmese armies entered Cachar, an area under British protection, and the British declared war. A British joint navy–army expeditionary force attacked and defeated Burmese forces at cities up the Irrawaddy River, but before the British attacked the Burmese capital at Ava, the Burmese surrendered. They ceded the Arakan to Great Britain and relinquished their claims on Assam and other border regions.

In 1852, the British, after their ships and trade had been subject to Burmese aggression, sent a joint expedition to Burma where it captured a number of Burmese cities. The British annexation of the province of Pegu in January 1853 ended the Second Burma War.

After the Second Burma War, Burma had been effectively reduced to the area around the capital Ava and its foreign policy was basically determined until 1879 by a British Resident. The Burmese felt they had been occupied and communicated with the French and Italians, mainly over trading issues. Burmese interference with the Bombay-Burma Trading Company caused the British to issue an ultimatum demanding the protection of British subjects and interests. The Burmese king rejected this ultimatum and the British quickly dispatched a three-brigade force that advanced on Ava before the Burmese had time to organize their defenses. Mandalay was occupied and the Third Burma War (1885) was over in less than one month. The British annexed Upper Burma on 1 January 1886.

The Burmese forces were not considered very formidable in open terrain, and seemed to be little more than "raw levies." They preferred to fight from blockades or other fortified defensive positions. The Burmese forces were generally tribal during the First Burma War and most were armed with spears and swords. They had a number of mixed and frequently outdated cannon in some of their fortifications. The Burmese had, however, developed a number of excellent war-boats for use on the many rivers. Occasionally the Burmese used elephants as a combination fighting vehicle and troop transport.

The Burmese forces possessed more firearms during the Second Burma War, when their army was said to number 50,000. By the Third Burma War, Burmese soldiers were less disciplined and motivated, and their army was only about 15,000 to 20,000 strong.

During the period of the Third Burma War, Burmese troops tried to copy British uniforms. They wore grotesque-looking spiked helmets, made of bamboo lacquer work and painted red, a jacket, and a pair of drawers that resembled pyjamas. The officers carried European swords, some of the men carried rudimentary guns, a few had spears, and others were armed with bamboo sticks. The Burmese cavalry was mounted on short ponies and armed with a *dah*, similar to a hatchet or wood chopper about 18 inches long. The Burmese had a limited number of artillery pieces, resembling small brass toys, each pulled by four men.

See also Burma War, First (1824–1826); Burma War, Second (1852–1853); Burma War, Third (1885); East India Company; India; Indian Army Operations

References: Bruce (1973); Callwell (1896); Farwell (1972); Haythornthwaite (1995)

Burma War, First (1824–1826)

Border disputes were the direct cause of the First Burma War. The Burmese attacked a British detachment at Shahpuri Island near the Chittagong River on 24 September 1823.

In January 1824, additional border tension was caused by two Burmese armies invading Cachar, an area in south-central Assam west of Manipur and under British protection. The British responded by declaring war on 5 March 1824.

The British plan was to drive the Burmese out of the territory in Assam they had taken, adopt a defensive posture there and on the Chittagong, and then send an expedition by sea to subdue the Burmese maritime provinces and, if possible, sail 600 miles up the Irrawaddy River to the capital of Ava. The Burmese disrupted these plans by assembling a 30,000-man army commanded by General Maha Bundula in the Chittagong area and attacking a small British force at Ramu on 17 May 1824.

The British gathered a formidable naval force, the ships of which carried over 200 guns. The Burmese Expeditionary Force, commanded by Brigadier General Sir Archibald Campbell, consisted of 10,644 soldiers, of whom 4,759 were British, with 42 artillery pieces. The force was divided into the Bengal Division (British 13th and 38th Regiments, 40th Bengal Native Infantry, and artillery), commanded by Colonel McCreagh, and the Madras Division (British 41st, 89th, and 102nd Regiments, 3rd, 8th, 9th, 10th, 17th, and 22nd Madras Native Infantry, 7th Madras Infantry, with Madras Foot Artillery and pioneers) with Colonel Macbean commanding. The force assembled at the end of April 1824.

Campbell's force landed at and captured Rangoon on 10 May 1824. The monsoon season began in May, and the British continued with their campaign. The British also attacked surrounding fortified areas, culminating in the capture of the Shwe Dragon Pagoda at Kemmendine on 10 June 1824. The heavy rains and debilitating jungle diseases, including dysentery, cholera, and malaria, took their toll on the British.

In July 1824, the British conducted a number of local attacks and seized Burmese blockhouses, establishing a moral supremacy in the process. The number of casualties from disease, however, continued to climb. Minor actions took place during the summer and fall.

Burmese King Bagyidaw recalled the army of Maha Bundula from Arakan, and by December 1824, about 60,000 Burmese soldiers had surrounded the British at Rangoon. A number of local skirmishes took place until the British conducted a counterattack on 7 December that soundly defeated and scattered the Burmese troops. From 1 December to 9 December the British had 30 soldiers killed and 220 wounded, while the Burmese were estimated to have lost about 5,000 men.

A Burmese deserter informed the British that Bundula had received reinforcements and had gathered a force of about 25,000 soldiers at Kokeen, north of Rangoon. Campbell realized he had to conduct a preemptive strike on the Burmese. Early on 15 December 1824, after leaving 3,000 men to hold Rangoon, he advanced toward Kokeen in two columns. The right column, of 540 British and Indian soldiers, was commanded by Brigadier General Willoughby Cotton. Campbell commanded the left column of 800 soldiers. The plan was for Cotton's troops to attack the Burmese position from the front, while Campbell's column would outflank the position and attack it from the rear.

The Burmese had built two strong blockades, each about 400 yards long and 200 yards wide, connected by a central trench. Campbell's force was met by a hail of Burmese fire as it emerged from the jungle, and Campbell ordered his signal guns fired to inform Cotton of his impending attack. Upon hearing the reply from Cotton, Campbell's men assaulted both stockades while Cotton's soldiers stormed the high stockade walls and engaged the Burmese with accurate fire. They then went in with the bayonet, and after about 20 minutes of intense combat, the remaining Burmese fled into the jungle. In the short but fierce fight, the British lost 136 killed or wounded, and the Burmese many more. The British troops involved in the battle included men from the 13th, 38th, 41st, and 89th Foot and Madras Europeans in one column, and from the 9th, 12th, 18th, 28th, 30th, and 34th Madras Infantry in the second column.

Campbell received reinforcements and then planned to advance on the Burmese capital of Ava. He commanded the land column, consisting of 1,300 British infantry, 1,000 sepoys (Indian infantry private soldiers), 2 cavalry squadrons, 1 horse artillery troop, and a rocket troop. Campbell's force was to advance parallel to the Hlaing River and then follow the Irrawaddy, linking up with the river column south of Danubyu, the site of another Burmese stronghold. The river column, commanded by Cotton, consisted of about 800 British infantry, a sepoy force, and artillery, all carried in a flotilla of 60 boats. A third small force, commanded by Major (later Major General Sir) Robert Sale, was to sail to and capture Bassein (about 100 miles west of Rangoon), then march roughly 60 miles through swampland to Danubyu.

Campbell's column began its march on 11 February 1825, bypassed Danubyu, and pressed on to Prome, hoping to meet Cotton on the river en route. Cotton was delayed, however, by Burmese strong points along the river. On 7 March 1825, Campbell heard the sounds of a large cannonade echoing from the south. Waiting one day, he was confident that Cotton's force had captured Danubyu, so he continued the advance northward. A few days later he learned Danubyu had not fallen to Cotton's troops, so Campbell had to march back downriver to link up with Cotton's force.

With his force united, Campbell planned to assault Bundula's fortress. British mortars and rockets began a preparatory barrage on 1 April 1825. Before the assault began the next morning, the British learned that Bundula had been killed by a rocket and the Burmese had fled silently into the jungle. The British occupied Danubyu unopposed on 2 April.

The British then continued their advance northward. Prome was entered on 25 April 1825 and Campbell decided to remain there during the rainy season. Over the summer months other British forces cleared the Burmese from Assam and made progress elsewhere, but by September 1825, while negotiations were ostensibly being conducted, a Burmese army had surrounded Prome.

On 1 December 1825, the British struck and caught the Burmese, then commanded by Maha Nemiao, off guard. The attack began with a heavy British naval cannonade that caught the attention of the Burmese, in conjunction with the movement of a sepoy force that appeared to be attacking a Burmese position. Concurrently, Campbell had divided his forces again into two columns and marched to the rear of the Burmese forces. The British attacked and defeated one of the three Burmese divisions, killing Nemiao in the process. Additional British attacks on 2 and 5 December, in dense jungle against heavily fortified strongholds, were highly successful, and the British had victory in their grasp.

The British continued their advance through the devastated countryside toward Ava. On 27 December 1825, under a flag of truce, Burmese envoys approached the British to negotiate a peace treaty to end the conflict. A two-week truce, to end on 18 January 1826, was agreed to by both parties. On 17 January, however, Campbell realized that the Burmese had been procrastinating and improving their defenses during the truce. On the morning of 18 January, Campbell again commenced hostilities by bombarding the Burmese defenses and afterward assaulting them. The Burmese seemed to have lost their stomach for fighting and retreated further toward their capital.

Campbell's force again renewed its march. On 8 February 1825, as the British reached a large opening in the jungle near Pagan, they found themselves confronted by a force of about 20,000 Burmese infantry and cavalry deployed in a crescent formation and commanded by Nawing Phuring. It was very unusual for the Burmese to abandon their stockades and fight in the open. The British attacked the Burmese flanks immediately, pushing the Burmese back to reinforced positions, and after five hours, the Burmese were finally routed.

King Bagyidaw finally agreed to accept the British terms. The Burmese surrendered the provinces of Arakan and Tenasserim, and renounced all rights of interference with Assam, Cachar, and Manipur. The king also had to pay the British an indemnity of one crore of rupees, then equal to the enormous sum of £1 million. The Treaty of Yandabo was signed and concluded the war on 24 February 1826. A reciprocal commercial treaty was signed later on 23 November 1826.

The First Burma War had been a very difficult war to fight, especially in the disease-ridden jungle. Of the 3,500 British soldiers, not including officers and sepoys, only 150 were killed in combat while almost 3,000 died from disease and sickness. Of about 150 officers, 16 were killed in action and 45 died from disease. While Britain had greatly expanded it territorial holdings, this war was, according to one commentator, "for the army beyond argument the most miserable, wretched and badly managed of all the wars to date that had made the British Empire" (Bruce 1973, p. 127).

See also Bengal Army; Burma; Burma War, Second (1852–1853); Burma War, Third (1885); East India Company, Military Forces; Madras Army; Rockets; Sale, Major General Sir Robert

References: Bruce (1973); Callwell (1896); Haythornthwaite (1995)

Burma War, Second (1852–1853)

Friction between the British and Burmese increased after Pagan Min became king of Burma in 1846. The Burmese seemed to ignore the Treaty of Yandabo, signed on 24 February 1826 that had ended the First Burma War and guaranteed the protection of British merchants and commerce. Burmese officials were harassing and unjustly taxing British merchants, and two British mariners were unlawfully imprisoned.

The British had the right to be protected from injustice, oppression, and extortion by their own government. Commodore Lambert, "a short-tempered and impetuous naval commander" (Bruce 1973, p. 132), was ordered to lead a squadron to Rangoon to investigate the situation. Lambert overstepped his orders, intimidated and humiliated relatively compliant Burmese officials, and illegally seized the king's royal yacht and began a blockade of the Rangoon River. The British then provoked the Burmese to open fire on the blockading ships. Events spiraled out of control and the British issued the Burmese king an ultimatum that he could not possibly comply with. The British ultimatum expired on 1 April 1852 without receiving an answer.

The British planned to strike early in April 1852, about six weeks before the monsoons began, and deliver a decisive blow against the Burmese. By 6 April 1852, the Bengal and Madras Infantry Brigades, under the overall command of Lieutenant General Henry Godwin (a veteran of the First Burma War, 1824–1826), had arrived by fleet at the mouth of the Rangoon River. The Bengal Brigade consisted of the British 18th and 80th Regiments and the 40th Bengal Native Infantry. The Madras Brigade included the British 51st Foot and the 5th, 9th, and 25th Madras Native Infantry Regiments. The force was supported by two companies of Bengal Artillery, three companies of Madras Artillery, and two of Madras Sapper and Miners. The entire force totaled about 6,000 soldiers.

The British first bombarded and occupied Martaban, north of Moulmein, capital of the British occupied province of Tenasserim, then returned to Rangoon by 8 April 1852. Three days later the naval flotilla sailed up the Irrawaddy River and bombarded the stockade at Rangoon and another on the opposite bank at Dalla. The following morning Godwin landed his troops, divided them into the customary two columns, and began a two pronged attack on the Rangoon stockade. One column was ambushed in the jungle but fought off the Burmese, and a British assault on the stockade was repulsed. Godwin brought up 8-inch howitzers and attacked again on 14 April. After a long artillery and small arms duel, Godwin's aide-de-camp led an assault party that entered a pagoda in the defenses and killed or scattered with the bayonet Burmese soldiers, leading to the capture of the Burmese stronghold. From 12 to 14 April, the British had 17 all ranks killed and 132 wounded.

The British attacked and seized Bassein on 19 May 1852, by which time the monsoon rains had begun and cholera was taking its toll. Learning that the Peguese had risen against their local Burmese rulers, the British sent a small force to Pegu and captured the town on 5 June 1852.

Additional British reinforcements arrived at Rangoon in September 1852. British ships sailed up river, bombarded the Burmese stockade at Prome, and the British occupied the deserted position on 10 October 1852. The British retook the town of Pegu after a short sharp fight on 21 November 1852.

The British annexed the province of Pegu shortly thereafter. To pacify the province, the British sent a 4,000-man force under General Steel to travel to the northern provincial boundary. Steel's march was practically unopposed, and he arrived at Toungee, on the northern border, on 22 February 1853.

After the British annexed Pegu, a number of Burmese officials resisted. One of these was Myat Htoon, commissioner of the Danchen district north of Danubyu. The British attempted to overthrow him by marching against his stockade in February 1853, but the Burmese ambushed this British force, killing or wounding more than 80 soldiers. Brigadier General Cheape, with a 1,100-man force supported by guns and rockets, was then given the mission. After a twenty-four-day-long fierce jungle battle, Cheape's force defeated the Burmese. The British lost 130 killed or wounded, including Ensign Garnet J. Wolseley, the future Field Marshal Viscount Wolseley, plus more than 100 dead from cholera.

As the British prepared to march on the Burmese capital of Ava, King Pagan Min was deposed by his brother Mindon, who wanted to end the war. The British were avaricious, and in addition to the province of Pegu, demanded hundreds of additional square miles that included valuable teak forests. The Burmese protested but had to accept the fait accompli, although King Mindon refused to sign the formal peace treaty. A ceasefire, ending the "inglorious" Second Burma War, was declared on 30 June 1853.

See also Bengal Army; Burma; Burma War, First (1824–1826); Burma War, Third (1885); East India Company, Military Forces; Madras Army; Wolseley, Field Marshal Garnet J.
References: Bruce (1973); Callwell (1896); Haythornthwaite (1995)

Burma War, Third (1885)

Anglo-French rivalry in southeast Asia was a major cause of the Third Burma War. Thibaw became king of Burma in 1878, and his weak rule encouraged corruption and bribery as well as French encroachment on what was considered a British sphere of influence.

The Burmese sent a delegation to Paris in 1883 to negotiate what appeared to be a commercial treaty. The British were wary that the French would also be supplying weapons, and especially modern artillery, to the Burmese. These concerns were heightened when the Burmese contracted with the French to build a railway from Mandalay to the Indian frontier and with news that the French had established a Burmese state bank. The French loans were to be repaid from royalties from Burmese oil and river customs charges.

In August 1885—during the period of June to December 1885 when Lord Salisbury's Tory government was in power—the council of ministers in Mandalay ordered a fine of 23 lakhs of rupees (£2,300,000) on the Bombay-Burma Trading Company for allegedly exporting more teak logs than they had actually paid for. In the context of the ongoing Anglo-French imperial and commercial rivalry, this arbitrary and insulting fine provided the British with an excuse to go to war.

The British issued an ultimatum on 22 October 1885 that gave King Thibaw until 10 November 1885 to accept a British envoy and British control of Burmese foreign relations, among other items. The British expected Thibaw to reject the ultimatum and organized a three-brigade force, under the command of Major General Harry Prendergast, V.C., to advance upon Mandalay via the Irrawaddy River and dethrone King Thibaw. On 7 November, King Thibaw proclaimed to his people that war was imminent and to be prepared to fight against and wipe out the "heretic" Britons.

Prendergast's force, consisting of 3,029 British and 6,005 Indian troops (with 2,810 followers), was organized into three brigades with artillery (67 guns) and support elements. As finally constituted, these units were 1st Brigade (commanded by Brigadier General H. H. Foord), consisting of 2nd Battalion, King's Liverpool Regiment, and the 21st and 25th Madras Infantry Regiments; 2nd Brigade (Brigadier General [later Field Marshal Sir] George S. White, V.C.), 2nd Battalion, Hampshire Regiment, and 12th and 23rd Madras Infantry Regiments; and 3rd Brigade (Brigadier General F. B. Norman), 1st Battalion, Royal Welsh Fusiliers, 2nd (Queens' Own) and 11th Bengal Infantry Regiments. Additional troops included a 600-man naval brigade and a body of volunteer cavalry. On 11 November 1885, instructions were received from London to begin the operation.

A flotilla of armed naval steamships towed the troops upriver in barges and lighters equipped with living quarters. The frontier into independent Burma was crossed on

15 November 1885 as the fifty-five-ship flotilla continued to steam up the Irrawaddy River. On the following day, Burmese artillery batteries in stockades on both sides of the river opened fire on the British. The British returned the fire, then landed infantrymen that quickly captured the stockades.

The heavily fortified town of Minhla was on the right bank of the Irrawaddy further up river and the fort of Gweg-Yaung Kamyo was opposite it. Prendergrast decided to attack both forts immediately. Early on 17 November 1885, several British and Indian battalions were landed a few miles south of each fort. As the British flotilla engaged each fort simultaneously, the British and Indian troops marched through the dense jungle and attacked their respective objectives. The Gweg-Yaung Kamyo was seized with little resistance, but the defenders of Minhla fought with determination. It took a number of British bayonet charges to finally dislodge the Burmese, who fled into the jungle. In the fighting that day, the British lost 1 officer and 4 men killed, and 4 officers and 27 men wounded.

Men of the naval brigade captured a Burmese stockade and silenced a battery of eleven heavy guns at Pagan on 22 November 1885. Two days later the British flotilla reached Myingyau, where a large Burmese force was entrenched. When the British bombarded the defenses, the Burmese initially returned fire with artillery and small arms but later slipped away at night, leaving the British advance unopposed.

As the flotilla steamed within sight of Ava on 27 November 1885, Prendergrast received a message from the king agreeing to surrender himself and his forces. When the British forces landed at Ava, they found that the Burmese Army had vanished. After destroying the Burmese artillery, the British continued their advance upriver and anchored off Mandalay the following day. British troops landed and, with bands playing, they marched to the royal palace and seized the Burmese king and queen. After barely two weeks of operations, the Third Burma War was over.

The British, on 1 January 1886, formally annexed Upper Burma and proclaimed that Burma would become a province of British India. The Burmese soldiers who had earlier fled into the jungle frequently became rebels or *dacoits* (bandits) and harassed the British and attacked their outposts. After four years of operations that required substantial British reinforcements, the Burmese rebellion was finally suppressed in 1890.

See also Burma; Burma War, First (1824–1826); Burma War, Second (1852–1853); Imperialism; India; Indian Army Operations; White, Field Marshal Sir George S., V.C.
References: Bruce (1973); Callwell (1896); Haythornthwaite (1995); Sewell (1985)

Burnaby, Lieutenant Colonel Frederick G. (1842–1885)

Lieutenant Colonel Frederick G. Burnaby was a successful, courageous soldier and traveler, whose accounts of his adventures gained him considerable renown. While unorthodox, his disdain for authority and frequently erratic behavior caused resentment among his superiors.

Burnaby, born on 3 March 1842 in England, was educated at Harrow and in Germany. He was commissioned into the Royal Horse Guards in 1859. Although considered a typical Englishman, Burnaby was tall (6 feet, 4 inches) and strong, and on one occasion reportedly carried two ponies, one under each arm, from an upstairs room of a building to a courtyard. He also had an insatiable yearning for adventure.

Burnaby had considerable time to travel and pursue leisure activities, frequently serving as a correspondent for newspapers. He traveled to the Sudan in 1875, covering part of Colonel (later Major General) Charles G. Gordon's expedition. At the height of winter amid the Great Game, he rode alone through Central Asia. When he arrived at Khiva, east of the Aral Sea, Burnaby found a telegram ordering him back to England. When he returned he wrote *A Ride to Khiva* (1876), which made him a popular hero and was reprinted eleven times in its first year of publication.

Other adventures and books followed, with Burnaby running unsuccessfully for Parliament in 1880 and ballooning alone across the English Channel in 1882. At the beginning of 1884, in response to a request from his old friend, Lieutenant General Valentine Baker Pasha, commanding the Egyptian Gendarmerie, Burnaby traveled to Egypt. He accompanied Baker Pasha to El Teb in the eastern Sudan, where in the face of dervish hordes the ill-trained gendermarie troops panicked and were soundly defeated on 4 February 1884. After the arrival of British troops, Burnaby fought in the battle on 29 February 1884 in which El Teb was captured.

Burnaby returned to England in April 1884. General (later Field Marshal Viscount) Lord Garnet J. Wolseley, appointed in the summer of 1884 to command the expedition to relieve

Gordon in Khartoum, asked for Burnaby's services, but Field Marshal H.R.H. Prince George F., Second Duke of Cambridge, vetoed the request. Burnaby told people he was traveling to Bechuanaland but instead traveled to Egypt. Upon his arrival, Wolseley appointed him an inspector on the Nile line of communications, although he was later attached to the Desert Column. On 16 January 1885, the Desert Column, with Burnaby as second in command to Brigadier General (later Major General) Sir Herbert Stewart, was intercepted before the wells of Abu Klea, and the following day formed a square and advanced against the enemy. The dervishes attacked a gap in the British square, which Burnaby may have helped widen by issuing his own commands to troops. Burnaby fought the attackers singlehandedly for a few moments before being fatally wounded by a spear thrust to the neck.

See also Abu Klea, Battle of; Baker Pasha, Lieutenant General Valentine; Cambridge, Field Marshal H.R.H. Prince George F., Second Duke of; Dervishes; Egyptian Army; El Teb, Battle of; Gordon, Major General Charles G.; Gordon Relief Expedition; Great Game; Stewart, Major General Sir Herbert; Sudan; Wolseley, Field Marshal Garnet J.

References: Alexander (1957); Barthorp (1984b); Brennan (2000); Lehmann (1964); Preston (1967); Symons (1965)

Butler, Lady Elizabeth

See Artists, War; Butler, Lieutenant General Sir William F.

Butler, Lieutenant General Sir William F. (1838–1910)

Lieutenant General Sir William F. Butler was a distinguished, innovative, and controversial British Army officer and a prominent member of the Ashanti Ring. He was also a well-known, prolific traveler and author.

Butler was born in Ireland on 31 October 1838, and after a Jesuit education, he was commissioned an ensign in the 69th Regiment in 1858. He served with his regiment in Ireland, India, and England before being posted to Canada in 1867, where he had the opportunity to satisfy his craving for travel. In 1870, Butler, who had already traveled extensively in Canada, was selected by Colonel (later Field Marshal Viscount) Garnet J. Wolseley to serve as intelligence officer of the Red River Expedition. Butler performed his duties well, and thereafter Wolseley considered him among his circle of outstanding subordinates.

In 1872, after the abolition of the purchase system, Butler was promoted to captain. He rejoined Wolseley in 1873, who was then commanding the expedition to Ashantiland, as intelligence officer, and also led a group of 1,400 indigenous Akims to try to intercept the main Ashanti Army. Butler became a confirmed member of Wolseley's Ashanti Ring, and he next served on Wolseley's staff in Natal in 1875.

After service at the War Office, Butler served in South Africa during the Zulu War (1879), but he did not see action. Butler again served on Wolseley's staff during the 1882 British expedition to Egypt. He also participated in numerous battles, including the assault on Tel el-Kebir (13 September 1882). During the 1884–1885 Gordon Relief Expedition, again commanded by Wolseley, Butler was responsible for organizing a 400-boat flotilla to carry soldiers up the Nile River to Khartoum, although it seems he, and many other Ashanti Ring members who were gaining higher rank, had difficulties working as a team member. Butler later accompanied the River Column on its advance, and he was instrumental in planning the successful operations at Kirbekan, where Major General William Earle, column commander, was killed in action on 10 February 1885.

In late 1885, Butler assumed command of a brigade on the Egyptian frontier and led it gallantly at the Battle of Ginnis, 30 December 1885. For his superb leadership, Butler was promoted to brigadier general and knighted in 1886, and the same year, he was involved in a notorious divorce trial. He served on half-pay from 1886 to 1888, then he was appointed to conduct an inquiry into the Army Ordnance Department. Butler commanded British troops in Egypt (1890–1893), then at Aldershot (1893), where the army was attempting to conduct innovative training. He commanded the South-Eastern District from 1893 to 1896.

In 1898, Butler was appointed commander in chief of British forces in South Africa. This was a tense time as friction between the British and the Boers increased, and Butler, while not favoring the Boers, opposed war. In July 1899, Butler followed his conscience and resigned, thus forfeiting the opportunity to command the British Army in war. He returned to Great Britain and was subjected to strong public criticism, but he was appointed to the Western Command, was promoted to lieutenant general in 1900, and retired in 1905.

Butler, who had married the distinguished war artist Elizabeth Thompson in 1877, wrote many superb books, including military biographies. His autobiography, *From Sketchbook and Diary*, was published in 1909. Butler died on 7 June 1910, the same day Wolseley wrote him, "I always looked upon you as a host in yourself, ready to undertake any difficult job, and the more dangerous it was the more you enjoyed it" (McCourt 1967, p. 259).

See also Artists, War; Ashanti Ring; Ashanti War, Second (1873–1874); Boer War, Second (1899–1902); Boers; Canada; Earle, Major General William; Egyptian Army; Ginnis, Battle of; Gordon Relief Expedition; Purchase System; Red River Expedition; Tel el-Kebir, Battle of; Wolseley, Field Marshal Garnet J.

References: Kochanski (1999); Lehmann (1964); Maxwell (1985); McCourt (1967); Pakenham (1979); Sixsmith (1970)

C

Camberley, Staff College

In 1802, the Royal Military College was founded by Colonel (later Major General) John Gaspard Le Marchant to train young men as infantry and cavalry subalterns in a Junior Department (which later became the Royal Military College, Sandhurst) and experienced officers in staff duties in a Senior Department. The Senior Department was formed at High Wycombe from a school privately founded in 1799 by a French émigré, General Jarry. The Junior Department moved to a new site in 1812 and became the Royal Military College, Sandhurst. The Senior Department moved to Farnham in 1814, and in 1821 it joined the Royal Military College, Sandhurst.

The poor performance of the British Army in the Crimean War (1854–1856) highlighted administrative, logistical, and staff weaknesses. In January 1856, a Council of Military Education was convened to look into revising officer education and training. Detailed proposals were made for the improvement of staff officer education, and on 17 December 1857 the Senior Department was renamed the Staff College. Admission to the Staff College was to be by competitive examination, and each two-year course was to consist of thirty students, twenty-five from the infantry, cavalry, and Guards, and five from the Royal Artillery and Royal Engineers. Initially, the Staff College did not attract the best officers.

The Staff College moved to its new building at Camberley, on the edge of the Sandhurst estate, in 1862. By 1865, at the end of the second year of Staff College the student was examined in, at most, seven subjects: military history, military administration and law, fortification, and military surveying and reconnaissance. The two additional subjects could be chosen from mathematics, modern languages (French, German, and Hindustani), and natural and experimental science.

The Franco-Prussian War (1870–1871) emphasized the need for comprehensive, realistic staff officer training. The course was revised in 1870 to make it more professional and practical, with less emphasis on mathematics. The period 1870–1890 also witnessed the greatest increase in student attendance. In 1870, forty students, twenty in their first year of study (Junior Division) and twenty in their second year of attendance (Senior Division) attended the Staff College. The establishment was raised to forty-eight students in 1884 and to sixty-four in 1886. In the late 1880s, students studied military history and geography, fortification and artillery, staff duties, administration and military law, military topography, reconnaissance, and one foreign language.

The reputation of the Staff College increased significantly in the 1890s, due mainly to qualified instructors and realistic training, including topics of strategy, mobilization, and imperial defense. The first "staff tour" took place in 1895.

The Second Boer War (1899–1902) showed that training needed to be conducted at a level higher than the regiment and with the Royal Navy. The establishment of the General Staff in 1906 generated new interest in and marked an improvement in the quality of staff work, as well as recognizing "the unique importance of the [Staff] College as the nursery of the General Staff" (Bond 1972, p. 240).

See also Boer War, Second (1899–1902); Crimean War; Esher Committee; Officers, British Army—Training and Education; Sandhurst, Royal Military College

References: Bond (1972); Harries-Jenkins (1977); Spiers (1992)

Cambridge, Field Marshal H.R.H. Prince George F., Second Duke of (1819–1904)

Field Marshal H.R.H. Prince George F., Second Duke of Cambridge, exerted significant influence on the reform and modernization of the British Army throughout the second half of the nineteenth century in his role as commander in chief, in which he served from 1856 to 1895.

Cambridge was born on 26 March 1819 in Hanover. His father was Adolphus, First Duke of Cambridge, the youngest of seven children of King George III and brother of Kings George IV and William IV. When he was born, the Second Duke of Cambridge was heir presumptive to the British throne until the birth of his cousin Victoria two months later.

Cambridge moved to England in 1830 and began his military career in 1838 with a one-year assignment to the Gibraltar garrison. In 1840, he was attached as a lieutenant colonel to the 12th Lancers. Two years later, he was gazetted (appointed) as colonel in command of the 17th Lancers. He commanded the Corfu garrison (1843–1845). At the age of twenty-seven, Cambridge was promoted to major general and served in various command positions in Ireland until 1852, when he was appointed inspector-general of cavalry. He succeeded to the dukedom on the death of his father in 1850.

In early 1854, Cambridge was appointed to command the 1st Division in the British expeditionary force sent to the Crimea. He commanded his formation at the Battles of the Alma (20 September 1854), Balaklava (25 October 1854), and Inkerman (5 November 1854). Although his performance was lackluster, contemporary sources refer to his gallant behavior. Whereas the regimental officers and soldiers had to persevere through the harsh winter of 1854–1855, Cambridge, ostensibly ill with dysentery and typhoid fever, was ordered home on 27 December 1854. Queen Victoria reportedly considered his departure from the Crimea "shameful" (Royle 2000, p. 301), and Cambridge's numerous attempts to receive another field command were denied.

Field Marshal Viscount Hardinge, officer commanding in chief of the army, suffered a stroke in July 1856 and Cambridge succeeded him. During his first 12 years in office, he advocated better military education, combined arms maneuvers, and supported the creation of a trained reserve.

The Duke of Cambridge was strongly opposed to many of the Cardwell Reforms, especially the confirmation of the primacy of civilian control of the army. The War Office Act of 1870 consolidated the War Office and the Horse Guards and required the commander in chief to physically move from the Horse Guards to the War Office, an unmistakable indicator of his new subordinate role as principal military adviser to the secretary of state. (The Duke of Cambridge, however, after moving to the War Office, was permitted to address his letters from the "Horse Guards, Pall Mall.") Cambridge also opposed the abolition of purchase (in which officers purchased their initial commissions and subsequent promotions to lieutenant colonel) and deplored the localization and linked-battalion systems (in which line regiments were linked with militia regiments).

From the 1870s until his retirement in 1895, Cambridge frequently opposed military reformers and one of their leaders, Field Marshal Viscount Garnet J. Wolseley. During this period the authority of the commander in chief was reduced further. Cambridge retired in 1895, was replaced by Wolseley, and spent the last years of his life involved with royal ceremonies and charitable causes. He died on 17 March 1904.

The Duke of Cambridge served as commander in chief of the British Army from 1856 to 1895. Although genuinely concerned about the British soldier, "At a time when Army reform was under discussion he was not just conservative but hopelessly reactionary, and not only opposed change, but quarreled with those who proposed it" (Barnett 1970, p. 334). He worked diligently to preserve the Crown's authority and control of the army, frequently against the tide of progress and reform.

See also Alma, Battle of the; Balaklava, Battle of; Cardwell Reforms; Commander in Chief, British Army; Crimean War; Hardinge, Field Marshal Henry; Horse Guards; Inkerman, Battle of; Purchase System; War Office; Wolseley, Field Marshal Garnet J.

References: Barnett (1970); Bond (1972); Hamer (1970); Kochanski (1999); Lehmann (1964); Longford (1963); Raugh (1987a); Royle (2000); Spiers (1992); St. Aubyn (1963); Strachan (1997); Wheeler (1914)

Cameron, General Sir Duncan

See Maori War, Second (1863–1869)

Campaign Medals

Campaign medals are military awards, generally consisting of an ornamental commemorative medallion suspended from a distinctive multicolored ribbon, presented to soldiers and sailors to recognize participation in a specific campaign or conflict. The recipient's name, rank, and regiment were usually impressed or engraved on the rim of the medallion.

During the late eighteenth and early nineteenth centuries, selected senior officers were given medallions to commemorate significant battlefield and naval victories. The first campaign medal issued by the British Government to all ranks was the Waterloo Medal, issued in 1816–1817 to recognize service at the Battles of Ligny, Quatre Bras, and Waterloo, 16–18 June 1815. (The general grant of campaign medals was by that time an established practice of the Honorable East India Company.) The Waterloo Medal became so popular, and was so highly valued by both officers and men that medals were subsequently awarded to recognize participation in all major campaigns. Bars (or clasps) with the names of specific engagements or battles were issued to be worn affixed to the respective campaign medal ribbon.

Naval, military, and India general service medals were also instituted, recognizing participation in various battles or campaigns over an extended period of time or in certain geographical locations. The India General Service Medal (1854–1895), for example, was instituted in 1854 and covered participation in many campaigns over a forty-one-year period. Twenty-three clasps were issued with this campaign medal, seventeen of which were for the almost continual fighting on the northern frontiers of India, with the remaining clasps for service during expeditions to Persia, Malaya, and Burma.

While the victory at the Battle of Waterloo was said to usher in the century-long "Pax Britannica" of no "major" wars, at least forty-three campaign medals with a total of 202 clasps were issued to soldiers by the British Government between 1815 and the beginning of World War I.

See also Awards and Decorations; East India Company; Victoria Cross
References: Dorling (1974); Farwell (1981); Gooding (1994); Joslin (1974)

Campbell, Brigadier General Sir Archibald
See Burma War, First (1824–1826)

Campbell, Field Marshal Colin, First Baron Clyde of Clydesdale (1792–1863)

Field Marshal Colin Campbell was a highly respected, charismatic, and brave British Army officer, truly "a soldiers' general," who served on active service in numerous campaigns for over a fifty-year period. His service culminated as commander in chief, India, during the Indian Mutiny (1857–1859). Campbell was born Colin Macliver on 20 October 1792 in Glasgow, Scotland. He adopted the name Campbell when his maternal uncle, Colonel Campbell, recommended him for a commission. Campbell was gazetted an ensign in the 9th Foot in 1808. He served in the Peninsular War, took part in the disastrous Walcheren Expedition in 1808, and fought in the campaign against the Americans at New Orleans in 1814–1815.

Service at Gibraltar and Barbados followed the Napoleonic Wars. Campbell was not wealthy, and this hindered his career during the era when officers purchased their promotions. He was, however, after being loaned money by a friend, able to purchase a majority in 1825, and in 1832, he purchased an unattached lieutenant colonelcy.

Campbell was appointed lieutenant colonel of the 9th Foot in 1835. He assumed command of the 98th Foot two years later, deployed that regiment to China in 1842, and saw active service in the First China War (1839–1842). Campbell was promoted to colonel and appointed commandant of Hong Kong.

As a brigadier general, Campbell commanded a brigade, then a division, during the Second Sikh War (1848–1849) and was knighted for his distinguished service. Campbell then became the commander of the Frontier Brigade, which was renamed the Punjab Irregular Force in 1851 (and the Punjab Frontier Force in 1865), and led expeditions against the Kohat Pass Afridis (1850), the Mohmands (1851–1852), and the Ranizais and Utman Khel (1852).

In 1852, Campbell returned to England and went on half pay until selected to command the Highland Brigade of the 1st Division in 1854 in the expeditionary force being sent to the Crimea. Promoted to major general in June 1854, he distinguished himself in the charge of the Highlanders at the Battle of the Alma (20 September 1854) and directed the "thin red line" of the 93rd Highlanders at Balaklava (25 October 1854). Campbell assumed command of the 1st Division in early 1855, but he departed the Crimea in November 1855 after quarrelling with his superiors and concerns that arose over the chain of command. Campbell was promoted to lieutenant general in June 1856 and returned to the Crimea to a promised corps command. But since the corps had not been formed, he returned to England a month later.

When the news of the Indian Mutiny and death of the commander in chief, India, reached England in July 1857, Campbell was offered the vacant position. He arrived in India a few months later. He demonstrated his superb organizational abilities in the November 1857 relief of Lucknow, defeat of Tantia Topi at Cawnpore on 6 December 1857, and the final capture of Lucknow on 23 March 1858. By then, Campbell, with age and many years of campaigning catching up with him, was quite methodical and earned the nickname of "Sir Crawling Camel" (Hibbert 1978, p. 334). It seems Campbell was concerned about his martial reputation and did not want to do anything to jeopardize his chances of receiving a peerage.

In May 1858, Campbell was promoted to general and elevated to the peerage as Baron Clyde of Clydesdale. After the Mutiny was suppressed, and in ill health, Campbell returned to England in 1860. He was promoted to field marshal in 1862 and died on 14 August 1863. "Lord Clyde has made a reputation in the military history of England," according to one source, "absolutely unrivalled in the records of the middle of the nineteenth century" (Farwell 2001, pp. 157–158).

See also Cawnpore, Siege and Relief of; Chillianwalla, Battle of; China War, First (1839–1842); Crimean War; India; Indian Army Operations; Indian Mutiny; Lucknow, Siege and Relief of; North-West Frontier; Punjab Frontier Force; Purchase System; Sikh War, Second (1848–1849); Tantia Topi

References: Cook (1975); Farwell (2001); Forbes (1895); Hibbert (1978); Nevill (1912); Royle (2000); Ward (1996); Watson (1991)

Canada

British North America—which became the Dominion of Canada in 1867—was a major component of the British Empire during the nineteenth century. Its unique cultural and political differences made Canada a difficult colony for the British to govern. The British Army served in Canada for many years, and when it engaged in active operations, it generally did so against internal rebellions.

British control over Canada began in 1760, when the French surrendered Quebec during the French and Indian War. Under the 1763 Treaty of Paris, "New France" became a British colony. A Royal Proclamation established a British civil government in Quebec and the boundaries of British North America. At this time, the population of British Quebec was 95 percent French Roman Catholic and 5 percent British.

In an attempt to assimilate the French population into British Protestant society, a number of measures were taken. In the wake of the American Revolution and the influx of British loyalists to Canada, one of the most significant was the Canada Act of 1791. This act reestablished colonial borders, replaced French property laws with a freehold tenure system, and established regional elective councils. In addition, the land surrounding the Great Lakes and the St. Lawrence River basin was divided into two parts, Upper Canada and Lower Canada. Upper Canada was the area located west of the Ottawa River around the Great Lakes (generally the current province of Ontario), and Lower Canada was centered on the St. Lawrence River, east of the Ottawa River. The British encouraged immigration, mainly to Upper Canada.

Both Upper and Lower Canada experienced significant population and economic growth after the War of 1812, and this increased the possibility of friction. A rebellion, led by Louis Joseph Papineau seeking greater political and fiscal power for French-Canadians in Lower Canada, broke out in 1837. British Army and militia units crushed the Papineau Rebellion within a few months, as they did "MacKenzie's Rebellion," which erupted in December 1837. A more serious outbreak took place in November 1838, when Dr. Robert Nelson was proclaimed president of the new Canadian Republic. British and militia forces dispersed and defeated the rebels in a number of short, sharp engagements. In response to this Canadian unrest, the British sent Lord Durham to investigate and report on the situation. Durham's subsequent recommendations were included in the 1840 Act of Union that reunited Upper and Lower Canada as the single province of Canada, under one governor and legislature.

With a united Canada, there were 426 militia battalions. Only required to assemble for one day per year, these units were not very effective, but they provided a foundation for further military expansion and increased proficiency. There was one regular unit, the Royal Canadian Rifle Regiment, raised in 1840. The 1846 Militia Act divided men into two age groups, 18–40 and 40–60, with the latter forming a reserve. The Militia Act of 1855 created a popular active militia of up to 5,000 volunteers who were paid for ten days' training each year.

External controversies, notably disputes with the United States over the border west of the Rocky Mountains and the New Brunswick–Maine boundary, came to the forefront in the 1840s. These issues were eventually resolved.

In November 1861, during the American Civil War, a U.S. Navy ship stopped and boarded the *Trent*, a British Royal Mail steamer, and apprehended two Confederate envoys en route to London. This episode caused a tremendous international furor and war between the United States and Great Britain seemed imminent. After reinforcements were sent, the British Army garrison in Canada totaled 17,000 soldiers.

Another threat soon faced Canada. The Fenian Brotherhood, an anti-British organization of Irish immigrants formed in the United States in 1858, was eager to attack British North America. Many of the Fenians had served in the American Civil War (1861–1865), and they were experienced and well organized.

Some 20,000 Canadian volunteers were mobilized by June 1866 to thwart a possible Fenian incursion. A force of about 800 Fenians crossed into Canada on the night of 31 May–1 June 1866 and forced back a defending Canadian unit. After a second skirmish, the Fenians, concerned about the arrival of Canadian reinforcements, returned to the United States. Canadian militia forces also repulsed two smaller Fenian raids in May 1870.

The 1866 Fenian attacks encouraged Canadians to support confederation. After discussions in London, the British North America Act was proclaimed on 1 July 1867. This act established the Dominion of Canada, then consisting of four provinces: Ontario, Quebec, New Brunswick, and Nova Scotia. Other provinces could join the Dominion at a future time. A federal government, consisting of an elected House of Commons and an appointed Senate, was established at Ottawa, and a governor-general was designated as the Crown's representative. Each province was to have its own seat of government, lawmaking body, and lieutenant governor. All but 3,500 British troops were withdrawn from Canada.

The immediate postconfederation period was an uncertain time for Canada, as incidents took place that aggravated existing cultural, linguistic, and political differences. The British North America Act did not apply to Rupert's Land, which was owned by the Hudson Bay Company and populated largely by the Metis people. They were Indian, French, and British, many of whom were traders and trappers. In 1869, Canada purchased Rupert's Land, which, along with the North-West Territories, became the province of Manitoba.

Many Metis believed that Rupert's Land was theirs by heritage. Under the leadership of Louis Riel, Metis of the Red River area declared a provisional government. The Red River Expedition, under the command of Colonel (later Field Marshal Viscount) Garnet J. Wolseley, was formed to suppress the Riel Rebellion. Wolseley's force, consisting mainly of seven regular infantry companies plus militia, traveled through 1,100 miles of wilderness to reach Fort Garry (near present-day Winnipeg), Riel's base, to find that the rebels had fled. Troops from Wolseley's force, except for a small element in Halifax, were among the last British troops to garrison Canada.

The Red River Expedition did not quell Metis unrest. With the exception of Newfoundland, all British possessions in North America were incorporated into the Dominion of Canada in 1878. Riel returned to Canada in 1884 and again led rebellious Metis against government forces. The railway permitted the mainly Canadian force organized to suppress the North-Western Rebellion to travel quickly to the disaffected areas. After a few fixed battles and more skirmishing, Riel surrendered on 15 May 1885. He was later convicted of treason and hanged in November 1885. This was the last campaign fought in Canada.

Canadian soldiers also served overseas in imperial campaigns. About 400 skilled Canadian boatmen, the *voyageurs* (who had served very ably on the 1870 Red River Expedition), participated in the Gordon Relief Expedition (1884–1885). Canada also raised four contingents totaling about 3,000 soldiers that fought in the Second Boer War (1899–1902). Canada had become a stalwart member of the British Empire.

See also Boer War, Second (1899–1902); Gordon Relief Expedition; Imperialism; MacDougall, Major General Sir Patrick L.; McNeill, General Sir John C., V.C.; Red River Expedition; Wolseley, Field Marshal Garnet J.
References: Barclay (1976); Barnett (1970); Haythornthwaite (1993); MacLaren (1978); Reid (1996)

Canton, Capture of (24 May 1841)
See China War, First (1839–1842)

Canton, Capture of (31 December 1857)
See China War, Second (1856–1860)

Cape Frontier Wars, Southern Africa
Nine interconnected conflicts took place in southern Africa between 1779 and 1878. These wars, called the Cape Frontier

Wars, or the Kaffir Wars (from the denigrating generic term for all blacks, meaning "infidel" in Arabic), were caused generally by Boer expansion and encroachment upon frontier indigenous tribes, with the British being frequently drawn in to protect the colonists.

The British first occupied the Cape of Good Hope area in South Africa in 1795. Initial conflict took place between the Boers as they spread eastward and encroached on Xhosa land, and a cycle of reprisals, generally involving land and cattle, began. Later conflicts focused on the ever expanding eastern frontier of Cape Colony, around the Great Fish River and the Amatola Mountains.

Cape Frontier Wars were fought in 1779, 1793, 1799–1802, and 1811–1812. Five Cape Frontier Wars were fought after 1815, in 1818–1819, 1834–1835, 1846–1847, 1850–1853, and 1877–1878.

The Sixth Cape Frontier War (1834–1835) began when Chief Maqoma of the Gaika tribe attacked Cape Colony at the end of 1834. White settlers retreated to Grahamstown and other defended posts. When word of the invasion reached the capital, Cape Town, the military commander, Lieutenant Colonel (later Lieutenant General Sir) Harry G. W. Smith, rode 600 miles in 6 days with a single orderly and arrived in Grahamstown on 6 January 1835. Smith organized and led the defense of Grahamstown, and with mainly local troops, including 3,000 Boers, drove Maqoma's force from the frontier. Governor Sir Benjamin D'Urban, with Smith as his second in command, led a four-column force into Xhosa territory in March 1835. After a brief conflict, the Xhosa returned cattle they had stolen and accepted a peace arrangement.

The "War of the Axe" is another name for the Seventh Cape Frontier War (1846–1847) because it reportedly started when indigenous locals were caught stealing an axe at Fort Beaufort. The thief was sent to Grahamstown for trial, but the escort was ambushed and the prisoner freed. After the Xhosa refused to return the prisoner, the British sent a force to punish and destroy a Xhosa settlement, but this force was repulsed. The British sent a mounted column that defeated the Xhosa at Guanga on 7 June 1846. Other engagements took place and the Xhosa chiefs eventually surrendered. By December 1847, when Smith returned as governor and commander in chief of Cape Colony, the war was basically over. Cape Colony's territory was extended to the Orange and Keiskamma Rivers, and the area between these rivers was annexed as British Kaffraria on 23 December.

Numerous cross-border engagements took place during the Eighth Cape Frontier War (1850–1853), which ended after a war of attrition basically destroyed the crops and cattle of the Xhosa. The power of the Xhosa was finally crushed in the Ninth Cape Frontier War (1877–1878). The last British commander in this later war was Lieutenant General (later General) Frederick A. Thesiger (later Second Baron Chelmsford), who may have thought the feeble resistance of the Xhosa characterized the fighting abilities of all African tribes. He would learn during the Zulu War (1879) that this was not true.

See also Boers; Chelmsford, General Frederick A. Thesiger, Second Baron; Commando System; Smith, Lieutenant General Sir Harry G.W.; Zulu War

References: Featherstone (1992a); Haythornthwaite (1995); Hulme (1968); James (1985); Mostert (1992)

Cardigan, Lieutenant General James T. Brudenell, Seventh Earl of (1797–1868)

The Seventh Earl of Cardigan is best remembered as having commanded the Light Brigade of the Cavalry Division in the quixotic Charge of the Light Brigade at the Battle of Balaklava (25 October 1854) during the Crimean War. An arrogant, confrontational martinet, although unquestionably courageous and a fine horseman, Cardigan has come to embody the worse abuses of the British Army purchase system by the wealthy aristocracy.

Born on 16 October 1797 in Buckinghamshire, James T. Brudenell was the only son of the Sixth Earl of Cardigan. He attended Oxford and became a Member of Parliament in 1818. While living in Paris, he eloped with the wife of a British Army captain, causing a sensational divorce trial.

Cardigan's army career began in 1824, when he purchased a cornetcy in the 8th Hussars. He continued to take advantage of the purchase system, buying promotion to lieutenant in January 1825, to captain in June 1826, to major in August 1830, and four months later to lieutenant colonel. Cardigan became the commander of the 15th Hussars in 1832. He was very quarrelsome and was involved in many incidents, including the illegal arrest of officers for breaches of social etiquette, dueling, libel, and a sensational court-martial. In 1836, he assumed command of the 11th Hussars (then Light Dragoons), reportedly for £40,000, and succeeded to the earldom when his father died the following year.

In April 1854, a few days after the British declaration of war against Russia that officially began the Crimean War, Cardigan was gazetted to brigadier general and appointed to command the Light Brigade of Cavalry (consisting of five regiments, totaling about 1,000 cavalrymen). He was to be subordinate to his detested brother-in-law, Major General (later Field Marshal) George C. Bingham, Third Earl of Lucan, commander of the Cavalry Division. (One officer noted, "two bigger fools could not be pulled out of the British Army" [Royle 2000, p. 132].) Cardigan, however, was given the impression his command was separate, and he would not be under Lucan's orders.

Cardigan joined his brigade at Varna on the Black Sea coast in June 1854. He led a reconnaissance patrol later that month, exceeded his orders, and was out of contact for over a week. Cardigan was frustrated by having been ordered to withdraw before making contact on 19 September 1854, the day before the Battle of the Alma.

Cardigan and the Light Brigade rode into immortality at the Battle of Balaklava, 25 October 1854. The "thin red line" of British and Turkish troops repulsed a Russian assault, and the Heavy Brigade charged and drove Russian cavalry back over the Woronzov Heights. The Light Brigade did not then act. Later in the morning, the British commander in chief, General (later Field Marshal) Fitzroy J. H. Somerset, First Baron Raglan, ordered Lucan to send cavalry to prevent the enemy from retreating with its guns. In the ensuing confusion, Cardigan bravely led the 673-man Light Brigade through Russian fire up the North Valley, the "Valley of Death." He was reportedly the first man in the Russian lines, and considering that he had done his duty, he turned around and returned to the British lines. Twenty minutes after the charge began, the Light Brigade suffered 113 men killed and 134 badly wounded.

Cardigan returned to England in January 1855 and was regaled as a hero even as he seemed to exaggerate his Crimean exploits. Appointed inspector-general of cavalry later that year, Cardigan was promoted to lieutenant general in 1861. Cardigan died on 28 March 1868 from injuries caused by falling off his horse. Upon Cardigan's death, the 11th Hussars thought so much of their former commander that they changed the timing of the last bugle call of the day from 10:00 P.M. to the minute he died. Others were less respectful, believing Cardigan "was, alas, unusually stupid; in fact [he was] an ass. The melancholy truth was that his glorious golden head had nothing in it" (Woodham-Smith 1953, p. 17).

See also Balaklava, Battle of; Charge of the Light Brigade; Crimean War; Lucan, Field Marshal George C. Bingham, Third Earl of; Purchase System; Raglan, Field Marshal Fitzroy J. H. Somerset, First Baron

References: David (1997); Harris (1973); Moyse-Bartlett (1971); Royle (2000); Selby (1970); Thomas (1974); Woodham-Smith (1953)

Cardwell, Edward T., First Viscount Cardwell of Ellerbeck (1813–1886)

Edward T. Cardwell was a mid-nineteenth-century Peelite-turned-Liberal British statesman. He served as secretary of state for war (1868–1874) and was responsible for the most significant administrative and organizational reform of the British Army during the Victorian era.

Cardwell, a merchant's son, was born in Liverpool on 24 July 1813. Considered intellectually gifted, he attended Winchester and Oxford and was called to the bar in 1838. He was first elected to Parliament in 1842. Cardwell held cabinet posts in the Aberdeen and Palmerston governments, rising to become colonial secretary (1864–1866).

The Liberals won the 1868 general election and William E. Gladstone became prime minister for the first time. He selected Cardwell, who had not previously demonstrated any interest in or knowledge of military affairs, to be his secretary of state for war. Cardwell was concerned with consolidating authority, reducing military expenditures, and increasing the effectiveness and efficiency of the British Army. Reduced manpower and the need for Britain to remain a world and Continental power, combined with the Liberal agenda to reduce privilege, also motivated Cardwell to reform the British Army. He also seemed to understand the implications of industrial power harnessed to mass armies, along with new military and staff organizations and methods, and how these factors required military modernization.

Cardwell phased cost reductions over the 1869–1870 and 1870–1871 Army Estimates. He withdrew 25,709 men from self-governing colonies, thus saving £2,330,800, slashed £641,370 from the stores vote, and reduced the size of infantry battalions to 560, later reduced to 520, other ranks. Cardwell's reductions were very popular.

Cardwell's Army Enlistment Act of 1870 replaced long service enlistment with short service, the latter requiring a soldier to enlist for twelve years—six on active and six in the reserves. Cardwell hoped to establish a reserve of 80,000 men and increase the quality of the enlisted soldier.

The War Office Act of 1870 consolidated the War Office and the Horse Guards, reduced overlapping responsibilities, and delegated its responsibilities to three distinct executive officers.

The Army Regulation Bill of 1871 contained provisions to abolish the anachronistic and abused purchase system, in which officers purchased their initial commission and subsequent promotions, and to transfer control of the militia from the county lords-lieutenants to the Crown. The purchase system was extremely controversial and stoutly defended by conservatives. Cardwell's main argument was that the purchase system prevented army reorganization. After a parliamentary struggle, he was able to persuade Queen Victoria to abolish the purchase system by royal warrant on 20 July 1871, to be effective on 1 November 1871.

The second component of the failed Army Regulation Bill, pertaining to the localization of the military system in territorial areas, was introduced separately and became the Localization Act of 1872.

Cardwell left office and was raised to the peerage in 1874. His physical and mental health deteriorated thereafter, and he died on 15 February 1886.

Cardwell and the "Cardwell Reforms" significantly changed the administration and organization of the British Army. Although not complete by the time Cardwell left office, these reforms included the introduction of short service enlistments; the reorganization of the War Office; the abolition of the outdated practice of officers buying their commissions; and the localization of the home army. Field Marshal Viscount Garnet J. Wolseley, a progressive officer who joined the War Office staff in 1871, later wrote that he could "think of no man whose memory and whose great services entitle him to be remembered by all ranks of the army, in the nation, the age and the empire at large" (Woodall 1986, pp. 68–69).

See also Army Estimates; Cardwell Reforms; Discipline and Justice, British Army; Gladstone, William E.; Horse Guards; Long Service; MacDougall, Major General Sir Patrick L.; Militia; Purchase System; Short Service; War Office; Wolseley, Field Marshal Garnet J.

References: Barnett (1970); Spiers (1992); Wheeler (1914); Woodall (1986).

Cardwell Reforms

The Crimean War (1854–1856) exposed the inadequacy of supply and commissariat departments, antiquated senior leadership, and general lack of training and preparedness of the British Army. Moreover, the private soldier, who had frequently suffered considerable privations in silence and had been ignored by society since Waterloo, became an object of concern as the increasingly literate public received uncensored and timely news directly from the battlefield.

A number of committees were appointed to study the need of Army reform in the wake of the Crimean War and the Indian Mutiny (1857–1859). The reform of the British Army became even more urgent after the Prussian Army crushed Austria in the 1866 Seven Weeks War and later defeated the French in the Franco-Prussian War (1870–1871). The united Germany demonstrated that it had arguably become the major military power on the European Continent.

Edward T. Cardwell became secretary of state for war after the Liberals won the 1868 general election. With little previous interest in or knowledge of military affairs, Cardwell was concerned with maintaining Great Britain as an imperial and European power in the wake of manpower shortages. Aware of the example of the American Civil War (1861–1865), Cardwell wanted to harness industrial power to technological and organizational reforms and to consolidate authority, reduce military expenditures, and increase the effectiveness and efficiency of the British Army. Moreover, he wanted to minimize scandals pertaining to the purchase system, and, as a Liberal, he wanted to reduce privilege and patronage as well as government expenditures.

Cardwell wanted to continue the momentum of reform. He gathered at the War Office a number of young, progressive officers, including Captain Evelyn Baring (later First Earl of Cromer), Major (later Major General Sir) George (Pomeroy-) Colley, and later Colonel (later Field Marshal Viscount) Sir Garnet J. Wolseley, to assist him.

The establishment of a professional army with a trained reserve was an urgent requirement for the British Army. Cardwell's Army Enlistment Act of 1870 replaced long service enlistment with short service, the latter requiring a soldier to enlist for twelve years—six with the colors and six in the reserves. (This was raised in 1881 to seven years with the colors and five years in the reserves.) Soldiers could extend their enlistment to complete a total of twenty-one years and become eligible for a pension.

Short service was instituted for a number of reasons. A shorter term of service was intended to appeal to more, and higher quality, soldiers. Many soldiers would not reenlist beyond their six years' active duty and be reassigned to the regular reserve. This would provide experienced manpower for the regular reserve. Moreover, money would be saved because fewer soldiers would remain on active duty long enough to become eligible for a pension. At a time of increasing imperial commitments, Cardwell was trying to help ensure a balance between the number of soldiers serving overseas and those serving at home, but the principal reason for enacting short service was to establish a 60,000-man reserve.

In 1869, the Northbrook Committee studied the tremendous duplication of effort in the British Army, with two separate headquarters (War Office and Horse Guards) and ill-defined and overlapping responsibilities. The War Office Act of 1870 consolidated the War Office and the Horse Guards. It also delegated its responsibilities to three distinct executive officers: the "officer commanding in chief" (Field Marshal H.R.H. Prince George F., Second Duke of Cambridge), responsible for the strictly military aspects of the army; the surveyor-general of the ordnance, responsible for supply and equipment; and the financial secretary, responsible to the secretary of state for war for the Army Estimates and all military financial matters.

The Duke of Cambridge initially resisted these changes, believing they would erode the queen's prerogative powers and diminish his own authority in the army. He eventually concurred with the constitutional supremacy of the secretary of state for war, and also gained responsibility for the Medical, Education, Chaplain-General's, and Topographical Departments.

The main component of the Army Regulation Bill of 1871 contained provisions to abolish the anachronistic and abused purchase system, in which officers purchased their initial commission and subsequent promotions, up to the rank of lieutenant colonel. The purchase system was extremely controversial and stoutly defended by conservatives; it was the rallying point for all who opposed British Army reform of any kind. Cardwell's main argument was that the purchase system prevented Army reorganization, and he believed it to be "the keystone of army reform" (Farwell 1972, p. 188).

Conservatives argued that the abolition of purchase would result in officers coming from the lower classes of society, especially those without land, who would be susceptible to revolution. Cardwell wanted officer promotions based upon merit, which would reduce promotion stagnation and increase the professionalism of the officers. After a parliamentary struggle, Cardwell was able to persuade Queen Victoria to abolish the purchase system by royal warrant on 20 July 1871, to be effective on 1 November 1871.

The second part of the failed Army Regulation Bill of 1871 pertained to the transfer of control of the militia from the county lords-lieutenants to the Crown. It was introduced separately and became the Localization Act of 1872. It "localized" the military system in territorial areas, where line regiments would be linked with militia regiments. This was especially important for recruiting purposes, which was accomplished by dividing Britain into 66 districts, following county boundaries as much as possible. Each district consisted of two regular battalions (one was generally on overseas service), two militia battalions, and volunteers. The Localization Act of 1872 also transferred control of the militia and volunteers from the lords lieutenant to the Crown.

Other Cardwell reforms included the abolition of enlistment bounties in 1869, the elimination of flogging except in wartime, and improvements to soldiers' pay and living conditions.

The Cardwell Reforms, although not perfect, included short service enlistments and the establishment of an organized reserve, the reorganization of the War Office, the abolition of the system of purchasing officers' commissions, and the localization of the home Army. These key reforms marked the end of the Wellingtonian era of the British Army and ushered in the more modern Cardwellian system. Prime Minister William E. Gladstone referred to Cardwell when he observed that, "I venture to affirm that no man who ever held the seals of office since the Secretaryship of War was established, has done so much for the reform and efficiency of the Army" (Erickson 1959, p. 76).

See also Army Estimates; Cambridge, Field Marshal H.R.H. Prince George F., Second Duke of; Cardwell, Edward T.; Correspondents, War; Crimean War; Gladstone, William E.; Horse Guards; Indian Mutiny; Long Service; Militia; Pomeroy-Colley, Major General Sir George; Purchase System; Short Service; Volunteers; War Office; Wolseley, Field Marshal Garnet J.
References: Bond (1962b); Dietz (1990); Erickson (1959); Farwell (1972); Gallagher (1975); Raugh (1984); Skelley (1977); Spiers (1992); Tucker (1963); Wheeler (1914); Woodall (1986)

Cathcart, Lieutenant General Sir George (1794–1854)

Lieutenant General Sir George Cathcart was a competent, conscientious officer who distinguished himself commanding British troops during the Eighth Cape Frontier War and the 4th Division during the Crimean War.

The third son of the Earl Cathcart, George Cathcart was born on 12 May 1794 and commissioned as a cornet in the 2nd Life Guards. He served as private secretary to his father, who was British ambassador to Russia, and was present at many of the Napoleonic battles in 1813. Cathcart entered Paris with the allied armies in 1814, and from 1815 to 1818 was aide-de-camp to Field Marshal Arthur Wellesley, First Duke of Wellington, at Waterloo and in Paris.

Cathcart's career was rather uneventful, as he exchanged into numerous regiments during the 1820s and 1830s, until his promotion to major general in 1851. He was then appointed governor and commander in chief of Cape Colony. Arriving in South Africa in 1852, Cathcart was responsible for concluding a campaign of attrition that wore down the Xhosa tribe. Hostilities ended in March 1853, and British Kaffraria was made a crown colony shortly thereafter. For his services in South Africa, Cathcart was knighted in July 1853 and appointed adjutant-general at the Horse Guards.

Cathcart commanded the 4th Division in the British expeditionary force that arrived in the Crimea on 14 September 1854. Even though he was not the senior division commander or senior to all of the staff officers, Cathcart held the "dormant commission," authorizing him to succeed to the command of the force in the event of the death or incapacitation of Field Marshal Fitzroy J. H. Somerset, First Baron Raglan, the commander. This was a secret piece of paper, signed by Queen Victoria, and known to only three people in the Crimea: Raglan, Field Marshal H.R.H. Prince George F., Second Duke of Cambridge (then commanding the 1st Division), and Cathcart, who carried the document in his pocket. This was a frequent source of friction, as Cathcart then seemed to consider himself the force second in command and expected to be consulted by Raglan.

At the Battle of the Alma (20 September 1854), Cathcart's 4th Division, along with the 3rd and the Cavalry Divisions, were in reserve. After the British victory, the force continued the march toward Sevastopol, which seemed undefended. Cathcart urged an immediate assault on Sevastopol, a suggestion brushed aside by the dogmatic Raglan.

On the morning of the Battle of Balaklava (25 October 1854) an aide-de-camp brought Cathcart the order to deploy his division to a supporting position. Cathcart complained that his men had spent the previous night in the trenches, and initially refused to move his formation. He eventually relented, and when the 4th Division finally arrived on the battlefield, he was ordered to seize a series of redoubts. The 4th Division occupied the first vacant redoubt and Cathcart refused to advance further, believing he would have to vacate them again anyway and return to the siege trenches before Sevastopol. While Cathcart refused to execute an order he deemed futile, another commander—Brigadier General James T. Brudenell, Seventh Earl of Cardigan—had no such scruples, and led the Charge of the Light Brigade that afternoon.

On the following day, and not related to the previous day's battle, Cathcart was informed by Raglan that the secretary of state for war had rescinded the dormant commission.

On 5 November 1854, the Russians attacked the British, and the 4th Division was ordered to support two divisions already fighting the Battle of Inkerman. In the rain and fog, Cathcart and a small element had moved too far to the east and were cut off by the Russians. A number of frantic assaults up the rugged hills were made to regain contact with the British. In one of these charges, Cathcart was shot in the chest and killed. His last words were, "I fear we are in a mess" (Kelsey 2002, p. 5).

See also Alma, Battle of the; Balaklava, Battle of; Cambridge, Field Marshal H.R.H. Prince George F., Second Duke of; Cape Frontier Wars, Southern Africa; Cardigan, Lieutenant General James T. Brudenell, Seventh Earl of; Charge of the Light Brigade; Crimean War; Inkerman, Battle of; Raglan, Field Marshal Fitzroy J. H. Somerset, First Baron; Wellington, Field Marshal Arthur Wellesley, First Duke of
References: Judd (1975); Kelsey (2002); Mawson (2001); Pemberton (1962); Raugh (1987a); Royle (2000)

Cavagnari, Major Sir Pierre L. N. (1841–1879)

Major Sir Pierre L. N. Cavagnari, an officer with extensive military experience in India, served as the British envoy in the Afghan capital of Kabul in 1879. His murder and the massacre of his mission on 3 September 1879 caused a resumption of the Second Afghan War.

The son of a French general and his Irish wife, Cavagnari was born in France on 4 July 1841 and raised and educated in England. He attended the East India Company's military "seminary" at Addiscombe and became an ensign in the 1st Bengal Fusiliers in 1858. During the Indian Mutiny he served in Oudh (1858–1859) and in 1861 was appointed assistant commissioner of the Punjab. In 1877, Cavagnari became deputy commissioner for Peshawar. He participated in seven North-West Frontier punitive expeditions.

In 1878, when the Russians sent a mission to Afghanistan, the British also formed a mission to visit Afghanistan. The British mission was headed by General (later Field Marshal) Sir Neville Chamberlain and included Cavagnari as political officer. The British mission marched out of Peshawar and encamped at Fort Jamrud, at the entrance to the Khyber Pass, on 21 September 1878. The following day Cavagnari, with a small military escort, rode ahead to coordinate passage. Cavagnari was stopped but met an Afghan general he knew, who told Cavagnari that force would be used to oppose the British march, and if they had not been friends, Cavagnari would have been shot.

This rebuff, plus the failure of Afghan ruler Sher Ali Khan to meet with a related British ultimatum, caused the British to invade Afghanistan and start the Second Afghan War on 21 November 1878. Cavagnari served as political officer of Lieutenant General Sir Samuel J. Browne's Peshawar Valley Field Force. He played a key role in negotiating the 26 May 1879 Treaty of Gandamak, which seemingly ended the Second Afghan War, with Yakub Khan, Sher Ali Khan's son and successor. Cavagnari received a knighthood for this achievement.

Cavagnari, while considered personally fearless but perhaps "unpleasantly ambitious and ruthless" (Barthorp 1982, p. 71), was appointed British envoy to Kabul. His mission included eighty others, including political assistants and a Corps of Guides military escort. The mission arrived in Kabul on 24 July 1879. In late August 1879, six undefeated Afghan regiments, resentful of their nation's surrender, the presence of foreigners, and owed three months' back pay, were transferred from Herat to Kabul. On 3 September 1879, amid rumors of disaffection, these Herati soldiers received only one month's pay. Enraged, they briefly attacked the British residency and then retreated.

The confrontation was not over, as the Afghan soldiers had only gone to get their weapons. Messages for assistance were sent to Yakub Khan, but they were apparently ignored. Some 2,000 Afghan soldiers returned and ferociously attacked the residency. Cavagnari was hit in the head by a ricocheting bullet; he then led a bayonet charge and died shortly thereafter. By the end of the day, only a few guides remained alive. They rejected Afghan pleas to surrender, fixed bayonets, and charged out of the residency to their deaths. (Three British soldiers who were messengers, and four on detached duty, survived the attack.) The massacre of Cavagnari and his mission sparked the renewal of hostilities.

See also Addiscombe, Military Seminary; Afghan War, Second (1878–1880); Afghanistan; Browne, General Sir Samuel J., V.C.; Chamberlain, Field Marshal Sir Neville B.; East India Company, Military Forces; Great Game; India; Indian Mutiny; Roberts, Field Marshal Frederick S., V.C.; Sher Ali Khan

References: Barthorp (1982); Miller (1977); Roberts (1897); Wright (1980)

Cavalry, British Army–Organization

There were only 31 cavalry regiments (each roughly equal to an infantry battalion) as against 144 infantry battalions in the British Army in 1870. Of the 31 cavalry regiments, 14 were in England, 1 in Scotland, 6 in Ireland, and 10 overseas, mainly in India.

British cavalry was divided into three classes—heavy, medium, and light—according to the size and weight of the horse and the rider. The 5 regiments of the Household Cavalry were in the heavy category and normally did not serve overseas. There were 13 medium regiments of dragoons and lancers and 13 light hussar regiments.

The cavalry regiment (at its peacetime strength) at the beginning of the Victorian period consisted of a headquarters (10 officers and 5 noncommissioned officers) and 6 troops, with each troop consisting of 1 captain; 1 lieutenant; 1 cornet, 1 troop sergeant major; 2 sergeants; 3 corporals; 1 trumpeter; 1 farrier; and 47 privates, for a regimental total of 363 officers and other ranks. The number of troops was raised from 6 to 8 during the Crimean War (1854–1856) and the Indian Mutiny (1857–1859), although the strength of these troops frequently fluctuated. It was common to group two troops into a squadron in about 1870.

In 1897, 3 squadrons within each cavalry regiment, each of 6 officers and 128 other ranks, were designated for active service. The fourth squadron was designated for depot duties and included an attached Maxim gun.

Establishments (personnel strengths) in the late 1890s varied according to the type, readiness status, and location of the cavalry regiment. Line cavalry regiments in the United

Kingdom had a higher establishment, and those that had recently returned from overseas duty were on the lower establishment and would rebuild their strength to the higher establishment. In the United Kingdom, the higher establishment cavalry regiment consisted of 26 officers, 2 warrant officers, 51 sergeants, and 617 soldiers ranked corporal and lower, for a total of 696 all ranks. The lower establishment consisted of 23 officers, 2 warrant officers, 45 sergeants, and 508 corporals and lower, totaling 578 all ranks. The Guard cavalry regiments were composed of 24 officers, 2 warrant officers, 53 sergeants, and 351 corporals and lower, for a total of 430 all ranks. Cavalry regiments serving in India consisted of 29 officers, 2 warrant officers, 54 sergeants, and 539 corporals and below, for a total of 624 all ranks. There were 488 all ranks in a cavalry regiment serving in Egypt, consisting of 21 officers, 2 warrant officers, 41 sergeants, and 424 corporals and below. A cavalry regiment serving in other colonies contained 24 officers, 2 warrant officers, 47 sergeants, and 520 corporals and privates, for a total of 593 all ranks.

In a larger formation or conflict, two or more cavalry regiments constituted a brigade and two brigades formed a division.

In 1889, there were 266,692 men in the British Army (including British troops in India and the reserves), of whom only 21,922, or 8.2 percent of the total, were in the cavalry and its reserves.

See also Cavalry, British Army—Tactics; Cavalry, British Army—Training; Cavalry, British Army—Weapons and Equipment; Crimean War; Indian Mutiny; Machine Guns
References: Bond (1965); Crouch (1983a); Ellis (1978); Grierson (1899); Knight (1996)

Cavalry, British Army—Tactics

The British Army cavalry was called the *arme blanche* (meaning the "white arm," a French term for sword), but it rarely served as the sword arm or the decisive arm of attack during the Napoleonic Wars or later. As a result of its limited use during the Napoleonic Wars, the British Army cavalry had lost the tactical initiative and was overshadowed by the dominant infantry.

The essence of the cavalry was its speed, mobility, and shock power, and to use the factors in conducting the decisive charge. The British generally employed cavalry on their flanks and were reluctant to employ massed cavalry. Cavalry was generally not placed in the center of the line because it would displace the infantry and reduce the strength of that sector of the line.

Cavalry attacked from the flank generally in echelon or in an oblique order. This tactic generally precluded the enemy from knowing the point of attack, and would draw the enemy's reserve frequently to the center of the threatened flank.

The column formation was simpler to execute, with the close column being used for assembly and the open column for maneuver. The column formation prevented the enemy from ascertaining the strength or depth of the column, and it permitted relatively simple extension or deployment in any direction. This formation also permitted easier command and control and exposed a smaller front to enemy musket fire.

Experience taught the British Army that the cavalry should charge in "rank entire" order, with all ranks on line. Advocates of the "rank entire" order generally tried to keep a second rank in support a hundred yards away. More conservative officers believed the cavalry should attack in three lines, with the second support line and third reserve line deployed in column, not in line.

In addition to attacking and guarding, screening, and protecting flanks, cavalry roles included reconnaissance, advance and rear guards, outpost duty, and skirmishing.

The adoption of the Minié rifle in the 1850s, and the lessons learned from European wars from 1859 to 1870 and American Civil War from 1861 to 1865, dramatically changed the traditional role of the cavalry on the battlefield—although many cavalry officers did not understand this transformation. The rifle was the main arm of the U.S. Army cavalry during the American Civil War, and dismounted fire, combined with the mobility provided by the horse, enhanced the cavalry's value. Increased accuracy, rates of fire, and lethality of weapons shifted the tactical advantage from the attacker to the defender. This decreased the cavalry's ability to conduct attacks and use their shock effect.

Practical experience in colonial campaigns, frequently in mountainous, jungle, or other terrain unsuitable for the charge, coupled with shortage of regular cavalry, gave rise to irregular cavalry, where carbines were the main weapons. This experience also emphasized the need to organize and conduct mounted infantry training. The inauspicious performance of the cavalry in the Second Boer War (1899–1902) did little to clarify its role. In 1903, it was directed that the cavalry's primary weapon would be the carbine or rifle, and the sword its secondary weapon. As a result, cavalrymen felt that they were being transformed into infantrymen. The cavalry continued to resist change and reform and paid the price of obstinacy on the battlefields of World War I.

> **See also** Boer War, Second (1899–1902); Cavalry, British Army—Organization; Cavalry, British Army—Training; Cavalry, British Army—Weapons and Equipment; Charge of the Light Brigade; Charge of the 21st Lancers; Infantry, British Army—Small Arms; Infantry, British Army—Tactics
> **References:** Bond (1965); Callwell (1896); Ellis (1978); Haythornthwaite (1895); Spiers (1992); Strachan (1985)

Cavalry, British Army–Training

Cavalry training in the British Army was relatively extensive and intensive. The new recruit was trained by his regiment or at the depot, if his regiment was posted outside the United Kingdom. He was first given training in drill and the use of arms on foot, gymnastics (about seventy fencing lessons), and stable work. After this preliminary two-month basic training period, the recruit began 90 to 120 hours of riding drill. Concurrently, he was given instruction in saddling, packing, and the use of arms while on horseback. Foot drill was conducted in the afternoons, and oral classes in the evening. After six to eight months of basic training, the cavalry recruit was given the same musketry training that an infantry recruit received, although the qualification standards were lower. Each winter, all cavalry troopers received three weeks of reinforcement training on foot drill and riding.

During the winter months when unit training was not being conducted, squadron officers taught their men reconnaissance and patrol duties, map reading and drawing, reporting, and similar soldier skills.

Each cavalry squadron was exempted from additional duties twice each year for a three-week period, during the winter and the spring, to receive squadron drill and field training from its own squadron officers. Training during the winter period (15 October to 15 March) consisted of "riding across country, manipulation of arms, fighting on foot, outpost duties, duties in the camp and in bivouac, fencing, and oral instruction" (Grierson 1899, p. 179). Training during the spring period (16 March to 31 May) was devoted to squadron drill and field duties. Each squadron was inspected by its regimental commander after spring training, and the results reported to the brigade commander. The brigade commander then inspected each regiment for training proficiency in April.

Marksmanship training for the cavalry soldiers would be conducted from March into the summer, and regimental drill would begin in June.

Cavalry regiments sent individual officers and men to additional training schools and courses, including sergeants and corporals to the riding school at Canterbury to be trained as riding masters, one officer and one sergeant each year to the six-week course at the musketry school at Hythe, and an officer once a year to attend the pioneer course at the engineering school at Chatham. Cavalry soldiers were also sent to the signaling school at Aldershot. Moreover, two officers were sent each year to the veterinary school at Aldershot for the month-long course in veterinary studies, and two farrier-sergeants and two farriers were sent to the same school each year for the two-months' course in horseshoeing and horse care.

> **See also** Aldershot; Cavalry, British Army—Organization; Cavalry, British Army—Tactics; Cavalry, British Army—Weapons and Equipment
> **References:** Bond (1965); Grierson (1899); Spiers (1992)

Cavalry, British Army–Weapons and Equipment

Cavalry tactics were continually debated during this era of rapid technological developments and advances in the lethality, accuracy, and rate of fire of rifles and other weapons. The way the cavalry was armed and equipped represented the predominant philosophy of cavalry employment.

Before the Crimean War (1854–1856), dragoons and hussars carried muzzle-loading carbines and occasionally pistols, in addition to swords. Lancers carried only swords, lances, and pistols. After the Crimean War, breech-loading Snider carbines were issued to the cavalry, and they in turn were superseded by the Martini-Henry in 1878, the Lee-Metford in 1892, and the Lee-Enfield in 1901. By 1880, all cavalrymen were armed with carbine and sword, and lancers also retained their lances.

In 1899, the cavalryman used a horse and a saddle. He wore a belt and a bandolier with an ammunition pouch, each containing fifteen cartridges. A small haversack was carried over his right shoulder and a water bottle (canteen) over his left shoulder.

The cavalrymen, while mounted, carried a flannel shirt, a pair of underwear, a towel, a cap, knife, fork, and spoon, pay book, and emergency ration. The soldier's cloak and an extra pair of boots were strapped over the saddlebags. A pair of riding breeches and puttees were rolled in a waterproof sheet and were buckled behind the saddle, underneath a hay net and nose feedbag. Cooking gear was positioned on the right-hand side of the saddlebags, while an extra pair of shoes and the picketing ropes for the horse were carried on each side of the saddle. The cavalryman was armed and equipped in a similar manner on the eve of World War I.

See also Cavalry, British Army—Organization; Cavalry, British Army—Tactics; Cavalry, British Army—Training; Infantry, British Army—Small Arms

References: Bond (1965); Crouch (1983a); Featherstone (1978); Grierson (1899)

Cawnpore, Siege and Relief of (1857)

Cawnpore, located about 260 miles east of Delhi, was an important station and thriving market town on the Grand Trunk Road between Delhi and Benares and on the south bank of the Ganges River. It served as the headquarters for the province of Oudh and was garrisoned by about 3,000 Indian troops and about 300 European troops, many of whom were invalids.

The Indian Mutiny began at Meerut on 10 May 1857, and the situation grew increasingly tense as news of the rebellion spread to other locations. The Cawnpore garrison commander, Major General Sir Hugh M. Wheeler, had a misplaced trust in his sepoys and underestimated the threat.

Wheeler had been warned about the loyalty of Nana Sahib, whose real name was Dhondu Pant, one of the adopted sons of the last Peshwa of Bithur, Baji Rao II. Rao had been dethroned by the British and his land was appropriated in exchange for a large annual pension. When Rao died in 1851, his pension stopped, and Nana Sahib, who retained the title of maharajah of Bithur, had worked tirelessly to get the British to restore the pension. During the early days of the mutiny, Nana Sahib was in Lucknow on business pertaining to his father's pension. Disgruntled at again being rebuffed by the British, Nana Sahib stated the situation at Cawnpore required him to urgently return to Bithur, which was about 6 miles from Cawnpore. He returned to Cawnpore with his own armed retinue and volunteered his services to Wheeler. Nana Sahib's men were assigned to guard the treasury.

A number of the native regiments in Cawnpore mutinied on the night of 5 June 1857. The 2nd Bengal Native Cavalry rode to the treasury, and with the assistance of Nana Sahib's men, plundered it. Nana Sahib was persuaded to lead the mutineers to Delhi, but the following morning, he returned to Cawnpore to lead the four rebellious regiments there.

On 6 June 1857, Nana Sahib's rebels attacked the ill-prepared British defenders of Cawnpore. After a desperate three-week siege, Wheeler accepted Nana Sahib's offer of safe passage by boat to Allahabad for the survivors in exchange for the surrender of the starving and outnumbered garrison. As the British were loading the boats, a murderous fusillade of musketry and grapeshot rang out from the opposite shore of the Ganges, and the group was attacked by a rebel cavalry troop. Wheeler was one of scores of British to be hacked, bayoneted, or shot to death, or burned alive in the boats. When this assault was over, the men were separated from the women and children and were all shot.

About 125 bedraggled women and children survived this massacre and were taken to a small house called the Bibighar, or the House of the Ladies. They were later joined by the wives and children of British officers from other mutinous garrisons.

Nana Sahib learned that a British relief force, commanded by Brigadier General (later Major General Sir) Henry Havelock, was advancing on Cawnpore. He decided, against the advice of many of his followers, to execute all the women and children hostages. Mutinous sepoys initially refused to shoot the British women, so five men—including two Muslim butchers—were sent into the Bibighar to kill the women and children. The slaughter was completed by evening, with the bodies of the dead, and reportedly some who were still living, dumped into a well or the Ganges River.

Havelock's force defeated the rebels on 16 July 1857, arriving in Cawnpore the following day and finding that the British women and children had been massacred. The floor of the Bibighar was covered with clotted blood and looked like a human slaughterhouse. There was a well-worn bloody trail from the Bibighar to the well, along which "thorny bushes had entangled in them scraps of clothing and long hairs. One of the large trees ... had evidently had children's brains dashed out against its trunk ... and an eye glazed and withered could be plainly made out ... smashed into the coarse bark" (Hibbert 1978, p. 209).

This unspeakable brutality infuriated the British soldiers, many of whom vowed vengeance against the mutineers. Before they were executed, captured rebels were forced, while being whipped, to kneel down and lick clean the floor of the Bibighar, which had been moistened with water earlier by people of the lowest caste. Others had pork and beef stuffed down their throats to break their caste. These gruesome acts humiliated the mutineers and religiously defiled them. While some mutineers were hanged, others were tied in front of the mouths of cannon and literally blown away. "It was a horrid sight," wrote one observer, "a regular shower of human fragments of heads, or arms, or legs, appeared in the air through the smoke; and when that cleared away, these fragments lying on the ground . . . were all that remained" (Wilkinson-Latham 1977, p. 26). This form of execution was especially feared, as it deprived the victims of an afterlife.

The British force left in Cawnpore was later besieged by rebels commanded by Tantia Topi and defeated in front of the city on 28 November 1857. A British relief force from Lucknow, commanded by Lieutenant General (later Field Marshal Lord Clyde) Sir Colin Campbell, decisively defeated the mutineers at Cawnpore on 6 December 1857.

The horrendous July 1857 massacre of women and children at Cawnpore symbolized the horror of the Indian Mutiny for the British and was undoubtedly a major factor in their desire for revenge. The rallying cry of "Cawnpore! Cawnpore!" motivated attacking British troops until the end of the mutiny.

See also Campbell, Field Marshal Colin; East India Company, Military Forces; Havelock, Major General Sir Henry; India; India, British Army in; Indian Mutiny; Nana Sahib; Tantia Topi
References: Brock (1858); Collier (1964); Edwardes (1963); Hibbert (1978); Hilton (1957); Ward (1996); Wilkinson-Latham (1977)

Cetshwayo kaMpande (c. 1832–1884)

Cetshwayo kaMpande was the last king of the united Zulu nation in South Africa. The Zulus considered him a courageous, strong, and fair ruler. When the British initiated war against the Zulus in 1879, he proved himself "a skilled politician, a competent battlefield commander, and a perceptive strategic thinker" (Knight 1999, p. 76).

Cetshwayo was born in about 1832 in southern Zululand, the eldest son of King Mpande kaSenzangakhona and of his "great wife" (or paramount wife of his many wives). The name Cetshwayo means "the slandered one," because rumors abounded at times that he was illegitimate. He served in a prestigious regiment in the Zulu Army and distinguished himself in battle against the Swazi in 1852. Cetshwayo's father, however, favored another son, Mbuyazi, to succeed him. This caused a tremendous rivalry that culminated in the Battle of 'Ndondakusuka (2 December 1856), where Cetshwayo and his followers slaughtered as many as 12,000 of their adversaries and followers. This was a remarkable victory for Cetshwayo. It was the only battle he commanded in person.

Mpande permitted Cetshwayo increasing control over the affairs of Zululand, and when Mpande died in 1872, Cetshwayo succeeded him as king. Cetshwayo permitted white representatives from Natal to crown him the following year, thus tacitly giving Natal the right to interfere in internal Zulu affairs, an ominous harbinger. He built a new royal homestead at oNdini (Ulundi) and sought to restore centralized royal authority.

As the British attempted to confederate South Africa in the late 1870s, they realized the independent Zulu kingdom was an obstacle to their plans. The British, who had previously supported the Zulus, engineered a territorial dispute as a basis for a confrontation with the Zulus. Cetshwayo was given an ultimatum to dismantle his army and turn over to the British those guilty of border violations.

Cetshwayo did not know how to react to the British demands. When the ultimatum expired on 11 January 1879, the British invaded Zululand. Cetshwayo conceived the basic Zulu strategy and issued a campaign plan but left the command of the Zulu field forces to trusted subordinates. A force of about 23,000 Zulus massacred the British at Isandlwana on 22 January although another Zulu force was repulsed that night at Rorke's Drift. Other engagements followed, and it became obvious that Zulu discipline could not overcome British firepower. The British routed the Zulus at the decisive battle of the war, Ulundi, on 4 July 1879.

Cetshwayo was apprehended on 28 August 1879 and sent as a prisoner to Cape Town. The Zulu kingdom's power was broken as Zululand was divided into thirteen independent chiefdoms, each overseen by a British resident. Cetshwayo traveled to London in 1882 and had a successful audience with Queen Victoria. He impressed the queen and society with his dignity, intelligence, and compassion, and one man who called him a "cruel and crafty gorilla" (Edgerton 1988, p. 162) in Parliament was shouted down in protest. He secretly returned to Zululand and was restored to a part of his old kingdom. Internecine warfare increased, and Cetshwayo's supporters were defeated in late 1883. Cetshwayo died on 8 February 1884, officially of a heart attack, although quite possibly by poisoning.

See also Chelmsford, General Frederick A. Thesiger, Second Baron; Imperialism; Isandlwana, Battle of; Rorke's Drift, Defense of; Ulundi, Battle of; Zulu War; Zululand
References: Edgerton (1988); Knight (1990); Knight (1995); Knight (1999); Laband (1995); Morris (1965)

Chamberlain, Field Marshal Sir Neville B. (1820–1902)

Field Marshal Sir Neville B. Chamberlain (no relation to Sir A. Neville Chamberlain, British prime minister, 1937–1940) was an officer of the East India Company's army and later the Indian Army. He was a superb leader, expert in hill warfare, and master of mobility who commanded numerous expeditions on the North-West Frontier and was wounded in action six times.

Born in Buenos Aires on 20 January 1820, Chamberlain was the son of Sir Henry Chamberlain, then consul-general in Brazil. At age fifteen, Chamberlain was sent to the Royal Military Academy, Woolwich, but when it appeared he would not pass the examinations, he was withdrawn and commissioned an ensign in the Bengal Native Infantry in 1837.

Chamberlain served in the First Afghan War (1839–1842) and the 1843 Gwalior campaign. He served in a number of staff positions, in peacetime and throughout the Second Sikh War (1848–1849). Chamberlain was posted to the Punjab after it was annexed in 1849, and as a local brigadier general, was appointed to command the 11,000-man Punjab Frontier Force in 1854. Chamberlain commanded numerous punitive expeditions against rebellious North-West Frontier tribes, including those against the Orakzais (1855), the Miranzai Expeditions (in 1855 and 1856), and against tribes near Dera Ghazi Khan (1857).

During the Indian Mutiny (1857–1859), Chamberlain initially commanded the Punjab Moveable Column. He later became adjutant-general and distinguished himself at the siege of Delhi.

Chamberlain was reappointed to the command of the Punjab Frontier Force in 1858 and commanded the punitive expeditions against the Waziris (1859–1860) and against the Mahsuds (1860). In 1863, he commanded a two-brigade force in the Ambela Campaign, which was characterized by fierce mountain fighting. He was promoted to major general and knighted for his services and leadership.

Promoted to lieutenant general in 1872 and full general in 1877, Chamberlain served as commander in chief of the Madras Army from 1876 to 1881. In 1878, when the Russians sent a mission to Afghanistan to extend their influence there, the British also formed a mission to visit Afghanistan. The British mission, headed by Chamberlain, marched out of Peshawar and encamped at the entrance to the Khyber Pass on 21 September. The Afghans would not permit the British mission to enter. This rebuff basically caused the British to invade Afghanistan on 21 November 1878 and start the Second Afghan War. Chamberlain departed India and retired in 1881, having been, according to some sources, responsible for inventing the game of snookers, a popular pocket billiards game.

Chamberlain was a courageous soldier and charismatic commander, considered by another senior officer as "the very soul of chivalry" (Farwell 2001, p. 181). Promoted to field marshal in 1900, Chamberlain died in 1902.

See also Afghan War, First (1839–1842); Afghan War, Second (1878–1880); Bengal Army; Cavagnari, Major Sir Pierre L. N.; East India Company, Military Forces; India, British Army in; Indian Army Operations; Indian Mutiny; Madras Army; North-West Frontier; Punjab Frontier Force; Sikh War, Second (1848–1849)
References: Barthorp (1982); Callwell (1896); Farwell (1972); Farwell (2001); Hibbert (1978); Nevill (1912)

Chaplains

Chaplains are the priests, ministers, rabbis, and other trained religious officials who serve as members of the military and provide religious services and spiritual comfort to its soldiers.

The Army Chaplain's Department was formed in 1796. All army chaplains belonged to the Church of England until 1827, when the first Presbyterian ministers were recognized. Eleven years later Roman Catholics were accepted as equals by their Protestant colleagues. In 1881, Wesleyan Methodists were recognized, and the first Jewish army chaplain was appointed in 1892.

Chaplains had been divided into ranks in 1816, and although they were commissioned first in 1859, they did not wear military uniforms until 1860. The chaplain general of the forces was authorized the rank of major general. There were four subordinate ranks of "chaplains to the forces": first-class chaplains were ranked as colonels, second-class chaplains as lieutenant colonels, third-class chaplains as majors; captain's rank was awarded to fourth-class chaplains.

In the 1850s, after concern in the army that some of the Roman Catholic priests in Ireland were preaching sedition to their troops, the War Office decided to exert better control over religious activities. To achieve this, the number of Anglican, Presbyterian, and Roman Catholic chaplains in the army would reflect the proportion of soldiers of each religion.

Most chaplains were generally more tolerated than appreciated, and some commanding officers were suspicious about them making the soldiers "too good." The traditional military view held that chaplains were useful for comforting the sick and wounded and "for keeping an eye on the rank and file," regardless of religious doctrine.

See also Religion
References: Brereton (1986); Farwell (1981); Skelley (1977)

Charasia, Battle of (6 October 1879)

While the Second Afghan War had seemingly ended with the signing of the Treaty of Gandamak on 26 May 1879, hostilities again broke out after the massacre of the British envoy and his escort at the British residency in Kabul on 3 September 1879.

The Kabul Field Force, commanded by Major General (later Field Marshal Earl) Sir Frederick S. Roberts, V.C., was formed to advance into Afghanistan. Consisting of a cavalry brigade of four regiments, two infantry brigades totaling seven battalions, and four batteries, the Kabul Field Force began its advance on 27 September 1879. The British units were armed with the new Martini-Henry rifle. Only one infantry brigade could move at a time due to transport shortages.

Roberts's force reached Charasia, about 10 miles from Kabul, on 5 October 1879. His advance was obstructed by a range of hills, stretching from east to west at elevations of about 220 to 500 yards, through which was only one pass, the Logar Defile. Roberts sent the transport back to Safed Sang to pick up the second brigade and encamped his force near the village of Charasia, planning to advance through the Logar Defile the following morning.

Roberts sent out a cavalry patrol early on 6 October 1879 to reconnoiter the Logar Defile. It was followed by a detachment of four companies of the 92nd Highlanders, half of the 23rd Pioneers, three field guns, and cavalry, commanded by Major (later Field Marshal Sir) George S. White, for the purpose of preparing the road through the defile for wheeled transport. The cavalry scouts discovered that several thousand Afghan tribesmen were positioned at the Logar Defile, in the adjacent hills, and threatening the British force. Moreover, Roberts learned that an Afghan force was situated between his 4,000-man, 18-gun force and his second brigade. Roberts realized he would have to attack before joined by his second brigade and reacted quickly.

White's detachment was tasked to fight and hold the enemy at the Logar Defile. At the same time the 2nd Brigade, commanded by Brigadier General T. D. Baker and consisting of the 72nd Seaforth Highlanders, 3rd Sikhs, 5th Punjab Infantry, 5th Gurkhas, and 23rd Pioneers, would attempt to outflank the Afghans, attack their weak right flank, and roll up their positions until the British reached the Logar Defile.

At about 11:30 A.M., the 72nd Highlanders, supported by a mountain battery and Gatling guns, led the 2nd Brigade attack up the steep slopes at the Afghan right. As they met fierce resistance, they were reinforced by the 5th Gurkhas and two companies of the 5th Punjabis. The Afghan commander shifted troops from his left to his right flank to meet the British attack, thus permitting White's detachment to advance and seize high ground on the Afghan left.

The 2nd Brigade's main attack met stubborn resistance. White sent two of his four companies of the 92nd Highlanders to assist the 2nd Brigade's attack, and when the two elements linked up, the balance tipped to the British side. The Afghans became unnerved and the battle turned into a rout, with the 9th Queen's Royal Lancers and the 5th Punjab Cavalry in hot pursuit. The Afghans had about 400 killed and many wounded, and abandoned about 20 guns.

The British victory at the Battle of Charasia cost Roberts's force about 83 soldiers killed and wounded. White won the Victoria Cross for his intrepid leadership and gallantry that day, and the route was open to Kabul, which Roberts entered on 8 October 1879.

See also Afghan War, Second (1878–1880); Afghanistan; Roberts, Field Marshal Frederick S., V.C.; Victoria Cross; White, Field Marshal Sir George S., V.C.
References: Barthorp (1982); Featherstone (1973); Forbes (1892); Roberts (1897); Tanner (2002); Young (1977)

Chard, Colonel John R. M., V.C. (1847–1897)

Colonel John R. M. Chard is best remembered for his service when a lieutenant and commander of the post of Rorke's Drift during its gallant defense against repeated Zulu attacks, 22–23 January 1879, during the Zulu War.

Chard was born on 21 December 1847 in Devonshire, England. He was commissioned a lieutenant in the Royal Engineers upon graduation from the Royal Military Academy, Woolwich, in 1868. Assignments in Bermuda and Malta followed before he returned to England in 1875. He left England with the 5th Engineer Company on 2 December 1878 for service in the Zulu War. Arriving at Durban on 4 January 1879, Chard was sent in advance to Helpmakaar to prepare for the arrival of his company. He arrived at Rorke's Drift on 19 January, and after Major Spalding's departure on 22 January, Chard was left in command of the post.

On 22 January 1879, Zulus devastated a British force at Isandlwana and that night attacked the small post of Rorke's Drift. Chard, assisted by Lieutenant (later Major) Gonville Bromhead of the 24th Regiment, hastily planned, organized, and led the defense of the post through numerous desperate and intense Zulu attacks until the following morning. Remarkably, the British garrison of 8 officers and 131 other ranks (including 35 sick in hospital) had held off the repeated assaults of about 3,000 to 4,000 Zulus. For his gallantry and leadership, Chard, and 10 others, were awarded the Victoria Cross. Chard was also given a supernumerary captaincy in the Royal Engineers and brevet majority, dated 23 January 1879. Chard thus became the first British Army officer to be promoted from lieutenant to major in a single day.

Chard was a somewhat unimpressive fellow, and many senior officers were amazed that he had been able to orchestrate and lead the stubborn defense of Rorke's Drift. Lieutenant General (later Field Marshal Viscount) Sir Garnet J. Wolseley, for example, who presented the Victoria Cross to Chard, reportedly found him "a hopelessly dull and stupid fellow, and Bromhead not much better" (Best and Greaves 2001, p. 123).

After the Zulu War, Chard served at Devonport, Cyprus, and other locations in England before sailing for Singapore in 1892, where he served for three years. Returning to Great Britain in 1896, he was promoted to colonel on 8 January 1897. Chard died of tongue cancer on 1 November 1897.

See also Bromhead, Major Gonville, V.C.; Isandlwana, Battle of; Rorke's Drift, Defense of; Victoria Cross; Wolseley, Field Marshal Garnet J.; Woolwich, Royal Military Academy; Zulu War
References: Best and Greaves (2001); Glover (1975); Knight (1990); Morris (1965); Stephen and Lee (1964–1865)

Charge of the Light Brigade

The Charge of the Light Brigade, a British cavalry action during the Battle of Balaklava in the Crimean War (1854–1856), has been romanticized and immortalized, primarily through an 1874 poem of the same name by Alfred, Lord Tennyson. The charge was not, as considered by many, a great and glorious venture, but rather a tremendous military blunder, arguably caused by the fog of war and incompetent senior commanders.

The Russians attacked the vulnerable British early on 25 October 1854, hoping to seize their supply port at Balaklava. Russian cavalry advances were repulsed by British infantry and by the Heavy Brigade of the Cavalry Division, the latter commanded by Major General (later Field Marshal) George C. Bingham, Third Earl of Lucan. The other element of the Cavalry Division, the Light Brigade, was commanded by Lucan's loathed brother-in-law, Brigadier General (later Lieutenant General) James T. Brudenell, Seventh Earl of Cardigan. The Light Brigade, even though only about 500 yards away, remained idle and did not assist the Heavy Brigade.

The entire situation that led to the Charge of the Light Brigade remains shrouded in controversy. Cardigan's subordinates became impatient with their forced inactivity, and a number questioned their commander. Cardigan had reportedly been ordered earlier by Lucan to remain in his position and be prepared to defend it against the Russians, and he did not intend to move.

General (later Field Marshal) Fitzroy J. H. Somerset, First Baron Raglan, British commander in chief, was then situated at a vantage point on the Sapoune Heights. He wanted to exploit the success of the Heavy Brigade, and at about 10:15 A.M., ordered Lucan to prepare his two brigades for an attack. Lucan positioned the Light Brigade in the North Valley facing east, with the Heavy Brigade in support, and waited for expected infantry support. At about 11:00 A.M., one of Raglan's staff observed the Russians taking guns from the redoubts captured earlier, to the right of the Light Brigade but out of sight of Lucan. Raglan did not want to lose any guns, and one of his staff officers wrote down his order: "Lord Raglan wishes the cavalry to advance rapidly to the front—follow the enemy and try to prevent the enemy carrying away the guns. Troop Horse Artillery many accompany. French cavalry is on your left. Immediate" (Royle 1999, p. 272).

This order was given to Captain Louis E. Nolan, an expert horseman but impetuous officer, to deliver to Lucan. As Nolan departed, Raglan admonished, "Tell Lucan the cavalry is to attack immediately" (Royle 1999, p. 273). When Nolan reached Lucan, the general, not able to observe the Russians taking away the guns but aware of Russian artillery on both sides of the North Valley, asked for a clarification of the orders. Nolan waved contemptuously down the valley. In the heat and confusion of battle, Lucan, perhaps realizing he may not have known the entire battlefield situation and knowing it was his duty to obey the order, rode over to Cardigan and ordered him to advance.

Cardigan hesitated and added, "But allow me to point out to you that the Russians have a battery in the valley in our front, and batteries and riflemen on each flank" (Judd 1975, p. 86). A sympathetic Lucan responded, "I know it. But Lord Raglan will have it. We have no choice but to obey" (Judd 1975, p. 86). Cardigan faced his men and said, "Well, here goes the last of the Brudenells!" (Judd 1975, p. 86) before giving the order to advance.

As Cardigan led his men at a trot down the "Valley of Death," Nolan, who had stayed to participate in the charge, rushed in front of Cardigan, waving his sword and gesturing wildly, perhaps trying to divert the direction of the charge away from the Russian guns. Nolan's motives will never be known, as Russian shrapnel ripped through his chest and killed him.

The Light Brigade stoically continued its advance as its ranks were thinned by deadly Russian enfilading fire coming from the elevated flanks as well as the front. Cardigan courageously rode at the center of his brigade. As the advancing cavalry reached and hacked its way through the Russian guns, Russian horsemen were seen formed behind them. Cardigan turned around and rode back to the British lines. In 25 minutes, the 673-man Light Brigade lost 113 men killed, 134 wounded, and more than 500 horses were killed or later destroyed.

The Charge of the Light Brigade was not a romantic, heroic assault against overwhelming odds, but an unnecessary bungle that destroyed the effectiveness of the Cavalry Division for the remainder of the war. As usual, recriminations began immediately. Cardigan stated accurately that he had simply obeyed orders, and, in Nolan's absence, most of the blame fell on Lucan's shoulders.

French General Pierre Bosquet, who observed the Charge of the Light Brigade, believed, *"C'est magnifique, mais ce n'est pas la guerre. C'est de la folie"* (Baumgart 1999, p. 130): "It was magnificent, but it was not war. It was madness." "There is one universal feeling of disgust throughout the whole Army at this murder," wrote one British Army officer who had also observed the Charge, "for it can be called nothing else" (Mawson 2001, p. 40).

See also Balaklava, Battle of; Cardigan, Lieutenant General James T. Brudenell, Seventh Earl of; Cavalry, British Army—Organization; Cavalry, British Army—Training; Crimean War; Lucan, Field Marshal George C. Bingham, Third Earl of; Raglan, Field Marshal Fitzroy J. H. Somerset, First Baron
References: Baumgart (1999); David (1977); Harris (1973); Kelsey (2003); Mawson (2001); Moyse-Bartlett (1971); Pemberton (1962); Robins (1997); Royle (1999); Selby (1970); Thomas (1974); Woodham-Smith (1953)

Charge of the 21st Lancers

The Charge of the 21st Lancers at the Battle of Omdurman (2 September 1898) produced heavy casualties, and it was a failure. The British public, however, viewed it as a courageous, self-sacrificial effort and idolized its participants.

The 21st Lancers, commanded by Colonel R. M. Martin, joined Major General (later Field Marshal Earl) Sir Horatio H. Kitchener's force in early August 1898. The regiment had never seen active service and was eager to vindicate itself in combat and eschew its satirical regimental motto, "Thou shalt not kill" (Keown-Boyd 1986, p. 209). Attached to the 21st Lancers as a supernumerary lieutenant was Lieutenant Winston L. S. Churchill of the 4th Hussars.

The main dervish attack against the Anglo-Egyptian defenses at Omdurman took place at dawn on 2 September 1898. In less than an hour, the dervish onslaught was repulsed, and the Mahdist formations were virtually destroyed.

Kitchener, the commander of the Anglo-Egyptian force, thought the battle was over. He was further convinced that no organized dervish resistance remained between his army and Omdurman. At 8:30 A.M., Kitchener ordered the 21st Lancers, which was patrolling near the high ground of Jebel Surgham, to "annoy them [the dervishes] as far as possible on their flank and head them off if possible from Omdurman" (Brighton 1998, p. 75).

The 21st Lancers rode southward and observed a number of dervishes in the open, blocking their advance on the Omdurman Road where it intersected with the Khor Abu Sunt (a dry watercourse running perpendicular to the Omdurman Road). Martin could not ignore this large body of dervishes and was probably eager to engage the enemy. He wheeled the regiment to approach, in columns, thus providing a target for the dervishes from the south, many of whom were armed with rifles.

When the 21st Lancers was 300 meters from the dervishes, Martin ordered the regiment to conduct a right wheel. All 16 troops then swung around and formed a long line and began to charge the dervishes. When less than 50 yards from the dervishes, the Khor, filled with about 2,000 veteran dervishes, became visible, and the British realized they had been lured into a trap. As soon as the cavalry reached the ravine, "horses plunged, blundered, recovered, fell; dervishes on the ground lay for the hamstringing cut; officers pistolled them in passing over, as one drops a stone into a bucket; troopers thrust until lances broke, then cut; everybody went on straight, through everything" (Steevens 1898, p. 273).

While a number of the cavalrymen fell or were hauled off their horses and brutally killed, the survivors regrouped on the far side of the Khor. Martin wanted to charge again to rescue any survivors, but he realized such an act would only increase casualties. The cavalrymen dismounted and fired at the dervishes, who retired in good order toward the Jebel.

The Charge of the 21st Lancers was over in less than an hour, and the 440-man regiment lost 21 officers and men killed and 71 wounded in it. Even though the charge was a failure, three lancers were awarded the Victoria Cross, and the episode captured the British imagination.

See also Cavalry, British Army—Tactics; Churchill, Sir Winston L. S.; Dervishes; Kitchener, Field Marshal Horatio H.; Omdurman, Battle of; Sudan; Victoria Cross

References: Brighton (1998); Churchill (1930); Harrington and Sharf (1998); Keown-Boyd (1986); Meredith (1998); Steevens (1898); Ziegler (1973)

Chelmsford, General Frederick A. Thesiger, Second Baron (1827–1905)

General Frederick A. Thesiger, Second Baron Chelmsford, was a British Army officer, considered by many to be professional and competent, although a bit aloof. His career culminated at, and he never held another field command after, the Zulu War (1879), where he was responsible for the tremendous British defeat at the Battle of Isandlwana (22 January 1879).

Thesiger was born on 1 May 1827. His father had a distinguished legal career, served as lord high chancellor, and was raised to the peerage as Baron Chelmsford of Chelmsford, Essex, in 1858. The younger Thesiger was determined to be a soldier and was gazetted to the Rifle Brigade in 1844. He served with his regiment in Nova Scotia until 1845 when he exchanged into another regiment. After duty in England, Thesiger served as aide-de-camp to the viceroy of Ireland in 1852 and later to another general officer.

Crimean War and Indian Mutiny service followed, and by 1858, Thesiger was a regimental lieutenant colonel. Promotion to colonel came in 1863, and in 1868, Thesiger became aide-de-camp to Queen Victoria. He was promoted to temporary brigadier general, commanded at Aldershot, and was promoted to major general in 1877.

In 1878, Thesiger became with local rank lieutenant general commanding the forces in South Africa and also succeeded his father as Second Baron Chelmsford. He performed relatively well in the Ninth Cape Frontier War (1878). He commanded British troops during the Zulu War but underestimated the discipline, organization, and fighting ability of the Zulus. The British, under his command, suffered a humiliating defeat at the Battle of Isandlwana. Chelmsford reportedly conspired with subordinates to blame the debacle on a column commander killed in action. General (later Field Marshal Viscount) Sir Garnet J. Wolseley was sent to replace Chelmsford, but Chelmsford defeated the Zulus at the decisive Battle of Ulundi (4 July 1879), before Wolseley's arrival. Chelmsford returned to England and appeared before a Court of Inquiry. He never again held another field command, but he was promoted to the permanent rank of lieutenant general in 1882 and to full general in 1888.

Chelmsford died of a heart attack while playing billiards in London on 9 April 1905. He will continue to be best known as the commander of British forces during the 1879 Zulu War when his men were massacred at the Battle of Isandlwana and he "was out-thought, out-manoeuvered, and out-generalled" (Lock and Quantrill 2002, p. 301) by the Zulu commander.

See also Cape Frontier Wars, Southern Africa; Cetshwayo kaMpande; Crimean War; Indian Mutiny; Isandlwana, Battle of; Rorke's Drift, Defense of; Ulundi, Battle of; Wolseley, Field Marshal Garnet J.; Zulu War; Zululand

References: Barthorp (1980); Edgerton (1988); England and Gardiner (1990); Knight (1990); Laband (1995); Lock and Quantrill (2002); Morris (1965)

Chenery, Thomas
See Correspondents, War

Chernaya, Battle of (16 August 1855)

The Russians besieged in Sevastopol during the Crimean War realized that, as the summer of 1855 wore on, they would have to take decisive action to avoid having to surrender in the face of growing allied forces. At a council of war held on 9 August 1855, the Russian commander, Prince Michael Gorchakov, decided to attack the French and Sardinian forces positioned on the Fedukhine Heights overlooking the Chernaya (Tchernaya) River.

The French, numbering 18,000 soldiers with 48 guns, were in defensive positions on the Fedukhine Heights overlooking the Chernaya River to the northeast. In addition, they had established positions on the far side of the Chernaya River protecting the Tractir Bridge, and also straddled the high ground on both sides of the road that crossed the bridge and continued across the Plain of Balaklava. There was a large gap on the French right flank before another mass of high ground was reached, occupied by about 9,000 Sardinian soldiers with 36 guns, also overwatching the Chernaya. Small infantry and artillery detachments were posted on the far side of the Chernaya on Telegraph Hill, and about 50 French and British cavalry squadrons patrolled the area. Additional French and Turkish forces were in reserve.

Gorchakov's field army, consisting of two corps, attacked the allied positions after a heavy artillery bombardment at dawn on 16 August 1855. General-Adjutant N. A. Read's two-division III Corps was on the Russian right with orders to bombard the Fedukhine Heights then cross the Chernaya River. On Read's left, Lieutenant General Pavel P. Liprandi's two-division VI Corps was to first seize Telegraph Hill, then await further orders.

Read's corps met ferocious resistance as it crossed the Chernaya ahead of schedule. Accurate French artillery and infantry forced the Russians, with Read killed, back across the Chernaya. Shortly thereafter, Gorchakov ordered Liprandi's corps to attack the Fedukhine Heights, and in doing so, the Russians exposed their flank to an accurate French and Sardinian crossfire.

By 10:00 A.M., amid the fog of war and with heavy casualties, a muddled Gorchakov sounded a general retreat. The Battle of the Chernaya represented the Russians' last major offensive operation, "the last hurrah of the Russian army during the Crimean War [and it] had proved as disastrous as it was fruitless" (Sweetman 2001, p. 71). The Russian forces suffered about 2,273 dead, 1,742 missing, and about 4,000 wounded. The allies sustained less than 1,700 casualties, and only 14 Sardinians were killed. The British liaison officer to the French, Brigadier General (later Field Marshal Lord) Hugh H. Rose was not present at the battle, and his lack of reporting caused the British to pay little attention to it. With the Russian field army defeated, however, the allies were able to concentrate their resources on ending the siege of Sevastopol.

See also Crimean War; French Forces, Crimean War; Rose, Field Marshal Hugh H.; Russian Forces, Crimean War; Sardinian Forces, Crimean War; Sevastopol, Siege of
References: Baumgart (1999); Palmer (1987); Royle (2000); Sweetman (2001)

Chesney, Lieutenant Colonel Charles C. (1826–1876)

Lieutenant Colonel Charles C. Chesney was a prominent military intellectual, prolific writer, historian, and educator who effectively taught students at both Sandhurst and the Staff College during the mid-Victorian era.

Born in Ireland on 29 September 1826, Chesney was commissioned a second lieutenant in the Royal Engineers after passing out of the Royal Military Academy, Woolwich, in 1845. He served in regimental postings and was stationed in New Zealand during the Crimean War (1854–1856).

In 1858, Captain Chesney was appointed professor of military history at the Royal Military College, Sandhurst. He was probably the first British officer to give the American Civil War serious attention, discussing it in his lectures in 1862. In 1863, Chesney wrote a series of articles on the campaign in Virginia and Maryland, and in the following year he wrote "Sherman's Campaigns in Georgia." As a contemporary writer thousands of miles away from the action, Chesney's American Civil War articles at the time were somewhat superficial and contained little analysis.

Chesney succeeded Colonel (later Lieutenant General Sir)

Edward B. Hamley as professor of military history at the Staff College in 1864. His teaching techniques were then considered unorthodox. He required his students to actually read and assess the various authorities on military topics. Chesney also gave a series of lectures on the Waterloo campaign that attracted widespread attention. He used multiple sources in chronicling and impartially assessing the Waterloo campaign, and he was the first English writer not only to point out weaknesses in Wellington's unit dispositions but also to give the Prussians a share of the victory. Chesney's *Waterloo Lectures,* arguably his most important work, was published in 1868.

After being promoted to lieutenant colonel in 1868, Chesney was posted to Aldershot. He also served on the Royal Commission on Military Education. In that same year, he wrote *The Tactical Use of Fortresses* and in 1870 coauthored *The Military Resources of Prussia and France.* After the conclusion of the Franco-Prussian War in 1871, Chesney was sent to Europe and wrote special reports on the siege operations conducted during the war.

In 1873, Chesney received the brevet rank of colonel and was appointed to command the Royal Engineers in the London District. An anthology of his articles was published as *Essays in Military Biography* in 1874. Frequently in poor health, Chesney caught pneumonia and died on 19 March 1876.

See also Camberley, Staff College; Hamley, Lieutenant General Sir Edward B.; Intellectuals, British Army; Sandhurst, Royal Military College; Woolwich, Royal Military Academy
References: Bond (1972); Luvaas (1964); Preston (1964)

Chillianwalla, Battle of (13 January 1849)

Lieutenant General (later Field Marshal Viscount) Sir Hugh Gough, commander in chief, India, commanded British forces during the Second Sikh War. His force in early January 1849 consisted of about 13,000 troops with 60 guns. Instead of waiting for reinforcements from Multan, Gough decided to attack the Sikh force of 30,000–40,000 men with 62 guns under Shere Singh before it was augmented by a Sikh and Afghan force that had just captured Attock.

On 13 January 1849, Gough's army approached the small village of Chillianwalla, located on the southeast bank of the Jhelum River about 85 miles northwest of Lahore. Gough's force encountered a picket on a mound near the town and drove it off. From this vantage point, Gough could see that the Sikhs were arrayed in a crescent-shaped battle formation on the edge of the jungle, with its left flank on high ground and its right flank anchored on two small villages. It was early afternoon, and Gough, who reportedly did not like to fight battles in the afternoon, decided to encamp his force and fight the Sikhs the following day.

The Sikhs, however, had different plans, and their artillery opened fire on Gough's force. The British artillery responded as Gough hastily ordered his units to deploy with two infantry divisions abreast. Major General Sir Walter Gilbert's 2nd Infantry Division (with two brigades, commanded by Brigadier Generals Mountain and Godby) was on the right, and Brigadier General (later Field Marshal Lord) Colin Campbell's 3rd Infantry Division (of two brigades, commanded by Brigadier Generals Pennycuick and Hoggan) was on the left. Another infantry brigade, commanded by Brigadier General Penny, was in reserve. Major General Sir Joseph Thackwell's Cavalry Division was split into its two brigades, with Brigadier General Pope's 2nd Cavalry Brigade with three troops of horse artillery covering the army's right flank, and Brigadier General White's 1st Cavalry Brigade covering its left flank. Artillery was placed between the infantry brigades and divisions.

After the Sikh and British guns had exchanged fire for about an hour, Gough, without adequate reconnaissance and only limited daylight remaining, ordered Campbell to "carry the guns in his front without delay at the point of the bayonet" (Featherstone 1992, p. 86). The 24th Foot advanced steadily through the jungle, with muskets unloaded and bayonets fixed, toward the Sikh positions, suffering 497 casualties (with 238 killed) of the 960 soldiers in the battalion. The overall British attack was characterized by insufficient reconnaissance; a lack of command, control, and coordination; poor orders and order transmittal; inadequate artillery support; and panicking cavalry, in addition to the normal fog of war. The Sikhs also attacked and fought ferociously.

As night fell and in considerable confusion, Gilbert and other senior officers decided on a "retrograde movement" (Featherstone 1992, p. 90). After losing their direction, the British were able to march south, away from the Sikhs. The Sikhs were not driven from their positions.

At Chillianwalla, British casualties totaled 602 men killed, 1,651 wounded, and 104 missing, or about 15 percent of the total force engaged in the battle. Sikh casualties may have been as high as 8,000. One source has stated that "British losses were so heavy that, coupled as they were with lack of water, Gough was compelled to retire and re-form his forces, thus rendering the action indecisive" (Young 1977, p. 67). These factors suggest a narrow Sikh victory at Chillianwalla.

When England learned of the high casualties at and results of the Battle of Chillianwalla, Gough was roundly criticized for his blundering leadership and "Tipperary tactics." He was relieved of command and replaced by General Sir Charles J. Napier. Before Napier reached India, however, Gough won the Battle of Gujerat (21 February 1849) and ended the Second Sikh War.

The gallantry of the infantry obscured the incompetent British military leadership at Chillianwalla. Indeed, Field Marshal Viscount Garnet J. Wolseley later wrote about Chillianwalla as "that unfortunate battle where British courage was a more distinguishing feature than either the strategical or tactical skill of the general commanding" (Symons 1989, p. 25). During the nineteenth century, the Battle of Chillianwalla was equated with military incompetence.

See also Campbell, Field Marshal Colin; East India Company, Military Forces; Gough, Field Marshal Hugh; Gujerat, Battle of; India; Napier, General Sir Charles J.; Sikh War, Second (1848–1849); Sikhs; Wolseley, Field Marshal Garnet J.
References: Amin (2000); Cook (1975); Crawford (1967); Featherstone (1989); Featherstone (1992); Symons (1989); Young (1977)

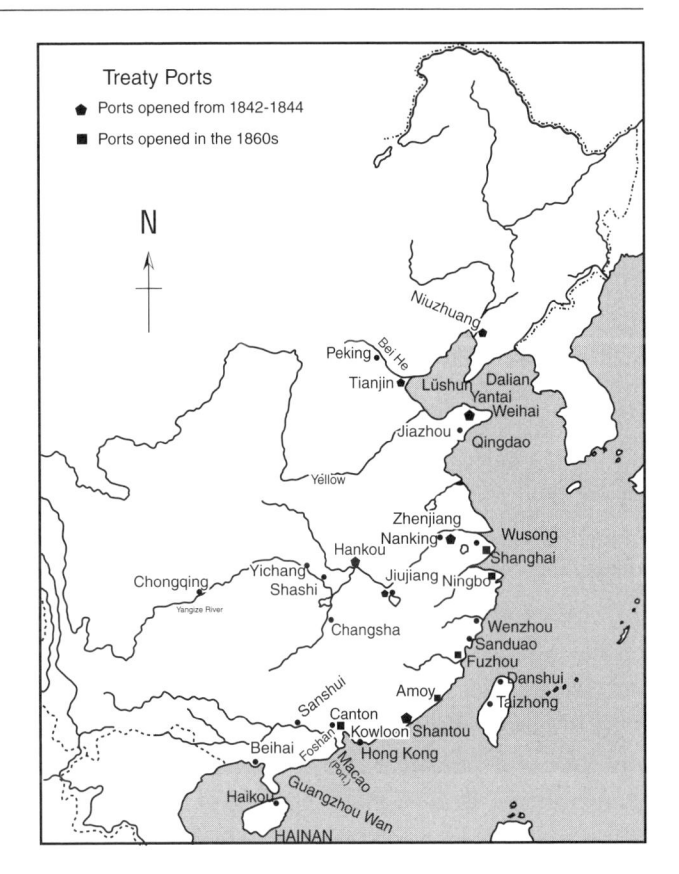

The China Seacoast

China

China was in a period of turmoil in the nineteenth century when its semimedieval government struggle against modernization failed to respond flexibly to Western encroachment, resulting in the demise of the Chinese dynastic system. The Chinese central government was ineffective, especially within the context of a market economy, and its military forces were outdated and weak, contributing to China's decline during this period.

At the end of the eighteenth century, China was shipping millions of pounds of tea to Great Britain via the East India Company. With its economy in a preindustrial stage, China did not want items from the West (all foreigners were considered "barbarians" by the Chinese), thus causing an unfavorable trade balance. By the early nineteenth century, the British were able to reverse this trade imbalance through the importation of opium from India. The Chinese attempted to abolish this trade which, coupled with cultural friction, led to the First China War (1839–1842), also called the Opium War because of the significant role of opium. The Chinese were humiliated and defeated in this conflict and forced to open additional ports to Western traders, pay a large indemnity, and cede Hong Kong to the British in what were later called "unequal treaties."

In October 1856, the Chinese seized the British-registered ship *Arrow*, igniting the Second China War. The British, and later the French, sent troops ostensibly to redress the situation and to secure more trading concessions. The Second China War ultimately ended with an Anglo-French victory in 1860. The Chinese were forced to permit a number of Western nations to establish diplomatic missions in China's capital, open ten new ports to foreign trade, remove many restrictions on foreign travel within China, permit missionaries the right to work and own property in China, and legalize the opium trade.

From 1860 to 1864, the Taipings fought the Manchu dynasty for control of China during the bloody second phase of the Taiping Rebellion. American adventurer Frederick Townsend Ward originally organized the "Ever Victorious Army" against the Taipings, which was commanded during the last year of the war by British Army Captain (later Major General) Charles G. Gordon. The Taiping Rebellion may have been the most destructive war in the entire nineteenth century, with about 20 million Chinese dying during 1850–1864 as a result.

There was significant internal unrest in China after the Taiping Rebellion, followed by attempts to modernize and reform the country. Antiforeign sentiment, manifested by members of the Society of the Righteous Harmonious Fists (the Boxers), rose as foreign trade and influence spread in China. The foreign legations in Peking were besieged by the Boxers during June–August 1900. Great Britain provided about 3,000 soldiers to the multinational force that marched on and captured Peking on 14 August 1900 and conducted punitive operations until the following May.

The Chinese were initially contemptuous of the British and other Western "barbarians" and grossly underestimated their military abilities. In 1842, at the end of the First China War, Chinese military forces were estimated at between 800,000 and 1.8 million organized in four classes, plus irregulars. Hereditary Manchus composed the first class, reportedly of 678 companies (divided into 8 divisions, or "banners"), while the second class consisted of 211 Mongolian companies. The third class consisted of 270 companies of other Manchu-allied Chinese, plus artillerymen. Many of the third class were cavalrymen, frequently called "Tartars" by the British. The fourth class, consisting of descendents of troops who had served in the army before the Manchu dynasty, numbered about 500,000 soldiers. Members of the various classes were distinguished by distinctive patches on their surcoats.

Many of the Chinese soldiers were armed with bows, arrows, and spears, and the artillery was outdated. By the Second China War, many Chinese soldiers were armed with smoothbore matchlock muskets, in addition to bows, crossbows, lances, and swords.

After the Taiping Rebellion, China recruited foreign military advisers and trainers to help modernize its army. Selected units were organized into brigades and battalions, and improvements were made, with limited success, in military training. The Chinese soldiers generally continued to carry traditional weapons, with the Boxers carrying primitive firearms and a variety of spears and halberds.

See also Boxer Rebellion; China War, First (1839–1842); China War, Second (1856–1860); Gordon, Major General Charles G.; Imperialism

References: Carr (1992); Featherstone (1989); Haythornthwaite (1995); Hibbert (1970); Hurd (1967); Lococo (2002); Selby (1968); Waller (1988); Wolseley (1862); Yu (2002)

China War, First (1839–1842)

The First China War (1839–1842), although characterized by British military administrative and logistical mismanagement, resulted in a British victory with far-reaching repercussions. The war, also called the Opium War, largely because it centered on British smuggling of the narcotic into China and Chinese attempts to curtail it, was the result of an arguably inevitable trading, diplomatic, and cultural clash.

The British East India Company conducted most trade with China through the southern port of Canton. The main item of trade was Chinese tea, which had become the British national drink. By the late eighteenth century, British ships transported millions of pounds of tea to Great Britain annually, but since the British had no goods the Chinese merchants or people wanted, almost all British ships returning to China carried silver bullion to pay for the tea.

The British, who first sent an official to Peking in 1793 to address this trade imbalance, refused to "kowtow" (to prostrate and touch one's face to the floor) when meeting the Chinese emperor. The British refused to participate in this "humiliation," and feelings of cultural superiority, both British and Chinese, festered through the following decades.

The East India Company, which established a monopoly over opium cultivation in India in 1773, used opium to reverse the trade imbalance with China. Although the East India Company technically did not ship opium on its own ships, it encouraged the trade because export taxes on opium from India provided more than 10 percent of India's revenue. Opium prices plummeted after 1819, and in 1833, the East India Company lost its monopoly and new trading groups entered the Chinese market. Importation into China of 135-pound chests of opium grew from about 5,000 in 1821 to 35,000 in 1837 (Christenson 1999, p. 1), thus swinging the balance of trade in favor of and the flow of silver to of the British. The Chinese paid about 34 million Mexican silver dollars to purchase opium in the 1830s.

With opium use rampant in China, the emperor tried to

abolish its smoking and trade in 1839. At the same time, he appointed a special commissioner, Lin Ze-xu, to enforce the Chinese laws at Canton. On 25 March 1839, Lin ordered the suspension of trade with all Western merchants and demanded they surrender their opium, which they did shortly thereafter. Lin burned the more than 20,000 chests of contraband opium.

In July 1839, a group of drunken British and American sailors killed a Chinese civilian at Kowloon. The Chinese demanded the British surrender the murderer, but British First Superintendent of Trade Charles Elliot refused to do so. In this power struggle, the Chinese forced all British merchant ships to retreat from Macao to Hong Kong. H.M.S. Volage, a 28-gun frigate, joined the British merchant ships anchored off Hong Kong on 31 August 1839. British merchant ships attempted to land at Kowloon for supplies four days later and were attacked by Chinese junks (warships). The junks were badly damaged, and other British warships sailed to join the Volage in protecting British trade interests.

On 3 November 1839, the Volage and the 18-gun H.M.S. Hyacinth approached the Chinese with a sealed letter demanding supplies and the resumption of trade. The Chinese returned the letter unopened and the British frigates attacked the Chinese ships, sinking five junks. An uneasy peace ensued and the opium trade resumed as the British assembled an expeditionary force.

A British naval force of 15 men-of-war and 5 armed East India Company steamers, under the command of Commodore Sir J. J. Gordon, carrying about 4,000 British and Indian troops, landed at Macao in June 1840. On 5 July 1840, the British bombarded and seized the port of Tinghai on Chusan Island (at the entrance to Hangchow Bay), and to put pressure on the Chinese, the British fleet blockaded Canton, other ports, and the mouth of the Yangtze River.

Negotiations followed, in which the British wanted the Chinese to open additional ports to trade and an indemnity for the opium destroyed by the Chinese. Concerned with increasing British demands, the Chinese broke off negotiations. The British responded by capturing the Chinese forts on either side of the Bogue on 7 January 1841 to open up the Pearl River and the route to Canton to British shipping. This operation, in which 38 British sailors were wounded and about 500 Chinese soldiers were killed, lasted only a few hours.

The Convention of Cheunpi was signed on 20 January 1841, with the Chinese ceding Hong Kong to the British in exchange for Tinghai, the reestablishment of Chinese merchants in Canton, and an indemnity of £6 million for the opium seized and destroyed in 1839. When the Chinese emperor learned of this humiliation, he ordered all his forces to assemble at Canton to repulse the British.

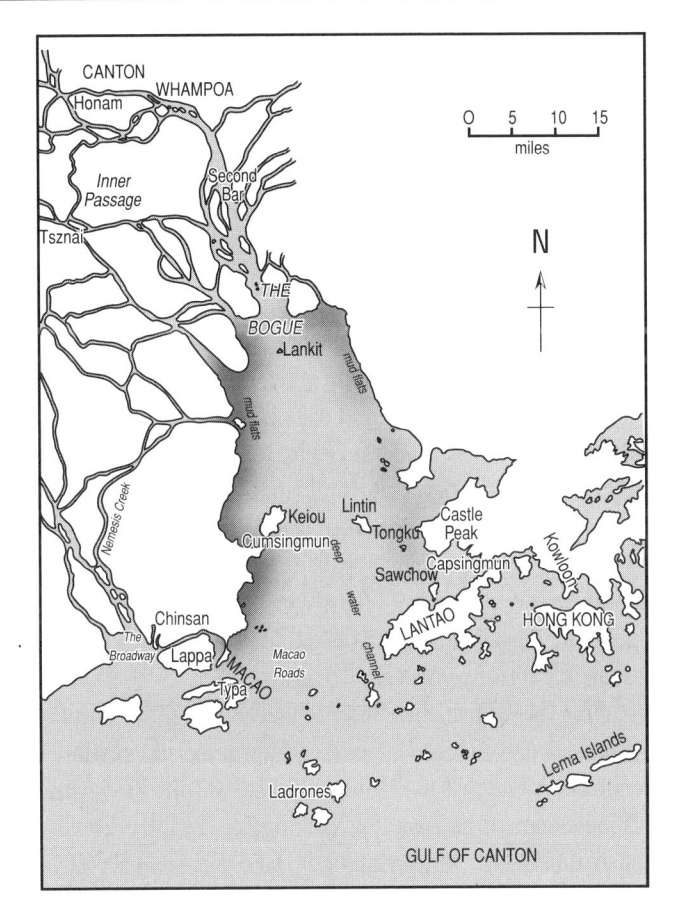

First China War, 1839–1842: Area of Operations

British operations under the command of Major General (later Field Marshal Viscount) Sir Hugh Gough took place sporadically until May 1841, when the British decided to attack Canton. The British plan was to first land the 26th Regiment and elements of the Madras artillery and sappers and miners near the warehouses in Canton's southwest suburbs. The main force, totaling about 2,400 soldiers and sailors, was landed on 24 May 1841 and captured the western forts at Canton. Gough's force was poised to attack the city the following morning when the Chinese requested a truce that Elliot agreed to. After various skirmishes in which the British lost about 15 soldiers killed and 112 wounded, the force returned to Hong Kong a few days later.

The British then decided to alter their strategy to conduct

operations up the coast of China, to the Yangtze River, and to threaten Nanking. Gough's 2,700-man force began operations on 20 August 1841. Amoy, on the Chinese coast opposite Formosa, was bombarded and captured on 26 August. Chinhai was captured on 10 October 1841, and Ningpo three days later, after which the British force, due mainly to administrative and logistical shortcomings, went into winter quarters.

After fruitless negotiations, the Chinese counterattacked on 10 March 1842 but were easily repulsed. The British then recommenced their northward offensive, capturing Chapu (south of Shanghai) on 18 May 1842, and Shanghai on 19 June 1842. The British continued up the Yangtze River, fighting their hardest battle at Chinkiang, in which the British suffered 34 dead, 107 wounded, and 3 missing, on 21 July 1842. The British were appalled by the grisly scene in Chinkiang. When many of the Chinese soldiers realized they would be defeated, they massacred their wives and children before committing suicide.

With the British then threatening Nanking, the Chinese "southern capital," the Chinese sued for peace and hostilities ended on 17 August 1842. On 28 August 1842, the British and Chinese signed the Treaty of Nanking, in which the Chinese opened five ports for foreign trade, paid an indemnity of 21 million Mexican silver dollars, and ceded Hong Kong to the British. The Treaty of Nanking and supplemental treaties were the first of the humiliating "unequal treaties" between China and the West and opened the formerly closed Chinese market to foreign trade. The opium trade, the ostensible cause of the First China War, was not mentioned in the Treaty of Nanking.

See also Boxer Rebellion; China; China War, Second (1856–1860); East India Company; East India Company, Military Forces; Gough, Field Marshal Hugh; Imperialism
References: Chrastina (n.d.); Christenson (1999); Clowes (1903); Farwell (1972); Featherstone (1989); Hibbert (1970); Masefield (1995); Napier (1995); Selby (1968)

China War, Second (1856–1860)

The Second China War (1856–1860) was perhaps the inevitable sequel to the First China War. The Chinese continued to resent Western intrusion in their country and felt the 1842 Treaty of Nanking was unfair and humiliating. Westerner traders, eager for increased profits, felt the Chinese were slow in implementing the terms of the 1842 Treaty. Opium smuggling continued.

The spark that ignited the Second China War was the seizure of the three-masted Chinese-owned but British-registered lorcha *Arrow* by Chinese officials, who also hauled down the ship's British flag on 8 October 1856 at Canton. After the Chinese refused to apologize for this incident, British ships commanded by Rear Admiral Sir Michael Seymour bombarded the four barrier forts guarding the approaches to Canton on 23 October. On 27 October, the Canton city walls were bombarded, and two days later, Seymour led a party of marines into the city.

Tensions increased over the winter months. On 24 February 1857, in Kwangsi Province, Chinese authorities gruesomely murdered a French missionary. The French could not ignore this atrocity and formed a military alliance and began planning an expeditionary force with the British.

The Royal Navy engaged and destroyed Chinese war junks over the summer months, but the Indian Mutiny delayed the arrival of reinforcements in China until December 1857. The bombardment of Canton began on 28 December 1857, and the following day, British troops (800 British and Indian troops, 2,100 Royal Marines, and 1,829 men in the naval brigade drawn from naval crews, commanded by Major General Charles Von Straubenzee) and a 950-man French naval brigade (under Rear Admiral Rigault de Genouilly) scaled the city walls. Three days later, the city was captured, at a cost of 13 British dead and 83 wounded, and 2 French killed and 30 wounded.

The British envoy, the Earl of Elgin, attempted to negotiate with the Chinese emperor in person but was rebuffed. The British fleet then bombarded the Taku Forts at the mouth of the Peiho River (leading to Peking) and forced them into submission on 20 May 1858. This paved the way for the 26 June 1858 Treaty of Tientsin, which opened more ports to foreign trade, allowed freedom of movement for merchants and missionaries within China, permitted the establishment of foreign diplomatic missions in Peking, and legalized the opium trade.

The British, in accordance with the Treaty of Tientsin, sent foreign diplomats to Peking, but they were denied entry. This treaty breach was unacceptable, and the British fleet, under the command of Admiral Sir James Hope, Seymour's successor, again attacked the Taku Forts on 25 June 1859 in a continuation of the war. British and French landing parties were repulsed and evacuated the following morning, with the British fleet, after losing three warships, withdrawing on 28 June. In this debacle, British casualties numbered 81 dead and 345 wounded.

The British and French then decided to send a joint expeditionary force to punish the belligerent Chinese. The British force, of about 11,000 British and Indian troops, was commanded by Lieutenant General (later General) Sir James Hope Grant. It consisted of the 1st Division, commanded by Major General (later Field Marshal) Sir Robert C. Napier; the 2nd Division, under the command of Major General Sir John Michel; a cavalry brigade; and artillery armed with the new Armstrong rifled breech-loading guns. The French troops numbered about 7,000 and were commanded by General Charles Montauban.

The allied force landed on 1 August 1860 near Pehtang, about 8 miles from the Taku Forts, and continued its advance on 12 August. Skirmishes took place near Sinho, and the British captured the fortifications at nearby Tangku on 14 August. Early on 21 August, 20 allied guns and 3 mortars began a fierce barrage, under cover of which about 2,500 British and 1,000 French troops began the assault on the Taku Forts, located on the banks of a tidal river. After scaling strong walls under fire, the allies had to use the bayonet to clear Chinese resistance from the first fort. One British soldier recalled that a French drummer was the first to scale the walls: "With an agility that seemed incredible, and a luck that appeared to be impossible, in view of the fury of the fire, he gained the summit of the parapet, and there, a solitary figure, he stood, firing rifle after rifle that was handed to him. He went on firing until death claimed him, for he was killed by a spear-thrust through the brain" (Knight 1999, pp. 180–181). The British had 17 soldiers killed and 184 wounded capturing the Taku Forts that day.

As the allies advanced up the Peiho River, a British negotiating party was attacked by the Chinese. The allies continued their advance, fighting and defeating Chinese forces at Chang-chia-wan on 18 September 1860 and at Pal-le-chiao three days later. The allies then planned to attack Peking.

The Chinese emperor's Summer Palace, located a few miles outside Peking, was looted by the French in early October 1860. To persuade the Chinese to surrender, the British emplaced their heavy artillery in protected positions ready to bombard the Peking city walls. Before a British ultimatum to the Chinese to surrender Peking expired, the Chinese opened the gates to the city on 13 October. Five days later, the British burned the Summer Palace to the ground in retribution and as a sign of strength. The Chinese, powerless to resist the British and French, ratified the Treaty of Tientsin on 24 October, although under the new name of the Treaty of Peking. The Chinese paid a large indemnity, ceded Kowloon to the British, and opened Tientsin to foreign commerce. A separate treaty with France was concluded two days later. "Thus ended the China War of 1860," wrote Lieutenant Colonel (later Field Marshal Viscount) Garnet J. Wolseley, who had served in the campaign, "the shortest, most brilliant, and most successful of all that we have waged with that country" (Wolseley 1862, p. 323).

See also Boxer Rebellion; China; China War, First (1839–1842); East India Company; East India Company, Military Forces; Gough, Field Marshal Hugh; Imperialism
References: Featherstone (1989); Hibbert (1970); Horowitz (2002); Hurd (1967); Knight (1999); Selby (1967); Selby (1968); Wolseley (1862)

Chinkiang, Battle of (21 July 1842)
See China War, First (1839–1842)

Churchill, Sir Winston L. S. (1874–1965)

Sir Winston L. S. Churchill, best known as the dynamic and pugnacious prime minister of Great Britain during World War II, lived during the final decades of Queen Victoria's long reign. His early life was dominated by the British Army and by journalism, and he was arguably the most famous soldier–war correspondent of the late Victorian era.

Born on 30 November 1874, Churchill was the son of Lord Randolph Churchill (who was the third son of the Seventh Duke of Marlborough) and an American-born mother. After being educated at Harrow and at the Royal Military College, Sandhurst, Churchill was commissioned into the 4th Hussars in 1895. He was highly ambitious, and his "plan was to round out his [military] training with direct experience of warfare and, simultaneously, to report to the world on what he saw" (Weidhorn 1974, p. 15). Churchill also intended to use his newspaper articles and books as a platform from which to launch a political career.

In 1895, taking advantage of family connections, Churchill was able to travel to Cuba, where an insurgency against Spanish rule had been in progress since the previous year. He sent letters back to England for publication in the *Daily Graphic*.

In September 1896, Churchill was posted to his regiment in India. The following year, while on leave, he learned of a punitive expedition being formed for action on the North-

West Frontier. Because all staff positions were filled, Churchill became a war correspondent to accompany the Malakand Field Force. He was resented by the professional soldiers who did not like his self-serving, journalistic motives. Churchill's *The Story of the Malakand Field Force: An Episode of Frontier War* was published in 1898.

The Anglo-Egyptian reconquest of the Sudan had begun in 1896, and Churchill was also eager to participate in the concluding phase of this campaign. He had already made a number of enemies within the British Army, and his "energetic pursuit of adventure had gained him the reputation of a medal-hunter and self-advertiser and his association with the newspapers was also a cause of suspicion" (Dyas 2002, p. 1). The commander of the Anglo-Egyptian force in the Sudan, Major General (later Field Marshal Earl) Sir Horatio H. Kitchener, was opposed to Churchill accompanying the force, but he was overruled by the adjutant-general at the War Office. Churchill was appointed a supernumerary lieutenant in the 21st Lancers and arrived in Cairo in August 1898 with an arrangement to provide news for the *Morning Post*. He was present at the Battle of Omdurman (2 September 1898) and participated in the Charge of the 21st Lancers, in which 21 officers and men were killed and 71 wounded. Churchill wrote the two-volume *The River War* (1899) based on his reports from the Sudan.

In September 1899, with war clouds looming over South Africa, Churchill was asked to be the *Daily Mail* correspondent in South Africa. He landed at Durban on 4 November 1899 and attempted to pay any soldier £200 to take him to besieged Ladysmith. He was later captured by the Boers, perhaps intentionally, and he escaped, thus becoming a national figure. Based on his Second Boer War reports, with which Churchill "reached both the climax and the end of his brief but incandescent career as a correspondent" (Woods 1992, p. xxvi), Churchill wrote *London to Ladysmith via Pretoria* (1900) and *Ian Hamilton's March* (1900).

The notoriety and fame Churchill achieved as a soldier and war correspondent helped him win election to Parliament in 1900. Churchill later served as prime minister (1940–1945; 1951–1955). He was knighted and received the Nobel Prize for Literature in 1953. Churchill, the soldier–war correspondent of the late Victorian era, died on 25 January 1965.

See also Blood, General Sir Bindon; Boer War, Second (1899–1902); Charge of the 21st Lancers; Correspondents, War; Kitchener, Field Marshal Horatio H.; Malakand Field Force; Omdurman, Battle of; Reconquest of the Sudan; Sandhurst, Royal Military College

References: Brighton (1998); Churchill (1898); Churchill (1900); Churchill (1930); Dyas (2002); Gilbert (1991); Jablonsky (1991); Kinsey (1987); Valiunas (2002); Weidhorn (1974); Woods (1992)

Civil-Military Relations

Civil-military relations between the civilian government and the British Army evolved considerably during the period 1815–1914. The trend was for increased civilian and Parliamentary control of the British Army at the expense of the Crown's prerogative and domination of the Army. This was in large measure caused by a greater public awareness of and concern for the soldiers of the British Army, the actions of reform and liberal movements to restrict the power of wealth and the aristocracy, and the desire to consolidate disparate military staff sections and conserve fiscal and other resources.

The Horse Guards, established in 1793, was the institution the Crown used to control the British Army. During the Napoleonic Wars, Parliamentary authority over the British Army declined and the commander in chief and the Horse Guards gained power. After 1815 and until the middle of the nineteenth century, the British Army "was deliberately ignored by the mainstream of the reform movement and purposely left under the control of the Crown because it was considered to be a useless institution" (Blanco 1965, p. 125). This was a period of relative stagnation, until the fetters of orthodoxy were broken by the death of Field Marshal Arthur Wellesley, First Duke of Wellington in 1852, and the need for military and organization reform was recognized and acted on.

The position of secretary of state for war was separated from that of the colonies in June 1854, the first time Great Britain had a full-time secretary of state devoted to military affairs. The post of secretary at war, responsible for the Army Estimates and other financial matters, was abolished, and its responsibilities, as well as those of about thirteen other departments, were consolidated under the secretary of state for war. Other Crimean War–era reforms helped consolidate the authority and responsibility of the secretary of state for war; for the first time, Parliamentary and civilian control of the army was achieved. The concept of dual control of the British Army had been effectively eliminated.

To reduce duplication of work, the War Office Act of 1870

merged the War Office and the Horse Guards, which was required to physically relocate to the War Office. Moreover, this act delegated War Office responsibilities to three distinct executive officers: the officer commanding in chief, the surveyor-general of the ordnance, and the financial secretary.

Industrialization, political reform, and economic displacement caused considerable unrest, and the British Army was frequently called on to assist the civil authorities in maintaining law and order. The 1840s was, for example, a tumultuous decade, with tension between England and Ireland and the potato famine in the latter. Troops were called out in the wake of bread riots and were employed in five different areas in 1847. In the following year, British troops fired on rioting mobs in Glasgow and elsewhere. In the 1880s, British Army units were sent to Ireland to assist the civil power, and frequently provided "large escorts for sheriffs, process-servers and bailiffs" (Hawkins 1973, p. 78). The British soldiers, who were better disciplined and more heavily armed than the local police, were able to "overawe" the local populace.

Another aspect of civil-military relations was the participation in both the House of Lords and the House of Commons of military officers. Army officers formed an especially conspicuous and influential group in the House of Lords, where in "1870, 1885 and 1898, there were 111, 132 and 182 officers in the Lords, comprising about 23, 27 and 35 per cent respectively of the total membership" (Spiers 1992, p. 162). In the Commons, military officers, in both political parties, totaled 102 Members of Parliament in 1870. This was about 16 percent of the total membership of the House of Commons.

After the retirement of Field Marshal H.R.H. Prince George F., Second Duke of Cambridge, from the position of commander in chief in 1895, additional measures were taken to strengthen civilian control over the military. Attempts were made to eliminate the position of commander in chief and replace it by a War Office Council.

When Field Marshal Viscount Garnet J. Wolseley succeeded the Duke of Cambridge as commander in chief in 1895, the responsibilities of the position were greatly reduced. The duties were also revised, and the commander in chief became in effect a chief of staff. Wolseley, however, while considering himself a servant of the Crown, never contested civilian control of the army. The position was further weakened and eventually eliminated in 1904.

At the end of the nineteenth and beginning of the twentieth centuries, the army, which had survived the change from dual and then to integrated control, "itself persistently brought the monarchy back into the frame, using it as a device to fend off governmental intervention" (Strachan 1997, p. 69). This was especially true during the 1914 Curragh Incident, when it appeared British Army officers would defy the civil authority. This situation also demonstrated the politicization of the army officer corps and strained civil-military relations.

Civil-military relations, tense at times and generally in a state of reorganization and evolution, permitted the development of a system that integrated civilian Parliamentary power with professional military knowledge "in such a way that the best interests of the state would be protected" (Hamer 1970, p. xi).

See also Army Estimates; Cambridge, Field Marshal H.R.H. Prince George F., Second Duke of; Cardwell Reforms; Commander in Chief, British Army; Curragh Incident; Horse Guards; War Office; Wellington, Field Marshal Arthur Wellesley, First Duke of; Wolseley, Field Marshal Garnet J.
References: Blanco (1965); Dietz (1990); Hamer (1970); Hawkins (1973); Spiers (1992); Strachan (1984); Strachan (1997)

Coastal Fortifications

Throughout the period 1815–1914 there were concerns that Great Britain would be invaded by enemy troops transported by naval forces. While ships of the Royal Navy could be used to help defend the British Isles, they were considered "much more susceptible to damage, were unsteady gun platforms, and they were vulnerable to hot shot" (Patridge 1989, p. 90). As a result, fixed fortifications were built on the coast and elsewhere to help defend Great Britain.

During the years 1792 to 1814, the invasion threat from Napoleonic France was always present. In addition to increasing the number of soldiers available for home defense, small forts and earthwork batteries were built on the coasts. Some seventy-three round Martello Towers with 24-pounder cannons had been built in Essex, Kent, and Sussex. French revolutionary actions in 1830 caused the Martello Towers to be repaired and rearmed with 32-pounder guns.

Coastal fortifications were also seen as a way to supplement military manpower shortages in Great Britain. In addition, by 1860, coastal fortifications received secondary importance to building fortifications to protect naval harbors of refuge and arsenals, notably on the Channel Islands and at Portsmouth, Plymouth, Pembroke, and Medway. All of the important coastal and harbor fortifications planned and constructed in the 1860s and 1870s were fully armed and manned by 1888 and served as a deterrent to possible invasion.

See also Home Defense; Mobilization Planning
References: Hibbs (2002); Partridge (1989); Spiers (1992); Strachan (1984)

Colenso, Battle of (15 December 1899)

After the Battles of Stormberg (10 December) and Magersfontein (11 December), the Battle of Colenso (15 December 1899) was the third of three demoralizing defeats suffered by the British during "Black Week" of the Second Boer War (1899–1902). It took place during operations to relieve Ladysmith.

The Boers began to besiege Ladysmith on 2 November 1899. General Sir Redvers H. Buller, V.C., commander in chief of the South African Field Force, assembled a 21,000-man force—the largest force commanded by a British general since the Crimean War—by 10 December 1899 at Frere for the purpose of relieving Ladysmith. The force consisted of four infantry brigades, a mounted infantry brigade, five field batteries and two naval guns, and a naval contingent. To get to Ladysmith, Buller's force would have to advance 10 miles across open country to the fast-flowing Tugela River, a major obstacle. High ground with a number of easily defensible peaks stretched from the bank of the Tugela northward for 5 miles. Ladysmith was 12 miles north of the Tugela. The town of Colenso was on the south bank of a loop in the Tugela, where a railroad bridge crossed the river. A wagon bridge crossed the Tugela less than a mile west of the railroad bridge.

Buller had originally planned to try to outflank Colenso by crossing the Tugela further upstream, but when he learned on 12 December 1899 of the British defeat at Magersfontein, he decided on immediate action and a frontal assault across the Tugela River. The British artillery bombarded the hills north of the Tugela for two days and revealed British intentions.

The 4,500-man Boer force, consisting of nine commandos (with one in reserve) with artillery under Commandant-General Louis Botha, was entrenched along a 7-mile front north of the Tugela, in a manner similar to their defenses at the Battles of Modder River (28 November 1899) and Magersfontein (11 December 1899). It concentrated on the Colenso bridges and other fording sites. Once the British attacked and tried to cross the Tugela, the Boers planned to enfilade the attacker by fire from a tenth commando, located on the Hlangwane Hill, south of the Tugela, on the British right flank. Moreover, the Boers would counterattack on their right flank.

Buller's plan was to attack with two brigades abreast in daylight and force a passage of the Tugela by sheer weight of numbers and seize the high ground north of Colenso. At 4:00 A.M. on 15 December 1899, the British force left its camp 3 miles south of the Tugela and marched northward. Major General H. J. T. Hildyard's 2nd Brigade was on the right, and was to conduct the main attack by crossing the Tugela at Old Wagon Drift, near the rail bridge. Major General Fitzroy Hart's 5th (Irish) Brigade was to the left, with orders to cross the Tugela at Bridle Drift, about 1 mile west of a second river loop. Colonel (later General) the Earl of Dundonald's mounted brigade guarded the right flank and was to seize Hlangwane Hill if possible. Major General G. Barton's 6th (Fusiliers) Brigade was in reserve to the right, and Major General (later General Sir) Neville G. Lyttelton's 4th (Light) Brigade was in reserve to the left. The artillery, under Colonel C. J. Long, who had commanded the artillery at the Battle of Omdurman (2 September 1898), was to support the infantry assault.

Hart's brigade got lost and marched into a salient in the Tugela and, when 200 yards from the river, the Boers opened fire. The roar of the Mausers sounded like "the sound of rain beating on a tin roof" (Pakenham 1979, p. 228). The Irish Brigade tried to deploy from close order, but Hart urged his men forward, and by 7:15 A.M., his disorganized brigade was receiving enemy fire from three directions and had suffered over 400 casualties. Buller ordered Hart to withdraw his brigade.

The aggressive Long, eager to support Hildyard's 2nd Brigade attack and to compensate for any inferior range of his artillery, galloped his 12 field and 6 naval guns forward, far ahead of his infantry escort and of even the 2nd Brigade. He deployed his guns and began firing at the Boers about 990 yards across the Tugela. Boer riflemen and artillery soon engaged the British in a tremendous firefight. After Long's artillery ran out of ammunition and about one-third of the artillerymen having become casualties, the remaining soldiers abandoned their guns.

When Buller was informed of this situation at about 8:00 A.M, and after only one of his brigades had attacked, he called off the entire operation. He then attempted to rescue Long and his guns, personally directing units and serving as an example of courageous leadership. He called for volunteers to save the guns, and a number of corporals and soldiers responded, followed by three officers of his staff. One of the three officers was Lieutenant Frederick Roberts, son of Field Marshal Lord (later Earl) Frederick S. Roberts, V.C. Numerous attempts were made to save the guns, and two guns were recovered.

Realizing the weariness of his troops in the hot sun, fighting against an unseen foe, coupled with the repulse of Dundonald's brigade, Buller realized the best course of action was to withdraw the entire force. By 3:00 P.M., most troops had retreated out of danger, and the transport of wounded to the rear began.

That evening, the tired and wounded Buller reported his "serious reverse" at Colenso and suggested that the besieged garrison of Ladysmith surrender if it could not hold out for another month. These actions led to Buller's supersession by Roberts, whose son died of his wounds received trying to rescue Long's guns and who would receive the Victoria Cross posthumously. Five others also received the Victoria Cross.

The failure at Colenso cost the British 1,138 casualties: 143 killed, 755 wounded, and 240 missing, most of whom were captured. This operation, a disaster due largely to Long's improper forward deployment and abandonment of his guns, followed a great British Army tradition: "courage matched only by stupidity" (Pakenham 1979, p. 240).

See also Boer War, Second (1899–1902); Boers; Botha, Commandant General Louis; Buller, General Sir Redvers H., V.C.; Commando System; Ladysmith, Siege of; Magersfontein, Battle of; Modder River, Battle of; Omdurman, Battle of; Roberts, Field Marshal Frederick S., V.C.; Stormberg, Battle of; Victoria Cross

References: Barnard (1970); Barthorp (1987); Lyttelton (1924); Pakenham (1979); Powell (1994); Raugh (1986); Symons (1963); Thornton and Fraser (1930); Trew (1999)

Commander in Chief, British Army

In 1793, at the time of the Terror of the French Revolution, it was decided to appoint a soldier as commander in chief to administer the British Army. The first British Army commander in chief was General (later Field Marshal) Lord Jeffrey Amherst. He was given authority over promotions, discipline, and supply. Two years later Amherst was replaced by Field Marshal H.R.H. Frederick, Duke of York, who established and organized a military staff.

The secretary of state for war was separated from the secretary of state for the colonies in June 1854, and all purely military departments came under his authority. Most of the other Crimean War–era reforms helped consolidate the authority and responsibility of the secretary of state for war. In May 1855, the power of the master-general of the ordnance was reduced considerably, with the position losing its autonomy and the incumbent being made subordinate to the commander in chief. Concurrently, the commander in chief assumed command of the Royal Artillery and Royal Engineers, which had formerly been subordinate to the master-general of the ordnance. Parliamentary and civilian control of the military was unquestionably achieved for the first time. The commander in chief then had only military responsibilities for the internal discipline, promotion, and training of the British Army. Even though the commander in chief was supposed to be responsible to the secretary of state for war, he remained outside the consolidated War Department, or War Office.

General (later Field Marshal) H.R.H. Prince George F., Second Duke of Cambridge (cousin of Queen Victoria), became commander in chief in July 1856. He inherited a weakened position that had only military responsibilities for the internal discipline, promotion, and training of the British Army. He was very dogmatic and generally resisted change to and reform of the British Army.

The War Office Act of 1870 consolidated the War Office and the Horse Guards. It also delegated its responsibilities to three distinct executive officers: the "officer commanding in chief" (Duke of Cambridge), responsible for the strictly military aspects of the army; the surveyor-general of the ordnance; and the financial secretary. The War Office Act of 1870 also required the commander in chief to physically move from the Horse Guards to the War Office, an unmistakable indicator of his new subordinate role as principal military adviser to the secretary of state. (The Duke of Cambridge, however, after moving to the War Office was permitted to address his letters from the "Horse Guards, Pall Mall.")

After Secretary of State for War Edward Stanhope enacted additional reforms in 1888, the commander in chief became responsible for all personnel and materiel issues for the army and auxiliary forces, in addition to the collection of intelligence and the construction and maintenance of fortifications.

The Hartington Commission report of 1889–1890 recommended eliminating the office of commander in chief after the Duke of Cambridge retired and replacing it with a War Office Council. A truncated War Office Council, without a chief of the staff, was in fact established, and in 1895 it was supplemented by an Army Board.

When the Duke of Cambridge retired in 1895 and was replaced by Field Marshal Viscount Garnet J. Wolseley, changes were made in the duties of the commander in chief, adding the responsibilities of a chief of staff.

The initial poor performance of the British Army in the field in South Africa after the Second Boer War broke out in October 1899 resulted in an inquiry into the whole organization and operations of the War Office. Additional reforms were enacted in November 1901.

The Elgin Commission investigated administrative shortcomings that had been revealed by the Second Boer War. It scrutinized the areas of planning, the reserve and manpower system, stores and supplies, and War Office organization. Lord Esher, a member of the Elgin Commission, wanted more substantive reform. He was able to get himself appointed to chair a new committee, the War Office Reconstitution Committee. The report of the Esher Committee, made in 1904, had a far-reaching impact on War Office and military reorganization. Significantly, the position of commander in chief was abolished and replaced by the chief of the general staff.

See also Adjutant-General, British Army; Cambridge, Field Marshal H.R.H. Prince George F., Second Duke of; Esher Committee; Horse Guards; Master-General of the Ordnance, British Army; Quartermaster-General, British Army; Roberts, Field Marshal Frederick S., V.C.; Stanhope, Edward; War Office; Wolseley, Field Marshal Garnet J.

References: Barnett (1970); Hamer (1970); Moyse-Bartlett (1974); Spiers (1992); St. Aubyn (1963)

Commando System

The commando system, instituted in 1715, was the "nonactive militia" method used by the Boers in South Africa to mobilize, organize, and man a military force.

The Boer lifestyle as farmers and hunters made the individual Boer a superb mounted infantryman generally armed with a German Mauser, a modern magazine rifle. The Boers, while frequently ill disciplined, were generally self-reliant, expert marksmen and horse riders with the ability to understand and use terrain to their advantage.

In both the Transvaal and the Orange Free State, every burgher (a male citizen) between the ages of 16 and 60, with very few exceptions based on occupation, was liable for unpaid military service. Age-groups were prioritized for service. Men between the ages of 18 and 34 were mobilized first, followed by those aged 35 to 50, and finally men 51 to 60 years old. The Boer citizen soldier, who fought in mufti, was expected to report for duty with 10 days' rations; a horse, saddle, and bridle; and a rifle with 30 rounds of ammunition. Many Boers regarded this service as voluntary rather than an imposed obligation, and there was said to be widespread service evasion.

The commando was the basic Boer military unit used to conduct operations. It was based on the numbers of Boers in the twenty-two electoral districts in the Transvaal and eighteen in the Orange Free State. Each electoral district was divided into wards, with five wards in the largest district and two in the smallest. Commandos varied in size, from 60 (from Springs) to about 4,000 (from Potchefstroom), based on the population of the respective district.

In keeping with the Boer spirit of individualism and independence, members of the commando elected their own commander and other officers. A commando was divided into field cornetcies of about 150–200 men each (corresponding to a ward), with an elected field cornet in charge. The field cornet, elected for three years in each ward, was probably the most important commando official. He was responsible for maintaining a register of service-eligible Boers and for ensuring they were always properly equipped. Upon mobilization, the field cornet was responsible for assembling the men of his ward, issuing ammunition and any other required equipment, and leading them to the commando assembly area, generally the district capital from which the commando took its name. Field cornetcies were subdivided into corporalships of about 25 men each.

During the Second Boer War (1899–1902), an estimated 41,650 Boers served in Transvaal commandos and 27,609 Boers served in commandos from the Orange Free State.

See also Boer War, First (1880–1881); Boer War, Second (1899–1902); Boers; Transvaal

References: Barthorp (1987); Belfield (1975); Featherstone (1989); Marix Evans (2000); Pakenham (1979); Reid (1996)

Communications

Communications between commanders and units, especially on active service and during maneuvers and exercises, was essential for effective command and control during operations. Signal and communications equipment became more sophisticated and dependable throughout this period, beginning with messengers, means in which both sender and receiver were required to be in visual contact with each other, to wireless telegraphy.

The traditional method of communications was by messenger. This method was not, however, infallible, due to strengths and weaknesses of individual messengers, distances and terrain required to traverse, and the possibility of being killed or captured by the enemy.

There were numerous applications of visual signaling in the British Army during active service or maneuvers. It would be essential for a higher headquarters to send orders, guidance, and intelligence information to subordinate or detached units. Similarly, subordinate units would be required to provide message acknowledgments, situation reports, and other information to their higher headquarters. Coordination would also be required between adjacent units, whether moving or in distant stationary positions.

"Flag waving," using a single flag, was an elementary means of visual communications. A 3-foot-square flag on a 5.5 foot pole was used for communicating over a distance of 5 to 7 miles, and a smaller flag, 2-foot-square on a 3.5 foot pole, was used for distances of 3 to 4 miles. The flagman would keep the flag moving rapidly when sending messages in International Morse Code to keep it unfurled and more visible to the receiver. The starting and resting position was 25 degrees from the vertical plane over the head of the flagman, who could work from either right to left or vice versa. A dot was made by swinging the flag from the resting position to 25 degrees from the vertical in the opposite direction and returning to the rest position without a pause. A dash was made by a longer flag swing, from the resting position to 115 degrees from the vertical plane in the opposite direction and returning, with a pause in the down position, to the resting position.

Two-flag semaphore signaling, adopted from the Royal Navy, could also be used easily, but its effectiveness was subject to distance, limited visibility and nighttime, and a fairly slow (five or six words per minute) transmission rate.

The heliograph, an instrument that uses the sun's rays for signaling, was first used by the British Army in India in the 1870s, on active service during the 1879 Zulu War, and extensively on the North-West Frontier. The heliograph could be used with either one or two mirrors. When the sun was in front of the heliograph, a single mirror, linked to a telegraph key, was used to reflect the sun's rays to the receiver. When the sun was behind the heliograph, a second mirror was used to reflect the sun's rays to the first mirror, then to the receiving station. Dependent on the sun (or moonlight, although with greatly reduced effectiveness), the heliograph could transmit messages 30 or more miles at a rate of 5–12 words per minute. During the Second Boer War, with ideal climatic and topographical conditions, a 5-inch mirror on a heliograph could be used to transmit messages 50 miles, and a 10-inch mirror to 100 miles.

Limelight lamps and Begbie lamps were also signaling instruments. Both lamps used shutters to flash dots and dashes in the International Morse Code to the receiving station. Messages could be read at a distance with the Mark III signaling telescope.

The electric telegraph and the code to use on it were invented in the 1830s by S. F. B. Morse. This system revolutionized communications, especially in the military, and was first used in the Crimean War (1854–1856). The telegraph line from allied capitals to the Crimea was completed in April 1855.

After the Abyssinian War (1867–1868), a Signal Wing was formed by the Royal Engineers at Chatham. In 1884, the Telegraph Battalion of the Royal Engineers was formed and participated in the Gordon Relief Expedition.

Signaling remained the responsibility of the Telegraph Battalion during the Second Boer War, during which 18,236 miles of wire were laid and 9,395 miles of existing wire repaired. Some 13,575,779 telegraphic messages were sent during the war.

Wireless telegraphy was first introduced in the field during the Second Boer War. The British Army experimented with Marconi equipment in South Africa, although ground conductivity and antenna-resonance problems did not permit successful results. The Royal Navy, however, was more successful in its experiments.

See also Boer War, Second (1899–1902); Crimean War; Engineers, British Army—Organization; North-West Frontier; Zulu War

References: Barker (1999); Boon (1985); Knight (1996); McEwen (2002); Morris (1965); Myatt (1983); Riall (2000); Royle (2000); Spiers (1992)

Concentration Camps

The British took increasingly harsh measures in 1900 to try to defeat the Boers in South Africa during the Second Boer War. In June, the British warned the Boers that farms near sabotaged railroad lines or from which British troops were fired on would be burned. A few months later it was announced that farms hiding and protecting combatant Boers would also be razed. Shortly thereafter, selected farms were designated for destruction and the policy of "land clearance" was implemented near the end of the year. These actions were intended to punish the Boers, individually and collectively, and to deprive the fighting Boers of food and shelter. Within weeks, numerous Boer families were homeless and many other refugees sought British protection from possible Boer reprisals. The British solution was to concentrate the displaced Boers in relative comfort and safety in protected "laagers" near the railways.

The British establishment of concentration camps for the Boer refugees was well intentioned, although there was an initial lack of command interest in the issue. Moreover, the British did not anticipate the large numbers of homeless Boers nor did they allocate adequate resources for the camps.

Conditions in the camps varied considerably. A superintendent, assisted by a storekeeper, clerks, a medical officer, a dispenser, a matron, and nurses, ran each camp. At first, the refugees were housed in prefabricated wooden huts, but the supply was soon exhausted. Large tents, and later bell tents, were used to house the internees. Extra medical care was frequently provided by camp inmates, who were paid for their assistance. Food was rationed, based on guidelines issued by medical authorities for the maintenance of health, and generally consisted of a pound of meal and about a half pound of meat per day, plus coffee and sugar. Additional food, clothing, and supplies were sold in camp shops at regulated prices. Attempts were made to find employment for as many of the refugees as possible, with many families being paid up to £20 a month for their work. Boers who had surrendered voluntarily were generally allowed to keep their livestock. Schools were set up in the camps for children.

Administrative difficulties soon arose and conditions in some of the camps became very bad. Health issues were a primary concern. While the living conditions and food in the camps were supervised carefully, medical authorities were still unaware of a number of items, including the possible vitamin deficiency of the diet due to a lack of fresh vegetables. Moreover, the Boers had normally lived on isolated farms or in widely separated villages and were unfamiliar with hygiene requirements of community living. The crowded conditions of the camps facilitated the exposure to and spread of contagious diseases to such a degree that simple illnesses became fatal. In addition, the winter of 1901–1902 was extremely severe, which exacerbated the situation.

Critical accounts of the conditions in the camps began to reach England early in 1901. Emily Hobhouse, a British social worker who had established the South African Women and Children Distress Fund, arrived in South Africa on 27 December 1900 to deliver supplies to the camps. She was shocked by the living conditions she saw, and on her return to London she produced a report that exposed the worst aspects of the refugee camps. Newspapers and public officials demanded inquiries and this helped lead to improvements.

Separate concentration camps were established for white and for black refugees. There were reportedly 27,927 deaths in the white camps during the war, of which 26,251 were women and children. Of the 115,700 people who were interned in black camps (which numbered at least 66, with perhaps as many as 80), there were 14,154 deaths recorded, of which about 8 percent were children.

The concentration camps of the Second Boer War must not be confused or equated with the German camps of World War II, although the former tainted the reputation of the British. For the most part, given the level of knowledge at the time and availability of resources, many British camp administrators had performed their duty the best they could. Many South Africans considered the operations of the camps a "crime"—although Boer Commandant-General Louis Botha had admitted during the war that "one is only too thankful nowadays to know that our wives are under English protection" (Pakenham 1979, p. 603)—and this has left an indelible impression on their memory.

See also Boer War, Second (1899–1902); Botha, Commandant-General Louis; Hobhouse, Emily; Kitchener, Field Marshal Horatio H.; Roberts, Field Marshal Frederick S., V.C.
References: Barthorp (1987); Lee (1985); Marix Evans (2000); Pakenham (1979)

Congreve, William
See Rockets

Contagious Diseases Acts of 1864, 1866, and 1869
See Military Medicine, British Army—Venereal Disease

Correspondents, War

War correspondents are relatively new to history. The Crimean War (1854–1856) was the first conflict in which an organized effort was made to have civilian correspondents report news directly to the civilian population of the home country. Many senior British Army officers were very distressed by this development, as they no longer held a monopoly on presenting their own version of news and events through their correspondence with the government and their campaign dispatches. Some generals also felt they were being robbed of martial glory by the war correspondents.

The war correspondent was generally looked upon with resentment, suspicion, and even disgust by senior British Army officers during the Victorian era. Field Marshal Earl Frederick S. Roberts, V.C., held a more positive view of war correspondents and was very conscientious in providing them accurate and timely information. "I consider it due to the people of Great Britain," declared Roberts, "that the press correspondents should have every opportunity for giving the fullest and most faithful accounts of what might happen while the army was in the field" (Farwell 1973, p. 205). Field Marshal Viscount Garnet J. Wolseley, at the other end of the spectrum, abhorred war correspondents, "those newly invented curses to armies, who eat the rations of fighting men and do no work at all" (Farwell 1973, p. 194). Wolseley's attitude toward war correspondents was more prevalent than Roberts's opinion in the British Army during the second half of the nineteenth century.

The electric telegraph was invented in the 1830s, and during the Crimean War, the electric telegraph cable was extended to the allied positions near Sevastopol. This permitted war correspondents to send instant reports bypassing military authorities directly to their newspapers. Coming from the battlefield, these reports were considered to be factual and honest. The newspapers were carried overnight by railroads to the breakfast tables of the increasingly literate middle class, who for the first time in history knew and cared about what their soldiers were doing and going through. Newspaper readership was further stimulated by the abolition of the newspaper tax duty in 1855. While the readership of the *Times* (London) was about 5,000 per day during the Napoleonic Wars, the circulation surged to over 40,000 per day during the Crimean War.

Civilian war correspondents participated in many of the colonial campaigns of the Victoria era, and in addition to reporting for their newspapers, many wrote books after their martial experiences. The most celebrated, although not the first or the only war correspondent in the Crimea, was William Howard Russell (1821–1907) of the *Times*. He accompanied the Guards Brigade to the Crimea in February 1854 and later wrote about the suffering of British soldiers during the harsh winter of 1854–1855, the poor military leadership, and the unsanitary, overcrowded hospital conditions, the latter reportedly inspiring Florence Nightingale to travel to the Crimea and improve medical conditions. The actual credit for initially arousing British public opinion about the conditions in the Crimea belongs to Thomas Chenery, the Constantinople correspondent of the *Times*, who wrote about the horrible conditions at Scutari in early October 1854. Russell was the major figure of early war reporting and later covered the Indian Mutiny, the American Civil War, the Austro-Prussian and Franco-Prussian Wars, and the 1879 Zulu War. Russell later failed to understand the urgency of war reporting and the need to "scoop" other papers in the competitive newspaper business.

Another leading war journalist was Archibald Forbes (1838–1900), a former private soldier who covered military campaigns during the last three decades of the nineteenth century. His rise as a journalist began with the Franco-Prussian War (1870–1871), which he covered for the *Morning Advertiser* from the German side, by which time Russell's effectiveness had begun to decline. (The Franco-Prussian War also saw the institution of the "pool" arrangement, in which newspapers would share reports of their respective correspondents.) Later as a *Daily News* special correspondent, Forbes reported from Serbia in 1876; the Russo-Turkish War, during the 1878 British occupation of Cyprus and in Afghanistan; and most notably in the 1879 Zulu War.

War correspondents during the 1873–1874 Ashanti expedition included a troika of interesting, successful reporters. Henry M. Stanley (1841–1904), a naturalized American who had recently "found" Dr. Livingstone (and fame) at Lake Tanganyika (allegedly uttering, "Dr. Livingstone, I presume?"), reported for the *New York Herald*, W. Winwood Reade represented the *Times*, and G. A. Henty (1832–1902) wrote for the *Standard*. The correspondents were all well armed in this jungle campaign, some with double-barreled shotguns. Stanley, who had fought in the American Civil War, shot Ashanti in battle as "cool and self-possessed as if he had been at target practice" (Lehmann 1964, p. 192). Stanley had earlier reported during the 1867–1868 Abyssinian War, and after his return from Ashantiland he wrote *Coomassie and Magdala: The Story of Two British Campaigns in Africa* (1874), before embarking on further African explorations. Reade wrote *The Story of the Ashantee Campaign* (1874), a compilation of his dispatches, and Henty authored *The March to Coomassie* (1874). Henty, later dubbed the "prince of storytellers" and "the boy's own historian," eventually wrote about 144 books and many stories. Wolseley understood the role of correspondents in providing information to a home audience but also realized he could give them false information, as he did during the Second Ashanti War and later during the 1882 expedition to Egypt, to deceive the enemy.

Two notable, adventurous war correspondents who covered the later colonial wars were Bennet Burleigh (c. 1840–1914), *Daily Telegraph,* and G. W. Steevens (1869–1900), *Daily Mail.* Burleigh covered the 1882 British expedition to Egypt, Gordon Relief Expedition (1884–1885), operations in the Sudan in 1898, and the Second Boer War (1899–1902). He also reported on early twentieth-century campaigns, including the Russo-Japanese War and the First Balkan War. Steevens wrote from Egypt in 1898 but died of typhoid in December 1899 during the siege of Ladysmith.

Army officers on campaign occasionally combined their military duties with service as a war correspondent. Lieutenant (later Major General Sir) (John) Frederick Maurice served as Wolseley's private secretary on the 1873–1874 Ashanti expedition, at the same time representing the *Daily News* as special correspondent. Maurice later wrote *The Ashantee War: A Popular Narrative* (1874). Perhaps the most famous soldier–war correspondent of this era was Winston L. S. Churchill. Churchill's "thirst for battle was born not just of a youthful yearning for adventure and a quest for medals but, above all from a determination to carve out a name and reputation for himself" (Woods 1992, p. ix). He also intended to use his newspaper articles and books as a platform from which to launch a political career. Churchill reported for the *Daily Graphic* in Cuba (1895–1896); on the North-West Frontier with the Malakand Field Force for the *Daily Telegraph* (1897); and for the *Morning Post* in the Sudan in 1898 and during the Second Boer War (1899–1900). Newspapers thought it was advantageous to have a serving officer, knowledgeable of military matters and with superb access to plans and leaders, be a war correspondent. Traditionalists correctly believed it was inappropriate for serving officers to act as war correspondents.

See also Abyssinian War; Artists, War; Ashanti War, Second (1873–1874); Boer War, Second (1899–1902); Churchill, Sir Winston L. S.; Communications; Crimean War; Gordon Relief Expedition; Indian Mutiny; Maurice, Major General Sir (John) Frederick; Nightingale, Florence; North-West Frontier; Photographers, War; Reconquest of the Sudan; Roberts, Field Marshal Frederick S., V.C.; Wolseley, Field Marshal Garnet J.; Zulu War

References: Barthorp (1995); Farwell (1973); Grey (1971); Haythornthwaite (1995); Knightley (1975); Laband and Knight (1996); Lehmann (1964); Luvaas (1964); Raugh (2001b); Russell (1966); Stearn (1990); Stearn (1991); Teulie (1995); Weidhorn (1974); Woods (1992)

Corrie Bird, Major General G.
See Tochi Field Force

Cotton, Major General Sir Willoughby
See Afghan War, First (1839–1842)

Crimean War (1854–1856)

The Crimean War (1854–1856) pitted Great Britain, France, the Ottoman Empire (Turkey), and later Sardinia against Russia. It was the only large-scale conflict Great Britain fought against a European adversary between 1815 and 1914. The British Army had advanced little since 1815 and fought the Crimean War with basically the same weapons, tactics, equipment, and doctrine—and in some cases even the same leaders—as it had fought at Waterloo. The failure of the British logistics and support systems, coupled with outdated and generally poor senior leadership, shocked the British out of their complacency and helped pave the way for long-overdue reforms in the British Army.

A religious squabble between Russian Orthodox monks and Roman Catholics over precedence and jurisdiction in the holy places of Turkish-ruled Jerusalem was the ostensible cause of the Crimean War. Russian Czar Nicholas I demanded the right to protect Christian holy places, while realizing this was an excellent opportunity to expand into

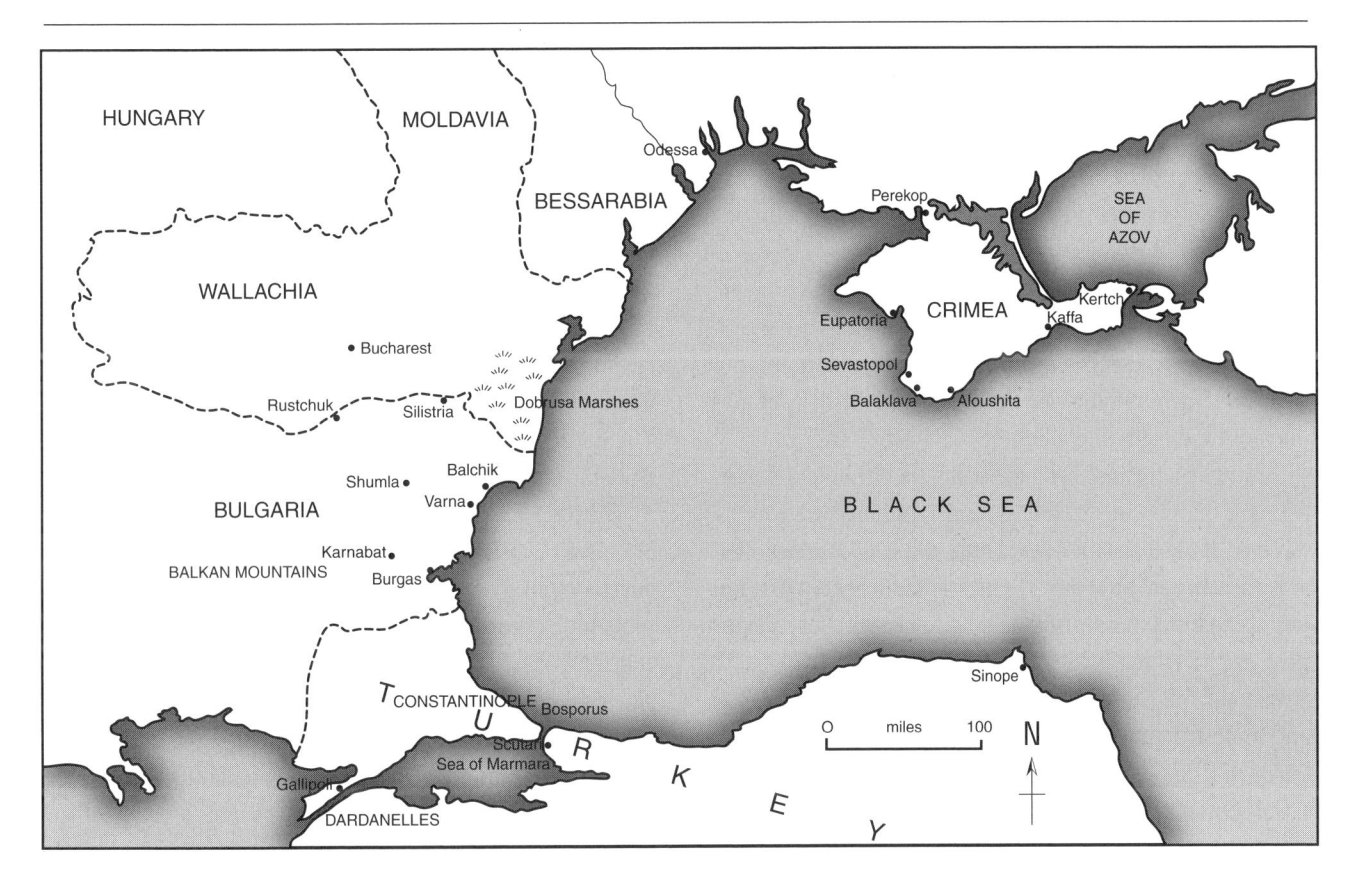

Crimean War, 1854–1856: Turkey and the Crimea

the territories of the weakening Ottoman Empire, the "sick man of Europe." To bolster his claims, Nicholas deployed troops to the Turkish provinces of Wallachia and Moldavia (in present-day Romania) in July 1853.

France, also concerned about the Holy Land in terms of national prestige, was reluctant to permit Russian expansion. Great Britain, desiring to maintain the balance of power in Europe, allied itself with France and Turkey.

Turkey declared war on Russia in October 1853 and sent its troops, under the command of Omar Pasha, to confront the Russians. On 4 November 1853, the Turks defeated the Russians at the Battle of Oltenitza in southern Romania.

Russian ships attacked the Turkish fleet in the harbor at Sinope on 30 November 1853. The technologically superior Russian ships destroyed the Turkish flotilla in a six-hour battle. Russia, for the first time, had used exploding shells in combat, and this seemed to threaten British naval supremacy. British newspapers sensationally reported the "massacre" at Sinope and inflamed public opinion against the Russians. An Anglo-French fleet was sent to the Black Sea.

After the Russians crossed the Danube River and invaded Bulgaria on 20 March 1854, the British and French both declared war on Russia on 28 March. They also formed a military alliance on 10 April 1854 and sent diplomatic notes to the czar demanding the Russian evacuation of Wallachia and Moldavia by 30 April. The Russians began to besiege Silistria on 14 April as they planned to advance to the Bosporus. The opening shots of the war were fired on 22 April, when British and French war ships bombarded the Russian port of Odessa.

British troops first began to deploy from England on 22 February 1854 and units continued to sail through the end of April 1854. By the end of May 1854, about 18,000 British and 22,000 French troops had assembled at Gallipoli. The hastily assembled British expeditionary force was commanded by General (later Field Marshal) Fitzroy J. H. Somerset, First Baron Raglan, a protégé of Field Marshal Arthur Wellesley, First Duke of Wellington. The force consisted of 5 infantry divisions (each generally containing 2 brigades of 3 regiments each), 1 cavalry division, 26 field guns, and limited supporting units, totaling about 26,000 soldiers. The British generally superannuated division commanders were as follows: 1st Division—Lieutenant General (later Field Marshal) H.R.H. Prince George F., Second Duke of Cambridge; 2nd Division—Lieutenant General (later General) Sir George de Lacy Evans; 3rd Division—Lieutenant General Sir Robert England; 4th Division—Lieutenant General Sir George Cathcart; Light Division—Lieutenant General (later General) Sir George Brown; and the Cavalry Division, Major General (later Field Marshal) George C. Bingham, Third Earl of Lucan. The French had four infantry divisions, each about twice the size of the British infantry division, and eight and a half field artillery batteries.

Before he left Great Britain, Raglan had been told that his primary mission was to protect Constantinople. He was also directed, if the Russians did not attack first, to conduct offensive operations: "No blow . . . struck at the southern extremities of the Russian Empire would be so effective for this purpose as the taking of Sebastopol" (Sweetman 2001, p. 30). Sevastopol was the home port of the Russian Black Sea Fleet, and its destruction would punish the Russians for the Sinope "massacre" and eliminate the Russian naval threat to British naval supremacy in the eastern Mediterranean.

In accordance with allied strategy and because of overcrowding, allied forces sailed to Varna, a Bulgarian port on the Black Sea, the following month. Preparations were made for the onward movement to the Crimean Peninsula. Logistical and sanitary shortcomings were recognized, and there was a cholera outbreak in midsummer. Allied leaders reconnoitered on the Crimean coastline later in the summer, and the allied force began landing at Calamita Bay, 30 miles north of Sevastopol, on 14 September 1854. After the entire force of about 63,000 soldiers and 128 guns was assembled, it began its advance to Sevastopol on 19 September.

In defensive positions on the south bank of the Alma River, the Russians tried to stop the allied advance and fought the unsuccessful Battle of the Alma on 20 September 1854. The victorious allies continued their march, but they probably missed opportunities of attacking Sevastopol from the north. Staff officers recommended Sevastopol be attacked from the south where the defenses were not yet completed. Accordingly, the allies conducted their march around the eastern flank of Sevastopol and established positions on the semi-circular heights south of the city.

The siege of Sevastopol began on 8 October 1854, and the allies formed a "corps of siege" to invest the Russian fortress and a "corps of observation" to protect their right flank from attack by a large Russian force that had departed Sevastopol on 25 September 1854. The first allied bombardment of Sevastopol began on 17 October.

On 25 October 1854, a Russian field army under the command of General Prince Alexander Sergeevich Menshikov attacked the British. The Russian goal was to attack through the weakly held British lines and capture Balaklava, the British base of operations and supply port, and in the process, lift the siege of Sevastopol. This battle, characterized by battalion- and brigade-sized operations, culminated in the famous but disastrous Charge of the Light Brigade. The battle was a tactical success for the Russians, but the British continued to hold high ground and Balaklava.

The Russians made another attack on 5 November 1854 hoping to crush the British forces in a large-scale double envelopment. This engagement, the Battle of Inkerman, was probably doomed to failure because of poor command and control and last-minute changes in plans on the Russian side. Soldiers on both sides generally fought tenaciously in numerous small-unit actions in the fog-enshrouded hills and ravines. Timely French reinforcements turned the tide of battle and made the Battle of Inkerman a costly allied victory.

With the onset of winter, British logistical, transportation, and medical shortcomings became painfully obvious as soldiers serving in the trenches before Sevastopol suffered tremendous hardships. These privations, previously unknown to the public at large, were brought to the attention of a horrified British public by, for the first time, war correspondents. A public outcry resulted in the initiation of further reforms, to include improvements in medical care and the dispatch of Florence Nightingale and acceptance of female nurses in battlefield medical treatment.

The allies continued their siege of Sevastopol over the winter months. The most significant action of the Crimean War in the early months of 1855, in addition to the ongoing siege of Sevastopol, was the unsuccessful Russian attack on Turkish forces at Eupatoria on 17 February 1855. In February 1855, the French received reinforcements and established a second corps that took over the right flank of the siege operation. The British then concentrated their efforts in the center of the siege line opposite the Great Redan.

The Russians aggressively made sorties in February and March 1855, and on 9 April 1855, the allies began their second large-scale bombardment of Sevastopol. This barrage lasted for ten days and, while causing significant casualties, was not overly effective, as the Russians worked indefatigably day and night to repair the damaged defensive positions. The third allied bombardment of Sevastopol began on 6 June 1855, and another artillery attack took place on 17 June preparatory to allied assaults on the Redan and the Malakov that failed disastrously.

The Russians made their last unsuccessful attempt to break the allied siege on 16 August 1855 at the Battle of Chernaya. The following day, the allies again bombarded Sevastopol for ten days, and again from 5 to 8 September 1855. The allies surprised the Russians by attacking at noon on 8 September, and the French seized the Malakov. The British attacked the Great Redan but were repulsed three times. The Russians, realizing the futility of further resistance, abandoned Sevastopol that night. The allied capture of Sevastopol was the last major operation in the Crimean War, although operations at Kinburn and at Kars continued until October and November 1855, respectively.

While the Crimea was the main theater of operations during the Crimean War, other actions took place in the Baltic and White Seas and Pacific Oceans.

On 30 March 1856, the Peace of Paris was signed, officially ending the Crimean War. In general terms, allied-occupied areas in the Crimea were to be returned to Russia, and Kars was to be returned to Turkey. The Black Sea was to be neutralized. Great Britain, concerned about India and its other colonial possessions, wanted a harsher treaty imposed on Russia. Fourteen years later, Russia reneged on the treaty and renewed its territorial expansion.

Great Britain sent out 111,313 officers and men to the Crimea, and lost 4,774 all ranks killed in action and died of wounds, in addition to another 16,323 who died of disease. The French suffered over 30,000 deaths out of over 300,000 soldiers sent to the Crimea, and the Sardinians sustained about 2,050 all ranks dead from their 15,000-man contingent. Overall Turkish losses have been calculated at about 140,000, and the Russian dead was at least 110,000.

The Crimean War, Britain's only conflict in Europe during 1815–1914, was a watershed in military history. Improved weapons were used for the first time, including rifled muskets and the Minié rifle, which presaged further weapons developments and the shift of the tactical advantage from the attacker to the defender. The British established a military railroad, and the telegraph permitted almost instantaneous communications between the home government and the commanders in the field. More importantly, the telegraph allowed war correspondents to report the horrors of war to an increasingly literate public. While limited military reforms had been initiated after the 1852 death of the Duke of Wellington and before the beginning of the Crimean War, the logistical, medical, and administrative shortcomings of the British Army and incompetence of elderly generals received unprecedented exposure. This paved the way for substantive British Army reform, including the abolition of purchase and the Cardwell Reforms.

> **See also** Alma, Battle of the; Balaklava, Battle of; Baltic Sea Operations, Crimean War; Brown, General Sir George; Cambridge, Field Marshal H.R.H. Prince George F., Second Duke of; Campbell, Field Marshal Colin; Cardigan, Lieutenant General James T. Brudenell, Seventh Earl of; Cardwell Reforms; Cathcart, Lieutenant General Sir George; Charge of the Light Brigade; Chernaya, Battle of; Correspondents, War; Eupatoria, Battle of; Evans, General Sir George de Lacy; French Forces, Crimean War; Inkerman, Battle of; Kars, Siege of; Lucan, Field Marshal George C. Bingham, Third Earl of; Nightingale, Florence; Pacific Ocean Operations, Crimean War; Purchase System; Raglan, Field Marshal Fitzroy J. H. Somerset, First Baron; Russian Forces, Crimean War; Sardinian Forces, Crimean War; Sevastopol, Siege of; Simpson, General Sir James M.; Turkish Forces, Crimean War; White Sea Operations, Crimean War
>
> **References:** Adye (1860); Airlie (1933); Calthorpe (1856); Clifford (1956); Hamley (1891); Judd (1975); Palmer (1987); Pemberton (1962); Raugh (1987a); Raugh (1988b); Royle (2000); Russell (1966); Warner (1972)

Cronje, Assistant Commandant-General Piet A. (1835–1911)

At the beginning of the Second Boer War (1899–1902), Piet A. Cronje commanded the South African Republic forces in the Western Transvaal. He began the siege of Mafeking, and after victories at Modder River and Magersfontein—largely attributable to competent subordinates—he was trapped at Paardeburg and on 27 February 1900 surrendered with 4,000 of his men.

Cronje was born in Colesberg in the Cape Colony in 1835 and accompanied his parents on the Great Trek north to the Orange Free State and Natal area. He participated in the 1848 Battle of Boomplaats, where the British defeated a Boer insurgency protesting the annexation of the Orange River Sovereignty. During the First Boer War (1880–1881), Cronje led the Boers in their successful siege of Potchefstroom and gained fame as the "lion of Potchefstroom." He was later elected to the *Volksraad* (Parliament) and served in numerous government positions. Cronje led the Boers who defeated Dr. Leander Starr Jameson and his raiders at Doornkop on 2 January 1896.

Cronje commanded the 6,000 men of the West Transvaal commandos at the beginning of the Second Boer War. This force was assembled along a 25-mile front on the Bechuanaland border near Mafeking, which they began besieging on 13 October 1899. To prevent the relief of Mafeking and Kimberley by the British, Cronje's forces then moved to the Modder River. At the suggestion of Jacobus De la Rey, the Boers altered their tactics. Instead of occupying the vulnerable high ground and taking advantage of the flat trajectory of their high velocity rifles, they dug in along the south bank of the Modder River. On 28 November 1899, the British predictably conducted a frontal assault and were pinned down by withering Boer fire all day. The Boers abandoned their positions that night, and the British won this costly battle.

The Boers then moved to Magersfontein to block the British relief of Kimberley. The British attempted a night attack, 11 December 1899, against the Boers, but a heavy rainstorm, combined with a lack of prior reconnaissance, poor navigation, and vacillating leadership, caused the British to deploy their forces and then try to change plans within 400 yards of the undetected Boer trenches. At about 4:00 A.M. the Boers opened fire into the bunched-up British formations, pinning them down until the afternoon. Observing flanking movements, some British soldiers thought a withdrawal was taking place, which soon turned into a rout. The British force was devastated and another key battle lost.

The British relieved Kimberley on 15 February 1900. Cronje then moved his force eastward to help block the expected advance on Bloemfontein. His long baggage train, encumbered with Boer families, was attacked by the British. Cronje, perhaps fatalistically, began to dig in his forces near Paardeberg Drift. The British began a series of attacks, the first ones unsuccessful, and almost retreated. On 27 February 1900—the anniversary of the British defeat at the 1881 Battle of Majuba—Cronje surrendered with 4,069 Boer fighters. This was the first significant British victory of the war.

Cronje was imprisoned at St. Helena until the end of the war. At the 1904 St. Louis World Fair, Cronje reenacted the last stand at Paardeberg and earned the opprobrium of his countrymen. He died in 1911.

See also Boer War, First (1880–1881); Boer War, Second (1899–1902); Boers; Boomplaats, Battle of; Jameson Raid; Mafeking, Siege of; Magersfontein, Battle of; Modder River, Battle of; Paardeberg, Battle of; Transvaal

References: Barthorp (1987); Marix Evans (2000); Pakenham (1979); Trew (1999)

Curragh Camp

The Curragh Camp (from the Irish *An Currach*, meaning "the race course," because the prominent race course hosting the Irish Derby and other famous horse races was nearby) was established as a permanent camp by the British Army in 1855. The Curragh, a vast unbroken plain about 6 miles long and 2 miles wide, is immediately east of Kildare town, County Kildare, and about 30 miles southwest of Dublin, Ireland.

Originally used as an assembly and training area for British Army troops deploying to the Crimean War, the Curragh Camp evolved into the most significant military station in Ireland and one of the finest British Army training grounds in the British Isles. The Curragh of Kildare Act of 1868 defined the camp as totaling 4,870 acres, divided into three main parts: brown lands (site of camp), 575 acres; blue lands (rifle ranges and training areas), 463 acres; and green lands (residue, used in maneuvers), 3,382 acres. These were known as Crown lands.

In the 1870s and 1880s, the British Army deployed two divisions and a cavalry brigade (totaling 25,000–30,000 troops) in Ireland. One of the two divisions, designated the Northern Command, had its headquarters at the Curragh Camp. The cavalry brigade was also stationed at the Curragh Camp. In 1888, training schools for mounted infantry were established at both the Curragh Camp and at Aldershot. Training at the Curragh Camp in the 1890s had become much more realistic and worthwhile and included night operations, lengthy marches, and deliberate battlefield maneuvers.

There were several rifle and machine-gun ranges at the Curragh Camp, in addition to maneuver areas. The gently rolling plains were ideally suited to cavalry training. Normally there were adequate permanent billets for about 20,000 soldiers, but during the summer months when additional training troops lived in tents, there would be accommodations for about 100,000 men.

The Curragh Camp gave its name to the Curragh "Incident" of March 1914, when a large number of British Army officers stationed there resigned their commissions rather than possibly obey orders that they believed were intended to coerce Ulster Unionists into a united Home Rule Ireland.

The Curragh Camp was turned over to the fledgling Irish Army in 1922.

See also Aldershot; Curragh Incident; Maneuvers, British Army
References: Beckett (1986); Irish Troops (1922); Spiers (1992)

Curragh Incident (March 1914)

A large number of British Army officers stationed at the Curragh Camp, Ireland, resigned their commissions in March 1914 when presented with an ultimatum in a scenario that could have involved coercing Ulster Unionists into a united Home Rule Ireland. The Curragh "Incident," as it became known, was a stark example of the high degree of politicization of the professional British Army and of a general distrust between the army and Liberal politicians.

The issue of Home Rule for Ireland had been festering for decades. The government of Liberal British Prime Minister Herbert H. Asquith (later the Earl of Oxford and Asquith) introduced the first Home Rule Bill on 11 April 1912, although members were split on excluding Protestant Ulster from the legislation. (The province of Ulster consisted of nine counties: Donegal, Londonderry, Antrim, Tyrone, Armagh, Down, Fermanagh, Monaghan, and Cavan.) Plans were reportedly made to establish a provisional government in the north of Ireland. The paramilitary Ulster Volunteer Force (UVF) was established, and the illegal arming, drilling, and training of civilians was being conducted, to resist Home Rule if necessary. The British Government began to be concerned with the safety of its armories in Ireland and the possibility of a civil war if Ulster would be forced to become a part of united Home Rule Ireland. Many British Army officers, discounting the possibility of sectarian conflict, were sympathetic to the Ulster Unionists.

In 1913, questions began to surface about the loyalty and reliability of the Army in obeying the orders of the civilian government if required to ensure the inclusion of Ulster in a united Ireland. A number of senior officers, including Field Marshal Earl Frederick S. Roberts, V.C., and Major General (later Field Marshal Sir) Henry Wilson, the director of military operations at the War Office, were actively fostering the idea that the army might not enforce Home Rule.

On 4 March 1914, the Cabinet proposed a provision in the Home Rule Bill for each county in Ulster to opt for exclusion from joining a united Ireland for three years, after which the county would have no choice but to come under the authority of the Dublin Parliament. Asquith changed the term of exclusion to six years, and the second reading of the Home Rule Bill was conducted on 9 March 1914.

The exclusion proposals were rejected and the police in Ireland reported possible UVF raids on British Army arms depots to seize weapons. Orders were issued to Lieutenant General Sir Arthur Paget, the general officer commanding, Ireland, to safeguard weapons at several designated locations in Ireland. Paget was then summoned to London for consultations on 18 and 19 March 1914 with the secretary of state for war, Colonel J. E. B. Seely, Field Marshal (later Earl) Sir John French, chief of the imperial general staff, and others. Paget was directed to reinforce his guards at selected "vulnerable" locations.

Paget telegraphed from London his instructions to issue live ammunition to guards, then returned to Dublin on 20 March 1914. He held a meeting with general officers in his command that included Major General (later General) Sir Charles Fergusson, commanding the 5th Division; Brigadier General (later General Sir) Hubert de la P. Gough, 3rd Cavalry Brigade commander; two infantry brigadier generals; the North Depots commander; and senior staff officers. Paget offered a number of hypothetical scenarios and gave the impression that a formal ultimatum would need to be given to all officers in view of imminent active operations against Ulster. This "ultimatum" offered officers domiciled in Ulster the choice of "disappearing" while operations were conducted. Any officers who refused to participate in the operations and did not live in Ulster would be dismissed from the army without entitlements or pension.

The senior officers were incensed at this ultimatum and proceeded to inform the officers in their subordinate units of the situation. The gravity of their decision and possible financial hardships gave some officers the impression they were being forced to barter their honor. Gough tendered his resignation, as did fifty-seven other officers in his brigade. Fergusson, mainly through force of personality and references to loyalty to the king, was able to maintain discipline within his division.

Gough and two of his regimental commanders were ordered to the War Office purportedly to ascertain the facts of the situation. He remarked that if his brigade had been ordered to go to Belfast, he would have done so without question. This was the crux of the issue, as Gough and his officers had not been issued an order but had been given an option in a theoretical scenario. It was determined, after numerous interviews and conferences, that there had been a "misunderstanding," caused mainly by Paget. Gough sought and actually received from Seely on 23 March 1914 a written guarantee that there would be no military coercion of Ulster before returning to Ireland that night. The incident seemed to be over. Two days later, however, the prime minister repudiated the guarantee, which in effect forced the resignations of Seely and French. The issue ended and was soon overshadowed by world war.

It cannot be determined satisfactorily if the Curragh Incident of March 1914 was "the product of accident and confusion, or of conspiracy and collusion" (Strachan 1997, p. 114), but it had the potential of dividing the army. It was a manifestation of the army's deep politicization.

See also Civil-Military Relations; Curragh Camp; French, Field Marshal John D. P.; Gough, General Sir Hubert de la P.; Roberts, Field Marshal Frederick S., V.C.

References: Beckett (1986); Farrar-Hockley (1975); Gough (1954); Jeffery (1985); Strachan (1997)

D

De la Marmora, General Alfonso
See Crimean War; Sardinian Forces, Crimean War

De la Rey, Assistant Commandant-General Jacobus (1847–1914)

Jacobus "Koos" De la Rey was one of the most dynamic and effective Boer leaders during the Second Boer War (1899–1902). He was an innovative, flexible tactician, responsible for the first and last Boer successes of the war—the capture of an armored train at Kraaipan on 12 October 1899 and the defeat and capture of Lieutenant General (later Field Marshal) Lord Paul S. Methuen at Tweebosch on 7 March 1902. He was without pretensions and admired by the Boers and the Britons.

De la Rey as born on 22 October 1847 in Winburg in what later became the Orange Free State. He had his first combat experience during the 1865 conflict with the Basutos, and at age nineteen, De la Rey became a field cornet, the youngest man known to hold this responsible appointment. In 1879, he participated in an expedition against Sekukuni and fought in the First Boer War (1880–1881). Elected a commandant in 1885, De la Rey became a member of the Transvaal *Volksraad*. He came into prominence as a member of Piet A. Cronje's force that captured Dr. Jameson's raiding force in 1896.

De la Rey expressed his reservations about provoking war with Great Britain in 1899, but when war broke out, he went along with the majority and acted as an "adviser" to the older Cronje in the Western Transvaal. De la Rey believed in swift attacks and thought that sieges wasted time and resources. He distinguished himself at Graspan (25 November 1899), where he observed that establishing vulnerable positions on hilltops was unwise when fighting an enemy with artillery superiority. He also realized that to maximize the effectiveness, flat trajectory, and range of their high velocity Mausers, it was best to engage the enemy from concealed positions at ground level. The Boers employed De la Rey's innovative tactics at the Battle of the Modder River (28 November 1899), where the British suffered heavy casualties but achieved tactical success. It was a bitter occasion for De la Rey, whose son was mortally wounded that day. De la Rey was responsible for selecting and preparing the defensive positions at Magersfontein, where the Boers crushed the assaulting British two weeks later.

Guerrilla warfare dominated the conflict by the end of 1900, with De la Rey commanding Boer operations in the Western Transvaal. De la Rey, unlike most of the other senior Boer commanders, trained his subordinate commando leaders to conduct autonomous operations. He also developed and used the tactic of charging on horseback. At Tweebosch on 7 March 1902, De la Ray captured the wounded British General Methuen. He treated Methuen kindly and even sent a message to Methuen's wife. De la Rey participated in the negotiations at Vereeniging and signed the peace treaty. Afterward De la Rey met a group of dejected Boer leaders and stated in halting English, "We are a bloody cheerful-looking lot of British subjects!" (Lee 1985, p. 206).

After the war, De la Rey became a senator in the first parliament of the Union of South Africa. He supported the nationalist movement and wanted to restore the Boer republics. Which side he would have taken during the 1914

Rebellion in South Africa was never known, as he was accidentally shot and killed at a police roadblock before it began.

See also Boer War, Second (1899–1902); Boers; Commando System; Cronje, Assistant Commandant-General Piet A.; Jameson Raid; Magersfontein, Battle of; Methuen, Field Marshal Paul S.; Modder River, Battle of; Transvaal
References: Lee (1985); Marix Evans (2000); Trew (1999)

De Wet, Chief Commandant Christiaan R. (1854–1922)

Chief Commandant Christiaan R. De Wet was an outstanding Boer guerrilla leader of the Second Boer War (1899–1902).

De Wet was born on a farm in the Orange Free State on 7 October 1854. He had little formal education, worked as a transport driver and butcher, and was one of the few Boers from the Orange Free State to fight in the First Boer War (1880–1881). He later farmed but also served in the parliaments of both the Transvaal and of the Orange Free State.

On 2 October 1899, nine days before the start of the Second Boer War, he and his three sons were summoned to military service. He was soon elected commandant of his commando. He demonstrated his leadership abilities at the Battle of Nicholson's Nek (30 October 1899), where his 300 men drove the British troops from their positions and took 800 prisoners.

De Wet was appointed field general under Assistant Commandant-General Piet A. Cronje in December 1899 and tried to persuade Cronje to invade Cape Colony. Cronje refused and later surrendered his force at Paardeberg on 27 February 1900.

De Wet reorganized the commandos in the spring of 1900 and instilled a new spirit of discipline into his men. With an uncanny sense of timing and location, De Wet conducted many hit-and-run raids on the British to disrupt their lines of communication and destroy their supplies. A notable example of this success occurred at Roodewal station, where De Wet captured £500,000 worth of British supplies on 7 June 1900. The British reacted to the Boer tactics by burning down Boer homesteads.

In July 1900, De Wet, with Orange Free State President Marthinus T. Steyn, was entrapped by the British in the Brandwater Basin area. De Wet and Steyn, with about 2,000 Boers, escaped, and the British initiated the unsuccessful large-scale operation called the "first De Wet hunt" to capture the elusive commando leader. Later in 1900, De Wet's forces invaded Cape Colony, and the British conducted other operations to try to capture him. His excellent intelligence system and mobility permitted him to continue to evade the British even after they established their blockhouse system.

Realizing the inevitability of Boer defeat, De Wet, as acting president of the Orange Free State, reluctantly signed the Treaty of Veereniging (31 May 1902), ending the Second Boer War. He then accompanied other Boer leaders to Europe, during which time he wrote *Three Years War*, his account of service and operations in the Second Boer War.

De Wet served in government positions until the creation of the Union of South Africa in 1910, when he retired from politics. He was a leader of the rebellion that broke out in the Orange Free State at the beginning of World War I, was captured, and was found guilty of treason. He was fined and sentenced to six years of imprisonment, but he was released after six months, an old man broken physically and spiritually. De Wet, one of the most able and charismatic Boer guerrilla leaders, died on 3 February 1922.

See also Bitter-Ender; Blockhouses; Boer War, First (1880–1881); Boer War, Second (1899–1902); Boers; Commando System; Cronje, Assistant Commandant-General Piet A.; Paardeberg, Battle of; Steyn, Marthinus T.; Transvaal
References: Barnard (1973); Belfield (1975); Lee (1985); Pakenham (1979); Pretorius (1977); Raugh (1994); Raugh (2001a); Riall (2000); Sixsmith (1974); Trew (1999)

Delhi, Siege and Storming of (1857)

The Indian Mutiny began at Meerut on 10 May 1857, and the rebels immediately marched on Delhi, ostensibly to restore British pensioner Bahadur Shah, the last of the Mughal emperors in India, to his throne.

The mutineers arrived in Delhi, where there were no European regiments, early on 11 May 1857. Most of the Indian troops joined the mutineers, and they butchered the Europeans they found. A few British officers and men defended the arsenal near the Kashmir Gate as long as they could; when their position became untenable, they blew themselves up with the arsenal, to deny the ammunition to the rebels and to inflict the heaviest possible casualties on them. European officers and families remained in their cantonment area outside the city, and after nightfall they fled to other cities. By the end of the day, the highly symbolic city of Delhi was in the hands of the mutineers.

The British identified Delhi as the center of the mutiny and concentrated their efforts on retaking it. The 3,000-man Delhi Field Force was commanded by General George Anson, but he died of cholera on 27 May 1857 and was succeeded in command by Lieutenant General Sir Henry W. Barnard. Joined later by other British and loyal Punjabi units, the Delhi Field Force fought a sharp engagement on 8 June 1857 at Badli-ke-serai, about 6 miles northwest of Delhi. The British drove about 30,000 entrenched rebels from their positions and occupied their old military cantonments on "the ridge" overlooking Delhi. Delhi was encircled by 7 miles of a 24-foot-high wall, reinforced by a number of bastions and 10 huge gates, all surrounded by a 25-foot-deep dry moat. The mutineers had 114 guns, mainly 24-pounders.

Barnard died of cholera on 5 July 1857, and Major General Reed succeeded him as commander. Reed, however, was not fit for command and resigned on 17 July 1857, when Brigadier General (later Lieutenant General) Sir Archdale Wilson became commander. The British force on the ridge waited for reinforcements before attacking Delhi.

Gurkhas and British Army units, as well as the Punjab Moveable Column commanded by the inspiring Brigadier General John Nicholson, arrived in Delhi by 14 August 1857 and increased the size of the Delhi Field Force by 4,200 men. The slow-moving British siege train reached Delhi on 4 September 1857, and the siting of the artillery began on 7 September. The following day, the British artillery barrage began, and the intense fire breached the Delhi city walls in a number of locations. The British force, divided into five columns, attacked Delhi early on 14 September. The first three columns (1st Column: 75th Foot, 1st Bengal Fusiliers, and 2nd Punjab Infantry, totaling 1,000 men; 2nd Column, consisting of 8th Foot, 2nd Bengal Fusiliers, and 4th Sikhs, 850 men total; and 3rd Column: 52nd Foot, Kumaon Regiment, and 1st Punjab Infantry, totaling 950 soldiers) were under Nicholson's overall command, and their mission was to seize the Water Bastion and then the Kashmir Gate. The 4th Column (Sirmur Battalion, Guides' Infantry, and a composite force of pickets, totaling 850 men, with 1,000 soldiers of the Kashmir Contingent in reserve), commanded by Major Charles Reid, was to cover the right flank of Nicholson's force and capture the suburb of Kishangunj. Brigadier General Longfield's 1,000-man 5th Column (61st Foot, 4th Punjab Infantry, and the Baluch Battalion) remained in reserve.

The British assault began on 14 September 1857 under a hail of rebel musketry fire and grapeshot, and a foothold was gained in the city after severe British losses, including the charismatic Nicholson. The Kashmir Gate was blown by sappers and created a significant breach in the walls. Confusion, poor coordination, and hard fighting followed. By the evening of 14 September, the British had established a foothold in the city, but at a cost of 66 officers and 1,104 men killed and wounded. After six days of determined (and occasionally drunken) urban fighting with no quarter given on either side, the British captured Delhi, suffering a total of 1,574 officers and men killed and wounded during the operation. The advance, according to many junior officers, was characterized by "the utmost incompetence" (Hibbert 1978, p. 310). The British victory was followed by looting, revenge, and the execution of mutineers.

Bahadur Shah was captured and his sons were shot after they surrendered to the British. The fall of Delhi was the turning point of the Indian Mutiny and ended mutineer dreams of a revived Mughal Empire. Moreover, it freed British troops to fight at Cawnpore and other locations.

See also Cawnpore, Siege and Relief of; East India Company, Military Forces; Gurkhas; India; India, British Army in; Indian Mutiny; Nicholson, Brigadier General John

References: Edwardes (1963); Collier (1964); Hibbert (1978); Hilton (1957); Leasor (1956)

Dervishes

The original name for the followers of the Mahdi in the Sudan was dervishes (from the Persian term *darawish* for "beggar"), a term later discarded in favor of *ansar* ("helpers"). Dervish, however, has become the most common appellation for those followers of the Mahdi and his successor, the Khalifa, in the Sudan (1885–1899).

The rapidly forming dervish army consisted of people from throughout the Sudan. The largest groups were the cattle-raising Baggara people from the desert area north of Kordofan, and the Beja of the eastern Sudan. The Beja, mainly because of the way they dressed their hair with mutton fat or butter to resemble a mop, were known as "fuzzy-wuzzies."

Many of the dervishes were religious fanatics, believing in Islamic fundamentalism, expansionism, and emancipation from foreign rule. They were also disciplined, courageous, and ferocious in battle.

The Mahdi's army was organized into three divisions, each under the command of one of his three caliphs and named after the color of its flag. The Black Flag, consisting of men from the western Sudan and the Baggara, was commanded by Khalifa Abdullah, who succeeded the Mahdi in 1885. Khalifa Ali wad Hilku commanded the Green Flag, whose soldiers came from the area between the Blue and White Niles, and the Red Flag, led by Khalifa Mohammed esh Sherif, came from the northern Sudan. There were no formal subordinate units, although the flags frequently became so large that they were divided into *rubs,* similar to battalions and having 800–1,200 men. *Rubs,* in turn, were frequently subdivided into four elements: an administrative unit and one element each of riflemen, swordsmen and spearmen, and cavalrymen.

The dervish army was mobilized only in time of war, but attempts were made to establish a standing army to garrison important towns. These soldiers, called *jihidiyya,* many of whom had worked for slave traders, were armed with rifles. They were organized into companies of 100 men and smaller platoons.

Initially, the dervishes used sticks, stones, double-edged swords, and spears as weapons, but as they defeated and massacred various Egyptian and British forces that had come to suppress them, they captured firearms and other equipment. The dervishes wore a white *jibbeh* (tunic) with colored patches sewn on it, representing poverty (considered a virtue), turban, skullcap, trousers, plaited straw belt, sandals, and beads.

The dervishes made excellent use of terrain, cover, and concealment. Generally, the swordsmen and spearmen, with another group of dervishes providing covering or suppressive fire, would sneak up as close as possible to the enemy. At the last minute they would charge, oblivious to incoming rifle fire, and then engage in ferocious hand-to-hand combat.

Dervishes armed with sticks, stones, and spears killed a group of Egyptian soldiers sent in the summer of 1881 to seize the Mahdi. He declared a jihad, or holy war, on 12 August 1881, and the dervishes annihilated an Egyptian force sent from Fashoda in June 1882.

The dervishes fought many other battles with the forces sent to the Sudan to eliminate them. When the forces were composed entirely of British troops, the dervishes started to lose battles, although they gained tremendous notoriety for breaking the British square at the Battle of Tamai, 13 March 1884. The British defeated the dervishes at the Battle of Ginnis (30 December 1885), and British-led Egyptian soldiers soundly defeated the dervishes, shattering the myth of their invincibility, at the Battle of Toski (3 August 1889). At the 2 September 1898 Battle of Omdurman, the Khalifa's army numbered over 40,000 against about 26,000 Anglo-Egyptians troops, and the dervishes suffered over 10,000 killed, about an equal number wounded, and about 5,000 captured. The British finally killed the Khalifa and defeated the dervishes at the Battle of Umm Diwaykarat (24 November 1899).

The British soldiers generally respected the savage courage and discipline of the dervishes. This sentiment was expressed by poet Rudyard Kipling in "Fuzzy-Wuzzy": "We've fought with many men acrost the seas, / an' some of 'em was brave an' some was not: / The Paythan an' the Zulu an' Burmese; / But the Fuzzy was the finest o' the lot" (De Cosson 1886, p. xiii).

See also Ginnis, Battle of; Gordon, Major General Charles G.; Gordon Relief Expedition; Khalifa; Mahdi; Omdurman, Battle of; Sudan; Tamai, Battle of; Toski, Battle of
References: Brook-Shepherd (1972); De Cosson (1886); Haythornthwaite (1995); Johnson (1965); Ludwig (1937); Robson (1993b); Slatin Pasha (1896)

Discipline and Justice, British Army

Discipline was harsh and punishment was severe in the British Army during the nineteenth century, especially before flogging was abolished in 1881.

Throughout the early nineteenth century, flogging was the bedrock of British Army discipline. There were three levels of courts-martial (regimental, district, and general) before 1829, each with almost unlimited powers. In 1829, regimental courts were restricted to maximum sentences of 300 lashes, and district and general courts to 500, totals reduced in 1833 to 200 and 300, respectively. In 1830, 5,946 British soldiers were court-martialed, of whom 1,754 were flogged; the number of courts-martial almost doubled to 9,628 in 1833, although the number of soldiers flogged decreased to 1,007. The maximum punishments of the three courts were further reduced in 1836, to 100 lashes for regimental courts, 150 for district courts, and 200 for general courts.

The lash had been a symbol of authority for centuries, and its use was designed not only to punish the disobedient soldier but also to warn others of the consequences of breaking the rules. The flogging was generally administered at sunrise in front of the malcontent's assembled unit, with the observing soldiers frequently angered and sickened by the spectacle. After the charges were read aloud, the reprobate was stripped to the waist and his hands tied to a post. Strokes of the lash were accompanied by a muffled drumbeat keeping count. The cat-o'-nine tails had nine lashes of whipcord sixteen inches long with three knots in each lash, reminiscent of a medieval torture instrument.

Conservatives wanted to retain flogging for major offenses, including mutiny, desertion, insubordination and violence, disgraceful conduct, and theft of army property. Imprisonment increasingly became an alternate punishment to flogging, and military prisons in Great Britain and overseas were built in the mid-1840s. Flogging was reduced to 50 strokes maximum in 1846, and the number of soldiers flogged that year fell to 652. In 1858, flogging was restricted to certain classes of offenses. In 1867, the only crimes punishable by flogging were mutiny and violence to superiors, and the following year, only to troops on active service. Even with its limited applicability, flogging had a detrimental impact on recruiting efforts. Corporal punishment, including flogging, was abolished by the Army Act of 1881.

One 1855 source observed that "according to the British military code, punishment, before the enemy, consists almost exclusively in flogging; and thus, the very punishment which is said, by its advocates, to be the only means of keeping up discipline in cases of great urgency, is the means of ruining discipline by destroying the *morale* and the *point d'honneur* of the soldier" (British Army 1855, p. 3). Senior military traditionalists did not seem to understand this contradiction.

While flogging was the most controversial aspect of the British Army's disciplinary system, the practice of branding was also condemned by humanitarians and others. Convicted soldiers were branded (actually tattooed) with one-inch letters, either a "D" for "deserter" on the left breast or a "BC" for "bad character" on the right forearm. The army justified this procedure "as a cheap method of identifying deserters, as an effective device for preventing multiple enlistments, and as a necessary means of protecting the public from criminals" (Blanco 1968b, pp. 137–138). Branding was abolished in 1871.

Soldier crime was a significant problem during the second half of the nineteenth century. Between 10,000 and 20,000 soldiers were court-martialed each year, the equivalent of 15 or 20 full-strength infantry regiments. This figure, however, reveals a reduction in the number of courts-martial and of the number and severity of punishments from the first half of the nineteenth century.

Many types of soldier criminal conduct were punished. Drunkenness was relatively common and after 1868 considered a minor offense, with commanding officers authorized to impose fines on guilty soldiers. In 1872, 51,501 fines were imposed for drunkenness on 26,111, or 28.1 percent, of the soldiers in the British Army, with the total decreasing to 26,243 fines for drunkenness on 14,165, or 12.1 percent, of the soldiers in 1898.

Thousands of soldiers deserted each year, many of whom were later captured. In 1862, there were 2,895 total desertions, or 1.4 percent of the army strength. This number increased to 5,861 (3.2 percent of the army) in 1872 but fell to 4,074 (1.9 percent of the army) in 1898.

The number of soldiers imprisoned also increased during this period. The annual average number of soldiers confined in military prisons was never less than 500, and frequently twice this number, throughout the period 1856 to 1899. In 1856, 6,376 soldiers (2.6 percent) of the British Army were imprisoned. In 1898, the number increased to 8,672 soldiers (4.0 percent of the army) confined.

Capital punishment was retained in the British Army, but only for the most serious crimes. The only civilian crimes punishable by death in 1861 were treason and murder. In the British Army, the death sentence could be given for treason and murder, and serious offenses committed while on active service, including desertion, mutiny, or violence to a superior officer. Execution was generally by hanging or by firing squad. Between 1865 and 1898, 37 soldiers were executed.

By the end of the nineteenth century, while discipline continued to be a required trait for all soldiers, punishments were less severe. In 1899, battalion and regimental commanders could punish privates by imprisonment with or without hard labor for a fortnight, and a company commander could imprison a soldier for seven days. For privates going absent without leave (AWOL), imprisonment could equal the number of days absent, not to exceed twenty-one days. Pay was also deducted for AWOL and drunken soldiers. Privates could be confined to barracks for up to twenty-eight days and required to serve additional tours of guard duty. Battalion and regimental commanders could only reprimand noncommissioned officers (NCOs); NCOs could be reduced in rank only by a regimental court-martial. Officers could be arrested, but not punished, by battalion and regimental commanders.

See also Army and Society; Rank and File, British Army—Enlistment; Rank and File, British Army—Social Background; Recruiting

References: Blanco (1968b); Brereton (1986); Burroughs (1994); de Watteville (1954); Grierson (1899); Skelley (1977); Strachan (1997); Stuart-Smith (1969)

Disraeli, Benjamin, First Earl of Beaconsfield (1804–1881)

Benjamin Disraeli was a British statesman who served twice as prime minister, first in 1868 and then from 1874 to 1880. He was initially a member of the Tory political party, whose members became known as Conservatives after 1834. In general terms, the Conservatives believed in moderate reform combined with a strong belief in traditional institutions, including private property. Disraeli's premierships were characterized by social reform and imperialist policies, the latter heavily influencing military strategy and operations.

Disraeli was born in London on 21 December 1804. After a private education and training as a solicitor, he became a novelist and developed an interest in politics. After a number of unsuccessful attempts to run for Parliament, he was elected in 1837 to represent Maidstone. A realist, he understood the inevitability of extending democracy and helped form the Young England group in 1842. Disraeli advocated a political alliance between the growing middle class and the aristocracy.

After holding a number of key governmental positions when the Conservatives were in power, Disraeli became Chancellor of the Exchequer and leader of the House of Commons in 1866. He championed a new Reform Bill, which was enacted in 1867. At this time, Disraeli may have thought that dispatching a British expedition to resolve the hostage situation in Abyssinia would help heal class divisions, show that Britain was a great military power, and demonstrate the popular appeal of imperialism. In reality, the Abyssinian War enabled Britain to extricate itself honorably from a failed Abyssinian policy. Disraeli became the prime minister when Lord Derby resigned in 1868. In the general election held later that year, Liberal William E. Gladstone became prime minister.

Disraeli again became prime minister in 1874. He was considered a "Big Englander" because of his imperialistic attitudes and policies through which he attempted to transform public sentiments into patriotic fervor. With great foresight, Disraeli had the British government purchase a controlling interest in the Suez Canal in 1875, thus forestalling French ambitions in the area while guaranteeing and shortening the route to India. Queen Victoria approved of Disraeli's imperialistic policies and desire to make Britain the most powerful nation in the world. In 1876, Queen Victoria, at Disraeli's suggestion, accepted the title of Empress of India. In return, she ennobled Disraeli as the First Earl of Beaconsfield.

Disraeli and Gladstone clashed over a number of issues in the late 1870s, including the 1876 Bulgarian Revolt, which led to the Russo-Turkish War (1877–1878). Disraeli represented Britain very well at the 1878 Congress of Berlin, which limited Russia's influence in the Balkans. Britain also received Cyprus, and Disraeli dispatched an Indian force to occupy the island and redirect British power back toward Europe. A resolute "forward policy" of defense against Russia was conducted, attempting to use Afghanistan as a buffer state between India and Russian encroachment. This, however, resulted in the Second Afghan War (1878–1880). The Zulu War (1879) was also fought when Disraeli was prime minister.

Disraeli and the Conservatives were defeated by the Liberals in the general election of 1880. Disraeli retired from politics and died on 19 April 1881.

See also Abyssinian War; Afghan War, Second (1878–1880); Civil-Military Relations; Egypt; Gladstone, William E.; Great Game; Imperialism; India; Suez Canal; Zulu War

References: Blake (1966); Bond (1960); Longford (1964); Pearson (1951); Preston (1969); Rodgers (1984); Somervell (1926); Spiers (1992)

Dongola, Capture of (23 September 1896)

The British reconquest of the Sudan began in March 1896, and its first objective was to recapture the province of Dongola.

The 9,000-man Egyptian Army, under the command of the sirdar, Major General (later Field Marshal Earl) Sir Horatio H. Kitchener, advanced south from Akasha and fought and defeated the dervishes at Firket on 7 June 1896. Egyptian losses were 113 killed or wounded while the dervishes suffered over 1,000 killed. Although a small engagement, it instilled confidence into the leaders and soldiers of the Egyptian Army.

The military railway that had been built to Wadi Halfa was then extended about 10 miles south of Firket. Over the summer of 1896, cholera broke out in the camps along the

Nile, killing over 600 men. Severe weather hindered preparations for the advance. A gunboat flotilla was assembled to support the advance.

As the town of Dongola, the capital of Dongola Province, was the obvious objective of Kitchener's force, the dervish governor established defensive positions at Kerma, on the east bank of the Nile, and at Hafir, a half-mile upstream on the Nile's west bank. On 18 September 1896, the dervish governor learned that the Egyptian Army was advancing on Kerma, and that night, he transported his force across the Nile to the defensive positions at Hafir.

Kitchener's force attacked Kerma at dawn on 19 September and found it deserted. The British gunboats discovered the dervishes on the opposite bank and opened fire on them, and after a heated artillery and small arms duel, Kitchener ordered the gunboats to proceed to Dongola, 35 miles upstream. That night the dervishes slipped away from the Hafir positions, and the following day Kitchener used the dervish boats to transfer his troops across the Nile.

On 22 September 1896 and through the evening, the Egyptian Army began its approach march to Dongola, anticipating action the next morning. When the Egyptian troops prepared for combat at dawn on 23 September, dervish cavalry was spotted in the distance, but they withdrew. The Egyptian Army advanced to Dongola and found that the dervishes were gone. The capture of Dongola was an anticlimax to the campaign. Kitchener pushed on and his forces occupied Debba and Merowe by the end of September, thus capturing all of Dongola Province and establishing positions near the dervish stronghold at Abu Hamed. The capture of Dongola Province, the first phase in the reconquest of the Sudan, met with enthusiastic approval in Great Britain. Anglo-Egyptian combat casualties were 47 killed and 122 wounded, but over a thousand lives had been lost to disease.

See also Dervishes; Egypt; Egyptian Army; Khalifa; Kitchener, Field Marshal Horatio H.; Railways; Reconquest of the Sudan; Sirdar; Sudan

References: Arthur (1920); Barthorp (1984); Keown-Boyd (1986); Neillands (1996); Pollock (2001); Rye and Groser (1917)

Dost Mohammed (1793–1863)

Dost (which means "friend") Mohammed, one of twenty-one brothers of the Afghan vizier (chief minister) Fateh Khan, seized power in Kabul, Afghanistan, in 1826 after years of instability and strife. He became the virtual king of Afghanistan. Dost Mohammed was concerned with solidifying his own power base as well as with external enemies, the Sikhs in the east and the Persians in the west.

Peshawar, in the Punjab, was ruled by the Afghans until 1834, when the Sikhs seized the city. The Persians threatened Herat in 1836, demanding tribute and hostages, and insisting that Herati coinage should bear the Persian imprint. The Afghan governor of Herat replied defiantly and waited for a Persian attack.

Dost Mohammed, however, requested assistance from the British to recover Peshawar from the Sikhs but was rebuffed. The Russian czar sent representatives to Herat and to Kabul, and the British responded by demanding Dost Mohammed cease negotiating with the Russians and give up all claims on Peshawar. Perceiving Dost Mohammed as obstructionist and possibly subject to Russian influence, the British decided to invade and occupy Afghanistan, depose Dost Mohammed, and replace him with the pliant pro-British Shah Shujah, a former ruler living in exile in India.

The British "Army of the Indus" departed India in December 1838 and began the debacle of the First Afghan War. The British finally reached Kandahar in April 1839 and captured the Afghan fortress at Ghazni, the key to Kabul, on 23 July 1839. Dost Mohammed fled to the Hindu Kush, surrendered on 3 November 1840 to the British, and was exiled to India.

The British had crowned Shah Shujah as amir of Afghanistan on 3 May 1839, and their continued presence in Kabul propped up his unpopular regime. On 2 November 1841, Afghans struck at the British Residency and defeated the British in an engagement at Beymaroo Hills on 23 November. On the verge of starvation, the British negotiated with the Afghans to depart the country and permit Dost Mohammed to return to Afghanistan.

Shah Shujah was assassinated in April 1842, and Dost Mohammed returned to his throne in Afghanistan early in 1843. Success, however, caused him to lapse into heavy drinking and debauchery, and he ruled in a tyrannical manner. He remained loyal to the British and supported them throughout the Indian Mutiny (1857–1859), before dying a natural death in 1863—a rare occurrence for an Afghan leader.

See also Afghan War, First (1839–1842); Afghanistan; East India Company, Military Forces; Great Game; India; Indian Mutiny; Sher Ali Khan; Sikhs

References: Fredericks (1971); James (1998); Judd (1973); Pottinger (1983); Tanner (2002); Waller (1990)

Dundas, Admiral Sir James W. D. (1785–1862)

Vice Admiral (later Admiral) Sir James W. D. Dundas, a veteran of the Napoleonic Wars, was the commander of the Mediterranean Fleet (and later the Black Sea Fleet) from the opening stages of the Crimean War through February 1855. He commanded the Baltic Sea Fleet during operations in 1855.

Dundas had extensive administrative experience working at the Admiralty as Fourth Naval Lord (1841), Second Naval Lord (1846), and First Naval Lord (1847–1852).

In 1853, Vice Admiral Dundas was commanding the Mediterranean Fleet, harbored at Malta. His ships, a potential symbol of British might and decisiveness, were the closest to the Black Sea area, where war was threatening between Russia and Turkey. After months of hesitation, on 22 December 1853 it was decided to send Dundas's fleet to the Black Sea. On 8 January 1854, a squadron under his second in command, Rear Admiral (later Admiral Lord) Sir Edmund Lyons, entered the Black Sea as a deterrent to possible continued Russian aggression. The first shots fired in anger by the allied forces in the Crimean War were by Dundas's British and French ships bombarding the Russian port of Odessa on 22 April 1854.

On 18 July 1854, Dundas attended a Council of War, convened by General (later Field Marshal) Fitzroy J. H. Somerset, First Baron Raglan, with his French counterparts to formulate allied strategy for the landings in the Crimea and beyond. A second conference was held the following month. On 17 October 1854, an allied sea and land bombardment was scheduled to take place on Sevastopol, but there were problems in coordinating with the French. The shelling was postponed, and the ships were too far offshore to be very effective. There was general dissatisfaction at the relative inactivity of the fleet under Dundas, mainly because the admiral was overly concerned about an underwater shoal and bringing his wooden ships within distance of the Russian land batteries.

Dundas, who was not very aggressive and had the nickname "Damn'd Ass," was replaced in February 1855. He took over command of the Baltic Sea Fleet of nineteen screw propeller-driven and one sixty-gun ship of the line. He set sail for the Baltic in March 1855 and spent most of the season reconnoitering Russian harbor defenses before returning to England in November 1855.

See also Baltic Sea Operations, Crimean War; Crimean War; Lyons, Admiral Sir Edmund; Raglan, Field Marshal Fitzroy J. H. Somerset, First Baron

References: Hibbert (1961); Judd (1975); Royle (2000); Sweetman (1993)

Durand, Sir Henry Mortimer (1850–1924)

Sir Henry Mortimer Durand was a member of the Indian Civil Service who served as foreign secretary of the government of India from 1884 to 1894. He is best remembered as having negotiated in 1893 the political boundary between India and Afghanistan, known then and since as the Durand Line.

Durand was born in Sehore, Bhopal State, India, on 14 February 1850. His father was in the British Army and later became Major General Sir Henry Marion Durand. The younger Durand was educated in England and entered the Indian Civil Service in 1870. During the Second Afghan War (1878–1880), Durand served as political secretary to Major General (later Field Marshal Earl) Frederick S. Roberts, V.C., in Kabul.

In 1884, Durand became foreign secretary of the government of India. The 1880s arguably marked the height of the Great Game, the rivalry between British India and Russia over imperialistic expansion into Central Asia. The following year, the Pendjeh Incident, in which Russian forces attacked the Afghan town of Pendjeh near the disputed northern Afghan boundary, took place. This episode almost caused a war between England and Russia before the crisis was defused through diplomatic efforts.

The boundary between Afghanistan and the North-West Frontier of India remained vague. The Afghan Amir Abdur Rahman, despite provisions in the 1879 Treaty of Gandamak that placed (in return for a substantial annual subsidy) the Khyber Pass, the Kurram Valley, and portions of Baluchistan under British administration, continued to claim the frontier area. The British thought he was encouraging tribal raiding in the frontier area. In the late summer of 1893, Abdur Rahman surprisingly proposed to the Marquess of Landsdowne, viceroy of India, that a conference be held in Kabul to agree to a formal and final delineation of the Afghan-Indian border.

Durand was sent to Kabul to attend this conference and negotiate with Abdur Rahman, considered "a catankerous and suspicious old savage" (Fredericks 1971, p. 239) by Landsdowne. An agreement was reached quickly and easily, perhaps facilitated by Durand offering to increase the amir's annual subsidy by £300,000. On 12 November 1893, the amir signed and sealed a treaty renouncing all claims to a band of territory extending from the Hindu Kush to the westernmost limits of Baluchistan. This large area contained the formerly contested lands of Bajaur, Dir, Swat, Buner, Tirah, the Kurram Valley, and Waziristan. As a result, the frontier tribesmen acquired a legal status, becoming "British protected persons." The Durand Line, as the delineated border between Afghanistan and India came to be called, marked the British Empire's longest land frontier next to the United States–Canada border. Over the following two years, a commission demarcated the boundary on the ground with a series of pillars.

The establishment of the Durand Line was considered a significant achievement and elicited congratulations from Queen Victoria. In many respects, however, it may be considered a factor in the Pathan uprising of 1897. The Durand Line has been criticized as "illogical from the point of view of ethnography, of strategy and of geography," mainly because it "splits a nation in two, and it even divides tribes" (Miller 1977, p. 241). Nonetheless, the Durand Line remains the border of Afghanistan and Pakistan, a successor state of British India.

In 1895, Durand was appointed minister to Persia. He advocated agreement with Russia for joint development of the country and continuation of the traditional policy of upholding the integrity and independence of Persia. Durand departed Persia in 1900 without regret, confessing that in Teheran he had "felt like a jellyfish in a whirlpool" (Greaves n.d., p. 3). Durand then served as British ambassador to Spain and then to the United States. He was recalled to London in 1906. Durand devoted himself to writing in England before dying on 8 June 1924.

See also Afghan War, Second (1878–1880); Afghanistan; Great Game; India; North-West Frontier; Penjdeh Incident; Roberts, Field Marshal Frederick S., V.C.

References: Barthorp (1982); Farwell (1989); Fredericks (1971); Greaves (n.d.); Mason (1974); Miller (1977); Stearn (1996a)

E

Earle, Major General William (1833–1885)

Major General William Earle is best known for his service as a general officer in Egypt and the Sudan.

Earle was born in Liverpool in 1833. After he was commissioned in the army, he served during the Crimean War and later in Nova Scotia. Earle served as military secretary to the viceroy of India, the Earl of Northbrook, from 1872 to 1876.

During the British expedition to suppress the Arabi Rebellion in Egypt in 1882, Earle, promoted to major general two years earlier, commanded the line of communication and base. As such, he was responsible for providing all logistical support to the force, a challenging duty in a desert environment. Earle performed his many tasks well, contributing to the expedition's success. He also earned the respect and appreciation of the force commander, General (later Field Marshal Viscount) Sir Garnet J. Wolseley.

In 1884, tentative plans were made to send an expedition to relieve Major General Charles C. Gordon in beleaguered Khartoum. Wolseley was then adjutant-general and made a number of command and personnel recommendations. He was willing to endorse Earle as commander with the rank of lieutenant general, but concerned that Earle—who "has not it in him to influence troops or to inspire them with any enthusiasm" (Preston 1967, p. 7)—had never before held a separate command. In August 1884, Wolseley was selected to command the expedition, and Earle was designated a prospective brigade commander.

Wolseley and much of the force arrived in Cairo in early September 1884 and departed on 27 September on the 1,630-mile advance to Khartoum. Earle conscientiously helped supervise operations on the line of communications.

On 11 December 1884, Wolseley received intelligence while nearing Korti that the Mahdi intended to starve out the Khartoum garrison. Wolseley, in an attempt to hasten the relief, divided his force into two elements. The Desert Column, commanded by Brigadier General (later Major General) Sir Herbert Stewart, was planned to travel overland and reach Metemmeh by 7 January 1885. The River Column, four battalions in boats under Earle's command, was to follow the Nile and reach Shendy, opposite Metemmeh on the Nile, on 1 February 1885. Earle would then establish a supply base.

The River Column, due largely to the cataracts on the Nile, was delayed in its advance. Earle was informed of the fall of Khartoum on 5 February 1885 and told to halt his force. Three days later Earle was told to resume the advance to Abu Hamed. On 10 February, Earle's scouts found dervishes in position at Kirbekan. With two of his four battalions nearby, Earle conducted an encircling attack around the dervish flank. During the battle, Earle was shot in the head and killed by an enemy hiding in a hut. The British won the battle.

See also Arabi Rebellion; Brackenbury, General Sir Henry; Crimean War; Dervishes; Gordon Relief Expedition; Lines of Communication; Mahdi; Stewart, Major General Sir Herbert; Sudan; Wolseley, Field Marshal Garnet J.
References: Barthorp (1984); Brackenbury (1885); Lehmann (1964); Maurice (1887); Preston (1967); Symons (1965)

East India Company

The East India Company, a trade entity that later governed a subcontinent, was formed on 31 January 1600 when

Queen Elizabeth I granted a royal charter to the "Governor and Company of Merchants of London Trading into the East Indies." Spain and Portugal had held the monopoly of the East Indian spice trade, and after the defeat of the Spanish Armada in 1588 and the death of Philip II, king of both Spain and Portugal, in 1598, the English wanted to break this monopoly. The East India Company had been granted its own monopoly, the exclusive right to trade with all the countries beyond the Cape of Good Hope.

The company's first ships arrived in India in 1608. The company defeated the Portuguese in India in 1612 and won trading rights from the Mughal emperor, Jahangir, in 1617. Initially, the company traded cotton, silk, indigo, and saltpeter for spices from South India. While the company extended trading operations within India, it also expanded trade relationships to the Persian Gulf, Southeast Asia, and South Asia. Considerable English communities developed in Calcutta, Bombay, and Madras. In 1634, the company was granted permission to trade through Bengal.

The trade monopoly of the original company was opposed by another company, which led to a consolidation of the two in 1708 as the "United Company of Merchants of England Trading to the East Indies" (the name it held until 1833). The Court of Proprietors, or shareholders, of the United Company annually elected twenty-four directors who worked through various committees to conduct the company's business. Company financial fortunes increased significantly in 1717, when the company was granted an exemption by the Mughal emperor from paying customs duties in Bengal.

In 1757, a military force led by Robert Clive defeated the forces of the Nawab (ruler) of Bengal, Siraj-ud-daulah, at the Battle of Plassey. This was a watershed event in the history of the company, as it then became a governing body, responsible for administering territory it conquered or annexed, in addition to a mercantile concern. This development, plus the company's reputation for plunder with increased military expenditures, forced the British Government to establish control over it. The 1773 Regulating Act raised the governor of Bengal (Warren Hastings) to the position of governor-general. This appointment, while made by the company's Court of Directors, became subject to the Crown's approval. In 1784, the India Act provided for a government-appointed Board of Control in London to supervise all company military, political, and financial activities.

By about 1800, despite new trading opportunities, most of the company's income came from land taxes. At about the same time, a lucrative trade had been established with China exporting tea for the British market while importing Bengali opium. In 1802–1803, opium exports were worth a million rupees, or about £250,000.

The company lost its trading monopoly in 1813, which was then placed under the Board of Control. The company continued its expansion, and Indian states came under company control by being conquered and incorporated into British India or by becoming allies that were ruled indirectly by British residents.

The powerful Maratha Confederacy was defeated in 1822, which established the British as the premier power in India. Sind was conquered in 1843, and the fertile Punjab plains were subjugated in the two Sikh Wars (1845–1846; 1848–1849). The company also adopted the notorious Mughal doctrine of lapse: upon the death of a local ruler who did not produce a male heir, the state became a part of the paramount power, in this case British India.

Increased indifference to the indigenous population, its religion, culture, and caste, coupled with the policy of lapse and harsh revenue policies, set the stage for a clash of cultures. Ignited by the "greased cartridge" controversy, the Indian Mutiny, which was characterized by brutality on both the Indian and British sides, erupted in 1857. Parliament passed the Act for the Better Government of India in 1858, in which the rule of India was passed from the company to the British Government effective 1 November 1858. The governor-general took on the additional title of viceroy and became answerable to the secretary of state for India, who was a member of the British Cabinet. The company was finally dissolved as a legal entity in 1874.

See also East India Company, Military Forces; India; India, British Army in; Indian Army Operations; Indian Army Organization; Indian Mutiny; Sikh War, First, (1845–1846); Sikh War, Second (1848–1849); Sind, Operations in

References: Farwell (1989); Gardner (1971); Haythornthwaite (1995); Heathcote (1974); James (1998); Mason (1974); Minney (1931)

East India Company, Military Forces

The East India Company was established by royal charter on 31 January 1600. King Charles II later gave the company almost sovereign powers when he granted it the authority to "coin money, command forts, raise an army, form alliances, make war and peace, and exercise criminal and civil jurisdictions" (Farwell 1989, p. 16).

The company, after first landing in India in 1608, raised its own army. In 1662, it formed armed groups of men to serve as factory (trading installation and warehouse) guards in Bombay and Madras, and six years later, Indian soldiers were first recruited into the company's forces. These served as the forerunner of the company's military forces. By 1708, the three presidencies of Bengal, Bombay, and Madras had been formed, and each had established its own military forces. The Bengal Presidency was the largest of the three, and its army commander in chief was also designated commander in chief, India, although in reality he exercised little control over the Bombay and Madras armies.

The company forces consisted of infantry, cavalry, artillery, and support units. Infantry battalions consisted of Europeans (mainly Irish) only, who were considered more reliable and disciplined than Indians. After battalions were filled with Europeans, additional battalions were still needed, and as the only manpower source was native Indians, there were many all-native battalions. The Bombay European Regiment was formed from independent companies in 1662, and European battalions in the Madras and Bengal Armies date from 1748 and 1756, respectively, from which time the company army can be said to have come into existence. Native battalions and regiments were also formed. The organization, equipment, and tactics of all East India company units were patterned after those of the British Army. Infantry battalions generally consisted of ten companies.

Company forces were reorganized in 1796, at which time they consisted of about 18,000 European and 84,000 Indian soldiers. The size of the company army expanded with the increase in company territory, and this also increased the demand for British officers. The company established its own military college for the training and commissioning of its officers in 1809 at Addiscombe Place near Croydon, Surrey.

The company's military forces experienced a high point probably between the beginning of the First Maratha War in 1775 and the initiation of the First Afghan War in 1839. During this period there were, however, in addition to military defeats, ominous rumblings of sepoy discontent. Perceptions of problems were frequently magnified when officers did not know their Indian soldiers well, and the sepoys did not have confidence and trust in their leaders. At Vellore, in 1806, sepoys became agitated because of a new order to replace turbans with hats (a sign of Christianity) and other uniform changes. The Madras infantry units there mutinied on 10 July 1806, killing 14 British officers and 114 other ranks of the British 69th Foot before their insurrection was brutally suppressed the following morning. Another uprising took place at Barrackpore in 1824, when Bengal Army troops in a recently reorganized battalion refused to deploy because of religious concerns about traveling by sea to Burma and monetary problems. British Army artillery opened fire on the mutineers and shattered their resistance. These mutinies began to establish a pattern, culminating in the Indian Mutiny (1857–1859).

The basic numbering sequence for the infantry battalions, cavalry regiments, and smaller units of the three presidency armies was established in 1824. In 1824, the Bengal Army consisted of two European infantry battalions, sixty-eight Indian infantry battalions, eight regiments of light cavalry, five regiments of irregular cavalry, three horse artillery brigades of four troops each, five battalions of artillery of four companies each, and one corps of sappers and miners. The Bombay Army contained two European infantry battalions, twenty-four native infantry battalions, three light cavalry and two irregular horse regiments, four horse artillery troops and eight foot artillery companies, and one corps of engineers and pioneers. There were two European infantry battalions, fifty-two sepoy infantry battalions, three light cavalry regiments, two horse artillery brigades (one European and one Indian), three battalions of foot artillery of four companies each, and two pioneer corps in the Madras Army. By 1830, the strength of the company military forces was about 37,000 Europeans and 223,000 Indians.

During the bloody Indian Mutiny, sixty-four Bengal regiments mutinied or were preemptively disarmed, while only two Bombay Army units, and none in the Madras Army, were disaffected. As a result, in accordance with the Act for the Better Government of India and effective 1 November 1858, the rule of India was passed from the company to the British Crown. The Crown took over direct control of the company's military forces. Mutineer regiments were disbanded, and others were renumbered as new units in the Indian Army.

All of the company's British officers accepted the Queen's commission, although this resulted in an excessive number of officers in the Indian Army. The European soldiers in the company's European regiments were told they would be transferred directly to British Army regiments. These soldiers were upset and demanded either a discharge or the same bounty given to new recruits. There were numerous acts of intransigence and insubordination, and the 5th Bengal European Infantry Regiment actually mutinied and was disarmed and disbanded. Of the company's 16,000 European soldiers (mostly Irish), 10,116 were discharged and shipped back to England. Of that number, 2,809 enlisted in the British Army—and many were sent back to India to serve with their British Army regiments. In 1861, the 12 European regiments of the company were absorbed directly into the British Army. The Royal Artillery absorbed 21 troops of horse artillery and 48 batteries of foot artillery from the Bengal, Bombay, and Madras Armies.

See also Addiscombe, Military Seminary; Bengal Army; Bombay Army; East India Company; India; India, British Army in; Indian Army Operations; Indian Army Organization; Indian Mutiny; Madras Army

References: Beaumont (1977); Farwell (1989); Haythornthwaite (1995); Heathcote (1974); Hervey (1988); Mason (1974); Roberts (1995)

Egypt

Egypt, linking Africa with Asia, became increasingly important to Britain, especially after the Suez Canal was built in 1869 and significantly shortened the sea route to India. Great Britain occupied Egypt in 1882 after suppressing the Arabi Rebellion and continued to do so through the end of this period.

Egypt was an Ottoman province at the beginning of this period. The commander of Ottoman forces was Mohammed Ali, who defeated the Mamelukes and consolidated his position in Upper Egypt. One of his goals was for Egypt to be independent of the Ottomans, and in 1831 he invaded Syria. As his forces neared Constantinople, Western powers, including Britain, anxious to maintain the status quo and preserve business interests, allied themselves with the Ottomans to drive out Mohammed Ali's forces. A British fleet bombarded Egyptian forces in Beirut in September 1840, with an Anglo-Turkish force landing and instigating an uprising in the Egyptian Army. Mohammed Ali was forced to return to Egypt, relinquish control of his conquered territories, and abandon trade monopolies. He was granted hereditary governorship of Egypt.

After Mohammed Ali died in 1849, a number of his successors were traditionalists and weak leaders. Ismail became

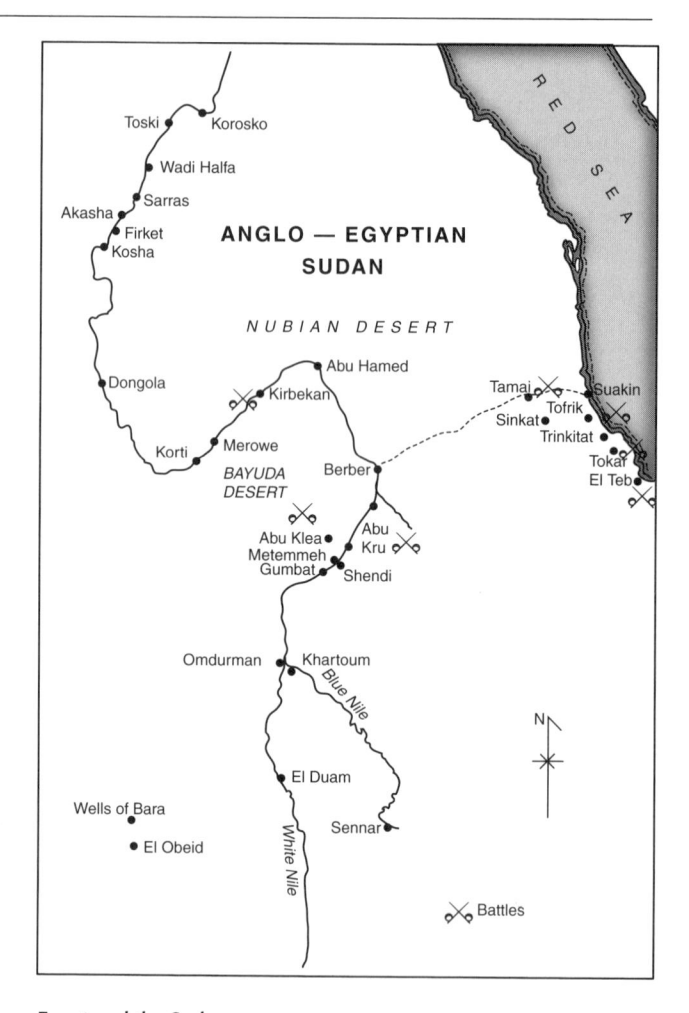

Egypt and the Sudan

khedive in 1863, and the French-built Suez Canal was opened in 1869. By 1875, Ismail's spending was causing serious financial difficulties, and to pay his creditors, he was forced to sell his shares in the Suez Canal Company. For £4 million, the British acquired a controlling interest in the Suez Canal. The British and French imposed a system of dual control over Egyptian finances and other Egyptian ministries, and were able to persuade the Ottoman sultan in 1879 to depose the obstructionist Ismail in favor of his more pliable son, Tewfik.

A number of factors—the steady loss of Egyptian sovereignty, heavy taxation, religious fundamentalism, and ethnic friction within the military—caused the 1882 Arabi Rebellion, led by Egyptian Army Colonel Ahmed Arabi Pasha. The British sent an expeditionary force, under the command of General (later Field Marshal Viscount) Sir Garnet J. Wolseley that suppressed the rebellion in September 1882. As a result, the British occupied Egypt, including its southern province, the Sudan (which it had controlled since 1821). Egypt became a part of the British Empire but was never officially a colony.

Great Britain occupied and administered Egypt until February 28, 1922, when it unilaterally declared Egyptian independence. Britain, however, retained responsibility for Egyptian defense, communications security, the protection of foreign interests, and the Sudan. In 1936, the Anglo-Egyptian Treaty was signed, allowing Britain to maintain a 10,000-man garrison in the Suez Canal Zone, and continuing its administration of the Sudan. The final evacuation of British troops from Egypt took place in 1956.

See also Arabi Pasha, Ahmed; Arabi Rebellion; Egyptian Army; Sudan; Suez Canal; Wolseley, Field Marshal Garnet J.
References: Chaille Long (1899); Ludwig (1937); Mansfield (1971); Metz (1991)

Egyptian Army

The fortunes of the Egyptian Army fluctuated considerably during this period, mainly because the country was subject to foreign domination.

The Egyptian Army, under Mohammed Ali until the mid-nineteenth century, fought campaigns on behalf of the Ottoman sultan in the Arabian Peninsula, Sudan, and Greece. When attempting to gain independence from the Ottomans, Mohammed Ali's army, reportedly numbering 250,000 soldiers, invaded Syria in 1831 and marched close to Constantinople before being pressured to withdraw by Western powers.

After 1850, Egypt's military strength declined. Ismail, who became khedive in 1863, sought assistance of American military officers to train and modernize the Egyptian Army. Between 1868 and 1883, over fifty Americans, many former U.S. Army or Confederate officers during the Civil War (1861–1865), served in the Egyptian Army. Many served in senior positions, such as Lieutenant General Charles P. Stone, who served as chief of the general staff of the Egyptian Army from 1870 to 1883. Others served as inspectors-general of cavalry and coastal defense, and some explored unknown regions. Stone tried to improve Egyptian efficiency by establishing a general staff and battalion training schools. Egypt's failure in its 1875–1876 campaign against Abyssinia and its indebtedness forced the departure of nine of the ten remaining Americans in 1878, as well as an 80 percent reduction of the Egyptian Army.

The downsizing of the Egyptian Army and the large number of officers and soldiers who were thrown out of work factored into the Arabi Rebellion in 1882. The remnants of the Egyptian Army were shattered by the British at the Battle of Tel el-Kebir (13 September 1882).

The British then occupied Egypt and raised and trained an entirely new Egyptian Army, under the overall command of Major General (later Field Marshal) Sir (Henry) Evelyn M. Wood, V.C., the first sirdar, in 1883. Wood selected 26 British officers, many of whom later achieved high rank, to assist him. These British officers frequently held ranks two higher than their British Army ranks.

The new Egyptian Army raised formally in 1883 consisted of 6,000 men who served four years in the army, four in the police, then four in the reserves. They were organized into eight battalions, with four battalions in each of the two brigades.

The Egyptian Army, by the end of 1885, consisted of 9 infantry battalions (totaling 25 British officers, 181 indigenous officers, and 4,646 men), 8 cavalry troops (1 British and 27 indigenous officers, 540 men), 4 artillery batteries (1 British and 18 indigenous officers, 403 men), and 3 Camel Corps companies (2 British and 7 indigenous officers, 203 men). The infantry and Camel Corps soldiers were armed with the Martini-Henry rifle and triangular socket bayonet, and the cavalry was armed with the Martini-Henry carbine and swords. The artillery consisted mainly of 7-pounder mountain guns.

The Egyptian Army grew as circumstances dictated. When the reconquest of the Sudan began in 1896, the Egyptian Army totaled 18,000 men and included Sudanese battalions. It ultimately comprised 18 infantry battalions.

The new Egyptian Army had its first real test of battle late in 1885, at Kosheh and Ginnis. At that time, one Egyptian or Sudanese infantry battalion, one Camel Corps company, and one field battery were attached to each British brigade. The British were very surprised by the proficiency and discipline of their Egyptian Army counterparts, especially the Sudanese.

The Egyptian Army bore the brunt of battle and campaigning during the 1896–1898 reconquest of the Sudan. In fact, of the 25,000 "British" soldiers at the Battle of Omdurman (2 September 1898), over 17,000 were Egyptians and Sudanese.

See also Arabi Pasha, Ahmed; Arabi Rebellion; Egypt; Ginnis, Battle of; Omdurman, Battle of; Reconquest of the Sudan; Sirdar; Sudan; Suez Canal; Tel el-Kebir, Battle of; Wood, Field Marshal Sir (Henry) Evelyn M., V.C.
References: Butzgy (1999); Johnson (1972); Ludwig (1937); Mansfield (1971); Metz (1991); Warner (1986)

El Teb, Battle of (4 February 1884)

Great Britain occupied Egypt and became responsible for its security in 1882 after defeating the Arabi Rebellion. The British also reorganized and provided leadership for the Egyptian Army. As the situation in Egypt-controlled Sudan became more chaotic with the rise of the Mahdi in 1881, the British realized they would have to eliminate this threat in their southern territory. A poorly trained and inadequately equipped Egyptian force under the command of Major General William Hicks Pasha was sent to defeat dervishes south of Khartoum. This force was annihilated by dervishes at Kashgil on 3–5 November 1883.

In late 1883, dervishes under the command of Osman Digna attacked Egyptian garrisons at Sinkat and Tokar and besieged Suakin, a key port on the Red Sea. A relief force, consisting of 1,000 men of the Egyptian Gendarmarie, 1,500 assorted black troops, and 450 Egyptian and Turkish cavalrymen, with two guns, under the command of Lieutenant General Valentine Baker Pasha, was sent to Suakin in mid-December 1883. Baker, who had been disgraced and discharged from the British Army in 1876, possibly desiring to restore his martial reputation, had his motley force transshipped to Trinkitat to conduct offensive operations.

Early on 4 February 1884, Baker Pasha's force, which included Lieutenant Colonel Frederick G. Burnaby, began its desert march to Tokar. The force was formed into a large square, with the cavalry screening the advance. As the force neared the village of El Teb, Baker, who was riding in front of the square with his staff, observed to his rear a few Arabs on horses and camels threatening the square's flanks. It seems that Baker ordered one cavalry troop to investigate the situation, but the entire cavalry force galloped out to flee the area.

Before Baker could enter the square, his soldiers began to panic and shot wildly at the charging dervish cavalry that was followed by thousands of armed dervish foot soldiers. The square disintegrated as the horrified Egyptians tried to run away from the dervish onslaught. "The sight," wrote Burnaby, "was one never to be forgotten, with some four thousand men running pell-mell for their lives, with a few hundred Arabs behind them, spearing everyone within reach" (Baker 1996, p. 140). By early afternoon, less than 500 men from Baker's force had escaped the massacre at El Teb and returned the 5 miles to Trinkitat.

The British response to this severe reverse was to send a force of two infantry brigades, a cavalry regiment, and other units under the command of Major General (later Lieutenant General) Sir Gerald Graham, V.C., from Egypt to Suakin. Graham's force fought a ferocious battle and defeated the dervishes at El Teb on 29 February 1884. British casualties were 35 killed and 155 wounded, with dervish losses estimated at over 2,000 killed in this second battle.

See also Baker Pasha, Lieutenant General Valentine; Burnaby, Lieutenant Colonel Frederick G.; Dervishes; Egypt; Egyptian Army; Graham, Lieutenant General Sir Gerald, V.C.; Hicks Pasha, Major General William; Kashgil, Battle of; Mahdi; Sudan
References: Alexander (1957); Baker (1996); Barthorp (1984); Keown-Boyd (1986); Neillands (1996)

Electric Telegraph
See Communications; Correspondents, War

Elphinstone, Major General William G. K.
See Afghan War, First (1839–1842)

Enfield Rifle
See Infantry, British Army—Small Arms

Engineers, British Army—Employment

The Royal Engineers were the primary support branch for the combat arms—infantry, cavalry, and artillery—and played an increasingly significant role throughout the Victorian era. Royal Engineer officers were also recognized for their professionalism and proficiency, and a number of them commanded military forces and expeditions.

Royal Engineers were responsible for the design and construction of fortifications and for developing methods to attack and defend them. During the first half of the nineteenth century, the challenge was to give military fortifications more positive features than simply to delay the enemy. Controversies included the type of fortifications to be built (angular or round) and how best to incorporate artillery into the defense. Tangential to this mission was the planning and construction of coastal and harbor defenses, fieldworks, entrenchments, and gun positions, as conducted during the Crimean War (1854–1856).

The Royal Engineers were also responsible for more mundane, but essential, tasks, including the construction and maintenance of barracks and all War Office buildings. Royal Engineer companies were also formed to conduct the ordnance surveys of Ireland and other areas and prepared topographic maps.

In 1846, the Royal Engineers conducted experiments to ascertain various aspects of the performance of the Brown Bess musket. The Royal Engineer report after these trials recommended that the British Army acquire more marksmanship firing ranges and instruct soldiers in judging distances and basic weapons marksmanship.

Many of the British Army's colonial wars were considered "engineer wars," as they were conducted in hostile environments where roads, bridges, and railways needed to be constructed and communications established between forces. Examples include the Second Ashanti War (1873–1874), the Gordon Relief Expedition (1884–1885), and the Second Boer War (1899–1902).

Royal Engineers were normally organized and employed in companies, with one field company usually supporting an infantry division and one mounted detachment supporting a cavalry division. Other engineer units provided general support to a force as a whole. As technology improved, specialized engineer units were formed to provide specific functions and support, such as the signal wing and the telegraph battalion of the Royal Engineers. Other specialized Royal Engineer units included railway, railway pioneer, bridging, survey, and balloon troops and sections.

See also Ashanti War, Second (1873–1874); Balloons; Boer War, Second (1899–1902); Coastal Fortifications; Communications; Engineers, British Army—Organization; Engineers, British Army—Training; Engineers, British Army—Weapons and Equipment; Gordon Relief Expedition; Home Defense; Maps; Railways

References: Grierson (1899); Haythornthwaite (1995); Spiers (1992); Strachan (1985)

Engineers, British Army—Organization

The Corps of Engineers and the Royal Regiment of Artillery were made separate entities in 1716. The Corps of Engineers was granted the title "Royal" in 1787, and its officers were called Royal Engineers. Soldier artificers were formed into the Corps of Royal Military Artificers in the same year, which was redesignated the Corps of Royal Sappers and Miners in 1812. In 1855, the Ordnance Department was abolished as a separate, independent establishment, and in 1856, the master-general of the ordnance's command of the Royal Engineers and the Royal Artillery was transferred to the commander in chief. The other ranks of the Corps of Royal Sappers and Miners were absorbed into the Corps of Royal Engineers.

The inspector-general of fortifications (a lieutenant general) served in the War Office and later on the War Office Council and the Army Board as the head of the Corps of Royal Engineers. In every military district, the senior Royal Engineer officer served as Commanding Royal Engineer (C.R.E.), with subordinate engineers supervising work in subdistricts of engineers.

The Royal Engineers consisted of the following subunits in 1899: one bridging battalion, one telegraph battalion, one mounted detachment field depot, two field parks with a training depot, one balloon section, eight field companies, eighteen fortress companies, two railway companies, twelve submarine mining companies, one coast battalion, four survey companies, and eight depot companies. The various units consisted of specialists and performed specific missions and tasks.

In war, one field company was attached to each infantry division for support, and one mounted detachment was attached to each cavalry division. If the organization included a corps, engineer units attached to it included one field company, one pontoon company, a staff and four sections of the telegraph battalion, a field park, a railway company, and a balloon section.

The Royal Engineer field company in war (as of 1899) consisted of 6 officers, 1 sergeant major, 1 quartermaster sergeant, 6 sergeants, 1 artisan, 2 trumpeters and buglers, 7 corporals, 7 second corporals, 12 acting corporals, 137 sappers and batmen, and 31 drivers and wagon men, for a total of 6 officers, 8 sergeants, and 197 men. The strength of the Royal Engineer mounted detachment was 4 officers, 1 sergeant major, 1 quartermaster sergeant, 5 sergeants, 2 artisans, 3 trumpeters and buglers, 4 corporals, 4 second corporals, 5 acting corporals, 74 sappers and batmen, and 24 drivers and wagon men, for a total of 4 officers, 7 sergeants, and 116 soldiers.

In 1861, the British Army totaled 221,604 officers and

men, 2 percent being Royal Engineers. In 1899, 3.6 percent of the army's 224,609 officers and men were Royal Engineers. There were 905 Royal Engineer officers in 1899, of whom 385 served in India. On 1 October 1899, there were 694 Royal Engineer officers and men serving in South Africa. The demands of the Second Boer War (1899–1902) required the service of over 7,000 engineer officers and men, supplemented by about 1,500 engineers from the militia and volunteers.

See also Boer War, Second (1899–1902); Commander in Chief, British Army; Engineers, British Army—Employment; Engineers, British Army—Training; Engineers, British Army—Weapons and Equipment; Master-General of the Ordnance, British Army; War Office
References: Grierson (1899); Hallows (1991); Skelley (1977); Sweetman (1984)

Engineers, British Army–Training

Royal Engineer training was conducted on an individual basis (for new recruits and officers) and collectively, for units. After 1830, annual training in siege operations was conducted at Chatham, the School of Military Engineering. Chatham also had training sites and provided training in pontooning, field fortifications, mining, and maneuvers.

New recruits in the Royal Engineers (except for drivers) were also required to be proficient in a trade. They were trained at the depot at Chatham (except for drivers, who were trained at Aldershot), where they underwent a year-long program of instruction in pioneer duties and infantry drill. During the summer, each depot company trained in a tent camp at Wouldham, near Chatham, where recruits were taught various camp duties, pioneering, and other skills. Engineer recruits also received considerable training in basic rifle marksmanship. Those new recruits, who enlisted to be telegraphers, photographers, lithographers, or cartographers, underwent an abbreviated pioneering course. The new recruit was required to pass an examination at the end of his depot training period before being assigned to a regular engineer unit.

Most British Army Royal Engineer officers received their precommissioning education and training at the Royal Military Academy, Woolwich. In the 1870s, a cadet at Woolwich studied mathematics, French, German, artillery, fortification, military surveying, landscape drawing, chemistry, military history, riding, gymnastics, and drill. After Woolwich graduation, Royal Engineer officers attended a two-year course at Chatham.

Every engineer company was required to conduct pioneer training for thirty days each summer. Railway companies were required to conduct only fifteen days' pioneering training each year.

See also Engineers, British Army—Employment; Engineers, British Army—Organization; Engineers, British Army—Weapons and Equipment; Railways; Woolwich, Royal Military Academy
References: Farwell (1981); Grierson (1899); Spiers (1992); Strachan (1984); Strachan (1985)

Engineers, British Army–Weapons and Equipment

The most common and versatile Royal Engineer units were the field company, which was attached to and supported each infantry division in war, and the mounted detachment, which was attached to each cavalry division in war. Each unit was equipped to permit maximum completion of its assigned engineer tasks.

The engineer field company included a support element (train) of four two-horsed entrenching tool carts, one one-horse cart for medical equipment, one field blacksmith, and two four-horsed pontoon wagons. There were also two carts for stores and baggage and one cart for provisions, each drawn by two horses. Five packhorses and carts were used to carry the following entrenching tools and related equipment: 111 shovels, 71 pickaxes, 9 spades, 39 large and 26 small axes, 43 bill hooks, 20 saws, 420 pounds of gun cotton, 1,000 sandbags, and 10 crowbars. The field company had the capability to construct, with the equipment and material it carried, one 75-foot light bridge for infantry or one 45-foot bridge that could be used by all arms.

The engineer mounted detachment, which was smaller, was more mobile than its infantry-support counterpart. It contained six two-horsed carts for baggage, provisions, and forage, and six four-horsed carts carrying entrenching tools and technical equipment. The latter six carts, plus six packhorses, carried 12 shovels, 18 pickaxes, 30 spades, 18 large and 6 small axes, 24 bill hooks, 15 saws, 436 pounds of gun cotton, 600 sandbags, and 6 crowbars.

The equipment of the dismounted engineers of the other ranks was similar to that of the infantry, and they were armed with infantry rifles and bayonets. The equipment of the mounted engineers of the other ranks was similar to that of the mounted field artillerymen. The mounted noncommissioned officers and trumpeters were armed with sabers and revolvers, the drivers with revolvers, and the mounted engineers with carbines and sword bayonets.

See also Engineers, British Army—Employment; Engineers, British Army—Organization; Engineers, British Army—Training; Infantry, British Army—Small Arms; Rank and File, British Army—Uniforms and Equipment
References: Grierson (1899); Haythornthwaite (1995)

Esher, Reginald B. B., Second Viscount (1852–1930)

Reginald B. B. Esher, Second Viscount, was a British public servant and historian best known for his post–Second Boer War efforts to reform the British Army.

Esher was born on 30 June 1852 and was educated at Eton College and Cambridge University. He served as a Liberal Member of Parliament from 1880 to 1885 and then withdrew from active politics, preferring to work behind the scenes to accomplish various goals. Esher refused editorship of a number of newspapers and declined government appointments, including undersecretary for the colonies (1899), undersecretary for war (1900), and governor of Cape Colony (1900).

Esher succeeded to the peerage in 1899 and became lieutenant and deputy-governor of Windsor Castle and keeper of the King's Archives in 1901. He established and nurtured a close relationship with the royal family, edited Queen Victoria's correspondence, and wrote a biography of King Edward VII.

In 1902, the Royal Commission on the War in South Africa, named the Elgin Commission after its chairman, the Earl of Elgin, was appointed to investigate administrative shortcomings that had been revealed by the Second Boer War. The Elgin Commission's primary recommendation was to modify the consultative machinery of the government.

Esher was a member of the Elgin Commission. He was offered the post of secretary of state for war in 1903 but did not accept it. He wanted more military reform conducted than the Elgin Commission recommended. As a confidant of King Edward VII, Esher was able to get himself appointed to chair a new committee, the War Office Reconstitution Committee (Esher Committee). The report of the Esher Committee, made in 1904, had a far-reaching impact on War Office and military reorganization. The Esher Committee found that there had been virtually no changes in War Office organization since the post–Crimean War reforms. The three key recommendations of the Esher Committee's report, which were all enacted, were the establishment of an Army Council on the model of the Board of Admiralty, the establishment of a general staff, and the division of departmental responsibilities in the War Office on more logical and defined principles.

Esher became governor of Windsor Castle in 1928 and died on 22 January 1930. The Esher reforms, combined with the extensive military reforms made under Richard B. Haldane, secretary of state for war from 1905 to 1912, helped prepare the British Army for service in World War I.

See also Boer War, Second (1899–1902); Civil-Military Relations; Commander in Chief, British Army; Esher Committee; Haldane, Richard B.; War Office
References: Barnett (1970); Bond (1972); Carver (1984); Esher (1938); Hamer (1970); Stone and Schmidl (1988); Wheeler (1914)

Esher Committee (1904)

The Second Boer War ended when the defeated Boers signed the Treaty of Vereeniging on 31 May 1902. Even before the British "victory," it had become obvious that the British Army could have been better prepared for the conflict. The British engaged in somber introspection as to why shortcomings in tactics, administration, logistics, organization, and leadership had prolonged the conflict.

A Royal Commission on the War in South Africa, appointed in 1902 and named the Elgin Commission after its chairman, the Earl of Elgin, investigated administrative shortcomings that had been revealed by the Second Boer War. This commission scrutinized the areas of planning, the reserve and manpower system, stores and supplies, and War Office organization. The primary recommendation of the Elgin Commission was to modify the consultative machinery of the government.

Lord Esher was a member of the Elgin Commission, although he dissented from its findings and opinion because he wanted more substantive reform enacted. As a confidant of King Edward VII and a political manipulator, Esher was able to get himself appointed to chair a new committee, the War Office Reconstitution Committee (Esher Committee). The report of the Esher Committee, made in 1904, had a far-reaching impact on War Office and military reorganization. The Esher Committee found that there had been virtually no changes in War Office organization since the post–Crimean War reforms. The three key recommendations of the Esher Report were the establishment of an Army Council on the model of the Board of Admiralty, the establishment of a general staff, and the division of departmental responsibilities in the War Office on more logical and defined principles.

The Army Council was to consist of seven members: the secretary of state for war, the first military member (operations and military policy), the second military member (recruitment and discipline), the third military member (supply and transport), the fourth military member (armaments and fortifications), a civil member (the parliamentary undersecretary for civil business other than finance), and another civil member (the financial secretary). The council was to meet frequently, and its decisions were to be collective.

The position of commander in chief was to be abolished and replaced by the chief of the general staff (C.G.S.). The War Office administration would be divided between the C.G.S., the adjutant-general, the quartermaster-general, and the master-general of the ordnance. The duties of the general staff were divided between the director of military operations (D.M.O.), director of staff duties (D.S.D.), and director of military training (D.M.T.). These changes helped delineate duties and responsibilities, and ensured the fundamental separation of training and administration.

Other contentious issues pertained to financial decentralization, the appointment of an inspector-general, and the reorganization of the army on a dual-service basis. There was considerable friction over some issues between the politicians and the soldiers. Nonetheless, as a direct result of the Esher Committee, the Army Council was created, and the office of commander in chief, the old War Office Council, and the Army Board were abolished, by Letters Patent issued on 6 February 1904. The United Kingdom was divided into seven districts and the commanding general of each was authorized an operations and an administrative staff. Each member of the Army Council was assigned an administrative director to handle more routine matters. An inspector-general of the forces was nominated. A Treasury Minute of 4 May 1904 formally reconstituted the Committee of Imperial Defense with a permanent secretariat. The general staff came into "recognizable existence" in October 1906.

"In its celerity, boldness and comprehensiveness," observed one prominent British military historian, "the work of the War Office (Reconstitution) Committee has no parallel in British military reform and few in any other branch of administration" (Bond 1972, p. 214).

See also Adjutant-General, British Army; Boer War, Second (1899–1902); Commander in Chief, British Army; Esher, Reginald B. B.; Horse Guards; Master-General of the Ordnance, British Army; Quartermaster-General, British Army; War Office

References: Barnett (1970); Bond (1972); Carver (1984); Hamer (1970); Stone and Schmidl (1988)

Eshowe, Siege of
See Zulu War

Eupatoria, Battle of (17 February 1855)

The most significant action of the Crimean War in the early months of 1855, in addition to the ongoing siege of Sevastopol, was the Russian attack on Turkish forces at Eupatoria on 17 February 1855.

Eupatoria, the town on Calamita Bay about 35 miles north of Sevastopol, was the primary disembarkation point for allied soldiers arriving in the Crimea from Varna. Many soldiers of the Turkish Army, under the command of Omar Pasha, were transported from the Danubian Principalities over the winter of 1854–1855. By mid-February 1855, about 35,000 Turkish troops were assembled at Eupatoria.

The Russians were concerned with this concentration of Turkish troops and feared an interdiction of their supply lines to Sevastopol. The Russian commander, Prince Alexander Sergeevich Menshikov, was prodded to attack the Turks after he received reinforcements. A 19,000-man Russian force, including 500 Cossacks and 108 guns, commanded by Lieutenant General Stephan A. Khrulev, assaulted Eupatoria early on 17 February 1855 after an artillery bombardment.

The defenders, including Turks, French, Tartars, and some marine artillery, received effective artillery support from offshore allied steamers. They repulsed the halfhearted Russian attack, which broke off after three hours when the Russians retreated. The Russians reportedly lost 769 soldiers in this ill-fated attack, while the defenders lost 401 soldiers, 364 of whom were Turks.

This Russian failure supposedly caused the czar "intense mortification and disappointment" (Warner 1972, p. 121).

Menshikov was relieved of command and replaced by Prince Michael Gorchakov.

See also Crimean War; Russian Forces, Crimean War; Sevastopol, Siege of; Turkish Forces, Crimean War
References: Baumgart (1999); Palmer (1987); Royle (2000); Warner (1972)

Evans, General Sir George de Lacy (1787–1870)

General Sir George de Lacy Evans was a soldier of distinction, although frequently vain and tactless, who saw considerable action during the Napoleonic Wars and the War of 1812. He later commanded the Spanish Legion during the Carlist War and served as an able division commander during the initial stages of the Crimean War. He spent most of his military career on half-pay and served in Parliament as a military reformer for almost three decades.

Evans was born in Ireland on 7 October 1787. He attended the Royal Military Academy, Woolwich, joined the army in India in 1806, and was appointed an ensign the next year. In 1812, he exchanged into the 3rd Dragoons in order to see active service in the Peninsular War, where he remained until 1814. He then served in the United States, but returned to Europe in time to participate in the Battle of Waterloo.

Evans went on half pay in 1818 and was elected to Parliament in 1830. He was not reelected in 1832 but won in another constituency in 1833 and, except for 1841–1846, continued to represent it until 1865. In Parliament, Evans was considered a "radical," advocating military reform, including the abolition of the purchase of officers' commissions and shorter enlistments for soldiers.

In 1835, Evans accepted the offer to raise in England and command, with the local rank of lieutenant general in the Spanish Army, a 10,000-man force to fight in Spain against the Carlists. Called the Auxiliary Legion, this largely inexperienced, ill-equipped force saw little action. Evans returned to England in time for the 1837 general election.

Promoted to major general by virtue of seniority in 1846, Evans was appointed a brigade commander for the large-scale training exercises held near Chobham in the summer of 1853. Largely the result of this experience and the exposure he gained, sixty-six-year-old Evans was appointed commander of the 2nd Division in the expeditionary force that deployed to the Crimea. At the Battle of the Alma (20 September 1854) Evans ensured his division maintained the momentum of the frontal assault and showed an appreciation of the effect of concentrated artillery fire. He was also wounded in the shoulder.

Thereafter Evans, enfeebled by old age and suffering from diabetes, rarely left his tent. On 26 October 1854, at an action known as "little Inkerman," Evans inspired and concentrated his troops, and launched a devastating counterattack against the Russians. He never commanded troops again, since he fell off his horse, which partly rolled over him, on 30 October.

When the Battle of Inkerman began on 5 November 1854, Evans got out of bed and rode to the battle. He realized he was unfit to command his division and permitted one of his brigade commanders to command the unit while he served as a source of inspiration to his soldiers. As his health further deteriorated, Evans was invalided from the Crimea a few weeks later. He continued to serve in Parliament but not on active duty and was promoted to general in 1861. Evans died on 9 January 1870.

See also Alma, Battle of the; Crimean War; Inkerman, Battle of; Maneuvers, British Army; Purchase System; Woolwich, Royal Military Academy
References: Judd (1975); Pemberton (1962); Raugh (1987a); Spiers (1983)

Fashoda Incident (1898)

The "scramble for Africa" and British and French imperial rivalry culminated in a confrontation between military forces in a desolate swamp at Fashoda, about 500 miles south of Khartoum on the Upper Nile River. This episode, involving national prestige and colonial encroachment, brought Britain and France to the brink of war.

Fashoda was a significant location because both the British and the French believed that whoever occupied the area could build a dam there that would control the Nile River waters and thus hold the key to controlling Egypt. The French also wanted to control Fashoda to unite their colonies from the Atlantic Ocean to the Red Sea and to drive a wedge between the British colonies of Egypt and Uganda. To accomplish their goal, the French sent three expeditions from various locations to converge from east and west at Fashoda.

The column of Captain Jean-Baptiste Marchand, consisting of seven French officers and about 120 Senegalese soldiers and boatmen, had struggled for over 4,000 miles through all types of terrain during a two-year journey before arriving at Fashoda on 10 July 1898. Marchand raised the French flag over the old fort at Fashoda and claimed the region for the French.

A large Anglo-Egyptian force under the command of Major General (later Field Marshal Earl) Sir Horatio H. Kitchener had been advancing from the Egyptian frontier southward up the Nile since 1896. The British campaign basically ended with the decisive defeat of the dervishes at the Battle of Omdurman (2 September 1898). Kitchener received instructions from Britain to immediately sail to Fashoda. He departed Omdurman on 10 September 1898, taking with him in five gunboats a 1,500-man force consisting of E Company, 1st Battalion, Queen's Own Cameron Highlanders; the 11th and 13th Sudanese infantry battalions; one battery of Egyptian artillery; and one section of four Maxim guns.

Kitchener arrived at Fashoda on 18 September 1898. The British greatly outnumbered the French and the situation was tense. Kitchener and Marchand met on a British gunboat at about 10:00 A.M. After a frosty introduction, both agreed that the ultimate decisions pertaining to the Fashoda situation would be made in London and Paris. Kitchener protested that the French presence at Fashoda violated Egyptian and British rights. Marchand replied that he could receive his orders only from Paris and was willing to fight to the death if necessary. Kitchener advised Marchand that he would not force him to lower the French flag or retire from Fashoda. In return, Marchand stated he would not object to Kitchener, the sirdar of the Egyptian Army, raising the Egyptian flag—but not the British flag—on the tree next to the fort.

The two senior officers celebrated after reaching this compromise. From another British gunboat, it was observed that "the two great men were slapping each other on the back, swapping anecdotes about beating the Dervishes and clinking glasses of whisky and soda" (Pakenham 1991, p. 548). In the afternoon, the French repaid Kitchener's hospitality with sweet champagne. Kitchener left the 11th Sudanese Battalion at Fashoda, then steamed the same day about 50 miles to the south where the Sobat River joined the White Nile. Kitchener posted another detachment there to observe any French activities. The following day Kitchener and his force sailed back past Fashoda, without stopping, to Omdurman.

Kitchener's and Marchand's adroit diplomacy had retrieved a potentially volatile situation. The French, embroiled at home in the Dreyfus Affair, attempted to negotiate with the British, but they realized they were in an untenable situation. Marchand was ordered to evacuate Fashoda and marched out of the fort there on 11 December 1898.

The Fashoda Incident was a moral victory for the British and a humiliating defeat for the French. While this colonial confrontation almost led to war, the resentment and anger soon faded. France yielded its claim to the Upper Nile region in March 1899 and was given part of the Sahara area as compensation. More importantly, this clash paved the way for Great Britain and France to become allies in the 1904 Entente Cordiale.

See also Dervishes; Egyptian Army; Imperialism; Kitchener, Field Marshal Horatio H.; Omdurman, Battle of; Reconquest of the Sudan; Sirdar; Sudan; Wingate, General Sir (Francis) Reginald

References: Baynes (1995); Daly (1997); Magnus (1959); Murray (1997); Pakenham (1991); Pollock (2001); Searight (1998)

Fenton, Roger
See Photographers, War

Ferozeshah, Battle of (21–22 December 1845)

The Sikh Khalsa crossed the Sutlej River on 11 December 1845 and the British declared war against them two days later, thus beginning the First Sikh War. After fighting the Sikhs at Mudki on 18 December, the British force, commanded by Lieutenant General (later Field Marshal Viscount) Sir Hugh Gough, commander in chief, India, marched to Ferozeshah.

A Sikh force of about 35,000 soldiers with 108 guns, under Lal Singh, was entrenched in a horseshoe-shaped position around the village of Ferozeshah. Gough, with typical impetuosity, wanted to attack the Sikhs immediately on 21 December 1845, before they could be reinforced by another Sikh army under Tej Singh. Gough's force at the time, however, numbered about 12,000 soldiers, and the reinforcements from Ferozepore he had requested the previous night, Major General Sir John Littler's 5,000-man, 21-gun division had not yet arrived.

Lieutenant General (later Field Marshal Viscount) Sir Henry Hardinge, the governor-general of India and Gough's political superior, had volunteered to serve as Gough's second in command two days earlier. When Hardinge learned that Gough intended to attack the strong Sikh positions before the arrival of Littler's division, he resumed his authority as governor-general and vetoed any attack until Littler's division had arrived. Gough had no option but to obey.

Littler's division arrived in the early afternoon, and the British force tried to deploy in an organized manner. This task was hindered by the absence of orders from Gough and the lack of information about enemy positions. Gough's army finally formed up with three divisions abreast and one in reserve. Major General W. R. Gilbert's division was on the right, Brigadier General Wallace's division in the center, and Littler's division was on the left, with Major General (later Lieutenant General) Sir Harry G. W. Smith's division in reserve. The 3rd Light Dragoons and the 4th Light Cavalry, with a troop of horse artillery, covered the right flank, and the 3rd Irregular Cavalry and the 8th Light Cavalry covered the left flank.

At about 4:00 P.M., the British began their artillery barrage, and the Sikh guns returned fire. British command and control was poor, and, inexplicably, one of Littler's brigades prematurely launched an attack on the left. It suffered heavy casualties and withdrew, exposing the flanks of other British units. The British then began a general advance, and Hardinge ordered Smith to send a unit to fill the gap caused by the withdrawal of Littler's brigade. Smith's unit repulsed a Sikh counterattack and continued attacking. In the smoke, confusion, and early darkness, Smith found himself with a few thousand men in the center of the enemy's position and withdrew at about 3:00 A.M. the following morning. Meanwhile, the rest of Gough's army had re-formed and encamped outside the Sikh positions. One participating officer observed that "never perhaps in the annals of Indian warfare has a British army on so large a scale been nearer to defeat which could have involved annihilation" (Crawford 1967, p. 43).

On the morning of 22 December 1845, after Smith's force had rejoined him, Gough launched another attack at the Sikh entrenchments only to find that most of them, and 73 guns, had been abandoned. After the British occupied the Sikh camp, Tej Singh's 30,000-man force arrived. After his artillery fired, he fought halfheartedly and then withdrew late in the afternoon. It was learned later that Tej Singh thought a British cavalry and artillery retreat was in fact a tactical maneuver to pass around his flank and cut him off from the Sutlej River. The Sikh retirement permitted the British to claim victory.

The Battle of Ferozeshah was perhaps the hardest fought engagement in India. The British barely won the Battle of Ferozeshah and suffered 696 dead and 1,729 wounded. Sikh losses were about 3,000 men and 72 guns. Hardinge, whose earlier veto of Gough's initial attack may have prevented a British disaster, believed that "India has been saved by a miracle . . . another such victory will cost us the Empire" (Featherstone 1973, p. 58).

See also Aliwal, Battle of; East India Company, Military Forces; Gough, Field Marshal Hugh; Hardinge, Field Marshal Henry; India; Sikh War, First (1845–1846); Sikhs; Smith, Lieutenant General Sir Harry G. W.; Sobraon, Battle of

References: Cook (1975); Crawford (1967); Featherstone (1968); Featherstone (1973); Featherstone (1992)

Forbes, Archibald
See Correspondents, War

French, Field Marshal John D. P., First Earl of Ypres (1852–1925)

Field Marshal John D. P. French, First Earl of Ypres, was an outstanding cavalry commander who led the Cavalry Division with distinction during the Second Boer War (1899–1902). He also served as chief of the imperial general staff immediately before World War I.

French was born on 28 September 1852 in Kent. His father was a retired naval officer, and the younger French joined the Royal Navy in 1866 although he resigned in 1870 and joined the militia. After tutoring, French passed the army entrance examination, was gazetted to the 8th Hussars in 1874, and shortly thereafter transferred to the 19th Hussars. He spent a number of years on regimental assignments, including secondment to a yeomanry regiment, and rejoined the 19th Hussars in Cairo in October 1884. French's baptism of fire came during the Gordon Relief Expedition, when his detachment, as part of the Desert Column, fought at the Battle of Abu Klea (17 January 1885) and covered its retreat from the Sudan.

The 19th Hussars returned to England in 1886. French commanded the regiment in England and in India from 1888 to 1893 and gained a reputation as an innovative cavalry leader and trainer. From 1893 to 1895, French was on half pay and was assigned to the War Office as a colonel in 1895. In May 1897, French assumed command of the newly organized 2nd Cavalry Brigade and, the following year, the 1st Cavalry Brigade.

French, as a local lieutenant general, was assigned to command the cavalry in Natal and arrived in South Africa shortly before the outbreak of war on 11 October 1899. His cavalry helped achieve victory at the Battle of Elandslaagte (21 October 1899) and avoided being besieged in Ladysmith. French was an indefatigable cavalry commander, driving his horsemen in the relief of Kimberley, the capture of Bloemfontein and of Pretoria, and later in "drives" to capture the insurgent Boers. French returned to England in July 1902. Whereas the unorthodox warfare of the Second Boer War ruined many reputations, French emerged from the conflict with two knighthoods and an assignment as 1st Army Corps commander at Aldershot.

French commanded the 1st Army Corps from 1902 to 1907, and it was apparent he was being groomed to command the British Expeditionary Force (BEF) in the event of a European war. He was appointed inspector-general of the forces and tried hard to instill drill and discipline into unit training and field maneuvers. In 1912, French became chief of the imperial general staff and was promoted to field marshal in 1913. As a result of the "Curragh Incident," he resigned in March 1914, and his career seemed to be over.

French was appointed commander in chief of the BEF when World War I began in August 1914, but he was relieved from command in December 1915. He served as commander in chief, home forces, 1916–1918, then as lord lieutenant of Ireland, 1918–1921. French was ennobled as a viscount in 1916 and as an earl after his final retirement. He died on 22 May 1925.

French was a good, but not a great, general, and in spite of a "colorful" personal life, he achieved the highest military rank and position. As a cavalry leader, however, French was "the most distinguished Englishman since Cromwell" (Holmes 1981, p. 366).

See also Abu Klea, Battle of; Boer War, Second (1899–1902); Cavalry, British Army—Training; Commander in Chief, British Army; Curragh Incident; Gordon Relief Expedition; War Office

References: Chisholm (1915); French (1931); Holmes (1981); Pakenham (1979); Sixsmith (1970); Symons (1963); Trew (1999)

French Forces, Crimean War

France and Great Britain became allied with the Ottomans (Turks) by declaring war on Russia on 28 March 1854.

In 1854, the French Army, experienced by fighting in Algeria since 1830, was considered the best-equipped, best-trained, and best-supplied military force in the world. All of the French infantry carried Minié rifles, and the French cavalry and artillery were considered outstanding. Its support services, including engineers, administration, medical corps, transport, and commissariat, had been reorganized and were efficient and effective. The French Army itself, and not civilian bureaucracies, was responsible for supporting its troops.

The initial French expeditionary force to the Crimea consisted of four infantry divisions (about 10,000 soldiers each), eight and a half field artillery batteries, and a cavalry detachment. By March 1855, French military strength in the Crimea had increased to 80,000, with many of the replacements having little military experience.

The first commander of the French force was 53-year-old Marshal Jacques Leroy de St. Arnaud. The average age of St. Arnaud and his four division commanders was 44.8 years, as compared to an average of 59 years of age for the British commander in chief and his five division commanders. As a whole, French officers were less aristocratic and more professional than their British counterparts, and commissioning from the ranks was fairly common.

French soldiers were conscripted for a six-year term of service. Instead of receiving the endless drill and harsh punishments of the British soldier, the French soldier received classes and training on history, hygiene, and physical readiness. They also learned the importance of individual initiative, audacity, and national pride. Like their British counterparts, many French soldiers were given to drunkenness and frequently contracted venereal diseases.

The best French troops were the highly skilled and courageous infantry Zouaves, named after the Algerian mountain tribesmen they had once fought. French Foreign Legion units also fought in the Crimea.

French regiments were uniquely accompanied by uniformed women known as *vivandieres* or *cantinieres*, some of whom were married to soldiers. They acted as sutlers and were in charge of unit canteens.

The French health and sickness record was initially much better than that of the British, but closer to the end of the war, when the British sickness rate fell, the French sickness rate soared. Typhus was the greatest scourge. During the first three months of 1856, during a period of relative inactivity, almost 53,000 French troops were admitted to the 14 French hospitals around Constantinople, and another 5,000 died on ships between Crimea and the Bosporus.

Some 300,000 French soldiers saw service in the Crimea, of whom 10,240 were killed in action with about another 70,000 dying from wounds or disease.

See also Crimean War; Russian Forces, Crimean War; Sardinian Forces, Crimean War; Turkish Forces, Crimean War
References: Edgerton (1999); Judd (1975); Palmer (1987); Raugh (1987a); Royle (2000); Warner (1972)

Fripp, Charles E.
See Artists, War

G

Gandamak, Action at (13 January 1842)
See Afghan War, First (1839–1842)

Gardner Machine Gun
See Machine Guns

Gaselee, General Sir Alfred
See Boxer Rebellion

Gatacre, Lieutenant General Sir William F. (1843–1906)

Lieutenant General Sir William F. Gatacre was a senior general who saw considerable active service during the final decade of Queen Victoria's reign, culminating in command of the 3rd Division during the Second Boer War.

Gatacre was born in 1843 and commissioned in the army in 1862. He served in India for many years, was an instructor at Sandhurst from 1875 to 1879, and participated in an expedition to Burma in 1889.

Gatacre commanded a brigade in the 1895 Chitral Relief Expedition on the North-West Frontier. On one occasion an attack was to be conducted on a rebel leader's fort. Gatacre thought the mission too risky, and argued with the force chief of staff over seniority. By the time the force commander arrived, the rebels had slipped away.

As a major general, Gatacre was sent to the Sudan in early 1898 and commanded a British brigade at the Battle of Atbara (8 April 1898) and a division at Omdurman (2 September 1898). While his soldiers fought well, Gatacre was considered an abrasive officer, "totally unable to delegate, he interfered constantly with his battalion commanders and insisted on being consulted on the slightest measure, right down to platoon level" (Neillands 1996, p. 191).

Gatacre arrived in South Africa in November 1899 in command of the 3rd Division. He was tasked with a small ad hoc force (as most of his division had been sent to Natal), to try to control as much of the northeastern section of Cape Colony as he could and prevent Boer advances from Stormberg. Even though instructed to remain on the defensive until reinforced, Gatacre was determined to seize Stormberg in a dawn attack after a night march. Gatacre failed to conduct a reconnaissance, at the last minute changed the route and direction of attack (or got lost en route), and then led tired troops in rugged terrain in an attempt to surprise the Boers.

In superb physical condition, Gatacre—nicknamed "Backacher" by his soldiers—expected his troops to also be in excellent shape and marched them as if they were impervious to fatigue. At daylight on 10 December 1899, Gatacre's column was caught unprotected in a pass with Boers on the high ground. The Boers opened fire on the British, some of whom were able to occupy nearby high ground, but most were exhausted and withdrew hastily. British casualties at Stormberg, one of the three significant British defeats constituting Black Week, were 28 killed, 51 wounded, and 634 captured.

On 10 April 1900, however, after Gatacre had failed to send his force to assist during an attack near Dewetsdorp, he was sacked and unnecessarily humiliated by Field Marshal (later Earl) Lord Frederick S. Roberts, V.C., commander in chief. Gatacre returned to England and commanded the Eastern District until he retired in 1904.

Gatacre, who "was as brave as a lion … No day was too hot for him, no hours too long, no work too hard" (Belfield 1975, p. 49), later worked for a rubber company, and died of fever in the jungles of Abyssinia in 1906.

See also Atbara, Battle of; North-West Frontier; Omdurman, Battle of; Reconquest of the Sudan; Roberts, Field Marshal Frederick S., V.C.; Sandhurst, Royal Military College; Stormberg, Battle of

References: Barthorp (1987); Belfield (1975); Farwell (1972); Neillands (1996); Pakenham (1979)

Gatling Gun
See Machine Guns

Gillespie, Major General Sir Rollo R.
See Gurkha War

Ginnis, Battle of (30 December 1885)

The Battle of Ginnis, fought between British and Egyptian troops and Mahdist forces on 30 December 1885, was the last engagement in the Sudan campaign involving British troops that began with the Battle of El Teb (29 February 1884). In addition, it was the first significant battle fought by the Egyptian Army after being reorganized and retrained by the British and was the last battle in which British soldiers wore scarlet serge uniforms.

The failure of its mission and other factors caused the Gordon Relief Expedition to be disbanded in the summer of 1885 and replaced by the two-brigade, 3,200-man Anglo-Egyptian Frontier Field Force. The Frontier Field Force manned forts and outposts in southern Egypt along the Nile River and the railroad from Aswan to Aksaha to prevent a dervish invasion of Egypt. The southernmost outpost was at Kosha. The overall commander of the Egyptian Army was Brigadier General (later Field Marshal Lord) Francis W. Grenfell, who had become sirdar (commander in chief) in April 1885. The 1st Brigade, Frontier Field Force commander was Colonel (later Lieutenant General Sir) William F. Butler and headquartered at Wadi Halfa, and the 2nd Brigade was commanded by Brigadier General Huyshe.

In late November 1885, scouts reported a buildup of dervish forces near the village of Ginnis, a few miles upriver from Kosha. The garrison at Kosha, consisting of the 79th Queen's Own Cameron Highlanders and the 9th Sudanese Battalion, was invested shortly thereafter. There were numerous skirmishes between the Anglo-Egyptian and dervish forces, and troops from the British Army of Occupation in Egypt, commanded by Lieutenant General (later General) Sir Frederick C. A. Stephenson were sent to reinforce the frontier region and relieve Kosha. Stephenson arrived on 19 December 1885 and assumed overall command of the operation, with Grenfell serving as division commander and Butler and Huyshe as brigade commanders.

Stephenson's 5,000-man force bivouacked the night of 29–30 December 1885 about 3 miles northeast of Kosha on the Nile River. At 5:00 A.M. on 30 December, the entire force began its advance. In the lead was the 1st Brigade that took up position in the ridge overlooking Ginnis, while the 2nd Brigade positioned itself to the east, overlooking Kosha. After a 15-minute artillery barrage that began at 6:10 A.M. and surprised the dervishes, the 2nd Brigade assaulted Kosha while its garrison attacked along the riverbank, supported by the gunboat *Lotus*. Kosha was cleared in less than a half hour, and the Kosha garrison troops and 2nd Brigade continued their advance toward Ginnis.

As the 1st Brigade attacked the Mahdist camp at Ginnis, dervishes counterattacked the Egyptian Camel Corps on the British left flank, but the Egyptians closed ranks and held their ground until the assault dissipated. The 1st Brigade charged into the village of Ginnis and into the main dervish camp. They were soon joined by the 2nd Brigade, and a bayonet charge broke the dervish will to fight and they withdrew. British and Egyptian cavalry conducted a weak pursuit. By 10:00 A.M., the Battle of Ginnis was over.

Anglo-Egyptian casualties at Ginnis were 10 all ranks killed and 41 wounded. The 6,000-man dervish force lost an estimated 400 killed and hundreds wounded. The new Egyptian Army had proven itself in battle. "The Soudanese troops had acted with dash and gallantry," Grenfell recalled, "and the Egyptians had done all that they were asked to do" (Grenfell 1925, p. 88). After the Battle of Ginnis, distant outposts were withdrawn and the Egyptian-Sudanese border fixed at Wadi Halfa.

See also Butler, Lieutenant General Sir William F.; Dervishes; Egypt; Egyptian Army; El Teb, Battle of; Gordon Relief Expedition; Grenfell, Field Marshal Francis W.; Sirdar;

Stephenson, General Sir Frederick C. A.; Sudan
References: Barthorp (1984); Clementson (1985); Grenfell (1925); Johnson (1977); McCourt (1967); Neillands (1996); Sly (1998)

Gladstone, William E. (1809–1898)

William E. Gladstone, mainly through his service as prime minister of Great Britain on four separate occasions (1868–1874; 1880–1885; 1886; and 1892–1894), exerted tremendous influence on domestic and foreign policies, including the reform and employment of the British Army. Gladstone was originally a member of the Whig political party, but in the middle of the nineteenth century, members became uncomfortable with their aristocratic connections and began referring to themselves as Liberals. This term was first used officially when Gladstone became prime minister in 1868.

The son of a wealthy merchant, Gladstone was born in Liverpool on 29 December 1809. He was educated at Eton and Oxford and was first elected a Member of Parliament in 1832. He served in numerous ministries in increasingly significant positions. When his party was not in power, he performed other duties, such as Lord High Commissioner Extraordinary to the Ionian Islands from 1855 to 1859. Of high morality and a devout Anglican, Gladstone worked to increase government efficiency, decrease income taxes, and extend the franchise.

The Liberals won the 1868 general election and Gladstone became prime minister for the first time. Gladstone supported his secretary of state for war, Edward Cardwell, and the Cardwell Reforms that significantly changed the administration and organization of the British Army. These reforms included the introduction of short service enlistments, the abolition of the anachronistic practice of officers buying their commissions, and the localization of the home army. During Gladstone's first premiership, British troops fought in the Second Ashanti War (1873–1874).

Benjamin Disraeli and the Conservatives returned to power in 1874, and Gladstone led the opposition. The reported massacre of Bulgarians by the Turks in 1876 and the subsequent 1877–1878 Russo-Turkish War caused an increase in Russophobia. The Conservatives implemented "forward policies" in South Africa and Afghanistan in 1878, but antagonism toward the Liberals did not prevent Gladstone from returning to power in 1880.

Although the Liberals were considered "Little Englanders" because of their disdain of imperialism, Gladstone was reluctantly required to send a British expeditionary force to Egypt in 1882 to quell the Arabi Rebellion. Two years later, after considerable delay, Gladstone's government sent a military force to rescue Major General Charles G. Gordon, who was besieged in Khartoum. For myriad reasons, the force failed to accomplish its mission, and public sentiment turned against Gladstone. Gladstone had been known as the "Grand Old Man"—"G.O.M."—and these initials were changed to "M.O.G."—"Murderer of Gordon." Gordon's death, as well as the 30 March 1885 Penjdeh Incident in Afghanistan, probably contributed to the fall of Gladstone's administration in June 1885.

The issues of further electoral reform and Home Rule for Ireland divided the political parties and caused a political seesaw for years. Gladstone formed a short-lived third ministry in 1886 and last served as prime minister from 1892 to 1894. Gladstone died on 19 May 1898 and was later buried in Westminster Abbey.

See also Arabi Rebellion; Ashanti War, Second (1873–1874); Cardwell, Edward T.; Cardwell Reforms; Disraeli, Benjamin; Egypt; Gordon, Major General Charles G.; Gordon Relief Expedition; Great Game; Imperialism; India; Penjdeh Incident; Purchase System
References: Blake (1966); Bond (1960); Bridge and Bullen (1980); Longford (1964); Morley (1903); Pearson (1951); Rodgers (1984); Somervell (1926); Spiers (1992)

Godwin, Lieutenant General Henry

See Burma War, Second (1852–1853)

Gorchakov, Prince Michael

See Chernaya, Battle of; Crimean War; Inkerman, Battle of; Russian Forces, Crimean War

Gordon, Major General Charles G. (1833–1885)

Major General Charles G. Gordon, probably best known for his exceptional ability to effectively command non-European troops, was an eccentric yet charismatic British Army officer and colonial administrator.

Gordon, born at Woolwich on 28 January 1833, was the son of Lieutenant General H. W. Gordon of the Royal Artillery. He entered the Royal Military Academy, Woolwich, in 1848 and was commissioned a second lieutenant in the

Royal Engineers after graduation in 1852. He served in Great Britain before being posted in late 1854 for duty in the Crimean War. In the trenches before Sevastopol, Gordon exposed himself to enemy fire many times, but he believed God protected him from danger. The only weapon he carried into battle was a light cane that became a symbol of his faith and courage in later years.

Gordon next served on a boundary commission in the Balkans before returning to England. In 1859, he volunteered to serve in the Second China War. British troops were sent to protect the European settlement in Shanghai against the so-called Taipings in 1862. In 1863, Gordon was appointed to command the Shanghai merchants' defense force, optimistically called the "Ever Victorious Army." Armed with his "wand of victory," Gordon was instrumental in crushing the rebellion in China. He returned to England in 1865 with a reputation as a master of unconventional warfare and the sobriquet of "Chinese" Gordon. He was also promoted to lieutenant colonel and decorated.

From 1865 to 1871, Gordon served at Gravesend, followed by two years as British commissioner on the Danube Commission. On the invitation of the Egyptian prime minister, he became governor of the Province of Equatoria, located south of the Egyptian Sudan. Gordon's mission was to facilitate British exploration in the area and suppress the flourishing slave trade. In 1877, after a brief return to England, he became governor-general of the Sudan and was involved in subduing the slave trade.

In 1880, Gordon served for a short time in India. The Chinese Government, concerned about an imminent war with Russia, requested Gordon's presence in Peking. The British Government ordered Gordon not to do so, but changed its mind. Gordon's short service in Peking seemingly averted war between China and Russia as well as an internal rebellion.

Gordon returned to England where he experienced his final significant religious experience. In 1881–1882, he commanded Royal Engineers on Mauritius and traveled to the Holy Land in late 1882 to contemplate ideas of fatalism, predestination, and other religious precepts. While in Palestine, Gordon was pressured by King Leopold of Belgium to accept the Congo command. Gordon believed he could finally suppress the slave trade. He also hoped and yearned for a speedy death. Gordon agreed to resign his British Army commission and accept the Belgian position.

During Gordon's absence from the Sudan, the Madhi—Muslim messiah—made his appearance in 1881 with the goal of regenerating Islam and destroying all unbelievers. Gordon turned down the Congo position because of the growing crisis in the Sudan, and he returned to London. In January 1884, he was selected by the British to travel to the Sudan to assess the seriousness of the situation and the possibility of evacuating Egyptian garrisons. Gordon's directive was ambiguous. After arriving in Cairo, he received supplementary orders to establish an organized government in the Sudan. He was also reappointed, at his request, as governor-general of the Sudan and planned to evacuate Egyptians from the Sudan. Gordon seemed to have forgotten his instructions, and his judgment became erratic. Gordon arrived in Khartoum, the Sudanese capital, in early February 1884. The situation was worsening, and by 12 March 1884, the Mahdi's hordes began the siege of Khartoum.

The British belatedly sent a relief force under the command of General (later Field Marshal Viscount) Lord Garnet J. Wolseley to save Khartoum and rescue Gordon. After struggling against fanatic dervishes, through the desert, down the Nile, and against supply shortages and time, the vanguard of Wolseley's force arrived near Khartoum on 28 January 1885, only to find that Khartoum had fallen, and Gordon killed, two days earlier.

Gordon was an enigmatic but dutiful and successful British Army officer and colonial governor. After his "martyrdom" in Khartoum, Gordon was considered "a hero of heroes. He was a soldier of infinite personal courage and daring, of striking military energy, initiative and resource; a high, pure and single character, dwelling much in the region of the unseen" (Morley 1903, 3:151). Gordon's character and ideals were unblemished, reflecting the highest values of the British Army and Victorian society.

See also China; Crimean War; Dervishes; Egypt; Gordon Relief Expedition; Imperialism; Mahdi; Slavery; Sudan; Wolseley, Field Marshal Garnet J.; Woolwich, Royal Military Academy

References: Buchan (1934); Butler (1907); Compton (1974); Elton (1954); Elton (1961); Garrett (1974); Gustafson (2002); Hanson (1954); Johnson (1982); MacGregor-Hastie (1985); Morley (1903); Raugh (1987b); Raugh (1988a); Strachey (1918); Waller (1988)

Gordon Relief Expedition (1884–1885)

The Gordon Relief Expedition was the ill-fated British operation in 1884–1885 to rescue Major General Charles G. Gordon, who was besieged in Khartoum by dervish forces. This was one of the most dramatic and legendary events in British imperial history, and its failure contributed to the downfall of the Liberal Government of William E. Gladstone in 1885.

Gordon, an eccentric British Royal Engineer officer, had served as governor of the province of Equatoria (south of the Egyptian Sudan) and governor-general of the Sudan in the 1870s. A deeply religious man, Gordon was eager to suppress the Sudanese slave trade. In 1881, an Islamic revolt led by the Mahdi that threatened Egypt had begun in the Egyptian Sudan. Various forces sent from Egypt to prevent Mahdist expansion were defeated.

It became clear to the British Government that all British and Egyptian citizens in the Sudan would have to be evacuated. Gordon, who was planning to resign his British Army commission to serve in the Congo, was interviewed by the British Cabinet on 18 January 1884. He was charged with traveling to the Sudan to investigate the possibility of evacuation, with the British Government deciding on a policy based on his recommendation.

Gordon departed for Cairo on 18 January 1884 and, after arriving, received supplemental instructions to establish organized government in the various Sudanese provinces. He was also reappointed as governor-general of the Sudan and reached Khartoum without incident in early February 1884. On 4 February, an Egyptian Gendarmarie force under the command of Major General Valentine Baker Pasha was annihilated by dervishes at El Teb. The British reacted by sending a force under the command of Major General (later Lieutenant General) Sir Gerald Graham, V.C., to the eastern Sudan. This British force defeated the Mahdists at El Teb on 29 February and was withdrawn in the following months.

Gordon requested from Khartoum that British troops be sent to Berber, but the British Government refused. On 12 March 1884, dervish forces began the siege of Khartoum. The British Government overestimated the influence of Egypt in the Sudan, underestimated the Mahdi's power, and failed to appreciate that British prestige was connected to Gordon's fate.

The British public, thinking that Gordon was being abandoned, pressured the government to debate sending a force to save him. While the government procrastinated, tentative plans were being made at the War Office, under the direction of the adjutant-general, General (later Field Marshal Viscount) Lord Garnet J. Wolseley, to send an expedition to rescue Gordon. A key planning factor was route selection. Wolseley preferred the 1,426-mile Nile River route from Cairo to Berber, while senior officers in Egypt recommended the 245-mile desert route from the Red Sea port of Suakin to Berber. As the government delayed, the dervishes captured Berber in late May 1884.

Throughout the summer, Wolseley urged the government to act. In June 1884, he wrote to the Marquis of Hartington, the secretary of state for war, "Time is the most important element in the question, and indeed it will be an indelible disgrace if we allow the most generous, patriotic, and gallant of our public servants to die of want or fall into the hands of a cruel enemy because we would not hold out our hands to save him" (Farwell 1972, p. 280). Finally, on 23 August 1884, Gladstone informed the queen he was sending Wolseley to Egypt to temporarily assume command of the British troops and oversee the preparations for any possible expedition.

Wolseley arrived in Cairo on 9 September 1884 and prophesied to his wife that he would rescue Gordon in Khartoum on about 31 January 1885. Wolseley finally received the order to proceed to the rescue of Gordon on 19 September, although he did not receive formal instructions until 8 October: "The primary object of the expedition up the valley of the Nile is to bring away General Gordon . . . from Khartoum. When that object has been secured, no further offensive operations of any kind are to be undertaken" (Cromer 1908, 1:581).

Wolseley had not been idle during the government's delays. Based on his successful Red River Expedition in 1870, he had developed a flotilla, under the command of Colonel (later Lieutenant General Sir) William F. Butler, of specially built whale boats manned by Canadian *voyaguers* for passage up the Nile. Butler arrived at Aswan, 600 miles from Khartoum, with his boats on 7 October 1884. All boats were at the foot of the Second Cataract by 18 October and reached the Third Cataract on 27 November 1884. From his headquarters at Wadi Halfa, Wolseley ordered Butler on 27 November 1884 not to advance further south, as other units would dash across the desert to defeat the Mahdi and save Gordon.

By 16 December 1884, Wolseley and his chief of intelligence, Colonel (later Major General) Sir Charles W. Wilson, had reached Korti, 400 miles downriver from Khartoum. Because Gordon could not hold out much longer, Wolseley divided his force (which eventually totaled about 11,000 troops) into two elements to attempt to accelerate the relief. The first element was the Desert Column, commanded by

Gordon Relief Expedition

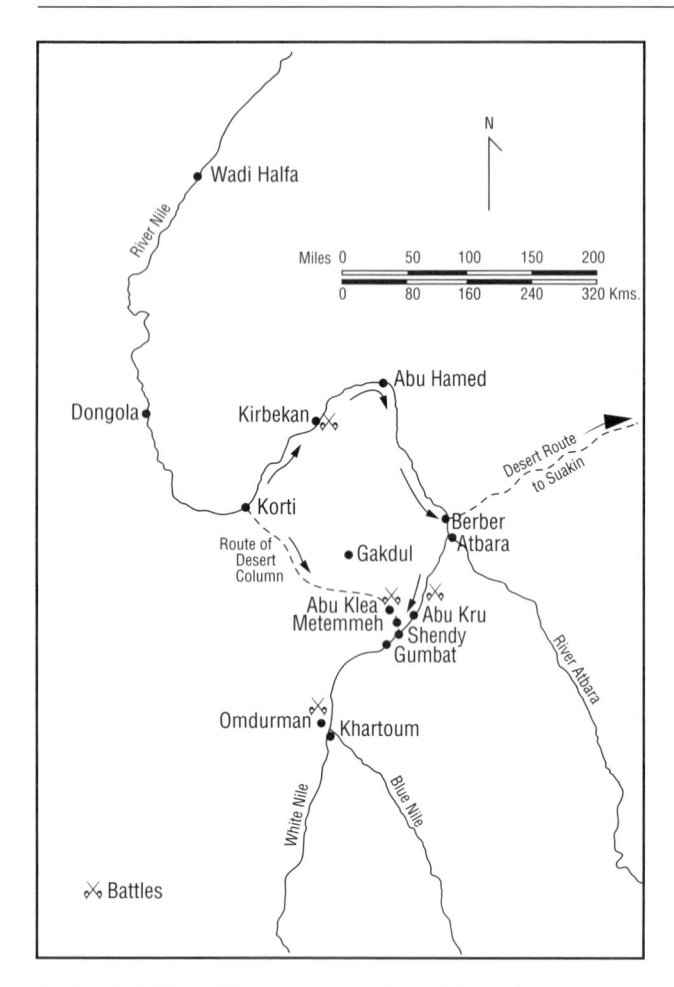

Gordon Relief Expedition, 1884–1885: Area of Operations
Source: Robin Neillands. *The Dervish Wars: Gordon and Kitchener in the Sudan, 1880-1898.* Reprinted with permission of A. M. Heath & Co., London.

Brigadier General (later Major General) Sir Herbert Stewart with Wilson accompanying it. Its task was to travel overland from Korti and reach Metemmeh on the Nile by 7 January 1885. Major General William Earle commanded the second element, the River Column (four battalions in boats), which was to follow the Nile and reach Shendi, opposite Metemmeh, on 1 February 1885. The River Column would then establish a supply base to be used in the final advance on Khartoum.

The River Column was delayed in its advance largely because of the Nile cataracts. Earle was informed of the fall of Khartoum on 5 February 1885 and told to halt his force, but he resumed the advance to Abu Hamed on 8 February. The British fought and defeated the dervishes at Kirbekan on 10 February, although Earle was killed in action.

The Desert Column fought the dervishes at the fierce Battle of Abu Klea on 17 January 1885. Wilson, a staff officer, seemed uncertain of what to do next. The Desert Column made a feeble attack on Metemmeh on 21 January when four steamers from Khartoum appeared on the Nile. Wilson spent the next day reconnoitering the area rather than taking the two steamers the 96 miles to Khartoum. Finally, early on 24 January, Wilson took two of the steamers and headed to Khartoum, which was sighted at midday on 28 January. Khartoum had fallen after a 317-day siege and Gordon had been killed two days earlier.

On 20 February 1885, all British troops were ordered to return to Korti. Graham's Suakin Field Force returned to Suakin on 12 March 1885, and the dervishes attacked and broke the British square, but were repulsed, at the Battle of Tofrek (22 March 1885). Concerns for imperial defense, especially with Russia on the northern border of India after the Penjdeh Incident (30 March 1885), provided a convenient excuse for the withdrawal of British forces from the Sudan in May 1885.

The news of the fall of Khartoum and death of Gordon was received in Great Britain with horror and indignation. Many people considered Gladstone, the "Grand Old Man"—G.O.M.—to be the "Murderer of Gordon," the M.O.G., and this contributed to the fall of his government later that year. Wolseley attempted to blame Wilson for the failure of the force, but the accusation was an effort to shift blame, and fifty-one-year-old Wolseley never received another field command. The Gordon Relief Expedition, in light of government procrastination and other difficulties, "was a campaign less against man than against time. Had British soldiers and camels been able to subsist on sand and occasional water, or had the desert produced beef and biscuit, the army might, in spite of its late start, have reached Khartoum in November" (Cromer 1908, 2:4). The Gordon Relief Expedition was indeed too late and failed in its mission.

See also Abu Klea, Battle of; Butler, Lieutenant General Sir William F.; Dervishes; Earle, Major General William; Egypt; El Teb, Battle of; Gladstone, William E.; Gordon, Major General Charles G.; Graham, Lieutenant General Sir Gerald, V.C.; Hicks Pasha, Major General William; Imperialism; Kashgil, Battle of; Mahdi; Penjdeh Incident; Red River Expedition; Slavery; Stewart, Major General Sir Herbert; Sudan; Tofrek, Battle of; War Office; Wilson, Major General Sir Charles W.; Wolseley, Field Marshal Garnet J.

References: Brackenbury (1885); Buchan (1934); Butler (1904); Clark (1985); Compton (1974); Cromer (1908); Elton (1961); Farwell (1972); Gleichen (1988); Harris

(1914); Lehmann (1964); MacLaren (1978); Preston (1967a); Preston (1978); Raugh (1987b); Raugh (1988a); Strage (1973); Symons (1965); Waller (1988)

Gough, General Sir Hubert de la P. (1870–1963)

General Sir Hubert de la P. Gough, relieved of command of the British Fifth Army in April 1918 in the wake of the German offensive of the previous month, is best known during the period 1815–1914 for his cavalry service during the Second Boer War and as the protagonist of the "Curragh Incident" of 1914.

Gough was born on 12 August 1870 in London. He was a member of a prominent military family, and his great-great uncle was Field Marshal Viscount Hugh Gough. His family was unique in that three of its members had received the Victoria Cross. Both his father, Charles, and his uncle, Hugh, were knighted generals and both received the Victoria Cross for gallantry during the Indian Mutiny. His younger brother was awarded the Victoria Cross for gallantry in British Somaliland in 1903.

Gough attended Eton and the Royal Military College, Sandhurst, and was gazetted a second lieutenant in the 16th Lancers in 1889. In 1890, he was assigned with his regiment to India. He used family connections to be assigned to the Tirah Field Force on the North-West Frontier, and later to South Africa after the outbreak of the Second Boer War in October 1899. Gough served in Colonel (later General) the Earl of Dundonald's 2nd Mounted Infantry Brigade, initially as a staff officer. As the commander of a composite squadron, Gough led the units relieving Ladysmith on 28 February 1900. He commanded a column before being wounded and returning to England in late 1901. After Second Boer War service, he was assigned to Aldershot and as a Staff College instructor before assuming command of the 16th Lancers in late 1906.

Gough became commander of the 3rd Cavalry Brigade at the Curragh in Ireland in 1911. This was a period of tension, and questions were asked about the reliability and loyalty of the army to obey the orders of the civilian government to forcibly include Ulster in a united Home Rule Ireland. A meeting of senior officers, including Gough, was held on 20 March 1914 at which hypothetical scenarios were discussed and the impression conveyed that a formal ultimatum would be given to all officers in view of imminent operations against Ulster.

In sum, many officers felt they were being forced to barter their honor. Gough and fifty-seven other officers in his brigade tendered their resignation. Summoned to the War Office, Gough explained that if his brigade had been ordered to Belfast, he would have gone unquestioningly. It was then determined that the entire situation was a "misunderstanding," and Gough returned to his unit. The secretary of state for war and chief of the imperial general staff, however, were forced to resign. The Curragh Incident revealed the deep politicization of the British Army.

During World War I, Gough commanded a brigade, two divisions, and the Fifth Army. He was relieved from command of the latter in April 1918, although he was exonerated in 1937. Gough published his memoirs, *Soldiering On*, in 1954, and died on 18 March 1963.

See also Boer War, Second (1899–1902); Curragh Camp; Curragh Incident; French, Field Marshal John D. P.; Gough, Field Marshal Viscount Hugh; Ladysmith, Siege of; Tirah Field Force; Victoria Cross; War Office
References: Beckett (1986); Farrar-Hockley (1975); Gough (1954); Pakenham (1979); Raugh (1986)

Gough, Field Marshal Hugh, First Viscount Gough of Chinkiangfoo in China and of Maharajpore and the Sutlej in the East Indies (1779–1869)

Field Marshal Hugh Gough was a brave, audacious soldier who fought numerous campaigns in China, India, and against the Sikhs. He was very popular with his soldiers even though his tactics were generally limited to high-casualty frontal assaults, frequently against static positions and artillery.

Gough, born in County Limerick in 1779, came from a distinguished military family. He was commissioned into the Limerick City Militia in 1793 and soon transferred to the regular army. Gough saw extensive and varied service throughout the Napoleonic Wars. He distinguished himself commanding his regiment throughout the Peninsular War, was severely wounded twice, and knighted in 1815. On half pay from 1817 to 1819, and again after 1826, Gough was promoted to major general in 1830. Seven years later, Gough was appointed to command the Mysore Division of the Madras Army.

In 1840, Gough became commander of the 4,000-man expeditionary force sent to China during the First China

(Opium) War. The Bogue Forts were captured on 26 February 1841 and Canton was stormed three months later. There was a pause in operations and combat resumed in 1842. After Chinkiang was captured on 21 July 1842 and Nanking was threatened, the Chinese sued for peace.

Gough returned to India and became commander in chief, Madras Army. He was appointed commander in chief, India, on 1 August 1843 and commanded the expeditionary in the short Gwalior campaign later that year. Gough's force defeated the Mahrattas at the Battle of Maharajpore (29 December 1843) by conducting an unimaginative frontal attack.

Gough commanded the British forces during the First Sikh War (1845–1846), during which he fought four battles employing Napoleonic tactics. Actions at the Battle of Ferozeshah (21–22 December 1845) were delayed due to command confusion. The governor-general, Lieutenant General (later Field Marshal Viscount) Sir Henry Hardinge, while Gough's political superior, was junior to Gough as a lieutenant general, and agreed to serve as Gough's second in command. On the second day of the battle, Gough rode out in his flowing white coat, reportedly to draw the enemy's fire from his soldiers, an example of "both his generosity of spirit and irresponsibility as a commander in chief" (Crawford 1967, pp. 43–44). The last and most successful of the four battles was at Sobraon (10 February 1846). The Sikhs sued for peace at Lahore, and Gough received a barony for his services.

Gough's performance during the Second Sikh War was characterized by bravery but little tactical skill. British casualties at the Battle of Chillianwalla (13 January 1849)—602 men killed, 1,651 wounded, and 104 missing—caused an uproar in England. Gough was superseded, but before his replacement arrived, he won the decisive Battle of Gujerat (21 February 1849), which ended the war.

Gough received a viscountcy when he returned to England but never received another command. He performed numerous ceremonial duties and was promoted to field marshal in 1862. Gough, who died on 2 March 1869, was said to have commanded in more battles than any other officer, except Field Marshal Arthur Wellesley, First Duke of Wellington, in the nineteenth century.

See also Chillianwalla, Battle of; China War, First (1839–1942); East India Company, Military Forces; Ferozeshah, Battle of; Gujerat, Battle of; Gwalior Campaign; Hardinge, Field Marshal Henry; India; Indian Army Operations; Madras Army; Sikh War, First (1845–1846); Sikh War, Second (1848–1849); Sobraon, Battle of; Wellington, Field Marshal Arthur Wellesley, First Duke of

References: Cook (1975); Crawford (1967); Farwell (1973); Featherstone (1968); Featherstone (1992); Featherstone (1995a); Symons (1989)

Graham, Lieutenant General Sir Gerald, V.C. (1831–1899)

Lieutenant General Sir Gerald Graham was a courageous, professional British Army officer who made his reputation as a dynamic commander in Egypt and in the Sudan. He was 6 feet, 4 inches tall, and "his appearance at once impressed one with a sense of physical grandeur and power" (Farwell 1972, p. 276).

Graham was born in London on 27 June 1831, and after attending the Royal Military Academy, Woolwich, was commissioned in the Royal Engineers in 1850. He served throughout the Crimean War, at the Battles of the Alma and of Inkerman, and many times in the trenches before Sevastopol. On 18 June 1855, when he led a ladder party during the assault on the Redan, Graham distinguished himself by his gallantry and was later awarded the Victoria Cross for this and other heroic actions. Graham, who was wounded twice during the Crimean War, also served in the Second China War and was severely wounded at the storming of the Taku Forts.

After a number of routine assignments, Graham was promoted to colonel in 1869. In 1877, he was assigned to the War Office, serving there until his promotion to major general in 1881.

Graham commanded the 2nd Brigade, 1st Division throughout the British campaign in 1882 to suppress the Arabi Rebellion in Egypt, including actions at Magfar (28 August 1882), Kassassin (9 September 1882), and at the Battle of Tel el-Kebir (13 September 1882). Graham emerged as one of the most experienced and trusted subordinates of the force commander, General (later Field Marshal Viscount) Sir Garnet J. Wolseley, and was knighted for his services.

After the Arabi Rebellion was over, Graham remained in Egypt with the British Army of Occupation. On 23 January 1884, Graham and others met the British representative, Major General Charles G. Gordon, who was going to Khartoum to assess the situation there. Graham and Gordon had known each other since they were both cadets at Woolwich.

A few days later Graham and others escorted Gordon part of the way on his train trip to Khartoum.

After dervish forces defeated the Egyptian gendarmerie at the Battle of El Teb (4 February 1884), Graham was ordered to lead a force, consisting of three British infantry battalions, elements of two cavalry regiments, and Indian units, to the eastern Sudan. Graham's force fought fierce battles with Osman Digna's dervishes at El Teb (29 February 1884) and Tamai (13 March 1884), the latter infamous because the British square was broken. Graham was then promoted to lieutenant general. His force was withdrawn in April and May 1884 but left behind a small garrison at Suakin. In 1885 Graham commanded the Suakin Field Force in a short campaign. The only notable battle was at Hashin on 20 March 1885.

Graham retired from the Army in 1890 and died on 17 December 1899.

See also Arabi Rebellion; Crimean War; El Teb, Battle of; Gordon, Major General Charles G.; Gordon Relief Expedition; Tamai, Battle of; Tel el-Kebir, Battle of; Victoria Cross; Wolseley, Field Marshal Garnet J.; Woolwich, Royal Military Academy

References: Barthorp (1984); De Cosson (1886); Lehmann (1964); Maurice (1887); Neillands (1996); Preston (1967); Symons (1965); Waller (1988)

Grant, General Sir James Hope (1808–1875)

General Sir James Hope Grant was an aggressive, albeit devout and respected, commander who saw considerable active service in Asia. He later served as an innovative reformer of military training.

Born in Scotland on 22 July 1808, Grant entered the army as a cornet in the 9th Lancers in 1826. As a captain, he was about to resign his commission because he could not afford life in an expensive regiment, when a general made a request for an officer-musician for an aide-de-camp. Grant, an expert cello player, received the appointment and served in the First China War. Grant also fought with his regiment during the First and Second Sikh Wars.

Promoted to brevet colonel in 1854, Grant commanded the Cavalry Brigade at the beginning of the Indian Mutiny. He fought at Delhi and the final relief of Lucknow (where he was appointed brigadier general), and commanded the garrison at Lucknow after the city was captured. He was ruthless in pursuing his duty; he once had twenty-five mutineers executed and on another occasion did not hesitate to have some fifty British soldiers flogged for looting. From April to August 1858, his cavalry force conducted mobile operations and defeated or scattered numerous rebel bands, and he played an important role in suppressing the mutiny.

Grant, as a local lieutenant general, commanded the 11,000-man British component of the Anglo-French expeditionary force sent to China in 1860. Grant was knighted for the British success in this short conflict, and in 1861 he was promoted to lieutenant general and appointed commander in chief of the Madras Army.

In 1865, Grant was assigned as quartermaster-general at the Horse Guards, and in 1870 became commander at Aldershot. In the wake of the Franco-Prussian War (1870–1871), Grant was instrumental in conducting large-scale training exercises at Aldershot in 1871 and 1872. Gazetted general in 1872, Grant died in London on 7 March 1875 while still in command.

See also Aldershot; China War, First (1839–1842); China War, Second (1856–1860); India; India, British Army in; Indian Mutiny; Madras Army; Maneuvers, British Army; Quartermaster-General, British Army; Sikh War, First (1845–1846); Sikh War, Second (1848–1849)

References: Cook (1975); Farwell (1972); Haythornthwaite (1995); Wolseley (1862); Wolseley (1903)

Great Game

The "Great Game" was the British term for the competition, initially clandestine, between British India and Czarist Russia to gather information about and exert influence and control over the vast, uncharted mountainous regions of Central Asia. The British played the Great Game to protect India, while the Russians wanted to keep the British from interfering with their "eastern destiny." The term "Great Game" was reportedly coined by an early British adventurer, Lieutenant Arthur Conolly of the 6th Bengal Native Light Cavalry, who posed as a Persian merchant and tried to reach Khiva in 1830. The Russian statesman Count Karl Nesselrode called the conflict "the tournament of shadows" (Farwell 1989, p. 106). The Great Game began early in the nineteenth century and continued until 1907.

In January 1801, Russian Czar Paul sent an army of 20,000 Cossacks to invade India. Even though the force met disaster at the Volga River, the Czar was not discouraged and tried, without success, to persuade Napoleon Bonaparte to conduct a joint Franco-Russian incursion into India via Afghanistan.

Central Asia during the Great Game

The specter of Russian invasion returned in the 1820s, as the Russians expanded southward after their victories in the wars against Persia (1825–1828) and Turkey (1828–1829). This began a decade of British exploration in Afghanistan and the surrounding area. British officers who participated in this early stage of the Great Game included Conolly, Lieutenant Alexander "Bokhara" Burnes, and Major Eldred Pottinger.

In 1838, anxious to block possible Persian and Russian encroachment, the British East India Company reached an agreement with Ranjit Singh, the Sikh ruler of the Punjab, and the pro-British Shah Shuja to restore the latter to the Afghan throne. This precipitated the First Afghan War the next year. This conflict witnessed ferocious fighting, including the British invasion of Afghanistan and an uprising in Kabul that resulted in the encirclement of the British force. While evacuating Kabul, this force—consisting of about 4,500 troops (of which 700 were British) and about 10,000 camp followers—was almost annihilated in the frigid mountain passes near Gandamak. A British punitive expedition tried to restore British influence, and the war ended in September 1842. The Russian threat receded.

Imperial rivalry subsided during the following decade. The Second Sikh War ended in 1849, and the British annexed the Punjab as a result. Before and after the Indian Mutiny (1857–1859), the British continued absorbing Indian states, and the Russians expanded further in Central Asia, conquering Samarkand in 1868, then Bokhara, Khiva, and, in 1875, Kokand. In England, the "Forward School" argued for military preparations, and the viceroy was directed to take "decided measures for counteracting the danger of the Russian advance in Central Asia and in particular for re-establishing our influence in Afghanistan" (Fredericks 1971, p. 187).

Afghanistan was in the throes of internal dynastic struggles in the late 1870s, and the Amir, Sher Ali Khan, tried to avoid involvement in the Anglo-Russian rivalry. The Russians, however, after their 1878 victory over the Turks, flexed their muscles and sent an uninvited mission to Afghanistan. As Sher Ali was struggling with his cousin Abdur Rahman Khan for the throne, he began to distance himself from the British and sought Russian assistance. The British demanded to send a similar mission to Afghanistan and, rebuffed, issued an ultimatum to Sher Ali. This demand went unanswered, and on 20 November 1878, the British invaded Afghanistan and started the Second Afghan War. British participation in this 1878–1880 war was very costly, although the British were able to establish the pro-British Abdur Rahman on the Afghan throne. The British also reorganized their political and military intelligence organizations.

The Great Game reached its peak during the 1880s, and the rivalry with Russia was more blatant, depending less on secrecy and disguise. Central Asia was "a vast adventure playground for ambitious young officers and explorers on both sides" (French 1994, p. 36). One of the leading British players during this period was Captain Francis Younghusband.

On 30 March 1885, while discussions were being held to fix the disputed northern boundary of Afghanistan, Russian forces attacked the Afghan town of Penjdeh in the disputed area, killing over 300 of the Afghan defenders. Afghanistan had been promised aid against aggression by the British, and the Pendjeh Incident almost sparked a war between England and Russia before the crisis was overcome through diplomacy. The Anglo-Russian Boundary Commission continued to meet, delineating the border between Afghanistan and Russia in 1887. Six years later, the boundary between Afghanistan and British India was fixed by the Durand Line.

Rumors of war persisted through the 1890s and into the twentieth century. Russia's defeat in the Russo-Japanese War (1904–1905) contributed to the revolution in St. Petersburg in December 1905. Weakened and humiliated, Russia, under French pressure, agreed to the Anglo-Russian

Convention of 1907, promising to respect India's frontiers. The Great Game was over.

See also Afghan War, First (1839–1842); Afghan War, Second (1878–1880); Afghanistan; Durand, Sir Henry Mortimer; East India Company; India; North-West Frontier; Penjdeh Incident; Sher Ali Khan; Sikhs; Tibet, Expedition to; Younghusband, Colonel Sir Francis E.

References: Farwell (1989); Fredericks (1971); French (1994); James (1997); Johnson (1998); Mason (1974); Preston (1969); Waller (1990)

Greaves, General Sir George R. (1831–1922)

General Sir George R. Greaves was a talented, courageous British Army officer. Although a member of the Ashanti Ring, Greaves also served in senior positions in India, culminating as commander in chief of the Bombay Army.

Greaves was born in England on 9 November 1831, the son of a British Army officer who had served in the Peninsular War. He spent most of his youth living in various European countries, but returned to England, attended Sandhurst, and was commissioned in 1849. Greaves served with his regiment in India from 1850 to 1861 and served on the North-West Frontier and in the Indian Mutiny. Service in New Zealand and participation in the Second Maori War followed, and Greaves returned to England in 1866 as brigade major.

In 1870, Greaves was appointed deputy assistant adjutant-general at the Horse Guards. Shortly thereafter, Colonel (later Field Marshal Viscount) Sir Garnet J. Wolseley was assigned to the Horse Guards, and he and Greaves "worked in the same room and became lifelong friends" (Greaves 1924, p. 121). When Wolseley was selected to command the expedition to Ashantiland in 1873, Greaves was designated his chief of staff. Field Marshal H.R.H. Prince George F., Second Duke of Cambridge, commander in chief, however, vetoed this and a number of other personnel appointments. Colonel (later General Sir) John McNeill became chief of staff, but he was seriously wounded in October 1873, at which time Greaves replaced him. After the Second Ashanti War, Greaves returned to the War Office.

In 1878, Wolseley was posted as first British high commissioner on Cyprus, and Greaves went with him as chief of staff. When Wolseley departed for South Africa in early 1879, Greaves became acting high commissioner and held that position (for which he received a knighthood) until appointed adjutant-general in India in October. Greaves unofficially served as chief of staff in India until 1884, during which time the Second Afghan War and many North-West Frontier campaigns had been fought.

Shortly after returning to England, Greaves was appointed chief of staff of the Suakin Field Force in the eastern Sudan. After this short operation, Greaves returned to India to command the Meerut Division, and in 1890, he became commander in chief of the Bombay Army. Greaves expected to succeed General (later Field Marshal Earl) Sir Frederick S. Roberts, V.C., as commander in chief, India, but the latter's term was extended and an officer junior to Greaves was named Roberts's successor. Bitterly disappointed, Greaves resigned his command in 1893. On returning to England, Greaves was promoted to general and offered other commands, but he retired to Wales.

Wolseley later wrote of Greaves that "no general could have had a better man at his side, and no one was ever better or more ably served than I was by him" (Wolseley 1903, 2:280). Greaves died in 1922, and his *Memoirs* were published posthumously in 1924.

See also Ashanti Ring; Ashanti War, Second (1873–1874); Bombay Army; Cambridge, Field Marshal H.R.H. Prince George F., Second Duke of; Horse Guards; India; Indian Mutiny; Maori War, Second (1863–1869); McNeill, General Sir John C., V.C.; North-West Frontier; Roberts, Field Marshal Frederick S., V.C.; Sudan; Wolseley, Field Marshal Garnet J.

References: Beckett (1992); Cavendish (1991); Greaves (1924); Kochanski (1999); Lehmann (1964); Maxwell (1985); Wolseley (1903)

Grenfell, Field Marshal Francis W., First Baron Grenfell of Kilvey (1841–1925)

Field Marshal Lord Grenfell of Kilvey was a highly versatile British Army officer best known for his staff and administrative abilities.

Grenfell was born in London on 29 April 1841 and commissioned into the army in 1859. For the following dozen years he served in garrisons in the United Kingdom and overseas, including Malta (1866–1867), Canada (1867–1869), and India (1869–1871). Due to a perceived lack of promotion and active service opportunities, Grenfell submitted his resignation paperwork in 1873. Before it was approved, however, Grenfell was offered the position of aide-de-camp to General Sir Arthur Cunynghame, general officer commanding Cape Colony. His duties were routine until the outbreak of the Ninth Cape Frontier War in 1877.

In 1878 Grenfell was a captain, but only four years later—after participation in the Ninth Cape Frontier War and the 1879 Zulu War, service in the Transvaal, followed by staff duty with the British expeditionary force sent to crush the Arabi Rebellion in Egypt in 1882—he was a full colonel and aide-de-camp to Queen Victoria. His rise was nothing less than meteoric, but perhaps even more importantly, his service had caught the attention of General (later Field Marshal Viscount) Sir Garnet J. Wolseley.

After the British had suppressed the Arabi Rebellion in September 1882, Grenfell remained in Egypt with the British Army of Occupation. When the British began raising and training a new Egyptian Army in early 1883, Grenfell was appointed second in command to Major General (later Field Marshal) Sir (Henry) Evelyn M. Wood, V.C., the first sirdar.

During the 1884–1885 Gordon Relief Expedition, the Egyptian Army secured the Nile line of communications. Grenfell, ranking as a brigadier general in the British Army, replaced Wood as sirdar in April 1885 and became a full general in the Egyptian Army. The Egyptian Army then established a frontier force, headquartered at Aswan, to prevent a Mahdist invasion of Egypt. Grenfell commanded a division under General Sir Frederick C. A. Stephenson at the Battle of Ginnis (30 December 1885). Grenfell later commanded the Egyptian Army against the dervishes at the Battle of Toski (3 August 1889), a victory that showed the high level of discipline and training of the Egyptian soldiers.

Grenfell returned to England in 1892 and served as deputy adjutant-general of reserve forces at the War Office. In 1897, he was asked to return to Egypt and command the British troops to facilitate the reconquest of the Sudan, then taking place under Major-General (later Field Marshal Earl) Sir Horatio H. Kitchener. Two years later, Grenfell became governor of Malta, was ennobled in 1902, and returned to England in 1903 to command the IV Army Corps.

Promoted to general in April 1904, Grenfell was appointed to the Irish Command the following month. He retired in 1908 and was promoted to field marshal the same year. Grenfell died in 1925, and his *Memoirs* were published later that year.

See also Arabi Rebellion; Cape Frontier Wars, Southern Africa; Egyptian Army; Ginnis, Battle of; Gordon Relief Expedition; Kitchener, Field Marshal Horatio H.; Reconquest of the Sudan; Sirdar; Stephenson, General Sir Frederick C.A.; Toski, Battle of; Wolseley, Field Marshal Garnet J.; Wood, Field Marshal Sir (Henry) Evelyn M., V.C.; Zulu War

References: Arthur (1920); Barthorp (1984); Farwell (1985); Grenfell (1925); Maurice and Arthur (1924); Preston (1967)

Gujerat, Battle of (21 February 1849)

After the Battle of Chillianwalla (13 January 1849), the arguably defeated British forces under Lieutenant General (later Field Marshal Viscount) Sir Hugh Gough withdrew from the battlefield to rest and await reinforcements. The Sikh forces, commanded by Shere Singh, remained encamped on the battlefield.

On 17 January 1849, Sikh and Afghan troops under Chuttur Singh arrived at Shere Singh's camp, with the combined Sikh army then totaling about 50,000–60,000 soldiers, 59 guns, and about 1,500 Afghan cavalrymen. Provisions became scarce in the local area and there were concerns about the arrival of British reinforcements under Major General William S. Whish, who had completed the capture of Multan on 22 January 1849. Then on 11–12 February 1849 Shere Singh "staged a brilliant deception, moving his entire force round Gough's right wing during the night, with the intention of crossing the Chenab and striking at him from the rear" (Allen 2000, p. 193). The Sikhs reached the banks of the Chenab River undetected, although British irregular forces were on the far side.

The Sikhs established a defensive position near Gujerat, about 70 miles north of Lahore. Whish's force from Multan linked up with Gough's army on 16 February 1849, increasing the British Army to about 24,000 soldiers with 96 guns, including three heavy batteries. By this time, Gough had also learned that as a result of the outcome of and heavy British casualties at the Battle of Chillianwalla, he was to be relieved and replaced. Rather than return to England disgraced and dishonored, Gough decided to attack the Sikhs before his replacement could arrive.

The Sikhs were deployed about 3,000 yards in front of and south of Gujerat, with their right flank against a dry nullah (streambed) and their left flank against the fortified town of Chota Kalra and a stream that ran into the Chenab River. The fortified town of Bara Kalra, where the Sikhs had emplaced two artillery batteries, was forward of the Sikh right. Additional artillery was interspersed along the Sikh line.

At 7:30 A.M. on 21 February 1849, the British advanced

against the Sikhs. The British deployed with Brigadier General Lockwood's Cavalry Brigade and Brigadier General Hearsay's Irregular Cavalry Brigade on the right flank against the stream. Three infantry divisions were abreast: Whish's on the right, with Brigadier General Hervey's brigade leading and Brigadier General Markham's brigade in support; Major General Sir Walter Gilbert's division was in the center, consisting of two brigades, Brigadier General Penny's on the right and Brigadier General Mountain's on the left, on line; and Brigadier General (later Field Marshal Lord) Colin Campbell's division arrayed on the far side of the dry streambed with two brigades on line (Brigadier General Carnegie's on the right and Brigadier General McLeod's on the left) and Brigadier General Hoggan's brigade in reserve. Brigadier General White's Cavalry Brigade protected the British left flank and siege artillery.

The British marched as if on parade. Gough halted his force at about 9:00 A.M., when it was fired on by Sikh artillery, then deployed his artillery and skirmishers forward to engage the enemy. After a two-hour cannonade, it appeared the British artillery had finally smashed that of the Sikhs. The British line pressed forward, with soldiers occasionally lying down to avoid Sikh fire. Fierce fighting took place. The British finally seized the villages of Chota Kalra and Bara Kalra after fighting house to house. The Sikhs intended to conduct their main counterattack down the dry streambed between Gilbert's and Campbell's divisions, but as they assembled, the Sikhs were caught by Campbell's artillery and suffered severe casualties. This broke up the Sikh main counterattack before it could be launched.

By 12:30 P.M., shaken by the intense British artillery bombardment, the Sikh infantry began to withdraw from the field in an orderly manner. The British cavalry pursued the Sikhs, and the retrograde movement turned into a rout. The British won this engagement and captured 53 Sikh guns. British losses were five officers and 91 other ranks killed and 24 officers and 646 other ranks wounded. Anesthetics were used on British soldiers for the first time at this battle. Sikh casualties were estimated as 3,100 killed and as many wounded.

The British maintained pressure on the Sikhs, who surrendered on 14 March 1849. The British then annexed the Punjab, and Queen Victoria received the Koh-i-noor diamond as a token of submission from the Sikh ruler. Gough, due to the distance between London and the Punjab, was able to salvage and add to his reputation, although he resented the criticism he received after Chillianwalla. Gough, who returned to England, wrote, "Thanks to a gracious God for not only covering my head in the day of battle, but for granting me . . . a victory, not only over my Enemies, but over my Country!" (Farwell 1972, p. 60).

See also Campbell, Field Marshal Colin; Chillianwalla, Battle of; East India Company, Military Forces; Gough, Field Marshal Hugh; India; Sikh War, Second (1848–1849); Sikhs
References: Allen (2000); Cook (1975); Crawford (1967); Farwell (1972); Featherstone (1989); Featherstone (1992); Smith (1987); Young (1977)

Gurkha War (1814–1816)

The mountainous border between India and Nepal was ill defined early in the nineteenth century, and the Nepalese (generically called Gurkhas) took advantage of this situation by frequently raiding villages in East India Company territory. These depredations culminated on 29 May 1814, when Gurkha troops of the Nepalese Army attacked three British police posts in the Butwal Valley, killing 18 police officers and wounding four. They also captured and killed barbarously the chief police officer—an Englishman.

In October 1814, the governor-general of Bengal sent an ultimatum to the Nepalese rulers to accept and adhere to the frontier. The ultimatum was refused and expired on 1 November 1814, when the British began building forts on the frontier. The Nepalese responded by ambushing and raiding the British.

The British declared war in November 1814 and sent a 22,000-man force, divided into four columns, through four mountain passes to invade Nepal. Only one of the four British column commanders, Major General David Ochterlony, appeared competent and led his force successfully.

The first significant engagement of the war was the siege of Kalunga, in October–November 1814. Some 600 Gurkhas steadfastly held off more than 4,000 British and Indian troops commanded by an arguably insane Major General Sir Rollo R. Gillespie during a 33-day siege. The British finally entered the Kalunga fort on 30 November 1814. In this operation, the British lost 75 soldiers killed (including Gillespie) and nearly 700 wounded, while the Gurkhas sustained about 720 casualties.

Ochterlony campaigned through the southern portion of the region, attacking Gurkha fortresses one at a time. Battles took place at Jitgurgh (14 January 1815) and at Deothal

(April 1815). The Gurkha leader, Amar Singh, realized it would be hopeless to continue the war and requested terms to cease the conflict. By the Convention of 15 May 1815, the Gurkhas withdrew east of the Kali River and ceded Kumaon, Garwhal, and Sirmoor to the British.

Throughout the fighting, the Gurkhas had proven themselves disciplined, determined, and courageous soldiers. One British officer observed that the Gurkhas "fought us in fair conflict like men, and, in the intervals of actual combat, showed us a courtesy worthy of a more enlightened people" (Farwell 1984, p. 30). Impressed by their adversaries, the British began recruiting Gurkha soldiers, and the Gurkha Corps (initially four battalions) was raised officially on 24 April 1815. This began the British Army's long association with the stalwart Gurkhas, which continues to this day.

Hostilities broke out again later in 1815. Ochterlony, then commanding the 17,000-man British force, advanced toward Makwanpore Fort on the road to Kathmandu. The British seized a village near the fort on 27 February 1816. The Gurkhas counterattacked repeatedly to regain the village against volley-fired muskets and grapeshot, until the Gurkha momentum ebbed. The Gurkhas left over 500 dead on the field of battle.

The Gurkhas knew they could not continue the war, which was ended by the 4 March 1816 Treaty of Segauli. This confirmed the Nepalese cession of Kumaon, Garwhal, and Sirmoor; established a British resident in Kathmandu; and gave the British the right to recruit Nepalese subjects into their army.

See also East India Company; East India Company, Military Forces; Gurkhas; India; Indian Army Operations

References: Farwell (1984); James (1997); James and Sheil-Small (1965); Mason (1974)

Gurkhas

The Gurkha soldier comes from Nepal, the 54,000-square-mile kingdom stretching about 500 miles along the northeastern border of India and back about 100 miles to the Himalayan Mountains. Gurkha is a generic term, although some limit its definition to those who live in the hills around Gurkha, a town about 25 miles northwest of Kathmandu. Gurkhas are of Mongolian origin and are considered by the British to comprise the military tribes of Nepal.

There are many tribes in Nepal. The Magars and Gurungs come from the western and central regions of Nepal, and provide most of the recruits to the contemporary British and Indian Gurkha regiments. The Khas or Chettri come from the Nepal Valley, and the Rais and Limbus come from the eastern section of the kingdom.

The British, who first became acquainted with the Gurkhas during the Gurkha War (1814–1816), were very impressed with these stalwart, determined, and loyal mountain troops and began recruiting Gurkha soldiers. The Gurkha Corps (initially four battalions) was raised officially on 24 April 1815—even before the first phase of the Gurkha War had ended with the Convention of 15 May 1815. A second phase of the Gurkha War was terminated by the Treaty of Segauli (4 March 1816), which gave the British the right to recruit Nepalese subjects into their army.

The term Gurkha is derived from *Gorkha,* which in turn comes from the words *go,* meaning "cow," and *rakh,* meaning "protector." The Gurkhas are Hindus, the "protector of cows." British soldiers generally call these Nepalese tribesmen "Johnny Gurkhas" or "Johnny Gurks." The Gurkha battle cry is "Ayo Gurkhali!" literally, "the Gurkhas are coming!"

These short, strong hillsmen, known for their selfless service and devotion to duty, were considered by many to be natural soldiers. The Gurkhas are also characterized by their skillful use of the *kukri,* a curved knife about 18 inches long with the cutting edge on the inside. The Gurkhas remained loyal to the British during the Indian Mutiny (1857–1859) and fought in many of the campaigns on the North-West Frontier. One British field marshal declared that "no soldiers in the Indian Army have been more valued than our ever-gallant and hard-fighting comrades from Nepal" (Farwell 1984, p. 15). Gurkhas continue to serve in the British and Indian Armies to this day.

See also East India Company; Gurkha War; India; Indian Mutiny; North-West Frontier

References: Cross (1986); Farwell (1984); James (1997); James and Sheil-Small (1965); Mason (1974)

Gwalior, Battle of (19 June 1858)

Final operations in central India during the Indian Mutiny (1857–1859) were conducted after the September 1857 capture of Delhi and the final Battle of Cawnpore in December 1857. Major General (later Field Marshal Lord Strathnairn) Sir Hugh H. Rose assumed command of the Central India Field Force on 16 December 1857. He fought a number of battles against the mutineers that culminated in the Battle of

Gwalior (19 June 1858), the last major battle of the Indian Mutiny.

When Rose became Central India Field Force commander, he was given the mission of clearing the countryside of insurgents and operating toward Jhansi, which he eventually reached on 21 March 1858. The walled city of Jhansi was finally captured on 3 April 1858, but the Rhani of Jhansi escaped and joined Tantia Topi.

Rose's force next advanced to Kalpi and defeated the mutineers there on 24 May 1858. He thought this was the final battle of the campaign, and plans were made to disband his force. The rebel leaders, however, would not surrender, and they decided to try to persuade the Maharaja Sindhia's troops in Gwalior, which had a strong fort, to revolt. The Maharaja tried to stop the advancing rebels, but most of his troops defected. The mutineers then occupied the town and fort of Gwalior and proclaimed Nana Sahib the chief of a revived Maratha dominion.

Rose had to act decisively, since the seasonal rains and flooding were imminent. He took a small force to Gwalior, where he would meet with other British forces by 19 June 1858. On 16 June, Rose's force found a strong rebel force at Morar and defeated it after fierce fighting. The following day other British forces fought at Kotah-ke-serai, where the Rhani of Jhansi was reportedly killed in action.

On 18 June 1858, Rose's force marched through great heat to Gwalior, and the next morning a 10,000-man enemy force was observed between Gwalior and Rose's force. Rose decided to try to cut off this large force from Gwalior, and he ordered the 86th Foot and 25th Bengal Native Infantry to attack the rebels' left flank, while the 95th Foot would conduct a diversionary attack against enemy artillery emplaced on a hill. The British attacks were successful, and soon they controlled the hills overlooking Gwalior. Rose realized the rebels were disorganized, and he attacked relentlessly with the Bombay Lancers in the van. By nightfall, most of the mutineers had fled, and the town was in British hands.

The Battle of Gwalior (19 June 1858) was the pinnacle of Rose's vigorous and relentless Central Indian campaign and last major engagement of the Indian Mutiny. The fortress of Gwalior was captured the following day in an extremely gallant small unit action.

See also Cawnpore, Siege and Relief of; Delhi, Siege and Storming of; India; Indian Army Operations; Indian Mutiny; Nana Sahib; Rhani of Jhansi; Rose, Field Marshal Hugh H.; Tantia Topi

References: Callwell (1896); Edwardes (1963); Gardner (1971); Hibbert (1978); Robson (1997)

Gwalior Campaign (1843)

In 1843, the East India Company was concerned about the turbulence and intrigue surrounding the succession and rule of an adopted child-heir in Gwalior, the stability of that state, and the potential threat of the Gwalior military to the British. There was apprehension that the Maratha resistance against company rule could be renewed, and it was reported that the dissidents in Gwalior were secretly seeking support from the Sikhs and other princely states. After the British humiliations in Kabul and at the Khyber Pass during the First Afghan War, the company's military reputation and credibility needed bolstering. The governor-general, Lord Ellenborough, attempted to discuss the situation with the Gwalior council of regency, but when he was rebuffed, company forces attacked Gwalior to suppress its military force.

Company armies were assembled at Agra, under the commander in chief, Lieutenant General (later Field Marshal Viscount) Sir Hugh Gough, and at Jhansi, commanded by Major General John Grey. The two forces, beginning their march on 17 December 1843, were to converge on Gwalior, Gough's from the north and Grey's from the south.

The Mahratta Army of Gwalior established strong defensive positions at Chonda on the Asun River. Due to the difficult terrain, Gough's force was divided into three columns. He intended to turn the enemy's left flank with his cavalry and infantry, threaten the enemy's left flank, with the main attack being a frontal assault.

Reportedly with no scouts in advance, Gough's force marched out of its assembly area early on 29 December 1843 and arrived at the village of Maharajpore. The Mahrattas had established new positions at this advance location, and this forced Gough to change his plan. What appeared to have been a flat plain between the forces was in fact ground devoid of cover and full of ravines. This made it impossible for the infantry, cavalry, and artillery to coordinate their actions, and when Gough's force came within 1,500 yards of the village, the well-trained Mahratta artillery opened up a murderous fire. Gough's response was simply, "On and at them!" (Featherstone 1992, p. 33).

Gough's three infantry and two cavalry brigades, totaling about 6,500 soldiers with 30 field guns, attacked the 17,000 Mahrattas. Amid the smoke, confusion, bad terrain, and fierce fighting, the British force was finally able to overcome its adversary. The British losses totaled 797 all ranks killed, wounded, or missing. The Mahrattas suffered over 3,000 men killed and wounded and lost 56 guns. Gough admitted to underestimating his foe. The Battle of Maharajpore was "a 'soldiers victory' won by the bayonet without the benefit of tactics, strategy or manoeuvring. Gough displayed no generalship whatsoever and gave but one order" (Featherstone 1973, p. 50).

On the same day, 29 December 1843, Grey's force reached the village of Punniar, about 12 miles south of the Gwalior Fortress. A Mahratta force suddenly attacked Grey's long baggage train. He sent half his horse artillery and a cavalry element to the rear of his column, and this saved the baggage.

In the afternoon, Grey's force was threatened by 12,000 Mahrattas positioned on high hills to the east. Grey ordered the 3rd Foot and sappers and miners to conduct a frontal assault, while the 39th Native Infantry attacked the Mahratta left flank. The 3rd Foot's determined assault was successful, and it drove the Mahrattas from their positions and captured 11 guns. At the same time, the 39th Native Infantry seized a hill that dominated the Mahratta position. After numerous volleys, the 39th rushed to the Mahratta positions and captured 2 guns, while the 2nd Brigade, which had been held in reserve by Grey, attacked and shattered the enemy right flank, capturing 11 more guns. The entire British force then advanced against the crumbling Mahratta defenses. The Mahrattas fled the field, abandoning their 16 remaining guns and more than 1,000 casualties. British total casualties at the Battle of Punniar were 217 all ranks and 11 horses.

These two decisive victories ended the short Gwalior campaign, and the Gwalior regency capitulated. Gough's and Grey's forces linked up at Gwalior a few days later, and on 31 December 1843 a treaty was signed that reduced the Mahratta Army, established a British resident in the capital, and provided for the British occupation of the Gwalior Fortress.

See also Afghan War, First (1839–1842); East India Company; East India Company, Military Forces; Gough, Field Marshal Hugh; India; Indian Army Operations

References: Featherstone (1973); Featherstone (1992); Haythornthwaite (1995); James (1998); Pollock (1957)

Haldane, Richard B., Viscount Haldane of Cloan (1856–1928)

Richard B. Haldane, Viscount Haldane of Cloan, was a British statesman, philosopher, and educator who is considered one of Great Britain's greatest secretaries of state for war.

Haldane was born in Edinburgh on 30 July 1856 and was educated at Edinburgh University and Göttingen University in Germany. He studied law in London and was called to the bar in 1879. He was first elected a Liberal Member of Parliament in 1885 and was reelected until 1911.

In the late 1890s, Haldane was a cofounder of the London School of Economics, and in 1902, he became a Privy Councillor. He became secretary of state for war in 1905 in the Liberal government of Prime Minister Henry Campbell-Bannerman. Haldane had no prior military experience and no preconceived plans to reform the British Army, other than the mandate to implement the report of the Esher Committee.

One of the key recommendations of the Esher Committee report was the establishment of a general staff, which was constituted by Army Order on 10 July 1906. After the Imperial Conference met in London in 1907, it was decided to reform the staffs of the military forces of the British Empire. Accordingly, the General Staff in London became the Imperial General Staff in 1908.

The general staff produced official military manuals, including the *Field Service Regulations,* which enumerated and standardized staff organization, administration, and operations.

Haldane spent much of 1906 studying the British Army. Concern about a possible German attack on France influenced military planning to strongly consider employment of the British Army on the Continent, but Haldane also needed to reduce the Army Estimates and ensure that drafts for overseas battalions were provided annually. At this time, there were 71 battalions at home and 85 abroad. Haldane rectified this imbalance to 74 battalions at home and abroad. He organized the home battalions into a new expeditionary force of six large infantry divisions (each of one Guards and 11 line battalions) and one cavalry division. The force structure of this new British Expeditionary Force was announced officially on 1 January 1907.

After organizing the regular British Army, Haldane turned his attention to the auxiliary forces. The Territorial and Reserve Forces Bill was introduced in 1907. In general terms, in 1908, the yeomanry and volunteer infantry battalions were merged to form the Territorial Force, under War Office supervision. At the same time, the militia ceased to exist and its units were transferred to the Special Reserve, where they retained their battalion designation in the regimental system, with the task of providing drafts for the regulars in wartime. The mission of the Territorial Force had been modified from overseas service to home defense.

Under Haldane's leadership, Officers Training Corps units, under War Office supervision, were established at civilian universities. This program helped provide a solution to the long-term problem of officer shortages.

By 1909, most of Haldane's military reforms had been completed. He was ennobled as Viscount Cloan in 1911 and served as secretary of state for war until 1912, when he was appointed lord chancellor. After World War I broke out in

1914, Haldane was falsely accused of pro-German sympathies and left the government. Although he later held office, Haldane is best remembered as having "pursued and achieved possibly the most critical reforms of the British military system: the creation of an expeditionary force capable of quick movement to the Continent; the development of the Territorial Army as an effective and well-trained reserve body; and the institution of a General Staff" (Sweet 2000, p. 1). Haldane died on 19 August 1928.

See also Boer War, Second (1899–1902); Civil-Military Relations; Commander in Chief, British Army; Esher Committee; Militia; Volunteers; War Office; Yeomanry

References: Barnett (1970); Bond (1972); Carver (1984); Haldane (1929); Hamer (1970); Hittle (1944); Koss (1969); Spiers (1980); Stone and Schmidl (1988); Sweet (2000); Wheeler (1914)

Hamilton, General Sir Ian S. M. (1853–1947)

General Sir Ian S. M. Hamilton, who participated in many campaigns and wars, was considered one of the brightest generals of the late Victorian and Edwardian eras. His dutiful service, significant accomplishments, and military reputation, however, have been overshadowed by his command of the disastrous Gallipoli campaign against the Turks in 1915.

Hamilton was born on Corfu, where his British Army officer father was stationed, on 16 January 1853. He was educated at Wellington College, in Germany, and attended a special course at the Royal Military College, Sandhurst, from which he graduated in 1872 and was commissioned as a second lieutenant in the 12th Foot in Ireland. After eighteen months of service, he transferred to the 92nd Highlanders, his father's old regiment, in India. Hamilton was not only ambitious, but was also a good sportsman and took an interest in improving unit marksmanship.

Hamilton's regiment was attached to the force commanded by Major General (later Field Marshal Earl) Sir Frederick S. Roberts, V.C., during the Second Afghan War (1878–1880) and his courage in action brought him to Roberts's attention. Roberts served as Hamilton's mentor for many years. Returning to Great Britain, Hamilton's regiment was diverted to South Africa, where Hamilton fought and was severely wounded at the ignominious Battle of Majuba Hill (27 February 1881). Recommended for the Victoria Cross, Hamilton was considered "too young" (Lee 2000, p. 17) to receive the award. He was selected to be aide-de-camp to Roberts, then commander in chief, Madras Army.

In 1884, while returning to England for leave, Hamilton participated in the Gordon Relief Expedition in the Sudan, then returned to India and service on Roberts's staff in 1886. Showing talent at staff work and with troops, Hamilton was promoted to colonel in 1891, reportedly the youngest in the British Army at the time. Hamilton held increasingly responsible positions in India, participated in the 1895 Chitral Relief Expedition, and commanded the 1st Brigade of the Tirah Field Force in 1897. He fell off his horse and broke his leg, missing the Battle of Dargai. He was given command of the 3rd Brigade shortly before the expedition ended.

Hamilton returned to Great Britain in 1898 and the following year was appointed assistant adjutant-general to General (later Field Marshal) Sir George White, quartermaster-general at the War Office. Both officers were assigned to South Africa in the fall of 1899 in anticipation of war against the Boers. As a local major general, Hamilton commanded the 7th Brigade at the Battle of Elandslaagte on 21 October 1899, and was again recommended for the Victoria Cross. This time he was considered too senior to receive the award. He served in besieged Ladysmith, then was promoted to lieutenant general and commanded a division under Roberts, then commander in chief, in field operations. When Roberts returned to Great Britain to serve as British Army commander in chief, Hamilton accompanied him as military secretary. Hamilton returned to South Africa in November 1901 to serve as chief of staff to General (later Field Marshal Earl) Sir Horatio H. Kitchener in the concluding phases of the guerrilla war. Hamilton, as a substantive lieutenant general, returned with Kitchener to England in July 1902.

In 1903, Hamilton was appointed quartermaster-general at the War Office. The following year he was attached as an observer to the First Japanese Army in Manchuria during the Russo-Japanese War and wrote about his experiences in *A Staff Officer's Scrap-Book*. Recalled to England in 1905, Hamilton then commanded Southern Command until 1909 and was promoted to general in 1907. He became adjutant-general in 1909 and in 1910 general officer commanding Mediterranean Command and inspector-general of overseas forces.

When World War I broke out in 1914, Hamilton was appointed to command the Central Force for Home Defense. The following year, he became commander of the Mediterranean Expeditionary Force with vague instructions to assemble a force in support of a naval assault on the Dardanelles. Hamilton had a premonition that the campaign would be ill-fated. With inadequate reinforcements, resupply, guidance, and political support, the Gallipoli campaign turned into a debacle, and Hamilton was relieved from command on 15 October 1915. His successor's recommendation for evacuation was approved.

Hamilton never held another command after Gallipoli. He became the lieutenant of the Tower of London in 1919 and immersed himself in regimental, veterans, literary, and other activities until his death in London on 12 October 1947.

See also Adjutant-General, British Army; Afghan War, Second (1878–1880); Boer War, Second (1899–1902); Gordon Relief Expedition; India, British Army in; Kitchener, Field Marshal Horatio H.; Madras Army; Majuba Hill, Battle of; North-West Frontier; Quartermaster-General, British Army; Roberts, Field Marshal Frederick S., V.C.; Sandhurst, Royal Military College; Tirah Field Force; Victoria Cross; White, Field Marshal Sir George S., V.C.

References: Hamilton (1905); Hamilton (1944); Hamilton (1957); Hamilton (1966); Lee (2000); Luvaas (1964); Pakenham (1979); Pollock (2001); Ransford (1967); Roberts (1897); Sixsmith (1970)

Hamley, Lieutenant General Sir Edward B. (1824–1893)

Lieutenant General Sir Edward B. Hamley was one of the most influential military theorists and intellectuals of the British Army after the Crimean War, although his impact was less progressive than originally realized. He also commanded the 2nd Division in the British expeditionary force sent to quell the Arabi Rebellion in Egypt in 1882.

Hamley, the son of a Royal Navy vice admiral, was born on 27 April 1824 in England. He was gazetted into the Royal Artillery in 1843 and served in Ireland and Canada. Apparently bored with the routine of regimental soldiering, Hamley began to write for publication after he returned to England. His first article, published in *Fraser's* magazine in 1849, was "The Peace Campaigns of Ensign Faunce."

Posted to Gibraltar in 1851, Hamley later served in the Crimean War (1854–1856), participating in every battle with the Royal Artillery. During this time, Hamley sent monthly reports that were published in *Blackwood's* magazine (and later as a book) and helped educate the British public.

The establishment of the Staff College in 1857 and Hamley's appointment as the first professor of military history provided him with the opportunity to continue writing and lecturing on military campaigns, strategy, and leadership, much as it had another intellectual, Major General Sir Patrick L. MacDougall. Hamley's major accomplishment during this tenure at the Staff College was to write *The Operations of War,* completed in 1866. In this study, which "enjoyed a remarkable success and established Hamley's reputation as Britain's leading authority on military thought" (Bond 1972, p. 87), Hamley tried to show that warfare could be studied rationally and that permanently valid principles could be derived from it.

A closer analysis of *The Operations of War* suggests that Hamley failed to understand the revolutionary impact that rifled firearms had on tactics, especially that these new weapons favored the defender and not the attacker. Hamley's traditional outlook and continued belief in the offensive found favor with the conservative British Army as a whole and many of its officers, although it did provoke opposition viewpoints. While *The Operations of War* was considered a classic study and became an established text, it contained no original theory and received greater recognition than it deserved. Indeed, "the 'Brown Bess' mentality which dominated most of [Hamley's] arguments produced a reactionary, or even regressive effect" (Preston 1964, p. 69).

In 1865, Hamley was assigned to the Council of Military Education and served on it until 1870 when he returned to the Staff College as commandant. Hamley improved and helped revive the curriculum and other aspects of the Staff College before relinquishing the position in 1877. After the 1878 Congress of Berlin, Hamley served from 1879 to 1881 as British boundary commissioner to help delineate the borders of various Balkan nations and Russia.

Hamley had been designated a commander in the fall 1882 maneuvers, but when Britain sent an expeditionary force to Egypt under the overall command of General (later Field Marshal Viscount) Sir Garnet J. Wolseley, he was appointed to command the 2nd Division. As part of his strategic deception plan, Wolseley temporarily gave false information to Hamley, which increased tensions between the two strong personalities, especially as Hamley seemed to consider himself an adviser to Wolseley. Hamley commanded the 2nd Division in the decisive battle of Tel el-

Kebir (13 September 1882). While he received a second knighthood and other recognition of distinction, Hamley believed he should have received more of the credit for the victory. One of Wolseley's followers later tried to correct any misperceptions: "Sir Edward Hamley, with all his theoretical knowledge of war, had completely lost touch of the practical working of large bodies of men, and that he was always so full of his own importance, that he could not be trusted to carry out orders that he received" (Kochanski 1999, p. 146).

Hamley retired in 1885 and then served in Parliament until his death on 12 August 1893. He is best remembered for *The Operations of War* and as a vigorous military intellectual and writer.

See also Arabi Rebellion; Camberley, Staff College; Crimean War; Intellectuals, British Army; MacDougall, Major General Sir Patrick L.; Tel el-Kebir, Battle of; Wolseley, Field Marshal Garnet J.

References: Bond (1972); Hamley (1891); Kochanski (1999); Lehmann (1964); Luvaas (1964); Preston (1964); Raugh (2001)

Hardinge, Field Marshal Henry, First Viscount Hardinge of Lahore and of King's Newton (1785–1856)

Field Marshal Henry Hardinge was a distinguished soldier-statesman who served in numerous responsible high-level military and government positions, culminating as British Army commander in chief after Field Marshal Arthur Wellesley, First Duke of Wellington.

Born on 30 March 1785, Hardinge attended Eton and became an ensign in the British Army in 1799. He served throughout the Peninsular War, where he was severely wounded twice and was attached to the Portuguese Army. Hardinge was knighted in January 1815. He lost his left hand at the Battle of Ligny (16 June 1815), by which time he had become a loyal subordinate and firm friend of the Duke of Wellington.

After staff service, Hardinge was elected a Member of Parliament in 1820 and retired on half pay as a colonel in 1827. He served as secretary at war in Wellington's ministry (1828–1830). In 1830 and 1834–1835, he was chief secretary for Ireland. From 1841 to 1844, Hardinge again served as secretary at war. He was promoted to major general in 1830 and to lieutenant general in 1841.

In 1844, Hardinge succeeded his brother-in-law, Lord Ellenborough, as governor-general of India. Hardinge arrived in India on 22 July 1844, where the commander in chief, India, was then Lieutenant General (later Field Marshal Viscount) Sir Hugh Gough. The Sikh Army in the Punjab was then very anti-British, and Hardinge made preparations to resist any Sikh attack. The Sikhs crossed the Sutlej River on 11 December 1845 and invaded British Indian territory. Hardinge declared war against the Sikhs on 13 December.

Hardinge was the political superior to Gough, but he was junior to Gough on the lieutenant general's list and voluntarily agreed to serve as Gough's second in command. This unusual command arrangement could have caused many problems, but it seems the well-liked Gough accepted Hardinge's advice—and Hardinge reportedly tempered Gough's aggressive attitude while covering up many of his mistakes. On the first day of the Battle of Ferozeshah, 21–22 December 1845, however, Hardinge was not satisfied with unit dispositions when Gough gave an order to attack. Hardinge reverted to his superior civil rank and countermanded Gough's order until a specific unit had arrived in its position. Hardinge then turned to Gough and stated, "Now the army is at your disposal" (Farwell 1972, p. 41). The British won the battle and the First Sikh War. Hardinge was rewarded with a viscountcy.

In early 1848, Hardinge returned to England. He became master-general of the ordnance in 1852, then succeeded the Duke of Wellington as British Army commander in chief when the latter died later that year. While Hardinge was viewed as a progressive and reformer, the mismanagement of the Crimean War while he was commander in chief tarnished his reputation.

In 1855, Hardinge was promoted to field marshal, and he resigned the commander in chief position due to failing health in July 1856. Hardinge, considered by contemporary opinion as "far above the ordinary run of English Generals" (Strachan 1984, p. 37), died on 24 September 1856.

See also Commander in Chief, British Army; East India Company; East India Company, Military Forces; Ferozeshah, Battle of; Gough, Field Marshal Hugh; India; Indian Army Operations; Master-General of the Ordnance, British Army; Sikh War, First (1845–1846); Sikhs; Wellington, Field Marshal Arthur Wellesley, First Duke of

References: Cook (1975); Crawford (1967); Farwell (1972); Featherstone (1968); Featherstone (1992); James (1998); Strachan (1984)

Havelock, Major General Sir Henry (1795–1857)

Major General Sir Henry Havelock was a British Army officer with long service in India, notably in charge of the force that conducted the first relief of Lucknow in September 1857 during the Indian Mutiny. Giving people an initial impression that he was "an old fossil dug up and only fit to be turned into pipe clay" (Hibbert 1978, p. 198), Havelock was a diligent and deeply religious officer.

Born in England on 11 April 1795, Havelock initially intended to be a lawyer but was commissioned a second lieutenant in the army in 1815. He served in Great Britain for eight years before exchanging into another regiment for service in India. Havelock arrived in India in 1823 and shortly thereafter served in the First Burma War. Lacking influence and funds to purchase promotions, he served as a lieutenant for twenty-three years before being promoted to captain in 1838. Havelock later served in the First Afghan War and the First Sikh War, and then returned to England for two years (1849–1851).

Back in India, Havelock was promoted to colonel in 1854. As a brigadier general, he commanded one of the two divisions under the overall command of Lieutenant General Sir James Outram that participated in the Persian War (1856–1857). The Indian Mutiny erupted in May 1857, and at the end of June 1857 Havelock assumed command of a column to march to the relief of Cawnpore. Havelock's force began its advance on 7 July 1857 and defeated the mutineers at Fatehpur on 12 July and near Aong the following day.

On 16 July 1857, the first significant battle of the Indian Mutiny took place as Havelock's force routed the mutineers under Nana Sahib blocking the Grand Trunk Road into Cawnpore. The next day the British entered Cawnpore to find the British women and children massacred. Havelock won a minor engagement at Bithur on 16 August 1857 attempting to relieve Lucknow, but he had to withdraw his forces and return to Cawnpore, which was in danger of being overwhelmed.

Outram arrived at Cawnpore with reinforcements on 15 September 1857. Since the force was then larger, he superseded Havelock in command. Outram, however, permitted Havelock to remain in command to complete the mission of relieving Lucknow. Outram occasionally interfered with Havelock by offering his "advice" but did not insist it be followed. After fierce resistance, the Lucknow residency was relieved on 25 September, and Outram officially assumed command from Havelock.

When the final relief of Lucknow took place on 17 November 1857, Havelock was informed that he had been knighted for his services. Worn out from the summer campaign, Havelock contracted dysentery and died in Lucknow on 24 November 1857. Before he died, but unknown to him, Havelock had been promoted to major general and created a baronet.

See also Afghan War, First (1839–1842); Burma War, First (1824–1826); East India Company, Military Forces; India; Indian Mutiny; Lucknow, Siege and Relief of; Nana Sahib; Outram, Lieutenant General Sir James; Persian War; Sikh War, First (1845–1846)

References: Edwardes (1963); Hibbert (1978); Hilton (1957); James (1997); Pollock (1957); Waller (1990); Ward (1996)

Hazara Field Force (1888)

The Black Mountain region, home to rebellious tribesmen for decades, was east of the Indus River at the northern end of the Punjab frontier. The Black Mountain consists of a main ridge running north to south at an average of 8,000 feet above sea level, with ridges and access trails projecting perpendicularly from its spine. The area was frequently the scene of raids and lawlessness. In 1852, a punitive expedition was conducted against the Hassanzais for the unprovoked murder of two customs officials. Hostile tribesmen instigated another expedition in 1868, and in 1884 a large skirmish took place between antagonistic tribesmen and a detachment of Sikh and Gurkha soldiers.

On 18 June 1888 a British reconnaissance patrol was fired on, and in the ensuing engagement, two British officers and four Gurkhas were killed. Tribal insolence increased afterward, and on 7 September 1888 a punitive force was organized. Ultimatums were sent to the Hassanzais, Akazais, Parari Saiads, and Tikariwals outlining terms for submission that would, if satisfied by 2 October 1888, save their villages from destruction.

The 9,500-man Hazara Field Force (as the force involved in this Black Mountain expedition was called) was commanded by Major General J. W. McQueen. The 1st Brigade was commanded by Brigadier General G. N. Channer, V.C., and the 2nd Brigade by Brigadier General W. Galbraith. Each of the two brigades was divided into two columns, and there was a fifth reserve column. The difficult terrain and lack of roads necessitated smaller, more mobile columns. The total force consisted of five British and nine native infantry battalions, one cavalry regiment, three mountain batteries, one engineer company, and four Gatling guns.

The 1st, 2nd, and 3rd Columns assembled at Aghi and the 4th Column at Darband. After road improvements and waiting—to no avail—for tribal compliance with the earlier ultimatum, the columns began their march on 4 October 1888. The soldiers carried a light load: no tents were taken; baggage was limited to half a mule for officers and 16 pounds for other ranks; each soldier carried 70 rounds of ammunition with another 30 rounds per rifle carried on mules, as well as rations for five days. The first three columns advanced on parallel ridges up the eastern side of Black Mountain, and the 4th Column threatened the tribes from the west. Little opposition was encountered on 4 October because the tribes had concentrated at Towara to oppose the advance of the 4th Column. The 4th Column fought a vicious engagement near Towara, as a group of tribesmen charged and tried to break the British line. The Gatling guns were swung into action, and 88 dead tribesmen were counted on the spot.

The first three columns spent the following days on the crest of Black Mountain, reconnoitering the area, improving communications, and destroying dissident tribal villages. The 4th Column razed a number of villages and confiscated grain and forage. The Hassanzais and Akazais had enough and requested an armistice on 19 October 1888, submitting fully to the British shortly afterward.

The first phase of the campaign was over and the second was about to begin. The Parari Saiads, Tikariwals, and later the Allaiwals all lived north of Black Mountain, an area untouched during the 1868 punitive expedition. This gave the tribes a false sense of security. McQueen's force, divided on 20 October 1888 into five columns, did not let the difficult terrain stand in the way of mission accomplishment. The advance continued amid frequent enemy sniping and desultory firing.

British progress was slow because of the jagged, steep, and inhospitable terrain. Only 2.5 miles were covered on 27 October 1888. The 1st and 5th Columns resolutely seized the Ghoraper Pass on 1 November 1888. The last 500 feet to the summit of the pass was almost impassable for baggage mules; even after extensive engineer work the following day, the mules spent 12 hours climbing the last mile of the road. Along the way, 14 mules fell off precipices and steep trails.

The principal Allaiwal village of Pokal was reconnoitered by the British on 2 November 1888 and destroyed the following day. The Allaiwals were persistent in its defense and suffered 80–100 killed in the process. The British columns then withdrew, and the entire force reassembled in the Agror Valley and at Darband on 13 November 1888. The objectives of the Hazara Field Force having been met, the force disbanded the following day with subordinate units returning to their peacetime duty stations.

The Hazara Field Force collected a significant amount of fines from the rebellious tribes and received promises that British subjects would not be injured and that no claims would be made on land east of the Black Mountain watershed. In addition, the Hazara Field Force surveyed 177 square miles of previously uncharted territory and constructed 222 miles of roads. British casualties were 25 killed, 7 dead from disease, and 54 wounded.

See also Gurkhas; India; Indian Army Operations; Machine Guns; North-West Frontier; Sikhs
References: Barthorp (1982); Featherstone (1973); Nevill (1912)

Heliograph
See Communications

Henderson, Colonel G. F. R. (1854–1903)
Colonel G. F. R. Henderson was an eminent military intellectual, theorist, historian, and the doyen of military educators of the late Victorian British Army.

Henderson, born on Jersey in 1854, was the son of a prominent educator. He won a history scholarship and attended Oxford, then entered Sandhurst. Henderson was commissioned a second lieutenant in the York and Lancaster Regiment in 1878. He served with his regiment in India, England, and Ireland, and participated in the 1882 British expedition to Egypt. He led his company at the Battle of Tel el-Kebir (13 September 1882). He was later posted to Bermuda and Halifax.

While stationed in Halifax, Henderson spent his leave touring the American Civil War battlefields in Virginia and Maryland and developed a lifelong interest in this watershed conflict. In 1886, after returning to England, Henderson anonymously published his study, *The Campaign of Fredericksburg*. This volume, written "with an intelligence and insight unusual in such literature and filled with thoughtful observations on the military significance of the campaign, . . . represented a skilful blending of personal knowledge of the terrain, careful study of the available resources, and a lively, readable style" (Luvaas 1964, p. 216). It emphasized the importance of leadership and discipline on the modern battlefield. This book was reviewed by Colonel (later Major General Sir) (John) Frederick Maurice, then in his second year as professor of military art and history at the Staff College. Maurice ascertained the author's identity and recommended the book to General (later Field Marshal) Viscount Garnet J. Wolseley, then adjutant-general at the War Office. *The Campaign of Fredericksburg* helped revive interest in the American Civil War and served to counter prevailing studies of the Prussian Army. Largely on the merits of this book, Wolseley appointed Henderson an instructor at Sandhurst in 1890.

Henderson, who had been contemplating leaving the army, enjoyed teaching and working with cadets. He founded the *Royal Military College Magazine* in 1891, but the War Office ordered it to be discontinued, reportedly because it was "too progressive" (Luvaas 1964, p. 221). In 1891, Henderson published *The Battle of Spicheren[,] August 6th 1870, and the Events That Preceded It: A Study in Practical Tactics and War Training*, a military history study used to train students in judgment.

This book resulted in Henderson's appointment in 1892 as Maurice's replacement at the Staff College. His stimulating lectures used military campaigns as examples of the practical application of various tactics. In 1898, Henderson wrote his monumental work, *Stonewall Jackson and the American Civil War*, which sealed his reputation as a military historian. In this study, to which Wolseley wrote the foreword, Henderson emphasized the strategic aspects of the war and the development of military leadership and command, as personified by Jackson.

Henderson was appointed director of military intelligence in South Africa in January 1900, but he held the position for only a few months before returning to England due to malaria and excessive fatigue. He died in 1903, and his collection of essays, *The Science of War*, was posthumously published in 1905. A protégé of Wolseley, inspiring teacher, and superb military historian, Henderson influenced the generation of British Army officers that served as the senior commanders in World War I.

See also Boer War, Second (1899–1902); Camberley, Staff College; Intellectuals, British Army; Intelligence; Maurice, Major General Sir (John) Frederick; Sandhurst, Royal Military College; Tel el-Kebir, Battle of; Wolseley, Field Marshal Garnet J.
References: Bond (1972); Fergusson (1984); Luvaas (1964); Preston (1964); Spiers (1992); Strachan (1997)

Henty, G. A.
See Correspondents, War

Hicks Pasha, Major General William (1830–1883)

Major General William Hicks Pasha served almost thirty years in the Bombay Army before retiring and joining the Egyptian Army, where he is best remembered for leading the force that was massacred by dervishes near El Obeid on 5 November 1883.

Hicks, born in 1830, was commissioned in the Bombay Army in 1849. He saw considerable action during the Indian Mutiny (1857–1859). During the Abyssinian War, Hicks served as brigade major of the 2nd Brigade, 1st Division, and participated in the capture of Magdala (13 April 1868). After respected but undistinguished service in the Indian Army, he retired as a colonel in 1880.

After the British occupied Egypt in 1882, he was employed by the Egyptian khedive as a major general, and in February 1883 was sent to Khartoum as chief of staff of the Egyptian Army in the Sudan. The Egyptian Army in the Sudan consisted mainly of demoralized soldiers who had been in Arabi's forces during the 1882 rebellion, had been imprisoned afterward, and as punishment had been marched in chains to the Sudan. One contemporary British Army officer observed that "the Egyptian officers are ignorant and incapable of grasping the meaning of the slightest movement. A third of the troops cannot use their rifles and would be more formidable if armed with sticks" (Neillands 1996, p. 68).

Hicks and his fellow British officers spent about one month trying to train their soldiers, then marched the 10,000-man force out of Khartoum on 29 April 1883. A few days later, Hicks's soldiers defeated and killed about 500 dervishes at Jebel Ard, south of Khartoum. The Egyptian force returned to Khartoum, where it stayed for about four months.

Hicks led his army out of Khartoum again on 9 September 1883, in the full heat of summer, and they left their forward base at El Duam on 27 September. Hicks's army marched toward El Obeid, which had been captured by the Mahdi in January 1883. Harassed by dervish patrols and running short of water, Hicks's force moved clumsily as a large hollow square (with about 6,000 camels in the center) through Kordofan. Morale, discipline, and cohesion plummeted, and on 3 November 1883 the force reached Kashgil, perhaps led into a trap by treacherous guides.

Mahdist forces were waiting at Kashgil and began a continuous fire on the large target. Hicks's army again advanced the morning of 4 November 1883; later that day or on the following one, the square was broken and wholesale slaughter began. Of Hicks's 10,000 Egyptian soldiers, only about 300 survived the bloodbath, and most survivors were captured by the dervishes. Hicks may have been lacking in competence but not in courage. In keeping with the Sudanese custom, the heads of Hicks and his other leaders were taken to the Mahdi.

The news of the veritable annihilation of Hicks's army shocked Cairo and shattered complacency in London, where the nature of the Sudanese quagmire was finally realized.

See also Arabi Rebellion; Bombay Army; Egypt; Egyptian Army; Indian Mutiny; Kashgil, Battle of; Magdala, Capture of; Mahdi; Sudan

References: Barthorp (1984); Daly (1997); Herbert (1983); Mansfield (1971); Neillands (1896); Slatin Pasha (1896)

Hlobane, Battle of (28 March 1879)

See Buller, General Sir Redvers H., V.C.; Wood, Field Marshal Sir (Henry) Evelyn M., V.C.; Zulu War

Hobhouse, Emily (1860–1926)

Emily Hobhouse was a British Liberal, pacifist, and self-appointed social worker who was one of the first to visit and report on the deficiencies of the refugee "concentration" camps in South Africa during the Second Boer War (1899–1902). Her complaints after her return to England prompted the government to establish the Fawcett Commission, which further investigated camp conditions and helped improve the sanitary and living conditions in them.

Born in 1860 in Cornwall, England, Hobhouse lived with her parents and took care of her invalid father until he died in 1895. She then traveled to the United States, where she reportedly became a social worker. Hobhouse returned to England after an unsuccessful marriage engagement.

Hobhouse became active in numerous social work and political reform movements, including the Adult Suffrage Society. Belonging to the radical wing of the Liberal Party, she opposed the Second Boer War that broke out in October 1899. Hobhouse spoke at several public meetings, denouncing the policies and activities of the British Government.

In late 1900, after the institution of British farm burning and land clearance policies in South Africa and the establishment of camps to house and protect displaced Boer refugees, Hobhouse began to learn details of poor treatment and unsatisfactory conditions in the camps. At about the same time, Hobhouse established the South African Women and Children Distress (or Relief) Fund, to provide food and clothing to those interned in the camps. Few people or groups, however, contributed to Hobhouse's fund.

Hobhouse traveled to South Africa to deliver supplies from her fund to the camps, arriving in South Africa on 27 December 1900. Sir (later Lord) Alfred Milner, high commissioner for South Africa, approved her visits. She visited several camps—all white camps—including those south of Bloemfontein, at Norvalspont, Aliwal North, Springfontein, Kimberley, and Orange River. Hobhouse complained to authorities at these camps about inadequate sanitary conditions and alleged insufficient rations.

Hobhouse, considered "pro-Boer" and a "screamer," returned to England in May 1901. She wrote a lengthy report exposing the worst aspects of the South African concentration camps and the harsh military methods employed by the British to end the war. Hobhouse tried to return to South Africa in October 1901 but was prohibited from doing so. Whether Hobhouse was motivated by social welfare concerns or was using the camps to advance her Liberal pacifist political agenda cannot be ascertained. Parliament appointed the all-female Fawcett Commission, excluding Hobhouse, to travel to South Africa and report on the conditions in the camps. The Fawcett Commission confirmed Hobhouse's main points and made a number of commonsense recommendations for camp improvement that were implemented shortly thereafter.

Hobhouse remained active in pacifist and social welfare organizations for the rest of her life. She died in Cornwall on 8 June 1926 and her ashes were buried in 1927 at the foot of the Women's Memorial in Bloemfontein, South Africa.

See also Boer War, Second (1899–1902); Concentration Camps; Kitchener, Field Marshal Horatio H.; Roberts, Field Marshal Frederick S., V.C.

References: Lee (1985); Marix Evans (2000); Pakenham (1979)

Home Defense

Home defense—the protection of the British Isles from foreign attack or invasion—was a mission of the British Army throughout this period. While imperial defense was the British Army's main strategic role in the nineteenth century, its rationalization and the allocation of troops to overseas stations had an additional purpose of releasing as many soldiers as possible for home defense duty.

Numerous coastal fortifications were built during the Napoleonic War years, and many of these forts and batteries were used through the mid-nineteenth century. They were considered important defenses in any possible war with France that dominated home defense concerns for decades. In 1828, for example, 33,556 soldiers were stationed at home. This number decreased to 28,277 by 1839 but increased to 52,460 in the following decade.

The issue of home defense rose to the forefront with the accession of Louis Napoleon to power in 1851. Concern that the French might use steamships as assault vessels led to the construction of numerous fortifications at key naval harbors and arsenals, including the Channel Islands, Portsmouth, Plymouth, Pembroke, Medway, and other locations.

Throughout the 1850s and early 1860s, the British Army in the United Kingdom was understrength and insufficient to man completed and projected fortifications. To augment the strength of the British Army, traditional reserve forces were revived and organized to accomplish peacetime and wartime tasks.

The Militia Act of 1852 revived the militia in numbers and effectiveness and also fixed the strength of the militia at 80,000 men to be raised by voluntary recruitment. In 1858, over 30,000 militiamen were mobilized for home defense. The militia system was strengthened and the British Army further modernized by the Cardwell Reforms of the early 1870s, which included the "localization" of the military system in territorial areas, where line regiments would be linked with militia regiments. The Localization Act of 1872 also transferred control of the militia and volunteers from the lords lieutenant to the Crown. During the Second Boer War (1899–1902), militia battalions, in addition to other tasks, provided home defense.

Elements of the Rifle Volunteer Corps (and some artillery and engineer units)—the volunteers—consisting of middle-class volunteers, were reestablished in 1859. In 1860–1863, the Rifle Volunteer Corps units were organized into administrative battalions, and the 1863 Volunteer Act legally established the force. In 1871, the War Office assumed administrative responsibility for the volunteer forces. In the 1880s and early 1890s, military debate frequently focused on home defense and the role of the volunteers.

The yeomanry, which was part-time cavalry, was called out on a number of occasions to assist the civil power between 1816 and 1867. The home secretary was responsible for the yeomanry until 1871, when control was passed to the secretary of state for war. In 1888, yeomanry units became liable for service anywhere within the United Kingdom for home defense duty.

In the late 1880s, further plans were developed for home defense. As a less expensive alternative to augmenting the Royal Navy or increasing the size of the British Army at home, it was decided to construct two rings of fixed defenses around London. Fortification lines were surveyed and plans drawn up, but little work was actually done. Sixty "Stanhope storehouses," named after the secretary of state for war, Edward Stanhope, were built, and were later used during the Second Boer War mobilization.

In 1908, the auxiliary forces were reorganized to provide a more effective and efficient system for reinforcing the regular army and providing home defense. The volunteers (infantry) and yeomanry were merged as the Territorial Force (later the Territorial Army). This provided a reserve force of fourteen infantry divisions and fourteen cavalry brigades that in peacetime served in the United Kingdom only and provided home defense, but in wartime could volunteer for overseas service.

See also Cardwell Reforms; Coastal Fortifications; Haldane, Richard B.; Militia; Mobilization Planning; Stanhope, Edward; Stanhope Memorandum; Volunteers; Yeomanry
References: Kochanski (1999); Partridge (1989); Strachan (1984)

Horse Guards

The headquarters of the British Army in the British Isles was known originally as the Horse Guards. It was established in 1793 when it was decided to appoint a soldier as commander in chief to administer the British Army. In 1795, Field Marshal H.R.H. Frederick, Duke of York (the son of King George III), became commander in chief. The Duke of York established a staff of three assistants: a military secretary, an adjutant-general, and a quartermaster-general. It was this organization, located in Whitehall, that became known as the Horse Guards. Through much of the nineteenth century, the Horse Guards attempted to retain total control over the army (except financial) against what was perceived to be civilian interference in military matters.

A number of significant reforms to streamline the effectiveness of the British Army and establish the primacy of civilian control over the military were undertaken in the early 1850s. In June 1854, the secretary of state for war was separated from the secretary of state of the colonies, the first time Great Britain possessed a full-time secretary of state solely for military affairs.

The commander in chief was supposed to be subordinate to the secretary of state for war, although he remained physically separated from the War Office at the Horse Guards. The War Office Act of 1870 consolidated the War Office and the Horse Guards and also required the commander in chief to physically move from the Horse Guards to the War Office, an unmistakable indicator of his new subordinate role as principal military adviser to the secretary of state. Even though the British Army commander in chief and his staff moved to the War Office in Pall Mall, the term "Horse Guards" was still frequently used to refer to the military component of the War Office.

See also Adjutant-General, British Army; Cambridge, Field Marshal H.R.H. Prince George F., Second Duke of; Commander in Chief, British Army; Master-General of the Ordnance, British Army; Quartermaster-General, British Army; War Office

References: Barnett (1970); Hamer (1970); Moyse-Bartlett (1974); Spiers (1992)

Hunter, General Sir Archibald (1856–1936)

General Sir Archibald Hunter was an inspiring leader, a superb troop trainer, and a skillful commander who made significant contributions to the British reconquest of the Sudan and operations during the Second Boer War.

Born on 6 September 1856, Hunter was gazetted to the 4th Foot after Sandhurst attendance in 1874. He served on Gibraltar and participated in the 1884–1885 Gordon Relief Expedition in the Sudan. Hunter served in the Egyptian Army from 1884 to 1899, gaining experience fighting against the dervishes while holding positions of increasing responsibility. He was severely wounded and was awarded the Distinguished Service Order (D.S.O.) for his leadership at the Battle of Ginnis (30 December 1885), and was again wounded while commanding a brigade at the Battle of Toski (3 August 1889).

Hunter continued to serve in the Sudan, where he was considered the "right-hand man" of the sirdar, Major General (later Field Marshal Earl) Sir Horatio H. Kitchener. After commanding the infantry at the Battle of Firket (7 June 1896), Hunter was promoted to major general in November 1896; he was reportedly the youngest British Army major general since Field Marshal Arthur Wellesley, First Duke of Wellington. Other major actions took place, notably the Battle of Atbara (8 April 1898), where Hunter initially advised Kitchener to delay his attack, and the Battle of Omdurman (2 September 1898), where Hunter commanded his division and maneuvered his troops and reserves with great skill. Hunter was knighted for his superb leadership in battle.

In May 1899, Hunter was assigned to India to command the Quetta Division. After the outbreak of the Second Boer War, he was appointed chief of staff to General (later Field Marshal) Sir George S. White, V.C., and played an indispensable role in the defense of Ladysmith. After the relief of Ladysmith, Hunter was promoted to lieutenant general and given command of the 10th Division. He led his division on numerous mobile operations, culminating at Brandwater Basin, where about 4,000 Boers surrendered on 30 July 1900. Hunter was invalided to England in January 1901.

Hunter commanded the Scottish District (later Command), from 1901 to 1903 and then was reassigned to India, where he commanded first the Western and then the Southern Army until 1908. He was promoted to general in 1905 while in India, and in 1910, Hunter was appointed governor and commander in chief of Gibraltar. He was not a success at Gibraltar, as his outspokenness and uncharacteristic discourtesy over a number of issues caused considerable friction with the civil population. Faced with possible dismissal, he resigned in 1913.

Shortly after the outbreak of World War I, Hunter was given command of Aldershot Training Center, and later of Aldershot Command, where he worked hard until late 1917 to train the troops needed for the front. In 1916, the prime minister stated that Hunter had "won the Battle of Omdurman in spite of Kitchener, and defended Ladysmith in spite of White" (Hunter 1996, p. 2). In spite of the high regard in which he was seemingly held, Hunter was very disappointed not to receive a combat command in World War I and to not have been promoted to field marshal. Hunter retired from the army in 1920.

Hunter served in Parliament briefly, was active in regimental affairs and charitable work, and died on 28 June 1936.

See also Aldershot; Atbara, Battle of; Boer War, Second (1899–1902); Dervishes; Egyptian Army; Ginnis, Battle of; Gordon Relief Expedition; Kitchener, Field Marshal Horatio H.; Ladysmith, Siege of; Omdurman, Battle of; Reconquest of the Sudan; Sandhurst, Royal Military College; Sudan; Toski, Battle of; White, Field Marshal Sir George S., V.C.

References: Griffith (1974); Hunter (1996); Magnus (1959); Pakenham (1979); Wickham Legg (1949); Ziegler (1974)

I

Imperial Service Troops

At no time did the East India Company, or later the British Crown, directly control the entire subcontinent of India. In the aftermath of the Indian Mutiny, about 562 semiautonomous princes ruled their own states under British guidance. These rulers maintained a large bodyguard, if not a small army, for their protection and prestige.

In 1885, when war with Russia over Afghanistan seemed imminent, many of these princes loyally offered troops to the service of the government of India and the British Empire. The Indian government's acceptance of this offer showed the princes that the British had faith in their loyalty. The government of India formed, from the princes' troop contributions, the composite Imperial Service Troops in 1889. Princes who joined this program agreed to raise and support units and train and equip them to Indian Army standards. Each ruler recruited his own troops from his own subjects, paid for them, and designated his own commanders. A British Army officer from the Indian Army establishment was attached to each native contingent to serve as military adviser.

The Indian rulers were serious in their pledges of troop contributions. During the 1895 Chitral Expedition, transport trains were organized by the maharajas of Gwalior and Jaipur, and Imperial Service Troops of the maharaja of Kashmir fought gallantly in the same campaign. The maharaja of Kashmir's army totaled 18,000 men with 66 artillery pieces. The maharaja of Jodhpur provided a cavalry force, and the maharaja of Ulwar trained 600 cavalry and 1,000 infantry soldiers for the Imperial Service Troops.

Many Imperial Service Troops also served overseas. Hyderabad sent contingents to Burma in 1888–1890 and to South Africa in 1902–1904. Alwar, Bikaner, and Jodhpur sent troops to China in 1900–1901 to help suppress the Boxer Rebellion, and Bikaner sent Imperial Service Troops to Somaliland in 1901–1904.

By 1912, the Imperial Service Troops consisted of over 20,000 soldiers contributed by the local Indian rulers. This program helped improve the readiness of the forces of indigenous rulers, increased interoperability between the Imperial Service Troops, Indian, and British forces, and enhanced Anglo-Indian relations and trust.

See also Boxer Rebellion; East India Company; Great Game; India; India, British Army in; Indian Army Operations; Indian Army Organization; North-West Frontier; Penjdeh Incident
References: Beaumont (1977); Farwell (1989); Haythornthwaite (1995); Heathcote (1974); MacMunn (1930); Roberts (1897); Sundaram (2002)

Imperialism

Imperialism was the policy of territorial expansion conducted with increasing success by European powers, especially Great Britain, between 1815 and 1914. There were many reasons for imperialism, including the search for raw materials and markets for Great Britain's manufactured goods during the Industrial Revolution; "Social Darwinism," in which the British felt superior to other peoples and thought it was their duty to "civilize" them by spreading their superior culture, religion, influence, and government; to retain the balance of power of European nations; to distract public opinion from domestic economic dis-

Imperialism

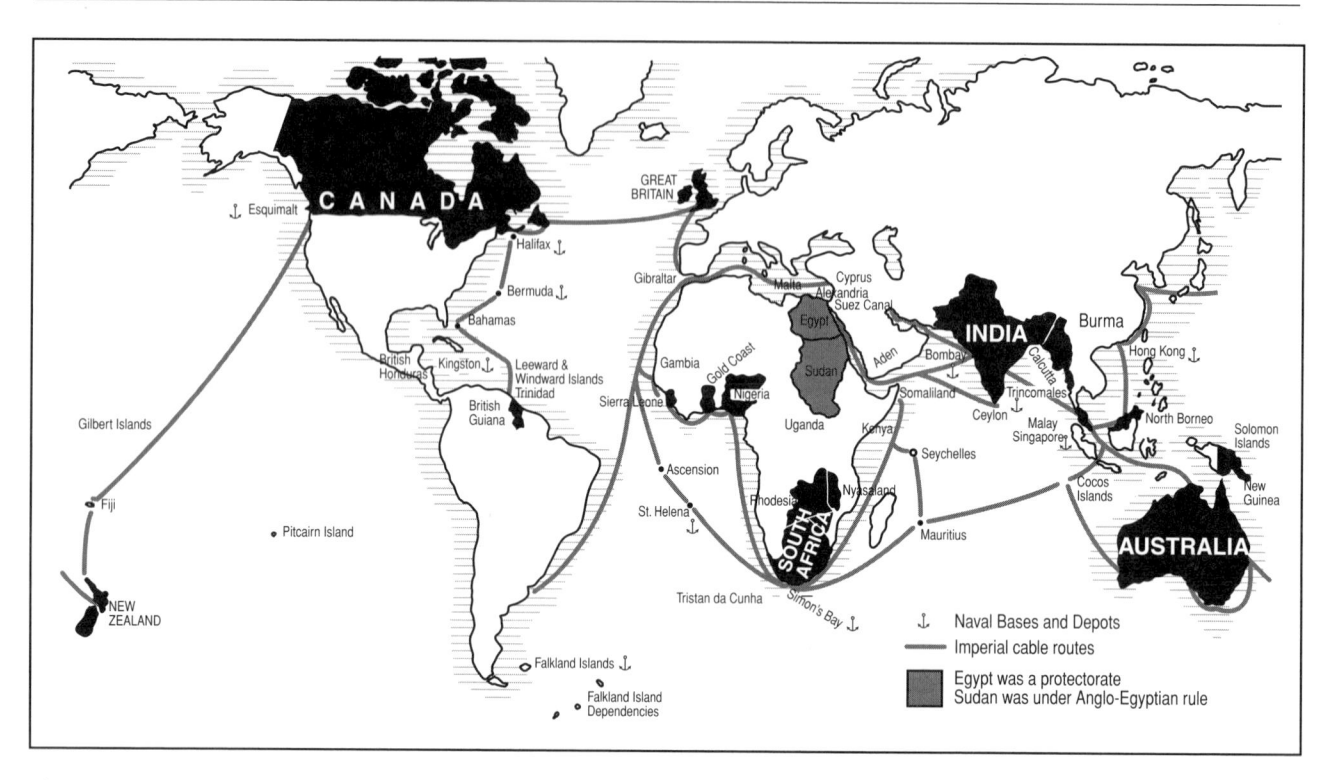

The British Empire, 1914

tress and social tension; rivalry among industrialized "great" powers; and the creation of allies. The British Army was also seen as a civilizing influence. As the instrument of British imperialism, the British soldier fought his nation's small wars and colonial campaigns and then administered those possessions.

The foundation of British imperialism, from the end of the fifteenth century to the middle of the nineteenth century, was mercantilism and the accumulation of wealth, which produced long-term economic growth. Mercantilism was a general economic policy in which new sources of raw materials were discovered and the contiguous areas colonized, and these colonies later became the markets for manufactured goods, especially during the burgeoning Industrial Revolution. A key element of this policy was maintaining a favorable balance of trade by regulating commerce, with low tariffs on imported raw materials and high tariffs on imported manufactured goods. The British sought tea and spices from the Far East, and when the Chinese, for example, were reluctant to accept British manufactures in exchange for tea, the British sold and smuggled opium to equalize the trade balance. This caused conflict and war, fought by the British Army. Until the middle of the nineteenth century, British imperialism focused on India and the Far East. Sea power was essential to conduct imperialism and maintain overseas colonies and markets. The period of mercantilism basically ended with the repeal of the Corn Laws in 1846, which ushered in a period of free trade.

The Indian Mutiny (1857–1859) transformed British Army units stationed in India into an army of occupation that assisted the civil power in the maintenance of British rule. Russian encroachment in Central Asia, dangerously close to British India, provided the British Army with a definite mission.

The 1860s was a period of tremendous turmoil, as the British textile industry was almost destroyed by the lack of cotton caused by the American Civil War. Numerous domestic and foreign pressures bore on Great Britain. France and Prussia—the latter soon to be a major component of a united Germany—began to challenge British hegemony. In 1867, Prime Minister Benjamin Disraeli launched an expedition to Abyssinia. During the first half of the nineteenth century, Africa, due to a lack of raw materials, the abolition of slavery, and perceptions of primitive cultures, had been generally neglected by Great Britain and other European nations. Disraeli timed this operation to distract attention from domestic woes, demonstrate the popular appeal of imperialism, and secure Abyssinia, to the south of Egypt, where the French would be completing the Suez Canal the following year. Disraeli wanted to forestall French influence in Africa while securing Britain's new lifeline, via the Suez Canal, to India and the Far East.

Imperialism became popular in the 1870s, as did the British Army. War and conflict, in the context of Social Darwinism, came to be seen as a natural occurrence in evolution and suggested British superiority in all areas. This ideology provided a rationale for war and conquest against "inferior peoples": "the destruction of their armies could be justified as a part of a constructive and civilising mission, a precursor to bringing them the unquestioned benefits of trade, technology, Christianity and British rule" (Spiers 1992, p. 185). The popular press, available to an increasingly literate public, encouraged these patriotic and militaristic sentiments as the British Army engaged in frequently romanticized colonial wars and campaigns.

A new wave of European rivalry and imperialism, the "scramble for Africa," began in 1876 when King Leopold II of Belgium established a private company to exploit the wealth of the Congo basin. France, which had lost the provinces of Alsace and Lorraine to the Germans in the Franco-Prussian War (1870–1871), was eager to regain lost prestige by gaining overseas colonies and supported a rival of the Belgians. In 1877, the British annexed the Transvaal in order to protect South Africa. The French occupied Tunisia in 1881, and two years later the British divided up Niger with France. In 1884, accelerating European imperialism in Africa, the Germans seized Cameroon, Togoland, and South West Africa, and Great Britain reacted by claiming more colonies. The rapid pace and relative ease of colonial conquest was aided by technological innovations, including machine guns.

Even though Britain continued to expand territorially, there were internal signs of decline, including decreasing exports, increasing imports, and a growing population. Moreover, the United States, for example, outproduced Great Britain in steel in 1880, in iron in 1890, and in coal production in 1900. Germany produced more steel than Great Britain in 1895.

Imperialistic rivalry between Great Britain and France culminated at Fashoda, in the south of Sudan, in September 1898. France withdrew from Fashoda in December 1898 and tension decreased.

The British conducted imperialism in Africa and around the globe, until the eve of World War I, to maintain their empire, taking South Africa and Egypt in order to protect India. Other areas were annexed to be able to compete economically with France and Germany, and to establish allies in the event of war with either country.

In 1860, the British Empire totaled about "9.5 million square miles; by 1909 the total had risen to 12.7 million. The British Empire [then] covered around 25 per cent of the world's land surface—making it three times the size of the French Empire and ten times that of the Germans—and controlled roughly the same proportion of the world's population: some 444 million people lived under some form of British rule" (Ferguson 2003, p. 1). The British Army, through its many colonial campaigns, had helped make the British Empire a success.

See also Abyssinian War; China; China War, First (1839–1842); Disraeli, Benjamin; Fashoda Incident; Gladstone, William E.; Great Game; India; Penjdeh Incident; Rhodes, Cecil J.; Slavery; Suez Canal

References: Barclay (1976); Beloff (1996); Ferguson (2003); Harcourt (1980); Headrick (1979); James (1985); O'Brien (1996); Pakenham (1991); Spiers (1992)

India

The British established their presence in India early in the seventeenth century when ships of the East India Company first reached its shores. By 1815, the company possessed the most powerful army in India. It also governed, directly or indirectly, Bengal, areas astride the Ganges River, and large areas in eastern and southern India, and it was continuing to expand its influence.

The defeat of the powerful Maratha Confederacy in 1822 established Britain as the paramount power in India. Sind was conquered in 1843, and the Punjab was annexed after the end of the Second Sikh War in 1849. There were few opportunities for additional British territorial expansion.

Under the East India Company, India was divided into three administrative entities—Bengal, Madras, and Bombay—called presidencies. Each presidency had its own governor and its own army under its own commander in chief. The Bengal Presidency, with its capital at Calcutta, was the largest of the three presidencies. The Bengal governor was made governor-general of Bengal in 1774, and in 1853 his control was extended over all political, civil, and military

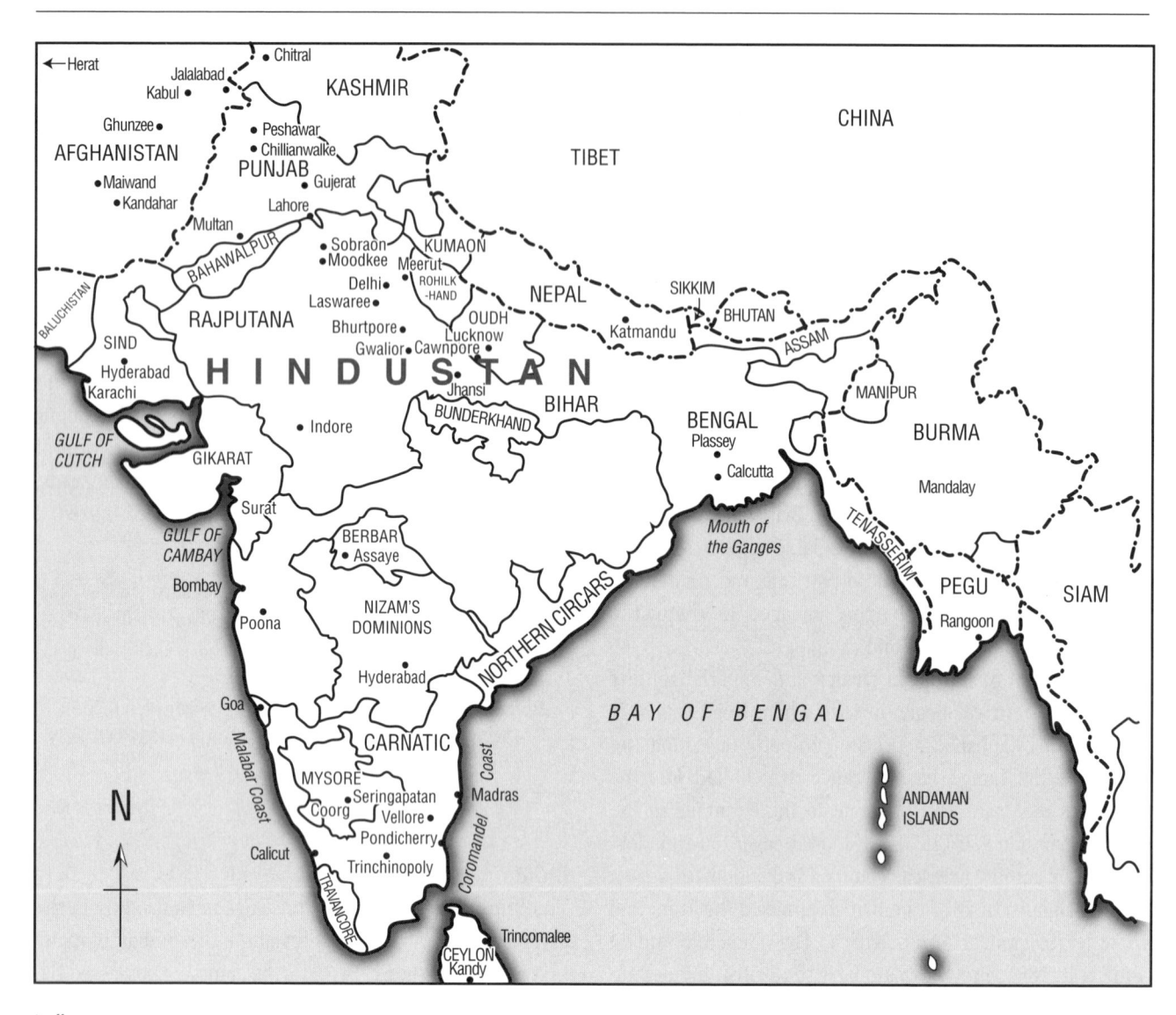

India

policy in India when he became the governor-general of India. When the British Government assumed all responsibility for the administration of India in 1858, the governor-general was also styled viceroy and became the representative of the sovereign.

The British ruled (in 1858) the Indian subcontinent, which covered an area of about 1.6 million square miles (six times larger than Texas), with every extreme of climate, topography, and vegetation. The heterogeneous population of about 400 million consisted of myriad races, languages, and cultures, most of whom were either Hindus or Muslims. Almost a quarter of the population of the subcontinent, however, did not live in British India, but in over 100 semi-autonomous princely states that had entered into alliance with the East India Company and later the Crown.

A key institution in India is the caste system, a concept very different from class. The Hindus were divided into about 3,000 groups, and people were forbidden to marry outside their group. Groups were further subdivided and it was usually prohibited to marry within the subdivision. Caste affected an Indian's entire life. "There are elaborate rules about eating, drinking, smoking and washing. Men from the higher groups must eat and smoke only with those of their own group and must not accept food or water from the lower—although there are almost always exceptions and some kinds of food are less subject to pollution than others"

(Mason 1974, p. 123). Anyone who broke caste rules became an "outcast" shunned by all. The outcast could only be cleansed by a long penance concluding with elaborate and expensive ceremonies. It is difficult to rank the castes exactly, but in general terms they were the Brahmins (priests), Rajputs (lords), Banias (merchants), and Sudras (serfs). Those outside the caste system were generally called "untouchables."

Perceptions and practices of caste in the three presidency armies were different. In the Bengal Army, notions of caste were included in the military recruiting patterns and organization. In the Madras and Bombay Armies, men in the ranks were considered relatively equal.

Caste concerns, primarily in the Bengal Army over the "greased cartridge" issue, helped ignite the Indian Mutiny in 1857. Other underlying issues in this cultural clash include harsh revenue policies, an apparent British indifference to indigenous religion and culture, and the policy of "lapse," according to which a state whose ruler did not have a male heir would come under control of the British when that ruler died. From the perspective of the British imperialist, "the Indians had for many years been the beneficiaries of a humane system of government, deliberately contrived to uplift them and modernise their country" (James 1999, p. 96).

The Indian Mutiny was marked by unimaginable brutality on both the British and Indian sides. As a result, the East India Company relinquished control of India to the British Crown in 1858.

As a key component of Britain's mercantile and imperial strategy, India imported British products worth £21 million in 1867, as much as Britain's largest foreign customer, the United States.

As India was "the brightest jewel in the British Crown," the British were constantly concerned about Russian encroachment in Central Asia, seemingly targeted at an invasion of India. The Great Game, as this imperial rivalry was called, spawned a "Forward School" of British strategy that argued for active measures to counter the potential Russian threat—and later resulted in the Second Afghan War (1878–1880).

In 1877, Queen Victoria was authorized by the Royal Titles Act to assume the additional title "Empress of India."

During the last few decades of the nineteenth century, the British Raj (British rule in India) was characterized by Indian attempts to participate in their government. The Indian National Congress was formed in 1885. Later in Bengal, armed revolutionaries conducted a campaign of terror and assassination that resulted in the partition of Bengal in 1905 and provoked resistance to British rule. The Muslim League was founded in 1907. India became independent on 15 August 1947.

See also Afghan War, Second (1878–1880); Bengal Army; Bombay Army; East India Company; East India Company, Military Forces; Great Game; Imperial Service Troops; Imperialism; India, British Army in; Indian Army Operations; Indian Army Organization; Indian Mutiny; Madras Army; North-West Frontier; Officers, Indian Army—Social Background
References: Heathcote (1974); James (1998); James (1999); Mason (1974); Ward (1996)

India, British Army in

The British Army in India consisted of two separate armies and was occasionally referred to as the "Army in India." The smaller of the two consisted of regular army units of the British Crown, serving a rotational tour of duty in India. The second and larger of the two was the army of the East India Company until 1858. The entire army in India was divided until 1895 into three separate armies under the control of the three presidencies into which British India was divided. These three armies were known as the Bengal Army (headquartered in Delhi), Bombay Army, and Madras Army, the latter two headquartered in the port city from which they took their names. Each of the three presidency armies included, until 1858, East India Company forces and British Army Crown forces. After 1858, East India Company control was abolished and the forces were amalgamated under Crown control. The Indian Army initially referred to those units of the East India Company, and after the Indian Mutiny, those forces including indigenous troops and British officers employed directly by the Government of India.

The 39th Foot was the first British infantry regiment sent to India in 1754, followed by the 84th Foot five years later. Four additional infantry regiments (74th–77th) were raised specifically for service in India in 1787. The first British Army cavalry regiment to serve in India was the 19th Light Dragoons, which was raised there in 1781. They formed the nucleus of a British Army force in India.

British Army officers frequently had mixed reactions when their regiments were ordered to India. Some wealthy, aristocratic officers, especially during times of peace, did not desire to serve in an unhealthy climate for extended periods and lead a relatively mundane garrison life, and they exchanged into regiments staying comfortably at home. Less wealthy officers frequently looked forward to a higher standard of living in India, where an officer's pay would stretch about 20 percent further than in England. The officers' social life centered around the regimental mess. For affluent officers, generous leave and few garrison duties enabled them to frequently hunt, ride, and engage in sports such as pig sticking and polo. Some officers tried to learn foreign languages (proficiency was rewarded by a small monetary allowance) and increase their military professionalism and knowledge, although other officers frequently looked down on such dedication. British Army officers generally did not socialize with their British counterparts in the Indian Army.

British Army other ranks were frequently bored with peacetime regimental soldiering in India but lacked the means to take advantage of the social and sporting activities that officers could afford. In the 1830s and 1840s, drill in many regiments was limited to nine hours per week. This gave the soldiers ample opportunity to wander around the regimental bazaar and adjacent towns. To pass the time, many soldiers got drunk. In 1835, for example, "the 674 customers of the 49th Regiment's canteen drank 7,217 gallons of *arrack* [a locally distilled and very strong rice liquor], 177 of brandy, and 144 of gin" (James 1998, p. 138). There were frequent deaths from alcoholism, as well as debilitating liver and related ailments that rendered soldiers ineffective for duty.

Venereal disease was another significant problem among British other ranks in India. A study made over a five-year period during the 1830s revealed a 32–45 percent venereal disease rate among British other ranks, as compared to 2–3 percent in Indian regiments. Military authorities in India, at a distance from religious moralists in Great Britain, were more realistic and circumspect in their attitudes toward prostitution. In India, brothels were inspected and operated, and prostitutes regulated, by military authorities. When brothels were closed temporarily in 1888, the venereal disease rate for British soldiers in India increased tremendously, and military brothels were reopened in 1899. The imposition of stricter controls reduced rates of venereal disease. Moreover, many regiments by that time operated their own brothels, with patrons restricted to British soldiers.

Later in this period sporting teams and competitions were developed, as were other activities, including musical concerts, to encourage moral, healthy behavior and conduct.

In the military reorganization that took place after the Indian Mutiny, the East India Company's European regiments were all amalgamated into the British Army. The 1st, 2nd, and 3rd Bengal European Light Cavalry Regiments became, respectively, the 19th, 20th, and 21st Hussars. Each of the three presidency armies also had three European infantry, light infantry, or fusilier regiments, and these were absorbed into the British Army as the 101st through 109th Regiments. Between 1860 and 1914, there were normally 50 British Army infantry battalions serving in India, which was generally at least one-third of the infantry strength of the entire British Army. (In 1879, for example, there were 82 British Army infantry battalions serving overseas, including India, and 59 at home.) In comparison, in 1865 there were 142 Indian Army infantry battalions and 42 cavalry regiments, in addition to support troops.

The strength of the combined British Army in India generally exceeded 200,000 soldiers throughout this period. In 1863, there were 205,000 Indian Army soldiers and 65,000 British soldiers, for a total of 270,000 soldiers serving in India. That number decreased to a total of 226,000 soldiers (153,000 Indian and 73,000 British) by 1887, and to 219,000 soldiers (142,000 Indians and 77,000 British) in 1903.

See also Bengal Army; Bombay Army; East India Company; East India Company, Military Forces; India; Indian Army Operations; Indian Army Organization; Madras Army; Military Medicine, British Army—Venereal Disease; Officers, British Army—Social Background; Sports and Recreation

References: Farwell (1989); Heathcote (1974); James (1998); Mason (1974); Raugh (1985); Raugh (1994); Spiers (1992); Wolseley (1878)

Indian Army Operations

The British Army in India—including its regular British Army units and its East India Company military forces/Indian Army units—fought in many wars of company and imperial expansion, punitive expeditions, and other campaigns. With few exceptions, composite units, consisting of both British and company/Indian Army units, were formed on a provisional basis for a specific mission, campaign, or punitive expedition. They were generally combined arms units, consisting of infantry, cavalry, and artillery, with support elements. When the operation's goal was accomplished, the provisional unit was disbanded. The requirement to secure India internally and defend it against external threats was the responsibility of the Army in India.

Campaigns prior to 1815 eliminated the French threat to the East India Company's domination of the area and helped the company seize and control additional territory. After 1815, numerous campaigns and wars were fought. The Indian Army, for example, fought against the Gurkhas in northern India and Nepal (1814–1816) and against the lawless Marathas (1817–1818).

For myriad reasons, including the establishment of friendly rulers in Afghanistan to help deter Persian and Russian encroachment, British and company troops of the "Army of the Indus" invaded Afghanistan in 1839. The British actually suffered a reverse in the First Afghan War (1839–1842). For similar reasons, the British launched and fought the Second Afghan War (1878–1880). The Persian War was fought in 1856–1857.

Sind was conquered and annexed by the company in 1843, and indigenous forces in Gwalior were suppressed the same year. Two wars (1845–1846; 1848–1849) were fought against the Sikh state of Punjab, the main independent power remaining in India. After the Sikhs were defeated in 1849, the British annexed the Punjab. After the Punjab was annexed, the border area between British India and Afghanistan became the North-West Frontier, a mountainous area of frequently hostile tribesmen. Beginning in 1849, the British sent numerous punitive expeditions and other field forces to discourage raiding, subdue hostilities, and maintain tranquility on the frontier. Expeditionary forces on the North-West Frontier ranged from approximately a brigade-size force, such as the one that fought the Waziris in 1852, to the 1897 Tirah Field Force that consisted of 34,506 British and Indian Army officers and other ranks, and 19,934 noncombatants.

Three wars were fought in Burma (1823–1826; 1852–1853; and 1885), mainly by troops of the Army in India. There were also a number of expeditions to the "North-East Frontier" that included Lushai, the Naga Hills, the Chin Hills, and Manipur.

East India Company and Indian Army units fought in various Asian conflicts. Indian troops served in the First China (or Opium) War (1839–1842), the Second China (*Arrow*) War (1856–1860), and in the 1900 Boxer rebellion in China. An Indian Army battalion also landed on Japan in 1863, with British Army units, to temporarily occupy a portion of that country. An expeditionary force from India was sent to Aden in 1865–1866, and another to Perak in Malaysia in 1875–1876.

The Indian Mutiny (1857–1859) was an especially bloody conflict frequently pitting company and British Army units against company battalions that had rebelled. After the Indian Mutiny, rebellious units were disbanded, company European regiments were merged into the British Army, and company authority transferred to the British Crown.

Army in India units also fought overseas with increasing frequency during this period. There was a long historical company precedent for overseas service, beginning with Madras Army troops defeating the Spanish and capturing Manila in 1762, and in the 1801 Egyptian campaign against the French.

Indian Army units were sent to Malta in April 1878 and participated later that year in the occupation of Cyprus—the first time Indian troops had been sent to Europe.

Indian troops also fought in a number of African campaigns. Many of the troops that fought in the Abyssinian War (1867–1868) were from the Bombay Army, dispatched to Africa because of their relative proximity to the area of operations. The British expeditionary force to Egypt in 1882 contained Indian units, as did the 1884–1885 Gordon Relief Expedition. Indian Army military forces also served in British East Africa between 1896 and 1901. Although the British Government redeployed medical units from India to South Africa, no Indian Army combat arms units were deployed to fight in the Second Boer War (1899–1902) because of possible racial repercussions.

See also Abyssinian War; Afghan War, First (1839–1842); Afghan War, Second (1878–1880); Arabi Rebellion; Boxer Rebellion; Burma War, First (1823–1826); Burma War, Second (1852–1853); Burma War, Third (1885); China War, First (1839–1842); China War, Second (1856–1860); East India Company, Military Forces; Gordon Relief Expedition; Great Game; Gurkha War; Imperialism; India; Indian Army Organization; Indian Mutiny; Japan, Operations against; North-West Frontier; Persian War; Sikh War, First (1845–1846); Sikh War, Second (1848–1849); Sind, Operations in

References: Beckett (1994); Farwell (1989); Fincastle and Eliott-Lockhart (1898); Haythornthwaite (1995); Mason (1974); Scudieri (1988)

Indian Army Organization

The Indian Army consisted of the troops of the East India Company prior to the Indian Mutiny (1857–1859). Afterward

Indian Army Organization

those units with indigenous soldiers and British officers were employed directly by the Government of India. Until 1895 the Indian Army (with its British Army components) was divided into three presidencies: Bengal (headquartered in Calcutta), Bombay, and Madras. The Bengal Presidency was the largest of the three, and its commander in chief served nominally until 1895 as commander in chief, India. In reality, the other two presidency armies were basically autonomous. The Bengal Presidency commander in chief was normally a full general, and the Bombay and Madras commanders in chief were usually lieutenant generals. After 1895, the commander in chief, India, was a full general.

Staff work was conducted in the presidency armies, and later in the consolidated Indian Army, in the same manner as in the British Army. The two principal staff officers, usually major generals, were the adjutant-general (responsible for discipline, training, and administration), and the quartermaster-general (responsible for equipment, barracks, and supplies). Deputies were normally colonels, and deputy assistants were majors. Each presidency also had its own staff corps, but these were consolidated in 1891 to form the Indian Staff Corps.

Prior to 1889, the three main armies were organized into administrative brigades and divisions, but they were rarely assembled as such and generally remained in regimental cantonments and garrisons scattered throughout India. This organizational structure was replaced in 1889 by one that divided each of the armies into first-class or second-class districts, commanded by a major general or brigadier general, respectively. The districts in turn were subdivided into first- or second-class stations, generally under the command of the senior officer, usually a colonel or lieutenant colonel (regimental or battalion commander), serving in it. Units were cobbled together to form four wartime divisions, but there were no divisional commanders or staffs designated or maintained.

In 1895, the three presidency armies were abolished and replaced by one Army of India, divided into four commands. These four commands were the Bengal, Bombay (including Sind and Baluchistan), Madras (including Burma), and the Punjab (including the Punjab Frontier Force).

General (later Field Marshal) Lord Horatio H. Kitchener, commander in chief, India, from 1902–1909, was instrumental in making sweeping organizational changes. To emphasize that there was one unified Indian Army, regiments were renumbered in a single sequence. In addition, it was realized that the Indian Army must be organized, led, and trained in peacetime as in war. Accordingly, the Indian Army was divided into three corps areas with divisions reconstituted and assigned to corps. The Northern Command was to consist of the 1st, 2nd, and 3rd Divisions, and three separate brigades; Western Command was assigned the 4th, 5th, and 6th Divisions, plus one separate brigade; the 7th and 8th Divisions were allocated to Eastern Command. The 9th Division and Burma Division were assigned directly to army headquarters. Due to financial constraints, this plan was only partially accomplished. Indian Army regiments were also rotated throughout the country and to the North-West Frontier.

The basic Indian Army and British Army unit was the infantry battalion and its counterpart, the cavalry regiment. During the Indian Mutiny, sixty-four Bengal regiments mutinied or were preemptively disarmed, whereas only two Bombay Army units, and none in the Madras Army, were disaffected. This was largely attributed to ideas of caste and class, and the organization of single-caste battalions in the Bengal Army. During the amalgamation and reorganization of Indian Army battalions after the mutiny, greater emphasis was placed on the reliability of the "martial races" from northern India, mainly Sikhs, Marathas, Dogras, and Garwhalis. Single-caste battalions in most cases were replaced by mixed battalions with various single-caste companies. A mixed battalion, for example, might consist of "one or two companies of Punjabi Muslims, one or two companies of Sikhs, and perhaps a company of Rajputs and one of Dogras, Pathans or Baluchis" (Mason 1974, p. 24). The aim of this structure was to prevent whole battalions from staging a mutiny again.

After the mutiny, each infantry regiment consisted of one battalion of eight companies. There were six British officers—the commander, second in command, adjutant, quartermaster, medical officer, and one staff officer—in the battalion headquarters, and two additional British officers, each of whom commanded a "wing" of four companies. Uniquely, there were a number of Indian "viceroy's commissioned officers" (VCOs) in the battalion. They were junior to British officers but carried swords, were saluted by Indian other ranks, and were addressed as *sahib* (from the Persian word for "sir"). The senior VCO in an infantry battalion was the *subedar-major*, who carried tremendous prestige and advised the commanding officer. Each company was commanded by a *subedar*, with a *jemadar* as second in command, and consisted of five *havildars* (sergeants), five *naiks* (corporals), 75 *sepoys* (*sipahi,* from the Persian word *sipah,* meaning an army), and two drummers. In the 1890s, the "wings" were replaced by four "double companies." These new subunits had a British Army major or captain in command, and the companies retained their Indian chain of command.

The postmutiny Indian Army cavalry was generally organized on the irregular *sillidar* system (from the Persian word *silahdar,* for "bearer of arms"). In general terms, the *sillidar,* in return for higher pay, contracted to provide and maintain his own horse and equipment. The Indian Army cavalry regiment was commanded by a British Army colonel, assisted by an adjutant and a small staff. The regiment was divided into three squadrons (increased to four in 1885), each with a British commander and second in command. Each squadron had two troops, and each troop was commanded by an Indian *rissaldar* (the cavalry counterpart to the infantry *subedar*) and assisted by a *jemadar*. Each troop further consisted of one *kot-dafadar* (irregular cavalry senior sergeant), eight *dafadars* (sergeants), seventy *sowars* (troopers, from the Persian *savar,* or "one who rides"), and one trumpeter. The cavalry troopers were armed with swords and carbines.

After the Indian Mutiny, field artillery was no longer controlled by Indians but remained under Royal Artillery authority. In 1885, the term "Native" was dropped from regimental titles.

In 1863, for example, there were 205,000 Indian Army soldiers. This total fell to 153,000 Indian Army soldiers by 1887 and to 142,000 in 1903. In 1906, the Indian Army consisted of 129 infantry and pioneer battalions, 40 cavalry regiments, 11 batteries of mountain artillery and one corps of frontier garrison artillery, and 33 companies of sappers and miners and support troops, totaling 158,344 Indian Army soldiers.

See also Adjutant-General, British Army; East India Company, Military Forces; India; India, British Army in; Indian Army Operations; Indian Mutiny; Kitchener, Field Marshal Horatio H.; Punjab Frontier Force; Quartermaster-General, British Army

References: Cunningham (2001); Farwell (1989); Haythornthwaite (1995), Heathcote (1974); Mason (1974); Wolseley (1878)

Indian Mutiny (1857–1859)

The Indian Mutiny was a series of generally unconnected military revolts of Indian soldiers, frequently accompanied by bloody atrocities and suppressed by the British with equal savagery, against the rule and authority of the East India Company. It was also perhaps the inevitable clash of British "civilization" with Indian customs, traditions, and religion. The Indian Mutiny was not an Indian national revolution or general uprising, as asserted by revisionist historians.

Most Britons in India stated they were surprised by the outbreak of the mutiny, although they should not have been. Signs of insurrection had included mutinies at Vellore in 1806, at Barrackpore in 1824, and several during the 1840s and early 1850s. There were indicators of increasing military, religious, social, and political friction, especially since the First Afghan War (1839–1842), when the company's forces were virtually annihilated. This largely destroyed the myth of company and European invincibility. Starting at about the same time, trust and respect between company officers and their soldiers, and vice versa, was steadily diminishing. Because steamships and railroads—also seen as a source of Western mysticism and radical change—brought more officers' families to India, British officers spent more time with their families and less with their soldiers.

Lord Dalhousie, the governor-general from 1848 to 1856, revived the Mughal doctrine of lapse, in which a local state whose ruler did not have a male heir would come under the control of the central government when that ruler died. The intent of the policy was to ensure better government and treatment for the peasants and to expropriate land from landlords who did not possess valid title to the land they claimed. In 1856, the king of Oudh was considered unfit to rule and deposed, and Oudh was annexed by the British. Oudh was the army's, and especially the Bengal Army's, primary recruiting ground, and high-caste Hindu sepoys feared that the social order would be upset further by the British. Many rulers became disenchanted, others worried about the fate of their own states, and Indians felt the British were trying to subsume their entire civilization and culture.

The British, from the Indian perspective, also interfered with indigenous customs and traditions. They abolished *suttee* (widow burning) and infanticide and legalized the remarriage of Hindu widows. This gave the perception, especially to British officers, that the Hindu religion was barbaric. Many sepoys felt that the British were attempting to break their caste, to defile them, destroy their social standing, and condemn them to an afterlife of damnation, especially by forcibly converting them to Christianity.

Indian Mutiny

The British enforced the Mahalwari system of taxation, which had an impact on sepoys of the Bengal Army who came from Hindi-speaking areas of northern India (excluding Oudh). Tax revenues increased over 70 percent during the first half of the nineteenth century, causing mounting agricultural debt and the mortgaging of land to moneylenders. In addition, products manufactured inexpensively by the British in England, under their mercantile system, were imported to India and sold at cheaper prices than local merchants could afford to match. These fiscal practices caused financial hardships among all classes of Indians.

The sepoys serving in "foreign" areas such as Sind and the Punjab received a supplemental monetary allowance, *batta*, to help pay for the local high prices of food. When the British annexed these areas, in 1843 and 1849, respectively, *batta* was abolished, despite the continued high prices of foodstuffs. To the sepoys, it seemed their reward for fidelity and victory had been the loss of their foreign service allowance, *batta*, and this was a significant source of resentment.

High-caste Hindus, who served mainly in the Bengal Army, were also concerned that they would lose their caste if they served outside of India. In July 1856 the General Service Enlistment Act was passed, which required all enlistees to serve overseas if required. This caused great consternation in the Bengal Army and seemed to indicate that any high-caste Hindus who joined the company's army would have to renounce their caste and follow orders, have their caste defiled, or simply not join the army.

There were many rumors and prophecies in this volatile environment. One prophecy stated that 100 years after the 1757 Battle of Plassey, the East India Company's rule would end. There was also a mysterious circulation of *chappatties* (Indian cakes) as a sort of chain letter, which Indians were fearful of breaking as they might be a harbinger of some significant event.

In May 1857, moreover, the combined total of regular British Army officers and men and soldiers in Company European regiments in India was about 40,000. The number of Indians in the three native armies totaled about 311,000, of whom 165,000 were in the Bengal Army. This very high ratio of one European to eight Indians (1:8) in the Army in India was caused partly by the need to send British Army regiments to fight in the Crimean War.

The spark that ignited these tensions, frustrations, and misunderstandings into full-fledged mutiny was the "greased cartridge" affair, another caste-related issue. In 1857, the old Brown Bess musket was replaced with the more accurate Enfield rifle. The greased Enfield cartridge contained both the ball and powder charge. The end of the cartridge had to be bitten off and the cartridge then rammed down the muzzle of the rifle. The sepoys believed that the greased cartridge was lubricated with a mixture of cow and pig fat. The cow is sacred to the Hindus, and the act of biting such a cartridge was viewed as an attempt to break their caste before being converted into Christianity. To the Muslims, the pig is an unclean animal, and touching pig fat means defilement.

Native regiments, especially high-caste Hindus in the Bengal Army who were treated with misplaced leniency and their lack of discipline tolerated, increasingly refused to accept the new cartridges. The 19th and 34th Bengal Native Infantry Regiments were disbanded in early 1857 for refusing to use the new cartridges. Unrest and tension simmered throughout the Bengal Army. On 24 April 1857, at Meerut (an important station about 40 miles northeast of Delhi, on the Grand Trunk Road that connected Calcutta in the east with the Punjab in the west), eighty-five native soldiers of the 3rd Bengal Cavalry refused the new cartridges. The malcontents were each tried and sentenced to ten years of hard labor. The Meerut regiments, believing that British Army units were marching to attack them, openly mutinied on 10 May 1857. The mutineers freed their comrades from jail, burned down garrison and barrack buildings, and attacked and killed British officers and their families. The insurgents then marched to Delhi, apparently hoping to reinstall the last king and revive the grandeur and glory of the Mughal Empire. This was the beginning of the violent "devil's wind" that blew across northern India.

The Indian Mutiny was largely confined to the Bengal Army. Sixty-four Bengal Army regiments mutinied or were preemptively disarmed, as compared with only two Bombay Army units and none in the Madras Army.

The Indian Mutiny broke out on 10 May 1857 and did not officially end until 8 July 1859. The mutiny itself can be divided into a number of campaigns. The first campaign consisted of the siege and capture of Delhi (June–September 1857). The second was the campaign in Oudh, including the defense of the Lucknow Residency (July–November 1857); the September and November 1857 relief of Lucknow; the defense (June 1857) and the three battles of Cawnpore (July, November, and December 1857); the final capture of Lucknow in March 1858; and the pacification of

Oudh and Rohilkand (April–June 1858). Operations in Central India were conducted in two phases, from June–November 1857 and January–June 1858. The Battle of Gwalior (19 June 1858) was the last major engagement of the Indian Mutiny. Final mopping-up operations took place from July 1858 until May 1859.

On 8 July 1859, Lord Canning, the viceroy and governor-general of Indian, issued a proclamation officially ending the Indian Mutiny and declaring peace.

See also Bengal Army; Bombay Army; Campbell, Field Marshal Colin; Cawnpore, Siege and Relief of; Delhi, Siege and Storming of; East India Company; East India Company, Military Forces; Grant, General Sir James Hope; Gwalior, Battle of; Havelock, Major General Sir Henry; India; India, British Army in; Lawrence, Brigadier General Sir Henry M.; Lucknow, Siege and Relief of; Madras Army; Nana Sahib; Nicholson, Brigadier General John; Outram, Lieutenant General Sir James; Rhani of Jhansi; Rose, Field Marshal Hugh H.; Tantia Topi

References: Amin (2002); Barthorp (1993); Broehl (1986); Collier (1964); Edwardes (1963); Hibbert (1978); Hilton (1957); Leasor (1956); Mason (1974); Mason (1985); Pollock (1957); Roy (2002); Sutcliffe (1995); Ward (1996); Wood (1908)

Infantry, British Army—Organization

The most numerous and significant component of the British Army through the Victorian era was the infantry, organized into regiments of one or more battalions each. In 1850, for example, there were 90,000 infantrymen, 12,000 cavalrymen, 7,000 artillerymen, and 1,200 engineers in the British Army, totaling 110,200 soldiers. In effect, the pay, weapons, uniform, and so on, of the infantry were those of the British Army, with the other arms serving as exceptions. The infantry battalion was the primary independent tactical element of the British Army.

The organization and strength of the infantry battalion fluctuated throughout this period. After the Napoleonic Wars, almost all regiments were reduced to single battalion units. The strength of most battalions was reduced to a total of 697 all ranks (officers and enlisted men), of whom 570 were private soldiers.

In 1822, the strength of battalions serving in India and the East Indies was fixed at 1,071, and they were organized into 10 companies, 9 service (overseas) and 1 recruiting company in the United Kingdom. Battalions serving elsewhere totaled 654 all ranks and were organized into 8 companies.

It was usually difficult to keep a battalion serving overseas up to full strength without an effective home depot organization. In 1825, to remedy this situation, infantry battalions were increased to 10 companies, of which 6 were to be service and 4 depot companies. The service element of the battalion consisted of 1 lieutenant colonel, 1 major, 6 captains, 8 lieutenants, 4 second lieutenants, 1 surgeon with an assistant, 4 staff sergeants, 36 color sergeants and sergeants, 24 corporals, 12 drummers, and 516 private soldiers, equaling 6 companies of 86 private soldiers each with officers and noncommissioned officers (NCOs). The depot element, frequently called the depot battalion, consisted of 1 major, 4 captains, 4 lieutenants, 4 second lieutenants, 1 surgeon, 26 staff sergeants and sergeants, 26 corporals, 8 drummers, and 224 privates, organized into 4 understrength companies of 56 privates each. When the battalion was formed in line, the right flank company was designated the grenadier company, and the left flank company was the light company. This distinction in flank companies was abolished in the 1860s.

From 1839–1840, infantry battalions received an increase in five private soldiers per company to help reduce shortages. In 1841, there were 78 infantry battalions serving overseas, 6 en route to or from overseas postings and 19 in the United Kingdom.

The infantry of the British Expeditionary Force to the Crimea in 1854, which included 3 Guards battalions, was organized into 4 infantry divisions and 1 light division, each division consisting of 2 brigades of 3 battalions. Battalions were increased to 16 companies, 8 service and 8 depot, giving each battalion the strength of almost 2 regular battalions. In June 1854, however, the depot element was reduced to 4 companies.

The Indian Mutiny (1857–1859) caused a further battalion reconfiguration. The 10th to the 25th Regiments were each directed to raise a second battalion consisting of 10 service and 2 depot companies, totaling 1,000 all ranks.

The Cardwell Reforms in 1872 linked single battalions in pairs and assigned regiments to specific geographical locations within the United Kingdom. All regiments then had a depot detachment, and in the case of two-battalion regiments, one battalion serving overseas and one at home. This scheme basically existed until the end of the Victorian era.

The strength of each battalion was dictated by its availability for foreign service. Since there were no reserves, the strength of the first 18 battalions on the foreign service roster was maintained at 820 rank and file, the next 18 battalions at 620 soldiers, and all others at 520.

In 1881, all regiments were given two battalions. The first twenty-five regiments remained intact, while the remainder were amalgamated into pairs to form the first and second battalions of the new regiments. Each regiment also had third and fourth battalions, consisting of militia, and a volunteer battalion. Each service battalion then consisted of a headquarters and eight companies each of about one hundred NCOs and men. Each company, commanded by a captain, was divided into two half companies, with a subaltern in charge of each. Each half company was further divided into two sections.

In 1913, as a result of lessons learned during the Second Boer War, the number of companies in an infantry battalion was reduced from eight to four, the so-called double-company system. Advances in weapons lethality meant that a larger company with more subunits was more maneuverable than a smaller one, especially when dispersion was required.

During large wars, such as the Crimean War and Second Boer War, three battalions were formed into a brigade, and two brigades were in a division. These were temporary formations, with commanders having little experience of higher-level command and control. Prior to World War I, brigades and divisions were made permanent formations.

See also Boer War, Second (1899–1902); Cardwell Reforms; Crimean War; Indian Mutiny; Infantry, British Army—Small Arms; Infantry, British Army—Tactics; Infantry, British Army—Training; Rank and File, British Army—Uniforms and Equipment

References: Knight (1996); Moyse-Bartlett (1974); Myatt (1983); Spiers (1981); Spiers (1992); Strachan (1985)

Infantry, British Army—Small Arms

Technological advances and weapons improvements had probably the greatest impact on the infantry, since they comprised the largest portion of the British Army and fought directly, using small arms, with its adversaries.

Most infantrymen from 1815 until the mid-1840s were armed with variations of the Brown Bess muzzle-loading, black-powder-firing smoothbore flintlock musket, considered a superb weapon in its day for close-order fighting and short-range and volley firing. It was a brass-mounted musket three-quarters of an inch in diameter with a 42-inch-long barrel and carried a 17-inch bayonet. Its total length was 4 feet, 7 inches, and it weighed nearly 10 pounds. The rate of fire was on average three rounds per minute by an experienced soldier, and its effective range was about 100 yards. The Brown Bess had no rear sight because it was not expected to be aimed. Since infantry fighting took place at that time in dense formations at close distances, the soldier would be marched into place, ordered to point his weapon at the opposing mass, and fire on command.

In the 1830s the Board of Ordnance decided in principle to change from the flintlock musket to one using the more reliable percussion system. The Brunswick rifle was adopted in 1836. It had a caliber of .704 inches, barrel length of 30 inches (fitted with a cross-handled sword bayonet), and was sighted to 300 yards. In practical terms, this rifle was considered unsuitable, mainly because the bore was too tight and there was insufficient power to keep the bullet spinning fast enough for a straight flight.

The smoothbore musket was officially replaced in 1851 by the Minié rifle, a weapon that revolutionized warfare. A problem with early rifles was loading the bullet into a rifled barrel. Captain Claude Minié of the Belgian Army solved this problem by developing a .702-caliber cylindrical-conoidal bullet. The base of the bullet was flat, exposing a maximum surface to the charge, and hollow, expanding from the explosion to fit the grooves of the rifle. The Minié rifle was 4 feet, 6 inches long and weighed 9 pounds. It was the first rifle to have a perfected sliding ladder rear sight. Its effective range was 800 yards, although targets at twice that distance could be hit. All of the British infantrymen in the Crimea (except for those in the 4th Division, who were still armed with old smoothbore muskets) reportedly carried Minié rifles.

In a period of rapid technological advances, the Minié rifle soon became obsolete. It was replaced in 1853 by the Enfield rifle, manufactured by American-made machinery at the Royal Small Arms Factory of Enfield. The Enfield rifle had a barrel 3 feet, 3 inches long, and the entire weapon was 4 feet, 6 inches long and weighed 8 pounds, 14 ounces. The bore was .577 inches, and the rifling was 3-grooved, rather than 4 like the Minié, which made the round more stable and permitted it to expand more easily. The ladder rear sight was sighted up to 1,200 yards, with the Enfield being a very accurate and reliable weapon. It remained, like its predecessors, a muzzle-loading rifle. The bullet and powder were sealed in a paper cartridge, which was thinly coated with grease to be waterproof and to lubricate the bullet. The new Enfield rifle with the greased cartridge, considered a potential source of defilement to both Muslims and Hindus, was a reason for the outbreak of the 1857 Indian Mutiny.

The success of the Prussian Army's bolt-action needle gun in the 1860s showed the obsolescence of the muzzle loader. A device designed by Jacob Snider of New York, consisting of a claw extractor fitted to the breech mechanism, partially pulled the new center-fire cartridge case out of the open breech, which was discarded by turning the rifle upside down. The army began to be equipped with this Snider-Enfield rifle in 1865, a design improved on two years later by the adoption of a better center-fire, brass cartridge.

The Snider-Enfield rifle was an interim weapon. In the late 1860s the Board of Ordnance tested 120 different actions on breech-loading weapons and 49 different cartridges before selecting the Martini-Henry in 1871. This rifle fired a black-powder, .45-caliber, center-fire brass cartridge with a lead slug. Rounds were loaded individually through the top of the breech. The rifle was 4 feet, 1.5 inches long and weighed 9 pounds. It was sighted for shooting at 500 yards, although it was accurate in trained hands to 1,000 yards and more. The Martini-Henry rifle (which underwent slight modifications in 1876 and 1879), with its smaller bore, greater range, lower trajectory, superior accuracy, and relative simplicity, was the best rifle issued to British soldiers up to that time. It was used with tremendous effectiveness during the many colonial campaigns of the 1870s and 1880s.

The British Army abandoned the single-shot principle when it adopted the bolt-action Lee-Metford rifle, which had an improved magazine and a barrel of .303 inches, in 1888. The magazine, which originally held 8 black-powder rounds, a number increased to 10 with the advent of cordite ammunition (changeover completed in 1893), fit beneath the breech. The Lee-Metford was 4 feet, 1 inch long and weighed 9 pounds. Sighted to 1,800 yards, the Lee-Metford also had a special sight that allowed reasonably effective collective fire to 2,900 yards.

In 1895 the Lee-Metford rifle was replaced by the Lee-Enfield, which had almost the same specifications as the former with an improved rifling system in the barrel.

The Lee-Metford and Lee-Enfield rifles were carried by the soldiers who fought and won the battles in the Sudan and South Africa. These two rifles remained the British Army's principal small arms through the Victorian period and beyond.

See also Bullets; Infantry, British Army—Tactics; Infantry, British Army—Training; Pistols; Rank and File, British Army—Uniforms and Equipment
References: Bailey (2002); Featherstone (1978); Haythornthwaite (1995); Knight (1996); Myatt (1983); Strachan (1985)

Infantry, British Army—Tactics

Infantry tactics evolved throughout this period from rigid, close-order formations of disciplined automatons under the direct command of generals to increasingly open, dispersed elements, where the leadership devolved down to company, platoon, and even section commanders. This was the result of technological advances that increased the lethality of small arms and artillery, coupled with other developments, including cordite (smokeless powder). Moreover, the advent of these more accurate and longer range weapons, notably the rifled musket, heralded a shift in tactical advantage from the attacker to the defender, a phenomenon not immediately understood.

The British Army needed to standardize its tactical doctrine, so that its infantry battalions, regardless of where they served, knew the same tactics and could operate and maneuver with each other. The 1824 *Field Exercise,* revised in 1833, encapsulated British tactics from the end of the Napoleonic Wars through the Crimean War: "advance in line—column—echellon (direct and oblique) and a ready formation into line at once during any movement are all a corps requires for action!" (Strachan 1985, p. 19). The line formation maximized the unit's firepower, and after volley firing, the unit would charge with bayonets fixed.

Set-piece battles were becoming increasingly anachronistic, especially when many battalions were frequently engaged in irregular colonial warfare in the 1840s and 1850s. The left flank company of each battalion, until the 1860s, was designated the light company. These soldiers could serve as skirmishers, deploying quickly and stealthily in front of the main body of the battalion to harass the enemy with aimed fire.

In 1851, the Minié rifle was authorized to replace the smoothbore percussion musket for British infantrymen, which in turn was replaced by the Enfield rifle in 1855. The Crimean War (1854–1856) and the Indian Mutiny (1857–

1859), however, were generally fought with conventional tactics, with the bayonet being used whenever possible.

The 1859 edition of *Field Exercises and Evolutions* recognized the need to revise tactics in the face of a longer range and more lethal rifle. All troops were to be trained in skirmishing techniques. Attacks were to be made in either column or line. They were to be preceded and screened, if possible, by a skirmish line, a line of supports (200 yards behind the skirmish line), and a reserve (300 yards behind the supports). In colonial warfare the tactics were frequently revised to meet the terrain and the enemy, with a larger screen of skirmishers and smaller main body of troops. The use of skirmishers was a major shift toward decentralizing command and control.

After the Franco-Prussian War, by which time breech-loading rifles had replaced muzzle-loading rifles and machine guns had been introduced, the British tactical manual was again revised. In 1877, a section of the infantry manual on "extended order" replaced skirmishing. A battalion was to attack in three elements: a firing line, supports, and reserves.

The first edition of *Infantry Drill* in 1889 preserved the traditional British line and recognized the battalion as the basic tactical unit. Revisions of the manual stated that "all movements in contact with the enemy should be covered by a screen of troops in extended order, supported normally by three lines—a firing line, generally moving in extended order, to engage the enemy and launch the assault, a second line of supporting soldiers to aid the assault, and a third line of reserves either to complete the success or cover a retreat" (Spiers 1992, p. 251).

Colonial warfare required different tactics. Generally the local commander, based on terrain and the enemy, had to modify regular tactics by weighing the importance of dispersal with concentration. The use of the close-order regimental square for defensive purposes was a feature of colonial warfare. The adroit use of cover and concealment, coupled with long-range rifles using smokeless powder, by the Boers in the Second Boer War (1899–1902), forced the British to reconsider their tactics. In general terms, the infantry battalion advanced in extended order to within about 500 yards of the enemy. The advance was continued employing fire and maneuver techniques, with one section providing suppressive fire on the enemy while the other moved about 30 or 40 yards, then the sections changed roles in a leapfrogging manner. Battlefield dispersal became more important, and when possible flank or rear attacks replaced costly frontal attacks, and night operations were conducted instead of daytime assaults. Mobility also became vital, and the British increasingly employed mounted infantry.

After the Second Boer War, improvements were made in musketry and machine-gun proficiency. A renewed emphasis was placed on tactical flexibility.

See also Boer War, Second (1899–1902); Crimean War; Infantry, British Army—Organization; Infantry, British Army—Training; Rank and File, British Army—Uniforms and Equipment

References: English (1981); Knight (1996); Myatt (1983); Spiers (1992); Strachan (1985); Travers (1979)

Infantry, British Army–Training

Infantry training changed considerably during this era, from harsh discipline and repetitive drill to ensure soldiers reacted instantly and precisely to commands in combat, to collective training emphasizing individual initiative in dispersed formations. Weapons and technological advances dictated tactics, and the goal of training was to learn and apply the evolving tactics.

Basic training of recruits was conducted within the home battalions by the noncommissioned officers, generally under the supervision of a junior officer, such as the adjutant. This individual training varied from regiment to regiment, and for much of this period consisted of little more than drilling interspersed with barracks and equipment maintenance and details.

By 1896, infantry recruit training had become standardized and was mandatory. The twelve-week program of instruction emphasized individual and squad drill, physical training, barrack room instruction, and basic musketry training and field firing.

Infantry unit training after the Napoleonic Wars was based on the comprehensive *Field Exercise and Evolutions of the Army* (1824). In practice, however, a battalion trained in three basic formations: line, for a short attack or engagement; various column maneuvers, for more extended movement and maneuver; and the battalion square, as a defense against cavalry. These basic drills remained in use mainly unchanged until the twentieth century.

The introduction of the Minié rifle in 1851, itself replaced by the Enfield rifle in 1855, and the Crimean War experience in 1854–1856 resulted in revisions in the 1859 edition of *Field Exercises and Evolutions*. The increased range and lethality of rifle fire was recognized, requiring all troops to be trained in skirmishing techniques. Skirmish lines were to precede all attacks, which were to be made in either column or line.

In 1877, a section of the infantry manual replaced skirmishing by "extended order." From the late 1870s, training became more flexible to allow for initiative, terrain, and other variables.

Mounted infantry training centers were established at Aldershot, the Curragh, and Shorncliffe in 1888. Mounted infantry were soldiers who rode horses into battle but dismounted to fight. Regiments were required to have one trained officer and thirty-two trained soldiers available to form an ad hoc mounted infantry detachment. These soldiers attended a ten-week course that included riding, stable duties, horse management, mounted infantry tactics, and field firing.

The first edition of *Infantry Drill* in 1889 was important for preserving the traditional British line and confirming that the battalion was to attack in three elements: a firing line, supports, and reserves.

Large-scale maneuvers had been conducted at the Chobham encampment in 1853, and in 1871 and 1872 after the scare caused by the Franco-Prussian War (1870–1871).

Training above the battalion level stagnated until the 1890s, when the importance of large-scale maneuvers was recognized and exercises revived. Battalions developed systematic annual plans for incremental, multi-echelon training. Infantry battalions received new soldiers after they had undergone about twelve weeks of basic training at the regimental depot. The new soldiers received advanced training in their battalion. During the winter months battalions conducted road marches and other conditioning drills. Each rifle company devoted itself to field and musketry training from 1 March to 31 October, which included (at larger camps), battalion drill and exercises in May and brigade-level combined arms training during the summer months. The culmination of this annual training cycle was the division-level autumn maneuvers, held generally in September and October. Large-scale maneuvers and exercises were conducted up to the eve of the Second Boer War (1899–1902) and afterward generally on an annual basis.

See also Aldershot; Crimean War; Curragh Camp; Infantry, British Army—Organization; Infantry, British Army—Tactics; Maneuvers, British Army

References: Crouch (1983b); Myatt (1983); Spiers (1992); Strachan (1985)

Ingogo, Battle of (8 February 1881)

The Natal Field Force, commanded by Major General Sir George Pomeroy-Colley during the first Boer War, returned to its camp at Mount Prospect to await reinforcements after being defeated by the Boers at Laing's Nek on 28 January 1881.

On 7 February 1881, the Boers started a flanking movement to sever the main road bringing reinforcements and supplies from Newcastle and ambushed an escort accompanying the mail. The Colonial Office was also pressuring Pomeroy-Colley to defeat the Boers quickly or end hostilities before they spread further. The next day Pomeroy-Colley, in an operation that should have been conducted by a subordinate officer, personally led a five-company force (five under-strength companies from the 3rd Battalion, 60th Rifles, numbering 273 all ranks; two 9-pounder and two 7-pounder guns; and a detachment of 38 mounted troops) escorting the mail wagon back to Newcastle to ensure the route was still open. He apparently also wanted to frighten the Boers in the area.

After a 5-mile march southwest, the column came to a double drift just to the west of the confluence of the Ingogo and Harte Rivers. Pomeroy-Colley detached F Company and two mountain guns and had them positioned on a spur overlooking the two fords.

About 2 miles further, as the force entered a plateau, Boer horsemen were spotted in the distance. The British artillery fired a few rounds at the Boers, hoping to frighten them. The Boers, however, charged at the British, and when they reached a ravine, they dismounted and began firing at their opponent. Other Boers, skillfully using the cover of the terrain and concealment of the 4-foot-high tambookie grass, began to encircle the British force on the plateau.

Pomerey-Colley realized he was in a precarious position and requested reinforcements from Mount Prospect. The Boers concentrated their fire initially on the artillery horses to immobilize the guns. At about 3:00 P.M., the reserve I Company was sent across open ground to reinforce an area where a Boer attack was expected. Boer sharpshooting reduced the company from 66 to 13 men within minutes, but the Boer firing then seemed to taper off because they were not strong enough to assault the British.

The Boers did receive some reinforcements, and at about

Inkerman, Battle of

5:00 P.M., a torrential downpour began. In the ensuing confusion, both sides purportedly used white flags of truce to their advantage, and both opponents ignored them. The Boers tried to collect their wounded and withdrew in the storm. The British, without food, water, and almost out of ammunition, took advantage of the noise and chaos caused by the storm to retreat to Mount Prospect. The rainstorm had swollen the Ingogo River, and it was only with great difficulty, and losing eight men and a number of horses in the process, that the flooded river was crossed and the British were finally able to return to their camp.

The Battle of Ingogo was considered a Boer victory, even though the British were able to withdraw. In this fiasco, the British lost 76 men killed and another 67 wounded, out of a total force of about 300. The Boers had about eight men killed and six wounded.

See also Boer War, First (1880–1881); Boers; Commando System; Laing's Nek, Battle of; Pomeroy-Colley, Major General Sir George

References: Barthorp (1987); Bond (1967); Droogleever (1991); Ransford (1967)

Inkerman, Battle of (5 November 1854)

In the Battle of Inkerman, during the Crimean War (1854–1856), the Russians attempted to break the British and French siege of Sevastopol by destroying their armies through a coordinated double envelopment. The ferocity, confusion, and carnage of the engagement gave it the sobriquet of "a soldiers' battle."

On 26 October 1854, the day after the Battle of Balaklava, a 5,000-man Russian force of six infantry battalions made a sortie from Sevastopol, a probing operation to check the strength of the British 2nd Division positioned on the Home Ridge. The Home Ridge was important terrain, as the Post Road that traversed the Inkerman Bridge over the Chernaya River ran over it before the road reached the Woronzov Road. The Russian force broke through forward British defensive positions before being turned back by artillery fire from Home Ridge. In this minor offensive, the Battle of "Little Inkerman," the Russians lost about 270 men killed and wounded and the British had about 100 casualties all ranks. After testing and finding a weakness in the British lines, the Russians built up their forces for a larger offensive and the British redeployed some of their units on the plateau before Sevastopol.

The British, concerned with the upcoming winter season, planned to attack the Russians on 6 November 1854. General Prince Alexander Sergeevich Menshikov, the Russian commander, had received reinforcements and his force, both inside and outside of Sevastopol, totaled about 107,000 men. The allies had about 70,000 soldiers. The British 2nd Division (3,500 men) remained on the Post Road, while the Guards Brigade (1,350 soldiers) encamped near a windmill about one-half mile south of the 2nd Division. The Highland Brigade was at Balaklava. Elements of the 3rd, 4th, and Light Divisions were to the west of the windmill, with one brigade to the northwest of the windmill on Victoria Ridge. British strength in this line of observation totaled about 8,600 soldiers.

The Inkerman Ridge was a heavily wooded spur that rose to the south of the Chernaya River, with Shell Hill near its center. Inkerman Ridge also contained numerous other ridges, including Home Ridge. The Careenage Ravine, to its south, divided it from the parallel Victoria Ridge. The Volovia, St. Clement, and Quarry Ravines ran south from the Chernaya River, with the Post Road traveling through the Quarry Ravine, to the positions of the British 2nd Division. French troops were positioned to the south, on Sapune Ridge.

The Russian plan of attack was for one 19,000-man force (under Lieutenant General F. I. Soimonov) to conduct the main attack from Sevastopol up Inkerman Ridge and position its artillery to the west of Shell Hill to fire on the British 2nd Division. Another 16,000-man Russian army (commanded by Lieutenant General P. I. Pavlov) would cross the Inkerman Bridge and advance through the Quarry Ravine to assemble to the east of Shell Hill and north of Home Ridge. When these two forces converged near Shell Hill, they would come under the unified command of General P. A. Dannenberg. Dannenberg's troops would then attack south toward the windmill. The largest Russian element, of about 22,000 men, commanded by General P. D. Gorchakov, would initially demonstrate in front of French General Pierre Bosquet's forces. When Dannenberg's army was attacking south over Home Ridge, Gorchakov's force was to attack from the east and help crush the British force in a pincer movement.

The Russian force, totaling about 60,000 soldiers with 234 guns, attacked in the early morning fog and drizzle on 5 November 1854. Poor timing and coordination and contradictory plans issued by subordinates immediately caused problems for the Russian attack. Soimonov's columns advanced up Inkerman Ridge, and in fierce fighting in which both he and his deputy were killed, Russian troops fell back toward their reserve units. Pavlov's units, which were supposed to arrive simultaneously on Inkerman Ridge, were delayed at the Inkerman Bridge. When Pavlov's men and remnants of Soimonov's force reached Shell Hill, Dannenberg assumed command. While bombarding the British with effective artillery fire, the Russians attacked in columns and captured one British redoubt.

As the British were being forced from positions near Home Ridge, especially the Kitspur and Sandbag Battery, the Guards Brigade arrived and entered the fray. Lieutenant General Sir George Cathcart, commanding the British 4th Division, went with one of his brigades around the right of the Guards. This brigade soon came under Russian fire, and Cathcart was shot and killed.

Raglan, positioned on Home Ridge, was better able to appreciate the seriousness of the British position as the fog began to lift at about 9:00 A.M. The British 2nd and 4th Divisions and Guards Brigade had suffered heavy casualties, and the Guards were beginning to retreat from the Kitspur. With no reinforcements available, Raglan requested immediate support from the French. Three battalions of French Zouaves and Algerians rushed to the Kitspur, helping turn the tide of battle and driving the Russians down the hill.

British artillery was dragged to Home Ridge and soon found the range of the Russian guns on Shell Hill. The British artillery, soon joined by French field pieces, began to destroy the Russian guns. An ad hoc force from the British Light and the 4th Divisions then assaulted Shell Hill.

At this time, about midday, Dannenberg basically gave up the battle. His forces retreated back down the Inkerman Ridge, leaving the allies in control of this terrain feature, and across the Chernaya River. A small Russian sortie from Sevastopol was the only successful Russian operation of the day.

The Battle of Inkerman was a costly allied victory, especially for the British. Its value was debated (although Raglan was promoted to field marshal), especially since the British had lost 597 all ranks killed and 1,860 wounded, while the French sustained 130 killed and 750 wounded. Even though the attacking Russians had suffered about 10,729 total casualties, they still held Sevastopol. "From the nature of the ground no generalship could prevail," noted one British source. "It is alone to the undying pluck of the officers and men that we are indebted for preservation" (Mercer 1998, p. 182). Bosquet, after observing the battlefield, where burial parties were still working three days after the engagement, reportedly exclaimed, "*Quel abattoir*" ("What a slaughterhouse") (Baumgart 1999, p. 136).

See also Balaklava, Battle of; Cathcart, Lieutenant General Sir George; Crimean War; French Forces, Crimean War; Military Medicine, British Army—Hospitals and Soldier Treatment; Nightingale, Florence; Raglan, Field Marshal Fitzroy J. H. Somerset, First Baron; Russian Forces, Crimean War; Sevastopol, Siege of

References: Baumgart (1999); Dreilinger (n.d.); Inkerman (1980); Judd (1975); Mercer (1998); Palmer (1987); Pemberton (1962); Royle (2000); Sweetman (1991); Warner (1972)

Intellectuals, British Army

The post-Waterloo British Army was considered a symbol of Napoleon's destruction that perpetuated a perceived legacy of invincibility. As a pillar of royal authority and the aristocracy, coupled with an entrenched bureaucracy, few efforts were made to alter the insular British Army. Since most officers were ill educated and many had purchased their commissions, their ignorance, lack of professionalism, and indifference did not encourage reform or change.

There were a number of military intellectuals, historians, and reformers in the pre–Crimean War British Army, although their efforts have been overshadowed by their counterparts of the latter half of the nineteenth century. One of these pre–Crimean War military reformers and intellectuals was General Sir William F. P. Napier (brother of General Sir Charles J. Napier), who wrote the *History of the War in the Peninsula,* considered by one authority to be "the finest military history in English and perhaps in any language" (Luvaas 1964, p. 14). Napier's adulatory history may have helped preserve the status quo to the detriment of army reform. Major General John Mitchell, frequently writing under the pseudonym Captain Orlando Sabertash, explored infantry and cavalry tactics and military organization. Another distinguished military thinker, Field Marshal Sir John Fox Burgoyne, was concerned with home defense, fortifications, and military administration.

The death of the dogmatic, revered Field Marshal Arthur Wellesley, First Duke of Wellington, in 1852, coupled with the abysmal performance of the British Army in the Crimean War (1854–1856), provoked criticism and demands for reform. While a few officers, as noted, had earlier advocated reform, the Crimean War marked a watershed in the military reform movement and paved the way for the Cardwell Reforms of the early 1870s.

The establishment of the Staff College at Camberley in 1857 and improvements in the process of officer education and the development of professionalism also helped sow the seeds of British military intellectualism that would continue to grow in the following decades.

A number of British Army officers personally observed, both officially and unofficially, military operations during the American Civil War (1861–1865). Among them were Lieutenant Colonel (later Field Marshal Viscount) Garnet J. Wolseley and Lieutenant Colonel (later General Sir) Arthur J. L. Fremantle, who also studied the campaigns of the Civil War and tried to derive lessons from them.

The unprecedented and unimaginable victories of the Prussians over the Austrians in 1866 and the French in 1870–1871, in which technological and scientific advances were harnessed to the Prussian war machine, contributed significantly to shocking the British Army out of its intellectual complacency. A number of army officers emerged as "intellectuals" to question the viability of British Army unit and staff organization, training, tactics, strategy, doctrine, and leadership. They also tried to understand the application of new developments, such as the railroad, rifle, and telegraph, to the evolution of tactics and the more efficient and effective conduct of war. These intellectuals also questioned or tried to place British military theory and doctrine within the Jominian and Clausewitzian paradigms.

There were a number of differences in the ideas and agendas of the British military theorists. Some intellectuals wanted to develop a purely British school of thought, while others were satisfied with adapting or emulating European examples. Other intellectuals were convinced that the role of the British Army was imperial policing, thus encouraging a "small wars" mentality, and others believed the British Army should prepare for a continental commitment. Indian military thinking frequently resulted in unique theories.

Lieutenant Colonel (later Major General Sir) Patrick L. MacDougall, the first commandant of the Staff College, was a very influential military intellectual. He can, in some respects, be "considered the founder of modern British military thought" (Preston 1964, p. 59). He wrote *The Theory of War* in 1856, and in 1863, *Modern Warfare as Influenced by Modern Artillery,* one of the first texts that incorporated lessons from the American Civil War. MacDougall also wrote *Modern Infantry Tactics* in 1873, the year he became the first chief of the Intelligence Branch at the War Office.

Another British Army intellectual closely associated with the establishment of the Staff College in 1857 was the future Lieutenant General Sir Edward B. Hamley, its first professor of military history. His conservative 1866 study, *The Operations of War,* met with unprecedented success, although its traditional outlook and frequently inaccurate perceptions provoked opposition viewpoints. Hamley returned to the Staff College as commandant in 1870 for a seven-year tenure and helped revise its curriculum.

In 1858, Captain (later Lieutenant Colonel) Charles C. Chesney was appointed professor of military history at the Royal Military College, Sandhurst. He included information from the American Civil War in his lectures in 1862 and was probably the first British officer to pay serious attention to this watershed conflict. Chesney succeeded Hamley as professor of military history at the Staff College in 1864, and he became prominent for his studies of Waterloo and other military topics.

Chesney's brother, Captain (later General Sir) George Chesney, wrote a fictional narrative called "The Battle of Dorking" in 1871, on the heels of the Franco-Prussian War. This article, chronicling a hypothetical successful German invasion of Great Britain, highlighted England's lack of preparedness and caused considerable alarm and controversy.

Wolseley was a prolific military historian and theorist, advocate of reform, and progressive intellectual in his own right. One of his more important contributions to the development of the British Army into a more modern force was using his authority as adjutant-general (1882–1890), except while in the Sudan (1884–1885), and as commander in chief (1895–1900), to appoint like-minded and visionary subordinates into key positions to further modernize the army. For example, Wolseley ensured the appointment of Major General (later General) Sir Henry Brackenbury as deputy quartermaster-general for intelligence in 1886. An advocate of more effective and professional officer education, Wolseley appointed Lieutenant Colonel (later Colonel) G. F. R. Henderson an instructor at Sandhurst in 1890. Wolseley had earlier selected Colonel (later Major General Sir) (John) Frederick Maurice to be professor of military art and history at the Staff College in 1885 and was instrumental in Henderson replacing him in 1892.

In India, one of the leading military intellectuals was Major General Sir Charles M. MacGregor, whose many writings culminated in *The Defence of India: A Strategical Study* (1884). General Sir George Chesney was also a prominent theorist and strategist of Indian issues.

Very few of these military intellectuals, however—even though most had participated in the "small wars" of empire—ever studied them. The most notable exception is Colonel (later Major General Sir) C. E. Callwell's *Small Wars: Their Principles and Practice,* first published in 1896 and one of the most original theoretical military studies published during the Victorian era. Other publications pertaining to expeditionary force and unconventional tactics and strategy include MacGregor, *Mountain Warfare: An Essay on the Conduct of Military Operations in Mountainous Countries* (1866); Captain G. J. Younghusband, *Indian Frontier Warfare* (1898); Miller Maguire, *Strategy and Tactics in Mountain Ranges* (1904); and W. C. G. Heneker, *Bush Warfare* (1907).

British Army intellectuals during this period made increasingly significant contributions to the revision of officer education and the study of military history, tactics, and strategy, adding to these debates through their writings, lectures, and influence. In terms of concrete reform in the British Army's unit and staff organization, tactics, and strategy, these intellectuals were less successful.

See also Brackenbury, General Sir Henry; Camberley, Staff College; Cardwell Reforms; Chesney, Lieutenant Colonel Charles C.; Crimean War; Hamley, Lieutenant General Sir Edward B.; Henderson, Colonel G. F. R.; Intelligence; MacDougall, Major General Sir Patrick L.; Maurice, Major General Sir (John) Frederick; Purchase System; Sandhurst, Royal Military College; Wellington, Field Marshal Arthur Wellesley; Wolseley, Field Marshal Garnet J.; Woolwich, Royal Military Academy

References. Bailes (1981); Biddulph (1939); Bond (1972); Callwell (1896); Fremantle (1863); Gallagher (1975a); Luvaas (1964); Luvaas (1965); Preston (1964); Preston (1969); Strachan (1978); Travers (1978); Younghusband (1898)

Intelligence

The British Army's intelligence system—the gathering, analysis, and dissemination of information of value—was not formalized until the establishment of the Intelligence Branch at the War Office in 1873. Prior to that time, the overt and covert collection of economic, political, and military information was conducted in a haphazard, ineffective manner.

An embryonic military intelligence organization, the Topographical and Statistic (T&S) Department, was established at the War Office in 1855 during the Crimean War. It focused on geography and mapmaking and was assigned miscellaneous duties, including producing the illustrations for the army dress regulations.

The momentum of War Office reform and reorganization generated by Edward T. Cardwell, secretary of state for war from 1868 to 1874, included the establishment of the Intelligence Branch, War Office, on 1 April 1873. The mission of the Intelligence Branch, patterned after the T&S Department's duties, was "to collect and classify all possible information relating to the strength, organization, etc., of foreign armies; to keep themselves acquainted with the progress made by foreign countries in military art and science, and to preserve the information in such a form that it can be readily consulted, and made available for any purpose for which it may be required" (Fergusson 1984, p. 45).

The Intelligence Branch was headed by a major general and included twenty-seven military and civilian personnel. The first chief of the Intelligence Branch (officially the deputy adjutant-general for intelligence) was Major General Sir Patrick L. MacDougall, who had been the first commandant of the Staff College when it was established in 1857 and was an eminent military intellectual and reformer. He participated in the development of imperial strategy and ensured the establishment of the Intelligence Branch as an integral component of the War Office.

One of MacDougall's assistant adjutant-generals was Captain (later Major General Sir) Charles W. Wilson. Wilson became executive officer of the T&S Department in 1869, and the following year, when the Ordnance Survey was separated from the T&S Department, Wilson, then only a captain, became director of the latter. He was instrumental in the reorganization of the department and establishment of the Intelligence Branch in 1873. In 1874, the Intelligence Branch was transferred from the adjutant-general's department to the quartermaster-general's department.

MacDougall was replaced by Major General (later General) Sir Archibald Alison in 1878. Alison departed in 1882, and no replacement was named until 1886. In 1886, Major General (later General Sir) Henry Brackenbury became the deputy quartermaster-general for intelligence, shortly thereafter redesignated director of military intelligence. The Intelligence Division, as it was then called, continued to be organized into four foreign sections (A, C, D, and E), one responsible for colonial defense (B), and one topographic and library section (F). Brackenbury bemoaned the lack of a general staff and was instrumental in collecting information and initially in developing home defense and mobilization plans. He also established intelligence coordination with the Colonial Office, the India Office, and the Foreign Office.

Later directors of military intelligence included Major General (later General) Sir Edward F. Chapman (1891–1896) and Major General Sir John Ardagh (1896–1901). The outbreak of the Second Boer War in October 1899 seemed to expose shortcomings of the Intelligence Division and weaknesses within the War Office that would lead to reorganization. The Department of Mobilization and Military Intelligence existed from 1901–1904 and consisted of a Mobilization Division and an Intelligence Division. The General Staff was formally established in 1906, with intelligence responsibilities falling under the Directorate of Military Operations after 1907.

See also Alison, General Sir Archibald; Balloons; Boer War, Second (1899–1902); Brackenbury, General Sir Henry; Cardwell, Edward T.; Intellectuals, British Army; MacDougall, Major General Sir Patrick L.; Maps; Mobilization Planning; War Office; Wilson, Major General Sir Charles W.

References: Fergusson (1984); Hamer (1970); Spiers (1992); Wheeler (1914)

Isandlwana, Battle of (22 January 1879)

The Battle of Isandlwana was one of the most humiliating defeats ever suffered by the British Army.

The British invaded Zululand on 11 January 1879 with three widely dispersed columns under the overall command of Lieutenant General (later General) Frederick A. Thesiger, Second Baron Chelmsford. The center column (No. 3), consisting of about 4,709 soldiers, was to cross the Tulega River at Rorke's Drift and conduct the main thrust directly toward Zulu King Cetshwayo kaMpande's royal kraal (homestead) at Ulundi. Chelmsford located his force headquarters with the center column. The left (No. 4) and right (No. 1) columns were to converge on Ulundi in support of the center column. Two smaller columns (Nos. 2 and 5) guarded the Zululand border.

On 20 January 1879, the center column reached Isandlwana, a distinctive, rocky outcrop rising about 300 feet above the plain and about 10 miles from Rorke's Drift. The British established a camp at its base. Intelligence reports suggested that Zulu forces were on their way to attack the British. The next day, Chelmsford sent out scouts who encountered Zulu soldiers near Mangeni, about 12 miles away. It was not realized that these were stragglers from the 23,000-man main Zulu Army.

Early on 22 January 1879, Chelmsford led a 1,600-man element (most of 2nd Battalion, 24th Regiment plus four guns) to find and engage the Zulu Army, leaving behind at Isandlwana about 1,700 British and African soldiers (1st Battalion, 24th Regiment and two guns) to guard the camp. Lieutenant Colonel Henry Pulleine was left in charge at the camp. He also ordered No. 2 column, commanded by Lieutenant Colonel Anthony W. Durnford, to advance to Isandlwana. Chelmsford, who had recently defeated the Xhosa during the Ninth Cape Frontier War, believed the Zulus would also avoid confrontation and conduct guerrilla warfare.

Durnford's column arrived at Isandlwana at about 10:30 A.M. He had seen Zulus in the area, and about an hour later he took his 500-man force to reconnoiter and stumbled on the main Zulu Army. The Zulus, taking advantage of concealment and the undulating terrain, reacted immediately and configured into the traditional "chest and horns" attack formation.

Durnford's column, about 4 miles from Isandlwana, began a fighting retreat back toward the camp. Pulleine assembled his 700 soldiers into a long line, with two light 7-pounder guns at the center, extended in open order with about a yard between each man. Auxiliaries also served in the line. Durnford's column rejoined Pulleine's right flank, by which time the British line consisted of about 1,300 men.

Fire from the British Martini-Henry .45-caliber breechloading rifles slowed down, but did not stop, the Zulu onslaught. After about 30 minutes, Durnford's soldiers ran out of ammunition and the right flank collapsed, permitting the Zulu left horn to outflank the British line and regain the initiative. The British line withdrew in disorder, and the Zulus rushed forward, stabbing and killing indiscriminately. The British resisted for a time in the saddle of the hill, running low on ammunition and holding off the Zulus with fixed bayonets. The British, with the Zulu right horn to their rear, were eventually overwhelmed and savagely killed. The Zulus disemboweled the enemy dead, supposedly to free their spirits.

It was dusk by the time Chelmsford realized the Zulus were attacking Isandlwana in strength, and he reassembled his force and returned to the camp. Of the 1,700 soldiers Chelmsford had left to guard the camp, 1,329 (858 white and 471

African soldiers) were killed. Very few white officers or men escaped the massacre. Perhaps as many as 3,000 Zulus were also killed. The battlefield defied description, although one Zulu warrior recalled that "the green grass was red with the running blood and the veld was slippery, for it was covered with the brains and entrails of the killed" (Knight n.d., p. 1).

See also Cape Frontier Wars, Southern Africa; Cetshwayo kaMpande; Chelmsford, General Frederick A. Thesiger, Second Baron; Rorke's Drift, Defense of; Zulu War; Zululand
References: Barthorp (1980); Bourquin (1985); Chadwick (1978); England and Gardiner (1990); Lock and Quantrill (2002); Knight (1990); Knight (n.d.); Morris (1965)

J

Jameson, Dr. Leander Starr (1853–1917)

Dr. Leander Starr Jameson was a colonial administrator in South Africa best known as the leader of the ill-fated Jameson Raid (29 December 1895–2 January 1896).

Born in 1853, Jameson trained as a physician and first traveled to Kimberley, Cape Colony, in 1878. He became associated with Cecil J. Rhodes and shared his imperialistic visions. After Rhodes received a charter from the British Government on 29 October 1889 for the British South Africa Company ("the Chartered Company"), Jameson became a company administrator.

Jameson served as administrator of Mashonaland (which became southern Rhodesia). In 1893, he led a force into adjoining Matabeleland, ostensibly to suppress the Matabele and stop their raiding and incursions into Mashonaland, but in reality to extend the influence of the Chartered Company.

In 1890, Rhodes became prime minister of the Cape Colony and envisioned British imperial holdings stretching "from the Cape to Cairo," with a federated South Africa. The Boer Transvaal Government opposed these plans. Rhodes conceived a plan that would be executed by Jameson to support an *uitlander* (foreigner) rebellion to force Transvaal compliance with this and other proposals.

Jameson, with a force of about 600 mounted troopers with machine guns and artillery, assembled near the Transvaal border. The revolt of disgruntled immigrants in Johannesburg that Jameson was supposed to support never materialized. On 29 December 1895, Jameson decided to dash to Johannesburg to instigate the rebellion. In sum, on 2 January 1896, Jameson's force was surrounded and after a pitched battle surrendered to the Boers.

Jameson and five of the Raiders were returned to England, tried, and imprisoned; Rhodes was forced to resign as prime minister of Cape Colony. After serving a fifteen-month prison sentence, Jameson returned to South Africa. He served in the Cape Colony Parliament from 1900 to 1902, was besieged in Ladysmith during the Second Boer War, and was premier from 1904 to 1908. Jameson played a significant role in the 1908–1909 South African National Convention that paved the way for the establishment of the Union of South Africa in 1910.

Jameson was made a baronet in 1911 and died in 1917.

See also Boer War, Second (1899–1902); Boers; Imperialism; Jameson Raid; Kruger, S. J. Paulus; Rhodes, Cecil J.; Transvaal
References: Barthorp (1987); Hensman (1900); Moritz (1998); Pakenham (1979); Trew (1999)

Jameson Raid (29 December 1895– 2 January 1896)

The Jameson Raid was an ill-fated attempt to support an uprising that would topple the Transvaal (South African Republic) Government to ensure foreign (mainly British) immigrants *(uitlanders)* were given full political rights. The raid was also intended to eliminate Transvaal resistance to plans to federate all of South Africa.

Uitlander grievances were subject to exploitation by British imperialists, such as Cecil J. Rhodes, the diamond and gold magnate. Rhodes stated that the *uitlanders*, "possessing more than half the land, nine-tenths of the wealth, and paying nineteen-twentieths of the taxes" (Hensman 1900, p. 1), should be allowed some voice in the government. He had earlier secured Bechuanaland (modern-day

Botswana) as a British protectorate and the charter for the British South Africa Company in 1889. In the following year, Rhodes became prime minister of the Cape Colony and envisioned British imperial holdings stretching "from the Cape to Cairo," with a federated South Africa.

The Transvaal was opposed to this strategy. Rhodes conceived a plan, apparently with the tacit approval of the Colonial Secretary, Joseph Chamberlain, and assisted by his colleague Dr. Leander Starr Jameson, to force Transvaal compliance. The plan was for an *uitlander* rebellion that would force the Transvaal to grant full political rights to them; then in the next election the *uitlanders* would vote for a government that would support Rhodes's scheme.

Jameson, with a force of about 600 mounted troopers, six Maxim guns, two 7-pounder mountain guns, and a 12.5-pounder artillery piece, assembled within the Cape Colony border. The *uitlander* revolt in Johannesburg was scheduled to take place near the end of December 1895, but it soon became apparent the rising "had fizzled out like a damp squib" (Hensman 1900, p. 5). On 29 December 1895, Jameson made the decision to dash to Johannesburg to instigate the *uitlander* rebellion.

When the raiders crossed into the Transvaal, they cut a number of telegraph wires to prevent early warning of their approach, but in the confusion apparently did not cut the wire to Pretoria. On 1 January 1896, Jameson and his men met Boer opposition at Krugersdorp, and on the following day, they were surrounded at Doornkop. The Jameson Raiders attempted to fight their way out of Boer encirclement and lost 16 men killed and 49 wounded before surrendering to the Boers—who had one man killed.

The fiasco of Jameson's unsuccessful raid had far-reaching repercussions. Jameson and five of the raiders were returned to England, tried, and imprisoned; Rhodes was forced to resign as prime minister of Cape Colony. Kruger's prestige was enhanced in South Africa as well as in Europe. A treaty of mutual assistance between the Transvaal and the Orange Free State was concluded in 1897, and both republics modernized the capabilities of their security forces. Finally, trust between Britain and the Boers was shattered, with some people believing that war was inevitable.

See also Boer War, Second (1899–1902); Boers; Imperialism; Jameson, Dr. Leander Starr; Kruger, S. J. Paulus; Rhodes, Cecil J.; Transvaal
References: Barthorp (1987); Hensman (1900); Moritz (1998); Pakenham (1979)

Japan

Japan's isolationist policies in the mid-nineteenth century were considered intolerable by expanding Western nations that needed Japan to provide safe harbors and coaling stations. A U.S. naval squadron commanded by Commodore Matthew Perry forced Japan to open its ports to American ships in November 1852. On Perry's second trip to Japan, the Treaty of Kanagawa was signed on 31 March 1854, allowing the Americans to use the small ports of Kakodate and Shimoda. This opened the door to Japan, and the merchants and gunboats of Great Britain and other European powers soon followed.

During this time the influence of the *daimyos* (feudal samurai lords who controlled various Japanese provinces) and the samurai (members of the hereditary warrior class) was waning. In an attempt to consolidate power, the shogun ("generalissimo") Iyesada attempted to form a more modern army with infantry, cavalry, and artillery. He organized 13,600 men into three combined arms divisions, although most men were armed with old muskets and swords. Only about a quarter of the infantrymen were armed with rifles. Many of the samurai refused to exchange their swords for firearms.

After the 1868–1869 Boshin Civil War and the Meiji Restoration, the position of shogun was dissolved and power restored to the emperor. An imperial army was established in 1871, and conscription was introduced the following year, which ended the samurai's unique place in society. Advances in military organization, training, and weapons continued. The Sino-Japanese War of 1894 marked the recognition of Japan as an imperial power. In 1900, Japanese soldiers fought with American and European forces during the Boxer Rebellion in China.

At the beginning of the twentieth century, the Japanese Army appeared well trained and had a sound infrastructure based on Western principles. The Japanese Army and Navy soundly defeated the Russians in the 1904–1905 Russo-Japanese War.

See also Boxer Rebellion; Imperialism; Japan, Operations against
References: Padfield (1981); Willmott (1982)

Japan, Operations against (1863–1866)

Western imperialist encroachment in Japan after 1854 further undermined a weakening political system and frequently caused friction between the foreigners and the

Japanese. Pressure was put on the shogun ("generalissimo," although another translation of the title is "great resister of the barbarian incursions" [Willmott 1982, p. 11]) by reactionary groups, and policies were established to expel foreigners from Japan.

In June 1863, the local *daimyo* (feudal lord) at Shimonoseki had his shore batteries fire at Western ships. A punitive expedition of allied ships was sent to demolish the *daimyo's* fortifications, destroy his ships, and disperse his followers. About three months later, a group of British travelers, ignorant of local customs and etiquette, forced their way through the procession of the *daimyo* of Satsuma on the road from Yokohama to Yedo (now Tokyo). Samurai killed one British merchant and wounded two others. The shogun could not compel the *daimyo* to turn the murderer over to the British. The British then sent a naval squadron (consisting of one frigate, one paddle-sloop, two gun vessels, one corvette, and one sloop) to exact revenge on the Japanese. On 15–16 August 1863, the naval squadron bombarded the shore batteries at Kagoshima, sank or captured a number of the *daimyo's* vessels, and opened fire on his palace.

Internal strife and hostilities against foreigners continued, and Japanese attacked the British legation at Yedo in late 1863. When the shogun was unable to guarantee British safety, the British minister requested troops to protect the legation. The vanguard of the force, two companies of the 2nd Battalion, 20th Foot, landed at Yokohama on 23 January 1864. The force eventually included the entire 2nd Battalion, 20th Foot; two companies of the 67th Foot; and detachments of Royal Marines, Royal Engineers, Royal Artillery, and the Baluch Regiment.

During 5–8 September 1864, in reprisal for continued hostility by the Chosu clan, an allied fleet of British, American, French, and Dutch ships again bombarded Shimonoseki. Early on 6 September, a landing force of two Royal Marine battalions and a naval brigade with a Dutch battalion landed to destroy the Japanese shore batteries. The sloop H.M.S. *Perseus* became grounded within range of a Japanese stockade, and the Royal Marines and naval brigade assaulted this stockade, climbed its 8-foot palisade, and captured the fort as the defending Japanese were abandoning it. The British ground troops, having lost seven killed and twenty-six wounded during the attack, blew up the stockade's ammunition magazine and spiked the guns in the batteries. This convincing demonstration of Western military superiority and audacity basically ended antiforeigner activities in Japan.

The entire British force protecting the British legation held a review on 20 October 1864, to which Japanese government and other officials were invited, to demonstrate British power. The Japanese were impressed. The last British troops were withdrawn from Japan in April and May 1866.

See also Imperialism; Indian Army Operations; Japan
References: Featherstone (1973); Haythornthwaite (1995); Padfield (1981); Willmott (1982)

Jervois, Major General William
See Perak, Punitive Expedition to

Joubert, Commandant-General Petrus J. (1831–1900)

Petrus "Piet" J. Joubert was the commandant-general of the forces of the South African Republic (Transvaal) during the First Boer War (1880–1881), and he commanded Boer forces in Natal early in the Second Boer War. Known as "Slim Piet," "slim" being a Boer word describing guile, Joubert was frequently reluctant to serve in war, but once called, he considered it his duty to serve.

Joubert was born in Cape Colony in 1831, and in 1838 his family participated in the Great Trek. They moved back to the Transvaal in 1843. In 1868, he was elected to the *Volksraad* (parliament) and in 1875 he was appointed acting state president of the Transvaal (South African Republic). Earlier, Joubert had led Boer forces in operations against neighboring black tribes.

The British annexed the Transvaal in 1877, and this action was met with widespread Boer dissatisfaction. Former Transvaal Vice President S. J. Paulus Kruger, accompanied by Joubert, traveled to London to protest the action, to no avail. Upon their return, they started gathering other nationalists to their side.

Confrontations were taking placed between the British and the disaffected Boers. On 13 December 1880, 4,000 Boers met and proclaimed the reconstitution of the Transvaal. At the same time they selected a triumvirate consisting of Kruger, former President Marthinus Pretorius, and Joubert to run the provisional government. Joubert was also elected commandant-general of the Transvaal forces. The formal proclamation of the republic was made on 16 December, and hostilities began by the Boers besieging the British in Potchefstroom and attacking other small British garrisons.

Joubert commanded the Boer forces that defeated the British at the Battles of Laing's Nek (28 January 1881) and Majuba Hill (27 February 1881). He was a charismatic leader, frequently ascribing battlefield victory to a "Higher Power."

After the First Boer War, Joubert became a rival of Kruger and twice ran against him unsuccessfully for president. After the 1895–1896 Jameson Raid, Joubert was responsible for purchasing new weapons to modernize the Transvaal military forces.

Initially against the Boer declaration of war against the British in 1899, Joubert fully supported Kruger once the decision was made. Joubert commanded the forces advancing into Natal, but he was cautious and defensive-minded, by then past his prime. On 30 October 1899, at the so-called Battle of Ladysmith, Joubert permitted a number of British troops to depart the city. The siege of Ladysmith is considered a blunder by some because it tied up thousands of Boers who could have been better employed continuing the offensive into Natal.

On 24 November 1899, Joubert was thrown from his horse and suffered serious internal injuries. Injured and demoralized by the driving rain and the realization that the Boers could not hold off the might of the British Army, Joubert ordered a general withdrawal to the Tugela River and handed over command to General Louis Botha. Joubert died of his injuries on 27 March 1900.

See also Boer War, First (1880–1881); Boer War, Second (1899–1902); Boers; Botha, Commandant-General Louis; Commando System; Jameson Raid; Kruger, S. J. Paulus; Laing's Nek, Battle of; Majuba Hill, Battle of; Transvaal

References: Barthorp (1987); Bennett (2001); Marix Evans (2000); Pakenham (1979); Ransford (1967)

K

Kabul to Kandahar March (August 1880)

News of the British disaster at Maiwand on 27 July 1880 reached Kabul the following day. The experienced Lieutenant General (later Field Marshal) Sir Donald M. Stewart commanded the North Afghanistan Field Force and permitted his subordinate, Lieutenant General (later Field Marshal Earl) Sir Frederick S. Roberts, V.C., to volunteer to lead a relief force to Kandahar.

The viceroy of India recognized something had to be done to retrieve the debacle and approved this proposal on 3 August 1880. He directed that Stewart's force would also withdraw via the Khyber Pass to India. Stewart magnanimously placed all resources at Roberts's disposal. The composition of Roberts's force was also published on 3 August.

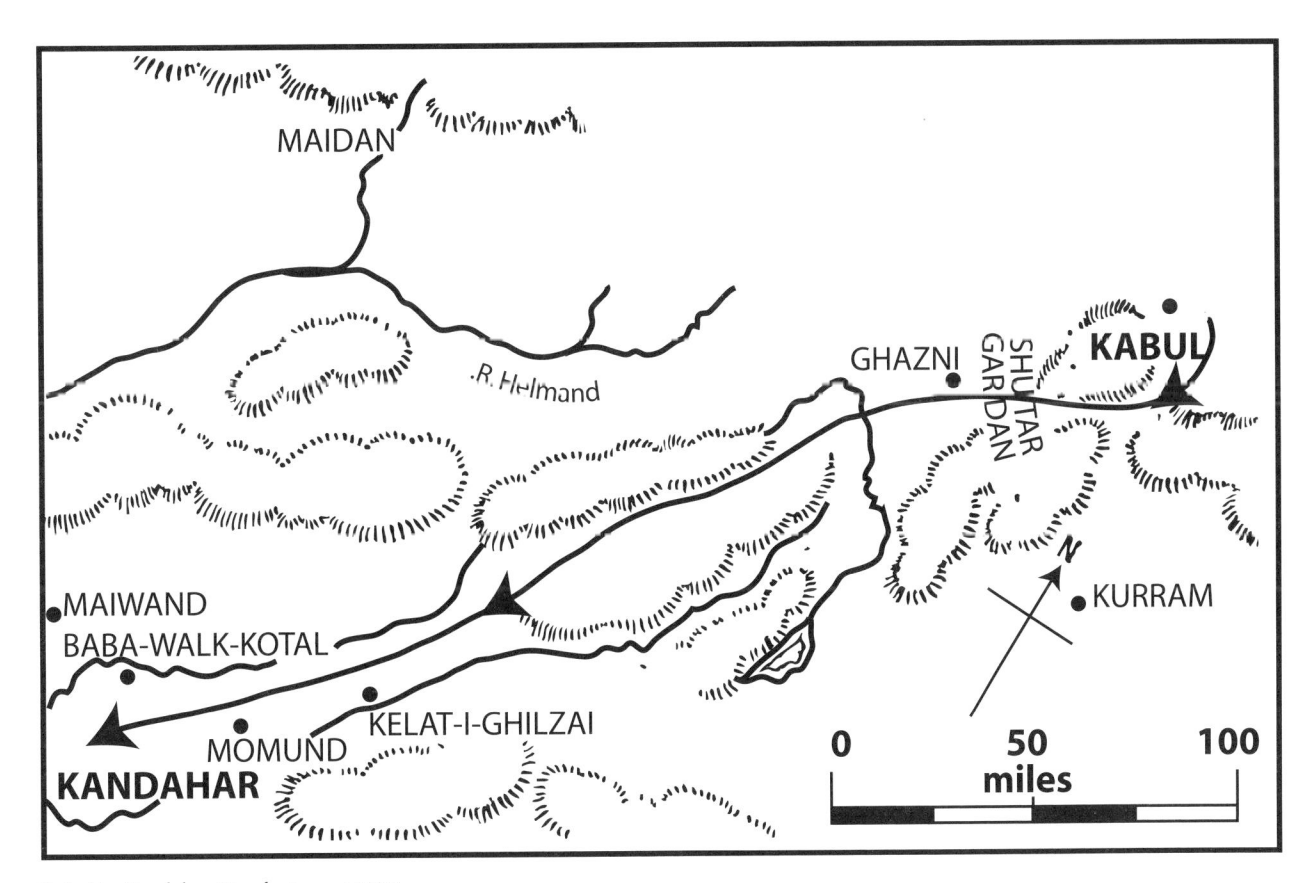

Kabul to Kandahar March, August 1880

It was to consist of three infantry brigades, each with a British battalion (60th Rifles, 72nd, or 92nd Highlanders), and a Sikh, a Gurkha, and a Punjab battalion. The Cavalry Brigade included the 9th Lancers. Only mule-borne artillery batteries were taken.

Equipment and baggage was reduced to a minimum. Each officer was permitted one mule for his equipment, with an additional mule for every eight officers for mess purposes. Rations for European troops consisted of tea, sugar, rum, and salt for thirty days and flour for five days; Indian troops received rations for five days. Cavalry horses and transport animals carried one day's grain in addition to their normal load. The strength of the newly formed Kabul-Kandahar Field Force was 10,148 combatants, 223 medical personnel, and 8,134 followers.

The Kabul-Kandahar Field Force began its march on 9 August 1880. Each day of the march, reveille was at 2:45 A.M., camp was struck, equipment was loaded by 3:40 A.M., and the head of the column began the march at 4:20 A.M. A ten-minute break was given each hour, and a twenty-minute halt was made at 8:00 A.M. for breakfast.

The 318-mile march, through waterless desert and great extremes of temperature, was completed on 31 August 1880 as the force reached the outskirts of Kandahar. Roberts attacked the Afghans the next day and defeated them at the Battle of Kandahar.

The Kabul-Kandahar March was considered by some "the most spectacular exploit of the war" (Tanner 2002, p. 216). While it was a good performance, it seemed to have been highly overrated, perhaps to deflect attention from the dismal defeat at Maiwand and the overall withdrawal from Afghanistan, and as an attempt to redeem British martial prestige. Stewart's thirty-two-day march from Kandahar to Kabul in April 1880, during which considerable fighting took place, was also very impressive. Roberts, who was carried for many days in a *doolie* (a type of ambulance) due to high fever, also considered the August 1880 march an overrated operation; his advance to Kabul in 1879 was "in every particular more dangerous, more difficult" (Fredericks 1971, p. 224). A special medal, the "Kabul to Kandahar Star, 1880," was struck and awarded to participants, one of the very few occasions a campaign medal commemorated an operation that did not include combat.

See also Afghan War, Second (1878–1880); Afghanistan; Campaign Medals; Indian Army Operations; Kandahar, Battle of; Maiwand, Battle of; Roberts, Field Marshal Frederick S., V.C.; Stewart, Field Marshal Sir Donald M.

References: Barthorp (1982); Featherstone (1973); Forbes (1892); Fredericks (1971); Hannah (1972); James (1998); Owen (1985); Roberts (1897); Tanner (2002)

Kambula, Battle of (29 March 1879)

See Buller, General Sir Redvers H., V.C.; Wood, Field Marshal Sir (Henry) Evelyn M., V.C.; Zulu War

Kandahar, Battle of (1 September 1880)

British Army Lieutenant General (later Field Marshal Earl) Sir Frederick S. Roberts's Kabul-Kandahar Field Force completed its 23-day, 318-mile march from Kabul to besieged Kandahar on 31 August 1880. The following day, Roberts's force fought and soundly defeated Afghan forces commanded by Ayub Khan, a contender for the Afghan throne.

Ayub Khan's forces were positioned on the high ground at and around the Baba Wali Kotal (Pass), northwest of Kandahar. British operations were conducted generally in accordance with Roberts's plan. The forces of Major General J. M. Primrose, which had been besieged in Kandahar, would bombard the Afghans positioned at the Baba Wali Kotal and conduct a frontal feint against them.

The Infantry Division of the Kabul-Kandahar Field Force, commanded by Major General J. Ross, contained three infantry brigades. The 1st Infantry Brigade, commanded by Brigadier General Herbert McPherson, consisted of the 92nd Highlanders, 23rd Pioneers, 24th Punjab Native Infantry, and 2nd Gurkhas. Brigadier General T. D. Baker's 2nd Infantry Brigade contained the 72nd Highlanders, 2nd and 3rd Sikh Infantry, and the 5th Gurkhas. The 3rd Infantry Brigade, with Brigadier General Charles Macgregor commanding, contained the 2nd Battalion, 60th Rifles, 15th Sikhs, 25th Punjab Native Infantry, and the 4th Gurkhas.

As Primrose's troops conducted their feint, the 1st Infantry Brigade seized the village of Guni Mulla and continued the attack around the Afghan right flank, which rested on a ridge. The 2nd Brigade conducted a wider flanking movement, and both brigades linked-up at Pir Paimal village. As the Afghan guns turned on them, both brigades continued their assault to the entrenched Afghan camp at Babi Wali. With bayonets fixed, the British and Indian troops stormed the Afghan positions, frequently before enemy guns firing at point-blank range. (The 3rd Infantry Brigade was in reserve.) The defeated Afghans fled, abandoning 32 guns and losing about 1,200 men, and were pursued by the British cavalry. The British suffered 58 killed and 210 wounded.

The Battle of Kandahar was the last battle of the Second Afghan War. Coming immediately after his vaunted Kabul to Kandahar March, this battlefield victory established Roberts as a great Victorian general and commander.

See also Afghan War, Second (1878–1880); Afghanistan; Kabul to Kandahar March; Maiwand, Battle of; Roberts, Field Marshal Frederick S., V.C.

References: Barthorp (1982); Featherstone (1973); Forbes (1892); Fredericks (1971); Roberts (1897); Tanner (2002)

Kars, Siege of (June–26 November 1855)

The frontier area of Transcaucasia was the scene of numerous, but generally neglected, battles between Russian and Turkish forces during the Crimean War (1854–1856). In 1855, the fortress city of Kars (located in Turkish Armenia, about 80 miles southeast of Batumi and roughly the same distance southwest of Tiflis) was stubbornly defended by Turkish troops until they were forced to surrender to the Russians on 26 November 1855.

The Turks had retreated into the fortress of Kars after being defeated by the Russians a number of times in 1853 and 1854. In August 1854, the British appointed Brigadier General (later Major General Sir) William Fenwick Williams to be liaison officer to Zarif Mustapha Pasha, the Turkish commander in Kars. When Williams and a small advisory team arrived in Kars on 24 September 1854, the low morale, inefficiency, corruption, and poor leadership became obvious.

Williams decided to assume command of the defense of Kars. Almost singlehandedly, he immediately began requesting supplies, building facilities, and training and disciplining his 17,000 Turkish troops. The Kars defenses were strengthened in early 1855 by a ring of eight forts and a system of interconnecting trenches and redoubts around the city.

A Russian army under the command of General Michael Muraviev advanced from Georgia into eastern Turkey in June 1855. After a series of probing attacks, the Russians blockaded Kars. The Turkish soldiers showed great courage and determination in defending against Russian attacks.

By 1 September 1855, supply shortages forced Williams to cut rations in half. Omar Pasha, commanding the Turkish forces in the Crimea, was unable to persuade his own or the allied governments to send troops to assist Kars. He eventually left the Crimea on 6 September, and after Sevastopol had fallen on 9 September, a large Turkish contingent followed Omar Pasha on 29 September.

The Russians determinedly attacked Kars on 29 September 1855 but were repulsed after sustaining about 7,500 casualties. Cholera and hunger devastated the Turkish garrison, and Williams, feeling betrayed by the allies, was forced to surrender Kars and over 18,000 Turkish officers and men on 26 November 1855. (The relief force under Omar Pasha was unable to reach Kars in time.) Williams was convinced the Turkish soldiers did not bear responsibility for their ultimate failure: "They fell dead at their posts, in their tents, and throughout the camp, as brave men should who cling to their duty through the slightest glimmering of hope of saving a place entrusted to their custody" (Royle 2000, p. 432). The fall of Kars was considered insignificant at the time, but it ended up being "a great sop to the Russians after the fall of Sevastopol" (Baumgart 1999, p. 184) and eventually paved the way for peace negotiations.

See also Crimean War; Russian Forces, Crimean War; Sevastopol, Siege of; Turkish Forces, Crimean War

References: Baumgart (1999); Edgerton (1999); Judd (1975); Royle (2000); Warner (1972)

Kashgil, Battle of (3–5 November 1883)

The Egyptian Government sent a large force under the command of Major General William Hicks Pasha to the Sudan in 1883 to suppress the uprising caused by the Mahdi and his dervish hordes. Many of the members of Hicks's Sudan Force were members of the Egyptian Army that had been disbanded after the 1882 Arabi Rebellion and later imprisoned. As part of their punishment, they had been marched in chains to the Sudan, and they were demoralized and relatively ineffective.

After a month of drilling and training, Hicks led his force out of Khartoum on 29 April 1883 and defeated a dervish force a few days later at Jebel Ard. Hicks's force killed over 500 dervishes at a cost of seven of his soldiers killed. This surprising victory showed that the dervishes could be defeated and gave the Sudan Force considerable confidence. Hicks led his force back to Khartoum to continue training and plan the next phase of his campaign.

On 9 September 1883, Hicks's 10,000-man force, which consisted of regular and irregular infantry and cavalry, 16 guns, 6 Nordenfeldt machine guns, and about 5,000 camels with 2,000 camp followers, advanced into the Kordofan Desert toward the Mahdi's headquarters at El Obeid. "Here we have nine thousand infantry," wrote an observer, commenting on the poor quality of the force, "that fifty good men could rout in ten minutes, [and] one thousand cavalry and bashi-bazooks [irregulars] that have never learned to ride" (Neillands 1996, p. 71), to face a Mahdist army estimated at 70,000.

Hicks's force established a supply base at El Duam on the Nile. Departing from this location on 27 September 1883, the Sudan Force took the longer of two proposed routes, believing it to have a better water supply. The force, led by guides who may have been Mahdist sympathizers, plodded clumsily in a large hollow square formation through the desert for over a month, harassed constantly by dervish patrols.

Discipline and cohesion broke down, and on 3 November 1883, the Sudan Force arrived at Kashgil, about 40 miles south of El Obeid. Dervishes, armed with thousands of rifles captured earlier, were waiting at Kashgil and poured a continual fire into the Egyptian square. Hicks's force continued to try to advance on 4 November, and either late that day or on 5 November the dervishes launched a main assault that shattered the square. The Egyptian soldiers made little effort to resist and were slaughtered. Fewer than 300 soldiers out of the 10,000-man force survived the massacre. Hicks, reportedly fighting courageously, was one of the last men killed. As was the Sudanese custom, Hicks and other leaders were decapitated and their heads given to the Mahdi.

The defeat of Hicks's force at Kashgil paved the way for the Mahdists to capture or besiege a number of Red Sea ports and further engulf the British in this Sudanese imbroglio.

See also Arabi Rebellion; Dervishes; Egypt; Egyptian Army; Hicks Pasha, Major General William; Mahdi; Sudan
References: Barthorp (1984); Keown-Boyd (1986); Neillands (1996)

Khalifa (?–1899)

The Khalifa, meaning "prince of the church" or "apostle," was Abdullahi ibn Mohammed, the handpicked successor to the Mahdi. When the Madhi died in 1885, the Khalifa continued his predecessor's policy of uniting the Sudan and transforming it into an Islamic state, the Mahdiya.

Abdullahi ibn Mohammed, from the cattle-grazing Baggara people of the southern Darfur Province, was older than the Mahdi, whom he first met in about 1880. While he was a capable administrator, the Khalifa was also cruel and cunning. Even though the Khalifa was the Mahdi's designated successor, he was only one of three caliphs chosen by the Mahdi, emulating the Prophet Mohammed. As a result, the Khalifa also had to overcome the opposition of the others and purged the Mahdiya of members of the Mahdi's family. He was not able to effectively consolidate power until 1891.

In the meantime, the Khalifa wanted to achieve the Mahdi's goal of conquering Egypt but was defeated by the British at the Battle of Ginnis on 30 December 1885. The Khalifa's fundamentalist rule was oppressive, with internal unrest and tense regional relations. In 1887, a 60,000-man dervish army invaded Abyssinia, and the Abyssinians invaded the Sudan two years later. The Khalifa's best general invaded Egypt but his force was soundly defeated by British-led Egyptian troops at the Battle of Toski (3 August 1889), ending the belief in dervish invincibility. The Belgians and the Italians also repulsed dervish invasions of their territories.

The British began their reconquest of the Sudan in earnest in 1896. A number of engagements were fought, culminating in the Battle of Omdurman, near Khartoum, on 2 September 1898. The 26,000-man Anglo-Egyptian force, commanded by Major General (later Field Marshal Earl) Sir Horatio H. Kitchener and fully utilizing its superior firepower, killed about 11,000 dervishes in the five-hour battle while losing 48 dead and about 400 wounded.

The Khalifa escaped and operations continued to subdue the dervishes. The British finally defeated the dervishes and killed the Khalifa and many of his key subordinates at the Battle of Umm Diwaykarat on 24 November 1899. The Mahdiya died with the Khalifa.

See also Dervishes; Ginnis, Battle of; Kitchener, Field Marshal Horatio H.; Mahdi; Omdurman, Battle of; Reconquest of the Sudan; Sudan; Toski, Battle of; Wingate, General Sir (Francis) Reginald
References: Brook-Shepherd (1972); Daly (1997); Ludwig (1937); Mansfield (1971); Metz (1992); Moore-Morris (1998b); Waller (1988)

Kipling, Rudyard

See India, British Army in; Military and Popular Culture; Roberts, Field Marshal Frederick S., V.C.

Kitchener, Field Marshal Horatio H., First Earl Kitchener of Khartoum and of Broome (1850–1916)

Field Marshal Horatio H. Kitchener was an enigmatic and controversial (yet frequently ruthless and generally successful) colonial campaign commander and imperial proconsul, best known for the defeat of the dervishes at the Battle of Omdurman (2 September 1898). He dominated British military affairs from the beginning of the twentieth century until his death during World War I.

Kitchener, the son of a retired British Army lieutenant colonel, was born in Ireland on 24 June 1850. He entered the Royal Military Academy, Woolwich, in 1868 and was commissioned a second lieutenant in the Royal Engineers in 1871. Shortly before being commissioned, he reportedly served on the French side for a short time during the Franco-Prussian War.

Kitchener was employed on survey and intelligence duties in Palestine (1874–1878) and Cyprus (1878–1882). He learned Arabic and assimilated into the Arab population, and gathered intelligence during the 1882 British expedition to Egypt to suppress the Arabi Rebellion. After the British occupied Egypt in 1882, the Egyptian Army was reorganized and led by British officers. Kitchener, after promotion to captain in 1883, was assigned as second in command of the Egyptian cavalry squadron.

During the Gordon Relief Expedition (1884–1885), Kitchener served in the intelligence section of the British expeditionary force, receiving brevet promotions to major and lieutenant colonel for his meritorious service. He served as governor of the Red Sea territories, headquartered at Suakin, from 1886 to 1888, then commanded the Egyptian cavalry and distinguished himself at the Battle of Toski (3 August 1889).

After serving as adjutant-general of the Egyptian Army (1890–1892), Kitchener succeeded Major General (later Field Marshal Lord) Sir Francis W. Grenfell as sirdar (commander in chief) of the Egyptian Army. He continued with military reorganization and rearmament, and in March 1896, the British authorized the Egyptian Army to begin the reconquest of the Sudan by advancing up the Nile River.

Kitchener realized that logistics and effective lines of communication were required to ensure success in the harsh desert environment, and he concentrated on establishing a logistical and transport infrastructure and advanced methodically. His 9,000-man force was assembled at Akasha, south of Wadi Halfa, by 4 June 1896. Three days later, Kitchener's soldiers defeated the dervishes at Firket. Disease and severe weather slowed down the advance in the summer of 1896, but an Egyptian force entered the city of Dongola on 23 September 1896 to find it deserted. The first phase of the campaign ended when Kitchener's army occupied Merowi and Korti.

To support Kitchener's continued advance, construction of the Sudan Military Railway began in early 1897. By 23 July 1897, 103 miles of track had been laid. This facilitated the Egyptian capture of Abu Hamed on 7 August 1897 and Berber on 5 September 1897. Kitchener's force remained in Berber, the start for the 1898 phase of the campaign.

On 4 January 1898, after it became apparent that the Egyptian Army needed British reinforcements to destroy the dervish army and win the campaign, Kitchener was appointed as the supreme commander of all Egyptian and British troops south of Aswan.

As the British reinforcements arrived, Kitchener's force advanced to Atbara, located about 200 miles north of Khartoum. When dervish forces were located on 30 March 1898, Kitchener became indecisive and wondered whether he should attack first or wait to be attacked. Kitchener finally resolved to attack, and the Anglo-Egyptian Army victory over the dervishes at the Battle of Atbara (8 April 1898) paved the way for the advance to Khartoum 200 miles to the south and the reconquest of the Sudan. Kitchener considered this his most important battle.

By mid-August 1898, Kitchener's force totaled about 8,200 British and 17,600 Egyptian and Sudanese soldiers, with artillery, machine gun, and naval gunboat support. The force began its final march to Omdurman on 28 August 1898. Three days later the army sighted the Kerreri Hills, high ground covering the approaches to Omdurman. On 1 September 1898, the 21st Lancers and the Egyptian cavalry reconnoitered the area and were astonished to find the dervishes advancing.

The Battle of Omdurman began early on 2 September 1898. By the end of the day, Kitchener's six-brigade force, with the effective support of Maxim guns, had repulsed a number of uncoordinated dervish assaults. The Anglo-Egyptian force won this decisive victory, largely as a result of the initiative and competence of Kitchener's subordinate commanders and its technological weapons superiority. Kitchener, however, did not position himself to see the entire battlefield. He generally centralized command in his own

Kitchener, Field Marshal Horatio H.

hands and did not properly use his staff, and issued a number of confusing and contradictory orders during the battle. These orders were frequently issued directly to brigade and battalion commanders, bypassing division commanders. Kitchener, as commander in chief, deserves credit for the victory, but if his brigade commanders had not used their own initiative successfully, "the glitter of Kitchener's post-battle reputation would have been dulled and his careless handling of Phase Two [of the battle] exposed" (Keown-Boyd 1986, p. 235). After the battle, Kitchener was raised to the peerage as Baron Kitchener of Khartoum ("K of K").

Shortly after the Battle of Omdurman, Kitchener led a force to Fashoda, about 500 miles south of Khartoum, to forestall French claims to the Nile. With the success of this mission, he stayed at Khartoum for one year as governor of the Sudan.

After the disastrous Black Week battles of December 1899 during the Second Boer War (1899–1902), Field Marshal Lord (later Earl) Frederick S. Roberts, V.C., was appointed commander in chief of the British forces in South Africa. Kitchener was designated his chief of staff on 18 December 1899 and arrived in South Africa the following month.

Even though the supply and transport system initially worked very well during the Second Boer War (1899–1902), Roberts and Kitchener tried to "reorganize" the supply and transport system in February 1900. The plan was to consolidate all supply and transport operations (except for those of the Cavalry Division and the frontline regimental transport) under centralized control. The result was a disaster, and within weeks the "old" supply and transport system, under the control of the Army Service Corps, was largely restored.

In Roberts's absence, Kitchener commanded British troops at Paardeberg on 18 February 1900, where he committed his troops to numerous futile frontal assaults against the entrenched Boers, failing to understand the lethality of an enemy armed with magazine-fed rifles using smokeless powder.

Roberts, after the capture of Bloemfontein (13 March 1900), Johannesburg (31 May 1900), and Pretoria (5 June 1900), seemed to believe the war was over. Although he initiated the policy of farm burning in June 1900, Roberts returned to England in November 1900 believing the British had won the war, and Kitchener succeeded him as commander in chief on 29 November.

Kitchener resorted to drastic methods, frequently criticized, to defeat the continued Boer insurgency. He increased farm burning, removed Boer families from their homesteads and resettled them in concentration camps, and constructed a large network of blockhouses, all designed to deprive the Boer guerrillas of subsistence and support. Mobile columns attempted to hunt down and isolate Boer forces. Kitchener's draconian measures finally wore down Boer resistance, and the war ended with the signing of the Treaty of Vereeniging on 31 May 1902.

Upon his return to England, Kitchener was made a viscount, knighted, promoted to full general, and given a £50,000 grant. He was also appointed commander in chief, India. His tenure was marked by a struggle with the viceroy over the control of the army, resulting in the viceroy's resignation in 1905. This permitted Kitchener to complete his plans for significant administrative reforms and organizational changes. The Indian Army was unified and divided into three corps areas with divisions reconstituted and assigned to corps.

When Kitchener departed India in 1909, he was promoted to field marshal and turned down the appointment of commander in chief, Mediterranean Forces. He was disappointed at not being appointed viceroy in 1910, but he accepted the position of agent and consul-general of Egypt in 1911, a position he held until 1914.

Kitchener received an earldom in 1914 and was on leave in England when World War I broke out in August 1914. He reluctantly accepted the position of secretary of state for war and advocated preparations for a long conflict. His autocratic manner with other members of the Cabinet and senior British Army officers caused friction, and his role in supporting continued operations at Gallipoli and elsewhere reduced his credibility. Kitchener, however, remained popular with the public and symbolized the war effort when he appeared on a recruiting poster. Kitchener drowned at sea on 5 June 1916 when the cruiser H.M.S. *Hampshire*, on which he was traveling to Russia, struck a mine and sank.

Kitchener was lauded as a hero and became a legend. His performance, however, suggests that he was frequently hesitant (especially at the Atbara in 1898), and on the most notable occasion when he was decisive (at the Battle of Paardeberg, 18 February 1898), Kitchener was dogmatic and unsuccessful. Kitchener generally centralized control in his own hands and was not an advocate of teamwork or of following the chain of command. He was more successful at improvisation, and his "two basic attributes were an unparalleled thoroughness, and an unparalleled drive" (Magnus

1959, p. 380). "Perhaps his enormous popularity with the general public was the most extraordinary fact about [him]" (Warner 1986, p. 206).

See also Arabi Rebellion; Army Service Corps; Atbara, Battle of; Blockhouses; Boer War, Second (1899–1902); Boers; Concentration Camps; Dervishes; Dongola, Capture of; Egypt; Egyptian Army; Fashoda Incident; Gordon Relief Expedition; Grenfell, Field Marshal Francis W.; Indian Army Organization; Khalifa; Omdurman, Battle of; Paardeberg, Battle of; Railways; Reconquest of the Sudan; Roberts, Field Marshal Frederick S., V.C.; Sirdar; Sudan; Toski, Battle of; Wingate, General Sir (Francis) Reginald

References: Arthur (1920); Ballard (1930); Begbie (1915); Daly (1997); Keown-Boyd (1986); Magnus (1959); Pakenham (1979); Pollock (2001); Rye and Groser (1917); Sixsmith (1974); Warner (1986); Ziegler (1974)

Kofi Karikari (1837–1884)

Kofi Karikari was the tenth *asantehene* (king of the Ashanti nation), and he reigned from 1867 to 1874. Under his leadership, the Ashanti attacked the Gold Coast in late 1872. This hostile incursion sparked the Second Ashanti War with the British. The Ashanti lost this conflict and Kofi Karikari was deposed in 1874.

Kofi Karikari, known to the British as "King Coffee," was born in 1837. In the mid-1860s, the Gold Coast was in turmoil. The Ashanti had been losing considerable income due to the suppression of the slave trade and because of blockades of other trading centers. In April 1867, the seventy-year-old Ashanti King Kwaku Dua I died unexpectedly in his sleep. His death ignited an internal struggle over his succession. After three months of bitter infighting, sacrifices, and assassinations, Kofi Karikari, Kwaku Dua I's grandnephew, was chosen *asantehene* by an electoral majority.

Kofi was thirty years old when he was elected king. He was of medium height, had a full beard, and was said to have been handsome except for smallpox scars on his face. Kofi made a number of enemies through his debauched lifestyle, which included making sexual advances to the wives of powerful men, and his profligacy with the kingdom's gold. Moreover, he was very inexperienced militarily and naive about royal intrigue. When Kofi was crowned, he is said to have promised, "My business shall be war" (Edgerton 1995, p. 95).

Kofi was confronted immediately by military crises, the first concerning the Fante blockade of the Elmina people living near the Dutch fort named Elmina. In 1868, the *asantehene* sent two large armies, commanding one himself, to relieve the Elmina people. Sporadic fighting continued until 1869.

The continuous warfare around Elmina disrupted trade so much that the Dutch ceded their fort at Elmina and other possessions on the Gold Coast to the British in 1872. Because the British refused to pay the Ashanti an annual tribute as the Dutch had done for many years, the Ashanti were incensed and eager for retribution. As a result, in December 1872 the Ashanti crossed the Prah River (the southern boundary of Ashantiland), defeating other tribes in their march to the sea, and were within a day's march of Elmina on 13 June 1873. A small Royal Marine detachment held off the attacking Ashanti. The British Government decided to send reinforcements, then an expeditionary force, under the command of Major General (later Field Marshal Viscount) Sir Garnet J. Wolseley.

Wolseley arrived at Cape Coast Castle on 2 October 1873. Irregular regiments of allied indigenous locals were raised and logistical preparations were made to receive British battalions. During this preparatory phase, confused correspondence passed between Wolseley and Kofi, and the Ashanti forces began to withdraw north slowly. Wolseley's plan was to use the British troops, starting in January 1874 at the beginning of the dry season, to march to Kumasi and destroy it as a sign of British strength and victory.

Wolseley's force began to advance toward Kumasi in January 1874. On 24 January 1874, Wolseley informed Kofi of his intention to march on Kumasi and issued an ultimatum to halt the conflict. Kofi then seemingly decided to lure the British further into the jungle to surround and destroy them. Skirmishing took place between the British and the Ashanti many times. The British were ambushed at Amoaful on 31 January but pushed on through their determined adversary and entered a largely empty Kumasi on 4 February 1874. Kofi had fled north and Wolseley razed Kumasi.

Wolseley threatened to hunt down Kofi, whose messengers finally caught up with Wolseley at Fomena on 13 February 1874. The *asantehene* stated he was anxious for peace and would agree to all the British demands in what became known as the Treaty of Fomena: payment of an indemnity of 50,000 ounces of gold, renunciation of suzerainty over a number of other tribes, cessation of rent payments on forts, free passage on all roads, and the suppression of human sacrifice. These conditions undermined the stability of the Ashanti Kingdom and the authority of the *asantehene*. As a result, Kofi was "destooled"(dethroned) in September 1874 and died in Kumasi ten years later.

See also Amoaful, Battle of; Ashanti; Ashanti War, Second (1873–1874); Imperialism; Wolseley, Field Marshal Garnet J.
References: Edgerton (1995); Featherstone (1989); Haythornthwaite (1995); James (1985); Keegan (1967); Lehmann (1964); Maxwell (1985)

Koosh-ab, Battle of
See Persian War

Kruger, S. J. Paulus (1825–1904)
S. J. Paulus Kruger was a soldier and statesman known as the founder of the South African nation. Called *Oom* ("Uncle") Paul because of his fatherly nature, Kruger served as president of the Transvaal (South African Republic) from 1883 to 1902. While seemingly an ignorant peasant, he was cunning and frequently underestimated.

Born on 10 October 1825 in the Cape Colony, Kruger had little formal education. In 1836, his family participated in the Great Trek, settling near Potchefstroom in 1838. Kruger soon became involved in public life and was elected a field cornet. He was present during the 1852 negotiations leading to the Sand River Convention that recognized Transvaal independence. In 1855–1856, he served on the commission that wrote the constitution of the new republic. During the unrest of the 1860s, Kruger served as commandant-general and played a prominent role in pacifying and unifying the Transvaal, although he resigned this position in 1873.

When the British annexed the Transvaal in 1877, Kruger and Petrus J. Joubert traveled to England to persuade the British to reverse their policy. Unsuccessful, Kruger and Joubert returned to the Transvaal and organized passive resistance. In 1880, friction between the Boers and the British increased. Finally, on 13 December 1880, about 4,000 Boers met and proclaimed the reconstitution of the Transvaal. They also selected a triumvirate, consisting of Kruger, Joubert, and former President Marthinus Pretorius to run the provisional government. Shortly thereafter, hostilities began, and the First Boer War, culminating in British defeat at Majuba Hill (27 February 1881), was over in about two months. Kruger then skillfully helped negotiate a peace settlement including limited independence.

Kruger was elected president of the Transvaal in 1883 (and was reelected three more times). The discovery of gold in 1886 on the Witwatersrand caused tremendous domestic problems, as large numbers of *uitlanders* (foreigners) migrated to the area. Kruger saw this as a threat to the separate identity of the Boers, "God's people," and was not willing to give full political rights to the mainly British immigrants, even though they were heavily taxed. In 1890, Kruger restricted the franchise to men resident in the Transvaal for at least fourteen years. At the same time he established a separate *Volksraad* to represent the mining interests, but this did not satisfy the foreigners. To try to topple the Transvaal, the British supported the ill-fated Jameson Raid in 1895–1896.

In 1898, Kruger was elected president for the fourth and last time. The following year a conference took place at Bloemfontein between Kruger and Sir (later Lord) Alfred Milner, high commissioner for South Africa and governor of the Cape Colony. Milner continued to press the cause of the *uitlanders,* and Kruger proposed a minimum seven-year residency requirement for enfranchisement. Milner refused the offer, tension increased, and both sides prepared for war, which was started on 11 October 1899 after a Boer ultimatum expired.

Kruger had hoped the Boers would conduct a series of rapid, preemptive strikes on the outbreak of war. The forces, however, lost momentum as they besieged various towns. He offered peace proposals to the British in March 1900 but was rebuffed. Kruger attended his last session of the *Volksraad* on 7 May 1900, then left Pretoria ahead of the advancing British troops. Too old for guerrilla warfare and revered as president, he traveled to Europe in October 1900. Promises of European support for the Boers never materialized, and Kruger died in exile in Switzerland on 14 July 1904. His body was buried in Pretoria later that year.

See also Boer War, First (1880–1881); Boer War, Second (1899–1902); Boers; Jameson Raid; Joubert, Commandant-General Petrus J.; Majuba Hill, Battle of; Transvaal
References: Marix Evans (2000); Pakenham (1979); Trew (1999)

Ladysmith, Siege of (2 November 1899–28 February 1900)

The Siege of Ladysmith, which confined over 13,000 British troops of the Natal Field Force for almost four months, completely disrupted British strategic plans during the Second Boer War. Its timely relief averted a tremendous military disaster.

A key component of Boer strategy at the beginning of the Second Boer War was to capture major rail junctions and disrupt the British lines of communication. Shortly after the outbreak of war on 11 October 1899, a 14,000-man Boer force commanded by Commandant-General Petrus J. Joubert began advancing from the Transvaal to Ladysmith, the principal town and main British supply base in northern Natal and the railhead from Durban on the coast. Another 6,000-man Boer force was assembling and planned to converge with Joubert's force at Ladysmith.

Lieutenant General (later Field Marshal) Sir George S. White, V.C., had been appointed general officer commanding Natal and landed at Durban on 7 October 1899. He decided to concentrate his forces forward at Ladysmith.

The British won an inconclusive victory at Talana Hill (20 October 1899), and the following day routed the Boers at Elandslaagte, only 10 miles from Ladysmith. White then ordered all his forces to Ladysmith. An engagement was fought at Rietfontein on 26 October, the same day the two Boer forces united and totaled about 24,000 men.

Instead of withdrawing 15 miles to the south of the Tugela River, White decided to attack the Boers before they could coordinate their efforts. White developed a plan involving a double envelopment at dawn after a night march, with secondary operations on both flanks, arguably "the greatest strategic mistake of the entire war" (Pakenham 1979, p. 155). The result was a debacle, with the British suffering about 360 casualties and another 1,000 soldiers captured. The Battle of Nicholson's Nek (30 October 1899)—the worst British defeat since the Battle of Majuba in 1881—was called Mournful Monday. White would have been relieved for incompetence had the Boers not surrounded Ladysmith on 2 November 1899.

Ladysmith was initially well provisioned, but disease struck, and the Boers humanely permitted the British to establish a hospital outside the town. The Boers attacked the British defenses on Wagon Hill on 6 January 1900 but were driven off. As the siege continued, disease, hunger, and misery increased. White also became ill and weak. About 810 garrison soldiers died during the siege, about 500 of them from disease.

General Sir Redvers H. Buller, V.C., commanding the British forces in South Africa, made numerous attempts to relieve Ladysmith. Buller's attack at Colenso (15 December 1899) failed, and he advised White to consider surrendering if Ladysmith could not hold out for another month. Other failed relief attempts occurred at Spion Kop (23–24 January 1900) and Vaal Kraantz (5 February 1900). Buller's force broke though Boer defenses on the Tugela River and launched a final assault on 27 February, thus avenging the Boer triumph at the Battle of Majuba 19 years earlier. The 118-day Siege of Ladysmith ended on 28 February 1900,

See also Boer War, Second (1899–1902); Buller, General Sir Redvers H., V.C.; Colenso, Battle of; De Wet, Chief Commandant Christiaan R.; Gough, General Sir Hubert de la P.; Joubert, Commandant-General Petrus J.; Lines of Communication; Majuba Hill, Battle of; Spion Kop, Battle of;

Vaal Krantz, Battle of; White, Field Marshal Sir George S., V.C.
References: Belfield (1975); Cassidy (2001); Griffith (1974); Nasson (1999); Pakenham (1979); Symons (1963); Teulie (1993)

Laing's Nek, Battle of (28 January 1881)

Laing's Nek was a strategic location, the only pass in the Drakensberg Mountain range through which an army could enter the Transvaal from Natal. After the First Boer War began on 16 December 1880 and a British column was basically wiped out at Bronkhorstspruit four days later, the British sent a force from Natal to suppress the insurgent Boers and relieve the encircled British garrisons.

Major General Sir George Pomeroy-Colley, British governor and commander in chief of Natal and the Transvaal, commanded the 1,400-man composite Natal Field Force that departed Pietermaritzburg on 10 January 1881. On 26 January 1881, a rainy day, Pomeroy-Colley's force arrived at a farm named Mount Prospect, about 3 miles south of Laing's Nek. He reconnoitered the area on the following day. The ridges converged onto the saddle of Laing's Nek, which the deceptively steep main road traversed, and were semicircular in shape with the ends enveloping the road and curving downhill toward Mount Prospect. The soldiers perceived that they were in a vast amphitheater. There were an estimated 2,000 Boers in defensive positions on Laing's Nek, commanded by Commandant-General Petrus J. Joubert.

Pomeroy-Colley attacked on 28 January 1881, with his force consisting of the headquarters and five companies, 58th Foot, totaling about 480 all ranks; the headquarters and four companies, 3rd Battalion, 60th Rifles, about 390 all ranks; about 140 mounted troops; the naval detachment of 80 all ranks with three rocket tubes; and artillery with four 9-pounder guns and two 7-pounder guns.

The commander planned to attack the extreme left of the Boer position on the ridge, then roll up their position in detail. The British assembled on the plain below the ridge, with the 58th to the right and the 60th to the left in a supporting position. After a short, ineffective artillery and rocket bombardment, the infantry—in the last assault of the "old red-coated army" and the last time British regimental colors were carried into battle—began their uphill frontal attack at about 10:00 A.M. The steep rise of the terrain had been underestimated and this delayed the infantry. The mounted troops were supposed to attack to the right of the 58th when the latter reached the crest of the ridge, but the cavalry charged prematurely. The first squadron reached the Boer trenches before being cut down, and the second squadron turned around and raced back downhill.

After destroying or dispersing the mounted troops, the Boers focused their attention on the infantry, still in close order, clambering steadily up the ridge about 400 yards away to their right. As the British suffered casualties, the acting 58th regimental commander was superseded by Colonel Deane, Pomeroy-Colley's chief staff officer, thus adding to the confusion. As the troops reached a glacis sloping to the summit about 50 yards away, Deane ordered the troops to fix bayonets and then charge. The Boers opened up a thundering fusillade of rifle fire and the British attack just withered away. One British officer gave the order to withdraw.

The 58th withdrew in an orderly manner, but for all practical purposes the battle was over. The attack was a dismal failure—Queen Victoria considered it "most distressing"—and the British casualties were 83 killed and 111 wounded, with the Boers losing 14 killed and 27 wounded. Pomeroy-Colley did not appreciate the lethality of well-aimed individual rifle fire and misunderstood the lessons of this battle, believing that bayonet charges were no longer effective and troops holding high ground would almost always defeat an attacking force. The British withdrew to Mount Prospect to await reinforcements.

See also Boer War, First (1880–1881); Boers; Bronkhorstspruit, Battle of; Commando System; Joubert, Commandant-General Petrus J.; Pomeroy-Colley, Major General Sir George; Rockets
References: Barthorp (1987); Duxbury (1980b); Ransford (1967)

Lances

See Cavalry, British Army—Weapons and Equipment

Land Transport Corps

The Crimean War (1854–1856) highlighted the tremendous bureaucratic and functional shortcomings of the British Army's logistical system.

At the beginning of the Crimean War, the Commissariat, a civilian organization under the direct control of another civilian agency, the Treasury, was responsible for providing land transport and nonmilitary supplies, such as food and forage, to the army in the field. The Commissariat was not subordinate to the military commander in the field.

One senior officer observed that nine-tenths of all supply problems in the Crimea were caused by a lack of transport. To remedy this situation, a Land Transport Corps under military control was proposed early in 1855. Recruiting problems forced the postponement until 24 June 1855 of the official activation of the Land Transport Corps. As a result, the Land Transport Corps had no effect on supply operations during the harsh winter of 1854–1855.

Near the end of the war, the 8,000 men of the Land Transport Corps were divided into battalions, with one transport battalion attached to each army division. Hasty recruitment had brought in men who lacked experience working with horses and were frequently averse to military discipline into the Land Transport Corps. When the Crimean War ended, a permanent land transportation unit was maintained under military control. In 1856, this permanent transport unit, based on the Land Transport Corps of the Crimean War, was redesignated the Military Train.

See also Animals, Transport; Army Service Corps; Crimean War; Lines of Communication
References: Royle (2000); Sweetman (1973); Sweetman (1984)

Lawrence, Brigadier General Sir Henry M. (1806–1857)

Brigadier General Sir Henry M. Lawrence was a soldier in the East India Company's army who was later seconded to the East India Company's civil service. Known for being tolerant of Indian customs and traditions, he was an effective administrator.

Lawrence, born in 1806, was the brother of John L. M. Lawrence, another key figure in the history of British India who served as viceroy from 1864 to 1869. Henry Lawrence was commissioned in the Bengal Army artillery in 1822 and fought in the First Burma War, the First Afghan War, and both Sikh Wars.

In 1847, Lawrence became the British resident in Lahore, the former Sikh capital. After the 1849 annexation of the Punjab, he became head of the provincial board of administration. He later resigned because of policy differences with his brother, John, who was also on the board. Lawrence was assigned to Rajputana in 1853.

In 1856, the British annexed the Kingdom of Oudh and caused great resentment among its inhabitants. Lawrence, considered a brilliant administrator, was assigned as British resident at Lucknow, the capital of Oudh, in early 1857. For myriad reasons, Indian regiments began to rebel in April 1857, and the following month Lawrence requested and received plenary powers.

Lawrence foresaw the mutiny spreading to Lucknow, and began to fortify the 33-acre residency compound on 23 May 1857. He gathered the European community of Lucknow and had a garrison of about 1,720 men, about half of whom were loyal sepoys. Earthen walls were constructed around the compound perimeter, trenches and gun pits dug, and booby traps set.

Near the end of June 1857, Lawrence, at about the same time he learned of the massacre of the Cawnpore garrison, was informed of rebels assembling northeast of Lucknow. By 29 June, the mutineers were reportedly at Chinhut, about 10 miles from Lucknow. Lawrence hastily gathered a 600-man force the next day and led it himself to attack the rebels. Supplies and water were inadequate, as was the reconnaissance, as the British stumbled onto a 6,000-man rebel force. Halfway through the engagement, Lawrence turned over command to an officer and returned to the residency, leaving behind almost 150 dead and wounded British soldiers. The defeated British straggled back to the residency, as all "of Lawrence's careful preparations [for defense of the residency] were put in jeopardy by his own bad leadership and inept organization" (Edwardes 1963, p. 71). The enemy followed and the siege began.

On 2 July 1857, a mortar shell burst in Lawrence's room, taking his left leg below the thigh. He died two days later. Lucknow held out until relieved on 25 September 1857.

See also Afghan War, First (1839–1842); Bengal Army; Burma War, First (1824–1826); East India Company; East India Company, Military Forces; Indian Mutiny; Lucknow, Siege and Relief of; Sikh War, First (1845–1846); Sikh War, Second (1848–1849)
References: Edwardes (1963); Gardner (1971); Heathcote (1974); Hibbert (1978); James (1997); Lee (2002); Mason (1974); Temple (1889)

Lee-Enfield Rifle
See Infantry, British Army–Small Arms

Lee-Metford Rifle
See Infantry, British Army–Small Arms

Lines of Communication

Lines of communication are the routes that connect a military force operating in the field with the bases that support it. The planning, establishment, and effective use of the lines of communication are essential components to battlefield success, especially in an undeveloped area. All supplies, ammunition, and reinforcements move on this line from a logistical base to the forward troops.

Occasionally lines of communication are established before the movement of the main force, with smaller supply points located in advance of the column of troops and at intervals along the route. Soldiers would consume these prepositioned stocks before using the rations and supplies they personally carried or supplies that were being transported by the regiment or in following supply columns. Lines of communication were also used for casualty evacuation and the return or retreat of the force.

The length of the lines of communication, the terrain and climate of the area of operations, and other factors could have a significant impact on the campaign or war. At times logistical factors could dictate the tactical plan. During a campaign, the lines of communication were frequently made a separate command, with a senior officer in charge.

Two colonial wars in which lines of communication played a decisive role were the Abyssinian War (1867–1868) and the Second Ashanti War (1873–1874).

See also Abyssinian War; Army Service Corps; Ashanti War, Second (1873–1874); Land Transport Corps; Railways
References: Bailes (1980); Chandler (1967); Keegan (1967); Spiers (1992)

Localization Act (1872)
See Cardwell, Edward T.; Cardwell Reforms; MacDougall, Major General Sir Patrick L.; Militia

Lockhart, General Sir William S. A. (1841–1900)

General Sir William S. A. Lockhart served in the Indian Army for over forty years. He was the Indian Army's premier expeditionary force commander on the North-West Frontier in the 1890s, known for his "uncompromising firmness and inexhaustible patience" (Farwell 1972, p. 319).

Lockhart, the son of a clergyman, was born in Scotland on 2 September 1841. He was commissioned into the East India Company's Bengal Native Infantry in 1858 and arrived in India during the mopping up operations of the Indian Mutiny (1857–1859). Lockhart saw extensive active service in the Bhutan War (1864–1866), Abyssinian War (1867–1868), and the Black Mountain Expedition (1868). Service as a staff officer in the Bengal Army followed, and from 1875 to 1877, Lockhart was an attaché with the Dutch Army and saw action in the Dutch East Indies. He participated in the Second Afghan War (1878–1880) and then served as deputy quartermaster-general for intelligence at Indian Army headquarters from 1880 to 1885.

Lockhart's superb leadership as a brigade commander during the Third Burma War (1885) earned him additional recognition and his first knighthood. Illness required his temporary posting to England, but he returned to India in 1890 and assumed command of the Punjab Frontier Force. With tribal unrest simmering on the North-West Frontier, Lockhart commanded the First and Second Miranzai Expeditions in 1891. After being promoted to lieutenant general, Lockhart commanded the Mahsud Expedition in 1894–1895.

After the Great Pathan Revolt broke out on the North-West Frontier in 1897, Lockhart commanded the largest punitive expedition ever deployed to the North-West Frontier, the Tirah Field Force, consisting of about 34,000 British and Indian Army officers and men and about 20,000 non-combatants. The mission of the Tirah Field Force was to invade the lands of the Afridis and the Orakzais and forcibly pacify and punish them. After fierce fighting in winter weather and inhospitable terrain, Lockhart skillfully proved his force could fight anywhere and was eventually able to suppress the tribal insurgents.

Lockhart, who was promoted to general in 1896, was appointed commander in chief, India, in 1898. He died in office on 18 March 1900. Known as a highly professional soldier, Lockhart was also respected by and popular with his tribal enemies, who called him "Amir Sahib."

See also Abyssinian War; Afghan War, Second (1878–1880); Bengal Army; Burma War, Third (1885); East India Company, Military Forces; India, British Army in; Indian Army Operations; Indian Mutiny; Miranzai Field Force; North-West Frontier; Punjab Frontier Force; Tirah Field Force
References: Barthorp (1982); Bruce (1975); Callwell (1896); Farwell (1972); Miller (1977); Nevill (1912)

Logistics
See Animals, Transport; Army Service Corps; Land

Transport Corps; Lines of Communication; Quartermaster-General, British Army; Railways

Long Service

Long service referred to a British soldier's period of voluntary enlistment prior to the Army Enlistment Act of 1870.

Prior to 1809 during the Napoleonic Wars, the term of enlistment was for life—as long as the army needed him or until he became physically unable to perform his duties. In 1809, the term of enlistment was reduced to 7 years in the infantry, 10 in the cavalry, and 12 in the artillery. Lifetime service was restored in 1829.

In 1847, in an attempt to attract higher-quality recruits, limited enlistment was introduced. This provision reduced terms of service to 10 years in the infantry and 12 in the other arms, with an option to extend enlistment to 21 years' service for the infantry and 24 years' service for the other arms, to qualify for a pension. Limited enlistment was generally not successful.

The British Army had difficulties procuring replacements during the Crimean War (1854–1856) and the Indian Mutiny (1857–1859). The American Civil War and Continental wars of the 1860s showed that the British Army was relatively weak. Attempts to form a military reserve in the 1860s were unsuccessful, the terms of long service deterring enlistment. Long service was blamed by many for recruiting shortfalls, low-quality enlistees, and the inability to establish a military reserve. As a result, long service was abolished and replaced with short service in the Army Enlistment Act of 1870.

See also Cardwell Reforms; Crimean War; Indian Mutiny; Rank and File, British Army—Enlistment; Recruiting; Short Service
References: Skelley (1977); Spiers (1992); Strachan (1984)

Lucan, Field Marshal George C. Bingham, Third Earl of (1800–1888)

The Third Earl of Lucan was a British Army cavalry officer who commanded the Cavalry Division during the Crimean War (1854–1856). Its most significant action was during the Battle of Balaklava (25 October 1854), when both the Heavy Brigade and the Light Brigade made courageous charges, the latter riding into military immortality as the Charge of the Light Brigade. He was an arrogant aristocrat who used his wealth to purchase his military ranks and commands, frequently over those more competent.

George C. Bingham was born in London on 16 April 1800, the eldest son of the Second Earl of Lucan. After being educated at Winchester, he was commissioned an ensign in the 6th Foot in 1816. After a series of rapid promotion purchases, regimental exchanges, and periods on half pay, Lucan became commander of the 17th Lancers as a lieutenant colonel on 9 November 1826, reportedly for £25,000. In 1828, Lucan was seconded to the Russian Army while it campaigned against Turkey, and he became familiar with the Russians and the terrain of the Balkans. Lucan commanded the 17th Lancers until 1837, when he again went on half pay. He succeeded to the earldom on his father's death in 1839.

As a sometime Member of Parliament, Lucan was promoted to colonel in 1841 and to major general ten years later. When the British began forming an expeditionary force for the Crimea, Lucan applied to be a brigade commander. On paper, he seemed a suitable candidate, and in February 1854, he was appointed to command the Cavalry Division. It consisted of the Light Brigade, commanded by his hated brother-in-law, Brigadier General (later Lieutenant General) James T. Brudenell, Seventh Earl of Cardigan, and the Heavy Brigade, under the command of Brigadier General James Y. Scarlett. Friction soon developed between Lucan and Cardigan, the latter believing his position to be basically independent. (One Light Brigade officer wrote, "We all agree that two greater muffs than Lucan and Cardigan could not be. We call Lucan the cautious ass and Cardigan the dangerous ass" [Thomas 1974, p. 210].)

The Cavalry Division was in reserve at the Battle of the Alma (20 September 1854). The cavalry played an important role at the Battle of Balaklava (25 October 1854). Early that morning, Russian cavalry forces advanced and were later thrown back by stalwart British and Turkish troops. Another Russian mounted force attacked, and the Heavy Brigade drove them back in confusion over the Woronzov Heights. The Light Brigade, however, remained out of action and was later positioned in the North Valley while the Heavy Brigade remained in the South Valley. Amid the fog of war and personality clash between Lucan and Cardigan, Lucan ordered the Light Brigade to charge. Cardigan led his 673-man Brigade into the North Valley, while Lucan, leading the Heavy Brigade to cover them, was wounded. The charge was a disaster for the Light Brigade, with Cardigan blaming

Lucan and Lucan blaming Captain Louis E. Nolan, an aide-de-camp who transmitted the order and was killed in the charge.

Lucan was censured for his actions at Balaklava and recalled to England in early 1855. His request to be court-martialed was refused and he "vindicated" himself in the House of Lords in March 1855. Afterward, Lucan was knighted. While he had no further active military employment, Lucan was promoted to lieutenant general in 1858, general in 1865, and field marshal in 1887. When Lucan died on 10 November 1888, he was the oldest soldier in the British Army.

See also Balaklava, Battle of; Cardigan, Lieutenant General James T. Brudenell, Seventh Earl of; Charge of the Light Brigade; Crimean War; Purchase System; Raglan, Field Marshal Fitzroy J. H. Somerset, First Baron

References: David (1997); Harris (1973); Judd (1975); Moyse-Bartlett (1971); Royle (2000); Selby (1970); Thomas (1974); Woodham-Smith (1953)

Lucknow, Siege and Relief of (1857–1858)

Lucknow was the capital of Oudh, the state annexed by the British in 1856 that caused great resentment among Indians. Some two-thirds of the Bengal Army was recruited in Oudh. The disaffection of Bengal Army units in Lucknow was made worse when the 7th Oudh Irregular Regiment refused the greased cartridges and was disbanded on 3 May 1857.

Brigadier General Sir Henry M. Lawrence, an experienced administrator, was assigned as British resident in Lucknow in early 1857. After Indian regiments began to mutiny, Lawrence received plenary powers in Lucknow. He foresaw the mutiny spreading to Lucknow, assembled the European community in the 33-acre residency, and began to fortify the residency on 23 May 1857. The Lucknow garrison totaled about 1,720 men, about half of whom were loyal sepoys. Trenches and gun pits were dug and earthen walls were constructed around the compound perimeter.

Lawrence learned near the end of June 1857 of the massacre of the Cawnpore garrison, around the time he was informed of rebels rallying at Chinhut, about 10 miles from Lucknow. On 30 June, Lawrence hastily gathered a 600-man force and led it to strike at the mutineers. This attack was poorly planned with little reconnaissance, and the British blundered into a 6,000-man rebel force. Halfway through the battle, Lawrence apparently had second thoughts about what he was doing, turned over command to another officer, and returned to the residency. He left behind almost 150 dead and wounded British soldiers, and the force later straggled back to Lucknow, hard pressed by the enemy and then besieged at the Lucknow residency. Lawrence was severely wounded on 2 July 1857 and died two days later.

Brigadier General (later Major General Sir) Henry Havelock led a 2,500-man Lucknow relief force that departed Allahabad on 7 July 1857. The force marched 126 miles in 9 days, during the hottest part of the summer, and defeated Nana Sahib's rebel troops at Fatehpur (12 July), Aong (15 July), and Cawnpore (16 July).

Lieutenant General Sir James Outram, commanding the Dinapore and Cawnpore Divisions, arrived at Cawnpore on 15 September 1857. As the senior officer, Outram had the duty to supersede Havelock in command, although he inappropriately waived this responsibility to permit Havelock to remain in command to receive the "glory" of relieving Lucknow. In this confusing command situation, Outram "advised" Havelock on operations. The 2,000-man relief force fought a grueling campaign from Cawnpore and finally relieved the Lucknow residency on 25 September, losing 31 officers and 504 men killed or wounded in the final assault. Outram officially assumed command the following day.

The small relief force was soon itself besieged in the Lucknow residency.

The final relief of Lucknow took place on 17 November 1857 by a force under the command of Lieutenant General (later Field Marshal Lord) Sir Colin Campbell. Outram was responsible for its evacuation and ordered to remain with about 4,000 men at the nearby Alambagh to wait for Campbell to return with a larger force. Outram's position was attacked six times by large rebel forces between November 1857 and February 1858. In March 1858, Outram's force advanced to Lucknow, and in a series of operations linked up with Campbell's 20,000 troops and cleared and captured the city on 23 March. In the final operation, the British sustained 127 officers and men killed and 595 wounded. After entering Lucknow, Campbell issued a proclamation in Latin, *Nune fortunatus sum*—which means "I am in luck now."

See also Bengal Army; Campbell, Field Marshal Colin; Cawnpore, Siege and Relief of; East India Company, Military Forces; Havelock, Major General Sir Henry; Imperialism; India; India, British Army in; Indian Mutiny; Lawrence, Brigadier General Sir Henry M.; Nana Sahib; Outram, Lieutenant General Sir James

References: Brock (1858); Collier (1964); Edwardes (1963); Edwardes (1973); Hibbert (1978); Hilton (1957); Lawrence (1990); Leasor (1957); Lee (2002); Pollock (1957); Seymour (1991); Watson (1991)

Lyons, Admiral Sir Edmund, First Baron (1790–1858)

Rear Admiral (later Admiral Lord) Sir Edmund Lyons was the second in command of the Mediterranean Fleet, and later the Black Sea Fleet, from the opening stages of the Crimean War through February 1855, when he assumed command of the Mediterranean Fleet.

In 1853, Lyons's superior was Vice Admiral (later Admiral) Sir James W. D. Dundas. Dundas had a reputation for being overly cautious, while Lyons was noted for being more aggressive. On 8 January 1854, Lyons led a British naval squadron into the Black Sea as a possible deterrent to continued Russian aggression against Turkey. Appropriately, Lyons was in H.M.S. *Agamemnon,* the Royal Navy's first screw battleship (built in 1849), armed with 91 guns and capable of 11 knots. Lyons was anxious to engage the Russian fleet and bombarded the Russian port of Odessa on 22 April 1854.

As seems to have been planned earlier, Lyons replaced Dundas in command of the fleet in February 1855. On 3 May 1855, an Anglo-French force sailed to conduct an amphibious operation and seize Kertch on the Sea of Azov, a conduit for supplies from Russia bound for Sevastopol. Within hours of landing, the French recalled the force. A second expedition sailed to Kertch on 22 May, and after a naval bombardment and unopposed allied landing, both sides of the strait leading into the Sea of Azov were secured. Ships of Lyons's fleet spent the next few weeks sweeping Russian ships from the Sea of Azov and destroying supply centers. Lyons reported that nearly 500 enemy vessels had been sunk, and enough flour and corn to feed 100,000 men for four months had been destroyed.

On 8 September 1855, the allies attacked Sevastopol. Lyons's ships were to support the attack, but a gale and rough seas allowed only six mortar vessels to contribute to the bombardment. The Russians, mainly due to the success of the French attack, evacuated Sevastopol the following day.

A 10,000-man force embarked on 7 October 1855 on seven Royal Navy ships and three French warships and two transports to destroy the Russian fortress of Kinburn, covering the confluence of the Rivers Bug and Dnieper. Said to have been the brainchild of Lyons, this expedition was a complete success.

Lyons was a British representative during the January 1856 Grand Council of War, which negotiated the end of the Crimean War.

See also Crimean War; Dundas, Admiral Sir James W. D.; Sevastopol, Siege of
References: Hibbert (1961); Judd (1975); Palmer (1987); Royle (2000); Sweetman (1993)

M

Macdonald, Major General Sir Hector A. (1853–1903)

Popularly known as "Fighting Mac," Major General Sir Hector A. Macdonald was highly competent and charismatic, one of only a few British Army generals who rose from the ranks on his own merit and professionalism.

Macdonald was born on a farm in Scotland on 13 April 1853. His father was a crofter and stonemason. While working as an apprentice draper, Macdonald joined the Inverness-shire Highland Rifle Volunteers. In 1870, he enlisted in the 92nd Gordon Highlanders, then serving in India. He was a diligent, disciplined soldier and served in the Second Afghan War. Macdonald, then a color-sergeant, distinguished himself in many engagements. In recognition of his gallant leadership, Macdonald was commissioned in his own regiment on 7 January 1880. At the time it was very rare for one of the other ranks to be commissioned a combatant officer.

Macdonald's regiment, the 92nd Gordon Highlanders, was returning to Scotland but was diverted to Natal in January 1881, where it fought in the First Boer War. At the Battle of Majuba Hill (27 February 1881), Macdonald commanded a twenty-man detachment and was one of the few to distinguish himself at this British defeat. He "behaved with the greatest coolness and courage, and to the last made every effort to turn the course of events" (Farwell 1985, p. 274). The Gordons alone suffered 44 killed and 52 wounded out of a total of 180 officers and other ranks. Unscathed, Macdonald was captured and paroled by the Boers.

In late 1884, Macdonald exchanged into the 1st Battalion to try to see active service in the Gordon Relief Expedition. The following year, he joined the Egyptian Constabulary, and in 1888 Macdonald transferred to the Egyptian Army. Macdonald commanded the 11th Sudanese Battalion in action against the dervishes and was awarded the Distinguished Service Order for his leadership at the Battle of Toski (3 August 1889).

Macdonald commanded a brigade during the attack on Firket (23 September 1896) during the Dongola Expedition. He commanded another brigade (consisting of the 9th, 10th, and 11th Sudanese Battalions) in the Battle of Abu Hamed (7 August 1897) and the fiercely fought Battle of Atbara (8 April 1898). These engagements culminated in the Battle of Omdurman (2 September 1898), where Macdonald's 1st Sudanese Brigade, bringing up the rear and on the extreme right flank of the army, fought off a frenzied dervish attack. As Macdonald's brigade bore the brunt of the dervish onslaught, Major General (later Field Marshal Earl) Sir Horatio H. Kitchener, the commander in chief of the Anglo-Egyptian force, directed his five other brigades to change front to meet the oncoming attack. As this maneuver was completed, another dervish force attacked Macdonald's brigade from the flank. With paradelike precision, Macdonald wheeled his brigade to meet and fought this new threat until another brigade was in position to support him. One newspaper correspondent reported that, "Beyond all else the double honours of the day were won by Colonel Macdonald and his Brigade . . . he achieved the victory off his own bat, proving himself a tactician and a soldier as well as what he has long been known to be, the Bravest of the Brave" (Neillands 1996, p. 210). While the actions of Macdonald and his soldiers were in large part responsible for the British victory at Omdurman, Kitchener gave Macdonald only the same credit he gave to the other brigade commanders.

213

After the reconquest of the Sudan and home leave, Macdonald assumed command of the Sirhind District in India. Shortly thereafter, he was reassigned to serve in the Second Boer War. Arriving in South Africa in January 1900 with the rank of local brigadier general, he assumed command of the demoralized Highland Brigade, which had been badly mauled and defeated at the Battle of Magersfontein (11 December 1899). He was wounded leading the brigade at Paardeberg in February 1900, and later that year, rumors emerged of Macdonald having a homosexual relationship with a Boer. This issue, combined with his force being disbanded and used for garrison duty, caused Macdonald to be reassigned to India in early 1901. He first returned to England and was knighted by King Edward VII.

Macdonald arrived in India in June 1901 but was sent on a goodwill tour to Australia and New Zealand. In January 1902, he was posted to command the British troops on Ceylon, but rumors of his sexual proclivities reached Ceylon before he did. A few months later, complaints were registered against him for habitual misbehavior with schoolboys. The governor of Ceylon confronted Macdonald with these allegations, even though there were no civil laws prohibiting homosexuality in Ceylon, but the general denied them. Perhaps to get Macdonald out of the way and to avoid a scandal, the governor recommended Macdonald return to England and seek counsel from his superiors. Macdonald, pleading innocent, was told to return to Ceylon and face a court-martial to clear his name. In Paris on 25 March 1903, Macdonald was stunned to see English-language newspaper headlines referring to "grave charges" made against him. Major General Sir Hector A. Macdonald, "the bravest of the brave," returned to his room and blew his brains out.

See also Afghan War, Second (1878–1880); Atbara, Battle of; Boer War, Second (1899–1902); Boers; Egyptian Army; Gordon Relief Expedition; Kitchener, Field Marshal Horatio H.; Magersfontein, Battle of; Majuba Hill, Battle of; Officers, British Army—Sources of Commissioning; Omdurman, Battle of; Reconquest of the Sudan; Sudan; Toski, Battle of

References: Barthorp (1984); Farwell (1985); Montgomery (1963); Neillands (1996); Royle (1982)

MacDougall, Major General Sir Patrick L. (1819–1894)

Major General Sir Patrick L. MacDougall was a leading intellectual in the post–Crimean War British Army. Many consider him the "founder of modern British military thought" (Preston 1964, p. 59).

MacDougall, born 10 August 1819, entered the British Army after completing the Sandhurst course in 1836. He served in a number of line regiments before being posted to Canada in 1844. In 1854, MacDougall returned to England to be superintendent of studies at the Royal Military College. After a short tour of duty in the Crimea, he returned to the Royal Military College. MacDougall wrote *The Theory of War* in 1856, "an appropriate moment for the distillation of the essential ideas of the classic European military writers" (Bond 1972, p. 84). This successful volume was followed in 1857 by his pamphlet *The Senior Department of the Royal Military College,* which highlighted his ideas on military education. These two volumes probably led to MacDougall's selection as the first commandant of the Staff College when it was established later in 1857.

MacDougall lectured at the Staff College on the campaigns of the great commanders, evaluating their military performance in accordance with the basic tenets outlined in his *The Theory of War*. He also wrote *The Campaigns of Hannibal* in 1858, revealing a keen understanding of the effectiveness of the various arms and their evolving tactics. MacDougall relinquished his Staff College post in 1861 and was then involved in planning Canadian defense strategy. He also visited Canada and studied some of the campaigns of the American Civil War. MacDougall became one of the first European military thinkers to incorporate lessons from this conflict into a military text, *Modern Warfare as Influenced by Modern Artillery,* written in 1863.

Returning to Canada in 1865, MacDougall served as adjutant-general of Canadian militia until 1869. One of his major initiatives was the formation of independent militia companies into battalions. He also formed seven brigades, each containing one regular and three militia battalions. MacDougall returned to England and served as deputy inspector-general of auxiliary forces at the War Office and chaired the Localization Committee in 1871–1872 to study the feasibility of linking battalions on a territorial basis.

When the Intelligence Branch at the War Office was formed in 1873, MacDougall became its first chief. He participated in the development of imperial strategy and ensured the establishment of the Intelligence Branch as an integral component of the War Office.

Also in 1873, after further study of American Civil War campaigns, MacDougall wrote *Modern Infantry Tactics,* suggesting that the experiences of the Franco-Prussian War confirmed his theories that modern firepower shifted the tactical advantage from the attacker to the defender.

MacDougall served as commander in chief of forces in British North America from 1878 to 1883 and retired two years later. He wrote little in retirement and died in 1894. MacDougall was one of the most respected and influential military reformers, writers, theorists, and intellectuals of his time.

See also Camberley, Staff College; Canada; Cardwell Reforms; Intellectuals, British Army; Intelligence; Sandhurst, Royal Military College; War Office

References: Bond (1972); Fergusson (1984); Kochanski (1999); Luvaas (1964); Preston (1964); Spiers (1992)

Machine Guns

Advances in weaponry were frequently focused on increasing firepower while reducing manpower; until metal cartridges were introduced, an effective multifiring weapon could not be developed.

The first viable machine gun was developed in 1862 by an American, Dr. Richard Gatling. In 1870, the British tested the Gatling gun and the French Montigny *mitrailleuse* breechloader, and after making improvements, the British Army adopted the Gatling gun the following year. The Gatling gun consisted of a number of breech-loading rifled barrels (ten barrels was preferred) grouped around and parallel to a shaft. The assistant gunner placed the ammunition in a hopper at the top of the gun, and the gunner turned a crank handle manually, with each barrel rotating and firing in succession, once in a revolution. The Gatling gun could fire more than 600 rounds per minute. It was mounted on a fixed artillery carriage, which precluded the gun from traversing and limited its effectiveness. The heavy .45-caliber bullet, "the high rate of concentrated fire plus its built-in psychological 'terror' factor, made it an ideal weapon for the Colonial Wars of the later nineteenth century" (Featherstone 1978, p. 58). Gatling guns, although they occasionally jammed, were used in the Second Ashanti War (1873–1874), the Zulu War (1879), and in the Sudan (1884–1885).

The Gardner machine gun replaced the Gatling gun in the Royal Navy in the 1870s. This gun had five barrels side by side, was also .45-caliber, and weighed, with a portable tripod, 369 pounds. Like the Gatling, the Gardner was hand cranked, with the rate of fire, which could reach 120 rounds per barrel per minute, controlled by the speed of the cranking. Ammunition in clips was loaded into the Gardner from the top.

The Royal Navy replaced both the Gatling and Gardner guns in 1880 with the four-barreled Nordenfeldt gun. In 1883, a five-barreled Nordenfeldt gun mounted on an infantry carriage was introduced. The Nordenfeldt fired more than 200 1-inch rounds per minute.

An American, Hiram Maxim, developed the Maxim gun, which was tested during trials in 1884. Maxim improved the model, reducing its weight to 40 pounds and increasing its rate of fire to 650 rounds per minute, and it was adopted by the British Army in 1891. The Maxim gun was considered revolutionary in design and operability, as "its recoil was used to load, fire and eject continuously while the trigger was held back; the cartridges were stored in a flexible belt and the gun was cooled by a water jacket around the barrel" (Featherstone 1978, p. 65). It was issued first to the cavalry and then to the infantry, but not to the artillery.

One of the most notable examples of the use and effectiveness of the Maxim guns was at the Battle of Omdurman (2 September 1898). Major General (later Field Marshal Earl) Sir Horatio H. Kitchener's 26,000-man Anglo-Egyptian force included 20 Maxim guns. During the first phase of the battle, the Maxim guns began firing when the attacking dervish hordes were about 2,000 yards away. (The Maxim guns were normally sighted up to 2,500 yards.) One British participant recorded that "all the time out on the plain on the other side bullets were shearing through flesh, smashing and splintering bone; blood spouted from terrible wounds; valiant men were struggling on through a hell of whistling metal, exploding shells, and spurting dust—suffering, despairing, dying" (Headrick 1979, p. 259). This battle—"the most signal triumph ever gained by the arms of science over barbarians" (Headrick 1979, pp. 259–260)—was a slaughter. In hours, over 10,000 dervishes were killed and perhaps 16,000 wounded, largely due to the effectiveness of the Maxim gun. British casualties were 48 killed and 434 wounded.

Machine guns reinforced a type of British moral superiority, as noted sardonically by Hilaire Belloc: "Whatever happens, we have got / The Maxim Gun, and they have not" (Bailes 1980, p. 88).

See also Dervishes; Infantry, British Army—Small Arms; Kitchener, Field Marshal Horatio H.; Omdurman, Battle of; Ulundi, Battle of

References: Bailes (1980); Callwell (1896); Featherstone (1978); Grierson (1899); Headrick (1979); Myatt (1983)

Madras Army

The Madras Army, established by the East India Company, was one of the three presidency armies in India. The other two armies were the Bengal Army and the Bombay Army, and all three were abolished in 1895 and replaced by a single Indian Army.

There were European companies in the Madras Army from an early period, and it is known that there were three in 1742 and seven in 1748, when they were formed into a single regiment. In 1824, the Madras Army consisted of two European infantry battalions, fifty-two Madras Native Infantry battalions, three irregular infantry battalions, three light cavalry regiments, one European and one native artillery brigade, three battalions (of four companies each) of foot artillery, and two pioneer corps.

The Madras Army soldiers showed exceptional discipline and loyalty throughout the Indian Mutiny, and unlike the other two presidency armies, no Madras Army units mutinied. This fidelity can probably be attributed to the recruiting methods the Madras and Bombay Armies shared. While the soldiers of these two armies were generally of a lower caste (and physically shorter), they were more concerned with gaining respect through their own merit and efforts, and much less interested in caste and class practices and traditions. This attitude also made Madras and Bombay Army soldiers more disciplined.

The postmutiny army reorganization had little impact on the Madras Army, other than the renumbering of units.

The strength of the Madras Army in 1876 totaled 47,144 officers and men, broken down into 33,968 Indian Army officers and other ranks and 13,176 British Army officers and men. The Madras Army was the second largest of the three presidency armies.

See also Bengal Army; Bombay Army; East India Company; East India Company, Military Forces; India, British Army in; Indian Army Operations; Indian Army Organization; Indian Mutiny

References: Beaumont (1977); Haythornthwaite (1995); Heathcote (1974); Hervey (1988); Mason (1974); Mason (1985); Wolseley (1878); Yong (2002)

Mafeking, Siege of (13 October 1899– 17 May 1900)

The Siege of Mafeking was a sideshow of the Second Boer War (1899–1902), but it grew in significance until it became a central event of the conflict, representing the triumph of British tenacity and heroism over the Boers.

Founded in 1885, the town of Mafeking was located at a rail junction 225 miles north of Kimberley inside the border of Bechuanaland and close to the border of the Transvaal (South African Republic). In 1899, about 1,500 whites lived in Mafeking, and the population of the adjoining black town, Mafikeng, swelled from about 5,000 to over 7,000 with refugees. Mafeking was highly symbolic to the Boers as the base for the failed Jameson Raid (1895–1896), which probably gave them an exaggerated idea of the value of the town.

Colonel (later Lieutenant General Lord) Robert S. S. Baden-Powell was sent to South Africa in July 1899. By early October 1899, he commanded a garrison in Mafeking totaling almost 700 Rhodesian troops. His mission was to protect the Cape Colony border, prevent any Boer raiding or attacks from the Transvaal, divert as many Boer troops as possible, and, if ordered, conduct raids into the Transvaal.

War was declared on 11 October 1899, and a 6,000-man Boer force commanded by Assistant Commandant-General Piet A. Cronje began besieging Mafeking on 13 October. Baden-Powell's preparations fortifying the town and demonstrations of strength, coupled with frequent raids, dummy guns, and various ruses, gave the Boers the impression the garrison was stronger than it actually was. Later in the month, the Boers brought up a 94-pounder siege gun to fire at the Mafeking garrison. In November 1899, Cronje took the majority of this force and moved to the south, leaving 1,500 Boers, under General J. P. Snyman, to continue the siege.

On 26 December 1899, the British launched an attack on a threatening Boer strongpoint that failed, at high cost, to seize its objective. As a British relief column neared Mafeking, the Boers conducted a daring but unsuccessful attack against the British. Finally, after a 217-day siege that cost the British 813 casualties, Mafeking was relieved on 17 May 1900.

World attention had been focused on this contest between the British and the Boers at Mafeking. Queen Victoria had written to Baden-Powell in April 1900 that "I continue watching with confidence and admiration the patient and resolute defence . . . under your ever resourceful command" (Pakenham 1979, p. 421). When Mafeking was relieved, unparalleled celebrations—not even rivaled by those at the end of the two world wars—broke out, especially in London, where the jubilant scenes were described as "mafficking."

The Siege of Mafeking boosted British morale. In addition, it diverted, especially during its first two months, thousands of Boers who could have been employed more effectively (and perhaps decisively) in further attacking Cape Colony. The siege also exposed the Boer weakness and unwillingness to sustain casualties by attacking defensive positions.

The success of the Siege of Mafeking can be attributed largely to the energetic, resourceful, and professional leadership of Baden-Powell. Contributing to the achievement were the armed Africans, although this was relatively unheralded at the time. Baden-Powell has been criticized for giving less food to unarmed blacks, perhaps to encourage them to leave the town, but he acted in accordance with contemporary practice and accomplished his mission.

See also Baden-Powell, Lieutenant General Sir Robert S. S.; Boer War, Second (1899–1902); Boers; Commando System; Cronje, Assistant Commandant-General Piet A.; Jameson Raid; Transvaal

References: Belfield (1975); Jeal (1989); Pakenham (1979); Plaatje (2003); Reynolds (1942); Webster (1970)

Magdala, Capture of (13 April 1868)

The mission of the British expeditionary force sent to Abyssinia in 1867–1868, under the command of Lieutenant General (later Field Marshal Lord) Sir Robert C. Napier, was to free the hostages held by Abyssinian Emperor Theodore and to punish him for his petulance and actions.

The advance party of the British force arrived at Zula on Annesley Bay, south of Massawa, on 21 October 1867. Most of the soldiers were ashore by December 1867, and Napier and his staff arrived on 2 January 1868. By this time, it had been ascertained that Theodore, with 8,000 warriors, his hostages, and artillery, was moving to his mountain fortress at Magdala. The British force deployed from Zula toward Magdala on 25 January 1868. The rough terrain and large support element made movement slow, with the main body arriving at Antalo, 200 miles from the coast, on 2 March 1868. After a reorganization of the force into assault (1st) and support (2nd) divisions and a ten-day halt, the force continued marching toward Magdala on 12 March 1868.

The force entered Dildi, from which they could see Magdala, on 24 March 1868. The rugged terrain required a meandering 60-mile march before the objective was reached. Magdala was an imposing fortress situated on a peak rising 300 feet above the southern end of the Islamgee plateau. Three of the sides were sheer, almost unscalable cliffs, although on the eastern flank the land rose gradually in three large terraces. There were two other peaks on the Islamgee plateau: Selassie to the north of Magdala, and Fala to the west of Selassie.

In early April 1868, Napier sent a formal demand for surrender to Theodore, but the ultimatum was ignored. On 8 April, the lead brigade was 12 miles from Magdala and halted to conduct final coordination. Two days later, the British advanced to reconnoiter the route to the Arogi plateau, the probable assault position for the attack on the Islamgee plateau. With a small escort, Colonel R. Phayre, deputy quartermaster-general, quickly reached the defile leading to the Arogi plateau. The infantry, however, due to the rock-strewn terrain and scorching heat, had lagged behind the rest of the force. Phayre apparently did not realize this when he signaled to Napier that the pass was undefended and then secured, and that the baggage animals and guns could be sent up the "King's Road" immediately.

The supply trains began to move forward, as did Napier, who observed that the infantry was not holding the vulnerable pass as he had been led to believe. He immediately ordered an engineer unit to secure the pass, and at about the same time Theodore's cannons thundered. Abyssinians began to stream down the slopes to attack. Theodore had observed what he thought was an unprotected baggage train and wanted to take advantage of his foe's vulnerability by sending 6,500 of his remaining soldiers to attack and loot the British supply column. Napier ordered his rockets to a firing position overlooking the Arogi plateau, but the bursting rockets did not stop the Abyssinians. British and Indian infantry battalions deployed into skirmishing order and opened fire at 150 yards. The British soldiers had the new Snider-Enfield breech-loading rifle, and after about an hour, their effective and rapid fire, combined with spirited counterattacks and artillery bombardments, defeated Theodore's soldiers. The Abyssinians lost about 700 killed and 1,500 wounded, while the British suffered 20 wounded (of whom 2 died later).

Theodore, his confidence shaken, tried to negotiate on 11 April 1868. Napier demanded Theodore immediately release the hostages. The emperor vacillated but freed all the hostages the following day. One objective of the campaign had been accomplished. Theodore, however, refused to surrender, obviously preparing a last-ditch defense.

Napier, concerned that Theodore might escape, launched his final assault on 13 April 1868 after an agreed-on armistice had expired. The only practical plan was to clear and occupy the high ground of Fala and Selassie, from which supporting fire could be provided and then, from the Islamgee plateau, conduct a frontal assault up a narrow path and through the front gate of the Magdala fortress. Against stalwart defenders, this operation would have been extremely difficult, if not impossible. By this time, however, Theodore was demoralized and his followers were deserting him.

The 1st Division assembled on the Arogi plateau as if on parade. The advance began at 8:30 A.M., with the sappers carrying scaling ladders in the van, followed by the 33rd Foot (Duke of Wellington's), climbing up a steep path from the west. Artillery pieces were positioned near the path to provide supporting fire. The advance continued to and through the saddle between Fala and Selassie. Three Indian infantry companies scrambled up a spur to their right and occupied Fala, and two companies of the 33rd Foot climbed Selassie. Both peaks were occupied after midday, and artillery was displaced to the forward slope of Selassie. British troops occupied the Islamgee plateau.

Shortly after 3:00 P.M., the British artillery started their bombardment of Magdala, and the final assault began about an hour later. Two companies of the 33rd Foot deployed in skirmishing order to the foot of the 300-foot high cliff face and began to fire to suppress the enemy overhead. The 10th Company, Royal Engineers, followed by K Company, Madras Sappers and Miners, carrying scaling ladders, powder charges to blow up the gates, picks, and so on, passed through them and began climbing the path as it began to rain. Six companies of the 33rd Foot, with a further two companies and other units in reserve, followed.

The lower of two gates was reached easily when it was discovered that the engineers had failed to bring or had lost their explosives and equipment. To maintain the impetus of the attack, two companies of the 33rd Foot shifted to the right to try to find another way into the bastion. A soldier used his bayonet to cut a hole in the thorn bush above the stone rampart and helped another soldier over the top. (Both soldiers later received the Victoria Cross.) In spite of heavy fire, more British soldiers entered the breach into the fortress and soon there were enough soldiers to attack the lower gate from the inside. The retreating Abyssinians failed to close the upper gate, which the British soon found undefended and poured through. Abyssinian resistance melted away, and the soldiers heard a single shot: Theodore had put his pistol in his mouth and killed himself. The Battle of Magdala was over. British casualties were two officers and 15 men wounded. Two days later, the engineers destroyed Theodore's artillery and the fortress itself. Napier's force had accomplished its mission.

See also Abyssinia; Abyssinian War; Animals, Transport; Lines of Communication; Napier, Field Marshal Robert C.; Theodore, Emperor; Victoria Cross

References: Bates (1979); Chandler (1967); Farwell (1972); Myatt (1970); Smith (1987)

Magersfontein, Battle of (11 December 1899)

The Battle of Magersfontein was a debacle, the second of three humiliating defeats for the British during what came to be known as Black Week. It also showed British inflexibility in adapting tactics to meet new battlefield conditions.

After the Pyrrhic British victory at the Battle of the Modder River (28 November 1899), the Boers, under the overall command of Assistant Commandant-General Piet A. Cronje, retreated north toward Kimberley. The Boers began initially constructing defensive positions on the high ground near Scholtz Nek and Spyfontein. Based largely on the Boer experience at the Modder River and the convictions of Assistant Commandant-General Jacobus De la Rey, the Boers moved further south and dug new positions at the foot of Magersfontein Hill, where they again would be less vulnerable to British artillery fire and could use the full range and effect of their Mausers.

The British 1st Division, commanded by Lieutenant General (later Field Marshal) Lord Paul S. Methuen, rested and received reinforcements after the Battle of Modder River. The 1st Division then had 13,000 soldiers. During this time, little was done to gather intelligence on the Boers, their intentions, and their disposition. Methuen's plan was for the Highland Brigade (commanded by Major General Andrew G. Wauchope) to advance at night across the open plain, deploy with three battalions abreast, and then assault the enemy positions at dawn. The 9th Lancers would advance on the right, with the 9th Brigade in reserve. Wauchope reportedly expressed his concerns about the plan to Methuen.

In the afternoon of 10 December 1899, the Highland Brigade marched forward to a slight rise known as Headquarters Hill, and at about 4:30 P.M., the British artillery bombarded the Magersfontein heights. This barrage wounded only three Boers, but warned the Boers (numbering about 8,000, including a Scandinavian contingent) that an attack was imminent.

After midnight, in a thunderstorm and over rough terrain, the 3,500-man Highland Brigade began its advance march, with its thirty companies arrayed one behind the other in mass of quarter columns. The 2nd Battalion, Black Watch, was in the lead, followed by 2nd Battalion, Seaforth Highlanders; 1st Battalion, Argyll and Sutherland Highlanders; and 1st Battalion, Highland Light Infantry.

Major G. E. Benson, the navigator, performed his duties very well, and on at least two occasions, he informed Wauchope that the point had been reached for deploying the brigade. Even though dawn was approaching, Wauchope disregarded this information and continued the advance, wanting to get as close as possible to the objective. Thick vegetation further prevented the brigade's lines being extended. Finally, at about 4:00 A.M., as daylight was breaking, the Highland Brigade, about 400 yards from the unseen Boer trenches, began to deploy into its attack formation.

At that point, the Boers opened fire, although many of their initial shots were fired high. Suddenly, sounding like machine guns, "from every side, . . . flashed out a line of fire, and an appalling sleet of missiles swept through the close locked ranks of the Highland Brigade" (Magersfontein n.d., p. 9). Units were in confusion, and Wauchope was soon shot and killed. For the following nine hours, the British were pinned down on the plain, and Methuen remained relatively inactive. One Englishman fighting with the Boers wrote, "You should see our entrenchments . . . we come out of our burrows and simply shoot them down like deer. . . . It is not war, but it is magnificent" (Belfield 1975, p. 48). Eventually, some of the British soldiers could no longer stand the strain and their nerves broke. Some soldiers panicked and ran away, while others cowered shamefully behind bushes. The Boers did not, as they had at the Modder River, leave their positions when the fighting was over.

The Battle of Magersfontein was an unmitigated disaster for the British, whose casualties totaled 902, as against 236 for the Boers. The Highland Brigade alone lost, in addition to Wauchope, 201 killed and 496 wounded. The British had yet to learn that bravery was not enough to stop well-armed rifle fire and win battles.

See also Boer War, Second (1899–1902); Boers; Cronje, Assistant Commandant-General Piet A.; De la Rey, Assistant Commandant-General Jacobus; Methuen, Field Marshal Paul S.; Modder River, Battle of; Wauchope, Major General Andrew G.
References: Baird (1907); Belfield (1975); Magersfontein (n.d.); Pakenham (1979)

Maharajpore, Battle of (29 December 1843)
See Gwalior Campaign

Mahdi (1844–1885)

A Sudanese religious leader named Mohammed Ahmed ibn Abdullah claimed in 1881 to be the Mahdi, a word derived from the Arabic for "divinely guided one," a messianic deliverer. He led the Sudanese in rebellion and fought numerous battles with Egyptian and British forces, culminating in the capture of Khartoum in 1885, in his quest to establish the *mahdiya,* the Mahdist state.

Mohammed Ahmed was born in 1844 near Dongola in the Sudan. He became attracted to religious studies, learned about the Koran in Khartoum, and preached its contents to other Sudanese.

The years 1877–1880 witnessed tremendous political, economic, and social turmoil in Egypt and the Sudan, with looming Egyptian bankruptcy, heavy taxation, and a disruption of the slave trade, a key element of the Sudanese economy and society. Religious fundamentalism increased during these years of discontent. Mohammed Ahmed preached that the Sudanese should get rid of the blasphemous foreigners ruling them, follow the path of God, and prepare for the coming of the Mahdi, who would purify the faith and offer salvation to the faithful. Another devout Sudanese, Abdullahi ibn Mohammed, met Mohammed Ahmed and became one of his most loyal followers.

In June 1881, Mohammed Ahmed publicly declared himself to be the Mahdi, and asserted that he, and not the Egyptian governor-general, would lead the Sudan. He had all the characteristics of the promised Mahdi, including a mole on his right cheek and a V-shaped gap between his two front teeth, features shared with Mohammed. Egyptian soldiers were sent to seize the Mahdi, but they were killed by his followers, called dervishes ("poor men"), a term later discarded in favor of *ansar* ("the helpers," men who had consecrated themselves to God in the hope of Paradise thereafter).

The Mahdi declared a jihad, or holy war, on 12 August 1881. His movement was very popular, especially among the common people. The Egyptians, concerned about this threat, sent a force from Fashoda that was annihilated by the dervishes in June 1882. Egypt was then involved with its own insurrection, during which time more followers flocked to the Mahdi's banner.

Various forces were sent to the Sudan to suppress the Mahdi's activities and regain territory his dervishes had captured. A 10,000-man Egyptian force was massacred near El Obeid on 3–5 November 1883, and another Egyptian force was wiped out near Tamanieb on 2 December 1883. The Egyptian Gendarmerie, commanded by Lieutenant General Valentine Baker Pasha, was soundly defeated at El Teb on 4 February 1884. The British then sent troops to the Sudan, and they frequently defeated the dervishes in ferocious fighting.

Major General Charles G. Gordon was sent by the British Government in January 1884 to assess the situation in the Sudan. Gordon was besieged in Khartoum by dervishes beginning in March 1884. A relief expedition, under the command of General (later Field Marshal Viscount) Lord Garnet J. Wolseley, was sent to the Sudan but failed to rescue Gordon from death at dervish hands on 26 January 1885.

British troops withdrew from the Sudan in March 1885, and the Mahdi died of typhus on about 20 June 1885. Before he died, the Mahdi had appointed Abdullahi ibn Mohammed, the Khalifa, as his successor.

See also Arabi Rebellion; Baker Pasha, Lieutenant General Valentine; Dervishes; Egypt; Egyptian Army; El Teb, Battle of; Gordon, Major General Charles G.; Gordon Relief Expedition; Khalifa; Slavery; Sudan; Wolseley, Field Marshal Garnet J.
References: Buchan (1934); Compton (1974); Elton (1954); Ludwig (1937); Mansfield (1971); Moore-Harell (2001); Waller (1988); Wingate (1892)

Maiwand, Battle of (27 July 1880)

The fall of the Conservative Government in England on 28 April 1880, during the Second Afghan War, resulted in a policy change to withdraw British forces from many locations, including Afghanistan. To fill the power vacuum upon their imminent departure and to maintain stability, the British selected Abdur Rahman to rule the country. He was proclaimed amir on 22 July 1880.

Ayub Khan, a brother of Yakub Khan then governing Kabul, believed he should rule Afghanistan, and he had been marching with a large force toward Kandahar to gain the throne by force since early July 1880. Former Afghan Army soldiers and religious followers flocked to Ayub Khan's cause.

On 2 July 1880, a British brigade, commanded by Brigadier General G.R.S. Burrows, began to advance from Kandahar to the Helmand River to prevent Ayub Khan's force from crossing it. Burrows's brigade consisted of the 66th Foot (minus two companies); 1st Bombay and 30th Bombay Native Infantry Regiments; 3rd Bombay Light Cavalry; 3rd Sind Horse; 2nd Company Bombay Miners and Sappers; E Battery, B Brigade, Royal Horse Artillery. This unit totaled 2,599 soldiers, six 9-pounder guns, and about 3,000 support and transport personnel.

Some 6,000 British-equipped local Afghans, manning a blocking position at Girishk, mutinied and joined Ayub Khan's advancing army, abandoning six of their artillery pieces to the British. With the Helmand River then indefensible, Burrows withdrew to Khushk-i-Nakhud, 50 miles from Kandahar. British intelligence ascertained that Ayub Khan's advance force was in Maiwand on 26 July 1880, and Burrows marched his brigade the following morning to that location to engage the Afghan force on the march.

The British first spotted the Afghan force, estimated at over 25,000 (with about 8,500 regular troops) with 30 guns, at about 10:00 A.M. on 27 July 1880. British artillery deployed forward and started firing on the Afghans. Burrows deployed his brigade in two lines, with the 1st Bombay Native Infantry to the left of the guns, four companies of 30th Bombay Native Infantry to the right of the guns, and the 66th Foot at the extreme right. The two cavalry regiments were positioned to the left rear of the line, and four companies of the 30th Bombay Native Infantry were in reserve.

The British, by deploying into a defensive combat position, forfeit the initiative. Ayub Khan's cavalry attacked the exposed British left flank and Afghan irregular infantry moved in a ravine to threaten the British right flank. The 66th, using their Martini-Henrys, repulsed the attacking *ghazis* on the right flank. Burrows ordered units on his left to advance and break up the impending Afghan attack, but heavy and accurate Afghan artillery fire limited their advance to about 500 yards.

The Afghans suffered considerably and then regrouped. At around 1:30 P.M. the British smoothbore artillery ran out of ammunition and withdrew. About an hour later, the Afghans, led by irregular soldiers, conducted an all-out attack on the British. Companies of the 30th, having lost all their officers, broke and ran to the 1st Bombay Native

Infantry, throwing the latter into confusion. A British cavalry charge was ineffective, and the horsemen retreated. Only the 66th maintained a semblance of order and discipline, and about 100 soldiers of the rearguard, surrounded by the Afghans, fought to the death. Realizing the situation was hopeless, Burrows ordered a withdrawal. The survivors straggled into Kandahar the following day.

The Battle of Maiwand was one of the worst British Army disasters of the Victorian era. The British lost about 962 soldiers killed and another 161 wounded. Afghan casualties are difficult to estimate, but some sources state they lost over 5,500 killed and 1,500 wounded. Ayub Khan's force then marched on and besieged Kandahar.

See also Afghan War, Second (1878–1880); Afghanistan; Bombay Army; Indian Army Operations; Kabul to Kandahar March; Roberts, Field Marshal Frederick S., V.C.

References: Barthorp (1982); Barthorp (1988); Featherstone (1989); Forbes (1892); Jalali and Grau (2001); James (1998); Maxwell (1979); Roberts (1897); Tanner (2002)

Majuba Hill, Battle of (27 February 1881)

The Battle of Majuba Hill ("mountain of doves"), the final and decisive battle of the First Boer War, was a humiliating British defeat.

After the outbreak of the First Boer War on 16 December 1880, the mission of the Natal Field Force, under the command of Major General Sir George Pomeroy-Colley, was to defeat the Boers who had proclaimed the Transvaal a republic and to relieve a number of British garrisons besieged by Boer forces. The only pass in the Drakensberg Mountains through which an army could travel from Natal to the Transvaal was at Laing's Nek. Accordingly, the Boers defended this pass.

The British conducted a frontal attack against the Boer positions on Laing's Nek on 28 January 1881 and were soundly repulsed. The British withdrew to nearby Mount Prospect to await reinforcements. On 7 February 1881, the Boers attempted to isolate the British force. On the following day, a five-company British force led by Pomeroy-Colley encountered and fought a large Boer force near the Ingogo River. In the ensuing engagement, the British lost seventy-six men killed and almost as many wounded.

After returning to the base camp, Pomeroy-Colley learned that the Boer positions at Laing's Nek had been strengthened considerably. Rather than divert forces (and military credit) to the newly arrived Major General (later Field Marshal) Sir (Henry) Evelyn M. Wood, V.C., and conduct a more complicated operation from Newcastle to Wakkerstroom, Pomeroy-Colley decided to outflank the Boer positions at Laing's Nek and seize the undefended mountain of Majuba. To the west of the Boer positions, Majuba was 2,000 feet higher than and dominated Laing's Nek. He believed that if 300–400 soldiers could occupy the summit of Majuba, they would be in an impregnable position and from this vantage point force the Boers to abandon their positions on Laing's Nek.

Pomeroy-Colley led an ad hoc 600-man force at 10:00 P.M. on 26 February 1881 to accomplish this goal. The force consisted of two companies of the 58th Foot (the Northamptons); two companies of the 3rd Battalion, 60th Foot (the King's Royal Rifles); three companies of the 92nd Foot (Gordon Highlanders); and 64 sailors. Although of battalion strength, this force did not have the cohesion of a single battalion and had no effective chain of command.

After a night march over steep, winding paths, and having detached about 200 soldiers in laagers en route, the last British soldier reached Majuba's unoccupied summit by 5:00 A.M. the following morning. A reserve force of 120 soldiers from all three regiments was designated and positioned in a central hollow area, and the remaining 250 or so men were deployed at 12-pace intervals around the triangular perimeter of the summit. Pomeroy-Colley, arguably overconfident, did not order his soldiers, who had not received any information as to the situation and plans, to dig defensive fighting positions.

When daylight broke, the summit was further reconnoitered, but it was not appreciated that a feature named Gordon's Knoll, near the northwest angle of the British perimeter, was actually higher than the rest of the plateau-like summit, and that the lower approaches to the summit from the north and northeast were hidden from the observation of the British soldiers. The soldiers were also not repositioned in any way, and there was no coordinated assault on Laing's Nek in conjunction with the occupation of Majuba Hill. At the same time, a certain "listlessness" is said to have overwhelmed Pomeroy-Colley.

The Boers, after seeing British soldiers on Majuba Hill, expected a British artillery barrage on their positions. When nothing happened, a number of Boers rode audaciously to the northern slopes of Majuba and, covered by supporting fire from comrades, began the ascent toward the British positions. At about 11:00 A.M., the naval detachment commander, standing next to Pomeroy-Colley, was mortally wounded. Pomeroy-Colley's control of the situation seemed to deteriorate rapidly thereafter, and he then lay down to sleep.

Shortly before noon about 60 Boers had gathered behind a ridge immediately beneath Gordon's Knoll. Alarmed at the increasingly heavy and accurate rifle fire, Lieutenant Ian S. M. Hamilton (later a knighted full general and commander of the Gallipoli operations in 1915), in charge of that sector, ran to inform Pomeroy-Colley of the danger. The general only acknowledged Hamilton's report and apparently took no action. About forty-five minutes later Hamilton reported that 400 Boers had infiltrated near his position. The staff seemed unconcerned, and Hamilton found Pomeroy-Colley asleep.

The assembled Boers, at about 12:45 P.M., stood up and concentrated their fire at close range on Gordon's Knoll, killing all but two or three of the soldiers there. The surviving British soldiers fled in panic, with the Boers occupying the knoll within a few minutes. The Boers then began pouring lethal fire into the main body of soldiers. Feverish confusion reigned as the Boers infiltrated to a fold in the ground about 45 yards from the British. The British had hoped that enfilading fire from Macdonald's Kopje (named after Lieutenant, later Major General Sir, Hector Macdonald, in charge of the position) on the left (west) flank of the summit would prevent such a Boer advance, but the British there were suppressed by accurate Boer sniper fire.

Some British officers, including Hamilton, realizing that the momentum of the battle was shifting against them, wanted to conduct a bayonet charge. Pomeroy-Colley refused permission. The Boers enveloped the British right flank, and many of the demoralized British soldiers, including the reserve, panicked, threw down their rifles, and stampeded to the rear. The Boers were close behind, shooting the fleeing soldiers. Only a half hour had gone by since the Boers had seized Gordon's Knoll.

Pomeroy-Colley, overwhelmed by the unexpected events, either tried to rally his men or surrender but was shot in the forehead and killed instantly. He was one of the 280 British soldiers, out of a force of about 365 on the summit, who became a casualty at the Battle of Majuba Hill. The Boers had only one man killed and a few wounded. "Poor Colley! What a gamble is the pursuit of Fame!" Hamilton later lamented. "The neglect of a mere military detail—an aberration of ordinary soldierly practice—by a brilliant Staff Officer whose career had given him no executive experience—was to turn glory into disgrace, vision into blindness, triumph into defeat" (Hamilton 1944, p. 133).

The British defeat at the Battle of Majuba Hill effectively ended the First Boer War. Less than two decades later, while fighting the same foe, the British battle cry was "Remember Majuba!"

See also Boer War, First (1880–1881); Boers; Hamilton, General Sir Ian S. M.; Ingogo, Battle of; Laing's Nek, Battle of; Macdonald, Major General Sir Hector A.; Pomeroy-Colley, Major General Sir George; Transvaal; Wood, Field Marshal Sir (Henry) Evelyn M., V.C.

References: Barthorp (1987); Bond (1967); Hamilton (1944); Lee (2000); Ransford (1967); Royle (1982)

Malakand Field Force (1897)

The ambush and murder in the Tochi Valley of the political agent, Mr. H. A. Gee, and the commander and other soldiers of his military escort in early July 1897 sparked the general uprising of the Pathan tribes on the North-West Frontier of India. A punitive expedition, the Tochi Field Force, was organized and sent to castigate the perpetrators from the Madda Khel of the Isazais tribe.

The wave of religious fervor, coupled with tribal concerns about growing British power and the possible loss of independence, spread quickly to the Swat Valley. A warning to prepare for tribal unrest was sent to the Malakand Brigade, commanded by Colonel W. H. Meiklejohn with elements in two garrisons astride the line of communication with Chitral. In the fort at Malakand were one squadron, 11th Bengal Lancers; No. 8 Bengal Mountain Battery; No. 5 Company Madras Sappers and Miners; and three infantry battalions: the 24th and 31st Punjab Infantry and the 45th Sikhs. Ten miles northeast of the Malakand Fort was the Chakdara Fort, established to protect the suspension bridge over the Swat River, and garrisoned by 180 soldiers from the 45th Sikhs and 20 from the 11th Bengal Lancers.

Late on 26 July 1897 word of the approach of tribesmen—Swatis, Utman Khels, Mamunds, Salarzais, and others, later joined by Bunerwals—was received at the Malakand Fort. A detachment of the 45th Sikhs was sent to delay their advance and, reinforced by the remainder of its battalion, successfully maintained its position until the tribesmen withdrew at about 2:00 A.M. During that time, however, a determined attack had been made on the north and center sectors of the Malakand Fort, with tribesmen successfully occupying an outbuilding and stealing ammunition until withdrawing at about 4:00 A.M.

Ferocious attacks against the Malakand Fort and desperate counterattacks by the British were conducted throughout the following four days and nights. A relief column under Colonel A. J. Reid arrived at the Malakand Fort on 31 July 1897, reinforcing the exhausted British defenders. Between the start of hostilities on 26 July 1897 and 1 August 1897, the Malakand garrison sustained 20 officers killed and wounded and 158 other ranks killed and wounded. Brigadier General (later General) Sir Bindon Blood, who was appointed to command an expeditionary force to punish the revolting tribes, arrived at Malakand on 1 August 1897 and assumed control of the operations. On 2 August 1897, a relief column from Malakand left for Chakdara. Meeting determined opposition along the way, this column was able to relieve Chakdara later that evening.

While the Malakand Fort had been under almost continuous attack from the tribesmen, the Chakdara Fort had also been holding out against tremendous odds. From 26 July until 2 August 1897, the disciplined, skilled Chakdara garrison, with 5 killed and 10 wounded, had killed an estimated 2,000 tribesmen. The tribesmen later admitted to having lost 3,700 killed, plus many more wounded.

The Malakand Field Force, under Blood's overall command, was quickly constituted and ready for operations on 7 August 1897. It consisted of three brigades plus divisional troops. The 1st Brigade, commanded by Brigadier General W. H. Meiklejohn, consisted of the 1st Royal West Kents, 24th and 31st Punjabis, and 24th Sikhs. The 1st East Kents, 35th Sikhs, 38th Dogras, and Guides Infantry composed Brigadier General P. D. Jeffreys's 2nd Brigade. Commanded by Brigadier General J. H. Wodehouse, the 3rd Brigade consisted of the 1st West Surreys, 2nd Highland Light Infantry, 22nd Punjabis, and 39th Garhwal Rifles. This force advanced up the Swat Valley, dispersing opposition, and received the submission of the Swat Valley tribes on 24 August 1897.

Before Blood had a chance to pacify other tribes and restore order in the area, he was ordered to advance into Bajaur and coordinate operations with the Mohmand Field Force, commanded by Brigadier General E. R. Elles. (On 6 August 1897, eleven days after the assault on the Malakand Fort, the Mohmands had attacked the border police fort of Shabkadr, 15 miles north of Peshawar.) Blood's brigades frequently operated independently in the systematic operations to punish the clans in the Mamund Valley. Numerous villages were destroyed and supplies were confiscated and used to feed the British transport animals while occasional attacks were made on the British camps.

On 21 September 1897, Blood's 3rd Brigade was attached to the Mohmand Field Force, and he reorganized his force before continuing operations. Twelve or fourteen villages were burned by the 2nd Brigade on 29 September. The Malakand Field Force attacked the villages of Agrah and Gat on 31 September, but it encountered surprisingly stubborn resistance as "it soon became apparent that large numbers of the enemy were concealed amongst the crags on the spur between the two villages" (Nevill 1912, p. 242). Fighting became desperate, and a British counterattack with bayonets fixed captured Gat. British casualties that day were 12 officers and men killed and 49 wounded.

The village of Badalai was destroyed on 3 October 1897, and active operations against the Mamunds ended although a settlement was not made until 18 October. The Malakand Field Force had accomplished its mission and was then dissolved.

Winston L. S. Churchill, who served as a war correspondent with the Malakand Field Force, immortalized the operations of this punitive expedition and the generalship of its commander through the publication of his book *The Story of the Malakand Field Force: An Episode of Frontier War*. In many respects, the Malakand operations (as noted on the dustjacket of the 1990 reprint of *The Story of the Malakand Field Force*) were similar to those of many other savage British campaigns on the North-West Frontier: "The danger and difficulty of attacking these fierce hill men is extreme. It is a war without quarter: They kill and mutilate everyone they catch and we do not hesitate to finish their wounded off."

See also Blood, General Sir Bindon; Churchill, Sir Winston L. S.; India; Indian Army Operations; Mohmand Field Force; North-West Frontier; Tochi Field Force

References: Barthorp (1982); Churchill (1898); Featherstone (1973); Fincastle and Eliott-Lockhart (1898); MacNeil (1997); Nevill (1912)

Maneuvers, British Army

British Army maneuvers were held during the second half of the Victorian era and immediately preceding World War I on a more frequent basis and on a larger scale as tactics became more complicated, weapons more lethal, and international relations more tense.

From the victory of Field Marshal Arthur Wellesley, the First Duke of Wellington, at Waterloo until his death in 1852, no British Army maneuvers were held. Many senior officers believed that "any attempt to tamper with the military machine that had defeated the French would be disastrous" (Blanco 1965, pp. 125–126). The British Army at this time was little more than a conglomeration of infantry battalions, cavalry regiments, artillery batteries, and support elements. The Prince Consort had been watching with growing concern the apparent lack of preparedness and development of the British Army. He wrote to General (later Field Marshal) Viscount Henry Hardinge, commander in chief of the British Army, and expressed his consternation.

Prince Albert may have been responsible for originating the exercises held near Chobham in 1853. This site was selected because it was in southern England, accessible by rail, and suitable as an assembly area for troops required to defend the southeast coast. The purpose of this exercise, according to Hardinge, was to "accustom the Officers, and Troops to move over rough and undulating ground, with that freedom, and ease, which should be practised before an enemy in the field—to take up ground in reference to its shape for defensive purposes—or to attack a position by such a combination of the three arms, as may be adapted to bring each into action in its proper place, and at the most appropriate moment" (Strachan 1984, p. 166).

The Chobham encampment also provided opportunities to test new ammunition wagons and new clothing and equipment. Fieldcraft was emphasized, and officers were encouraged to reflect on the impact of the new rifled musket on tactics.

The ad hoc "division" was selected as the unit for encampment because it was a self-contained combined arms formation. From June to July 1853, the division consisted of two infantry brigades (of three battalions each), a cavalry brigade, a brigade of guards, and supporting artillery and engineers. On 14 July 1853, all the troops were replaced by new soldiers and units. Some of the field maneuvering conducted was not realistic, and communications systems were antiquated. Deficiencies in training and equipment were highlighted, and plans were made to correct these shortcomings and hold annual maneuvers. Overall, the Chobham exercise was a tremendous success. Land at Aldershot was purchased and the British Army's first and largest permanent training camp was established in 1854.

The Crimean War (1854–1856) curtailed plans for training at Aldershot and the British "victory" in that conflict and success in the Indian Mutiny (1857–1859) conveyed an unrealistic and inflated perception of the British Army's proficiency. The decisive Prussian victory over the French in 1870–1871 and the unification of Germany shocked the British out of their complacency, as the need for systematic training became painfully apparent. British Army maneuvers involving three divisions were held in the fall of 1871 at Aldershot. Field Marshal H.R.H. Prince George F., Second Duke of Cambridge, then British Army commander in chief, reported "the various weaknesses of the infantry: poor outpost duty, failure to use ground cover, and exposure to enemy fire before being fully deployed" (Kochanski 1999, p. 58). Similar maneuvers were held in 1872 and 1873, but with the fading of the war scare and government concern about expenses, overconfidence returned. In 1873, it was decided that individual soldiers and smaller units needed more training and that individual arms would be trained and maneuver separately.

British Army training above the battalion level stagnated until the 1890s. The 1890s witnessed a realization that peacetime training was essential to wartime success and a revival in training and maneuvers. Two divisions participated in autumn maneuvers in 1891 at Aldershot, the largest exercise in almost two decades. The British Army conducted its first "Staff Tour (Ride)" in 1895, and the following year maneuvers were conducted that included five divisions and sixteen militia battalions. In July 1897, a mobilization exercise was conducted that required an emergency mobilization of the 1st Brigade, 1st Division.

In 1898, after the government purchased 41,000 acres of Salisbury Plain, the British Army was able to hold exercises involving two corps maneuvering against each other. From 1–7 September 1898, the "Home" or "Red" Army, commanded by General H.R.H. the Duke of Connaught, maneuvered against General Sir Redvers H. Buller's "Invading" or "Blue" Army. Each force was equal in strength, consisting of an army corps of three infantry divisions, a cavalry brigade, and support elements. The maneuver area was roughly 48 miles square; 53,600 soldiers, with 9,400 horses and 242 guns and machine guns, took part in the training. The overall maneuvers, however, were based on faulty tactical scenarios that did not properly take into account the increased lethality of smokeless rifle fire. The red-coated British infantry made frontal assaults and attacked enemy fortifications, the cavalry charged its opponents, and the artillery dashed about the sham battlefield to support the infantry. Field Marshal Viscount Garnet J. Wolseley, then British Army commander in chief, reported that "it would be optimistic to say that the fullest tactical value was obtained from each day's operation" (Kochanski 1999, p. 228). Generalship was poor and tactics were inappropriate, and the true results of these maneuvers were seen the following year in South Africa, when Buller was fighting against Boers and suffered three significant defeats during Black Week (December 1899).

After the Second Boer War, numerous reforms were made to standardize the organization and enhance the effectiveness of the British Army. A training system was established in which multi-echelon unit training was conducted each year, culminating in the Autumn Maneuvers. Before 1909, different divisions had theoretically been mobilized each year for annual maneuvers, but they were all dependent on the voluntary duty of reservists. These divisions were thus composed of men, horses, and equipment "borrowed" from other formations. The 1909 maneuvers consisted of four infantry divisions and one cavalry division, totaling 44,000 soldiers. British Army maneuvers, especially after the Boer War, helped prepare and train the British Army for the conflagration of World War I.

See also Aldershot; Boer War, Second (1899–1902); Buller, General Sir Redvers H., V.C.; Cambridge, Field Marshal H.R.H. Prince George F., Second Duke of; Crimean War; Hardinge, Field Marshal Henry; Indian Mutiny; Infantry, British Army—Training; Wellington, Field Marshal Arthur Wellesley, First Duke of; Wolseley, Field Marshal Garnet J.

References: Blanco (1965); Bond (1972); Kochanski (1999); Spiers (1992); Stone and Schmidl (1988); Strachan (1984)

Maori War, First (1843–1848)

The First Maori War (1843–1848) was caused by conflicts between the Maoris and settlers primarily over disputed land sales.

Armed clashes between Europeans and Maoris became more frequent in the 1830s. To help restore and maintain law and order, and amid rumors that the French were developing plans to colonize New Zealand, the British appointed a resident in 1833. The British resident, however, had limited authority and little success. In England, the New Zealand Company, formed in 1839 to colonize New Zealand, failed to receive Colonial Office approval to operate. Concerned that this commercial enterprise would not be in the best interests of the Maoris and their land, and in order to bring stability to New Zealand, the British Government then appointed a British Consul, Captain William Hobson.

Hobson arrived in New Zealand in January 1840, raised the British flag, and began negotiations with Maori chiefs. The result was the Treaty of Waitangi, signed on 6 February 1840, by British representatives and about forty-five Maori chiefs. New Zealand then became a British colony, with the first British garrison (detachments of the 80th and 96th Regiments) arriving soon thereafter.

Friction over land ownership between Europeans and Maoris increased. The Maoris believed in the sanctity of their land as perpetual tribal property, and they did not understand the concept of buying and selling and private ownership of land. In June 1843, armed European settlers trying to enforce a disputed land sale confronted a Maori chief and his followers near Wairau. The Maoris refused a demand to surrender and a skirmish broke out, resulting in the death of the chief's wife and 15 Maoris and settlers. The 30 European survivors fled the area, but the Maoris caught 11 and executed them on the spot, in a customary act of revenge *(utu)* for Maoris killed initially. This confrontation is regarded as the first engagement of the Maori Wars.

In July 1844, Maori Chief Hone Heke Pokai, to protest his disillusionment with the British administration, cut down the flagpole he had erected on Maiki Hill at Kororareka for the display of the British flag. He again cut down re-erected flagpoles on 9 January 1845 and on 11 March 1845 (giving rise to the name the "Flagpole War" for this series of confrontations). On 11 March, Hone Heke also attacked the settlement, killing ten soldiers and seamen and setting fire to many buildings. This action resulted in a split among Maori tribes, with some siding with the British, and a call for British reinforcements.

The British reinforcements were mainly from the 58th, 96th, and 99th Regiments. An infantry force with attached marines and a Congreve rocket detachment, commanded by Lieutenant Colonel William Hulme, attacked Hone Heke's *pa* (earthwork stockade) at Puketutu on 8 May 1845. The British, unfamiliar with these strong defensive positions, were driven back with heavy losses.

Hone Heke's men attacked the *pa* of pro-British Chief Tamati Waka Nene on 12 June 1845 unsuccessfully. Similarly, the British, with men from the 58th and 99th Regiments and naval personnel, were unable to capture the *pa* of Hone

Heke's ally Kawati on 1 July 1845. This attack cost the British forty casualties, although they captured and destroyed the *pa* after it was abandoned that night.

Hone Heke built a new *pa* at Ruapekepeka, which was attacked by the British on 11 January 1846. Artillery was used to breach the stockade and the assaulting British found the *pa* almost empty; the Christian Maoris, who never expected the British to attack on a Sunday, were attending a church service. The Maoris were unable to recapture the fort and dispersed quietly.

Confrontations with other Maori tribes and settlers were increasing elsewhere. Maoris attacked the British garrison at Boulcotts Farm (in the Hutt Valley north of Wellington) on 16 May 1846. The *pa* of one of the offending chiefs was bombarded by the British on 6 August 1846, and Maori raids ended in this area.

The continued settler encroachment on Maori land provoked Maoris to attack the British stockade at Wanganui on 16 April 1847 and again on 19 May 1847. In an indecisive engagement at nearby St. John's Wood on 19 July 1847, the British suffered two men killed, and one officer, ten soldiers, and one friendly Maori wounded. Other Maori casualties were unknown. In February 1848, after the British pursued a policy of clemency, Maori chiefs involved in the fighting at Wanganui approached the British and declared their willingness to cease all hostilities. This ended the First Maori War.

See also Maori War, Second (1863–1869); Maoris; Rockets; Taranaki War

References: Barthorp (1979); Featherstone (1989); Haythornthwaite (1995); Knight (1996)

Maori War, Second (1863–1869)

British colonization of New Zealand continued after the Taranaki War (1860–1861), with the number of colonists increasing rapidly from 59,413 in 1858 to 218,637 in 1867 (Farwell 1972, p. 177). Further measures were taken that deprived the Maoris of their lands. In 1862, the General Assembly passed the Native Lands Act to facilitate the purchase of Maori land and prevent tribal leaders from attempting to block the sales. The construction of a military road by the British toward the Waikato region, on the northwestern coast of the North Island, was considered provocative and a harbinger of further white encroachment. Tensions mounted and violence flared up in 1863, with sporadic clashes taking place until 1869. These hostilities were part of the continuing struggle between the Maoris and the white settlers.

On 4 May 1863, the Maoris ambushed a British military patrol of the 57th Foot on Maori land at Oakura. There was only one British survivor. The British assembled considerable forces under the command of General Sir Duncan Cameron to launch a punitive expedition against the Maoris. On 6 July 1863, the government announced a new policy of "creeping confiscation," in which the military would occupy and settle Maori land. Six days later Duncan's force, supported by river gunboats, began the Waikato campaign. The British stormed a Maori *pa* (earthwork stockade) at Koheroa later in July 1863 and continued a guerrilla campaign with the Maoris.

Cameron's 1,300-man force, consisting of soldiers from the 12th, 14th, 40th, and 65th Regiments, with artillery, engineers, naval personnel, and locally raised militia, attacked the Maori *pa* located at Rangiriri on 20 November 1863. After a combined land and naval gunboat bombardment, the British made their first assault on the fortification and seized the first line of defensive trenches. Three subsequent attacks were repelled, but the following morning the Maoris, surrounded and out of ammunition, surrendered. Maori losses were 36 men and women killed, with 183 taken prisoner, and the British suffered 38 all ranks killed and 92 wounded.

Cameron continued with his offensive. Skirmishes were fought until Maoris were surrounded on 30 March 1864 in the Orakua *pa*. After an initial repulse, Cameron decided to besiege the stockade. Anxious to minimize casualties on both sides, Cameron asked the Maoris to surrender. In a famous shout of defiance, the Maoris responded, "Friend, we shall fight you for ever and ever!" (Haythornthwaite 1995, p. 290). Three days later the Maoris broke out of the encircled *pa* and escaped into the bush, thus ending the Waikato campaign. Ostensibly as reparations, the British confiscated Maori land.

Maoris also took up arms in the Bay of Plenty area, and Cameron sent reinforcements to this area. Some 1,700 soldiers from the 43rd and 68th Regiments, plus naval personnel, attacked the 300 Maoris at the Gate *pa* on 29 April 1864. After ferocious close quarter fighting, the British were repulsed, losing over 120 men killed and wounded. That night the Maoris again vanished.

Cameron departed for other service, leaving Lieutenant Colonel H. H. Greer in command. Greer's soldiers, mainly from the 43rd, 68th, and 1st Waikato Regiments, successfully stormed the Te Ranga *pa* on 21 June 1864. This was the last large battle in this area.

The last stage of the war has been called the Hau Hau campaign from the movement that inspired it. Maori adherents of this new faith combining Christian and Maori theology with nationalism were instructed to yell "Hau! Hau!" to make them invulnerable to bullets. Beginning in April 1864, they engaged in guerrilla warfare mainly with locally raised units, such as the Forest Rangers, because the British were withdrawing their regular forces. A few battles were fought, notably at the Otapawa *pa,* captured by the British on 14 January 1866, and in September and November 1868, by which time the Hau Hau had begun ritual cannibalism.

The followers of another Maori chief, Te Kooti Rikirangi Te Turuki, murdered seventy people, settlers and Maoris, at Poverty Bay on 10 November 1868. He built a *pa* at Ngatapa, which was captured on 2 February 1869. This engagement, in the minds of many, ended the Second Maori War, although minor raids and skirmishes took place until 1872.

See also Maori War, First (1843–1848); Maoris; Taranaki War
References: Barber and Clayton (1989); Battle of Rangiriri (n.d.); Farwell (1972); Featherstone (1973); Haythornthwaite (1995); Knight (1996); Knight (1999); Waitangi Tribunal (1996)

Maoris

The Maoris are the indigenous people of New Zealand, having reportedly migrated from Polynesia in the fourteenth century. Captain James Cook claimed New Zealand for Great Britain in 1769, and colonization, as well as confrontation with the Maoris, began slowly. During the mid-nineteenth century, fighting was sporadic, frequently intense, and was part of a continuous struggle between the colonizing Europeans, mainly British, who greedily wrested the land from the Maoris. This avarice and cultural clash provoked the First Maori War (1843–1848), the Taranaki War (1860–1861), and the Second Maori War (1863–1869).

The Maoris claimed ownership of all of the North Island, as well as much of the South Island, of New Zealand. They were skillful, brave, and ferocious warriors, whom Sir John Fortescue considered "among the most redoubtable fighting men encountered by the Victorian soldier" (Featherstone 1989, p. 115). Organized into tribes and clans, Maori society was very warlike, with conflict a routine part of Maori life. Their daily life was governed by a strict code of conduct, called *tapu,* and customs and traditions. The prestige of the tribal chief, or *manu,* and the collective ownership and sanctity of their land was paramount. A tribal incursion into another tribe's land was considered an insult to the chief and his *manu,* with the offended tribe desiring revenge *(utu),* which in turn led to intertribal conflict. A secondary cause of these conflicts was *muru,* or plunder. These wars occasionally ended with the victors eating the vanquished to supplement their meat-deficient diets.

The Maori warriors, with heavily tattooed faces, were originally armed with primitive spears, clubs, and axes. The white man *(pakeha)* introduced firearms to the Maoris, and this new weapon caused wholesale massacre among rival tribes. The Maori wars of 1818–1833 are called the Musket Wars, as various tribes used the new weapons to seek *utu* with other tribes. Relentless intertribal warfare reportedly caused 65,000 Maori casualties up to 1840.

The Maoris displayed unsurpassed engineering skills in rapidly constructing *pas,* which were earthwork stockades. The typical *pa* was about 90 yards long and 50 yards wide, with projecting flanks. The *pa* was typically surrounded by a 5-foot-deep ditch and 3 rows of palisades, with each row of palisades made of logs and tree trunks each 15 feet high and 9–20 inches in diameter. Layered flax leaves, serving as a type of armor, covered the palisades. An intricate, interconnected trench system zigzagged between the palisades, permitting the Maoris to enfilade likely avenues of approach. Rifle pits and firing positions punctuated the covered trench lines, into which chambers were dug to provide cover to the defenders during a bombardment.

See also Maori War, First (1843–1848); Maori War, Second (1863–1869); Taranaki War
References: Featherstone (1989); Haythornthwaite (1995); Knight (1996); Ryan (1986)

Maps

Maps represent a portion of the earth's surface, generally written or printed on paper, and include natural and man-made features; they are generally produced in variable scales. Accurate maps, which were of limited availability in the nineteenth century, greatly assist the successful completion of military maneuvers and operations.

The Ordnance Board, formally constituted in 1597, was responsible for armaments, munitions, and the maintenance of castles and forts. Over the centuries its responsibilities evolved. Under the purview of the Ordnance Board, a military survey of the Scottish Highlands was begun in the

1740s. When Britain feared a possible invasion from France in the 1790s, the Board of Ordnance began a survey and mapped England's vulnerable southern coasts. This led to the creation of the Ordnance Survey in 1791.

The Board of Ordnance ordered a survey of Ireland in 1824, and 13th and 14th Royal Engineer Survey Companies were raised for this mission. The board became increasingly dominated by army officers and was closely linked to the army. It was abolished and merged with the War Office in 1855.

The head of the Topographical and Statistical Section of the War Office also became the director general of the Ordnance Survey. In 1870, the library and map collections were considered "deficient," but this was later improved. Training of military surveyors during this period was conducted at a number of locations, including the Tower of London. A school for training military surveyors and cartographers was established in 1833 by Lieutenant Denison at Chatham (this school was the predecessor of the current Royal School of Military Survey at Hermitage). Many officers and noncommissioned officers were seconded to the Ordnance Survey for survey work in British colonies and on boundary commissions around the world. An example is the Anglo-Russian Boundary Commission that delineated the northern boundary of Afghanistan (1885–1887).

Inaccurate maps hindered military operations, notably in the Second Boer War (1899–1902), when columns and especially lines of communications often stretched over hundreds of miles of unmapped territory in the Transvaal and Orange Free State. The inadequacy of maps was a contributing factor in the defeat of the British force at the Modder River on 28 November 1899. A blueprint used as a map at the Tugela River the following month included a statement that "vacant spaces indicate that data . . . is wanting rather than that the ground is flat" (Pakenham 1979, p. 216). Four mapping sections were deployed to South Africa and mapped 15,000 square miles in support of operations. A rudimentary mobile map production system was also developed during this period.

See also Boer War, Second (1899–1902); Engineers, British Army—Employment; Intelligence; Modder River, Battle of
References: Fergusson (1984); Marix Evans (2000); Pakenham (1979)

Marchand, Captain Jean-Baptiste
See Fashoda Incident

Martini-Henry Rifle
See Infantry, British Army—Small Arms

Master-General of the Ordnance, British Army

The master-general of the ordnance was generally a senior officer in the British Army. The historical title was first associated with Lord Dartmouth in 1683. While the master-general of the ordnance was a soldier, the appointment was basically political in nature since it carried with it a seat in Parliament until 1828 and frequently a cabinet position. The master-general of the ordnance was initially independent of the British Army commander in chief in terms of military discipline and of the Treasury in financial matters. The master-general of the ordnance was responsible, as defined in 1851, for "the provision, custody, and supply of every description of warlike stores, whether for sea or land service; ordnance, carriages, small arms, ammunition, pontoons, tents, and camp-equipage, entrenching tools: everything, in short, which is required to arm a fleet or fortress, or to equip an army for the field" (Strachan 1984, p. 232).

The master-general of the ordnance commanded the ordnance forces: the commissioned and noncommissioned ranks of the Royal Artillery, officers of the Royal Engineers, and other ranks of the Corps of Royal Sappers and Miners. He also commanded the Royal Military Academy, Woolwich, which trained ordnance cadets. In conjunction with the commander in chief, the master-general of the ordnance prepared the defense of the United Kingdom and was solely responsible for supervising the construction and maintenance of fortifications throughout the British Empire. His deputy and immediate subordinate was the lieutenant-general of the ordnance, although this position was discontinued in 1831.

The master-general of the ordnance also had civil responsibilities as he presided over the Board of Ordnance and through it controlled the Ordnance Department. The Ordnance Department provided certain and numerous supplies to the British Army and the Royal Navy.

Before the Crimean War, it became apparent that the civil and military functions of the master-general of the ordnance, combined with his rapidly increasing responsibilities, exposed weaknesses in the ordnance system and operations. The Crimean War exacerbated these inadequacies. In 1855, the cabinet decided to end the Ordnance Department as a separate and independent establishment. The civil responsibilities of the master-general of the ordnance were transferred to the secretary of state for war. The master-general of the ordnance's command of the Royal Artillery and Royal Engineers was transferred to the commander in chief, and a reduced position of master-general of the ordnance, bereft of any civil responsibilities, was also made subordinate to the commander in chief.

See also Artillery, British Army—Organization; Commander in Chief, British Army; Crimean War; Engineers, British Army—Organization; Horse Guards; War Office; Woolwich, Royal Military Academy

References: Barnett (1970); Hamer (1970); Moyse-Bartlett (1974); Strachan (1984); Strachan (1997); Sweetman (1984)

Maurice, Major General Sir (John) Frederick (1841–1912)

A member of the Ashanti Ring, Major General Sir (John) Frederick Maurice was a highly talented but controversial military intellectual, theorist, historian, editor, and educator. He was also Field Marshal Viscount Garnet J. Wolseley's "lifelong friend, apologist and amanuensis" (Preston 1967, p. 244).

Maurice, born on 24 May 1841, was the eldest son of the social reformer Frederick Denison Maurice. He was educated at the Royal Military College, Sandhurst, and commissioned in the Royal Artillery in 1862. After postings in England, Scotland, and Ireland, Maurice entered the Staff College in 1870. While in attendance and in the wake of the Franco-Prussian War (1870–1871), he learned the Second Duke of Wellington was sponsoring an essay contest on "The System of Field Manoeuvres Best Adapted for Enabling Our Troops to Meet a Continental Army," with £100 for first prize. Maurice won the essay contest, defeating another entrant—Wolseley—whom he quoted in his treatise.

Maurice's essay had no real impact on the British Army, but it helped his career. Wolseley selected Maurice, then serving as an instructor in tactics at Sandhurst, to be his private secretary on the 1873–1874 Ashanti expedition. As a result, Maurice became a trusted member of the Ashanti Ring and later wrote *The Ashantee War: A Popular Narrative*.

After serving in Canada (1875–1877) Maurice returned to England and a posting in the Intelligence Department. When Wolseley was sent from Cyprus to South Africa in 1879 to command the forces during the latter phases of the Zulu War, he took Maurice with him as intelligence officer. During the subsequent campaign to capture Sekukuni, Maurice demonstrated gallantry on the battlefield and was shot in the chest.

After recovering, Maurice served as a brigade major in Cork. Wolseley again summoned him to the staff of the British expeditionary force sent to Egypt in 1882. Maurice became the official historian of this campaign and *The Military History of the Campaign of 1882* in Egypt was published in 1887. This study was criticized for being too favorable to Wolseley. Maurice also served on Wolseley's staff during the 1884–1885 Gordon Relief Expedition.

In 1885, Wolseley, returning to his position as adjutant-general, appointed Maurice professor of military art and history at the Staff College. He accepted the position reluctantly, but he became a superb teacher. He oriented his rigorous and stimulating military history courses so the student would "improve his judgement as to what ought to be done under the varied conditions of actual war" (Bond 1972, p. 136). Maurice was also Wolseley's most articulate advocate of a British, rather than an Indian-based, strategy of imperial defense. Maurice was a prolific author and lecturer, although prone to be absentminded and argumentative.

Maurice was succeeded at the Staff College in 1892 by Lieutenant Colonel (later Colonel) G. F. R. Henderson, and was posted to successive artillery commands at Aldershot, Colchester, and Woolwich. Although Maurice retired in 1902, he succeeded the ailing Henderson as official historian of the Second Boer War. Frequently considered "the second pen of Sir Garnet," Maurice died in 1912.

See also Arabi Rebellion; Ashanti Ring; Ashanti War, Second (1873–1874); Camberley, Staff College; Gordon Relief Expedition; Henderson, Colonel G. F. R.; Intellectuals, British Army; Intelligence; Sandhurst, Royal Military College; Wolseley, Field Marshal Garnet J.; Zulu War

References: Beckett (1992); Bond (1972); Fergusson (1984); Luvaas (1964); Maurice (1872); Maurice (1887); Maurice and Arthur (1924); Maxwell (1985); Preston (1967); Spiers (1992)

Mauser Rifle
See Commando System

Maxim Gun
See Machine Guns

McNeill, General Sir John C., V.C. (1831–1904)

General Sir John C. McNeill was a courageous and charismatic British Army officer who was an experienced member of the Ashanti Ring. He later commanded troops in the Sudan.

McNeill was born in Scotland on 29 March 1831. He was educated at St. Andrew's and Addiscombe, the East India Company's Military Seminary, near Croydon. In 1850, he was gazetted into the 107th Bengal Infantry Regiment of the Indian Army. During the Indian Mutiny, he served as aide-de-camp to Major General Sir Edward Lugard.

In 1864, McNeill was serving as aide-de-camp to General Duncan Cameron during the Second Maori War on New Zealand. On 30 March 1864, McNeill and a small escort party were ambushed by Maoris. The British soldiers galloped to evade the attacking Maoris when McNeill realized one of the soldiers in the escort was not with them. McNeill turned around, caught the missing soldier's horse, then helped the soldier mount and led him away from the intense Maori small arms fire. For saving the life of the private soldier at the risk of his own while under enemy fire, McNeill was awarded the Victoria Cross, Britain's foremost gallantry award.

McNeill was reassigned to Canada, and during the 1866 Fenian disturbances, he commanded the Tipperary Flying Column. Shortly thereafter he became military secretary to the governor-general of Canada. Colonel (later Field Marshal Viscount) Garnet J. Wolseley, serving as deputy quartermaster-general in Canada, was given command of the Red River Expedition to quell "rebels" protesting the incorporation of the Red River Colony into the Dominion of Canada. McNeill became Wolseley's chief of staff during this operation that was a logistical triumph and laid the foundation of Wolseley's reputation.

McNeill was selected—but not as first choice—to be Wolseley's chief of staff in the 1873–1874 expedition to Ashantiland. In a skirmish with the Ashanti on 14 October 1873, McNeill was severely wounded in the wrist and evacuated to England.

During the 1882 British expedition to Egypt, McNeill, as a colonel, served on the staff of Major General H.R.H. the Duke of Connaught and Strathearn, who commanded the 1st Brigade of the 1st Division. McNeill was knighted for his services in Egypt.

After the fall of Khartoum on 26 January 1885, the Suakin Field Force was organized, under the command of Lieutenant General Sir Gerald Graham, V.C., to crush dervish resistance in the Suakin area. McNeill, as a major general, commanded the 2nd Brigade. The British defeated dervishes at Hashin on 20 March 1885, and Graham decided to establish staging depots en route to Tamai, occupied by another large dervish force. McNeill was given this mission, and two days later, he took a 3,300-man two-brigade force to establish these depots. McNeill was ignorant of intelligence forecasts, had no artillery and inadequate cavalry, and was burdened with last-minute changes in instructions and considerable transport. While establishing a zareba (a redoubt enclosed by a hedge of thorny mimosa bushes) near Tofrek, McNeill's unit was surprised by a fierce dervish force, and it was only the dogged determination and courage of the British soldiers that saved the force. Total British casualties included 149 soldiers, 176 camp followers, and 501 camels, and 1,500 dervishes were killed. McNeill, who was criticized by both Wolseley and Graham for a lack of security and inadequate cavalry, never held another field command.

McNeill later served as equerry to Queen Victoria and aide-de-camp to King Edward VII. McNeill died at St. James's Palace in London on 25 May 1904.

See also Addiscombe, Military Seminary; Arabi Rebellion; Ashanti Ring; Ashanti War, Second (1873–1874); Bengal Army; Canada; Dervishes; Indian Mutiny; Maori War, Second (1863–1869); Red River Expedition; Tofrek, Battle of; Victoria Cross; Wolseley, Field Marshal Garnet J.

References: Beckett (1992); De Cosson (1886); Greaves (1924); Kochanski (1999); Lehmann (1964); Maxwell (1985); McNeill (1999); Preston (1967); Robson (1993b)

McQueen, Major General J. W.
See Hazara Field Force

Menshikov, Prince Alexander Sergeevich
See Balaklava, Battle of; Crimean War; Eupatoria, Battle of; Inkerman, Battle of; Russian Forces, Crimean War

Methuen, Field Marshal Paul S., Third Baron (1845–1932)

Field Marshal Lord Methuen was a highly proficient and professional British Army officer who was relentless in pursuing mission accomplishment. He was an unacknowledged junior member of the Ashanti Ring.

Methuen was born on 1 September 1845 in England, the eldest of three sons of the Second Baron Methuen. After being educated at Eton and serving two years in the Royal Wiltshire Yeomanry, Methuen joined the Scots Fusilier Guards as a lieutenant in 1864 and progressed steadily in his regiment. He served on Major General (later Field Marshal Viscount) Sir Garnet J. Wolseley's staff during the Second Ashanti War (1873–1874) and was Wolseley's headquarters commandant during the 1882 British expedition to Egypt. Methuen also saw active service during the Bechuanaland Expedition (1884–1885), commanding Methuen's Horse.

Promoted to major general in 1888, Methuen commanded the Home District from 1892 to 1897 and succeeded to his father's barony in 1891. He then served as press censor at the Tirah Field Force headquarters on the North-West Frontier in 1897 and was promoted to lieutenant general in 1898.

When the Second Boer War began in October 1899, Methuen was designated the commander of the 1st Division. He had learned his profession in colonial campaigns and his tactical knowledge was outdated, but his enthusiastic performance in South Africa, while mixed, was better than that of most other division commanders. Methuen arrived in South Africa in November 1899 and commanded his division as one element of a three-pronged attack on the Boers. The plan for the 1st Division was to advance and relieve Kimberley, then return to the Cape with all rescued noncombatants. En route to his objective, Methuen won minor victories over the Boers at Belmont (23 November 1899), Graspan (25 November), and Modder River (28 November). However, in trying to dislodge the Boers from trenches at Magersfontein, Methuen attempted a night attack on 11 December 1899—perhaps trying to replicate Wolseley's success at Tel el-Kebir (13 September 1882), which he had observed. The attack turned into a horrible defeat with 948 British casualties (210 killed and 728 wounded). On 14 December 1899, the War Office directed General Sir Redvers H. Buller, V.C., commander in chief, South Africa, to relieve Methuen, but Buller countermanded this directive.

While most officers of his rank had been replaced or returned to England, Methuen remained active in South Africa until the end of the war. On 7 March 1902, his force, consisting mainly of newly recruited yeomanry and irregulars, was defeated by the Boers at Tweebosch. In addition to being wounded, Methuen suffered the humiliating experience of surrendering to the Boers.

After the Second Boer War, Methuen commanded the IV Army Corps (1904–1908) and served as general officer commanding in chief, South Africa (1908–1912). He was promoted to field marshal in 1911 and served as governor of Malta from 1915 until retirement in 1919. Methuen, considered "chivalrous, kindly, generous, with the highest standards of duty and expecting others to be imbued with the same ideals" (Wickham Legg 1949, p. 615), died on 30 October 1932.

See also Arabi Rebellion; Ashanti Ring; Ashanti War, Second (1873–1874); Boer War, Second (1899–1902); Buller, General Sir Redvers H., V.C.; Magersfontein, Battle of; Modder River, Battle of; North-West Frontier; Tirah Field Force; Wolseley, Field Marshal Garnet J.; Yeomanry

References: Barthorp (1987); Kochanski (1999); Miller (1996); Pakenham (1979); Sixsmith (1970); Symons (1963); Wickham Legg (1949)

Military and Popular Culture

The British Army had a marked impact on the popular culture of Great Britain, especially during the second half of the nineteenth century. The popular culture—a mass phenomenon consisting of the body of popularly and customarily held beliefs and values, patterns of behavior, and ideas and images—was a part of an evolving society and culture. There were a number of forms of popular culture, including newspapers, books, literature, poetry, art, music, and advertising.

The overwhelming majority of soldiers in the other ranks of the British Army were from the working class, and the army, like civil society, was heavily stratified. As the British Army was basically a microcosm of the civilian working class, it generally reflected the same beliefs and values.

The British Army was generally despised, or at least neglected, until the Crimean War era. An increasingly literate British public was able to receive timely, uncensored news almost directly from the battlefield, where war correspondents observed military activities, wrote their stories, and sent them via the telegraph—bypassing military authorities—directly to their newspaper in London. The tremendous privations of the other ranks, logistical shortcomings, and incompetent leadership horrified the public, which clamored for military reform.

Renewed interest in the army coincided with the "new imperialism" that began in the 1870s. There were many reasons for this resurgence of imperialism, including Great Britain's need of raw materials and markets for its manufactured goods. Viewed in the context of Social Darwinism, war and conflict came to be seen as a natural occurrence in evolution and suggested British superiority in all areas. This ideology provided a rationale for war and conquest against "inferior peoples," as well as competition with other colonial powers.

The instrument of British imperialism was the British Army, and the British soldier fought his nation's small wars and colonial campaigns, helped extend the empire, and administered these distant possessions. The popular press encouraged these patriotic and militaristic sentiments as the British Army engaged in frequently romanticized colonial wars and campaigns. The exploits of the heroic British Army encouraged patriotism and jingoism and helped popularize imperialism.

This renewed interest in the British Army and imperialism was reflected in many forms of popular culture. In the journalistic field, war correspondents and war illustrators accompanied military expeditions and reported for their respective newspapers. Numerous books, factual and fictional, were written about military commanders, their soldiers, and their wars and battles. The courage, as well as the foibles and everyday life of the stalwart British soldiers, was memorialized by writers and poets, notably Rudyard Kipling in India. War artists painted exquisite scenes of heroic military operations and battles that were displayed in salons and in royal exhibitions. Military subjects were popular in the area of sheet music and songs, and advertisers frequently used on their products logos and symbols depicting leading military commanders and battle scenes.

One outstanding contemporary example of a successful British Army commander becoming a highly visible and influential component of various forms of popular culture was Field Marshal Viscount Garnet J. Wolseley. After his triumph in the Second Ashanti War (1873–1874), Wolseley became a popular hero in England. Prominent actor George Grossmith made himself up as Wolseley to sing "The Modern Major-General" in Gilbert and Sullivan's *The Pirates of Penzance* and caricatured his mannerisms and dress, and it became a national habit, in an emergency, to "send for Wolseley" (Morris 1973, p. 402). "All Sir Garnet" became the universal tonic for every national ailment, and "cough syrup and boot-polish manufacturers, as well as music-hall lyricists, who used his brand name to admonish the public, helped to perpetuate the legend of his enduring effectiveness" (Preston 1967a, p. xiii). The press sang praises of Wolseley, whom Prime Minister Benjamin Disraeli gave the sobriquet of "our only General" (Lehmann 1964, p. 283).

While Wolseley was in Cyprus in 1879, the Zulu War broke out. After the disastrous debacle at Isandlwana (22 February 1879), at which some 800 European and 500 native troops were wiped out, Wolseley was chosen by the government to restore the situation. The popular magazine *Punch* expressed this sentiment:

When Wolseley's mentioned, Wellesley's brought to mind
Two men, two names, of answerable kind:
Call to the front, like Wellesley, good at need,
Go, Wolseley, and like Wellesley, greatly speed.
(Lehmann 1964, p. 245)

This play on the similarity between Wolseley's name and that of Field Marshal Arthur Wellesley, First Duke of Wellington, reassured the British public that all would be well.

During this same period, "our only other General" was Field Marshal Earl Frederick S. Roberts, V.C. The exploits of his men and his achievements in India were recorded by Rudyard Kipling, who also wrote two poems about Roberts.

During the second half of the Victorian era, the British Army became accepted and admired. It was the instrument for gaining and extending the British Empire, and its exploits fanned the flames of patriotism and jingoism, popularizing imperialism at the same time. The British Army's leaders, soldiers, and battles became a permanent part of Britain's popular culture.

See also Artists, War; Correspondents, War; Crimean War; Imperialism; Roberts, Field Marshal Frederick S., V.C.; Wellington, Field Marshal Arthur Wellesley, First Duke of; Wolseley, Field Marshal Garnet J.; Zulu War

References: Brereton (1986); Farwell (1981); Haythornthwaite (1995); Knight (1996); Lehmann (1964); Morris (1973); Preston (1967a); Raugh (1989)

Military Medicine, British Army–Enlistment Physical Standards

The physical standards for soldiers to enlist in the British Army fluctuated considerably during this period, although they decreased when there was a sudden demand for new soldiers, as in time of war. Physical standards were lowered later in the nineteenth century as the available manpower pool shrank and as the number of recruits coming from urban areas increased.

Prior to the Crimean War (1854–1856) many of the recruits came from rural areas and were considered healthier and more robust than their counterparts decades later. There was frequently no proper physical examination for recruits, or it was superficial, although they were required to declare any physical disability.

In 1861, the age limits of new recruits were 17 to 25 years with a minimum height of 5 feet, 8 inches. The minimum height was set at 5 feet, 6 inches in May 1869, but after the introduction of short service and recruiting shortfalls, the requirement was lowered in August 1870 to 5 feet, 4 inches. The height standards changed frequently, occasionally rising to 5 feet, 6 inches for infantry recruits, but they were usually lowered. From 1883 to 1889 the standard was only 5 feet, 3 inches, but it was 5 feet, 4 inches from 1889 to 1897, when it fell again, finally to 5 feet, 3 inches in 1900, during the Second Boer War.

In 1884, the minimum weight for new recruits was set at 115 pounds, and the minimum chest measurement for recruits under 5 feet, 6 inches in height was 33 inches. Ironically, as the standard of living and health of most Britons improved with economic, demographic, and medical improvements, the British Army was forced to lower its standards and enlist smaller and younger men. Even then, recruits not meeting the physical standards could be enlisted on a conditional basis as "special enlistments." These "specials," which increased from 18 percent to 36 percent of all enlistments during the 1890s, were anticipated to meet the minimum physical standards within four months after enlistment. Even with lowered physical standards, the number of recruits rejected by medical examinations increased from 4,600 men in 1861 to 23,370 in 1898.

In 1901, by which time all recruits received thorough physical examinations by army doctors, the most common physical reasons for rejection were: inadequate chest measurement, 6.4 percent; defective vision, 4.2 percent; and being underweight, 3.4 percent.

See also Boer War, Second (1899–1902); Crimean War; Rank and File, British Army—Enlistment; Recruiting

References: Brereton (1986); Moyse-Bartlett (1974); Skelley (1977); Spiers (1992); Strachan (1984)

Military Medicine, British Army—Hospitals and Soldier Treatment

The medical treatment of British Army soldiers improved considerably from 1815 to 1914 as public awareness grew and medical and scientific advances were made.

During the first half of this period, sick or wounded soldiers were treated by their regimental medical officer, with two assistant surgeons and assisted by an enlisted dispenser, at their regimental hospital. This regimental hospital was a tent in the field or a separate barrack block in garrison and could generally hold up to thirty soldiers. If the soldier had a serious injury or disease while in garrison, he was sent to a general hospital in Chatham, Dublin, or Cork, or later to Woolwich and Netley. General hospitals, with permanent staffs, could hold between 200 and 300 soldier inpatients.

The Crimean War (1854–1856) exposed the inadequacy of the British Army medical services. In the Crimea, tactics dictated that attacks continue, regardless of casualties, to maintain the momentum of the offensive. Only after the battle was over would the wounded receive any type of treatment. Generally, the bandsmen, who had no medical training, would carry the wounded to the regimental hospital tent in the rear. By that time, many wounded soldiers who could have lived with prompt treatment had already died or were suffering from infection. Regimental surgeons, generally overwhelmed after a large battle when there were thousands of casualties, did the best they could with rudimentary instruments. Sword and bayonet wounds were sewn up, bullets were probed for and extracted, and severely damaged limbs were quickly amputated, hacked off with a large knife or saw. Even though chloroform had been introduced as a general anesthetic in 1847, the British Army inspector-general of hospitals reportedly forbade its use, "on the grounds that pain was a stimulant to recovery" (Baylen and Conway 1968, pp. 16–17). As a result, soldiers were frequently given a slug of rum or whiskey or, if that was unavailable, had a rag stuffed in their mouth or were told to "bite the bullet" before surgery.

Evacuation from the regimental hospitals to ships 3 miles from the battlefield was tortuous and difficult, in large measure because the British Army commander in chief had deliberately instructed that no regimental hospital equipment or field ambulance units were to accompany the original expedition. Some local wagons were acquired, and seamen also carried the wounded in hammocks slung on poles.

Ships took these wounded and ill soldiers to Scutari, where the largest base hospital could accommodate 1,086 patients. Conditions were unsanitary, the soldiers were overcrowded, and equipment, medicine, and supplies were in short supply. Florence Nightingale headed the Scutari hospital female nursing staff and made significant improvements over the winter of 1854–1855.

Medical care and treatment improved after the Crimean War, especially while on active service. There were fewer gunshot wounds during the colonial wars, and most wounds were slashing and stabbing wounds. Regimental surgeons, who were better trained and had supplies of anesthesia, tried to repair injured limbs rather than immediately amputate them.

Various reorganizations and more sophisticated equipment permitted the British to treat and evacuate their wounded more efficiently and effectively during the Second Boer War (1899–1902). Each rifle company had one noncommissioned officer and two trained stretcher bearers attached to it, and these personnel evacuated the wounded to the battalion aid station. Stretcher bearers from the stretcher bearer company took the wounded to the next echelon of treatment, the brigade field hospital, which had five officers and forty other personnel. It was intended for the temporary treatment of up to 100 patients.

Medical facilities for more serious cases were not mobile. Next was the stationary hospital, organized for 100 patients on stretchers, whose personnel included 4 officers and 41 other ranks. The general hospital, normally at the end of the line of communications, had 166 personnel assigned to it, including 20 medical officers, 1 quartermaster, and 145 other ranks, all belonging to the Royal Army Medical Corps. There were also 8, and later 20, female nurses assigned to each general hospital. General Hospital No. 2 in Pretoria, for example, had 1,200 beds. The British also operated 4 hospital trains and 10 hospital ships during the Second Boer War.

See also Boer War, Second (1899–1902); Crimean War; Military Medicine, British Army—Medical Personnel; Military Medicine, British Army—Sanitation; Nightingale, Florence; Royal Army Medical Corps

References: Baylen and Conway (1968); de Villiers (1984); Edgerton (1999); Kaufman (2001); Skelley (1977); Spiers (1992); Watt (1992)

Military Medicine, British Army—Medical Personnel

After the Napoleonic Wars, the British Army relied on regimental surgeons, two assistant surgeons, and a dispenser, to provide medical care to its soldiers at the regimental level. Military medical personnel became better trained, performed more functions, and made greater contributions to the army as medical and scientific advances were made.

Little progress in the medical field was made until the Crimean War (1854–1856), a large conflict the Army Medical Department was woefully ill prepared for. A hospital corps of about 600 trained wagon drivers, stretcher bearers, and hospital orderlies was established in April 1854 for Crimean service. In 1854, there were 667 medical officers serving on the staff or with regiments; an additional 174 were contracted for the Crimea. This allocated one doctor to every 144 men, hypothetically sufficient for a force of 25,000—although the British force grew to over 60,000 soldiers, who suffered from unimaginable privation, grievous wounds, and cholera without adequate medical supplies or facilities.

Having read of these horrible conditions and soldier suffering in the Crimea, Florence Nightingale volunteered to head a female nursing staff at the military hospital at Scutari. She initially recruited thirty-eight female nurses to serve with her. Nightingale made significant improvements in hospital, bedding, and clothing cleanliness; diets; and medical supply availability and organization. Her assistance improved hospital conditions for the soldiers in the Crimea, especially over the first harsh winter of 1854–1855.

After the Crimean War, the Army Hospital Corps was established in 1857. It consisted of soldiers who enlisted specifically for medical service and attended a special two-month course at Aldershot. In 1883, there were 2,000 men in the Army Hospital Corps. The Army Nursing Service was formed in 1861.

Administrative reforms were made in 1873 to consolidate precious medical personnel and resources, make them more efficient, and standardize medical treatment. Medical officers were removed from regimental control and assigned to either one of the two general hospitals (at Netley and Woolwich) or base hospitals, under control of the Army Medical Corps. Improvements were made in the pay and status of medical officers.

After inadequacies in medical personnel competence and treatment were revealed in the British expedition to Egypt in 1882, a select committee recommended additional training for medical noncommissioned officers and men. The committee also recommended improvements in training and an expansion of the female nursing service. (Seven female nurses had accompanied the British force to South Africa in 1879, and 32 served in Egypt and the Sudan between 1882 and 1885.) The number of female army nurses was expanded from 60 in 1890 to 72 in 1898. The Royal Army Medical Corps (RAMC), consolidating all male medical personnel and activities, was formed in 1898.

The Second Boer War (1899–1902) was the first conflict in which each soldier was issued a first aid dressing. Each company had attached to it one medical noncommissioned officer and two stretcher bearers to take the wounded soldiers to the battalion aid station. The battalion aid station was the lowest level at which a surgeon or physician served. About 800 army nurses also served in the Second Boer War, serving no closer to the front lines than in ambulance trains and at railheads. About 8,500 medical personnel, of whom about three-quarters were contracted civilians, served in the Second Boer War.

Queen Alexandra's Imperial Military Nursing Service was formed and replaced the Army Nursing Service in 1902.

See also Boer War, Second (1899–1902); Crimean War; Nightingale, Florence; Royal Army Medical Corps
References: de Villiers (1984); Kaufman (2001); Skelley (1977); Spiers (1992); Summers (1988)

Military Medicine, British Army—Sanitation

Reformers discovered during the Crimean War that the British soldier was living in a filthy environment, and that his unsanitary environment would need to be improved to ensure soldier fitness for duty and productivity.

Florence Nightingale, whose prestige in 1856 was immense as a result of her work in Crimean hospitals, and Secretary at War Sidney Herbert were largely responsible for the establishment of the army Sanitary Commission in 1857. They compared army and civilian sanitary and living conditions to show the generally miserable state of the soldier's health and that his mortality was twice that of the average male in England. This unhealthy, unsanitary environment, more than anything else, contributed to the high rate of sickness and disease in the army. Barracks had been built without adequate ventilation, heating, lighting, water, and sewage disposal, and were frequently overcrowded, often including soldiers' wives and families. The commission's 1857 report recommended 600 cubic feet of living space for each soldier, while the existing regulations required 450 cubic feet, which compared atrociously with the 480 or more cubic feet allowed paupers in Scottish poorhouses.

Efforts to improve the soldiers' environment were only partially successful. Public and political interest waned in the 1860s, the government wanted to minimize expenditures, and the Army Sanitary Commission was allowed to lapse. Progress in soldiers' health continued, and in 1873 the regimental medical officer was required "to be particular in observing the married soldiers' quarters and is to report to the Commanding Officer if they are not kept in a proper state of cleanliness" (Maitland 1950, p. 113). By the mid-1880s, most serious sanitary and other problems in barracks had been corrected. Improvements had also been made in the soldiers' diet, more facilities for personal hygiene were provided, and more opportunities for washing clothes and bedding were made available.

British participation in the Second Boer War (1899–1902) revealed a continued lack of understanding of various aspects of sanitation, notably the importance of clean drinking water. Soldiers frequently drank contaminated water, which caused massive outbreaks of typhoid fever. Of the 556,653 British soldiers who served in the Second Boer War, 57,684 contracted typhoid. The British lost 7,582 soldiers killed in action, but 8,225 died from typhoid.

Scientific and medical advances led to a better understanding of the connection between infectious diseases, notably tuberculosis, respiratory ailments, and fevers, and environment. After the Second Boer War, the British Army founded a School of Sanitation at Ash Vale, near Aldershot, and barracks improvements and renovations were made through 1906.

See also Boer War, Second (1899–1902); Military Medicine, British Army—Venereal Disease; Nightingale, Florence
References: Burroughs (1980); de Villiers (1984); Maitland (1950); May (1984); Skelley (1977); Smith (1971)

Military Medicine, British Army—Venereal Disease

Venereal diseases, in spite of increased awareness, improved sanitation, temperance, and more facilities and opportunities for soldier recreation, plagued the British Army throughout the nineteenth century.

Florence Nightingale, nurse and pioneer medical reformer, was appalled at the high incidence of venereal disease in the Crimea, where it was the fourth major cause—

after malnutrition, tuberculosis, and dysentery—of disablement and hospitalization. After the Crimean War programs were initiated to improve sanitation, even though the issue of venereal disease was a delicate social problem generally ignored by society, and the British Army attempted to control venereal diseases. In 1859, for example, there were 422 admissions to army hospitals caused by venereal disease for every 1,000 soldiers, and the following year 369 cases per 1,000 men. There was a very bad outbreak of venereal disease in 1862 in Great Britain among troops recently returned from India, where the disease was rife.

The government was pressured to enact medical reforms. The first Contagious Diseases Act was passed in 1864, requiring compulsory hospitalization for women thought to be prostitutes in military areas. The 1864 act was generally ineffective, and the Act for the Better Prevention of Contagious Diseases was passed two years later. The 1866 act, among other provisions, enlarged military areas in which women suspected of prostitution could be detained for medical examination and decreed more severe penalties for brothel keepers.

In about 1860, the army estimated that venereal diseases caused 33 percent of all hospitalizations. This rate decreased to 29 percent in 1864 and to 20 percent in 1867. A third act in 1869 again enlarged the military areas and required incarceration for suspected prostitutes. The Contagious Diseases Acts were later considered degrading and were repealed in 1886.

In 1873, the army decided to dock the wages of soldiers found to have venereal diseases, and this resulted in a large decrease in reported cases in 1873–1874. In 1875, however, it was discovered that soldiers were failing to report their disease and trying to treat it themselves.

Venereal diseases were more rampant in the British forces serving in India, even though brothels were inspected and operated and prostitutes regulated by military authorities. The clamor of religious moralists in Great Britain caused military brothels to be closed temporarily in 1888. The venereal disease rate for British soldiers in India then skyrocketed, from 361 hospital admissions for every 1,000 soldiers in 1887 to 438.1 per 1,000 in 1890–1893, at which time the rate for soldiers in Britain was "only" 203.7 per 1,000.

Military brothels were reopened in India in 1899. The imposition of stricter controls resulted in a decrease in the venereal disease rate of 536 hospital admissions per 1,000 British soldiers in India in 1895 to 67 per 1,000 in 1909.

Many regiments by that time operated their own brothels, with patrons restricted to British soldiers.

See also Crimean War; India, British Army in; Military Medicine, British Army—Sanitation; Nightingale, Florence
References: Blanco (1967); Farwell (1989); Skelley (1977); Smith (1971)

Military Music

Military forces have been accompanied by music for millennia. Music has been used to instill discipline and aid drill and precision movements, to give orders and signals during maneuvers and in combat, to instill confidence on the battlefield, to entertain and enhance morale, and to overawe an adversary.

In Britain, one fife and one drum were authorized in the 1500s for each company of 100 infantrymen. This seems to have been the beginning of military and regimental bands, probably under the influence of the French Army. The first bands were formed in the early eighteenth century and consisted of a small number of musicians who played instruments such as horns, bassoons, and drums. Scottish regiments generally also had pipers, albeit unofficially, in their bands beginning in 1633. Bands were usually maintained privately by the officers of each regiment.

The official British Army trumpet and bugle calls, or "sounds," were first codified and issued in 1798. These included reveille to wake the soldiers at 6:00 A.M., through lights out at 10:15 P.M. The regulation bugle calls were reputedly composed not by an Englishman, but by the Austrian composer Franz Joseph Haydn.

While the British Army was on active service in the Crimean War (1854–1856), a grand review was held in honor of Queen Victoria's birthday. The bands of the various regiments were massed and played "God Save the Queen." The music was played in many different arrangements and in differing keys, and it became obvious that some type of organization and standardization was needed for the military bands. As a result, the British School of Music was established in 1857 at Kneller Hall, Twickenham.

The ceremony of playing "Long Reveille" was also instituted during the Crimean War. This was probably the first example of a performance of the Massed Pipes and Drums of the Highland Brigade, also notable because pipers had been officially recognized as such in 1854.

Regiments generally had their own music and their own

slow march and quick march as well. The Leicestershire Regiment's band, for example, always played "Wolfe's Lament" before the national anthem. The Grenadier Guards had "The British Grenadier," a popular tune that was adopted by other regiments. Many regiments had tunes that reminded them of their home counties, such as the Lincolnshire Regiment's "The Lincolnshire Poacher" and the Suffolk Regiment's quick march, "Speed the Plough." Regimental bands also gave concerts for their soldiers.

British soldiers frequently sang songs, especially while marching (such as during the long treks of the Second Boer War), to help make the time go by quicker and to raise their morale. Many soldiers' songs, however, are too crude or ribald to appear in print.

See also Boer War, Second (1899–1902); Communications; Crimean War; Discipline and Justice, British Army; Military and Popular Culture

References: Brereton (1986); Farwell (1981); Keeling and MacLellan (1973)

Militia

The militia was the oldest of the auxiliary forces, tracing its roots back to King Alfred in the ninth century. It first appeared in the statute books in 1558. The militia had a formal statutory existence from 1558 to 1604, 1648 to 1735, 1757 to 1831, and from 1852 to 1908.

Initially, the militia was responsible to the county high sheriff, and later to the lord lieutenant, thus being a truly "territorial" force. Militia officers were generally required to be local landowners. Service in the militia was usually voluntary, with certain categories of people, including peers, soldiers, clergy, and so on, being exempt from service.

The Militia Act of 1852 revived the militia both in numbers and effectiveness. It also fixed the strength of the militia at 80,000 men to be raised by voluntary recruitment. During the Crimean War (1854–1856) many militia regiments performed useful services in garrison duty in the Mediterranean Sea, replacing regular battalions that deployed to active service in the Crimea.

An important requirement for modernization of the British Army as contained in the Cardwell Reforms of the early 1870s was the "localization" of the military system in territorial areas, where line regiments would be linked with militia regiments. This was especially important for recruiting purposes. This was accomplished by dividing Britain into sixty-six districts, following county boundaries as much as possible. Each district consisted of two regular battalions (one was generally on overseas service), two militia battalions, and volunteers. The Localization Act of 1872 also transferred control of the militia and volunteers from the lords lieutenant to the Crown.

The linked battalion system was completed in 1881 with the amalgamation of many regular regiments. At that time militia battalions were redesignated as the 3rd (and sometimes 4th) battalion of regular infantry regiments, without changing their militia status.

Service in the militia was also an alternate method of achieving an army career, because most direct commissions were given to militia officers. In the latter decades of Queen Victoria's reign, about 150 new officers were commissioned each year after having served at least fifteen months in the militia.

During the Second Boer War (1899–1902) militia battalions not only provided home defense and garrisoned Mediterranean bases, but they also served and fought well in South Africa.

In 1908, the yeomanry and volunteer infantry battalions were merged to form the Territorial Force, under War Office supervision. At the same time, the militia ceased to exist and its units were transferred to the Special Reserve, where they retained their battalion designation in the regimental system, with the task of providing drafts for the regulars in wartime.

See also Boer War, Second (1899–1902); Cardwell Reforms; Crimean War; Haldane, Richard B.; Home Defense; Officers, British Army—Sources of Commissioning; Volunteers; Yeomanry

References: Barnett (1970); Farwell (1981); Mills (1996)

Minié Rifle

See Bullets; Infantry, British Army—Small Arms

Miranzai Field Force (1891)

The Orakzai tribe of the Pathans, like many other North-West Frontier tribes, became increasing hostile toward the British after the outbreak of the Second Afghan War in 1878. The Orakzais had an earlier history of belligerency and banditry and had begun minor hostilities in 1855 that were suppressed.

In 1891, after the Orakzais had become more defiant and

conducted numerous cross-border raids, the British sent a punitive expedition, commanded by Brigadier General (later General) Sir William S. A. Lockhart, to the Miranzai Valley. Lockhart's force was divided into three columns, commanded by Colonel A. McC. Bruce, Lieutenant Colonel A. H. Turner, and Lieutenant Colonel C. C. Brownlow, respectively. After a delay caused by bad weather, the force assembled at Gwada in the Khanki Valley on 29 January 1891. The three columns conducted mobile operations and destroyed villages so quickly that the Orakzais came to terms and agreed to the construction of three fortified posts on the Samana Ridge and roads connecting them, overlooking the Miranzai Valley. With its mission apparently completed, the force was disbanded the following month.

During the construction of the positions on the Samana Ridge, hostile Orakzai tribesmen attacked the working parties' military escort on 24 April 1891. The tribesmen were concerned that the British would annex the area and decided to conduct a preemptive strike. British reinforcements were sent to the area and the Miranzai Field Force was reformed for a second expedition. Again commanded by Lockhart, the force consisted of three columns and a cavalry brigade. Colonel Sym commanded the 1st Column, and the 2nd and 3rd Columns were commanded by the same officers from the first expedition. Colonel Biscoe commanded the Cavalry Brigade.

The Miranzai Field Force for the second expedition was assembled and prepared for operations by 16 April 1891. Little opposition was encountered although the troops suffered in the heat with a shortage of water while occupying the Samana Ridge on 17 and 18 April. A short but fierce engagement was fought at Gulistan on 20 April, resulting in a British victory and one man killed and four wounded. The Orakzais lost about 200 men.

Lockhart's force doggedly pursued the Orakzais throughout April and the first week of May, with the tribesmen surrendering at Gulistan on 9 May 1891. The Miranzai Field Force was broken up for a second time later in late May, although one native mountain battery and three infantry regiments remained to ensure that the outposts were constructed on Samana Ridge.

See also Afghan War, Second (1878–1880); India; Indian Army Operations; Lockhart, General Sir William S. A.; North-West Frontier

References: Barthorp (1982); Haythornthwaite (1995); Miller (1977); Nevill (1912)

Mobilization Planning

The British Army did not have any mobilization plans when the Prussians mobilized its reserves with unprecedented rapidity and decisively defeated the French in the Franco-Prussian War (1870–1871). The British took steps, initially ineffective, to develop their own mobilization and deployment plans.

In 1875, the British produced a mobilization plan in which the home forces were organized into brigades, divisions, and army corps, each with its own staff organization and headquarters. The plan included assembly areas for reservists and logistical centers. This plan was based on an army of eight corps, for which available regular and auxiliary infantry troops were sufficient to provide unit cadres; there were insufficient cavalry, artillery, and other support troops to fill the proposed eight corps. The 1875 mobilization plan was ineffective, as shown in the chaotic partial mobilization exercise involving two corps in 1876. The 1875 plan was ignored when one corps was mobilized in 1878.

The prevailing method of operations was that when an expeditionary force was needed overseas, a commander was designated, available units were hastily assembled, organized into provisional brigades, equipped, and sent to their destination. Such ad hoc arrangements could only work in the case of small, colonial wars.

After the 1882 British expedition to Egypt, the Gordon Relief Expedition in the Sudan (1884–1885), and the war scare with Russia in 1885 over the Penjdeh Incident, the recently appointed director of military intelligence, Major General (later General) Sir Henry Brackenbury, drew up realistic mobilization plans. He conducted a systematic analysis of all military forces available and how they could best be organized. Brackenbury arranged the force structure so that after units for home defense and colonial garrison duty were allocated, there would be enough troops remaining to organize and fill two army corps of regular soldiers, plus a cavalry division and supply and support troops. This scheme, which became the standard for later plans, was controversial at the time, because it revealed the British Army's lack of readiness and would require significant expense to accomplish. The two army corps mobilization plan was endorsed by the secretary of state for war, Edward Stanhope, and it was a key component of his 1888 Stanhope Memorandum, which enumerated and prioritized British Army missions. In early 1888, mobilization planning had increased significantly and was transferred from the Intelligence Branch directly to the office of the adjutant-general.

Mobilization for the Second Boer War, while unprecedented and generally successful, was hindered by a number of factors. Officers designated to be unit commanders and staff officers upon mobilization did not always hold those positions in peacetime, and there was a staff shortage in many units. On other occasions, mobilization plans were altered for no reason other than to organize "fancy" brigades, such as Scotch or Irish brigades.

In late 1901, during the Second Boer War, the Mobilization Division was again amalgamated with the Intelligence Division. The new organization was headed by a lieutenant general, designated the director general of mobilization and military intelligence. One of the Esher Committee recommendations carried out in 1904 was to transfer the Mobilization Division of the Intelligence Department to the Directorate of Military Training.

See also Arabi Rebellion; Boer War, Second (1899–1902); Brackenbury, General Sir Henry; Esher Committee; Gordon Relief Expedition; Home Defense; Penjdeh Incident; Stanhope Memorandum; War Office

References: Fergusson (1984); Hamer (1970); Kochanski (1999); Spiers (1992); Wheeler (1914)

Modder River, Battle of (28 November 1899)

The Battle of Modder River (28 November 1899) showed that leaders and tactics, in light of advanced weapons technology, needed to be flexible to meet changing battlefield conditions.

The British forces in South Africa were divided into three main forces in November 1899 to accomplish three different missions. The westernmost force, the 10,000-man 1st Division commanded by Lieutenant General (later Field Marshal) Lord Paul S. Methuen, was given the task of relieving Kimberley. On 21 November, his force began the 75-mile advance north from Orange River Station, encountering Boer forces and winning engagements at Belmont (23 November) and Graspan (25 November). The next significant obstacle on the march was the Modder River, about 21 miles south of Kimberley.

On 27 November 1899, 1,500 Boers led by Assistant Commandant-General Piet A. Cronje had arrived from Mafeking and joined Assistant Commandant-General Jacobus De la Rey's force, about 3,500 men with six Krupp guns. De la Rey, who had fought at Belmont and Graspan, began to appreciate the need to alter conventional tactics.

The Boers had been placing their artillery on the crests of steep hills, believing them impregnable. But in fact these crests were easily identifiable targets and highly vulnerable to counterbattery fire, and the slopes of the hills protected the attacker. Moreover, plunging fire from rifles greatly reduced their range and effectiveness. The horizontal, flat trajectory of the Mausers would increase their lethality and permit them to fire to the limit of their 2,200-yard range. De la Rey decided to place his force in the bed of the Riet River (and centered on the railroad bridge that crossed over it), near its confluence with the Modder River. This was in essence a large and deep trench, and its southern lip provided ideal cover and concealment for a firing line.

Early on 28 November 1899, with inadequate intelligence, Methuen hurriedly ordered an attack. He also had inaccurate maps and believed the rivers could be easily forded. The British advanced at about 7:00 A.M. on a 3-mile front, with the 9th Brigade on the left (west) of the railway line and the Guards Brigade on the right, toward the Modder Bridge at the river junction. When the British were 1,200 yards from the unseen enemy positions, the Boers, using smokeless powder, opened fire prematurely with a hail of bullets. The British were pinned down in the scorching heat, with the Guards Brigade unable to advance. Shortly after noon, elements of the 9th Brigade moved around the Boer right flank. Boers on the right flank, subject to friendly fire from the north river bank, retreated, and a further British advance was halted.

Methuen, who had exercised little command and control over the battle, was wounded at about 4:00 P.M. The operation became even more disorganized as darkness fell and the firing faded away. The British postponed a planned attack, and the Boers decided to abandon their positions that night.

The Battle of Modder River was a costly victory for the British, who lost 70 all ranks killed and 413 wounded, as compared to Boer casualties of about 150. Methuen, with little enemy intelligence, faulty maps, and inadequate communications, rode bravely around the battlefield like a junior officer, but he failed to exercise proper command and control of the operation. Most importantly, the Battle of Modder River demonstrated the futility of frontal assaults against an entrenched enemy.

See also Boer War, Second (1899–1902); Boers; Cronje, Assistant Commandant-General Piet A.; De la Rey, Assistant Commandant-General Jacobus; Mafeking, Siege of; Methuen, Field Marshal Paul S.
References: Belfield (1975); Miller (1996); Nasson (1999); Pakenham (1979)

Mohammed Ahmed bin Seyyid Abdullah
See Mahdi

Mohmand Field Force (1897)
The general uprising by Pathan tribes on the North-West Frontier that began in July 1897 sparked many smaller tribal insurgencies and hostilities.

On 7 August 1897, about 5,000 Mohmands entered British territory and attacked the border post at Shabkadr Fort, about 18 miles north of Peshawar. The garrison held out for over twelve hours until the Peshawar Movable Column, commanded by Colonel Woon, arrived and reinforced it. The next day Woon marched his force to attack the tribesmen on the plateau near the fort, but before this was accomplished, Brigadier General E. R. Elles arrived from Peshawar and assumed command of operations. As the Mohmands advanced on the British, two squadrons of the 13th Bengal Lancers conducted an audacious cavalry charge and disrupted the enemy attack.

To pacify the Mohmands, it was decided to form the two-brigade Mohmand Field Force, commanded by Elles. The 1st Brigade was commanded by Brigadier General R. Westmacott and consisted of the 1st Battalion, Somerset Light Infantry; 20th Punjabis; and 2nd Battalion, 1st Gurkhas. Brigadier General C. R. Macgregor commanded the 2nd Brigade, composed of the 2nd Battalion, Oxfordshire Light Infantry; six companies of the 37th Dogras; and the 9th Gurkhas. Divisional troops included the 13th Bengal Lancers, Jodhpur Lancers, two mountain batteries, three Maxim machine guns, and supporting elements. Elles was instructed to coordinate operations with the Malakand Field Force, commanded by Brigadier General (later General) Sir Bindon Blood.

The Mohmand Field Force began its advance on 14 September 1897 over barren terrain through intense heat to Gandab. After reconnoitering the area, the Mohmand Field Force linked up with Blood's Malakand Field Force on 20 September, and Blood's 3rd Brigade (commanded by Colonel Graves) was attached to Elles's force. Two days later, the Mohmand Field Force attacked enemy positions on the Badmanai Pass. The Mohmands defended gallantly at first but could not withstand the British onslaught, supported by artillery and a Maxim gun, and fled before the British reached their positions. The British lost one killed and six wounded; Mohmand casualties are unknown.

Continuing the advance on 23 September 1897, the Mohmand Field Force met little opposition other than occasional sniping, and it destroyed many villages in its path. The razing of additional villages produced signs that the tribesmen were willing to come to terms, which were negotiated on 28 September. The Mohmands were fined and required to surrender many of their weapons. The mission of the Mohmand Field Force had been accomplished, and it was disbanded, with some units sent to the Malakand and Tirah Field Forces. The Mohmand Field Force, which lost four soldiers killed and twenty-five wounded during its operations, had traveled to areas never before visited by British forces and demonstrated that cross-border depredations would not be tolerated.

See also Blood, General Sir Bindon; India; Indian Army Operations; Malakand Field Force; North-West Frontier; Tirah Field Force
References: Barthorp (1982); Featherstone (1973); Haythornthwaite (1995); Miller (1977); Nevill (1912); Pioneer (1898)

Morse Code
See Communications

Mudki, Battle of (18 December 1845)
See Sale, Major General Sir Robert; Sikh War, First (1845–1846)

Multan, Siege of (1848–1849)
See Gujerat, Battle of; Sikh War, Second (1848–1849)

N

Nana Sahib (c. 1821–?)

Nana Sahib was a leader of the mutineers at Cawnpore, after initially supporting the British. His most infamous act was to order the slaughter of about 200 British women and children in Cawnpore in July 1857.

One of the adopted sons of the last Peshwa of Bithur, Baji Rao II, a Mahratta monarch, Nana Sahib's real name was Dhondu Pant. He was born in about 1821. Baji Rao II had been dethroned by the British, who took his land in exchange for a pension of about £80,000 per year. When Baji Rao II died in 1851, his pension stopped, and Nana Sahib attempted repeatedly, without success, to have the pension reinstated. He retained the courtesy title of Maharajah of Bithur.

Mutinies of native regiments occurred throughout early 1857, at about the same time Nana Sahib traveled to Lucknow to meet with the British financial commissioner about his father's pension. Nana Sahib, rebuffed by the British, stated that events in Cawnpore required him to return quickly to nearby Bithur. The British were suspicious, but Nana Sahib returned to Cawnpore with his own armed retinue and offered his services to the British. Nana Sahib's men were assigned to guard the treasury.

As the word of the massacre at Meerut and other mutinies reached Cawnpore, the situation grew tense until finally, on the night of 5 June 1857, some of the Cawnpore native regiments mutinied. They broke into the treasury, reportedly assisted by some of Nana Sahib's men. A deputation of mutineers approached Nana Sahib and asked him to lead the mutineers to Delhi. Disgruntled by the years of British refusals to reinstate his father's pension and other slights, Nana Sahib, ambitious and eager to regain his father's greatness, apparently decided it was no longer to his advantage to side with the British. Nana Sahib intended to lead the mutineers to Delhi but returned to Cawnpore to lead four mutinous regiments.

On 6 June 1857, Nana Sahib's rebels attacked the British defenders of Cawnpore. Outnumbered, the besieged British negotiated to surrender to Nana Sahib on 27 June, with plans for the survivors to be evacuated by boat. When the boats were loaded, a murderous fusillade rang out from the opposite shore. When the firing stopped, the men were separated from the women and children and all shot. About 125 women and children survived this massacre, and joined later by others, over 200 were crammed into a small house called the Bibighar, or the House of the Ladies.

A British relief force, commanded by Brigadier General (later Major General Sir) Henry Havelock, advanced on Cawnpore. Nana Sahib decided to execute all his hostages, who were butchered and dumped into a well. Havelock's force defeated the rebels on 16 July 1857, and Nana Sahib reportedly galloped away toward Bithur. After pretending to commit suicide in the Ganges River, Nana Sahib was never seen or heard from again. He may have died from fever in Nepal in 1859.

See also Cawnpore, Siege and Relief of; Havelock, Major General Sir Henry; India; Indian Mutiny; Rhani of Jhansi; Tantia Topi

References: Edwardes (1963); Featherstone (1992b); Hibbert (1978); Mason (1974); Ward (1996)

Napier, Admiral Sir Charles (1786–1860)

Charles Napier was a distinguished British naval officer with over a half century of service on the high seas. He is probably best known as commander of the Baltic Fleet from 1854 to 1855, during the Crimean War.

Born in Scotland on 6 March 1786, Napier entered the Royal Navy as a midshipman in 1799. Napier participated in numerous operations against the French during the Napoleonic Wars and fought against the Americans during the War of 1812.

In the early 1830s he served successfully as a vice admiral in the Portuguese Navy. Reinstated in the Royal Navy in 1834, he was promoted to commodore in 1839. Napier participated in the storming of Sidon in September 1839 and Acre the following month.

Napier was promoted to vice admiral in May 1853. The Russians attacked Turkey that summer, and the Turks declared war on Russia on 5 October 1853. The British (and later the French) fleets entered the Black Sea to bolster Turkey. War fever broke out in these countries, with British troops sailing in February 1854 and French soldiers a few weeks later for Turkey.

Napier was appointed commander of the hastily assembled Baltic Fleet and sailed for the Baltic on 10 March 1854. With British and French expeditionary forces en route to Turkey, Napier's mission was to seal the Baltic, destroy the Russian fleet, and protect Danish and Swedish shipping and territory from Russian attack.

War was declared on 28 March 1854. His fleet arrived at the entrance to the Gulf of Finland on 17 April 1854. When the weather deteriorated, Napier's fleet withdrew to Stockholm. He reconnoitered defenses at Hango and Sveaborg but found them to be too strong for his guns. Leaving ships at Sveaborg, Napier sailed for Kronstadt, arriving on 26 June 1854. Thirty Russian ships were anchored nearby. After a careful reconnaissance, it was determined that only shallow-draught ships could approach the Russian fortress.

Napier sailed back to Sveaborg and received word that 10,000 French soldiers with 10 guns would be sent on British ships to attack either Sveaborg or Bomarsund, guarding the best entrance to the large harbor on Aland. The allied force began bombarding Bomarsund, the more vulnerable of the two fortresses, on 13 August 1854, and it surrendered shortly thereafter. This success, however, achieved very little.

Napier wanted to continue operations, but the French fleet began to withdraw from the Baltic on 4 September 1854. The Royal Navy maintained the blockade on the Russians until the end of October 1854 then returned to port at Spithead. Napier was brusquely ordered, "you are hereby required and directed to strike your flag, and come on shore" (Judd 1975, p. 170).

This humiliating relief of command was the culmination of a long controversy between Napier and the Admiralty. Napier was eventually exonerated, and the Admiralty offered him award of the Knight Grand Cross—the highest class—of the Order of the Bath. As a sign of his contempt, Napier refused this honor.

Napier, called "Fighting Charlie" by his admirers and "Black" or "Dirty Charley" by others because of his swarthy complexion and sloppy dress, was promoted to admiral in 1858. He died in London on 8 November 1860.

See also Baltic Sea Operations, Crimean War; Crimean War
References: Judd (1975); Palmer (1987); Royle (2000); Warner (1972)

Napier, Field Marshal Robert C., First Baron Napier of Magdala and Carynton (1810–1890)

Robert C. Napier was a distinguished officer of the Indian Army who served with distinction in numerous campaigns in India and in China. He is best remembered as the commander of the British expedition to Abyssinia in 1867–1868.

Napier was born in 1810 in Colombo, Ceylon. His father was Major Charles F. Napier, who was mortally wounded while attacking the fort of Cornelis—the middle name given to the younger Napier—in Java shortly after his son was born. Napier was educated at Addiscombe, the College for East India Company military cadets, and was commissioned into the Bengal Sapper and Miners in 1828. In addition to participating in numerous campaigns, he also planned and supervised many military and civil construction projects in India and designed the Napier system of cantonments.

Napier saw considerable action during the First Sikh War (1845–1846). He fought at the Battles of Mudki and Ferozeshah and had a horse shot out from underneath him in each battle. Severely wounded at Ferozeshah, Napier recovered in time to participate in the Battle of Sobraon. During the Second Sikh War (1848–1849), he was present at the Siege of Multan and the Battle of Gujerat. In 1852, Napier commanded the right column in the Black Mountain expedition, and the following year he fought in another small campaign on the North-West Frontier.

Napier's star began to rise during the Indian Mutiny (1857–1859). Initially, he served as adjutant-general and military secretary to Major General (later Lieutenant General) Sir James Outram at Lucknow; as a brigadier general, he developed the plan to recapture the city. In the march to Gwalior, Napier was second in command to General (later Field Marshal) Sir Hugh H. Rose. Napier commanded the division in later operations in India. He also commanded the 2nd Division in the war against China in 1860 and was promoted to major general.

In 1865, Napier assumed command of the Bombay Army. Two years later, after being promoted to lieutenant general, he was appointed to command the expedition sent to Abyssinia to free hostages of Emperor Theodore. The Abyssinian campaign, although expensive, was a model of superior leadership and excellent planning. For his service, Napier was ennobled as the First Baron Napier of Magdala (the site of his greatest battle in Abyssinia) and Carynton and received the thanks of Parliament and two knighthoods.

From 1870 to 1876, Napier served as commander in chief, India, and was promoted to general in 1874. He served as governor of Gibraltar from 1876 to 1883, and was promoted to field marshal upon his retirement in 1883. Napier served as constable of the Tower of London from 1886 until 1889.

While Napier was undoubtedly an outstanding general, he had many interests outside soldiering. He painted in watercolors and enjoyed poetry. Napier also loved children. His first wife bore six children, and his second wife, nine. Napier died of influenza in London in 1890.

See also Abyssinian War; Addiscombe, Military Seminary; Bengal Army; Bombay Army; China War, Second (1856–1860); East India Company, Military Forces; Indian Mutiny; Magdala, Capture of; North-West Frontier; Outram, Lieutenant General Sir James; Rose, Field Marshal Hugh H.; Sikh War, First (1845–1846); Sikh War, Second (1848–1849); Theodore, Emperor

References: Bates (1979); Chandler (1967); Farwell (1972); Haythornthwaite (1995); Myatt (1970); Nevill (1912)

Napier, General Sir Charles J. (1782–1853)

General Sir Charles J. Napier was a professional soldier best known for the controversial conquest of Sind in 1843.

Napier was born in London in 1782, in a family that had important social and political connections. He was gazetted an ensign in 1794 and purchased higher ranks until he was a major in 1806. In 1807, Napier served in the short Danish campaign, and subsequently served with distinction in the Peninsular War and was severely wounded twice. He was posted with his regiment to Bermuda in 1812 and fought in the United States in 1813. In 1814, believing his active service was over, he went on half pay and missed the Waterloo campaign.

In 1819, Napier was posted to Corfu, and three years later he was reassigned to Cephalonia, an Ionian Island, as governor and military resident, and in 1825, he was promoted to colonel. In 1830, he had an argument with the high commissioner of the Ionian Islands and retired. Even though promoted to major general in 1837, Napier did not return to active duty until 1839, when he was appointed commander of the northern district of England. This was a period of Chartist disturbances, and Napier was responsible for maintaining law and order.

Napier was thereafter posted to India, and in September 1842, he was reassigned to Sind, an area east of the Indus River and Baluchistan that had served as a staging and transit area during the First Afghan War (1839–1842). Napier's task was to negotiate with the Sindian amirs a treaty more stringent than that of 1838. The amirs refused and attacked the British residency in Hyderabad on 15 February 1843. Napier considered this a pretext for war and soundly defeated the numerically superior Sindians in battle at Miani (17 February 1843) and at Dubba, near Hyderabad (24 March 1843). The British then annexed the 50,000-square-mile region of Sind. Napier's reportedly famous message of "*Peccavi*," Latin for "I have sinned," was more likely a *Punch* invention.

Napier's actions were very controversial, especially when they became known in Great Britain. It seems Napier had thwarted Sindian attempts at negotiation and reconciliation, and had intentionally provoked war, which in turn resulted in the unwarranted confiscation of private property. Major (later Lieutenant General Sir) James Outram, who had served at Hyderabad, argued that Napier had in fact destabilized Sind. The issue reached Parliament and resulted in the recall of the governor-general of India, although Napier, quarrelsome as ever, remained in Sind until 1847.

Napier returned to England but was recalled after the Battle of Chillianwalla (13 January 1849) to command troops in the area. The Second Sikh War ended before Napier returned to India, however, and he remained there for only a short time. After having a disagreement with the governor-general, he resigned. Napier died in 1853. Four years later his brother, General Sir William F. F. Napier, wrote *The History of*

General Sir Charles Napier's Conquest of Scinde to defend the conquest of Sind.

See also Afghan War, First (1839–1842); Outram, Lieutenant General Sir James; Purchase System; Sikh War, Second (1848–1849); Sind, Operations in
References: Farwell (1972); James (1997); Mason (1974); Napier (1857); Napier (1973); Rice (2002)

Nepal
See Gurkha War; Gurkhas

New Zealand
See Maori War, First (1843–1848); Maori War, Second (1863–1869); Maoris; Taranaki War

Nicholson, Brigadier General John (1822–1857)

Brigadier General John Nicholson was a dynamic, charismatic, and indefatigable Bengal Army leader, worshiped by some locals as a god named Nikalsain. He distinguished himself during the Indian Mutiny and was killed leading the attack on Delhi.

Nicholson was born in Ireland in December 1822 and was educated at Dungannon College. He received a Bengal Army cadetship in 1839 and served in the First Afghan War. Nicholson participated in the defense of Ghazni and was taken prisoner when the garrison surrendered on 1 March 1842, although he escaped by bribing a guard. He was later appointed political officer in various regions and was assigned to the British force during the Second Sikh War. After this conflict, Nicholson became deputy commissioner of the Bannu district, where he earned a reputation as a strict but fair disciplinarian. He reportedly personally pursued criminals and displayed their severed heads on his desk.

When the Indian Mutiny broke out in May 1857, Nicholson was deputy commissioner of Peshawar. Actions were taken immediately to disarm suspect native regiments, secure arsenals, and safeguard key positions. Nicholson was given command of the Punjab Moveable Column and advanced toward Delhi, disarming wavering sepoys and hanging mutineers en route.

Nicholson's column reinforced British forces, commanded by Brigadier General Archdale Wilson, on the Delhi Ridge on 14 August 1857. On 7 September 1857, the British began preparations for besieging Delhi, which they eventually stormed. The attack on Delhi, with Nicholson leading the main column and designated the overall assault force commander, began early on 14 September. The Kashmir Gate was captured, but a number of attempts to seize the Lahore Gate were unsuccessful. Nicholson then waved his sword above his head and faced his soldiers to exhort them to follow him. As he did so, his back was momentarily presented to the rebels, who shot him. His wound was fatal, although he lingered until 23 September.

See also Afghan War, First (1839–1842); Bengal Army; East India Company, Military Forces; Delhi, Siege and Storming of; Indian Mutiny; Sikh War, Second (1848–1849)
References: Edwardes (1963); Hibbert (1978); Hilton (1957); Leasor (1956); Waller (1990)

Nightingale, Florence (1820–1910)

Florence Nightingale was a leading progressive and reformer who sought to improve medical and sanitation conditions in the British Army, notably at the Scutari General Hospital during the Crimean War (1854–1856) and within British society as a whole.

Nightingale was born of wealthy British parents on 12 May 1820 in Florence, Italy. At age seventeen, Nightingale believed she was called by God to some unnamed great cause. She rejected many suitors, against her mother's wishes, and at age twenty-five declared she wanted to become a nurse. Her parents opposed this idea, as nursing was then considered beneath her class.

In London, Nightingale met Elizabeth Blackwell, the first woman to qualify as a doctor in the United States. This bolstered Nightingale's determination and in 1851 her father gave her permission to train as a nurse. After nursing studies in Germany, Nightingale served as resident lady superintendent of a hospital of invalid women in London.

The Crimean War broke out in 1854. The first large engagement of the war, the Battle of the Alma (20 September 1854), resulted in over 3,000 allied, mostly British, casualties. This high number of casualties, coupled with an outbreak of cholera two months earlier, overburdened the inadequate British medical system. The horrendous suffering was revealed to the British public via the pages of *The Times*. Nightingale read of these disgraceful medical conditions and volunteered to create a nursing service in the Crimea. The British Government accepted her proposal, and she was appointed Superintendent of the Female Nursing Establishment of the English General Hospitals in Turkey.

Arriving at the Scutari General Hospital with thirty-eight nurses in early November 1854, Nightingale met with a mixed reception. Many in the military considered her an interloper and were concerned that she had direct communications with the secretary for war in London. Nightingale, who had access to other funding sources, immediately set to work improving the filthy conditions of the hospital by washing sheets and blankets, establishing hygiene instructions to be given to the orderlies, improving patient diets, and streamlining the feeding process. She also organized the nursing services at Scutari. Additional contingents of female nurses arrived, and many served in the Crimea, although they were not under Nightingale's control. By her initial efforts, as well as skillful manipulation of the press and influential people, Nightingale emerged from the Crimean War with the reputation as the omnipresent "Lady with the Lamp" ostensibly checking on soldiers in the hospital wards at night. Perhaps more accurately, Nightingale "has monopolised the public imagination, and blotted out most of the history of Crimean War nursing" (Summers 1988, p. 47).

Nightingale returned to England as a heroine. She was instrumental in establishing the army Sanitary Commission in 1857 and helping improve the sanitation and quality of life in soldiers' barracks. She spent the rest of her life trying to improve standards of nursing and advocating women's rights. In 1895, she went blind and died an invalid in London on 13 August 1910.

See also Alma, Battle of the; Crimean War; Military Medicine, British Army—Medical Personnel; Military Medicine, British Army—Sanitation
References: Kaufman (2001); Palmer (1987); Royle (2000); Simkin (n.d.); Strachey (1918); Summers (1988)

Nordenfeldt Gun
See Machine Guns

North-West Frontier

The North-West Frontier was the border region between British India and Afghanistan created by the annexation of the Punjab in 1849 after the Second Sikh War. This barren and mountainous region was about 400 miles long, from the Pamir Mountains in the north to Baluchistan in the south, and about 100 miles wide, from the Hindu Kush ("killer of Hindus") Safed Koh-Sulieman ranges of mountains in the west to the Indus River in the east. From the Second Sikh War until the end of the nineteenth century, there were at least forty-two major campaigns on the North-West Frontier involving British troops.

The relatively well-defined western flank of the North-West Frontier, the Hindu Kush-Safed Koh-Sulieman mountain ranges vary in height from about 20,000 feet in the north to about 5,000 feet in the south. (This border between Afghanistan and the North-West Frontier, called the Durand Line, was delineated in 1893 after Sir Henry Mortimer Durand, foreign secretary to the Government of India, negotiated an agreement with the Afghani amir, Abdur Rahman.) The terrain resembles "a tangled mass of mountains and valleys, like an exaggerated Switzerland" (Nevill 1912, p. 2). Even at the turn of the twentieth century, this rugged region was largely unmapped. This mountainous, rough terrain, with precipitous peaks and narrow defiles, was ideal for tribal warfare characterized by ambushes, sniping, and other irregular warfare tactics.

The indigenous inhabitants of the North-West Frontier were generically called Pathans, a Pushtu-speaking Islamic race of fierce, independent warriors. The Pathans were said to number about 200,000 "of the most turbulent and finest fighting material in the world, unrestrained by civilised government and fired by fanaticism" (James 1997, p. 400). The Pathans were divided into tribes, which were further divided into clans *(khels)*.

There are a number of key passes, generally defiles or river courses, through the mountains leading from Afghanistan, through the North-West Frontier, to the Punjab. These significant terrain features, coupled with the ruggedness of the mountains, tended to frequently compartmentalize and isolate the homelands of the numerous tribes living there.

From north to south, the mountain passes or breaches of the North-West Frontier, as well as the tribes living in their vicinity, are listed below. (The first eight passes are all snowbound in winter.) Some tribes were more bellicose than others; the numbers listed in parentheses after a tribe's name indicates the approximate fighting strength of that tribe in about 1910.

1. Kilik Pass (15,600 feet). Due north of Hunza, leads across the extreme east of Afghan territory into

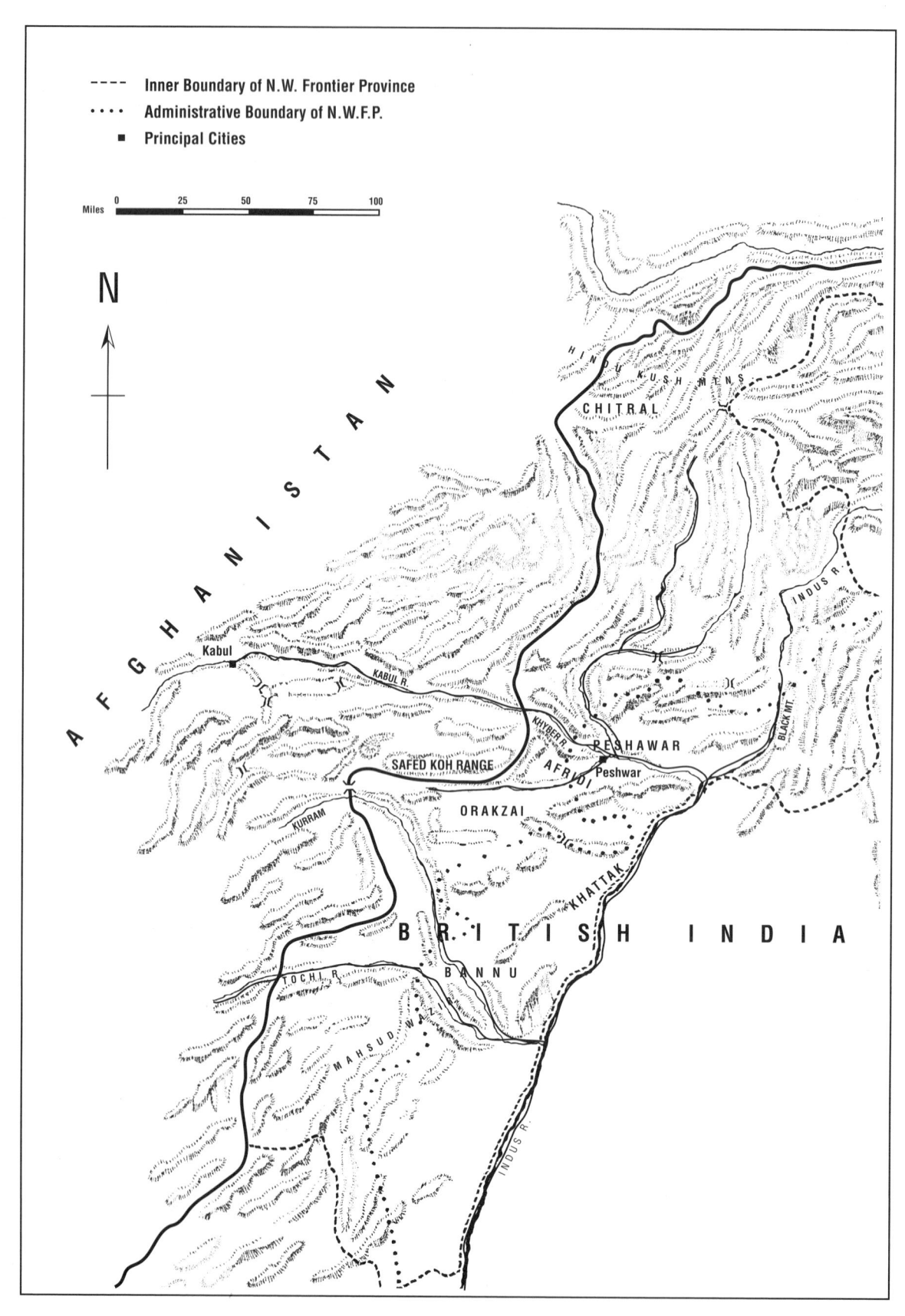

North-West Frontier of India

Russian Turkestan. The Kanjutis (5,000) lived in Hunza and Nagar.

2. Baroghil Pass (12,400 feet). Due north of Yasin, it leads to the center of the projecting finger of Afghan territory. Gilgitis (3,000), Punialis (400), and Yasinis (1,200) lived in this area.
3. Dorah Pass (14,800 feet). Northwest of Chitral, leads into Afghanistan.
4. Shawal Pass (14,100 feet). Southwest of Chitral, leads into Kafiristan.
5. Kuner River. Breaks through the mountains 50 miles south of Chitral. Chitralis (7,000), "treacherous, cruel, avaricious, revengeful" (Nevill 1912, p. 4) lived in this area.
6. Burzil Pass (13,800 feet). On the road between Srinigar and Gilgit.
7. Shandur Pass (12,250 feet). On the road from Gilgit to Chitral.
8. Lowarai Pass (10,250 feet). On the road from Nowshera to Chitral.
9. Binshi Pass (8,020 feet). On the road between Dir and the Afghani town Asmar. The Yusafzais, a large and important tribe, inhabited the area from the Black Mountain in the east to the Afghani border in the west. Subtribes include the Swatis (11,800), Tarkaris (39,000), Utman Khel (10,000), Bunerwals (8,000), Chagarzais (5,000), and Isazais (5,300).
10. Kabul River. The Mohmands (25,000) lived in this rocky and arid area. They were divided into nine clans, with the Safis in the north and the Shilmanis in the south. Their most martial clan was the Baizais. A separate clan was the Mullagoris (600), living south of the Kabul River.
11. Khyber Pass. This was the most important and most famous pass between India and Kabul. The nomadic Afridis (30,100), the most powerful of the frontier tribes, lived in the area bounded on the north by the Khyber Pass, on the east by Peshawar, on the south by the Mastura Valley, and on the west by the Safed Koh Mountains. They were said to have been "endowed with many martial qualities, but are rapacious, untrustworthy, and lawless by nature. They are constantly at feud with one another, but are always ready to unite in defence of their independence" (Nevill 1912, p. 7). The Afridis were divided into eight clans: Zakha Khel (5,000); Kuki Khel (5,000); Malikdin Khel (4,500); Kambar Khel (5,000); Kamrai Khel (700); Sipah (1,400); Aka Khel (2,000); and Adam Khel, including the Jowakis (6,500).
12. Kurram River. This area was inhabited by the Orakzais (30,000), which had seven clans, including the Massuzai, Chamkannis, Bizotis, and Rubia Khel. The Zaimukhts (4,000) and the Turis (7,000) also lived in the area.
13. Kaitu River. This passed through the territory of the relatively "lawless" Darwesh Khel Waziris.
14. Tochi River. Provided a direct route to Ghazni from Bannu, also passing through the territory of the Darwesh Khel Waziris.
15. Gomal River and Pass. A route generally used by camel caravans, with the Waziris (56,000) living to the north and the Zhob Valley tribes to the south. There were four Waziri clans: Darwesh Khel (29,000); Mahsuds (14,000); Dawaris (6,500); and Bhittanis (6,500).
16. Khojak Pass. Close to the Afghan border and on the road between Quetta and Kandahar.
17. Harnia Pass. Defile through which a railway runs.
18. Bolan Pass. Once a formidable obstacle, later traversed by a road and a railroad. The Baluchi tribes, of which the Zhob Valley inhabitants are a branch, live in the vicinity of the Khojak, Harnia, and Bolan Passes.

Internecine warfare and raiding formed a major part of the lives of the North-West Frontier tribes. After the Punjab was annexed in 1849, the British and Indian armies were brought into contact with the lawlessness of these tribes, which provoked numerous punitive expeditions and campaigns. In the eight years from the end of the Second Sikh War in 1849 to the Indian Mutiny, there were at least twenty British expeditions against tribes of the North-West Frontier. Between 1899 and 1906, local intelligence sources enumerated 602 raids and disturbances on the North-West Frontier (in 1901, the North-West Frontier had been organized as a province).

For the British officer, duty on the North-West Frontier was considered superb, realistic training, with slim chances of becoming a casualty. "The Frontier," according to one source, "remains a source of perpetual joy to the soldier, but to the politician a problem yet to be solved" (James 1997, p. 403).

See also Afghanistan; Buner Field Force; Durand, Sir Henry Mortimer; East India Company; Hazara Field Force; India; Indian Army Operations; Indian Mutiny; Malakand Field Force; Miranzai Field Force; Mohmand Field Force; Sikh War, First (1845–1846); Sikh War, Second (1848–1849); Sittana Field Force; Tirah Field Force; Tochi Field Force
References: Barthorp (1982); Featherstone (1989); Featherstone (1995); Fincastle and Eliott-Lockhart (1898); Hamilton (1966); James (1997); Miller (1977); Nevill (1912); Younghusband (1898)

Ntombe Drift, Battle of (12 March 1879)
See Zulu War

Officers, British Army—Pay

British Army officer pay rates were established in 1797 and changed very little throughout the period 1815–1914. Officer pay, especially in the era when an officer was generally required to purchase one's commission and subsequent promotions, was ordinarily insufficient to meet myriad expenses. It was considered more of an honorarium or a retaining fee, "less a wage for service done than a fund to enable the service to be performed; rather the tools of a trade than the profits of a trade" (Harries-Jenkins 1977, p. 85). A large private income was generally required for an officer, especially in more "expensive" regiments, such as the Foot Guards, Life Guards, and Horse Guards.

Officer pay varied on the basis of rank, service, type of regiment, and duty station, and frequently included additional emoluments, such as staff, subsistence, and horse maintenance allowances. In 1815, for example, the per diem pay for a lieutenant colonel was 31s in the Life Guards, 23s in the cavalry, 17s in the infantry, and 18s 1d in the horse artillery. For a captain, the per diem pay was 16s in the Life Guards, 14s 7d in the cavalry, 10s 6d in the infantry, and 11s 1d in the horse artillery. A lieutenant in the Life Guards received 11s per diem, 9s in the cavalry, 6s 6d in the infantry, and 6s 10d in the horse artillery.

Officers were able to go on the "half-pay" list and technically receive the difference in the value of their half- and full-pay commissions. The purpose of the half-pay system was to retain the services of the officer in case of a national emergency or military expansion, but in reality, it served as a means to retirement. Before 1830, any officer could transfer to the half-pay list, but after 1830, three years' service was required.

Officers' expenses included mess and band subscriptions, uniform costs, and a frequent loss of allowances, in addition to a loss of interest from the purchase value of the officer's commission. A private income of £50 to £100 per year was considered essential for an officer under the rank of major prior to the Crimean War (1854–1856).

Around 1854, annual pay for officers in the Royal Horse Guards was £94 for a lieutenant, £206 for a captain, £350 for a major, and £427 for a lieutenant colonel. In the Dragoon Guards and dragoons, a lieutenant received £70 yearly; a captain, £190; a major, £270, and a lieutenant colonel, £364. In line infantry regiments, the annual pay of a lieutenant was £41, £106 for a captain, £189 for a major, and £265 for a lieutenant colonel.

Daily officer pay around 1899 for a lieutenant colonel was £1 3s 6d in the Household Cavalry, £1 1s 6d in the cavalry, 18s in the infantry, and £1 4s 9d in the horse artillery. A captain's daily pay was 13s 6d in the Household Cavalry, 13s in the cavalry, 11s 7d in the infantry, and 15s in the horse artillery. A lieutenant in the Household Cavalry received 9s per day, 7s 8d in the cavalry, 6s 6d in the infantry, and 8s 10d in the horse artillery.

It 1850, it was observed that British Army officers "were the worst-paid and hardest-working of public servants" (Harries-Jenkins 1977, p. 86). This trend changed little prior to World War I.

See also Officers, British Army—Retirement; Officers, British Army—Social Background; Officers, British Army—Uniforms and Equipment; Officers, Indian Army—Pay; Purchase System; Rank and File, British Army—Pay

References: Farwell (1981); Grierson (1899); Harries-Jenkins (1977); Haythornthwaite (1994); Historical Sketch (2002); Strachan (1984)

Officers, British Army—Retirement

There was no adequate system for British Army officer retirement prior to about 1840. Before 1840, an officer would go on the half-pay list as a means to retirement, but this would cut him off from future promotion prospects.

After 1840, in an attempt to organize a retirement program, permission to go on half pay was restricted to those officers with at least eighteen years of service. In 1852, the service requirement was increased to twenty-one years, to align it with the pension plan of the other ranks.

An officer who had purchased his initial commission or any of his later promotions could retire from the British Army at any time, regardless of his length of service. Provided that he had not been found guilty of any misconduct, the retiring officer received the value of the commission he was selling. An officer who had not purchased his commission or any of his promotions was allowed to retire by selling his commission after a certain period of service. This provided the officer with a sizable financial nest egg for retirement, and permitted the government to save money on military pensions. For an officer who had been commissioned from the ranks, every two years served in the ranks counted as one year in commission and was the basis for selling his commission.

A Royal Commission in 1875 examined issues relating to promotions and retirement in the postpurchase British Army. Shortly thereafter, terms of retirement were regulated in which lieutenants and captains, if not promoted, would be required to retire at age 40 on £200 per year, forfeiting £10 for every year of service less than 20. A major was mandatorily retired at age 48 with a pension of between £250 and £300 a year, depending on years of service. Lieutenant colonels and colonels were retired at age 55 on annual pensions of £365 and £420, respectively. Major generals were retired at age 62 with £700 per annum, and lieutenant generals and full generals at 67 with £850 and £1,000 per year, respectively. There was limited flexibility in the officer retirement system, as a lieutenant or captain with 12 years of service could voluntarily retire with a £1,200 gratuity, and a major after 20 years of service could retire with an annual pension of £250. Although military pension expenditures increased from about £737,000 in 1884 to about £1 million in 1894, the officer retirement system preserved promotion by seniority within the regiment and helped sustain the flow of promotions in the postpurchase British Army.

See also Officers, British Army—Pay; Officers, Indian Army—Retirement; Purchase System; Rank and File, British Army—Retirement

References: Historical Sketch (2002); Spiers (1992); Strachan (1984)

Officers, British Army—Social Background

The social composition of the British Army officer corps remained virtually unchanged during the period 1815–1914. It was characterized mainly by financial exclusivity and was influenced heavily by the landed and not the commercial classes. Whereas the rank and file came from a variety of backgrounds, "the officers have been described, perhaps not unjustifiably, as a 'military caste,' many of them descended from generations of ancestors who had held commissions" (Barnes 1968, p. 38).

In large measure the social stratification of British society reproduced itself in the structure of the military. Officers generally served for honor, prestige, and social status—a manifestation of the ideal of service in the aristocratic tradition. Moreover, because members of the aristocracy and landed gentry were the "leisured class, they were also the fighting class, duty-bound and historically conditioned to protect civil society from invasion and disruption" (Cannadine 1990, p. 264).

During the nineteenth century, the landed interest was a relatively open group. As wealthy families lost their fortunes and vacated their estates, individuals who had accumulated wealth from involvement in industry and commerce moved onto the land. Military service as an officer was a means of gaining respectability.

The socioeconomic background of British Army officers during this period can be stated in general terms. In 1830, 21 percent of the officers came from the aristocracy, 32 percent from the landed gentry, and 47 percent from the middle class. By 1875, the percentage of aristocratic officers had decreased slightly to 18 percent of the total, while 32 percent again came from the landed gentry, and 50 percent from the middle class. In 1912, 9 percent of the officers came from the aristocracy, 32 percent from the landed gentry, and 59 percent from the middle class. The middle-class officers frequently came from the yeoman, who owned 100 to 3,000 acres of land, or the small proprietors, who owned between 1 and 100 acres. These two groups formed a considerable part of the landed interests.

Even though the Royal Military College, Sandhurst, provided for a minority of British Army officer accessions, it is revealing that between 1810 and 1869 over half of its entrants were sons of army or navy officers. In 1820, 67 percent of the new Sandhurst cadets had army or navy officer fathers. In 1880 and 1890 (and the number decreased thereafter), over half of the new cadets at the Royal Military Academy, Woolwich, had fathers who were army or navy officers.

Officers generally came from the classes that provided the "natural" leaders of society, and the officers were the natural leaders of the British Army. A fundamental principle was that they would spare no efforts in looking out for the health and welfare of their men. Officers in many cases acted in a paternalistic manner, and there was a general acceptance of the values of *noblesse oblige*. Conversely, the other ranks generally behaved deferentially toward their officers and accepted their leadership, just as, in most cases, they accepted the status quo in social stratification. The noncommissioned officers and other ranks expected their officers to lead by example, be courageous, and possess self-confidence. Occasionally there was friction between an officer and his soldiers if the former had been commissioned from the ranks.

The abolition of the purchase system in 1871 did not significantly alter the social composition of the British Army officer corps. The tremendous expansion of the British Army in World War I and simultaneous demand for additional officers irrevocably altered the social composition of the British Army officer corps.

> **See also** Army and Society; Officers, British Army—Sources of Commissioning; Officers, Indian Army—Social Background; Officers, Indian Army—Sources of Commissioning; Purchase System; Rank and File, British Army—Social Background; Sandhurst, Royal Military College; Woolwich, Royal Military Academy
>
> **References:** Barnes (1968); Cannadine (1990); Harries-Jenkins (1977); Otley (1970); Raugh (1986); Raugh (1994); Razzell (1963); Sherriff (1968); Simpson (1985); Spiers (1980a)

Officers, British Army—Sources of Commissioning

British Army officers were commissioned through the purchase system, through graduation from the Royal Military Academy, Woolwich, or the Royal Military College, Sandhurst, by direct appointment without purchase or through the militia, and by promotion from the ranks.

Prior to 1871, most commissions and subsequent promotions in the infantry and the cavalry, up to and including lieutenant colonel, were purchased. This was called the purchase system. Costs of initial commissions and promotions were officially regulated, but due to availability, regiment, location, and other factors, costs were usually "over regulation" and at least twice the regulation price.

Sandhurst graduates were a minority of newly commissioned officers; for example, between 1834 and 1838, less than 20 percent of the new officers came from Sandhurst. After 1842, officers who entered the army via Sandhurst did not purchase their commission.

Only 2,411 of the 5,120 officers on full pay in January 1848 had purchased all their commissions, although an additional 1,555 had bought one or more. In 1850, only 82 of 204 majors had purchased all their commissions. Of 141 infantry lieutenant colonels, 67 had not purchased that rank and 5 had not bought a single commission. In 1855, 1,378 commissions were granted in the army, of which 315 were purchased and 1,063 were not.

Sandhurst was closed when the purchase system was abolished in 1871. First commissions, for a short period, were awarded by written competitive examination, although in 1877 the examination became the basis for appointment to a reopened Sandhurst rather than for a commission. Sandhurst was not able to provide all the new officers required by the British Army, and militia subalterns who had participated in two annual drills, had held their rank for at least fifteen months, and were under twenty years of age were able to enter the British Army by passing a competitive examination. During the period 1885–1906, Sandhurst and Woolwich graduates numbered 9,021, or about 55 percent, out of a total of 16,472 officers commissioned.

There were relatively few promotions from the ranks. In the mid-1830s, fewer than 20 noncommissioned officers were commissioned each year, most of them to be regimental adjutants, quartermasters, or riding masters. Between 1830 and 1839, 182 noncommissioned officers were commissioned, and between 1840 and 1847, 264 were commissioned. During the period 1885–1899, the number of noncommissioned officers commissioned as second lieutenants in the infantry, cavalry, artillery, engineers, and Army Service Corps ranged from a low of 9 in 1897 to a maximum of 41 in 1888.

See also Officers, British Army—Social Background; Officers, British Army—Training and Education; Officers, Indian Army—Sources of Commissioning; Purchase System; Sandhurst, Royal Military College; Woolwich, Royal Military Academy

References: Grierson (1899); Harries-Jenkins (1977); Spiers (1980a); Spiers (1992); Strachan (1984)

Officers, British Army—Training and Education

The majority of British Army officers during the period 1815–1914 came from the aristocracy and the landed gentry. As a result, "their claims to command were based on character and social standing rather than expertise and professional training; they were at ease leading troops who were mostly from rural and humble backgrounds; and they regarded their occupation as the natural extension of familiar country pursuits" (Cannadine 1990, p. 265).

Until the Crimean War, little was done to train and educate officers, since character was preferred to ability. Moreover, the purchase system did not require professional training or qualifications for advancement.

In the 1850s, as the Crimean War was beginning, plans for the proper professional education of junior officers and for a system of staff training was approved. The first branch to establish training for newly commissioned officers was the Royal Engineers. In the 1850s, a course was established at Chatham where the engineer officer would receive instruction in surveying, reconnaissance, architecture, and historical siege operations, as well as practical training in siege operations, mining, bridging, pontooning, and infantry battalion movements. This course lasted about two years. The artillery established a professional course shortly afterward, while the only compulsory professional training for new infantry and cavalry officers was to pass a drill examination within two years of being commissioned.

The poor performance of the British Army in the Crimean War (1854–1856) highlighted administrative, logistical, and staff weaknesses. Detailed proposals were made for the improvement of staff officer education, and on 17 December 1857 the Senior Department was renamed the Staff College to educate staff officers. The Staff College increased in importance during this period.

Prior to 1849, those aspiring to be commissioned officers did not have to take any type of educational or professional competence examination. Most officers commissioned prior to 1849 "were singularly ill-educated and, in so far as they had received any formal education at all, this would be of a very limited character, as, for example, through private tuition" (Otley 1973, p. 192). In 1849, all officer candidates were required to take elementary educational examinations in English, mathematics, and Latin. Between 1855 and 1858, entrance examinations to Sandhurst and Woolwich were made more demanding.

After the abolition of purchase in 1871, standardized competitive examinations were administered to those who wanted a commission. After Sandhurst, commissioning from the militia was the most important route to become an officer. After about 1874, there was systematic recruitment for officers from universities, and after 1894, those with university degrees were commissioned directly into the British Army.

See also Camberley, Staff College; Crimean War; Militia; Officers, British Army—Social Background; Officers, British Army—Sources of Commissioning; Officers, Indian Army—Social Background; Officers, Indian Army—Training and Education; Purchase System

References: Cannadine (1990); Otley (1973); Spiers (1992); Strachan (1984)

Officers, British Army—Uniforms and Equipment

A newly commissioned officer would have to provide his own uniforms, cases, furniture, mufti, servant's outfit, and other expenses on joining his regiment. These uniforms and other items cost about £200 for an infantry officer, but the more expensive uniforms, saddle equipment, civilian clothing, and the purchase of two chargers cost between £600 and £1,000 for a cavalry officer, depending on his regiment.

By the late 1890s, infantry officer uniforms were like those of the other ranks, except that their tunics were embroidered with gold on the collars and facings. In the less formal uniform, officers wore caps similar to those of their men and dark blue serge frocks.

Officers wore common rank insignia. Second lieutenants wore shoulder straps without any insignia, while lieutenants had one star (or "pip") and captains had two stars on their shoulder straps. Field grade officers (major, lieutenant colonel, and colonel) wore a crown, and in addition the lieutenant colonel wore one star and the colonel two stars. (British Army officer rank insignia was later revised, so that second lieutenants wore one star, lieutenants wore two stars, and captains wore three stars.)

Each regiment had its own distinct color, which was the same color as its facings, the cuffs, lapels or collars, and the turn back of the coat.

See also Officers, British Army—Pay; Rank and File, British Army—Uniforms and Equipment
References: Grierson (1899); Harries-Jenkins (1977); Spiers (1992)

Officers, Indian Army—Pay

It was much less expensive to serve in the Indian Army in India than in the British Army, a key consideration for less wealthy officers. Indeed, "pay for a British subaltern with a British regiment in India was better than in Britain by a proportion not absolutely constant but usually around 20 per cent; in the Indian Army, for those who made India a career, it was about 50 per cent better" (Mason 1974, pp. 372–373). In the Indian Army, many infantry officers could generally live on their pay, although this was not possible in Indian Army cavalry regiments.

In 1855, the pay of East India Company's officers, including maximum allowances, was (rupees [Rs] figures are pay per month and pound figures are the daily rate) for horse artillery and cavalry colonels, Rs 1,478 (£4 16s 7d), and for foot artillery, engineer, and infantry colonels, Rs 1,295 (£4 5s 0d). Horse artillery and cavalry lieutenant colonels received Rs 1,157 (£3 16s 0d), while foot artillery, engineer, and infantry lieutenant colonels received Rs 1,032 (£3 7s 11d). Majors in the horse artillery and cavalry received Rs 929 (£3 1s 0d), while those in the foot artillery, engineers, and infantry were paid Rs 789 (£2 11s 11d). Depending on branch, captain pay ranged from a high of Rs 563 (£1 11s 5d) to Rs 415 (£1 7s 2d), and lieutenant pay ranged from Rs 365 (£1 4s 0d) to Rs 257 (16s 10d). Pay for cornets, second lieutenants, and ensigns ranged from Rs 311 (£1 0s 5d) to Rs 203 (13s 2d). The pay of a subaltern in the British Army in 1862 was about £95, and his minimal annual expenses were estimated at £157.

Additional allowances were paid for those serving in designated command and staff positions, including that of adjutant. Foreign language proficiency pay was an additional allowance for those who qualified as a translator in designated languages.

A lieutenant serving in the Bengal Army in 1831 had living expenses of about Rs 275 per month. This typically included Rs 40 for house rent, Rs 59 for servants, Rs 45 for meals, Rs 35 for wine, Rs 6 for cigars, Rs 6 for candles, Rs 17 for horse feed, and Rs 8 for contributions to pension funds. The pay, with allowances, for a subaltern at the time was only about Rs 365 month.

See also East India Company; East India Company, Military Forces; India, British Army in; Indian Army Organization; Officers, British Army—Pay; Officers, Indian Army—Retirement; Officers, Indian Army—Social Background; Rank and File, British Army—Pay
References: Beaumont (1977); Farwell (1989); Heathcote (1974); Mason (1974); Raugh (1985)

Officers, Indian Army—Retirement

Officers of the East India Company's military forces and, after 1858, the Indian Army employed directly by the government of India, did not purchase their commissions or subsequent promotions. As a result, their retirement system was considerably different from that of British Army officers who, prior to the abolition of the purchase system in 1871, could retire by selling their commission.

Retirement conditions and pensions, as is standard, varied according to the rank and length of service of the Indian Army officers. Every officer who had served in India for twenty-five years, in accordance with the rules of the East India Company, could retire on the full pay of the rank he held, calculated at infantry rates. Captains and field grade officers (majors, lieutenant colonels, and colonels) who retired on medical grounds, regardless of length of service, received pensions equal to half pay of their ranks. Lieutenants with more than thirteen years of Indian service, and cornets, second lieutenants, and ensigns with more than nine years of Indian service, could also retire with a pension equal to half pay of their rank. Subalterns with six years of Indian service retiring on medical grounds would receive the half pay of an ensign.

There was no mandatory retirement age for Indian Army officers. Officers frequently remained on active duty hoping to be promoted again because the higher rank would sizably increase their pension. This also resulted in many superannuated officers remaining on active duty. The average promotion time for a cornet or ensign to be promoted to lieutenant was seven years, and from lieutenant to captain a total of fifteen years. At promotion, a captain was about forty years old and might be willing to serve another ten years to reach the rank of major before retiring. Many officers retired as majors, receiving their pension as well as a lump sum from a subscription fund. Other officers, expecting to be promoted to lieutenant colonel six years later, would remain on active duty hoping for the promotion and increased pension that would accompany it.

Military and civil officers in each of the three presidency armies of the East India Company contributed to funds that would be used to supplement official benefits on an officer's retirement. Officers paid a lump sum on joining the fund and on each subsequent promotion. A colonel joining the fund would pay an initial sum of rupees (Rs) 4,350 on joining and Rs 723.12 on promotion. A lieutenant would pay Rs 450 on joining the fund and Rs 150 on promotion. A married colonel would pay a monthly subscription of Rs 62.8, an unmarried colonel Rs 28.2, and married and single lieutenants Rs 10 and Rs 5.10, respectively. On retirement, an officer would also receive a lump sum from this fund.

After 1858, Indian Army officers retired on half pay. As promotion in the Indian Army was based on length of service and not on seniority, officers could expect to be promoted to lieutenant colonel after twenty-six years of service, when many officers would retire.

See also East India Company; East India Company, Military Forces; Indian Army Organization; Officers, British Army—Pay; Officers, British Army—Retirement; Officers, Indian Army—Pay; Purchase System
References: Heathcote (1974); Mason (1974)

Officers, Indian Army—Social Background

British Army officers generally came from a more aristocratic and wealthier background than their counterparts in the East India Company's military forces and the Indian Army.

A number of studies have shed light on the social background of Indian Army officers. During the period 1758–1774, of 448 Indian Army officers, 1.5 percent came from the aristocracy, 6 percent from the landed gentry, and 92.5 percent from the middle class. From 1775 to 1804, of 626 Indian Army officers, 3 percent came from the aristocracy, 13.5 percent from the landed gentry, and 83.5 percent from the middle class. Of 950 Indian Army officers studied between 1805 and 1834, 5 percent came from the aristocracy, 19 percent from the landed gentry, and 76 percent from the middle class. Over this approximately 80-year period, 1758–1834, the number of Indian Army officers with an aristocratic background increased from 1.5 to 5 percent, those from the landed gentry increased from 6 to 19 percent, and those from the middle class declined from 92.5 to 76 percent. These figures stabilized thereafter. In comparison, in 1830 some 21 percent of the British Army officers came from the aristocracy, 32 percent from the landed gentry, and 47 percent from the middle class.

The class origin of officers in the Bengal Army from 1820 to 1834 was also studied. Of the 1,403 officers studied whose fathers were not employed in India, 419 were military officers, 307 were in clerical orders, 118 were merchants, 96 were in the legal profession, 68 were tradesmen, 75 were in the medical profession, and others, in decreasing numbers, were bankers, customs officials, farmers, members of parliament, clerical workers, craftsmen, and others. During the same period, of 542 Bengal Army officers whose fathers worked in India, 252 were Indian Army officers, 96 were civil servants, and 38 were in the medical profession, with decreasing numbers of others.

Another study was made of the class origins of those cadets at Sandhurst from 1890 to 1895 who joined the Indian Staff Corps. Of 129 cadets identified, 40 had fathers employed in India and 89 had fathers residing in the United Kingdom. Of the 40 with fathers in India, 29 had fathers in the Indian Army, 9 in the Indian Civil Service, and 2 in other occupations. Of the 89 cadets whose fathers were in the United Kingdom, 57 were British Army officers, 5 were naval officers, 5 were surgeons, 4 were private gentlemen, 4 were clergymen, 2 each were civil engineers, gentlemen farmers, and doctors, while 8 were others.

Indian Army officers came predominantly from the less affluent sections of the British middle class and probably would not have been able to purchase their commissions had they been required to do so.

See also East India Company; East India Company, Military Forces; Indian Army Organization; Officers, British Army—Social Background; Officers, British Army—Sources of Commissioning; Officers, Indian Army—Pay; Officers, Indian Army—Sources of Commissioning; Rank and File, British Army—Social Background; Sandhurst, Royal Military College
References: Farwell (1989); Heathcote (1974); Hervey (1988); Razzell (1963)

Officers, Indian Army—Sources of Commissioning

There were numerous ways to be commissioned an officer in the East India Company army and later the Indian Army.

The usual method was for the aspirant to obtain a nomination from a director of the company. After appearing with supporting documentation before an appropriate committee, the candidate, if selected, would be appointed a cadet and arrangements made for him to attend training in the United Kingdom or be sent directly to India.

During the first decade of the nineteenth century, forty of the approximately 100 cadetships at the Royal Military Academy, Woolwich, were reserved for East India Company cadets. To meet the increased demand for ordnance officers, an ordnance company was formed at the Royal Military College, Sandhurst, in 1803, in which twenty vacancies were reserved for East India Company cadets.

To train more British officers for its own expanding military forces, especially in technical branches such as the artillery and engineers, the East India Company established its own military college, the Addiscombe Military Seminary, in 1809. The course of instruction lasted two years and closely followed that of the Royal Military Academy, Woolwich. Newly commissioned company engineer and artillery officers received additional training at the British Army schools at Chatham and Woolwich, respectively. Those who wished to join the company infantry as cadets could do so by going directly to India. Company cavalry lieutenants received direct appointments and did not attend Addiscombe.

After the East India Company's authority was transferred to the British Crown in 1858, it was decided that Woolwich and Sandhurst would be sufficient to train new officers for both the British Army and the Indian Army, and Addiscombe was closed in 1861. During Addiscombe's 52-year existence, some 2,000 infantry, 1,100 artillery, and 500 engineer officers were commissioned into the East India Company military forces.

The Royal Military College, Sandhurst, was closed after the purchase system was abolished in 1871. It was reopened in 1877 and trained practically all of the Indian Army's new officers. These new officers were commissioned into the Indian Staff Corps, which served as a manpower pool for Indian Army officers.

See also Addiscombe, Military Seminary; East India Company; East India Company, Military Forces; Indian Army Organization; Officers, British Army—Sources of Commissioning; Purchase System; Sandhurst, Royal Military College; Woolwich, Royal Military Academy
References: Farwell (1989); Heathcote (1974); Hervey (1988); Mason (1974); Spiers (1992)

Officers, Indian Army—Training and Education

Newly commissioned British officers assigned to the Indian Army were not assigned immediately to an Indian Army regiment but spent a year on the Unattached List in a British Army battalion serving in India. This year-long apprenticeship of sorts permitted the new officer to learn and practice leadership, become familiar with Indian soldiers, acclimatize to the region, and learn the local languages (Urdu and/or Gurkhali) of the soldiers he would lead.

In 1870, forty students attended the British Army Staff College at Camberley. Beginning in 1877, six selected Indian Army officers were authorized to attend Camberley, a number increased to eight (out of a course total of sixty officers) in 1886. The results were disappointing because, among other factors including expense, Staff College certification was not required for staff service or promotion in India. Attitudes changed with the increased professionalization of both the British Army and the Indian Army, and by the 1890s, "the best bloods and best all-around men began to compete" (Mason 1974, p. 364) for Staff College attendance.

To enhance the training of Indian Army staff officers, a temporary Staff College was established at Deolali in 1905. Initially, twenty-four officers—approximately two-thirds from the Indian Army and one-third from the British Army in India—attended the course. The Staff College moved to its permanent site at Quetta in 1907.

In actuality, other than training for one year in a British Army battalion and until the establishment of the Staff College at Quetta, Indian Army officers at the beginning of the twentieth century received little military training after leaving the Royal Military College, Sandhurst.

See also Camberley, Staff College; East India Company; East India Company, Military Forces; Indian Army Organization; Officers, British Army—Sources of Commissioning; Officers, British Army—Training and Education; Officers, Indian Army—Sources of Commissioning; Sandhurst, Royal Military College
References: Bond (1972); Farwell (1989); Heathcote (1974); Hervey (1988); Mason (1974); Spiers (1992)

Officers, Indian Army—Uniforms and Equipment

After the Indian Mutiny (1857–1859), the Indian-style clothing and uniforms of the irregular regiments, especially the infantry, came into general use. While there were regimental differences, in general terms, the turban and loosely cut knickerbockers and puttees replaced the shako and light trousers, and a loose tunic replaced the coatee.

Between 1861 and 1864, khaki uniforms were worn for hot-weather duties by all British and Indian troops. Khaki uniforms were replaced by white cotton uniforms, but khaki was reissued during the Second Afghan War (1878–1880). From 1880 until World War I, colored serge uniforms were worn in cold weather and white for hot weather parades, except on operations.

Uniforms and field equipment generally cost the newly commissioned Indian Army officer about Rs 2,000. This was a considerable amount of money, and the subaltern usually had to borrow this money, with interest of about 10 percent per year.

See also East India Company; East India Company, Military Forces; Indian Army Organization; Officers, British Army—Uniforms and Equipment; Officers, Indian Army—Pay
References: Farwell (1989); Heathcote (1974); Hervey (1988)

Omdurman, Battle of (2 September 1898)

Anglo-Egyptian forces crushed dervish power at the Battle of Omdurman, the climactic battle of the reconquest of the Sudan. It was also the last great colonial battle of the British Empire.

Major General (later Field Marshal Earl) Sir Horatio H. Kitchener's Anglo-Egyptian army defeated the dervishes at the Battle of Atbara (8 April 1898) and destroyed the last remaining dervish force outside Omdurman. The Anglo-Egyptian forces then encamped to await additional reinforcements, logistical preparations, and the arrival of the campaigning season in August. The Sudan Military Railway reached Fort Atbara in early July 1898. By mid-August 1898, Kitchener had received an additional British brigade and assembled about 8,200 British and 17,600 Egyptian and Sudanese troops, 44 guns and 20 machine guns on land, and a flotilla of gunboats armed with 36 guns and 24 machine guns.

The arrival of a second British infantry brigade resulted in the formation of the British Division, commanded by Major General (later Lieutenant General Sir) William F. Gatacre. The 1st British Brigade (1st battalions of the Cameron Highlander, Royal Warwickshire, Seaforth Highlander, and Lincolnshire Regiments) was commanded by Brigadier General (later Major General) Andrew G. Wauchope. Brigadier General (later General Sir) Neville Lyttelton commanded the 2nd British Brigade (1st battalions of the Grenadier Guards and of the Northumberland Fusiliers, and the 2nd battalions of the Rifle Brigade and of the Lancashire Fusiliers). Additional British reinforcements included the 21st Lancers, two field batteries with 5-inch howitzers and 9-pounder Maxim-Nordenfeldt guns, and a four-gun Maxim battery. Seven gunboats reinforced the troops.

The Egyptian Division, commanded by Major General (later General Sir) Archibald Hunter, had also been reinforced by a fourth brigade. The 1st Egyptian Brigade (12th, 13th, and 14th Sudanese and 8th Egyptian Battalions) was commanded by Colonel (later General Sir) John G. Maxwell, and the 2nd Egyptian Brigade (9th, 10th, and 11th Sudanese and 2nd Egyptian Battalions) was under Colonel (later Major General Sir) Hector A. Macdonald. The 3rd Egyptian Brigade (3rd, 4th, and 7th Egyptian Battalions) was commanded by Colonel D. F. Lewis, and the newly arrived 4th Egyptian Brigade was commanded by Lieutenant Colonel John Collinson.

The Khalifa's 52,000-man army, a third of which was armed with rifles and the remainder with swords and spears, assembled on the plains at Omdurman on the west bank of the junction of the White and Blue Niles.

Kitchener's force began its final march to Omdurman on 28 August 1898. Three days later, the army sighted the Kerreri Hills, a low ridge running perpendicular to the Nile and running westward about 2 miles into the desert. This high ground covered the approaches to Omdurman, and about 3 miles further south was another hill, Jebel Surgham.

On 1 September 1898, the 21st Lancers and the Egyptian Cavalry reconnoitered the area and were astonished to find the dervishes advancing south of Jebel Surgham. On the same day, in a demonstration of Anglo-Egyptian firepower, the gunboats blasted the Khalifa's forts and the Mahdi's tomb. As these operations were taking place, the infantry was building a camp near the village of El Egeiga, on the Nile between the Kerreri Hills and Jebel Surgham.

Five of the six infantry brigades were arranged in an arc facing the west and with their rear to the Nile, with the sixth (Collinson's) in reserve. From north to south, these brigades were commanded by Lewis, Macdonald, Maxwell, Wauchope, and Lyttelton, with the 21st Lancers closing the gap on the south with the Nile. Maxims and artillery were positioned between the brigades. By nightfall, the dervishes had not advanced further, and Kitchener's soldiers spent an uneasy night in their positions. The Anglo-Egyptian soldiers stood to at 3:30 A.M. on 2 September 1898. The advancing dervish horde was first observed at about 6:00 A.M. From this point onward, the battle is usually divided into three phases.

The first phase began when Osman Azrak's 8,000 dervishes attacked directly eastward to the Anglo-Egyptian center, supported by another 4,000-man force on his right, at dawn. The dervishes, conducting a frontal assault over open ground against an adversary with modern weapons, began to suffer significant casualties when the British guns began firing at a range of about 2,900 yards. Maxim guns opened up at 2,000 yards. Two other dervish forces under the Green Flag moved northward toward the Kerreri Hills, as they believed wrongly that the Egyptian troops were north of that high ground. Egyptian Cavalry stopped this force from attacking the British right flank.

After about forty-five minutes, after Kitchener's troops had fired about 200,000 rounds of small arms ammunition and at least 1,000 artillery rounds, the dervish onslaught was halted and the Mahdist units virtually annihilated. This ended the first phase of the battle and a lull followed.

After the main dervish assault, Kitchener thought the attack was over, with no organized dervish units remaining between his army and Omdurman. At about 8:30 A.M., the 21st Lancers—which had never been in combat before—was ordered forward to Jebel Surgham to prevent withdrawing dervishes from reaching Omdurman. Kitchener apparently did not know that a 12,000-man dervish force was assembled south of the Jebel. The 21st Lancers moved south, between the Jebel and the Nile, and observed dervishes in the open. These were men dervish leader Osman Digna had purposely positioned on the northern edge of the Khor Abu Sunt (a dry watercourse running east-west from Jebel Surgham), in which he hid 2,000 battle-hardened dervishes. The 21st Lancers took the bait, charged across the broken ground, and at the last moment, when they reached the edge of the *khor* (dry watercourse), realized they had fallen into a trap. Many Lancers charged through the dervishes, but others were knocked to the ground, where they were hacked to death in the fierce fighting. Survivors regrouped on the far side of the *khor*, ready to charge back through the dervishes. Common sense prevailed as the Lancers dismounted and began firing into the dervishes, who retreated toward the Jebel. The charge of the 21st Lancers was a glorious disaster, and the regiment, numbering about 440, suffered 21 officers and men killed, 71 wounded, and 199 horses killed or wounded in the short melee.

As the 21st Lancers were in action, Kitchener's brigades advanced out of their encampment and wheeled southward toward Omdurman, 7 miles away. From left to right, the brigades were those of Lyttelton, Wauchope, Maxwell, Lewis, and Macdonald, with Egyptian Cavalry and the Camel Corps protecting the right flank. Difficulties in command and control caused confusion, and a large gap opened between Lewis's and Macdonald's brigades as the force advanced southward.

As the Anglo-Egyptian army neared the Jebel Surgham, it received shots from the high ground. To the south of the Jebel, and unknown to Kitchener, was the Khalifa's 17,000-man Black Flag reserve force. The Khalifa ordered the Black Flag to attack Macdonald's brigade. As this attack began, the Green Flag began its own uncoordinated attack from the Kerreri Hills. Macdonald calmly wheeled his brigade around to meet the new threat, and Wauchope marched his brigade to fill the gap between Macdonald's and Lewis's brigades. Macdonald's brigade, with eighteen guns and eight Maxims, shattered the attack of the Green Flag. Maxwell's brigade, with Lewis on his right and Lyttelton on his left, cleared the Jebel of dervishes and halted the Black Flag attack by 11:30 A.M. This ended the second phase of the battle. The third phase of the battle consisted of the advance to and entry into Omdurman, completed by the end of the day.

The Battle of Omdurman destroyed Mahdist power (even though the Khalifa escaped), reestablished Anglo-Egyptian power in the Sudan (which was confirmed at Fashoda later that month), and avenged the martyrdom of Gordon. In many respects, the battle was a slaughter, in which Anglo-Egyptian casualties were 48 killed and 434 wounded; over 10,000 dervishes were killed and perhaps 16,000 wounded by the superior British firepower and technology. Kitchener's victory seemed to be attributed more to luck than tactical ability and leadership. Indeed, one war correspondent present at the battle commented that Kitchener's triumph at the Battle of Omdurman "so crushingly and so cheaply was the gift of luck and the Khalifa" (Steevens 1898, p. 292).

See also Atbara, Battle of; Charge of the 21st Lancers; Dervishes; Egyptian Army; Fashoda Incident; Gatacre, Lieutenant General Sir William F.; Hunter, General Sir Archibald; Khalifa; Kitchener, Field Marshal Horatio H.; Macdonald, Major General Sir Hector A.; Machine Guns; Railways; Reconquest of the Sudan; Sudan; Wauchope, Major General Andrew G.

References: Barthorp (1984); Harrington and Sharf (1998); Hunter (1996); Keown-Boyd (1986), Meredith (1998); Neillands (1996); Pollock (2001); Steevens (1898); Ziegler (1974); Zulfo (1980)

Opium War

See China War, First (1839–1842)

Outram, Lieutenant General Sir James (1803–1863)

Lieutenant General Sir James Outram, considered "the Bayard of India," was a generally competent and professional Bombay Army officer and conscientious administrator who held high command during the Persian War of 1856–1857 and the Indian Mutiny.

Outram was born on 29 January 1803 in England and was educated at Aberdeen. He received an Indian cadetship in 1819 and arrived in India in 1820. For his first fifteen years of service he trained native infantry soldiers, developing an excellent rapport with them. He served in Gujerat from 1835 to 1838, participated in the First Afghan War, and then was posted as political agent in Sind. Outram opposed the policies of his superior, General Sir Charles J. Napier, believing that he provoked the amirs into war and the British conquest of Sind.

After additional political and military assignments in India, Outram was appointed resident at Lucknow. Two years later it was his duty to execute the annexation of Oudh, when he became the first chief commissioner of the troubled province. In 1857, with the rank of lieutenant general, Outram commanded the British expedition to Persia. His forces routed the Persians at the Battle of Koosh-ab (8 February 1857), and shortly thereafter the Persians fled the battlefield at Mohumra. On 5 April 1857 Outram learned a peace had been negotiated, and he returned to India two months later as the Indian Mutiny broke out.

Outram was appointed to command the Dinapore and Cawnpore Divisions on 4 August 1857, and arrived at Cawnpore with reinforcements on 15 September 1857. He superseded Brigadier General (later Major General Sir) Henry Havelock, who had fought a number of battles and was advancing to relieve Lucknow. Outram foolishly, since responsibility could not be delegated to a subordinate (although some considered it an act of magnanimity), permitted Havelock to remain in command to receive the glory of relieving Lucknow. Outram occasionally interfered with Havelock by offering his "advice" but did not insist it be followed. After fierce resistance, the Lucknow residency was relieved on 25 September and Outram officially assumed command from Havelock.

It soon became apparent to Outram that the rebel force was so large he could not force his way out of Lucknow, and his relieving force became besieged. The final relief of Lucknow by a force under the command of Lieutenant General (later Field Marshal Lord) Sir Colin Campbell took place on 17 November 1857. Outram was responsible for its evacuation and ordered to remain with some 4,000 men at the nearby Alambagh to wait for Campbell to return with a larger force. Between November 1857 and February 1858, Outram's position was attacked six times by large rebel forces. In March 1858, Outram's force advanced to Lucknow, and in a series of operations linked up with Campbell's troops and cleared and captured the city on 23 March.

Outram resumed his position as chief commissioner of Oudh, but strain and ill health forced his return to England in 1860. Outram died in France on 11 March 1863 and was buried in Westminster Abbey.

See also Afghan War, First (1839–1842); Bombay Army; Campbell, Field Marshal Colin; East India Company, Military Forces; Havelock, Major General Sir Henry; India; Indian Army Operations; Indian Mutiny; Lucknow, Siege and Relief of; Napier, General Sir Charles J.; Persian War; Sind, Operations in
References: Edwardes (1963); Hibbert (1978); James (1997); Waller (1990)

Paardeberg, Battle of (18–27 February 1900)

The Battle of Paardeberg took place after the siege of Kimberley was lifted and ultimately resulted in the first important British victory of the Second Boer War (1899–1902).

The British relieved the besieged town of Kimberley on 15 February 1900. Assistant Commandant-General Piet A. Cronje, Boer commander, realized his forces were vulnerable and decided that night to abandon his position near Magersfontein and follow the Modder River to Bloemfontein, the capital of the Orange Free State, 90 miles to the east. Cronje's force consisted of about 5,000 burghers (many with families), about 500 wagons, and thousands of reserve horses. On 17 February, the British detected Cronje's laager near Paardeberg Drift, 30 miles upstream from the Modder River Station. While the wagons remained on the north bank of the Modder, Boer forces had dug positions on both sides of the river.

Lieutenant General (later General Sir) Thomas Kelly-Kenny, commanding the British 6th Division, wanted to surround Cronje's force and bombard it into submission. Field Marshal Lord (later Earl) Frederick S. Roberts, V.C., commander in chief, was detained elsewhere and ill, so he delegated his authority to his chief of staff, Major General Lord (later Field Marshal Earl) Horatio H. Kitchener. This caused considerable resentment, as Kelly-Kenny was senior in rank to Kitchener. However, Kitchener, who was backed by Roberts, impatiently ordered Kelly-Kenny to use his division and immediately attack Cronje's force.

Kitchener's plan of attack was for Kelly-Kenny's division to conduct a frontal assault from the south bank of the Modder River against the entrenched Boers. At the same time, the 9th Division's Highland Brigade would attack upstream from the south bank, while the 19th Brigade (also of the 9th Division) would cross the Modder and attack upstream from the north bank. A mounted infantry unit, with two infantry battalions, would also attack downstream along the north bank. Kitchener wanted to conduct this huge pincer movement and defeat Cronje's force before it could move or be reinforced.

Kitchener's attack, ordered by verbal messages, began early on 18 February 1900. The 6th Division advanced across an open plain toward the Modder River, suffering many casualties, to find the river in flood. The 6th Division halted at the river while the Highland Brigade joined its left flank. Kitchener, however, seems to have ordered the Highland Brigade to conduct a frontal assault against the Boers. The Highland Brigade was pinned down in the scorching sun by Boer sharpshooters, just as it had been at the Battle of Modder River (28 November 1899). In the early afternoon, Kitchener ordered a limited left flank attack, then a right flank assault—giving up high ground to the Boers in the process—as Kelly-Kenny resisted his directives to continue the frontal attack.

Chief Commandant Christiaan R. De Wet, whose Boer force was about 15 miles south of the Modder, attacked and captured the hill south of the Modder that was the key to the entire ridgeline. Control of this hill made the British position untenable while providing an avenue of escape for Cronje.

By sunset, it became clear that Kitchener's chaotic battle, consisting of uncoordinated and haphazard frontal assaults, had failed. It was "the most severe reverse, judged by the British losses, of any day in the entire war" (Pakenham 1979, p. 356). The British lost 24 officers and 279 men killed, 59 officers and 847 men wounded, and 61 all ranks missing, for a total of 1,270 casualties—more casualties than the total sustained during the 1896–1898 reconquest of the Sudan. Neither Kitchener nor Roberts had ever fought against a European-type foe armed with modern weaponry. The Boers sustained about 100 men killed and 250 wounded.

Roberts arrived on the battlefield on 19 February 1900. He vacillated about what course of action to take and considered retreating. On 21 February, De Wet's men abandoned the hill they occupied, and the British regained their nerve and sense of purpose. Less than 100 of Cronje's Boers had escaped via De Wet's position. On 27 February 1900—the nineteenth anniversary of the Boer victory at the Battle of Majuba—Cronje and 4,069 of his men surrendered. The British won the Battle of Paardeberg despite the incompetence of Kitchener and Roberts, and this was the greatest British success in the war to date. The Boers realized they could no longer use conventional means to defeat their adversary, planting the seeds for a protracted guerrilla war.

See also Boer War, Second (1899–1902); Boers; Cronje, Assistant Commandant-General Piet A.; De Wet, Chief Commandant Christiaan R.; Kitchener, Field Marshal Horatio H.; Majuba Hill, Battle of; Modder River, Battle of; Reconquest of the Sudan; Roberts, Field Marshal Frederick S., V.C.
References: Belfield (1975); Carver (1999); Nasson (1999); Pakenham (1979); Pollock (2001); Reid (1996)

Pacific Ocean Operations, Crimean War

The Royal Navy, in addition to conducting significant operations in the Black and Baltic Seas during the Crimean War, conducted secondary operations in the Pacific Ocean and the White Sea.

British naval operations in the North Pacific in 1854 centered on Petropavlovsk, the Russian Far Eastern naval base on the Kamchatka Peninsula. A six-ship Anglo-French flotilla, commanded by Rear Admiral David Price, was following a number of Russian vessels, including the frigate *Aurora,* and hoped to capture them before they reached the safety of Petropavlovsk.

The Russian ships reached their heavily protected anchorage before the allied fleet, which arrived at Petropavlovsk on 29 August 1854. The next morning, before an assault on the naval base was to begin, Price went to his cabin and shot himself, perhaps in remorse for failing his mission. Price's death did not stop the operation. The combined attack began, but the British accidentally shelled a French landing party and a second landing force was ambushed by the Russians. The allied flotilla withdrew on 5 September 1854. It took many months for news of this disaster to reach England.

Three British naval squadrons operated in the Pacific Ocean in 1855. One squadron under Rear Admiral Henry W. Bruce operated in the North Pacific, and a second squadron, operating in Chinese waters, was under the command of Admiral Stirling. A third squadron was later assembled at Hong Kong under Commodore Elliot. None of these three flotillas made much of an impact on the war effort.

See also Baltic Sea Operations, Crimean War; Crimean War; White Sea Operations, Crimean War
References: Judd (1975); Palmer (1987); Royle (2000)

Pasha, Omar
See Crimean War; Turkish Forces, Crimean War

Peiwar Kotal, Battle of (2 December 1878)

The 6,500-man, 18-gun Kurram Valley Force, commanded by Major General (later Field Marshal Earl) Frederick S. Roberts, V.C., was one of three British columns that marched into Afghanistan at the beginning of the Second Afghan War on 21 November 1878.

After marching through the Kurram Valley, Roberts's force found its advance blocked by Afghans (estimated at eight regiments) with artillery at the Peiwar Kotal (Pass), about 3,800 feet above the valley floor. On 28 November 1878, elements of the 29th Punjabis attempted to rush the Afghan position but were forced back. Roberts then reconnoitered the area for two days before deciding on a plan of action.

At 10 P.M. on 1 December 1878, Roberts led a 2,263-man assault force (consisting of the 2nd and 29th Punjabis, the 5th Gurkhas, half the 72nd Highlanders, the 23rd Pioneers, a mountain battery, and four artillery pieces on elephants) on a 12-mile trek up a steep path that ended at the Spingawi Kotal to the left of the Afghan position. The column took a wrong turn and had to retrace its steps and lost even more time ascending in a boulder-strewn streambed. As dawn approached, the force had not reached its objective and was almost compromised when two shots were fired, reportedly by traitorous Pathan sepoys. Roberts halted the column and put the Gurkhas and a Highlander company in the lead.

At first light, the Gurkhas and Highlanders pressed forward, orienting on enemy rifle flashes and "pausing only to bayonet the defenders" (Tanner 2002, p. 207). By 8:00 A.M. on 2 December 1878, the British had secured the head of the Spingawi Kotal. Heavy fighting followed, and at about 1:00 P.M., the British found a location to emplace their artillery and fire on the Afghans. The tide of battle was turning. As the British rolled up the Afghan position and threatened its rear, the 8th King's Regiment and the 5th Punjab Infantry conducted a frontal assault. The Afghans abandoned their positions and guns, and they left about 300 dead on the field. British casualties were about 21 dead and 75 wounded.

The victory at the Battle of Peiwar Kotal initiated Roberts's reputation as a field commander and cleared the route to Kabul.

See also Afghan War, Second (1878–1880); Afghanistan; Gurkhas; India; Indian Army Operations; Roberts, Field Marshal Frederick S., V.C.

References: Barthorp (1982); Featherstone (1973); Forbes (1892); Fredericks (1971); Roberts (1897); Tanner (2002); Young (1977)

Peking, Siege of (20 June–14 August 1900)
See Boxer Rebellion

Penjdeh Incident (30 March 1885)

The Anglo-Russian imperial rivalry of the nineteenth century known as the Great Game consisted of attempts to control the vast uncharted areas of Central Asia. The Russians wanted to expand southward, and the British were committed to ensure that the Russians did not invade India in the process.

In an attempt to establish Afghanistan as a buffer or a client state to prevent further Russian expansion, the British fought and won the Second Afghan War (1878–1880) and established a pro-British government under Abdur Rahman Khan. After promising to protect the northern border of Afghanistan against foreign encroachment, the British evacuated the country in 1881.

The Russians, meanwhile, had not been idle. In 1884, they seized Merv, a Turkmeni settlement in Central Asia only a few miles north of the ill-defined Afghan border. In response to this provocation, the Afghan amir, Abdur Rahman, sent 500 additional troops to reinforce the garrison at nearby Penjdeh, a desert oasis at the confluence of the Kusidi and Murghab Rivers.

General Sir Peter Lumsden, part of a commission established to finalize the Russo-Persian border, arrived at Sarakhs near the Persian-Afghan border in October 1884. He was told his Russian counterpart had been delayed until the following spring. During the winter of 1884–1885, the British received intelligence from various sources that the Russian pacification of Turkmenistan, the last independent Muslim principality in Central Asia, was a prelude to a large-scale invasion of what was presumed to be Afghan territory. There were indications that the Russian threat would be directed toward the Afghan town of Penjdeh. In February 1885, the Russian government expressed an interest in fixing the northern Afghan border, and the Anglo-Russian Boundary Commission was established to officially demarcate the northern Afghan border. This apparent cooperation was only a subterfuge, as the Asiatic section of the Russian Foreign Ministry and the Russian Army planned to continue their advance southward and seize as much territory as possible while the Boundary Commission was still negotiating. Shortly thereafter, the Russians claimed that Penjdeh was a part of the Merv area and thus Russian territory.

To support the Russian claim, General Komarov, the commander of the Russian forces, deployed his troops forward near the banks of the Kushk River. A few small skirmishes between the Russians and Afghans ensued as patrols and pickets made chance contact with each other. On 25 March 1885, the Russians began to make threatening troop movements in order to provoke the Afghans into action to make them appear as the aggressors. At this stage, the Afghans had 3,099 troops, including 416 Kabul and 867 Herati irregular cavalry, a mule-drawn artillery battery of four guns, and a field battery of four 6-pounder cannons. The Russian force consisted of 3,300 infantrymen, 272 cavalry, and 11 artillery pieces.

The Russian infantry conducted a reconnaissance in force on 27 March 1885, which pushed back the Afghan outpost pickets. The Afghans established new observation posts, which the Russians disingenuously considered "aggressive" and used as the pretext for a Russian attack. On 29 March, Komarov issued an ultimatum to the defenders of Penjdeh to withdraw or risk being driven out of "Russian" territory by force. Lumsden was in the vicinity and, realizing

Perak, Punitive Expedition to

a battle was inevitable, withdrew but left behind a small group of officers to negotiate with the Russians. All British attempts to reach a compromise with the Russians were unsuccessful.

At 6:30 A.M. on 30 March 1885, Russian troops advanced on the Afghan defenses until fired upon. The Russians returned well-aimed fire that "broke" the Afghan cavalry. The Russians continued their advance, eventually reaching the Afghan trenches where bitter hand-to-hand fighting took place. According to Lumsden, two companies of Afghans fought hard and "died in their trenches to a man" (Johnson 1999, p. 10). The remainder fled, and the Russians occupied Penjdeh. Afghan casualties numbered between 300 and 800, while the Russians suffered 48 killed and wounded.

The British were alarmed, and because of the British guarantee to protect Afghanistan's borders, war appeared inevitable. After considerable saber rattling, the crisis was eventually overcome by diplomacy and the Russians withdrew. A boundary commission was established that handed Penjdeh back to the Russians in exchange for Afghan control of the strategic Zulfikar Pass, and the border between Afghanistan and Russia was delineated in 1887. This entire crisis pointed out the vulnerability of India, and while war was averted, the solution seemed to be a humiliation for Great Britain.

The Penjdeh Incident had many significant consequences for the British, who increased the strength of British and Indian forces in India, conducted additional contingency planning for a forward defense, and expanded the road and rail network in India to ensure the rapid mobilization and deployment of forces.

See also Afghan War, Second (1878–1880); Afghanistan; Great Game; Imperialism; India; India, British Army in; Indian Army Operations

References: Farwell (1989); Fredericks (1971); French (1994); James (1997); Johnson (1999); Roberts (1897)

Perak, Punitive Expedition to (1875–1876)

The punitive expedition to the state of Perak on the Malayan Peninsula was one of the many lesser-known campaigns of the Pax Britannica, in which British and imperial soldiers fought with equal gallantry and distinction but are seldom chronicled in history books.

The East India Company established the British settlements of Penang, Malacca, and Singapore (the Straits Settlements) between 1786 and 1825 and governed them until 1858, when they came under the India Office. In 1867 they were transferred to the Colonial Office and were constituted a separate Crown Colony. The value of the Straits Settlements lies primarily in the commercial and strategic link they provided by serving as the nexus between the Indian subcontinent and the Chinese trade, as well as to the defense of India.

There was immediate friction between the newly established imperial policies, local traditions, and trade disputes with other European powers, notably the Dutch. Finally, in September 1873 Britain abruptly reversed its nonintervention policy, mainly in order to control the lucrative tin mining and other commercial ventures and exclude the Dutch from trading activities.

Sir Andrew Clarke became governor of the Straits Settlements on 4 November 1873. Shortly thereafter, J. W. W. Birch became the British resident at Perak. There were numerous misunderstandings over the role of religion in government, and Birch proposed to reform the revenue collection system, the administration of justice, and debt slavery. The local chiefs were highly concerned about this threat to their livelihoods. While posting notices containing new detailed tax and customs regulations, Birch was assassinated in the village of Passir Salak on 2 November 1875.

When the news of Birch's murder reached Penang on 3 November 1875, Lieutenant Colonel (later General Sir) A. E. H. Anson, the lieutenant governor, dispatched a force of over ninety soldiers under Captain Innes to investigate the murder and protect other British officials. This contingent reached the British residency at Bandar Bahru on 6 November and joined a force under Major Dunlop. They attacked the rebel stronghold at Passir Salak the following day. After a short skirmish, the rebel force withdrew. British casualties were four killed (including Innes), and thirteen wounded. Dunlop conducted a second attack on 15 November on the rebel strongholds at Kampong Pisang and Passir Salak, although both had been abandoned. The successful assault on Passir Salak seemed to have ended the Perak War before the reinforcements from Hong Kong entered the fray and even before the Indian contingent reached Perak.

Not knowing the success of Dunlop's small force, the governor, Major General (later Lieutenant General Sir) William Jervois (who had succeeded Clarke in May 1875), frantically cabled London for reinforcements from India and Hong Kong. By early December 1875 the British force (in addition to Dunlop's force in the field) consisted of 300 men of the 80th Foot (reinforcements from Hong Kong), under Major General F. Colborne, and a 1,500-man Indian contingent commanded by Brigadier General J. Ross. Jervois intended to invade Perak by dividing his force into a northern column (Ross's troops) and a southern column (Colborne's contingent). The overall plan of this punitive expedition was to conduct a large pincer movement to capture Birch's murderers, who were reportedly at Blanja. On 14 December 1875 Colborne's forces arrived at Blanja and found it deserted.

There were concurrent indications of a native uprising in Sungei Ujong, north of Malacca. British forces near Rassa, in Sungei Ujong, consisted of Lieutenant Hinxman and 45 soldiers of the 10th Foot. Reinforcements soon brought Hinxman's force to 6 officers and 177 soldiers. On 7 December 1875, Hinxman's troops attacked through rugged terrain without fire support and captured a rebel fort at Paroe. This sharp engagement cost the British 42 casualties.

Anson brought reinforcements to Sungei Ujong, and by 12 December 1875, he had over 500 soldiers, artillery, and more than 120 rockets. He divided his force into a 1st Division (9 officers and 160 men, commanded by Lieutenant Colonel Hill) and a 2nd Division (8 officers and 365 men, under Lieutenant Colonel Clay). The plan was for Hill's force to travel through dense, uncharted jungle and swamp and attack three enemy strongholds at the Bukit Putus Pass from the rear, while Clay's 2nd Division, starting on 20 December 1875, would march directly to the pass and attack the forts from the front.

Clay's Division was spearheaded by a fifty-man element led by Captain Channer. After halting to remove felled tree obstacles, Channer saw smoke and heard voices of the unsuspecting rebels. Taking advantage of the element of surprise, Channer and his force moved quietly through the dense jungle to the southwest corner of the first stockade. Channer audaciously seized the initiative and, with two Gurkhas, stormed the stockade. Channer shot with his revolver the first insurgent he encountered of the two dozen or so there, and each Gurkha shot a rebel as the remainder of Channer's force followed. The surprised enemy fled the stockade, and after Channer's force concentrated its fire on the other two stockades, the enemy fled them, too. This ended the fighting, with one Gurkha killed and three wounded, and an unknown number of Malay casualties. Channer later received the Victoria Cross for his intrepidity in action that day.

The destruction of the stockades at the Bukit Putus Pass on 20 December 1875 basically ended operations in Sungei Ujong. In Perak, Ross's soldiers participated in a savage firefight on 4 January 1876 at Kota Lama, where the British soldiers fought with fixed bayonets and the Malays steadfastly with spears. In retaliation, Kota Lama was destroyed on 20 January. Active operations in the Perak War were veritably over even though it took months to round up the remaining insurgent ringleaders and complete the pacification.

The military operations in Perak and Sungei Ujong during the Perak War were generally conducted professionally, effectively, expeditiously, and perhaps most importantly to Whitehall, economically. As of 6 April 1876, after active operations had ended and pacification was continuing, Jervois reported that the entire war had cost only £71,074. As a result of the Perak War, the British were able to extend complete control over the west coast states of the Malay Peninsula from Perak in the north to Malacca.

See also East India Company; Imperialism; India; Indian Army Operations; Rockets; Victoria Cross
References: Burns and Cowan (1975); Cowan (1961); Parkinson (1960); Raugh (2000); Sadka (1968)

Persia

Persia (probably derived from the Persian word *Fars* or *Pars*, a term now applied to the southern province of Iran, the country's current name) was a large plateau-like kingdom with the Arab Mesopotamia to the west, the mountains of Afghanistan to the east, the Persian Gulf to the south, and the Caucasus Mountains in the north. This region was part of the playing field of the Great Game, the imperial rivalry in which Great Britain attempted to protect India from Russian encroachment, while Russia tried to expand its spheres of strategic influence in achieving its "eastern destiny."

The Qajar dynasty assumed power in Persia in 1795. The Persians fought two disastrous wars with Russia (which ended in 1812 and 1828, respectively) and were forced to cede territory to the victor. In the 1830s, the Qajars tried to replace their army, based on tribal levies, with a standing army organized, disciplined, and equipped along European lines and trained by Russian and Polish officers.

The Persian Army that faced the British in the Persian War (1856–1857) had lost much of its proficiency and discipline. Only 20,000 soldiers, out of a nominal total strength of 86,700, were reportedly fit for duty. Discipline was unbearable, pay was poor, equipment and weapons were outdated, and medical facilities nonexistent. Regular troops included the shah's (king's) guard, usually stationed in the capital, Teheran, and other regiments in key towns and provinces. At Koosh-ab, for example, there were nine infantry regiments and one guards battalion. Irregular troops, consisting mainly of cavalrymen, were mobilized only in wartime.

The artillery was said to be the most proficient of all the arms in the Persian Army although its effectiveness was plagued by a large variety of caliber weapons, even within regiments, poor maintenance, and ammunition shortages.

As shown by its performance during the 1856–1857 Persian War, the Persian soldiers suffered considerably from poor leadership and other factors and were easily demoralized. During one Persian retreat during the campaign, it was reported that an 800-man Persian infantry regiment cornered a single British mounted lancer, who audaciously charged and scattered the entire Persian unit.

See also Afghanistan; East India Company; Great Game; Imperialism; India; Persian War

References: Featherstone (1989); Haythornthwaite (1995); Metz (1989); Waller (1990)

Persian War (1856–1857)

The British, even while fighting the Crimean War (1854–1856), continued to be concerned about Russian expansion into Central Asia in the Great Game, considered the main threat to British India. After conquering the Syr Darya Valley, Russian influence reached Persia's frontier in 1854. Afghanistan, an important buffer state from the British perspective, seemed threatened. The 30 March 1855 Treaty of Peshawar created an Anglo-Afghan alliance against Persia to thwart further Russian expansion.

In September 1855, Persian troops, reportedly with Russian assistance and after ignoring a British warning, occupied the key Afghan town of Herat, a nexus of trade routes about 400 miles west of Kabul. Persia formally annexed Herat on 25 October 1856. After the Persians refused to evacuate the town, the British declared war on 1 November 1856. This was the last war fought mainly by East India Company troops.

Within days a British force sailed from India to Persia. Commanded by Major General Foster Stalker, the 5,670-man force from Bombay conducted an unopposed amphibious landing 10 miles south of Bushire on the Persian Gulf on 5 December 1856. Two days later the British seized the weakly defended fort at Reshire, the last defensive position before the port of Bushire. Bushire was bombarded by naval gunfire on 12 December, and British infantry assaulted through a breach made in the city walls. Fighting ceased at noon as the Persians surrendered.

The British Government decided to extend operations in Persia and double the size of the British force. A new force commander, Lieutenant General Sir James Outram, arrived in Bushire on 27 January 1857, and a second division, commanded by Brigadier General (later Major General Sir) Henry Havelock, arrived the same month. Outram believed his force was threatened by Shooja-ool-Mool's 7,000-man Persian army located 46 miles away at Borasjoon.

Outram immediately marched his 4,500-man force to Borasjoon, only to find the Persian Army retire without firing a shot. The British withdrew to Bushire but were attacked by a 6,900-strong Persian army near Koosh-ab on 8 February 1856. The 3rd Bombay Cavalry and the Poona Horse, with artillery support, charged the Persians while the British infantry deployed into tactical formations. A Persian infantry regiment formed a defensive square, but the British cavalry opened a gap in the square through which additional cavalry poured. By this time, the British infantry began its deliberate march toward the Persian line, which broke and fled, leaving about 700 dead on the battlefield. The British lost 10 dead and 62 wounded at Koosh-ab.

After leaving a force at Bushire, Outram's 4,900-man force was towed up the Euphrates River in troopships to the new Persian position at Mohumra. At dawn on 26 March 1856, the British fleet began bombarding the Persian defenses, and about six hours later, the British made an unopposed landing. After the British formed their line of battle and advanced upon the Persians, the latter again fled the battlefield. Outram sent three river steamers with 300 soldiers up the Karum River after the withdrawing Persians. When the Persians saw the small British flotilla, and a gunboat shell landed near their commander, they withdrew again. On 5 April, Outram learned that a peace had been negotiated and the Persians agreed to evacuate Herat.

This ended the Persian War, and the British force was withdrawn, soon thereafter to fight in the Indian Mutiny. The frontier between Persia and Afghanistan was restored. The Persian shah (king) reportedly ordered the seizure of army officers who had run away at the Battle of Mohumra, and had them publicly humiliated by being dragged by rings in their noses. This small war was supposedly unpopular with Britons at home, and a contemporary article in the London *Times* began, "Where Herat is, we neither know or care" (Farwell 2001, p. 36).

See also Afghanistan; East India Company; East India Company, Military Forces; Great Game; Havelock, Major General Sir Henry; India; Indian Army Operations; Indian Mutiny; Outram, Lieutenant General Sir James; Persia

References: Brock (1858); Farwell (2001); Featherstone (1973); Featherstone (1989); Haythornthwaite (1995); Kempton (1993); Royle (2000)

Photographers, War

Photography was invented in the 1820s and generated tremendous enthusiasm and curiosity, especially for its truthfulness in recording exact images and accurate depictions. Its wartime use began in the early Victorian military campaigns and became more frequent as time passed.

The first rudimentary camera was made in 1827 by Joseph Nicephore Niepce. He became a partner of Louis Daguerre in 1829, and the latter soon developed a method of developing photographic plates by immersing them in a salt solution and making the image permanent. These permanent images, called Daguerreotypes, first appeared in 1839 and aroused great interest. At about the same time William Henry Fox Talbot developed the Calotype, which was of inferior quality to the Daguerreotype but could be reproduced in an unlimited number of positive prints.

Britain's first war photographer was probably John Mac-Cosh, a British Army surgeon serving in India. An amateur photographer stationed in the Himalayas, he began taking photographs in 1844 and photographed a number of people and scenes from the Second Sikh War (1848–1849) and the Second Burma War (1852–1853).

At the beginning of the Crimean War in early 1854, the British public was generally patriotic and eager for pictures of the war. James Robertson (c. 1813–1881), an Englishman working as chief engraver at the mint in Constantinople and neophyte photographer, recognized this need. As allied troops arrived in Constantinople in April and May 1854, he took photographs and sent them to the *Illustrated London News*, where they were used as the basis for accurate engravings. Robertson later photographed the fall and destruction of Sevastopol in September 1855. In 1857, during the Indian Mutiny, he was appointed official photographer to the British forces in India.

Times war correspondents Thomas Chenery and William Howard Russell aroused public opinion in Britain in the fall of 1854 with reports of the dreadfully unsanitary medical conditions and soldier suffering in the Crimea. To restore public confidence in the conduct of the war, it was decided to use the new medium that never lied to record actual conditions in the Crimea. Roger Fenton (1819–1869), an unsuccessful painter who had studied law but had frequently photographed the Royal family, was sent to the Crimea in March 1855 to record combat conditions in the Crimea. He took with him a wine merchant's wagon converted into a darkroom.

Fenton had the opportunity to record the realistic horrors of war, but he failed to do so. The lengthy exposure times and other limits of photographic techniques prohibited action scenes, which means all of his photographs of people and objects were stationary, and perhaps posed. Political and financial concerns probably overrode all other considerations. Fenton had the support and sponsorship of the Royal family and British government, and he probably realized he should not take photographs detrimental to the government's war effort. He was also probably concerned about postwar exhibitions and selling his photographs with the assistance of a publisher and did not want to offend the public in this regard. As a result, Fenton took photographs of allied military leaders, the camp life of soldiers, scenes in and around Balaklava and before Sevastopol, but did not take any images of combat or its aftermath.

Suffering from cholera, Fenton returned to Britain in the late summer of 1855 after taking about 350 photographs. The fall of Sevastopol on 9 September 1855 ended most of the fighting and the British and French seemed destined to win the war. Exhibitions of Fenton's photographs were held in October 1855, and the public was intrigued, while some people may have been repulsed, by the vividness of his images of camp life and other subjects from the Crimea. All of his photographs did not sell, however, and it seemed the British public wanted to forget the earlier horrors of war. Moreover, the development process of Fenton's photographs caused them to fade with time. Fenton's photographs were important in setting a precedent in war photography, which added a new element to the battlefield.

It was technically not possible to reproduce photographs in mass until the invention of the halftone screen in 1880. Until then, photographs served as models for war artists, illustrators, and engravers. George Eastman's invention of the Kodak camera and film in the 1880s made it much easier for individuals to own cameras and take war photographs.

See also Artists, War; Burma War, Second (1852–1853); Correspondents, War; Crimean War; Indian Mutiny; Sikh War, Second (1848–1849)
References: Bowie (1989); Bruce (1973); Fabb and Carmen (1975); James (1981); Knightley (1975); Leggat (1999); Leggat (2000); Rainbird (1999); Royle (2000); Sweetman (2001)

Pistols

Pistols, due to their unreliability, short range, and single-shot capability, were seldom used by British Army officers and cavalrymen until improved designs in the 1850s made them more practical and effective. "It is the opinion of every Officer Commanding a Cavalry Regiment," noted a Board of General officers in 1828, "and of, it may be added, every old soldier who has had experience of European Warfare, [that the pistol] is seldom, if ever, found of any use" (Strachan 1985, p. 62).

Interest in the pistol was generated at the Great Exhibition in 1851, where the pistols of Colt and of Deane and Adams were on display. The Colt revolver had six chambers, weighed 4 pounds, and was of relatively small caliber, with sixty balls to the pound. It had to be recocked after every shot. The Deane and Adams pistol had five chambers, which allowed a larger caliber (thirty-two balls to the pound), and it weighed 2 pounds, 14 ounces. The biggest advantage of the Colt was that it was machine-made and all of its component parts were interchangeable. After trials, the British Army adopted the Colt in 1854.

Pistol improvements, notably the Smith and Wesson invention of the hinged frame that permitted quick loading and the development of an effective center-fire cartridge, were made in the 1860s. Officers were encouraged to purchase pistols that fired .45-caliber ammunition. The Webley 1867 Royal Irish Constabulary model and the Adams Mark II were popular revolvers used throughout the 1870s.

The Board of Ordnance in 1880 designated the .477 Enfield pistol for use by senior Royal Artillery sergeants, and seven years later, replaced it with the .455 Webley.

During the Second Boer War (1899–1902), the British Army discontinued the policy of permitting officers to purchase pistols of their choice and recommended the six-chambered, .441-caliber Webley. Those who carried pistols at this time included infantry and cavalry officers, warrant officers, and staff sergeants. Infantry and artillery drivers were armed with pistols only.

See also Cavalry, British Army—Weapons and Equipment; Engineers, British Army—Weapons and Equipment; Infantry, British Army—Small Arms
References: Grierson (1899); Knight (1996); Strachan (1985)

Pollock, Major General Sir George
See Afghan War, First (1839–1842)

Pomeroy-Colley, Major General Sir George (1835–1881)

Major General Sir George Pomeroy-Colley was considered a "brilliant" British Army officer, and his outstanding abilities and promise had been recognized early by his inclusion in Major General (later Field Marshal Viscount) Sir Garnet J. Wolseley's Ashanti Ring of young, competent, and progressive officers. While a superb staff officer and instructor, Pomeroy-Colley had little command experience.

Pomeroy-Colley (his original surname was "Colley," but he hyphenated his name later in life) was born into an Anglo-Irish family in 1835. At thirteen he entered the Royal Military College, Sandhurst, passed out at the top of his class, and in 1852 was commissioned without purchase an ensign in the 2nd Foot. Promoted without purchase to lieutenant to 1854, he was posted to his regiment in Cape Colony, South Africa, where he served as a border magistrate.

In 1860, Pomeroy-Colley served as a company commander in the Second China War and then returned to England to attend the Staff College. Pomeroy-Colley's intellect was readily apparent when he completed the normal two-year course in less than ten months, achieving on the examination the highest score then on record. His exceptional theoretical knowledge soon led to his appointment as professor of military administration at the Staff College.

Wolseley selected Pomeroy-Colley to serve as director of transport during the Second Ashanti War (1873–1874). This operation, in a disease-ridden jungle environment, heavily depended on logistics and transportation. Pomeroy-Colley's superb achievements in West Africa earned him a secure place in Wolseley's fledgling Ashanti Ring and promotion to colonel. Wolseley believed, "He was a man in a thousand, with an iron will and of inflexible determination" (Farwell 1972, p. 243).

In 1875, when Wolseley was appointed governor of Natal, Pomeroy-Colley accompanied him as a staff officer and had a good opportunity to reconnoiter the terrain of the area and gain an appreciation for Boer attitudes. Pomeroy-Colley then became military secretary to the viceroy of India, but when Wolseley was appointed to command the forces during the later phases of the Zulu War, 1879, he rejoined Wolseley as chief of staff. The conclusion of the war in Natal, coupled with renewed fighting in Afghanistan, required Pomeroy-Colley's return to India.

Pomeroy-Colley was promoted to major general in April 1880 and succeeded Wolseley as governor and commander in chief of Natal and the Transvaal and high commissioner for South-East Africa. There was considerable Boer discontent in the Transvaal, which had been annexed by Britain in 1877, and friction increased over taxation and other issues.

The First Boer War broke out on 16 December 1880. The initial action of the war took place four days later, when the Boers intercepted a British column at Bronkhorstspruit, east of Pretoria. In the short engagement that followed, the British suffered heavy casualties and the survivors surrendered. This was a humiliating defeat for the British.

At this time Pomeroy-Colley commanded about 3,500 British troops in the Transvaal and in Natal. While Pomeroy-Colley was considered a brilliant staff officer and administrator, this was his first independent field command. Pomeroy-Colley also seems to have overestimated the fighting abilities of the British while underestimating that of the Boers.

Pomeroy-Colley's 1,400-man composite Natal Field Force departed Pietermaritzburg on 10 January 1881 to quell the Boer unrest and relieve the British garrisons in the Transvaal. On 28 January 1881, Pomeroy-Colley's force conducted a frontal attack uphill, intending to turn the Boer position at Laing's Nek, a key pass in the Drakensberg Mountains on the route to the Transvaal. Accurate Boer marksmanship halted the British, who again sustained a large number of casualties. The attack was an abject failure. Pomeroy-Colley seems to have found it unimaginable that a bunch of Boer farmers had defeated well-trained and disciplined British soldiers.

The British withdrew to Mount Prospect, 3 miles south of Laing's Nek. On 7 February 1881, however, the Boers started a flanking movement to isolate the British force. The next day Pomeroy-Colley, under Colonial Office pressure to defeat the Boers quickly, personally led a five-company force to ensure the route was still open. This was an act that should have been conducted by a subordinate officer. Some 8 miles south of Mount Prospect, near the Ingogo River, the British fought a large Boer force and had many casualties.

Back at the base camp, Pomeroy-Colley, eager to redeem his tainted reputation before a peace settlement was reached, learned that the Boer positions at Laing's Nek had been strengthened considerably. He decided to seize the undefended mountain of Majuba that dominated Laing's Nek.

To accomplish this plan, Pomeroy-Colley led his force in a night march, 26–27 February 1881, over steep and winding paths. The last British soldier reached Majuba's unoccupied summit by 5:00 A.M. on 27 February. Pomeroy-Colley, arguably overconfident, did not order his soldiers (who had not received any information as to the situation and plans) to dig defensive fighting positions. At the same time, a certain "listlessness" is said to have overwhelmed Pomeroy-Colley, and there was no coordinated assault on the Nek.

In sum, the Boers advanced stealthily up the hill to the British positions. After about five hours, during which time heavy rifle fire was exchanged, about 400 Boers had reached positions within striking distance of the summit. By using skillful fire and movement and infiltration techniques, the Boers occupied Majuba. They poured heavy fire into the confused and demoralized mass of British soldiers, many of whom panicked and stampeded to the rear.

Pomeroy-Colley seems to have been dazed by the rapidity of events and sudden reversal of fortune. Whether trying to rally his men or surrender, Pomeroy-Colley was shot in the forehead and died instantly. He was one of the 285 British soldiers, out of a force of about 365 on the summit, killed or wounded at the ignominious Battle of Majuba Hill. In his quest to redeem his reputation, Pomeroy-Colley may have become unbalanced and achieved a sort of immortality different from that which he had sought.

See also Ashanti Ring; Ashanti War, Second (1873–1874); Boer War, First (1880–1881); Boers; Camberley, Staff College; China War, Second (1856–1860); Majuba Hill, Battle of; Sandhurst, Royal Military College; Wolseley, Field Marshal Garnet J.

References: Barthorp (1987); Bond (1967); Bond (1972); Farwell (1972); Maxwell (1985); Ransford (1967)

Pratt, Major General Thomas
See Taranaki War

Prendergast, Major General Harry, V.C.
See Burma War, Third (1885)

Prior, Melton
See Artists, War

Punjab Frontier Force

The British victory over the Sikhs in the First Sikh War (1845–1846) permitted the extension of British influence in the Punjab. The British quickly realized that the stalwart Sikh soldiers were formidable warriors and began to raise military units in the Punjab.

Lieutenant (later Colonel) Harry Lumsden formed the first unit in the Punjab, the Corps of Guides, in December 1846. It was intended to serve as a scout element, and was the first unit to wear dust-colored, or khaki, uniforms, to blend in with the local terrain. Other infantry and cavalry units were soon formed, including in 1846–1847 the 1st through the 4th Sikh Regiments as the "Infantry of the Frontier Brigade." In 1851, the "Frontier Brigade" became the "Punjab Irregular Force," to which was added the Corps of Guides. The nickname "Piffers" originated with the initials of the Punjab Irregular Force—PIF—and was retained after the unit was redesignated the Punjab Frontier Force in 1865.

The Punjab Frontier Force was a strong force at this time, consisting of the Corps of Guides, ten infantry regiments, five cavalry regiments, and a number of light field and mountain artillery batteries. The Punjab Frontier Force, or elements and lineal descendents thereof, participated in at least seventeen of the hard-fought campaigns on the North-West Frontier between 1851 and 1908.

Prior to 1886, the Punjab Frontier Force was unique in being the only unit not to come under the command of the commander in chief, Bengal, who was also the commander in chief, India. In 1886, control of the Punjab Frontier Force was transferred from the direct command of the lieutenant governor of the Punjab and of the government of India to the commander in chief, India.

The Punjab Frontier Force was disbanded and its subordinate battalions and regiments were redesignated in the 1903 reorganization of the Indian Army. Selected infantry battalions and cavalry regiments that had been part of the Punjab Frontier Force were permitted to bear "Frontier Force" after the unit title.

See also Bengal Army; Chamberlain, Field Marshal Sir Neville B.; India; Indian Army Organization; Lockhart, General Sir William S.A.; North-West Frontier; Sikh War, First (1845–1846); Sikhs

References: Cook (1975); Farwell (1989); Haythornthwaite (1995); Mason (1974); Nevill (1912)

Punniar, Battle of (29 December 1843)
See Gwalior Campaign

Purchase System

The purchase system was introduced when an English standing army was formed in 1683 to prevent another government similar to the military regime of Oliver Cromwell and his major generals. Prospective officers were required to purchase their initial military commissions in the infantry and cavalry and subsequent promotions through the rank of lieutenant colonel. The purchase system, however, could be manipulated and abused by wealthy officers, and it became outdated and was abolished in 1871 when professionalism and competence became more important than wealth as officer qualifications and as a prelude to further army reform.

Aristocrats and gentry, men of property with a stake in the country and in maintaining the status quo, and not military adventurers, were generally the only men who could afford such substantial sums. The purchase price of a commission also served as a type of guarantee of good behavior, since men dismissed from the service forfeited their commission prices. As one of the most important lessons of the English Civil Wars and Cromwell Commonwealth, the Crown and Parliament resolved to ensure the officers—the leaders and decision makers—of the army were of the class that had everything to lose and nothing to gain by conducting or supporting a military revolution.

Those who held the King's or Queen's commissions—the commissioned officers—were expected to be, quite simply, "officers and gentlemen." This implied, in addition to wealth (which at the time generally meant owning estates and land), good breeding. Being a gentleman was considered a prerequisite for being an army officer.

It was believed from the time of the Restoration until about the end of the nineteenth century that "war [was] the occupation of the nobility and gentry" (Cannadine 1990, p.

264). Because the aristocrats and gentry were large landowners, they were generally considered the "leisured class," since they derived their wealth from their land and did not have to work for a living. They were also, in this patriarchal society, the fighting class, duty-bound to protect the "subordinate," lower classes of civil society from foreign invasion and depredation: "Honor and glory, courage and chivalry, gallantry and loyalty, [and] leadership and horsemanship were quintessential patrician attributes, inculcated in the country house and learned on the hunting field" (Cannadine 1990, p. 264). The claim to command of the aristocracy and gentry was based on character and social standing, rather than on concepts of military proficiency or tactical expertise. They were considered, and considered themselves, the natural leaders, of society, their estates, and of the army. Their role as leaders in the army was thought to be a natural extension of the leadership they consistently demonstrated on family land, leading troops from more humble and generally agrarian backgrounds.

The purchase system, from the government perspective, also made good fiscal sense. The pay of officers was very low, barely covering minimal living expenses. From 1713 to about 1763, for example, officer pay remained basically unchanged, regardless of inflation. A private income was necessary for officers, especially those in the more fashionable regiments. Moreover, the purchase system permitted the government to save money on costly military retirement pensions. The retiring officer, up to and including the rank of lieutenant colonel, would be able to sell his commission and probably realize a large profit, which would serve as his pension fund.

Initial officer commissions, and occasionally promotions, were sometimes obtainable without purchase. Sons of career army officers, as a tribute to the father's military service and a reflection of inadequate financial resources, could petition the commander in chief and request to be commissioned without purchase. Field Marshal Viscount Garnet J. Wolseley received his commission in this manner in 1852. Occasionally an officer could be promoted free as recognition of gallantry or distinguished conduct in battle. In addition, if a serving officer was killed in action or died, it could be possible for the next senior officer in the regiment to fill the vacancy without purchase. The dead officer, or his widow, forfeited and did not receive reimbursement for any commission or promotion purchases. Similarly, an officer promoted above the rank of lieutenant colonel lost all money paid for his commission and promotions.

The purchase system initially worked relatively well in the English, then the British, Army. The government did not want a repeat of the Cromwellian military dictatorship, desired stability, and was eager to save money on its standing army. The rigid social class structure also permitted the purchase system to operate somewhat effectively. As the nineteenth century progressed, questions were posed pertaining to a system in which those with social status, land, and money were able to buy promotions over the heads of officers with more experience, expertise, and proven battlefield leadership abilities. Abuses of the purchase system became exposed as a result of the debacle of the Crimean War and other campaigns.

Under the purchase system, only the wealthy could expect to be promoted to major or to be a regimental (battalion) commander as a lieutenant colonel. One of the biggest injustices of the system was the enormous price of each promotion. The War Office issued in 1821 an official tariff regulating the prices of initial commissions and subsequent promotions in the various types of regiments. A higher demand versus lower supply, coupled with bribery, caused the actual "overregulation" prices of commissions and promotions to be much higher than the official tariffs. In 1850, the purchase prices of commissions were:

Line Regiments—lieutenant, £700; captain, £1,800; major, £3,200; lieutenant colonel, £4,500
Dragoon Guards and Dragoons—lieutenant, £1,190; captain, £3,225; major, £4,575; lieutenant colonel, £6,175
Horse Guards—lieutenant, £1,600; captain, £3,500; major, £5,350; lieutenant colonel, £7,250
Foot Guards—lieutenant, £2,050; captain, £4,800; major, £8,300; lieutenant colonel, £9,000

To buy or sell commissions at any rate other than the official tariff was considered a misdemeanor, but by the mid-nineteenth century, such regulations were ignored and openly evaded. In 1856, it was stated before the Commission on the Purchase of Commissions in the Army that the common overregulation prices for the rank of lieutenant colonel were £7,000 in line regiments, £13,000 in the Foot Guards, and £14,000 in the cavalry.

Lieutenant General James T. Brudenell, Seventh Earl of Cardigan, was an aristocrat who came to embody the worst abuses of the British Army purchase system by the wealthy aristocracy. Born in 1797, Cardigan began his army career in 1824 when he purchased a cornetcy in the 8th Hussars. He continued to take advantage of the purchase system, buying promotion to lieutenant in January 1825, to captain in June 1826, to major in August 1830, and four months later to lieutenant colonel. In 1836, he assumed command of the 11th Hussars (then Light Dragoons), reportedly for £40,000. Cardigan is best remembered as having commanded the Light Brigade of the Cavalry Division in the Charge of the Light Brigade at the Battle of Balaklava (25 October 1854) during the Crimean War.

Cardigan's brother-in-law, Field Marshal George C. Bingham, Third Earl of Lucan, used his wealth to purchase his military ranks and commands, frequently over those more competent. He was born in 1800 and was commissioned an ensign in the 6th Foot in 1816. After a series of rapid promotion purchases, regimental exchanges, and periods on half pay, Lucan became commander of the 17th Lancers as a lieutenant colonel on 9 November 1826—reportedly for £25,000. He commanded the 17th Lancers until 1837, when he again went on half pay, and was promoted to colonel in 1841 and to major general ten years later. Lucan commanded the Cavalry Division during the Crimean War.

The purchase system permitted the mediocre and incompetent to attain high rank and command positions. Wealthy aristocrats, as in the cases of Cardigan and Lucan, often used their means to further their careers, and changed regiments as often as necessary, having little interest in their temporary affiliations. To avoid overseas duty and active service, officers occasionally exchanged regiments or went on half pay.

In 1856, a Royal Commission concluded that the purchase system was "vicious in principle, repugnant to the public sentiment of the present day, equally inconsistent with the honour of the military profession and the policy of the British Empire, and irreconcilable with justice" (Farwell 1981, p. 57). The purchase system was the rallying point for all those opposed to military reform of any kind. After lengthy debates, Queen Victoria signed the Royal Warrant on 20 July 1871 that abolished the purchase system, effective 1 November 1871.

See also Army and Society; Cardigan, Lieutenant General James T. Brudenell, Seventh Earl of; Cardwell, Edward T.; Cardwell Reforms; Crimean War; Lucan, Field Marshal George C. Bingham, Third Earl of; Officers, British Army—Pay; Officers, British Army—Retirement; Officers, British Army—Sources of Commissioning; War Office; Wolseley, Field Marshal Garnet J.

References: Barnett (1970); Cannadine (1990); Farwell (1981); Harries-Jenkins (1977); Maurice and Arthur (1924); Moyse-Bartlett (1974); Raugh (1984); Skelley (1977); Woodham-Smith (1953)

Q

Quartermaster-General, British Army

The quartermaster-general was one of the three original British Army staff positions, in addition to the military secretary and adjutant-general, created by Field Marshal H.R.H. Frederick, Duke of York, commander in chief, in 1795. This staff, originally located in Whitehall, became known as the Horse Guards.

At the end of the Napoleonic Wars, the major duties and responsibilities of the quartermaster-general included quartering, encamping, and moving troops.

The duties and responsibilities of the quartermaster-adjutant evolved considerably between 1815 and 1914, especially after the War Office and the Horse Guards were consolidated under the provisions of the War Office Act of 1870.

By 1853, the duties and responsibilities of the quartermaster-general were defined more specifically and were considered "less demanding" than those of the adjutant-general. The quartermaster-general was responsible for the march, embarkation, and disembarkation of troops; for the siting of encampments; and for the billeting and accommodation of troops. He had responsibility for the defense of Great Britain, which included maintenance of military establishments, as well as for the defensive plans of military camps and barracks. The quartermaster-general formed information and survey branches with a military plans and papers department. At this stage, there remained some redundancy between the duties and responsibilities of the quartermaster-general and those of other departments. There were, like the adjutant-general, three officers with subordinates to assist the quartermaster-general at the Horse Guards. There were a deputy quartermaster-general in Edinburgh and assistant quartermaster-generals in the United Kingdom districts required to submit monthly reports to the quartermaster-general at the Horse Guards.

The Army Council, in addition to a general staff, was established in 1904 as a result of recommendations of the War Office Reconstitution, or Esher, Committee. The Army Council was to consist of seven members. The third military member was the quartermaster-general, responsible for transport, remount, railway, supply, and veterinary services; barrack administration; maintenance of authorized food and material reserves; contracts; and the administration of votes (in the Army Estimates) for these services. In sum, all aspects of material supply other than actual manufacture fell within the purview of the quartermaster-general. The quartermaster-general's key subordinates were the director of transport and remounts, the director of movements and quartering, the director of supplies and clothing, and the director of equipment and ordnance stores.

See also Adjutant-General, British Army; Army Estimates; Commander in Chief, British Army; Horse Guards; Master-General of the Ordnance, British Army; War Office
References: Barnett (1970); Bond (1972); Hamer (1970); Moyse-Bartlett (1974); Spiers (1992); Sweetman (1984)

Quetta, Staff College
See Officers, Indian Army–Training and Education

Raglan, Field Marshal Fitzroy J. H. Somerset, First Baron (1788–1855)

Field Marshal Fitzroy J. H. Somerset, First Baron Raglan, was a senior British Army officer and a protégé of Field Marshal Arthur Wellesley, First Duke of Wellington. His career culminated in command of British forces in the Crimean War (1854–1855).

Raglan, born on 30 September 1788 at Badminton, was the youngest of eleven children of the Fifth Duke of Beaufort. He was educated at Westminster School and commissioned as a cornet in the 4th Light Dragoons in 1804. As an aristocrat, he purchased his promotions quickly and received prestigious assignments. He served as aide-de-camp to Wellington during the Peninsular War and became his military secretary in 1810. Staff service did not prevent Raglan from participating in combat duty, and he distinguished himself with gallantry at numerous engagements. Raglan was noted for being courageous, industrious, tactful, and calm in the most difficult situations. He married Wellington's niece in 1814.

Raglan served as Wellington's military secretary at the Battle of Waterloo (18 June 1815). Raglan's right elbow was shattered by a sniper shot, and his arm was amputated on the battlefield. As his arm was tossed away, he reportedly called out, "Hey, bring my arm back. There's a ring my wife gave me on the finger" (Hibbert 1961, p. 3).

After the Napoleonic Wars, Raglan continued to serve Wellington in numerous diplomatic and military missions. In 1827, Wellington became British Army commander in chief, and Raglan, then a thirty-nine-year-old major general, became his secretary. Raglan continued to serve Wellington loyally, frequently doing the aging duke's work.

In 1852, Wellington died, and Raglan, who had hoped to succeed him, became master-general of the ordnance and was given a peerage as the First Baron Raglan.

On 7 February 1854, as war with Russia over the Ottoman Empire became imminent, Lieutenant General Lord Raglan was appointed "General Officer Commanding the Forces eastward of Malta" (Sweetman 2001, p. 22). He was promoted to general on 20 June 1854 and led the 26,000-soldier British expeditionary force to the Crimean Peninsula, landing at Calamita Bay on 14 September 1854. After assembling, the allied British-French force began its advance to the south toward Sevastopol, the objective.

The Russians, defending on the southern bank of the Alma River, contested the allied advance on 20 September 1854. In the ensuing battle, Raglan appeared with his staff along the British line, thus inspiring his soldiers while observing the operation. At 3:00 P.M., he ordered the infantry to advance and moved to a forward position to observe and direct the attack. The Battle of the Alma was an allied victory.

Raglan wanted to advance to Sevastopol immediately, but he conceded to his French counterpart who wanted to march around Sevastopol's eastern flank and attack the fortress from the south. This was probably an error in judgment, derived from Raglan's conciliatory nature.

Raglan decided to besiege Sevastopol on 28 September 1854, and the siege began on 8 October 1854. The first heavy allied bombardment took place on 17 October. The Russians tried to break the allied siege of Sevastopol while it was still in its early stage. Their field army attacked on 25 October to destroy the British force and its supply base at Balaklava. Raglan's performance at this battle is best noted for the set of muddled orders that resulted in the Charge of the Light Brigade.

At the Battle of Inkerman (5 November 1854), Raglan remained characteristically calm in the middle of numerous small unit engagements. His timely request for French reinforcements helped ensure an allied victory in the battle. After this engagement, Raglan was promoted to field marshal.

The severe Crimean winter set in after the Battle of Inkerman, and the British transport, logistical, and medical shortages became increasingly significant. The situation was exacerbated when a tremendous storm hit on 14 November 1854, sinking twenty-one ships. The British soldiers did not have adequate winter clothing, meals, or shelter. Raglan visited the soldiers and trenches frequently, but the often sensationalistic reports of war correspondent William Howard Russell of the *Times* frequently contained unconfirmed reports and personal attacks against Raglan.

While the commissariat was responsible for many of the problems in the Crimea, the *Times* accused Raglan and his staff of incompetence and mismanagement. The government also tried to shift its responsibility to Raglan. The Earl of Aberdeen's government fell on 29 January 1855 and was replaced by Viscount Palmerston's ministry. Raglan was accused of not visiting his troops, but he produced evidence from an aide-de-camp's journal that he had visited his soldiers forty times in the previous two months. He was told that a change in leadership would satisfy the public, but he continued to loyally perform his duties.

The weather and supply situation began to improve in February 1855 as the siege of Sevastopol continued. A general assault on Sevastopol was planned for 18 June 1855, the anniversary of the Battle of Waterloo. The attack was to be preceded by an intense two-hour artillery bombardment. At the last moment, the new French commander decided to attack at daybreak, two hours earlier than originally planned. Raglan reluctantly accepted his decision and "either through pride or ignorance" (Pemberton 1962, p. 192) employed only 8,000 British troops while the French used 25,000 in the assault.

The attack was an unmitigated disaster for the British, and Raglan felt a deep personal responsibility for it. He became demoralized, and his physical resistance declined to the point that by about 25 June 1855 he had contracted cholera. Raglan died on 28 June and was buried in Wales.

Raglan was loyal, courageous, and a superb administrator. He was, however, relatively inexperienced as a field commander, at times lacked resolve, and frequently tried to placate his contemporaries and allies rather than make tough decisions. After he died, one captain observed that Raglan "was distinguished for nothing but his amiable qualities" (Pemberton 1962, p. 208).

See also Alma, Battle of the; Balaklava, Battle of; Charge of the Light Brigade; Correspondents, War; Crimean War; Inkerman, Battle of; Master-General of the Ordnance, British Army; Purchase System; Sevastopol, Siege of; Simpson, General Sir James M.; Wellington, Field Marshal Arthur Wellesley, First Duke of
References: Hibbert (1961); Pemberton (1962); Raugh (1987a); Royle (2000); Sweetman (1993); Sweetman (2001)

Railways

The construction and use of railways by the British Army, frequently as lines of communication, gained increased importance during the Victorian era.

The first railway built by the military was constructed in 1855 during the Crimean War. It was 7 miles long and built between Balaklava and the heights above Sevastopol. This railway was used to haul siege equipment and other supplies to the trenches and to evacuate the wounded in the first hospital train.

During the Abyssinian War (1867–1868), a short railway was built, using steam locomotives for the first time. During this campaign, about 24,000 men and 13,000 tons of supplies were transported by rail across a 10-mile stretch of inhospitable coastal desert.

Colonel (later Field Marshal Viscount) Sir Garnet J. Wolseley studied the lessons of the Franco-Prussian War (1870–1871) and on 29 January 1873 delivered a lecture entitled "The Use of Railroads in War" at Aldershot. Published as a separate pamphlet, this lecture helped stimulate British military interest in railways. Wolseley later commanded the ill-fated 1884–1885 Gordon Relief Expedition. A railway from the Red Sea port of Suakin to Berber on the Nile River was under construction when it was decided to evacuate the Sudan.

Courses on military railways were conducted at the School of Military Engineering in the 1880s, and the first *Manual of Military Railways* was published in 1889. In 1896, a railway control office providing liaison officers and controllers between railway operators and force commanders was established at Chatham.

A military railway was built to facilitate the reconquest of the Sudan (1896–1898). It was built south to Wadi Halfa, where one line continued to parallel the Nile to the Third Cataract. Construction began on 1 January 1897 on a second line, the Sudan Military Railway, by the Railway Battalion of the Egyptian Army under the supervision of Royal Engineer Lieutenant Percy Girouard. This line crossed about 225 miles of Nubian Desert to Abu Hamed and eventually to Berber. This railway line served as an indispensable line of communication for the force.

Railways were crucial as lines of communication over the vast distances of South Africa during the Second Boer War (1899–1902). (It was, for example, 650 miles from Cape Town to Kimberley, and 1,000 miles from Cape Town to Pretoria.) Railway companies and a railway pioneer regiment were raised and deployed. Three British columns advanced during the initial British offensive, and two of them, to Bloemfontein and Kimberley, were supplied by rail. Field Marshal Lord Frederick S. Roberts later used the railway as the main line of communication as his force struck east to Bloemfontein.

The Imperial Military Railways organization, under the command of Lieutenant Colonel Girouard, was formed and eventually contained 18,000 personnel. By August 1900, for example, the British had moved 177,000 men, 86,000 animals, and about 500,000 tons of freight by rail. By the end of the Second Boer War, the British used 19 armored and many hospital trains in South Africa. Thousands of blockhouses were built to protect the railways.

See also Blockhouses; Boer War, Second (1899–1902); Crimean War; Lines of Communication; Reconquest of the Sudan; Wolseley, Field Marshal Garnet J.
References: Bailes (1980); Bates (1979); Moore-Morris (1998a); Pakenham (1979); Royle (2000); Wolseley (1873)

Ramnagar, Battle of (22 November 1848)
See Sikh War, Second (1848–1849)

Ranjit Singh
See Afghanistan; Sikhs

Rank and File, British Army—Enlistment

Enlistment was the voluntary engagement to serve as a soldier for an indefinite period or for a specified number of years. The number of years, or term, of an enlistment generally decreased during this period.

Field Marshal Arthur Wellesley, First Duke of Wellington, frequently called the other ranks "the scum of the earth" (Blanco 1968a, p. 217); early in the nineteenth century, soldiering was perhaps considered the least respectable of professions. Soldiers were generally treated as outcasts from society. The majority of new enlistees were considered the "utterly lazy class . . . the drunken, dissolute, the debauched, the ticket-of-leave men" (Blanco 1968a, p. 219). A minority of men enlisted for the adventure.

The prospective soldier generally enlisted in a regiment and not in the British Army as a whole. He was frequently enticed by regimental recruiters and pensioners with the offer of drink and the Queen's shilling, the bounty for enlisting.

To attract a higher-quality soldier during the Napoleonic Wars, the term of enlistment in 1809 was reduced from "life"—basically until the soldier's services were no longer needed or he was physically unable to perform his duties—to seven years in the infantry, ten in the cavalry, and twelve in the artillery. Lifetime service was restored in 1829.

Limited enlistment was introduced in 1847 in an attempt to equate military service with other working-class occupations and attract a higher-quality soldier. The terms of service were reduced to ten years in the infantry and twelve in the other arms, with the possibility of reenlistment for an additional eleven or twelve years. The terms of this act became effective in 1857, ten years after the first enlistment, and were shown to be a relative failure, with recruiting becoming very difficult.

In the late 1850s and 1860s enlistments failed to meet the army's needs. This situation was made worse by threats of war with France in 1859 and insecurity caused by the Prussian military mobilizations and quick victories in the 1860s. Physical and other standards were reduced and bounties increased during this period to increase enlistments.

To correct these enlistment shortfalls, Secretary of State for War (later Viscount) Edward T. Cardwell introduced the Army Enlistment Bill of 1870, which became an act that same year. The Army Enlistment Act of 1870 was responsible for introducing the concept of "short service." While the initial term of army service was kept at twelve years, under normal conditions the soldier would spend the first six years on active duty "with the colors," and the second six years with the regular reserve. (In 1881 this was changed to seven years with the colors and five in the reserves.) Soldiers could extend their service to complete a total of twenty-one years on active duty and receive a pension, but short service was intended to attract a better-quality recruit and reduce expenses (because more soldiers would depart the service before becoming pension eligible), and a trained reserve would be established and maintained. Short service was controversial for the remainder of the nineteenth century, and its flaws were accentuated by government budgetary constraints.

The main provisions of the army Enlistment Act of 1870 remained in effect through the Second Boer War. In 1904, terms of service were reduced to three years with the colors, followed by reenlisting on active duty or being discharged to the reserve for nine years. The impact was that in infantry battalions the number of soldiers who had been in the army for more than three years was less than 3 percent. This system seemed to deprive the army of soldiers at their peak of military and physical training and when they were prepared to become noncommissioned officers. The following year, the enlistment terms were changed to nine years with the colors and three with the reserve. In 1906, enlistment terms were amended to seven years active duty followed by five in the reserve.

See also Army and Society; Cardwell, Edward T.; Cardwell Reforms; Long Service; Rank and File, British Army—Social Background; Recruiting; Short Service; Wellington, Field Marshal Arthur Wellesley, First Duke of

References: Blanco (1965); Blanco (1968a); Brereton (1986); Denman (1996); Moyse-Bartlett (1974); Skelley (1977); Spiers (1992); Strachan (1984)

Rank and File, British Army—Pay

The pay of the British soldier, especially considering the harshness of drill and discipline and potential hardships of combat and foreign service, was very low. It was fixed in the 1790s and increased only slightly through the end of the nineteenth century.

The minimum pay of the infantry private was about 1 shilling per day. The cavalry trooper received 1s 3d per day and guardsmen slightly more. That figure was very deceptive and inaccurate, since every soldier's pay was subject to stoppages or deductions. These stoppages included the cost of food, tailoring, laundry, haircuts, cost of medical treatment if sick, barracks damage repairs, and replacements for lost equipment. Army pay was also low compared with civilian pay. In 1832, for example, the weekly wage of an agricultural worker was calculated at 12s, and that of the artisan as 33s. In Leeds in 1838 the weekly wage of the skilled laborer was over £1, while the private soldier's pay remained 1s per day.

In the 1830s, a sergeant major would have received 3s per day pay, plus a room, fuel allowances, the use of a soldier servant, and free education for his children.

The pay of an infantry private in 1856 was 1s 1d per day. He could earn extra pay by serving as an officer's servant or a mess waiter. In the artillery and engineers he could supplement his base pay with "working pay," by engaging in tasks outside his normal duties, such as road and bridge construction. Good conduct pay also supplemented regular pay.

In the 1870s, a sergeant major's basic pay was roughly 4s per day.

The pay of the infantry private rose to 1s 2d per day, before stoppages, in 1890. An analysis of the pay of 696 privates at Aldershot that same year showed that out of an annual pay of £18 0s 5d, the average private's pay was stopped £7 3s for uniforms, footware, laundry, haircuts, and so on. The Royal Pay Warrant of 1893 generously decreed that after all stoppages had been deducted, "a residue of at least 1d a day shall be left to the soldier" (Brereton 1986, p. 100). At the same time, the daily pay of the infantry corporal was 1s 8d; the cavalry corporal, 2s; the infantry sergeant major, 5s; and the cavalry sergeant major, 5s 4d. In 1899, the average weekly wage of an unskilled laborer in London was 29s 2d.

See also Army and Society; Officers, British Army—Pay; Rank and File, British Army—Retirement; Recruiting

References: Bond (1962); Brereton (1986); Skelley (1977); Strachan (1984)

Rank and File, British Army—Retirement

One incentive to join the British Army was a relative security of tenure with retirement and a pension after twenty-one years of service. Temporary disability pensions were awarded to those invalided for wounds or illness incurred in military service, and permanent pensions to those who had served at least fourteen years with the colors and had been invalided due to military service. These pensions, however, were generally inadequate for the retired or disabled soldier.

In the late 1820s it was established that long and good service, and not disability, was to be the basis of a pension. After serving twenty-one years, or twenty-four in the cavalry, the pensioner received 1s a day, or 10d per day if discharged at his own request. Wounds and higher rank permitted a higher financial reward.

The basis to some extent for a pension reverted to disability in 1833. A private soldier discharged after twenty-one years received 6d per day, which could rise to 1s per day after additional service or because of disability. This did not please soldiers, who were often worn out after serving for twenty-one years, frequently in inhospitable foreign stations. Few soldiers could physically endure service that long. In the 1830s, only about a dozen men per regiment served for that length of time, and in 1845, only two of the 27,000 soldiers in the United Kingdom had served the twenty-seven years required to earn a pension of 1s per day (Strachan 1984, p. 69). Consequently, a soldier literally limped through his last years of service or drank or otherwise induced disability. The basic pension of 1s per day for twenty-one years of service was restored in 1847.

In the 1880s, normal pension rates started at 8d to 1s 6d per day for a private to 3s per day for a sergeant major. Pensions were generally paid quarterly in advance, a system that encouraged wastefulness. In 1892, the maximum rate of long-service pensions for noncommissioned officers was established at 5s per day. After the Second Boer War (1899–1902) the minimum rate for retired privates was raised to 1s per day.

Retired soldiers without dependents could apply to become an in-pensioner at one of two large military hospitals located in Chelsea and Dublin. The former had facilities for about 500 and the latter for about 150 in-pensioners, and a total of about 200 were admitted annually.

A number of organizations were established to help pensioners after retirement gain employment rather than end up as destitute beggars. The Army and Navy Pensioners and Time-Expired Men's Employment Society, founded in 1855 and supported by private contributions, helped old soldiers find work. The Incorporated Soldiers and Sailors Help Society taught useful trades to former soldiers and provided sponsors to assist in finding employment. One of the most successful was the Corps of Commissionares, founded in 1859 by Captain Edward Walker, to provide pensioners jobs as watchmen, messengers, doormen, servants, valets, and similar positions.

See also Army and Society; Officers, British Army—Retirement; Rank and File, British Army—Pay
References: Brereton (1986); Farwell (1981); Skelley (1977); Strachan (1984)

Rank and File, British Army—Social Background

The rank and file of the British Army came from the lowest segment of British society, frequently forced into the army by starvation, unemployment, and poverty, and occasionally as an alternative to prison. *Blackwood's Edinburgh* magazine observed in 1859 that "the soldier with us, as an abstract idea is a hero ... but as a social fact ... is a pariah" (Blanco 1965, p. 127).

Of 120 soldiers who enlisted in the 13th Light Infantry Regiment in 1839, two-thirds had been unemployed; 2 were respectable men who had fallen on hard times; 16 thought the army was an easy life; 8 were "shady characters" who joined the army as a last resort; 1 was a criminal; 2 had fallen out with their families; 8 were discontented with civilian life; 1 was ambitious; and 2 had no reason. In the same year, new recruits into the 80th Foot had these trades prior to enlistment: 64 had been laborers, 9 servants, 6 tailors, 6 potters, 4 collies, and 24 "others" (Neuberg 1989, p. 26).

In the 1860s, about half the new recruits were from England and Wales, a third from Ireland, and the rest from Scotland. A small minority of the new soldiers were interested in adventure and some were former students and "gentlemen," but a large majority were of the "utterly lazy class ... the drunken, dissolute, the debauched, the ticket-of-leave men" (Blanco 1968, p. 219).

This trend continued through this period. In 1900, it was calculated that 90 percent of all new army recruits came from the working classes, 7 percent were shop men or clerks, 3 percent were boys, and 1 percent from the "servant keeping class" (Farwell 1981, p. 85). One officer made an estimate of the social origins of the men in his battalion on the eve of World War I, identifying various strata of the working class. He stated 5 percent came from the upper working class, 24 percent from the working class, and 70 percent from the real lower class.

See also Army and Society; Officers, British Army—Social Background; Rank and File, British Army—Enlistment; Recruiting
References: Blanco (1965); Blanco (1968a); British Soldier (1859); Denman (1996); Farwell (1981); Neuberg (1989)

Rank and File, British Army—Training and Education

Soldiers in the British Army were trained as individuals and as members of a unit. Many soldiers, coming from the lowest class of society, were also poorly educated, and they had an opportunity to raise their level of literacy while in the army.

The primary function of a home battalion was to train recruits and send them to service battalions overseas. Noncommissioned officers conducted the recruit training, which varied in length, content, and quality, based on the recruit's regiment and arm of service. In general, recruits received instruction in basic drill, equipment and barrack maintenance, physical training, and musketry instruction. Recruit training, especially during the first half of this period, was frequently inadequate and interrupted by policing duties and drill. After completing his recruit training, the new soldier would participate in collective training as a member of his unit and be shipped to a service battalion overseas.

The soldier's education was initially regarded as reprehensible in some quarters, although its importance became increasingly realized as weapons became more sophisticated and tactics decentralized control and responsibility. As tactics became more dispersed, more noncommissioned officers would have to be literate to write down orders, instructions, etc.

Illiteracy in the armed forces was said to have declined from 51 percent in 1785–1814 to 32 percent in 1815–1844. This can partially be attributed to the establishment of regimental schools in 1812 for soldiers' children, although adult attendance became more widespread. The 1841 census recorded that 60 percent of those in the army aged 16 to 25 (excluding officers) were literate, and 78 percent of those aged 26 to 35 (including officers) were literate.

The principal chaplain of the British Army was appointed the first inspector of military schools in 1846. He was responsible for establishing a standardized system of education and selecting and appointing schoolmasters. In the 1850s, schoolmasters were classed as warrant officers.

Regimental schools were very popular. In February 1854, the average school attendance per regiment was 166, of whom only 39 were recruits. Six regiments had over 300, and three of these over 400, soldiers attending school. By 1857, 20.5 percent of other ranks (the majority in the infantry) were totally illiterate, 18.8 percent were able to read but not write, 56 percent could read and write, and 4.7 percent were classified as having a superior education.

In 1861, army certificates of learning were established, and these, providing three standards and linked to promotions, encouraged education.

The Education Acts of 1870 and 1872 gave impetus to civilian and, in turn, military education and literacy. The educational attainments of the rank and file of the British Army increased considerably during the second half of the nineteenth century. In 1861, for example, it was calculated that 19.0 percent of the rank and file could not read or write, 19.7 percent could read only, 53.9 percent could read and write, and 7.4 were considered possessing a superior education. By 1899, only 1.9 percent of the rank and file could not read or write, 2.2 percent could read only, 10.5 percent could read and write, and 85.4 percent were evaluated as possessing a superior education.

See also Artillery, British Army—Training; Cavalry, British Army—Training; Engineers, British Army—Training; Infantry, British Army—Training

References: Skelley (1977); Smith (1987); Smith (1988); Strachan (1984)

Rank and File, British Army— Uniforms and Equipment

The uniform and equipment of the British soldier—the red coat—changed very little between Waterloo and the Crimean War. The centralization of clothing manufacture and issuance, plus the increased participation in colonial campaigns, the effectiveness of rifled muskets, and concern for soldier comfort, brought about uniform and equipment changes later in this period.

Until 1854, soldiers' uniforms were provided by the regiment, and commanding officers were not above making a profit by having uniforms made of coarser and inferior materials, and so on. An arbitrary amount for uniforms was charged against the soldier. If this amount was insufficient, the soldier was charged more. If the deduction was less than the actual expense, the commanding officer kept the profit.

Uniforms varied between regiments and arms of the service. In general terms, each soldier had two types of dress: full dress, for ceremonial occasions; and undress, a more relaxed style used for work. Every recruit received on enlistment a complete set of clothing and other items of "kit." Coatees (later tunics), trousers, and boots were expected to last one year (two years in India); greatcoat, three years; and other equipment, twelve years. After his first uniform and equipment issue, the soldier paid for his kit items, including underclothing, fatigue or undress uniform, knapsack, mess tin, blacking, and so on. New uniforms were generally issued on 1 April of each year.

An 1855 source described the general uniform: "The old swallow-tail coatee, disfigured by ugly facings, still distinguishes the British from every other soldier. The trowsers are tight, and uncomfortable. The old cross-belt system for fixing bayonet-scabbard, pouch and knapsack, reigns supreme in almost all regiments" (British Army 1855, p. 3). The soldiers' red coat was denigrated, "which makes their soldiers look like dressed-up monkeys" (British Army 1855, p. 3). The headgear was the "bell-topped shako," and trousers were dark blue/gray for winter issue, and white linen for summer wear (although in 1846, except for service in hot climates, lavender trousers replaced white).

Service in the Crimean War (1854–1856) resulted in significant uniform changes. A tunic was issued in place of the tight coatee, and the trousers were looser. Haversacks, smaller than the knapsacks, were issued to all soldiers.

Soldiers who served during the Indian Mutiny (1857–1859) were the first ever to wear relatively comfortable uniforms. Beginning in the 1840s, soldiers had discolored their white summer undress uniforms, and the result was called *khaki*, after the Urdu word for dust. Local blue dungaree trousers were also worn.

A uniform specifically designed for campaign service was introduced in the 1870s. It consisted of a gray/green plain loose frock, matching trousers, and a light cork sun helmet.

The amalgamation of battalions in 1881 resulted in the replacement of traditional facing colors with national ones. At the same time, a seven-button frock coat was authorized for home service, and a five-button undress frock coat for overseas service. The army was also transitioning from colored to khaki uniforms, with the engagement at Ginnis in the Sudan (30 December 1885) being the last major battle fought by soldiers wearing scarlet. In 1897, khaki was adopted as the universal dress for all arms overseas. The khaki uniforms worn in the Second Boer War were the culmination of improvements made in the preceding decades.

Individual equipment was assigned to the rank and file, who generally had to carry all their gear. An infantry knapsack, consisting of a large black canvas box, was introduced in 1808 and used until 1871. In the 1860s a small wooden water bottle, carried on a leather strap, was issued. In 1871, the new valise equipment replaced the Napoleonic era knapsack. The varnished canvas valise, connected to suspenders and waist belt, was worn on the small of the back. A mess tin was carried above the valise, above which the greatcoat was folded flat and strapped to the shoulder belts. Two 20-round ammunition pouches were worn on each side, and the bayonet was worn at the left rear of the waistbelt. A small haversack was worn over the right shoulder and a new design wooden canteen worn over the left shoulder.

The Slade-Wallace pattern equipment was introduced in 1888, modifying the valise equipment. The larger valise was replaced with a smaller, lighter version, worn higher on the back, and the mess tin and great coat were strapped to the waistbelt. Ammunition pouches were also reconfigured.

The soldiers in the Second Boer War were equipped with the Slade-Wallace pattern gear. This equipment, with ammunition, weighed about 25 pounds, the lightest equipment a British soldier had yet worn into action.

See also Artillery, British Army—Weapons and Equipment; Boer War, Second (1899–1902); Cavalry, British Army—Weapons and Equipment; Crimean War; Engineers, British Army—Weapons and Equipment; Ginnis, Battle of; Indian Mutiny

References: British Army (1855); British Soldier (1859); Featherstone (1978); Haythornthwaite (1995); Knight (1996)

Reade, W. Winwood
See Correspondents, War

Reconquest of the Sudan (1896–1898)

The British, after occupying Egypt in 1882, realized they needed to protect the Nile River headwaters on which the Egyptian agricultural economy and population depended. In the mid-1890s, the British Government became concerned about forestalling French and Italian claims to the Upper Nile region. Moreover, the defeat of an Italian army by Abyssinians at Adowa in March 1896 could have encouraged a possible alliance between the anti-British Abyssinian Emperor Menelik and the Khalifa, which the British wanted to prevent. The British occupation of the Sudan would preclude another power from controlling the Nile water flow and possibly destabilizing Egypt, which in turn could threaten the Suez Canal, Britain's imperial link with India. In addition, such a program could capitalize on the public's desire to "avenge Gordon," the British general murdered by dervishes in Khartoum in January 1885.

Reconquest of the Sudan

In March 1896, the British authorized the Egyptian Army, under the command of the sirdar, Major General (later Field Marshal Earl) Sir Horatio H. Kitchener, to begin the advance up the Nile. Kitchener concentrated on establishing a logistical and transport infrastructure and advanced methodically. The reconquest of the Sudan was a three-year campaign, divided into annual phases. The first phase was the recapture of the province of Dongola in 1896. The second phase was to include the construction of the Sudan Military Railway from Wadi Halfa to and the capture of Abu Hamed, but actually concluded with the occupation of Berber. In 1898, the Anglo-Egyptian army returned to the Sudan and crushed the dervish forces at Omdurman near Khartoum.

The Egyptian Army was mobilized, and by 4 June 1896, Kitchener had assembled a 9,000-man force, consisting of 10 infantry battalions, 15 cavalry and camel corps squadrons, and three artillery batteries at Akasha, south of Wadi Halfa and near the dervish positions at Firket. All soldiers were Egyptian or Sudanese with the exception of a few hundred men from the North Staffordshire Regiment and some Maxim machine-gunners. On 7 June, Kitchener's forces defeated the dervishes at Firket.

Disease and severe weather slowed down the advance in the summer of 1896. A land force, supported by a flotilla of Nile gunboats, entered the city of Dongola on 23 September 1896 to find it deserted. Kitchener's forces occupied Merowi and Korti, which ended the first phase of the reconquest of the Sudan.

Kitchener knew logistical support and an effective line of communication in the barren desert would be a key to his success, and he was eager to continue the advance to seize Abu Hamed and Berber. On 1 January 1897, construction of the Sudan Military Railway began. Its 225-mile route was straight across the Nubian Desert from Wadi Halfa to Abu Hamed. By 23 July 1897, 103 miles of track had been laid, but the line was vulnerable to dervish raids from Abu Hamed.

Kitchener ordered Major General (later General Sir) Archibald Hunter to advance from Merowi and eliminate the dervish threat at Abu Hamed. Hunter's force, consisting mainly of a Sudanese brigade, traveled 146 miles in eight days and attacked Abu Hamed on 7 August 1897. After the dervishes lost Abu Hamed, they also unexpectedly abandoned Berber. Kitchener was concerned about extending his forward positions ahead of the railway, but his forces advanced and occupied Berber on 5 September 1897. The railway reached Abu Hamed on 31 October 1897, and Kitchener's advance forces remained in Berber, which would be the start point for the concluding phase of the campaign.

Intelligence suggested that the Khalifa was assembling his forces for a possible attack on Berber, and it became apparent that the Egyptian Army would need British reinforcements before it could destroy the dervish army and win the campaign. On 4 January 1898, Kitchener was appointed supreme commander of all Egyptian and British troops south of Aswan. The first khaki-clad British brigade, under the command of Major General (later Lieutenant General Sir) William F. Gatacre, arrived in the Sudan in late January 1898.

As the British reinforcements arrived, Kitchener sent one Egyptian Army brigade forward to the Atbara fort, located on the northeastern side of the confluence of the Atbara and Nile Rivers about 200 miles north of Khartoum. As the dervishes marched north to a possible engagement with the Anglo-Egyptian forces, Kitchener assembled his forces near the Atbara fort. When the location of the dervish forces was pinpointed on 30 March 1898, Kitchener was not sure if he should attack first or wait to be attacked.

Kitchener resolved to attack, and his army advanced closer to the enemy on 4 April 1898. At dawn on 8 April, the Anglo-Egyptian force conducted a frontal attack with three infantry brigades on line and one brigade in reserve. In less than an hour, with the Sudanese troops having fought especially well, Kitchener's force won the battle. Anglo-Egyptian casualties were 81 all ranks killed and 478 wounded; over 3,000 dervishes were killed.

After the Battle of Atbara, logistical preparations continued for the final advance to Omdurman, the Sudan Military Railway was extended further, and additional reinforcements arrived. By mid-August 1898, Kitchener's 25,800-man force consisted of the British Division, commanded by Major General (later Lieutenant General Sir) William F. Gatacre, with two British infantry brigades, and the four-brigade Egyptian Division, commanded by Major General (later General Sir) Archibald Hunter. Cavalry, artillery, Maxim guns, and gunboats also supported the force.

Kitchener's army began its final advance to Omdurman on 28 August 1898. On 1 September 1898, advance elements stumbled onto the attacking dervishes north of Omdurman, and the main body of the Anglo-Egyptian force established a camp on the Nile River near the village of El Egeiga.

The Battle of Omdurman began at about 6:00 A.M. on 2 September 1898, and consisted of three phases. The first phase included the dervish main attack against the Anglo-Egyptian center, but this frontal assault was halted and the dervishes were annihilated by a combination of rifle, artillery, and Maxim gun fire. At the same time, two other large dervish forces under the Green Flag moved north to the Kerreri Hills, believing that enemy troops were located in the area. Egyptian Cavalry blunted the advance of this force before it could attack Kitchener's right flank. The first phase ended at about 8:00 A.M.

Kitchener thought the battle was over and sent the 21st Lancers south to cut off any fleeing dervishes before they could reach Omdurman. This resulted in the charge of the 21st Lancers, the most famous single action of the battle, and perhaps of the entire reconquest of the Sudan. This cavalry action was a failure and resulted in large casualties, but the Lancers' heroism, for which three Victoria Crosses were awarded, was revered by the British public and press.

As the 21st Lancers engaged the enemy, the main body of the army marched out of its encampment and wheeled southward toward Omdurman. As it did so, the Khalifa's 17,000-man Black Flag reserve force attacked the Anglo-Egyptian right-flank brigade, commanded by Colonel (later Major General Sir) Hector A. Macdonald, which had lost contact with its nearest brigade. At about the same time, the dervish Green Flag made an uncoordinated attack from the Kerreri Hills to the north. Macdonald calmly wheeled his brigade to meet the threat from the north, crushed the dervish attack, then wheeled again and helped shatter the Black Flag onslaught. By 11:30 A.M., the second phase of the battle was over. The third phase of the engagement consisted of the march to Omdurman, which was completed by nightfall. Anglo-Egyptian casualties at the Battle of Omdurman numbered 48 killed and 434 wounded. The dervishes lost about 10,000 killed and perhaps twice that number wounded.

The Battle of Omdurman was the decisive engagement of the reconquest of the Sudan. Even though the Khalifa escaped from Omdurman and was killed at the Battle of Umm Diwaykarat on 24 November 1899, the Mahdist state had been destroyed at Omdurman and the Nile watershed secured. Gordon had been avenged.

See also Atbara, Battle of; Dervishes; Dongola, Capture of; Egypt; Egyptian Army; Fashoda Incident; Gatacre, Lieutenant General Sir William F.; Gordon Relief Expedition; Hunter, General Sir Archibald; Imperialism; Khalifa; Kitchener, Field Marshal Horatio H.; Macdonald, Major General Sir Hector A.;

Mahdi; Railways; Sirdar; Sudan; Suez Canal; Wingate, General Sir (Francis) Reginald

References: Barthorp (1984); Caie (1998); Daly (1997); Hunter (1996); Keown-Boyd (1986); Magnus (1959); Neillands (1996); Steevens (1898)

Recruiting

The British Army remained a volunteer force throughout this period. Recruiting enough soldiers to fill its ranks, especially in time of conflict or with increasing imperial demands, was always a challenge and generally a failure.

During the first half of this period, when the army averaged 100,000 men, the normal number of casualties per year, including discharges, was only 13,140, but the recruiting system produced an average of only 12,885 new soldiers. In times of conflict, this recruiting shortfall was magnified. In March 1855, for example, during the Crimean War, about 90,000 men were required, but only 4,514 were recruited. Recruiting became more difficult during the 1850s and 1860s with Irish depopulation and increased civilian employment in farming and industrial sectors.

The recruiting administration was divided into seven military districts that were linked to seven major cities in the nation (Belfast, Bristol, Cork, Dublin, Leeds, Liverpool, and London). Each district was manned by an inspecting field officer, a medical officer, and an adjutant paymaster. Each district was subdivided into thirty smaller areas, each under the command of a subaltern.

The subaltern supervised pensioners who did the actual recruiting and received a fee for every man they recruited. The pensioners intentionally went to taverns and similar establishments to find their recruits, who were "only obtained by cajollery, by misrepresentation and by immoderate drinking" (Blanco 1968a, p. 219), in many cases only after consuming a gallon of beer. In 1859, for example, £1 7s 6d was shared between the recruiter (the pensioner) and his supervisor, the subaltern. Such a system, in which the best recruiters were probably homelessness and hunger, encouraged fraud, deception, and drunkenness. Occasionally regiments preparing for overseas service would send sergeants into their local area to recruit new soldiers.

In 1867, the recruiting system was centralized under the control of an inspector-general. Efforts were made to make recruiting methods uniform and more honest, and the number of pensioners employed as recruiters was greatly reduced. Recruiters were instructed to remove their offices from inns and drinking places.

Long service—always an impediment to recruiting—was ended in 1870 and replaced with short service. At the same time enlistment bounties, which had always encouraged fraud and desertion, were abolished.

Short service, coupled with small pay raises and reforms that included the abolition of flogging, did not end recruiting difficulties. Height and weight standards were frequently reduced to increase recruitment.

Recruiting difficulties were largely responsible for the decision in 1881 to further amalgamate battalions so that each regiment had two active battalions, third and fourth militia battalions, and frequently a volunteer battalion. These regiments formed a subdistrict and recruited a number of their new soldiers locally.

The increase in battalions serving overseas and a reduction in the number of home battalions also caused recruiting difficulties. Shifting demographics and the competition for labor also caused personnel shortages. Proposals to increase pay and improve service conditions were ignored, with many people thinking that the army would not again be of vital importance. The Second Boer War (1899–1902) proved them wrong, as did the First World War, when conscription was adopted in 1916.

See also Army and Society; Cardwell Reforms; Discipline and Justice, British Army; Long Service; Military Medicine, British Army—Enlistment Physical Standards; Rank and File, British Army—Enlistment; Short Service

References: Anderson (1967); Blanco (1968a); Bond (1962a); Burroughs (1994); Skelley (1977); Strachan (1984)

Red River Expedition (1870)

The Dominion of Canada was established on 1 July 1867, and the new Canadian government sought to protect the vast area, consisting mainly of Rupert's Land, that stretched from Lake Superior to the Rocky Mountains. Canada purchased Rupert's Land from the Hudson Bay Company for £300,000 in 1869, planning to make it part of the new province of Manitoba.

The economic center of Rupert's Land was along the Red River south of Lake Winnipeg. The area was populated by Metis, a people of traders and trappers, many of mixed white and Indian blood, who had developed their own distinct French-speaking Roman Catholic culture. The Metis, who were not consulted about the government's plans, were concerned about losing their land and their way of life.

Louis Riel became a leader of the Metis and declared a provisional government in December 1869. The Canadian Government seemed willing to make concessions to the Metis, but after they apprehended and shot a government surveyor in March 1870, it was decided to send a military force to restore order in the area.

Colonel (later Field Marshal Viscount) Garnet J. Wolseley, then serving as deputy quartermaster-general of the British forces in Canada, was selected in April 1870 to command this force. The British, in the process of withdrawing their troops from Canada, agreed to provide a regular battalion as the force nucleus. The force consisted of 1st Battalion, 60th Rifles (377 men); 20 Royal Artillerymen with four 7-pounder guns; 20 Royal Engineers; and Army Service Corps (12 men) and Army Medical Corps (8 men) detachments. The Canadian government provided two militia battalions, the 1st Battalion, Ontario Rifles, and the 1st Battalion, Quebec Rifles, each of 378 soldiers. The total strength of the Red River Expedition, including 21 staff members, was 1,214 all ranks.

Wolseley selected a number of young officers for his force, many of whom would figure prominently in his future campaigns. These officers included Lieutenant Colonel (later General Sir) John McNeill, V.C., Captain (later General Sir) Redvers Buller, and Lieutenant (later Lieutenant General Sir) William F. Butler. Wolseley took with him only the officers he considered the best and most able, and these officers formed the embryo of his Ashanti Ring.

There was no direct route to Fort Garry and speed was essential to surprise and suppress Riel and his insurgent followers. Wolseley decided to follow an old trading route through a series of rivers and lakes westward from Fort William (Thunder Bay) on Lake Superior to Lake Winnipeg. The force was organized into 21 brigades. Each brigade consisted of 6 boats each with a crew of 10 to 12 men all ranks, plus 12 *voyaguers* (Canadian boatmen) and a pilot. Each boat carried each man's individual equipment, 60 days of provisions, cooking utensils, blankets, waterproof sheets, and a chest containing the soldiers' Snider rifles.

The route of the Red River Expedition was about 1,200 miles long. The force departed Toronto by rail on 21 May 1870, traveled 94 miles to the port of Collingwood, then boarded steamships for the 534-mile voyage to Thunder Bay, where they arrived on 25 May. The force was then

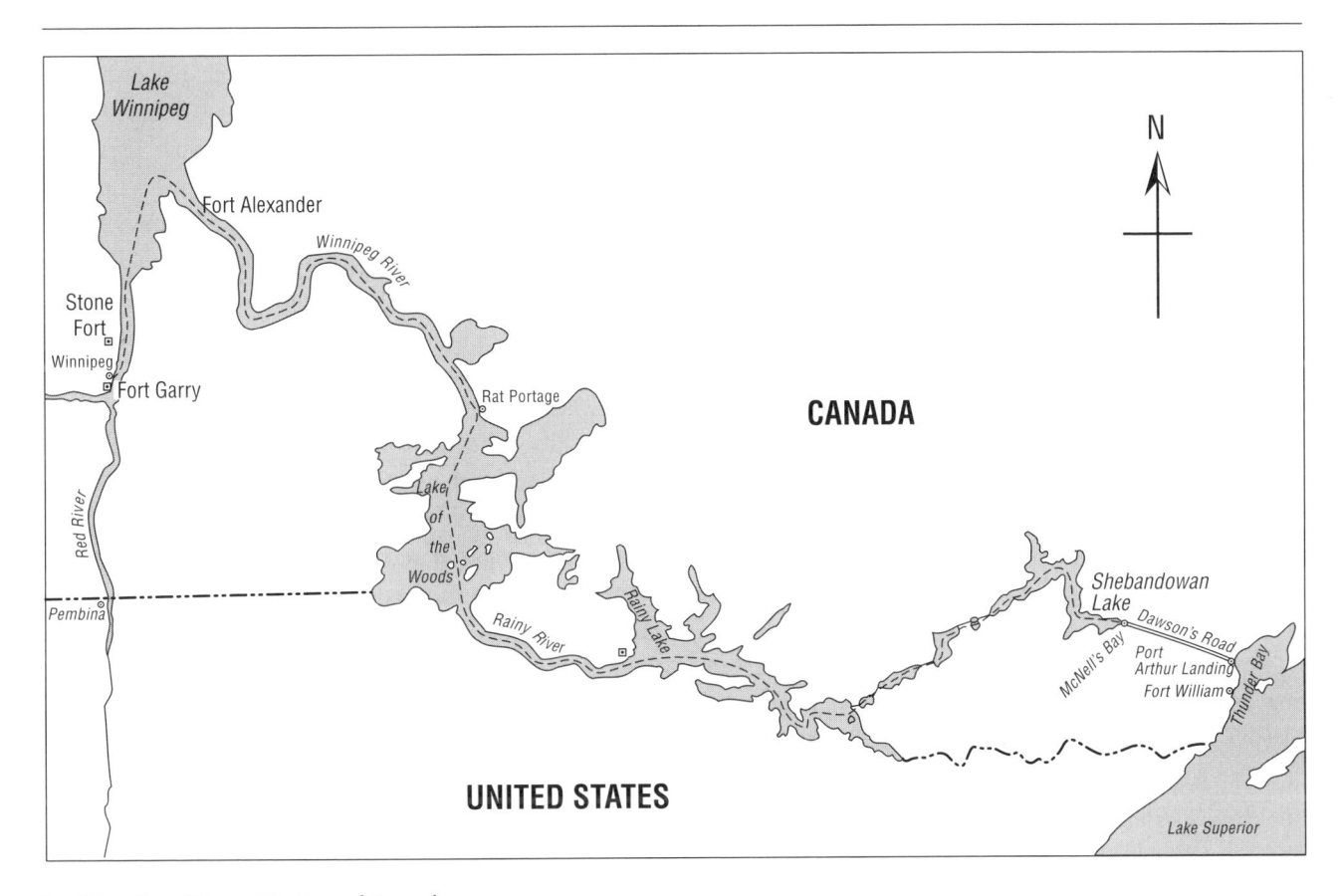

Red River Expedition, 1870: Area of Operations

delayed by constructing a 48-mile road through the wilderness to Lake Shebandowan, which was finally reached on 16 July 1870. The force then rowed, sailed, and poled their boats though a chain of rivers and lakes, and carried them over dozens of portages, the remaining 532 miles to Fort Garry. Forty days later (the number of days accurately predicted by Wolseley), lead elements of the force reached Fort Garry, only to find that Riel and his followers had abandoned the place. After restoring order, the expedition departed Fort Garry starting on 2 September 1870, and the entire force was back in Canada by 18 October 1870.

Wolseley was disappointed not to see action, but the Red River Expedition—the last British military expedition in North America—was a success in terms of mission accomplishment and low cost. This was in large measure due to Wolseley's superb leadership, attention to detail, flexibility, and determination. This achievement, for which Wolseley was knighted, brought him to the attention of his superiors and marked him as an officer of great promise and potential.

See also Ashanti Ring; Buller, General Sir Redvers H., V.C.; Butler, Lieutenant General Sir William F.; Canada; Lines of Communication; McNeill, General Sir John C., V.C.; Wolseley, Field Marshal Garnet J.

References: Kochanski (1999); Lehmann (1964); Low (1883); Manore (1987); Maxwell (1986); McCourt (1967); Raugh (1989); Red River Difficulty (1870); "With the Army Service Corps" (n.d.); Wolseley (1903)

Religion

Religion played a role to varying degrees in the life of every British soldier. Some regiments, such as the 19th Hussars and the 12th Lancers, were known for being more pious than others and had their bands play hymns at night. The soldiers of the Norfolk Regiment, in contrast, were known as the Holy Boys, not because of their devoutness but because prior to an overseas posting each soldier was given a Bible, which he sold for beer.

Early in this period every recruit was required to declare

a religious affiliation—Anglican, Presbyterian, or Roman Catholic. Although many of the officers considered themselves Christians, they were not overly zealous, with religion being even less important to the other ranks. Most other ranks in Highland regiments were Protestants, but almost all Irish soldiers were Roman Catholics. Some soldiers had no real religious preference, but because church parades were compulsory and the regimental band went to the Anglican service, many soldiers went to the Church of England services. Soldiers appear to have hated Sundays the most because the compulsory church parade required half the day of preparation. Many soldiers abhorred it when religion was forced on them. One soldier who had served in India wrote, "Ninety-five per cent of the battalion heartily detested Church Parade and would do anything in reason to get out of it" (Brereton 1986, p. 95).

Religious organizations were instrumental in establishing Soldiers Homes—mission centers containing baths, sleeping quarters, meeting halls, games and smoking rooms, a tea and coffee bar, and other comfortable facilities. The first Soldiers Home was founded at Chatham by Wesleyans in 1861. The Soldiers Homes were well patronized and were believed to have contributed significantly to the decrease in crime between 1856 and 1899. Religious organizations were also influential in advancing temperance and moderate behavior.

See also Army and Society; Chaplains
References: Brereton (1986); Farwell (1981); Skelley (1977)

Retreat from Kabul (January 1842)
See Afghan War, First (1839–1842)

Rhani of Jhansi (c. 1828–1858)

The Rhani of Jhansi was a courageous heroine of the Indian Mutiny, reportedly killed in battle while leading her followers.

Born in about 1828, Lakshmi Bai Manu was said to have been very athletic for a girl and enjoyed reading and learning. In 1842, when about fourteen years old, Lakshmi Bai married Gangadhar Rao, Maharaja (king) of Jhansi, and she became the Rhani (queen) of Jhansi. In about 1851, the Rhani had a son who died as an infant. The maharaja was not well and was worried about a successor to the throne. He adopted a son and wrote to the British governor-general requesting the Rhani be permitted to govern the state while she was alive. The maharaja died in November 1853. This request was denied and the British annexed Jhansi in 1854.

Even though the Rhani was awarded a generous life pension and allowed to keep the palace, and the adopted heir was authorized to inherit the maharaja's personal estate when he came of age, she did not want to relinquish the fort or any other possessions. The Rhani was, like the Nana Sahib, an embittered and alienated Indian aristocrat whose way of life was being shattered by the "progressive" British.

The garrison at Jhansi mutinied on 5 June 1857. The British officers there took refuge in the fort and surrendered three days later after receiving a promise of safe conduct. When they emerged, they were killed, possibly on orders of the Rhani, although this has never been proved.

Major General (later Field Marshal Lord Strathnairn) Sir Hugh Rose assumed command of the Central India Field Force on 16 December 1857. Operating from Indore, Rose was given the mission to clear the countryside of insurgents and operate toward Jhansi. Rose's force fought a number of battles and had received reinforcements before arriving outside Jhansi, which contained about 11,000 rebels, on 21 March 1858.

After bombarding the city, Rose first had to fight the force of Tantia Topi at the Betwa River on 1 April 1858 to prevent him from relieving the besieged mutineers in Jhansi. After defeating Tantia Topi, Rose's force assaulted the walled city early on 3 April and fought its way to the palace. During the ensuing bloodbath, the Rhani escaped and joined Tantia Topi.

On 17 June 1858, at Kotah-ke-serai (near Gwalior), the British again attacked the rebels. The 8th Hussars engaged the enemy cavalry, and in a fierce fight killed the Rhani of Jhansi, who was dressed as a man and had been wielding a sword with lethal effect. Rose described her as "the best and bravest military leader of the rebels" (Hilton 1957, p. 192).

See also East India Company; Gwalior, Battle of; India; Indian Mutiny; Nana Sahib; Rose, Field Marshal Hugh H.; Tantia Topi
References: Edwardes (1963); Hibbert (1978); Hilton (1957); Mason (1974)

Rhodes, Cecil J. (1853–1902)

Cecil J. Rhodes was a successful capitalist, ardent imperialist, and prime minister of the Cape Colony from 1890 to

1896. He was forced to resign the prime ministership because of his support of the ill-fated Jameson Raid (29 December 1895–2 January 1896). Rhodes influenced many of the events that led to the outbreak of the Second Boer War in 1899.

Rhodes was born in England in 1853. Suffering from a lung illness, Rhodes was sent in about 1866 to join his brother Herbert, who was cotton farming in Natal. The farming was not profitable, so Rhodes and his brother moved to Kimberley, where diamonds had been discovered in 1867. Rhodes was a shrewd businessman and realized that a company that monopolized output would effectively control the diamond market.

By age twenty, Rhodes had become very wealthy and returned to England to study at Oxford University. He frequently returned to Kimberley to oversee his business, and his activities in forming the De Beers Mining Company in 1880 delayed his graduation until 1881. While a student, Rhodes's imperialistic ambitions began to take shape, and he envisioned British imperial holdings stretching "from the Cape to Cairo," with a federated South Africa.

Rhodes returned to Kimberley in 1881 and became a member of the Cape Colony parliament. In 1885, he persuaded Britain to annex Bechuanaland (modern-day Botswana) in an attempt to curtail Boer territorial expansion. Three years later, Rhodes controlled all diamond production in Kimberley. He secured the charter for the British South Africa Company (the "Chartered Company") in 1889, with a mandate to administer the territory now known as Zimbabwe and Zambia.

Rhodes's ambitions were partially realized when he became prime minister of Cape Colony in 1890. He used this position to further British imperial interests, extending the influence of the Chartered Company in Mashonaland by force in 1893.

Rhodes exploited the grievances of the many foreign immigrants *(uitlanders)* who had flocked to the Transvaal in 1886 after the discovery of gold. The *uitlanders* did not receive full political rights. To ensure the Transvaal granted the franchise to these foreign immigrants (many of whom were British), Rhodes planned to overthrow the Transvaal Government by an *uitlander* rebellion in Johannesburg supported by external forces led by Dr. Leander Starr Jameson. The newly enfranchised *uitlanders* would then vote in the next election for a government that supported Rhodes's goal of a federated South Africa. Jameson's force was surrounded and surrendered to the Boers; the Jameson Raid was an embarrassing fiasco traced back to Rhodes.

The uproar and controversy caused by the unsuccessful Jameson Raid forced Rhodes to resign as prime minister of Cape Colony and lose his position as chairman of the Chartered Company. His political career was ruined. Trust between Britain and the Boers was shattered, and armed confrontation seemed inevitable. During the Second Boer War, Rhodes was besieged in Kimberley, where his sense of self-importance caused him to frequently interfere with the military chain of command, priorities, and operations.

Rhodes, who died in 1902, is little remembered today. The territory administered by the Chartered Company was named Rhodesia in 1895, but was renamed Zimbabwe in 1979. Rhodes's greatest legacy was his endowment to establish the Rhodes scholarships to provide academic opportunities at Oxford for scholars from the British Commonwealth, the United States, and Germany.

See also Boer War, Second (1899–1902); Imperialism; Jameson, Dr. Leander Starr; Jameson Raid; Kruger, S. J. Paulus; Transvaal

References: Barthorp (1987); Hensman (1900); Pakenham (1979)

Rifled Muzzle-Loader
See Artillery, British Army—Weapons and Equipment

Rifles
See Infantry, British Army—Small Arms

Roberts, Field Marshal Frederick S., V.C., First Earl Roberts of Kandahar, Pretoria, and Waterford (1832–1914)

Field Marshal Frederick S. Roberts, V.C., was a distinguished Indian Army officer. He was very popular with his soldiers and was known as "Bobs." Roberts served as commander in chief, India (1885–1893), in South Africa during the Second Boer War (1899–1900) and was the last commander in chief of the British Army (1901–1904).

Roberts was born in Cawnpore, India, on 30 September 1832. His father was an Indian Army officer who later became General Sir Abraham Roberts. After being educated in England and completing the Addiscombe course,

Roberts was commissioned in the Bengal Artillery of the East India Company on 12 December 1851. His first assignment was in Peshawar, where he served in a field battery as well as aide-de-camp to his father, then commanding the Peshawar Division.

In 1856, Roberts became deputy assistant quartermaster-general on the staff, and thereafter, saw basically no more regimental service. He saw extensive service in the Indian Mutiny, initially as a staff officer in the Punjab Moveable Column, and later in the Delhi Field Force. He fought in operations at Delhi, Cawnpore, Lucknow, and elsewhere. Roberts especially distinguished himself in action near Khodagunge on 2 January 1858, when he chased two insurgents who had captured a standard, cut down one of them, and retook the standard. Later the same day, he saved the life of a trooper who was being attacked. For his gallantry that day, Roberts was awarded the coveted Victoria Cross.

Roberts continued to serve in logistics positions and participated in the 1863 Umbeyla expedition to the North-West Frontier, the Abyssinian War (1867–1868), and the expedition into Lushai, between southeast Bengal and Burma, in 1871–1872. In 1875, Roberts was promoted to colonel and became quartermaster-general of the Bengal Army.

At the outbreak of the Second Afghan War in 1878, Major General Roberts was selected to command the 6,500-man, 18-gun Kurram Field Force. This was one of three Indian Army field forces that advanced into Afghanistan simultaneously in November 1878.

Roberts's force, after marching through the Kurram Valley, found its advance blocked by artillery-equipped Afghans at the Peiwar Kotal (Pass). Late on 1 December 1878, Roberts led a large column on a flanking movement that advanced to the left of the Afghan position. The following morning, his troops assaulted the high ground and eventually defeated the Afghans, thus clearing the route to Kabul. Roberts demonstrated superb leadership, used the terrain to his advantage, and employed his troops in a flank attack. The victory at the Battle of Peiwar Kotal established his reputation as an able commander. The Kurram Field Force was withdrawn from Afghanistan in early 1879.

After the British envoy to Kabul, Major Sir Pierre L. N. Cavagnari and his mission were massacred in Kabul on 1 September 1879, the British again invaded Afghanistan. Roberts commanded the newly formed Kabul Field Force, which began its advance on 27 September. On 5 October 1879, the force found its advance halted at Charasia, about 10 miles from Kabul. Roberts again used a flanking movement the following day when his force soundly defeated the Afghans, and he entered Kabul on 8 October. After martial law was established, the Kabul Field Force occupied the fortified Sherpur Cantonment near Kabul.

The Afghans began to increasingly resent the British occupation, and after tensions rose, they began to besiege the British in Sherpur beginning on 14 December 1879. The British defended their cantonment against a strong Afghan attack on 23 December.

Afghanistan was in turmoil in 1880, and after the Conservative Government in England fell on 28 April 1880, the "forward policy" and the British occupation of Afghanistan were about to end. An Indian brigade was soundly defeated at the Battle of Maiwand (27 July 1880) and withdrew to Kandahar. Roberts was then directed to lead a relief force from Kabul to Kandahar, 318 miles away. His 10,000-man force began its march on 9 August 1880, traveled over mountainous terrain and waterless desert, and reached Kandahar on 31 August. The next morning, Roberts's force attacked and soundly defeated the Afghans at the Battle of Kandahar, which basically ended the Second Afghan War. Roberts's achievements, especially the Kabul to Kandahar March, caught the British public opinion and overshadowed concurrent military operations in Africa. Roberts was awarded a baronetcy.

Roberts was then appointed to be commander in chief of the Madras Army and served in this position until he became commander in chief, India, in 1885. During his seven years in command in India, Roberts was instrumental in further developing North-West Frontier defenses and communications. By this time, Roberts had attracted an informal group of officers called the Roberts Ring, a counter to the Ashanti Ring, which believed in forward defense and long service. In 1892, Roberts was raised to the peerage. He departed India in 1893 after spending forty-one years on the subcontinent. Roberts was diligent in looking after the health and welfare of his soldiers. He was fortunate in having a poet and novelist, Rudyard Kipling, record and popularize his achievements and those of his men.

Roberts succeeded Field Marshal Viscount Garnet J. Wolseley as commander in chief, Ireland, in 1895. In December 1899, the same month his son was killed in action, Roberts was appointed commander in chief, South Africa. After a disastrous attempt to reorganize the supply and transport system in February 1900, Roberts's strategy capture enemy capitals. He captured Bloemfontein (13 March 1900), Johannesburg (31 May 1900), and Pretoria (5 June 1900), when his offensive began to lose steam. Roberts did not understand the unconventional tactics of the Boers, and he did not secure areas behind the British advances, thus making them vulnerable to guerrilla warfare. Roberts also misunderstood the changes in tactics and warfare caused by improved weapons and other technological developments, including smokeless powder.

Roberts initiated the policy of burning Boer farms in June 1900; failing to understand the nature of Boer warfare, he thought the war was basically over. Roberts relinquished command in November 1900 and replaced Wolseley as British Army commander in chief in January 1901. He also received an earldom. Roberts was the last soldier to hold the position of commander-in chief before it was abolished in 1904.

After his retirement in 1905, Roberts became an outspoken advocate of military preparedness, training, and marksmanship. Roberts was devoted to his Indian troops, and he traveled to the Western Front of France in November 1914 to visit them. He caught pneumonia and died on 14 November. "The story of [Roberts's] life," observed one senior officer, "is thus completed as he would have wished himself, dying in the middle of the soldiers he loved so well and within the sound of the guns" (Callwell 1927, p. 1: 187).

See also Abyssinian War; Addiscombe, Military Seminary; Afghan War, Second (1878–1880); Afghanistan; Ashanti Ring; Boer War, Second (1899–1902); Boers; Cavagnari, Major Sir Pierre L. N.; Charasia, Battle of; Commander in Chief, British Army; East India Company; Great Game; Indian Army Operations; Indian Army Organization; Indian Mutiny; Kabul to Kandahar March; Kandahar, Battle of; Lucknow, Siege and Relief of; Madras Army; North-West Frontier; Peiwar Kotal, Battle of; Quartermaster-General, British Army; Sherpur, Battle of; Victoria Cross; War Office; Wolseley, Field Marshal Garnet J.

References: Barthorp (1982); Bruehl (1986); Brooke-Hunt (1914); Callwell (1927); De Watteville (1938); Forbes (1892); Hannah (1972); Hibbert (1978); Jerold (1901); Miller (1977); Myatt (1970); Pakenham (1979); Raugh (1986); Roberts (1897); Wessels (2000)

Rockets

Military rockets, initially little more than glorified fireworks, became more accurate and lethal and were used by the British in many colonial campaigns.

Indian troops initially used rockets against the British. In 1788, Indian Hyder Ally formed a rocketeer contingent of 1,200 men. His son, Tippoo Sultun, fired a huge barrage of rockets at the British soldiers during the 1792 Battle of Seringapatam, followed by an assault of 36,000 men. Even though the Indian rockets were relatively primitive, their sheer numbers, noise, and light disoriented the British soldiers.

The Briton largely responsible for refining the design of rockets and introducing them into the British military arsenal was William Congreve. In 1804, he began studying rockets, and his first design was a larger, elongated version of the Indian rocket designed to be fired from ships to set fires on enemy shore targets. These rockets, weighing 18, 24, 32, 42, 100, or 300 pounds, were named Congreve rockets after their designer.

The rocket most widely used in battle weighed 32 pounds and had a gunpowder charge (the propellant) housed in a casing 3 feet, 6 inches long by 4 inches wide. Each 30-pound rocket was called a "stick rocket" because it was normally mounted on a stick 15 feet long and 1.5 inches wide for stabilization. They were inexpensive to produce and were made in large numbers. Many stick rockets employed a conical, metal warhead that embedded itself in its target before oozing a slow-burning incendiary mixture. Congreve also developed a rocket that ejected shot, similar to shrapnel. The Congreve rockets had a range of about 3,000 yards.

The British used their rockets during the Napoleonic Wars and the War of 1812 with the United States. On 13–14 September 1814, a tremendous barrage of Congreve rockets was fired at Fort McHenry in Baltimore. One witness was Francis Scott Key, who wrote of the Congreve "rockets' red glare" in his poem "The Star Spangled Banner," which later became the U.S. national anthem.

Congreve rockets were employed in large numbers in 1825–1826 during the First Burma War. The 12-pounder Congreve rocket was employed in the Crimean War (1854–1856) and the Indian Mutiny (1857–1859). The more accurate and reliable Hale rocket was developed in the 1860s. The Hale rocket had a more accurate trajectory because of flanges at the vent, which deflected the gas and caused the rocket to spin in flight. They were produced in 9-pound (field) and 24-pound (bombardment) varieties. Fired from a trough on a tripod, the Hale rockets were not very accurate and had a maximum range of about 1,500 yards.

Hale rockets were used during the Abyssinian War

(1867–1868), Second Ashanti War (1873–1874), and most notably at Isandlwana and Ulundi during the Zulu War (1879). Rockets had basically become obsolete by the 1880s, but the British retained them longer than most nations, ostensibly for the psychological shock effect when employed against indigenous populations.

See also Abyssinian War; Artillery, British Army—Weapons and Equipment; Ashanti War, Second (1873–1874); Burma War, First (1824–1826); Crimean War; Indian Mutiny; Zulu War

References: Harris (1999); Haythornthwaite (1995); Lethbridge (2000); McCaig (2000); Stearn (1996b)

Rorke's Drift, Defense of (22–23 January 1879)

The heroic defense of Rorke's Drift during the Zulu War (1879) took place only hours after the disastrous and bloody Battle of Isandlwana (22 January 1879). This action represented the epitome of bravery and endurance of the British soldier.

There were only two passable tracks from Natal into Zululand, and one of them crossed the Buffalo River at Rorke's Drift. This track continued to run eastward via Isandlwana to Ulundi. There were two buildings about one-half mile from Rorke's Drift that had originally been Jim Rorke's farm, with high ground to the south. These buildings had been requisitioned by the British and were being used as a base hospital and supply depot for the center column (No. 3) of the invasion force.

Lieutenant (later Colonel) John R. M. Chard, who had arrived at Rorke's Drift on 19 January 1879, was in command of the post. He was assisted by Lieutenant (later Major) Gonville Bromhead, commander of Company B, 2nd Battalion, 24th Foot, which had been designated to protect the base. The garrison at Rorke's Drift consisted of about 8 officers and 131 other ranks, including 35 sick in hospital.

In the early afternoon of 22 January 1879, firing was heard at Isandlwana, 6 miles directly to the east of Rorke's Drift. Horsemen fleeing from Isandlwana stopped long enough to shout that the British force there had been overrun and massacred. Chard directed that immediate measures be taken to fortify the post, and 200-pound mealie (corn) bags and large biscuit boxes were used to construct walls and redoubts. Firing loopholes were hastily smashed in the hospital, and one solder later observed that "we were pinned like rats in a hole" (Smythe n.d., p. 2). A basic perimeter was constructed in about an hour.

At about 5:00 P.M., a soldier spotted the Zulus approaching and shouted, "Here they come! Black as hell and thick as grass!" (Glover 1975, p. 98). The 4,000 Zulus were members of three regiments that had been in reserve in Isandlwana and had seen only limited action. They were eager to prove themselves as warriors. About 500 Zulus rushed to the south wall of the British post in their initial assault, but they were stopped by the British rifle fire. As more Zulus rushed to encircle the station, a general assault began.

About an hour later, Chard ordered the abandonment of the wall in front of the hospital. The men in the hospital were fighting the Zulus and withdrawing room by room when the thatched hospital roof was lit on fire, and they fell back on a new wall built in front of the storehouse. By 10:00 P.M., the British soldiers were within the wall protecting the storehouse. Relentless Zulu assaults continued until after midnight and then began to slacken as the attackers became exhausted. Sporadic assaults continued as the attackers had to struggle over the heaps of Zulu bodies to get close to the British. "All we saw was blood," one Zulu warrior later recalled (Edgerton 1988, p. 105).

By 4:00 A.M., the area was silent and the attack was apparently over. The Zulus reappeared at about 7:00 A.M., but they only rested for a short time before moving to the east. About 400 dead Zulu littered the ground, and the British lost 17 killed and 10 seriously wounded.

The defense of Rorke's Drift was a triumph of British courage and skill over tremendous odds, but it was a relatively small victory. Eleven of the Rorke's Drift defenders, including Chard and Bromhead, received the Victoria Cross, the largest number for a single engagement in British history. These awards were spread out over an extended period, to maintain public interest and support. The epic of Rorke's Drift also helped restore British military prestige after the humiliating defeat at Isandlwana—and divert attention from it.

See also Bromhead, Major Gonville, V.C.; Cetshwayo kaMpande; Chard, Colonel John R. M., V.C.; Isandlwana, Battle of; Ulundi, Battle of; Victoria Cross; Zulu War; Zululand

References: Barthorp (1980); Chadwick (1978); Edgerton (1988); Glover (1975); Knight (1990); Morris (1965); Smythe (n.d.)

Rose, Field Marshal Hugh H., First Baron Strathnairn of Strathnairn and Jhansi (1801–1885)

Field Marshal Hugh H. Rose, Lord Strathnairn, held numerous military and diplomatic postings, culminating as commander in chief, Ireland, from 1865 to 1870.

Rose was born on 6 April 1801 in Berlin, where his father was minister plenipotentiary at the Prussian court, and also educated there. He was commissioned an ensign in the 93rd Sutherland Highlanders in 1820 and purchased a number of promotions in rapid succession. Rose served with his regiment in Ireland, Gibraltar (1833–1836), and Malta (1836–1839). In 1839, he purchased an unattached lieutenant colonelcy, and the following year was selected for special service in Syria. At this time, British and allied naval and land forces were involved in expelling the Egyptian Army of Mohammed Ali from Syria to prevent it from seizing Constantinople. Rose distinguished himself in this operation and then served as consul-general for Syria from 1841 to 1848.

Rose then served as secretary of the British Embassy in Constantinople, and during the Crimean War (1854–1856) he served with the local rank of brigadier general as the primary British liaison officer with the French headquarters. He spoke and wrote French well, and his other skills permitted him to gain the confidence of French commanders and provide insightful reports to the British. Rose was promoted to major general and knighted for his Crimean service.

When the Indian Mutiny broke out in May 1857, Rose was posted to India and assumed command of the Central India Field Force on 16 December 1857. He divided his force into two brigades and began operations to eliminate all insurgents the following month. Acting decisively and moving quickly, Rose's force fought its way to Saugor, which was relieved on 3 February 1858, and to the rebel-held fort at Gathakot, which was abandoned the night of 11–12 February and destroyed by Rose's troops.

Rose's force crushed the rebels at Madanpur on 4 March 1858 while en route to his next objective, Jhansi, which was reached on 21 March. While bombarding Jhansi, Rose's force had to fight the 20,000-man relief force under Tantia Topi. The British refused to lift the siege of Jhansi, and Rose detached a portion of his force and attacked both flanks of the insurgent force after it had crossed the Betwa River. Rose's force won the Battle of Betwa River on 1 April 1858, and then he turned his full attention back to Jhansi, which was stormed and captured on 3 April. Rebel forces were also defeated at Kunch (1 May 1858) and Kalpi (22 May 1858). By that time, Rose had defeated the mutineers in thirteen engagements in five months. Rose became ill, but when he learned the Gwalior forces had defected to the mutineers, he remained to finish the campaign.

Tantia Topi and the Rhani of Jhansi fled and then established a new base of operations in the Gwalior fortress. Storming parties stealthily climbed to the fortress early on 19 June 1858 and were able to open many of the gates without detection, then assaulted and engaged the remaining garrison in brutal hand-to-hand combat. Tantia Topi escaped, the Rhani of Jhansi had been killed the previous day, and Rose occupied Gwalior. This brought the Central Indian campaign to a close, although mopping up operations continued until 1859.

Rose was promoted to lieutenant general and appointed commander in chief of the Bombay Army in 1860. The following year he became commander in chief, India, serving in that position until 1865. From 1865 to 1870, Rose was commander in chief, Ireland. He was ennobled in 1866 and promoted to general in 1867 and to field marshal in 1877. Rose died in 1885.

See also Bombay Army; Chernaya, Battle of; Crimean War; Egyptian Army; French Forces, Crimean War; Gwalior, Battle of; India; Indian Mutiny; Purchase System; Rhani of Jhansi; Tantia Topi

References: Edwardes (1963); Haythornthwaite (1995); Hibbert (1978); Palmer (1987); Robson (1997); Royle (2000)

Royal Army Medical Corps

The Royal Army Medical Corps (RAMC) was formed on 23 June 1898 from the Army Medical Staff (consisting of officers) and the Army Medical Staff Corps (medical noncommissioned officers). The formation of the RAMC was intended to consolidate all male medical personnel in the British Army to streamline effectiveness and efficiency.

The formation of the RAMC also settled a number of grievances held for decades by military surgeons and physicians. After 1873, when medical officers had been removed from regimental control and assigned to one of two general hospitals or to station hospitals, there had been concern about loss of regimental privileges, prestige, and low pay. Rates of medical pay were increased in 1879, although medical ranks were abolished and medical officers were categorized as noncombatants in the 1880s. With the formation of the RAMC, military ranks were reinstituted and medical officers were made eligible for honors.

The formation of the RAMC had little impact on the medical organization in the field. The first engagement for the newly formed RAMC was the Battle of Omdurman (2 September 1898) in the Sudan. General medical arrangements and treatment of the 434 wounded British soldiers was considered satisfactory and an improvement over those of previous campaigns.

On 1 October 1899, shortly before the outbreak of the Second Boer War, the strength of the RAMC (all ranks) was 3,707, with another 1,009 men in the reserve. This number of medical personnel, however, proved inadequate during the Second Boer War. By the last year of the Second Boer War, 1902, the strength of the RAMC in South Africa reached 8,500, of whom about three-quarters were contracted civilians. Over 300 RAMC personnel lost their lives in South Africa. They also won six Victoria Crosses for gallantry.

Reforms took place in the British Army, including the RAMC, after the Second Boer War. These included moving the Royal Army Medical College from Netley to Millbank in London in 1907 and the establishment of an RAMC Territorial Force. To augment the number of trained nurses in an emergency, volunteer aid detachments were also formed.

See also Boer War, Second (1899–1902); Military Medicine, British Army—Medical Personnel; Reconquest of the Sudan; Victoria Cross

References: Hallows (1991); May (1984); McLaughlin (1972); Skelley (1977); Spiers (1992)

Royal Warrant (30 October 1871) Abolishing Purchase
See Cardwell Reforms; Officers, British Army—Sources of; Purchase System

Russell, William Howard
See Correspondents, War

Russian Forces, Crimean War

The peacetime strength of the Russian Army during this era was about 700,000 soldiers, although in 1853 it had increased to about 1 million men. The Russian Army consisted of 188 infantry regiments, 32 rifle battalions, and 48 frontier battalions (responsible for garrisoning distant Russian provinces). There were close to 60 cavalry regiments, 310 artillery batteries, 11 engineer battalions, and 6 half battalions of engineers with bridging equipment. The elite of these forces were the Imperial Guard and the Grenadiers. It was the world's largest army, and many observers thought it was the best. The colorful uniforms and unparalleled precision of Russian soldiers on parade were very impressive.

The first commander of the Russian forces in the Crimea was Prince Alexander Sergeevich Menshikov, a "bluff soldierly man with little imagination" (Royle 2000, p. 33). In February 1855, Menshikov was replaced by Prince Michael Gorchakov.

The Russian Army, however, was deficient in tactical and musketry training and field soldiering. Moreover, out of the total strength of 1 million soldiers, only a fraction could be deployed to and actually fight in the Crimea. The 48 frontier battalions consisted of about 150,000 troops, and they needed to remain in their garrisons; Cossack irregulars consisted of about 250,000; and another 200,000 were committed fighting Chechens and others in the Caucasus. Since there were no railroads south of Moscow, the Russians needed to maintain and defend long lines of communications. Even though the Russian Army was operating on interior lines, the British and French could bring reinforcements and supplies to the Crimea by sea faster than the Russians could by land.

The Russian officer corps was relatively diverse, with about one out of every six officers coming from wealthy, noble families. Over 80 percent of the Russian officers were "the semiliterate sons of petty nobles who had failed secondary school and entered the army as 'Junkers,' hoping to salvage a career" (Edgerton 1999, p. 59). These Junker officers had served in the ranks and were frequently jealous of other officers and brutal to their soldiers. Senior officers occasionally detested each other and were incompetent. Russian artillery and engineer officers, however, were considered well trained and professional.

The Russian other ranks were mainly illiterate serfs, many overage, who were conscripted for twenty-five years. Russian soldiers were armed with smoothbore muskets, including some from 1814. Immediately before the war began, an inspection in one infantry regiment revealed that 1,400 out of 1,991 muskets had significant defects. Russian tactics were to advance in close order—a lucrative target for French and British soldiers armed with Minié rifles—fire one volley, then charge with the bayonet. The Russian soldiers frequently fought very doggedly and courageously despite their hardships.

Some 17,800 Russian forces were besieged in Sevastopol in late September 1854, a number increasing to 45,000 soldiers and 9,000 naval gunners by June 1855. Most of the war involved the surrounding allied troops trying to capture Sevastopol, while additional Russian forces attempted to break through the allies and relieve the surrounded Russians.

The Russians are estimated to have suffered in the Crimean War 256,000 deaths, with 128,700 killed in action and the rest from disease.

See also Crimean War; French Forces, Crimean War; Sardinian Forces, Crimean War; Sevastopol, Siege of; Turkish Forces, Crimean War

References: Edgerton (1999); Judd (1975); Palmer (1987); Raugh (1988b); Royle (2000)

S

Sabers
See Cavalry; British Army—Weapons and Equipment

St. Arnaud, Marshal Jacques Leroy de
See Crimean War; French Forces, Crimean War

Sale, Major General Sir Robert (1782–1845)
A brave soldier who served in uniform for forty-seven years, Major General Sir Robert Sale, nicknamed "Fighting Bob," was a hero of the First Afghan War (1839–1842).

Sale, born in 1782, saw considerable active service in India, during the First Burma War, and in Mauritius. He commanded the 1st Brigade in the expeditionary force, dubbed the Army of the Indus, marching from Ferozepore to Kabul at the beginning of the First Afghan War (1839–1842). The fortress of Ghazni guarded the approach to Kabul. Sale led a storming party on 23 July 1839 to blow up a main gate as a prelude to a general British assault on the fortress at Ghazni, but in confusion at a key moment ordered a retreat. A subordinate, however, used his initiative and encouraged the attack to continue until successful. While courageous, the assault on Ghazni was one example of Sale's blundering.

The British entered Kabul the following month, where Sale became the second in command. In late 1841, Sale's brigade was ordered back to India, but it met resistance and had to seek refuge in Jalalabad, where it fought off numerous Afghan attacks. The remaining Kabul garrison and families, about 4,500 troops and 12,000 camp followers, were forced to evacuate Kabul in January 1842 and were massacred attempting to return to India.

On 7 April 1842, Sale marched his 5,000-man brigade out of Jalalabad to engage an approaching Afghan force and to lift the siege of the fortress. Sale was successful, and Jalalabad was reached on 16 April by the "Army of Retribution" marching from India.

Sale, as the quartermaster-general in India in 1845, attached himself to the leading infantry at the Battle of Mudki (18 December 1845) during the First Sikh War (1845–1846). Sale was killed in the battle.

See also Afghan War, First (1839–1842); Burma War, First (1824–1826); East India Company, Military Forces; India; Sikh War, First (1845–1846)
References: Cook (1975); Farwell (1972); Featherstone (1968); Waller (1990)

Sandhurst, Royal Military College
The British Army's weak performance during the early campaigns of the French Revolutionary Wars suggested the need to better train and educate junior officers. The Royal Military College was founded in 1802 by Colonel (later Major General) John Gaspard Le Marchant to train young men as infantry and cavalry subalterns in a Junior Department (which later became the Royal Military College, Sandhurst), and experienced officers in staff duties in a Senior Department (later the Staff College, Camberley).

The Junior Department began at Great Marlow with the mission to educate the sons of officers who intended to follow their father's profession and serve in the army. This attempt to create a self-perpetuating officer class was short-lived. After 1803, Gentlemen Cadets thirteen to fifteen years old and with a more varied social background nominated by the commander in chief were admitted. A new site was first occupied in 1812, when the Junior Department became the Royal Military College, Sandhurst.

In its early years, the Sandhurst course did little to develop military professionalism and was more theoretical than practical. Sandhurst was spending too much time on remedial and classical education. Proficiency in six subjects (mathematics, fortification, military surveying, and three optional subjects chosen from French, German, siege operation, landscape drawing, military drawing, Latin, general history, and geography) was required to receive a commission. "Character" training continued to be a vital component of the curriculum. Sandhurst graduates were a minority of newly commissioned officers; for example, between 1834 and 1838, less than 20 percent of the new officers came from Sandhurst. After 1842, officers who entered the army via Sandhurst did not purchase their commission.

In 1849, examinations became a prerequisite for receiving a commission. Between 1855 and 1858, the minimum age for entrance to Sandhurst was raised to sixteen. As Sandhurst attracted better-educated candidates, entrance examinations became more rigorous. As these changes were made, some of the petty, irksome rules intended for schoolboys rather than young men were not eliminated. This led to the "Cadet Mutiny" of 1862, in which the cadet battalion withstood a three-day siege in one of the earthworks used for fortification training, until the commander in chief, the Duke of Cambridge, had to personally restore order.

When the purchase of commissions was abolished in 1871, Sandhurst, seemingly obsolete, was closed. First commissions were then awarded by written competitive examination. In 1877, Sandhurst was reopened, when the examination became the entrance examination for appointment to Sandhurst.

The length of the Sandhurst course varied with the demand for new officers. In 1912, Sandhurst was increased in size to eight companies.

See also Addiscombe, Military Seminary; Camberley, Staff College; Officers, British Army—Sources of Commissioning; Officers, British Army—Training and Education; Woolwich, Royal Military Academy

References: Harries-Jenkins (1977); Otley (1973); Spiers (1992); Strachan (1984)

Sardinian Forces, Crimean War

On 26 January 1855, the united Kingdom of Piedmont-Sardinia joined the British, French, and Turkish allies in fighting the Russians in the Crimean War. Its motive was largely political. The Sardinian prime minister, Count Cavour, was eager to have his country represented at a peace conference following the war. At this conference, Piedmont-Sardinia would effectively be speaking on behalf of other states in the still disunited Italy.

The Sardinian Army totaled 45,000 men in peacetime, a figure increased to 85,000 in time of war. It consisted of infantry, rifles, cavalry, artillery, engineers, a wagon train, and gendarmes. Sardinian soldiers were conscripted, and infantrymen were required to serve eight years on active duty with eight years in the reserve.

The Sardinian contingent in the Crimea War consisted of 15,000 soldiers under the command of forty-year-old General Alfonso de la Marmora. The Sardinians, organized in provisional regiments, arrived in the Crimea in May 1855 and were attached to the British force. They made an impression on the war-weary veterans already in the Crimea, wearing "bandit-looking hats with large plume of black cocks' feathers" (Judd 1975, p. 135). Within a month of their arrival, however, 5 percent of the Sardinian advance party had succumbed to cholera.

The Sardinians served in the trenches before Sevastopol and distinguished themselves at the Battle of Chernaya (16 August 1855) and in the attack on the Malakov (8 September 1855). The Sardinians, called the "Sardines" by the admiring British, and their commander "General Marmalade" redeployed to Genoa during the last week of April 1856 (Palmer 1987, pp. 235–236).

The Sardinian contribution to the Crimean War was relatively minor, although its forces sustained about 1,000 dead from all causes. As a result, Piedmont-Sardinia earned a place at the Paris Peace Conference. The ratification of the Treaty of Paris on 27 April 1856, which formally ended the Crimean War, showed little sympathy for Piedmont-Sardinian national aspirations. In 1859, Piedmont-Sardinia renewed its struggle for Italian independence. France, its forces under the personal command of Napoleon III, joined Piedmont-Sardinia to drive Austrian forces from north Italy. Italy gradually united around Piedmont.

See also Chernaya, Battle of; Crimean War; French Forces, Crimean War; Russian Forces, Crimean War; Turkish Forces, Crimean War

References: Edgerton (1999); Judd (1975); Palmer (1987); Royle (2000); Warner (1972)

Scott, Colonel Sir Francis
See Ashanti Expedition

Semaphore Signaling
See Communications

Service Support, British Army
See Animals, Transport; Army Service Corps; Land Transport Corps; Lines of Communication; Quartermaster-General, British Army; Railways

Sevastopol, Siege of (8 October 1854–9 September 1855)

The Crimean War, in large measure, was fought over the issue of maintaining the balance of power in Europe and preventing Russian expansion into the Ottoman territories. The allies needed to punish the powerful Russian Black Sea Fleet, based at Sevastopol, for its atrocious role in the Sinope "massacre," 30 November 1853, and destroy this threat to British naval supremacy. As a result, the capture of Sevastopol became a major objective of the war.

The allies landed their troops at Calamita Bay, on the Crimean coast, beginning on 14 September 1854. After the British, French, and Turks assembled their forces, they began the southward march toward Sevastopol on 19 September. The next day, the Russians, defending on the south bank of the Alma River, attempted to halt the allied advance at the Battle of the Alma. After a hard fight, the allies continued their advance. Opportunities were probably missed by not attacking Sevastopol from the north before the city's defenses were better prepared, and the allies made a flank march around Sevastopol on 25–26 September.

General (later Field Marshal) Fitzroy J. H. Somerset, First Baron Raglan, British commander in chief, made the decision to besiege Sevastopol on 28 September 1854, when he directed that the siege trains be landed on shore. The allies held a war council on 7 October 1854, and the siege of Sevastopol began the next day.

The city defenses were strengthened considerably, mainly under the direction of Lieutenant Colonel (later General Count) Franz E. I. Todleben. Many of the Russian ships were intentionally sunk to block the mouth of Sevastopol Harbor, and the guns were removed for use in the defense of Sevastopol. Ramparts were quickly constructed, and there were six main redoubts on the Sevastopol perimeter. From west to east these redoubts were the Quarantine Bastion, the Central Bastion, the Flagstaff Bastion, the Redan, the Malakov, and the Little Redan. By the middle of October 1854, the Russians had in their defensive positions 342 guns, of which 118 were heavy caliber and able to reach the allied siege lines.

The first allied bombardment, using 126 land-based and other naval guns, began on 17 October 1854. This bombardment was poorly coordinated, and all 30 major allied ships were damaged. The barrage continued until 25 October and was a failure.

The Russians attempted to break the siege of Sevastopol by attacking on 25 October 1854 (the Battle of Balaklava) and 5 November 1854 (the Battle of Inkerman). The former was a tactical success for the Russians, but the latter was definitely a tactical and strategic defeat for the Russians.

The allies were very slow in preparing their siege positions. "They call it a siege," one British officer wrote home, "It's more like a garden party. We shan't get anywhere like this" (Judd 1975, p. 80). Over the winter months, logistical mismanagement and dubious leadership caused the British soldiers to suffer unimaginable privations. Shelter and clothing was inadequate, the diet monotonous, medical care poor, and transportation entirely insufficient to move supplies from Balaklava Harbor to the soldiers.

Even though more and better supplies began to arrive for the British soldiers early in 1855, the strength of the British Army had declined significantly, with only about 11,000 men physically fit for duty and 23,000 sick and wounded at the beginning of February 1855. In that month, the plan for the allied conduct of the siege was changed, with the numerically superior French forming a second corps to take over the right sector of the siege works, especially in front of the Malakov and the Little Redan. The first French corps remained in the left sector, and the British were to concentrate their operations in front of the Great Redan. This began the period of the "new siege."

Attacks took place periodically. The Russians captured the Mamelon, a small hill about 400 yards in front of the Malakov, on the night of 22 February 1855. They also made a sortie against the French on 22 March 1855 and temporarily held some of the French line.

The allies began their second large-scale bombardment of Sevastopol on 9 April 1855. For ten days, 382 French and 138 British guns fired about 165,000 rounds into the fortress city, and were answered by 998 Russian artillery pieces that fired 90,000 rounds. The Russians worked indefatigably and repaired the damage each night, although they abandoned the destroyed Flagstaff Bastion. This bombardment caused significant casualties on all sides, including 6,131 Russian, 1,587 French, and 263 British casualties.

The French, under a new commander, conducted a fierce but successful night attack on 22 May 1855 on Russian defenses between Quarantine Bay and the Central Bastion. This operation cost the French 2,303 men.

The third allied bombardment of Sevastopol began on 6 June 1855, enabling the British to advance to the Redan and the French to capture the Mamelon. Allied artillery again pounded the Russian defenses on 17 June, preparatory to an allied assault the next day in which the British planned to capture the Redan and the French to seize the Malakov. Confusion and Russian preparedness caused the attack to fail disastrously, with the British sustaining about 1,500 casualties and the French twice that number. Demoralized and ill, Raglan died on 28 June.

The last Russian attempt to break the allied siege by field operations was the Battle of Chernaya (16 August 1855). Sardinian forces, which had arrived in the Crimea on 8 May 1855, assisted the French in defeating the Russians in this engagement.

The allies, then with over 800 guns, responded by intensifying their bombardment of Sevastopol. Beginning on 17 August 1855, the allies continually bombarded the defenses for ten days, and again from 5 to 8 September 1855, causing more than 7,500 Russian casualties during the latter period alone. At noon on 8 September, the allies attacked the defenses. The British, numbering 11,000 troops, attacked and were repulsed from the Great Redan three times, having seemingly lost their nerve and discipline. The French were able to surprise the Russians and seize the Malakov, a decisive position. That night, the Russians, after losing 12,913 men, withdrew across a floating bridge to the north side of Sevastopol Bay and abandoned their defense of Sevastopol. The allies, having suffered about 10,040 casualties in the attack, entered the ruins of Sevastopol on 12 September.

Other than operations at Kinburn and at Kars in October and November 1855, respectively, the allied capture of Sevastopol marked the end of major operations in the Crimea. The adversaries seemed to have lost heart for a continuation of combat.

See also Chernaya, Battle of; Crimean War; French Forces, Crimean War; Kars, Siege of; Raglan, Field Marshal Fitzroy J. H. Somerset, First Baron; Russian Forces, Crimean War; Sardinian Forces, Crimean War; Turkish Forces, Crimean War

References: Baumgart (1999); Bell (1956); Judd (1975); Mansfield (1973); McCormick (1855); Palmer (1987); Pemberton (1962); Robins (2003); Royle (2000); Strachan (1978); Warner (1972)

Seymour, Admiral Sir Edward H.
See Boxer Rebellion

Shah Shujah
See Afghan War, First (1839–1842); Afghanistan; Dost Mohammed

Sher Ali Khan (1825–1879)

Sher Ali Khan was the ruler of Afghanistan from 1863 until deposed by a brother in 1866, and again from 1869 to 1879, at a time when his nation was the playing field of the Great Game between Russia and Great Britain.

Sher Ali was born in 1825, the third son of Dost Mohammed Khan. Dost Mohammed, as amir of Afghanistan, signed an alliance with Great Britain in 1857. When he died in 1863, Sher Ali, whom he had selected to succeed him, became amir. Dynastic struggles, as well as conflicts between other relatives and tribes, broke out. In spite of internal dissension and strife, Sher Ali was a relatively progressive ruler who created a national army and postal system, established the basis of collecting land taxes, and published the nation's first newspaper.

At the same time, Sher Ali was under pressure from external sources, mainly Great Britain and Russia, each wanting to expand their imperial influence in Central Asia and Afghanistan. The Russians conquered a number of Central Asian cities, including Samarkand in 1868, Khiva in 1873, and Kokand in 1875.

The British unsuccessfully tried to persuade Sher Ali to accept a British ambassador and soldiers to train his army.

Sher Ali seemingly attempted to maintain Afghan neutrality. In 1878, when he heard the Russians intended to send a mission to his kingdom, he wrote and urged them not to come. The Russians sent their uninvited mission to Afghanistan. The British, concerned that the Russians would extend their influence to Afghanistan, demanded similar representation and sent an ultimatum to Sher Ali. This demand went unanswered, and on 21 November 1878, the British invaded Afghanistan and started the Second Afghan War.

Sher Ali Khan, characterized as "not only a savage, but a savage with a touch of insanity" by the viceroy of India (Fredericks 1971, p. 191), attempted to escape the British forces and traveled north seeking Russian support. The Russians told him not to come, and Sher Ali Khan died, supposedly heartbroken, at Mazar-i-Sharif on 21 February 1879. He was succeeded as amir by his son, Yakub Khan.

See also Afghan War, Second (1878–1880); Afghanistan; Cavagnari, Major Sir Pierre L. N.; Dost Mohammed; Great Game; Roberts, Field Marshal Frederick S., V.C.
References: Fredericks (1971); James (1997); Roberts (1897)

Shere Singh
See Chillianwalla, Battle of; Gujerat, Battle of; Sikh War, Second (1848–1849)

Sherpur, Battle of (23 December 1879)
Major General (later Field Marshal Earl) Sir Frederick S. Roberts, V.C., was given command of the hastily formed Kabul Field Force in September 1879 when hostilities again broke out in Afghanistan. Roberts's force began its advance on 27 September and defeated a large Afghan force at Charasia, on the route to Kabul, on 6 October 1879. The 7,000-man Kabul Field Force occupied the large, heavily fortified Sherpur Cantonment near Kabul.

Roberts ruthlessly applied martial law, and Afghans increasingly came to resent the presence of a foreign occupying force. Rebel Afghan troops began to converge on Kabul. British troops were sent on 11 December 1879 to disperse an Afghan column, but the 300 British soldiers rode unwittingly into a group of about 10,000 Afghans and had to hurriedly retreat, leaving behind four guns. Heavy fighting continued for the following three days. By 14 December, the British force was effectively besieged.

On 22 December 1879, Roberts learned from a spy that the Afghans were planning a full-scale attack on the Sherpur Cantonment the next morning. Roberts was informed of the exact enemy plan, and that the attack would be initiated by the lighting of a beacon fire on the nearby Asmai Heights. Accordingly, the British forces remained vigilant and manned their defensive positions on the 15-foot cantonment walls through the night.

Just before dawn on 23 December 1879, a large flare was expectedly fired from the Asmai Heights, and Afghan musket and artillery fire poured into the east and south walls of the British defenses. *Ghazis* (Muslim warriors) with scaling ladders charged across the snow as the 28th Punjabis and Guides on the east wall opened fire on the attackers. The 67th Foot and 92nd Gordon Highlanders on the south wall then commenced firing, and all British guns concentrated their fire on the advancing masses. Waves of relatively uncoordinated assaults were mowed down, and there was a lull in the attacks at about 10:00 A.M., although attacks began again an hour later. Roberts was able to send four guns with a cavalry escort outside the cantonment to shell Afghan assembly areas, and by 1:00 P.M., the Afghans were fleeing. The 9th Lancers, Guides, and 5th Punjab Cavalry conducted an energetic, although not especially creditable, pursuit. Three lancers were reportedly assigned to each Afghan straggler, who was killed after being run down.

The result of the Battle of Sherpur was basically a foregone conclusion, as the Afghans were unable to cross the open areas in the face of superior and disciplined British rifle and cannon fire from a well-defended position. Of the 100,000 Afghans purportedly involved in the attack, about 3,000 dead littered the battlefield. British casualties sustained between 15 and 23 December 1879 were, according to Roberts, 2 officers, 9 other ranks, and 7 followers killed, and 5 officers, 41 soldiers, and 20 followers wounded.

See also Afghan War, Second (1878–1880); Afghanistan; Charasia, Battle of; Roberts, Field Marshal Frederick S., V.C.
References: Barthorp (1982); Featherstone (1973); Forbes (1892); Roberts (1897); Tanner (2002); Young (1977)

Short Service
Short service replaced long service as the term of voluntary enlistment in the British Army by the Army Enlistment Act of 1870.

Long service, in which a soldier had been generally

required to enlist for "life" (twenty-one years), or for ten or twelve years with an option to extend enlistment to twenty-one or twenty-four years to become eligible for a pension, was not effective in attracting quality soldiers or forming a military reserve.

As a result of British experiences and recruiting shortfalls in the 1850s and 1860s, it was determined to replace long service with short service. Secretary of State for War (later Viscount) Edward T. Cardwell was responsible for introducing short service in the army Enlistment Act of 1870. The initial term of service for the soldier was kept at twelve years, but the soldier would spend the first six with the colors, and the second six years in the regular reserve. (This was raised in 1881 to seven years with the colors and five years in the reserves.) Soldiers could extend their enlistment to complete a total of twenty-one years and become eligible for a pension.

Short service was instituted for a number of reasons. A shorter term of service was intended to appeal to more, and higher quality, soldiers. Many soldiers would not reenlist beyond their six years of active duty, and would be reassigned to the regular reserve. This would provide experienced manpower for the regular reserve. Moreover, money would be saved because fewer soldiers would remain on active duty long enough to become eligible for a pension. At a time of increasing imperial commitments, Cardwell was trying to help ensure a balance between the number of soldiers serving overseas and those serving at home.

Short service was controversial in many respects. It required more recruits annually, and allowed experienced men to leave the army before reaching their potential. The youth and lack of physical readiness made many new soldiers unfit for the rigors of overseas and active service. The army's efficiency, however, was the prime consideration, and the principle of short service remained in the British Army.

See also Cardwell, Edward T.; Cardwell Reforms; Long Service; Rank and File, British Army—Enlistment; Recruiting
References: Skelley (1977); Spiers (1992); Strachan (1984)

Sikh War, First (1845–1846)

Ranjit Singh, "the lion of the Punjab," was able to effectively unite the Sikh sects in the Punjab and build a well organized, trained, and disciplined Sikh army called the *Khalsa*. Ranjit declared himself maharajah of the Punjab in 1801 and attempted to maintain friendly relations with the British. In 1839, however, when the British wanted to oust Dost Mohammed from the Afghan throne, Ranjit, while their nominal ally, would not permit the British to take the direct route to Kabul through the Punjab, so they had to launch the expedition from Sind.

In 1839, Ranjit, a strong unifying factor for the Sikhs, died, and the Punjab slid toward anarchy with various factions fighting for control of the state. In 1843, a small child, reportedly Ranjit's son, acceded to the throne. At about the same time, Sikh soldiers elected and formed soldiers' councils called *panchayats* within their regiments. The British conquest of Sind in 1843 basically cut off the Sikh route to the sea via the Indus and encircled the Punjab. Fearful of a British attack, the Sikhs continued to build up the *Khalsa* and were emboldened to strike by the disastrous British performance in Afghanistan during the First Afghan War.

In July 1844, Lieutenant General (later Field Marshal Viscount) Sir Henry Hardinge became governor-general of India. The commander in chief, India, at the time was Lieutenant General (later Field Marshal Viscount) Sir Hugh Gough. As the *Khalsa* became more anti-British and bellicose, the British quietly made unobtrusive preparations to defend against an expected Sikh attack. Garrisons near the Punjab (Ferozepore, Ludhiana, Ambala, and Meerut) were reinforced with 22,911 soldiers and 28 guns, from a total of 17,612 men and 66 guns under the previous governor-general to a total of 40,253 men and 94 guns. Fifty-six boats that could be used to cross the Sutlej River, plus a pontoon train from Sind, were also positioned at Ferozepore.

The Sikh *Khalsa*, reportedly concerned about British troop movements, crossed the Sutlej River on 11 December 1845. This was considered a violation of the 1809 Treaty of Amritsar, and Hardinge declared war on the Sikhs two days later.

On 18 December 1845, Gough's exhausted 12,000-man force, which had marched over 120 miles from Ambala in less than 6 days, was surprised near Mudki by a Sikh force of about 13,000 men and 22 guns. Gough decided to attack immediately, brushing aside criticism of impetuosity, and then began "the last of the wars in which the army, still geared to Waterloo and the Napoleonic Wars, went into battle with an Order of Battle and the old-style dress, with their leaders Peninsular veterans" (Featherstone 1968, p. 52). The attack was hastily organized, and the British infantry, advancing in echelon of brigades from the right, had to

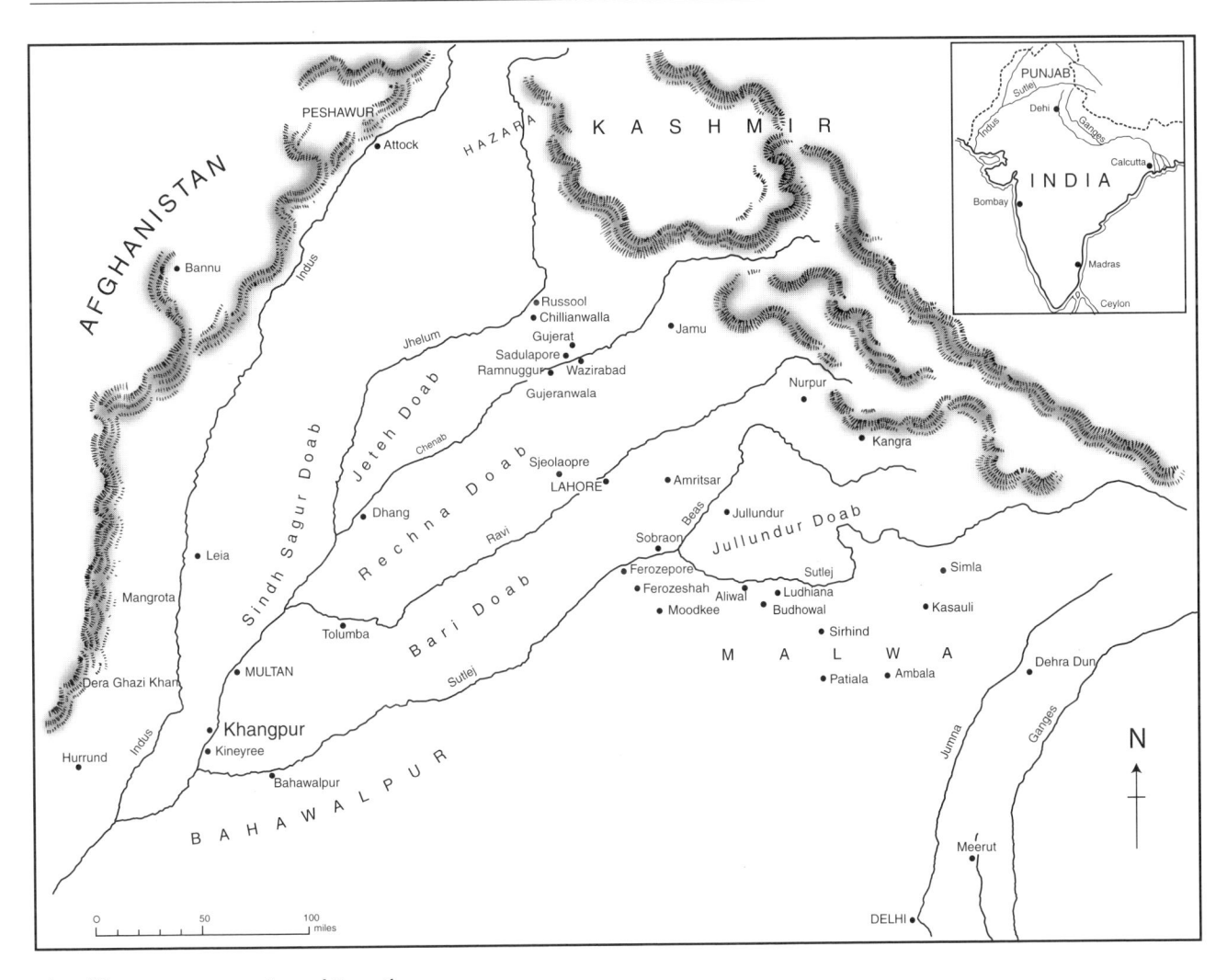

First Sikh War, 1845–1846: Area of Operations

march across plowed fields toward the Sikhs, who were positioned on the edge of a jungle. An artillery duel between Sikh and British guns took place at the same time, as confusion and chaos reigned. Eventually, British bravery, discipline, and cold steel carried the day, and thus "ended one of the most untidy actions the British Army in India had ever fought" (Cook 1975, p. 49). The British suffered 872 casualties, including two major generals killed in action. The Sikhs, who also had high casualties and lost seventeen guns, marched to Ferozeshah to join another large Sikh force in an entrenched camp there.

On 19 December 1845, Hardinge, Gough's political superior but junior to him as a lieutenant general, volunteered to serve as Gough's second in command. This unusual command arrangement generally worked well.

Gough's force marched to Ferozeshah and encountered a Sikh force of about 25,000 troops commanded by Lal Singh on 21 December 1845. A fourth British division increased Gough's army strength to 16,700 men with 69 guns before the battle. The British attacked with three divisions on line and one in reserve, and in the tremendous confusion, both sides sustained heavy casualties. Most of the Sikhs abandoned their positions overnight, and the British were able to occupy the vacated entrenchments the following morning. A second Sikh army, commanded by Tej Singh, arrived, and fought half-heartedly before withdrawing that afternoon. The British barely won the Battle of Ferozeshah, and suffered 696 dead and 1,729 wounded. Sikh losses were about 3,000 men and 72 guns.

Gough then decided to rest and await reinforcements

from Sind, but detached a force eventually totaling 10,000 men and 32 guns under Major General (later Lieutenant General) Sir Harry G. W. Smith to protect his lines of communication and the British garrison at Ludhiana. On 28 January 1846, Smith's force, with his cavalry and horse artillery in the lead, encountered the Sikhs in an entrenched camp near Aliwal. The Sikhs were caught by surprise and had no time to deploy their artillery. Smith coordinated the attack of his infantry, cavalry, and artillery, and Sikh resistance was smashed. With the Sutlej River to their rear, the Sikhs could not reform effectively and were routed, losing about 3,000 men and 67 guns. The British won a complete victory at a cost of 589 casualties.

After the Battle of Aliwal, only one large Sikh force remained south or east of the Sutlej River, at Sobraon. The Sikh position was well entrenched and defended by about 30,000 soldiers and 67 guns, abutting and with a pontoon bridge across the Sutlej River, with additional artillery on the far side of the river. Gough's force of 15,000 men with 70–80 guns, including Smith's troops, attacked Sobraon on 10 February 1846. After an inadequate artillery bombardment, Gough's troops again conducted a frontal attack. The fighting was severe, and the Sikhs fought savagely, largely because the Sutlej had risen seven feet overnight and some of the pontoons had been removed from the bridge across the river. The Sikhs were eventually thrown into the Sutlej, and suffered 8,000–10,000 casualties at Sobraon, compared to about 2,300 British casualties in this badly managed battle.

The British victory at Sobraon basically ended the First Sikh War, although the British, who had lost about half their European soldiers in four battles, were still in a somewhat precarious position as the Sikhs were still able to field a 40,000-man army. The overall moral effect on the Sikhs, however, seems to have been decisive, and they accepted the terms of the Treaty of Lahore. These terms restricted the size of the *Khalsa* to 25 infantry battalions and 12,000 cavalrymen, and forced them to surrender 25 guns. Other indemnities and the surrender of territory were required, as was the stationing of British troops in Lahore until the end of 1846. The First Sikh war, according to one officer, was a "tissue of mismanagement, blunders, errors, ignorance and arrogance" (Farwell 2001, p. 759)—but the British won.

See also Afghan War, First (1839–1842); Aliwal, Battle of; East India Company; East India Company, Military Forces; Ferozeshah, Battle of; Gough, Field Marshal Hugh; Hardinge, Field Marshal Henry; India; Sikh War, Second (1848–1849); Sikhs; Sind, Operations in; Smith, Lieutenant General Sir Harry G. W.; Sobraon, Battle of

References: Carleton (2002); Cook (1975); Crawford (1967); Farwell (2001); Featherstone (1968); Featherstone (1989); Featherstone (1992); Fredericks (1971); Haythornthwaite (1995); Nijjar (1976)

Sikh War, Second (1848–1849)

The hard-fought First Sikh War between the British and the Sikhs was officially ended on 11 March 1846 with the signing of the Treaty of Lahore. Among the treaty's sixteen articles was one awarding Kashmir, a Sikh possession since 1819, to Ghulab Singh, a chief who had not participated in the fighting and had engaged in diplomacy with the British during the war.

The Sikh governor in Kashmir refused to surrender his authority, and a Sikh force with a few British officers was sent to Kashmir, which surrendered without fighting. Ghulab Singh entered Kashmir city on 9 November 1846.

On 20 April 1848, an internal squabble in Multan, in the Punjab, resulted in the death of two British officers. A large-scale rebellion followed and quickly spread throughout the Punjab. The British later decided to send a force from Lahore to capture Multan. Commanded by Major General William S. Whish, this force reached Multan on 18 August 1848. After receiving reinforcements, this force eventually totaled 28,000 British, Indian, and Sikh soldiers. The allied Sikh contingent, about 4,300 strong, was commanded by Shere Singh.

The strong citadel at Multan was defended by about 12,000 insurgent Sikhs commanded by Mulraj. Whish, on 4 September 1848, demanded Multan surrender within twenty-four hours—to which the besieged Sikhs responded with cannon shot close to Whish's headquarters. The British were able to seize Multan's forward entrenchments on 10 and 12 September. The situation was completely changed on the morning of 13 September when Shere Singh deserted the British and joined the Multanis.

Whish then decided to withdraw and await reinforcements. Shere Singh departed Multan with its Sikh and Hindu defenders on 9 October 1848 to join his father, Chuttur Singh, who had joined the rebellion in the northwest Punjab. A 20,000-man British field force under the command of Lieutenant General (later Field Marshal Viscount) Sir Hugh Gough, commander in chief, India, and consisting of twenty-one infantry battalions, twelve cavalry regiments, and eleven artillery batteries, finally crossed the Sutlej River on 9 November 1848.

Gough sent his Cavalry Division, commanded by Brigadier General C. R. Cureton, to counter the Sikh threat to Lahore. Cureton's force found the Sikhs near the village of Ramnagar on the Chenab River, about 70 miles northwest of Lahore, on 22 November 1848. The British conducted a number of gallant cavalry charges, but the Sikhs had skillfully used the terrain to their advantage, with one British cavalry regiment attacking and floundering in the deep sand of the river bank while under intense Sikh fire. The British were repulsed and contact was then broken off, with the Sikhs on the north bank of the Chenab River and the British on the south bank. Cureton was killed in the engagement, as were twenty-five others killed or missing and fifty-nine wounded.

The Sikhs fortified the far bank of the Chenab River, forcing Gough and his Army of the Punjab to find an alternate crossing point over the Chenab. The British finally forced a crossing at Sadulpore on 3 December 1848.

Meanwhile, Whish's reinforcements began to arrive at Multan on 10 December 1848. The British then recommenced the siege, capturing Multan on 3 January 1849 and its citadel on 22 January. This crushed the Sikh insurrection in the immediate area.

Gough learned on 10 January 1849 that the town of Attock had fallen to Chuttur Singh's besieging force and 5,000 allied Afghans. This meant Chuttur Singh's army was en route to link up with Shere Singh's force. Gough decided to strike before the two Sikh forces united and before Whish's troops joined his own, and on 12 January 1849, he advanced his 13,000-man force to confront Shere Singh's 30,000–40,000 Sikhs and 62 guns at Chillianwalla.

Gough knew the Sikhs had established a crescent-shaped position on high ground within the edge of a jungle and with the Jhelum River to their rear. The village of Chillianwalla was about 1 mile in front of and basically in the center of the Sikh positions. The British were organizing their camp near Chillianwalla on 13 January 1849 when forward-deployed Sikh cannons opened fire. The British cavalry had failed to reconnoiter the area, and the British had walked into a carefully organized trap. Gough had little option but to conduct another frontal attack.

Gough ordered his artillery to respond to the Sikh bombardment and ordered his forces to deploy. Two infantry divisions (each with two brigades) abreast, with cavalry on the flanks and artillery distributed along the line, attacked the Sikhs. The jungle reduced the effectiveness of the British artillery, and the broken terrain reduced the effectiveness of the cavalry. The fighting was ferocious, and the poorly commanded British cavalry on the far right panicked, leading to the loss of many British guns.

At nightfall, the British withdrew, leaving to the Sikhs a number of guns and three British regimental colors. The high British casualties, coupled with lack of water, forced Gough to retire and attempt to reform his army. The Battle of Chillianwalla was basically a stalemate, although it seems Gough exaggerated its results. British casualties in this extremely fierce battle totaled about 2,350, or about 15 percent of Gough's total force, while the Sikhs probably suffered about 8,000 casualties.

England was appalled when it learned of the Battle of Chillianwalla and the tremendous British casualties sustained there. The governor-general of India wrote that, "the conduct of the battle was beneath the contempt even of a militiaman like myself" (Cook 1975, p. 180). Authorities immediately took steps to relieve Gough and replace him with General Sir Charles J. Napier, but before Napier reached India, Gough had won the Battle of Gujerat (21 February 1849), which ended the Second Sikh War.

The British sustained heavy casualties fighting in their second conflict with the Sikhs, considered by many to have been the most formidable foe in India. The *Khalsa* surrendered to the British and its soldiers were disarmed. The British annexed the Punjab as a result of their victory in the Second Sikh War.

See also Chillianwalla, Battle of; East India Company, Military Forces; Gough, Field Marshal Hugh; Gujerat, Battle of; India; Napier, General Sir Charles J.; Sikh War, First (1845–1846); Sikhs

References: Carleton (2002); Cook (1975); Crawford (1967); Featherstone (1968); Featherstone (1989); Featherstone (1992); James (1998); Nijjar (1976)

Sikhs

The Sikhs were members of a monotheistic reformist religion propounded by Guru Nanak (1469–1539). Guru Nanak was born in the Punjab, the border area between Islam and Hinduism. Nanak gave his followers the name "Sikh," which means "disciple" or "learner." The Sikh religion failed to promote harmony between Islam and Hinduism, and instead provoked hostility, causing Sikhism to develop, under the tenth guru, Govind Singh, a political and martial character. His followers were known as the *Khalsa*, meaning the "'pure." Sikhism had a wide appeal to people in the area because, although there were some group divisions, it did not have caste or class distinctions.

The "Punjab," which means the "Land of Five Rivers," lies in a triangle formed by the winding Indus River on two of its sides, with the Sutlej River forming the base of the triangle. The Five Rivers—from north to south, the Jhelum, Chenab, Ravi, Beas, and Sutlej—subdivide the Punjab into separate provinces.

The Sikhs rose as a political power in the void left by the collapse of the Mughal Empire. Ranjit Singh, "the lion of the Punjab," emerged as a dominant chief and was able to unify much of the Punjab under Sikh control and with its capital in Lahore. In 1803, the Sikh state of Patiala came under control of the East India Company. This was confirmed by the 1809 Treaty of Amritsar, which defined the Sutlej River as the boundary between Sikh and British territory.

The Sikhs developed a formidable army, which came to be called the *Khalsa*, and which was the last significant threat to the British in India. Ranjit Singh initially found the Sikh army to be a large mass of brave but ill-trained horsemen, and began improving the infantry and artillery. He recruited numerous French veterans of the Napoleonic Wars, as well as British and even American officers, to train his army. The *Khalsa* was divided into a regular army, irregular units, and a feudal levy. In 1833, the Sikh regular army was divided into twelve combined arms brigade groups (*derahs*), each of three or four infantry battalions, one or more cavalry regiments, and one or two artillery batteries. Each *derah* totaled about 4,000 soldiers. Infantry battalions consisted of 800–900 soldiers and were divided into eight companies. The artillery was numerous and superbly trained, and Sikh guns were heavier than British guns.

In 1845, on the eve of the First Sikh War, the *Khalsa* reportedly consisted of 150,000 soldiers, with 54,000 regular infantry, 6,000 regular cavalry, and 11,000 artillerymen, with the remainder being irregulars.

See also East India Company; East India Company, Military Forces; Sikh War, First (1845–1846); Sikh War, Second (1848–1849)

References: Carleton (2002); Cook (1975); Featherstone (1968); Featherstone (1989); Fredericks (1971); Haythornthwaite (1995); Nijjar (1976)

Simpson, General Sir James M. (1792–1868)

General Sir James M. Simpson is best known as the reluctant successor to Field Marshal Fitzroy J. H. Somerset, First Baron Raglan, as commander in chief of the British Army in the Crimea in 1855.

Simpson, born in 1792, was commissioned an ensign and lieutenant in the Grenadier Guards in 1811. During the Peninsular War, he saw service at the siege of Cadiz and relief of Seville. He later fought in the 1815 campaign, and was wounded severely at the Battle of Quatre Bras (16 June 1815). In 1826, as a lieutenant colonel, Simpson commanded the 29th Foot on Mauritius, and in 1842 took the regiment to India. Four years later he returned to England, and in 1851 Simpson was promoted to major general.

Public outrage over the suffering of the ill-prepared and poorly supplied British Army in the Crimea over the harsh winter of 1854–1855 resulted in a change of government in January 1855. To help improve the effectiveness of the army in the Crimea and reduce criticism of Field Marshal Lord Raglan, the commander, Simpson, then serving as commandant at Chatham, was selected to be Raglan's chief of staff. Simpson, who arrived in the Crimea in March 1855, had instructions to communicate directly with London. This initially caused suspicion and resentment until Simpson sent reports to London supporting Raglan and describing the difficulty of his position.

Raglan died on 28 June 1855, and Simpson succeeded to the command. This was a period of stalemate and war-weariness in the siege of Sevastopol, and also marked the ascendancy of the French in the allied coalition. The French did not respect Simpson as they had Raglan, who had possessed dignity, authority, and fluency in French. It appears Simpson also suffered from depression and did "nothing to disguise his bewilderment at commanding an army which he had never wanted to lead in the first place" (Royle 2000, p. 402). Within weeks Simpson was asking to be relieved of command. A former secretary of state for war visited the Crimea in the summer of 1855 and reported that Simpson was a "raving lunatic" (Royle 2000, p. 404).

The French successfully stormed the Malakov, a key bastion in Sevastopol's defenses, on 8 September 1855, coinciding with the British failure to seize the Great Redan. The Russians evacuated Sevastopol the following day. This highlighted Simpson's weakness and ineffectiveness as a commander. By the end of September 1855, Simpson had finally decided to resign, writing, "The turmoils of a command like this are too much for my age and health" (Palmer 1987, p. 224). The Cabinet in London accepted his resignation on 3 October 1855, and he was replaced on 11 November 1855 as commander by General Sir William Codrington.

Simpson returned to England, retired from the army, and died in 1868.

See also Crimean War; Raglan, Field Marshal Fitzroy J. H. Somerset, First Baron; Sevastopol, Siege of

References: Baumgart (1999); Farwell (2001); Hibbert (1961); Palmer (1987); Royle (2000); Sweetman (1993)

Sind, Operations in (1843)

Sind was a 50,000-square-mile area east of the Indus River and Baluchistan. It was annexed by the East India Company in 1843 by a force commanded by General Sir Charles J. Napier that defeated the Sindian army at two battles. This was a controversial episode, as it seems the British intentionally provoked war as an excuse to annex the region.

In 1838, when threatened by Sikhs in the Punjab, the Sindian amirs accepted a British treaty of alliance. This treaty permitted the appointment of a British resident, who would basically handle Sindian foreign affairs. It was also important to the British to have an additional buffer between Afghanistan and India in case of further Russian encroachment in the region.

During the First Afghan War (1839–1842) the British lines of communication traversed Sind. The situation deteriorated as the British suffered reverses in Afghanistan and the Sindians became resentful of the British. Napier was sent to Sind to present a more restrictive treaty to the amirs, which was known would probably not be accepted.

While Napier thwarted attempts at negotiation by the amirs over the winter of 1842–1843, he prepared for war, knowing he would have to defeat the Sindian forces before the onset of the hot season in April. As a further provocation, Napier, at the end of January 1843, marched his 3,000-man army toward Hyderabad where the amirs were assembling their followers. The amirs attacked the British residency in Hyderabad on 15 February 1843. Napier considered this a pretext for war.

Early on 17 February 1843, Napier's scouts discovered the amir's soldiers in defensive positions near Miani, south of Hyderabad. The enemy soldiers were numbered at 11,000, which was only about half their strength. Napier quickly organized his infantry into three elements and with the 22nd Foot, the only British regiment, in the lead, advanced in echelon. The Sindian soldiers also rushed forward, but the Anglo-Indian force's better aimed volley fire and the bayonet, coupled with close-range artillery firing grapeshot, decided the day. The victorious British lost 39 dead and 231 wounded, and the Sindians about 2,000.

While some of the amirs surrendered at the Battle of Miani, others continued to resist. Napier's reinforced army of 5,000 soldiers attacked 20,000 entrenched enemy soldiers at Dubba, near Hyderabad, on 24 March 1843. Napier led the final charge himself, and his troops captured the enemy position at a cost of 267 casualties. The enemy suffered thousands killed. The British—actually the East India Company—then annexed Sind.

Napier's actions were condemned in England, although British rule was portrayed as an improvement for the local population. In actuality, the British were more concerned about monopolizing tariffs on the Indus River, and ensuring that Sind was a part of India. The latter was important so the British would no longer have to pay their indigenous soldiers *batta,* a type of foreign service allowance, although with religious implications the British did not fully appreciate. Resentment at the loss of *batta* was a factor in causing the Indian Mutiny (1857–1859).

See also Afghan War, First (1839–1842); East India Company, Military Forces; India; Indian Mutiny; Napier, General Sir Charles J.; Outram, Lieutenant General Sir James

References: Farwell (1972); James (1997); Mason (1974); Napier (1857); Rice (2002)

Sirdar

The term "sirdar" was derived from a Perso-Indian title and denoted the British commander in chief of the Egyptian Army during the period 1882–1937. From 1899 until 1924, the sirdar also served as governor-general of the Sudan. The position of sirdar also symbolized the British domination of Egypt.

The British occupied Egypt after it crushed the Arabi Rebellion in 1882. It became obvious that the disaffected Egyptian Army would have to be disbanded. In early 1883, Major General (later Field Marshal) Sir (Henry) Evelyn M. Wood, V.C., became the first sirdar of the Egyptian Army. Wood, with a handpicked cadre of twenty-six British Army officers to assist him, raised the new Egyptian Army in 1883. This new force totaled 6,000 men organized into eight infantry battalions (in two brigades), two cavalry regiments, four artillery batteries, and a camel company. British Army officers serving in the Egyptian Army, including the sirdar, generally served at two ranks higher than their permanent British Army rank.

Wood was replaced as sirdar in March 1885 by his second in command, Brigadier General (later Field Marshal Lord) Francis W. Grenfell. In 1892, Colonel (later Field Marshal Earl) Horatio H. Kitchener succeeded Grenfell as sirdar. After reconquering the Sudan and destroying the power of the Mahdi at Omdurman in 1898, Kitchener was rewarded with a peerage and, in January 1899, appointment to the dual position of governor-general of the Sudan as a result of the Anglo-Egyptian Condominium Agreement. Colonel (later General) Sir (Francis) Reginald Wingate replaced Kitchener as sirdar in December 1899 and held the position for seventeen years until he was replaced by Major General Sir Lee O. F. Stack in 1916.

The 1936 Anglo-Egyptian Treaty formally ended the British occupation of Egypt, which gained control of its own security forces for the first time since 1882. The last British sirdar was Major General Sir Charlton W. Spinks, whose last day of duty as commander in chief of the Egyptian Army was 12 January 1937.

See also Arabi Rebellion; Egypt; Egyptian Army; Grenfell, Field Marshal Francis W.; Kitchener, Field Marshal Horatio H.; Mahdi; Reconquest of the Sudan; Sudan; Wingate, General Sir (Francis) Reginald; Wood, Field Marshal Sir (Henry) Evelyn M., V.C.

References: Daly (1997); Farwell (1985); Grenfell (1925); James (1993); Mansfield (1971); Raafat (2001); Rizk (2000)

Sittana Field Force (1858)

The only disturbances on the North-West Frontier during the Indian Mutiny (1857–1859) were caused by "Hindustani Fanatics," or from the Pathan perspective, *mujihadin*, or "warriors of God." The Hindustani Fanatics originally came from Hindustan, or Bengal, where their founder, Ahmad Shah, had attracted many followers. They fought the Sikhs and eventually settled at Sittana on the west bank of the Indus River and south of the Black Mountain. They were joined in 1857 in Sittana by sepoys from the 55th Bengal Native Infantry who had mutinied at Mardan and had survived a subsequent retaliatory attack by Colonel (later Brigadier General) John Nicholson's forces.

After the 55th Bengal Native Infantry had mutinied, Mardan was garrisoned by forces under the command of Major J. L. Vaughan. The Hindustani Fanatics in the area began to plunder and raid in the name of God (Allah) and caused other unrest, and on three separate occasions in 1857, Vaughan led punitive expeditions to quell these disturbances. On 2 July 1857, Vaughan led elements of the 5th Punjab Infantry and two guns of the Peshawar Mountain Battery, augmented by a detachment of the 2nd Punjab Cavalry, to the village of Shekh Jana, the center of the disorder. His force attacked the insurgents, drove the survivors into the surrounding hills, and burned the village before returning to Mardan.

Less than two weeks later, the Hindustani Fanatics caused a disturbance at Narinji. Since it was difficult to reach Narinji and surprise was of the utmost importance, Vaughan stockpiled supplies at another village, diverting attention from his real objective. Vaughan's force conducted a night march and reached Narinji at dawn on 21 July 1857, completely surprising and driving out its defenders. As the Hindustani Fanatics conducted a number of fierce counterattacks, the British destroyed the lower part of the village and later withdrew without opposition. British losses in the punitive raid were 5 killed and 21 wounded; the enemy suffered at least 50 killed.

Another outburst of violence took place at Narinji the following month. The composite British force was much larger this time, totaling almost 1,500 soldiers (including 2 24-pounder howitzers and 4 mountain guns; 50 soldiers each from 3 British regiments; 800 infantrymen from 4 native regiments; 325 police and levies; and 150 cavalrymen from the 2nd Punjab Cavalry). Again, Vaughan led the force on a night march, arriving at Narinji before sunrise. He opened the battle with his artillery, then one 300-man element flanked the village to the British right and attacked the enemy rear while another detachment moved around the left flank and cut off escaping rebels. This double envelopment intercepted the enemy's retreat and secured the upper portion of the village, while another force under Vaughan conducted a frontal assault and occupied the lower portion of the village. The entire village was destroyed without British casualties. At least 3 tribesmen were captured and later executed.

The British assistant district commissioner was attacked less than three months later while encamped at Shekh Jana. This grievous insult to British authority demanded a large-scale punitive expedition. In the spring of 1858, a 4,877-man force under the command of Major General Sir Sydney Cotton was assembled near Nowshera to punish the Hindustani Fanatics and their accomplices. This Sittana Field Force was divided into four relatively mobile columns. The 1st Column was the largest and remained under Cotton's command. It consisted of six artillery pieces; infantrymen from the 2nd North Staffordshires, 9th and 18th Punjab Infantry, 21st Native Infantry, and the Guides; cavalrymen from the 7th Irregular Cavalry, Guides Cavalry, and Peshawar Light Horse; and sappers and miners. Lieutenant Colonel H. Renny commanded the 2nd Column, which consisted of soldiers from the 2nd Loyal North Lancashires, 8th Punjab Infantry, 18th Irregular Cavalry, and sappers and miners. Commanded by Major A. T. Allen, the 3rd Column included elements of the 81st Foot, 98th Foot, 8th and 9th Punjab Infantry, 21st Native Infantry, and Guides Infantry; 7th and 18th Irregular Cavalry and Guides Cavalry, plus sappers and miners. The 4th Column consisted of five guns and infantry from the 2nd Sikh, 6th Punjab, and 12th Punjab Infantry, and was commanded by Major J. R. Becher.

The entire force occupied Salim Khan on 25 April 1858, and thereafter the columns operated independently, destroying villages and strongholds of the Hindustani Fanatics. On 3 May 1858, Cotton's column reached Khabal. One last Hindustani stronghold remained at Sittana. Cotton's plan was to employ the 1st and 4th Columns together in an enveloping attack on Sittana early on 4 May. The attack was executed according to Cotton's plan, and the Hindustani Fanatics were caught in a deadly crossfire from the soldiers of the two columns. The battle soon degenerated into hand-to-hand combat, in which "every Hindustani in the position was either killed or taken prisoner" (Nevill 1912, p. 41).

Prior to departing the area, Cotton sent an ultimatum to nearby clans demanding they not assist or ally themselves with the remaining Hindustani Fanatics. The clans willingly complied with this mandate, and the Sittana Field Force marched back to Nowshera.

During this punitive expedition, the British used the Enfield rifle for the first time and with great effect on the North-West Frontier. The Enfield rifle "was found most effective and evidently made a great impression, both on the minds of the enemy as well as on those of the native chiefs who accompanied the force" (Nevill 1912, p. 43).

See also Bengal Army; East India Company, Military Forces; India; Indian Army Operations; Indian Mutiny; North-West Frontier
References: Barthorp (1982); Featherstone (1973); Nevill (1912)

Slavery

Slavery was a significant issue for British colonial policymakers during the nineteenth century. Evangelicals and other idealists advocated releasing slaves from bondage, restoring to them their birthright as free people, and converting them to Christianity. Britain abolished the slave trade in 1807, although slaves continued to work on plantations in the British West Indies and elsewhere.

Great Britain induced other governments to follow its lead in abolishing the slave trade. As Britain gained more influence and colonies around the globe, its abolition of the slave trade was considered an example of its humanity, enlightenment, and morality. In 1833, the British national conscience helped persuade a reformed House of Commons to abolish slavery.

British public opinion demanded the suppression of slavery, and it was frequently the military that was called upon to execute such seemingly simple, but actually complicated, policies. In 1877, for example, Great Britain signed an agreement with the Egyptian ruler to suppress the slave trade in all Egyptian territories, including the Sudan (the present Sudan and part of today's northern Uganda, Eritrea, Ethiopia, and northern Somali coast). A British aim of eliminating the slave trade in the Sudan was also to replace it with legal trade to attempt to benefit the British economy.

In the case of the Sudan, British attempts to eliminate the slave trade, while at the same time trying to spread Christianity, were frequently made in ignorance of local social and economic conditions and of Islam. These policies, executed by European Christians employed by the Egyptian Muslim khedive, frequently antagonized slave traders and their allies and disrupted indigenous society, the economy of which depended heavily on slavery. Moreover, many subordinate Egyptian administrators received monetary rewards from slave traders to cast a blind eye to the officially illegal practice, which undermined the authority of their European superiors.

During the second half of the nineteenth century cabinet ministers and others wanted Britain to rid itself of unprofitable colonies on the west coast of Africa, but humanitarians and others wanted the military to end the slave trade there and bring "enlightenment" to the area. There were numerous military expeditions and operations against local slave traders in West and Central Africa into late in the 1890s.

See also Egypt; Gordon, Major General Charles G.; Sudan
References: James (1999); Moore-Harell (2001); Waller (1988)

Smith, Lieutenant General Sir Harry G. W. (1787–1860)

Lieutenant General Sir Harry G. W. Smith, while not one of the most senior or competent of Queen Victoria's generals, served ably as a division commander, notably during the First Sikh War (1845–1846) and later as governor and commander in chief of Cape Colony.

Born on 28 June 1787 in Cambridgeshire, Smith was named Henry, but he preferred to be called Harry. He was commissioned a second lieutenant in the 95th Regiment in 1805. After participating in the expedition to Montevideo and Buenos Aires in 1806, he served through the Peninsular War, from Salamanca in 1808 to Toulouse in 1814. He fought in the United States in 1814–1815 and returned to Europe in time to take part in the Battle of Waterloo.

Post-Napoleonic service included duty in France, Scotland, Nova Scotia, and Jamaica before being assigned to the Cape of Good Hope in 1828. When Smith received word at the end of 1834 of the outbreak of the Sixth Cape Frontier War, he immediately rode the 600 miles from Cape Town to Grahamstown in six days, arriving on 6 January 1835. He led a force in offensive operations that defeated the Xhosa, and when Queen Adelaide Province was formed, Smith became the governor.

In 1840, after an acrimonious departure from Cape Colony, Smith became adjutant-general in India with the local rank of major general. He participated in the 1843 Gwalior campaign and was knighted for his leadership at the Battle of Maharajpore (29 December 1843).

Smith served throughout the First Sikh War (1845–1846) under Lieutenant General (later Field Marshal Viscount) Sir Hugh Gough. Smith commanded a division at the Battles of Mudki (18 December 1845) and of Ferozeshah (21–22 December 1845), and frequently criticized Gough's leadership. On 16 January 1846, Gough ordered Smith to take a force to protect the lines of communication and the British garrison at Ludhiana. After a reorganization conducted on 26 January, Smith's force totaled about 10,000 men and 32 guns. Anticipating the Sikhs to cross the Sutlej River at the Aliwal ford, Smith, with his cavalry and horse artillery leading, advanced to meet the enemy on 28 January.

Smith's force surprised the 20,000-man, 67-gun Sikh Army early on 28 January 1846 at Aliwal. He deployed his units and skillfully coordinated and controlled his infantry, cavalry, and artillery assets—unlike Gough's bloody, unimaginative frontal assaults. After repeated attacks, the Sikh squares broke, and their soldiers attempted to cross the Sutlej River. Smith's victory was complete and his casualties relatively light, while the Sikhs lost about 3,000 men and all 67 guns. British Army historian Sir John Fortescue called the Battle of Aliwal "the battle without a mistake" (Featherstone 1992, p. 57), and Smith received a baronetcy with the distinct words "of Aliwal" added to the title.

On 8 February 1846, Smith's force rejoined Gough's main army. Smith commanded his division at the Battle of Sobraon (10 February 1846).

In 1847, Smith returned to South Africa as governor and commander in chief of Cape Colony. The "War of the Axe," another name for the Seventh Cape Frontier War, was basically over by this time, and Smith was criticized for the arrogant manner in which he concluded the conflict. He commanded an expedition against disaffected Boers and defeated them at the Battle of Boomplaats (29 August 1848). Military forces in the area were reduced, and continued friction with the Xhosa led to the outbreak of the Eighth Cape Frontier War in 1850. He was, perhaps unfairly, recalled in 1852. Smith declined command of the Madras Army but commanded the Western Military District (1853–1854) and the Northern and Midland Military Districts (1854–1859). He was promoted to lieutenant general in 1854.

Smith, the hero of Aliwal, was a respected leader, especially in South Africa. The town of Harrismith in the Orange Free State was named after him, and Aliwal North after his victory in the First Sikh War; Ladysmith in Natal was named after his wife. Smith died on 12 October 1860 in London, and his autobiography was first published in 1901.

See also Aliwal, Battle of; Boers; Boomplaats, Battle of; Cape Frontier Wars, Southern Africa; East India Company, Military Forces; Ferozeshah, Battle of; Gough, Field Marshal Hugh; Gwalior Campaign; Sikh War, First (1845–1846); Sobraon, Battle of
References: Berkeley (1899); Cook (1975); Farwell (1972); Featherstone (1968); Featherstone (1992); Smith (1901)

Smuts, Assistant Commandant-General Jan Christian (1870–1950)

Jan Christian Smuts was a skillful South African lawyer who became a prominent Boer military leader during the Second Boer War.

Smuts was born on 24 May 1870 in the Cape Colony. He was educated in South Africa and at Cambridge and read for the Bar. Returning to South Africa in 1895, Smuts established a law practice in Johannesburg. He was considered a brilliant lawyer, writer, and orator, and was appointed state attorney in 1898. At the Bloemfontein Conference (31 May–5 June 1899), Smuts persuaded President S. J. Paulus Kruger to make considerable concessions over the *uitlander* franchise issue to the British representative, Sir (later Lord) Alfred Milner, but a compromise could not be reached.

War broke out on 11 October 1899, and Smuts remained at his administrative post. After the British entered Pretoria on 5 June 1900 and regular military operations transitioned to guerilla warfare, Smuts joined the commando of Assistant Commandant-General Jacobus De la Rey operating in the western Transvaal. He proved an able field leader and administrator.

Smuts believed that the Boers' best chance of winning the war lay in invading British territory and inciting rebellion among Afrikaners, and persuaded De la Rey to give him the opportunity. On 16 July 1901, Smuts's commando, divided into four groups, began their march through the Transvaal. He barely escaped capture on a number of occasions, and after a 300-mile ride his commando entered Cape Colony. After proclaiming himself "commander in chief," Smuts intended to proclaim a new Boer republic in the western Cape Colony, but a lack of support caused this plan to fail. By the winter of 1901–1902 Smuts controlled a large, albeit empty, part of the northwestern Cape Colony.

Smuts reorganized Boer forces in the area and tried to encourage insurrection, but the war was nearing its end. The British requested Smuts to attend the peace negotiations, where he played a key role in persuading the other Boer leaders to accept the peace with the hope of a future constitution. The Treaty of Vereeniging, signed on 31 May 1902, ended the Second Boer War.

Smuts's subsequent career was remarkable. During World War I, he served in the Imperial War Cabinet, was prime minister of South Africa for many years, and was promoted to field marshal in the British Army in 1941. Smuts died on 11 September 1950.

See also Boer War, Second (1899–1902); Boers; Commando System; De la Rey, Assistant Commandant-General Jacobus; Kruger, S. J. Paulus; Transvaal
References: Carver (1999); Lee (1985); Pakenham (1979); Smuts (1952); Wickham Legg and Williams (1959)

Snider-Enfield Rifle
See Infantry, British Army—Small Arms

Sobraon, Battle of (10 February 1846)

The Sikhs were defeated by the British at the Battle of Aliwal (28 January 1846), then retreated to Sobraon, their last position on the British side of and bridgehead over the Sutlej River. Lieutenant General (later Field Marshal Viscount) Sir Hugh Gough, commander in chief, India, received reinforcements and was reunited with the Major General (later Lieutenant General) Sir Harry G. W. Smith's force. He then marched toward Sobraon.

The Sikh force of about 30,000 men and 67 guns was positioned in an entrenched semicircle about 3,000 yards long, with each flank abutting the Sutlej River to the north. Gough's plan was to initiate the battle with an artillery barrage, then the main attack, by Major General Robert Dick's 13-battalion division, would be conducted against the Sikh right flank. At the same time, Smith's and Major General Gilbert's smaller divisions would make feints against the enemy's left and center, respectively.

The British artillery barrage began at about 7:00 A.M. on 10 February 1846. The barrage was not very effective because of inadequate ammunition—reportedly caused by the commander's impatience to attack—and the strength of the 16-foot-thick enemy breastworks. The British artillery ammunition was expended by about 10:00 A.M., to which Gough supposedly reacted: "Thank God! Now I can be at them with the bayonet!" (Featherstone 1973, p. 59).

Dick's division then attacked, even though the two feints had yet to be developed. After an initial success, the Sikhs counterattacked and repulsed Dick's division. Smith's and Gilbert's attacks were also beaten back with heavy casualties. After a third attempt, Dick's soldiers were able to break into the Sikh positions, and this gave the other two divisions the chance to gain a foothold there. The fighting was savage, with no quarter given or asked. The Sikhs were especially desperate, as the Sutlej River had risen and their pontoon bridge to safety had been damaged. Sappers cut a hole in the Sikh fortifications on their right, and the 3rd Light Dragoons filed through and charged the enemy while the three infantry divisions converged on the Sikh bridgehead and routed the remaining defenders. "The sluggish waters of the Sutlej," according to one source, "were clogged with human carcases" (Crawford 1967, p. 48).

The Battle of Sobraon severely damaged the power of the *Khalsa* and was the final engagement of the First Sikh War. British casualties were 320 all ranks killed and 2,063 wounded. The Sikhs lost all their artillery and their casualties were estimated at about 8,000–10,000 killed and drowned.

Gough's generalship at Sobraon was again characterized by impetuosity, mismanagement of the artillery, and poor command and control over his divisions. Fortunately, the British troops fought well, and their Indian allies performed in a determined manner. The governor-general, Lieutenant General (later Field Marshal Viscount) Henry Hardinge, believed the victory at Sobraon to have been "one of the most daring ever achieved" (Young 1977, p. 98).

See also Aliwal, Battle of; East India Company, Military Forces; Gough, Field Marshal Hugh; Hardinge, Field Marshal Henry; India; Indian Army Operations; Sikh War, First (1845–1846); Sikhs; Smith, Lieutenant General Sir Harry G. W.
References: Cook (1975); Crawford (1967); Featherstone (1968); Featherstone (1973); Featherstone (1992); Young (1977)

Soldier's Pocket Book for Field Service

In 1861 Lieutenant Colonel (later Field Marshal Viscount) Garnet J. Wolseley was ordered to Canada as assistant quartermaster-general. He spent the next decade in Canada, during which time he was able to devote himself more to the study of the profession of arms and the testing of his theories of military organization and training. After his promotion to full colonel in 1865, Wolseley started collecting and collating practical military information for the use of regimental officers and soldiers that would answer any question in the field and on active service and would supplement the *Queen's Regulations* and the *Field Exercise*.

In the book he subsequently wrote, *Soldier's Pocket Book for Field Service,* Wolseley included in Part I detailed information on the roles, responsibilities, and equipment of the combat branches and support services. Part II included the composition of an army, transportation, and related matters. The details of a force in action, from marching and deploying to actual tactics, were covered in Part III. The last section included, among other items, engineer and communications tasks, as well as a cipher code for operational field use. Other subjects described included information on the care and feeding of elephants, menus, exchange rates for foreign currency, burials at sea, the management of spies, and journalists.

The *Soldier's Pocket Book for Field Service,* first published in 1869 and printed through 1889 in five editions, appealed to the rank and file and brought Wolseley to the attention of Edward T. Cardwell, the progressive and reform-minded secretary of state for war. On the other hand, by advocating the treatment of soldiers with respect and as individuals, and for his other blunt and realistic comments, Wolseley offended many aristocrats and other traditionalists who were concerned with maintaining through strict discipline a rigid social hierarchy. In 1874 Wolseley also prepared a special edition of the *Field Pocket Book for Auxiliary Forces*. This detailed, worthwhile guide was the forerunner of modern Field Service Regulations and predated the War Office's *Field Service Pocket Book* by four decades.

See also Cardwell, Edward T.; Rank and File, British Army—Training and Education; Wolseley, Field Marshal Garnet J.
References: Blumenson and Stokesbury (1975); Farwell (1972); Kochanski (1999); Lehmann (1964)

Soldiers Homes
See Religion; Sports and Recreation

Spion Kop, Battle of (23–24 January 1900)

The Battle of Spion Kop was a disastrous attempt by the British to relieve the besieged garrison at Ladysmith.

After the unsuccessful Battle of Colenso (15 December 1899), General Sir Redvers H. Buller, V.C., had been replaced as commander in chief of the South African Field Force and became commander of British troops in Natal. Buller's force was strengthened by the arrival of the 5th Division (10th and 11th Brigades), under Lieutenant General (later General) Sir Charles Warren, in January 1900. This permitted Buller to execute the plan he had initially considered before Colenso: attacking to cross the Tugela River further upstream preliminary to relieving Ladysmith.

Buller intended to cross the Tugela at Potgieter's Drift to the west of Colenso, then cross the Brakfontein Ridge and advance the 18 miles northeast to Ladysmith. Vaal Krantz dominated the eastern end of the Brakfontein Ridge, which rose in the west to the peak of Spion Kop and extended 3 miles further along the Tabanyama range.

Buller's force consisted of five infantry brigades (one remained at Colenso), one mounted brigade, eight artillery batteries, ten naval guns, and support elements. On 16 January 1900, British troops crossed the Tugela at Potgieter's Drift and established themselves on the north side of the river, at the foot of the Brakfontein Ridge, occupied by about 7,000 Boers under the overall command of Commandant-General Louis Botha. Buller decided to send about two-thirds of his force, under Warren, to cross the Tugela 5 miles upstream at Trikhardts Drift, where there were fewer Boers. Warren's 13,000-man force (with 36 guns) was to form a second bridgehead across the Tugela, then advance north through the hills, west of Spion Kop, onto the plain, and threaten to outflank Potgieter's Drift. At that point, Buller would lead the remainder of the force, about 8,000 soldiers with 22 guns, across the river and hills to join Warren's force, and together they would advance to Ladysmith.

Warren's attack was ponderously slow, giving the Boers time to reinforce their right flank. His soldiers began crossing Trikhardts Drift on 17 January 1900, and on 23 January, Buller rode to Warren and directed him to launch an attack. Warren decided to attack the precipitous Spion Kop at night, arguably the key to the entire Boer position commanding the wagon road and to Ladysmith. The attacking force consisted of 2,000 men of Major General E. R. P. Woodgate's 11th Brigade, 200 soldiers of Lieutenant Colonel Alec Thorneycroft's mounted infantry, and engineers with 20 shovels and picks. It assembled at Three Tree Hill, about 6 miles southwest of Spion Kop, at 8:30 P.M. on 23 January.

After moving slowly in the foggy dark over the rocky path, the lead British element reached the foot of Spion Kop and was challenged by a Boer sentry. The British fixed bayonets and charged, and at a cost of ten men, they occupied the hill. Trenches were dug on what was thought to be the forward crest of the summit.

In the early morning of 24 January 1900, the Boers attacked up the gentle slope from the north but were repulsed by the British. The fog cleared at about 8:30 A.M., and the British realized that their trenches were too shallow and incorrectly placed and should have been sited 200 yards further forward (north). The British, not knowing the topography, had failed to seize Conical Hill, about 800 yards to their front, or Aloe Knoll, 400 yards to their right. The Boers seized these two hills and began to enfilade the British trench while their artillery pounded the British. The battle was a scene of confusion and carnage.

Warren received a request for assistance, dispatched a number of soldiers, then he forwarded the message to Major General (later General Sir) Neville Lyttelton near Potgieter's Drift. Lyttelton, without consulting Buller, sent two battalions and mounted troops in the direction of Spion Kop.

On the hill, the Boers wanted the British to surrender. Thorneycroft, appointed the commander after the death of senior officers, refused to permit any more soldiers to surrender (170 British soldiers had already surrendered), and led his troops to a line of rocks behind the trench. At this crucial moment, reinforcements sent by Warren reached Spion Kop. With fixed bayonets, they charged the startled Boers and, with Thorneycroft's men, occupied the trench. By mid-afternoon, the situation had stabilized. Lyttelton's reinforcements attacked the Twin Peaks, respectively 2,000 and 3,000 yards to the east of Spion Kop later that day, but withdrew from them after dark.

The demoralized Boers abandoned Spion Kop after nightfall. In the nighttime uncertainty, Thorneycroft, without communications with Warren, also ordered the British to withdraw from the hill. During the retrograde, Thorneycroft met a rescue force of 1,400 infantrymen with sappers and gunners but refused to go back to the peak, and the entire element returned to Warren's camp. The British abandoned Spion Kop, with corpses stacked three deep in the shallow trench. The Boers were amazed the following morning to return and find that the summit was in their possession.

The Battle of Spion Kop was another dismal defeat for the British, who retreated south of the Tugela River. The hilltop battlefield, an "acre of massacre" (Pakenham 1979, p. 310), was a horrible scene of death and destruction. Official British casualty figures at Spion Kop were 322 men killed, 585 wounded, and 300 captured, although these numbers, especially of men killed, seem very low. The number of Boers killed probably exceeded 150. Ladysmith continued to be besieged by the Boers.

See also Boer War, Second (1899–1902); Boers; Botha, Commandant-General Louis; Buller, General Sir Redvers H., V.C.; Colenso, Battle of; Ladysmith, Siege of; Warren, General Sir Charles
References: Barnard (1971); Pakenham (1979); Ransford (1969); Symons (1963); Trew (1999)

Sports and Recreation

Opportunities and facilities for increasingly healthy and wholesome soldier sports and recreational activities improved significantly during this period. In the 1840s, some attempts, including the establishment of regimental libraries and savings banks, and sporting activities such as cricket, had been made to treat the soldier more like a human being. The Crimean War (1854–1856) marked a watershed in the reform of the British Army as an institution and in the concern for the health and welfare of the soldiers as individuals.

Various on- and off-duty sports and other activities were conducted to relieve soldier monotony and improve physical health and standards of conduct and morality by providing alternatives to drunkenness, gambling, and visiting prostitutes.

Cricket became popular in the army in the 1860s, and within decades was being played by officers and other ranks, separately and together on the same teams. Sports, except for those activities played mounted on a horse, provided a temporary egalitarian effect on the sporting field.

Other ranks began to participate in sporting events and play games in the last quarter of the nineteenth century. Boxing and wrestling were two popular sports in Britain as well as in India. Cross-country running, rugby, tug of war, and hockey became favorite activities.

Interregimental athletic competitions became increasingly popular and enhanced unit esprit de corps and individual physical fitness, as did interunit competitions in basic soldiering skills, including marksmanship.

Officers and enlisted soldiers participated in theatricals, as actors and in production roles. Regimental band concerts also attracted soldiers.

Officers, largely due to their higher income and role in society, had many other types of recreation available to them. Many of these activities depended on the horse and revolved around hunting, which helped train an officer in terrain appreciation, tracking, and horsemanship, and helped give him additional confidence in his leadership skills. Polo, tennis, badminton, croquet, billiards, yachting, and riding to hounds were popular. Polo, pig-sticking, and tent staking were frequent pastimes in India, where it was not unusual for an officer to receive many months' leave each year to hunt. The game book of the 2nd Gordons, for example, reveals how popular hunting was in India; regimental officers between 1902 and 1912 shot "674 big game of thirty-six species, including three elephants, six tigers, twelve panthers and eighty-four boars. They also shot 27,293 small game, including 4,256 pigeons, 7,549 ducks and 9,354 snipe" (Farwell 1981, p. 207).

Soldiers Homes were established by religious organizations to provide wholesome environments and activities for off-duty soldiers. First founded by Wesleyans in 1861, Soldiers Homes were mission centers containing baths, sleeping quarters, meeting halls, games and smoking rooms, a tea and coffee bar, and other comfortable facilities normally not available to the barracks dweller. The Soldiers Homes were well patronized and were believed to have contributed significantly to the decrease in crime between 1856 and 1899.

Religious organizations crusaded against alcoholism and drunkenness and in 1893, a number of churches united and formed the Army Temperance Association. Two years later, the group claimed 8,641 members, and the membership quickly grew to 20,000. This organization had a large impact on reducing drunkenness and crime and enhancing morality among the other ranks of the British Army.

See also Army and Society; Chaplains; Crimean War; Officers, British Army—Social Background; Rank and File, British Army—Social Background; Religion
References: Brereton (1986); Farwell (1981); Neuberg (1989); Spiers (1992); Strachan (1984)

Staff Organization
See Adjutant-General, British Army; Camberley, Staff College; Commander in Chief, British Army; Esher Committee; Horse Guards; Quartermaster-General, British Army; War Office

Stalker, Major General Foster
See Persian War

Stanhope, Edward (1840–1893)
Edward Stanhope served as secretary of state for war from 1887 to 1892. He was noted for his sense of responsibility and integrity and served during a crucial period in the modernization of the British Army.

Stanhope, the second son of the Fifth Earl Stanhope, was born in 1840. He attended Oxford and was elected a Fellow of All Souls in 1862. He traveled to the United States and visited both Union and Confederate headquarters during the American Civil War. Becoming a lawyer in 1865, Stanhope was elected a Conservative Member of Parliament in 1874. Service in the Board of Trade (1875–1878) and at the India Office (1878–1880) gave him experience, and he became vice president of the Board of Trade in 1885 and colonial secretary the following year. In the government shuffle that took place following the controversy surrounding the British Army's two corps mobilization plan, Stanhope became secretary of state for war in January 1887.

Stanhope's tenure was filled with concerns over home defense and mobilization plans, disputes over strategic priorities, internal War Office reorganizations, and many other issues. Stanhope was responsible, in the Stanhope Memorandum, for providing a definite, prioritized mission list for the British Army. The Stanhope Memorandum provided "more direction in the last third of the nineteenth century than at any previous period in British military history" (Beckett 1982, p. 299).

A conscientious, devoted public servant, Stanhope remained secretary of state for war until July 1892, when the Salisbury government resigned. Overworked and frequently in poor health, Stanhope died, apparently of gout, in December 1893.

See also Civil-Military Relations; Home Defense; Mobilization Planning; Stanhope Memorandum; War Office
References: Barnett (1970); Beckett (1982); Beckett (1984); Hamer (1970); Spiers (1992); Wheeler (1914)

Stanhope Memorandum

The late Victorian British Army did not have a viable plan for mobilizing its home-based forces until a systematic assessment of all British Army forces available was conducted in 1886 by Major General (later General) Sir Henry Brackenbury, then director of military intelligence. Edward Stanhope, who became the secretary of state for war in January 1887, endorsed the two army corps mobilization plan developed by Brackenbury.

As adjustments were made to British Army units to ensure compliance with the two army corps mobilization plan, the adjutant-general, General (later Field Marshal) Viscount Garnet J. Wolseley, requested a definitive, prioritized mission statement for the British Army. Wolseley submitted a list of recommended military priorities in January 1888 and again on 8 June 1888. On 8 December 1888, Stanhope first issued the Stanhope Memorandum to comply with Wolseley's request and to clarify the role and purposes of the army. It generally reiterated the list of recommended military priorities Wolseley had submitted, with one major exception.

The prioritized missions of the British Army, according to the Stanhope Memorandum, were (1) the effective support of the civil power in the United Kingdom; (2) to provide reinforcements for India; (3) to provide garrisons for all home and overseas fortresses and coaling stations; (4) to provide and mobilize two army corps for home defense (Wolseley had requested three army corps); and (5) to deploy one army corps to fight in a European war. The Stanhope Memorandum was criticized by some as reflecting outdated priorities and hindering imperial strategy planning, as it did nothing to increase the size of the army and seemed to discourage the assumption that the army be prepared to fight on the Continent of Europe. There was also concern that the British Army was trying to usurp the historical role of the Royal Navy in defending the British Isles.

The Stanhope Memorandum was issued to provide guidance in the formulation of strategic and military policies. It was originally circulated only to the Cabinet, but was reissued on 1 June 1891 and apparently did not become public knowledge until published as a parliamentary paper in 1901.

See also Brackenbury, General Sir Henry; Home Defense; Mobilization Planning; Stanhope, Edward; War Office; Wolseley, Field Marshal Garnet J.
References: Barnett (1970); Beckett (1982); Beckett (1984); Bond (1972); Kochanski (1999); Spiers (1992)

Stanley, Henry M.
See Correspondents, War

Steevens, G. W.
See Correspondents, War

Stephenson, General Sir Frederick C. A. (1821–1911)

A highly competent senior officer, General Sir Frederick C. A. Stephenson was commander of the British Army of Occupation in Egypt after the 1882 Arabi Rebellion and commander at the last battle of the Gordon Relief Expedition in 1885.

Stephenson, born in 1821, saw active service in the Crimean War. After the outbreak of war in China in 1857, Stephenson, as a lieutenant colonel, commanded the troops on board H.M.T. *Transit*—one of the officers on board was Lieutenant (later Field Marshal Viscount) Garnet J. Wolseley—which was shipwrecked on 10 July 1857. Stephenson served in China until 1860.

After the Arabi Rebellion in Egypt was suppressed by a British force commanded by Wolseley in 1882, Stephenson, as a lieutenant general, commanded the British Army of Occupation. After the bloody defeat of the Egyptian Gendarmerie by dervish forces at the Battle of El Teb (4 February 1884) Stephenson was ordered to send a force, commanded by Major General (later Lieutenant General) Sir Gerald Graham, V.C., to the eastern Sudan.

By March 1884, Major General Charles G. Gordon, who had been sent to assess the situation in the Sudan, was in a desperate situation in Khartoum. Tentative plans were being made to send an expedition to rescue him. Wolseley, then adjutant-general at the War Office, favored the 1,426-mile Nile River route from Cairo to Berber, while Stephenson and Major General (later Field Marshal) Sir (Henry) Evelyn M. Wood, V.C., sirdar of the Egyptian Army, preferred the 245-mile route across the desert from the Red Sea port of Suakin to Berber. Wolseley's prestige and earlier success on the 1870 Red River Expedition resulted in the choice of the Nile route in August 1884.

Stephenson was the obvious choice to lead the force to relieve Gordon, but it was decided he should not command an expedition he felt certain would fail. Wolseley was then designated to supersede Stephenson in command of all troops in Egypt, and in October 1884 he would also take command of the relief force. Stephenson considered resigning but did not, and served in a support role during the Gordon Relief Expedition. When Wolseley returned to England on 27 June 1885, after the conclusion of the Gordon Relief Expedition, the command of troops in Egypt (not including the Egyptian Army) reverted to Stephenson.

Stephenson commanded the troops that defeated the Khalifa's dervish troops at the Battle of Ginnis (30 December 1885). This was basically the last engagement of the Khartoum campaign, after which the British withdrew totally from the Sudan and fixed the Egyptian-Sudanese border at Wadi Halfa. Stephenson remained in command of the troops in Egypt until 1888.

Stephenson, of whom Wolseley wrote, "A more devoted or gallant soldier, a more perfect gentleman, an abler commanding officer or a better fellow never breathed" (Wolseley 1903, p. 1: 231), died in 1911. His book *At Home and on the Battlefield: Letters from the Crimea, China and Egypt, 1854–1888*, was published in 1915.

See also Arabi Rebellion; Crimean War; Egypt; Ginnis, Battle of; Gordon, Major General Charles G.; Gordon Relief Expedition; Graham, Lieutenant General Sir Gerald, V.C.; Khalifa; Red River Expedition; Sudan; Wolseley, Field Marshal Garnet J.; Wood, Field Marshal Sir (Henry) Evelyn M., V.C.

References: Barthorp (1984); Neillands (1996); Preston (1967); Symons (1965); Wolseley (1903)

Stewart, Field Marshal Sir Donald M. (1824–1900)

Field Marshal Sir Donald M. Stewart served almost his entire military career in India, and is best known for his superb leadership during the Second Afghan War (1878–1880).

Born in Scotland on 1 March 1824, Stewart was educated at schools including Aberdeen University. He entered the Bengal Army in 1840, and served on the North-West Frontier in 1854 and 1855 in punitive expeditions against the Mohmands, Afridis, and other tribes. His service during the Indian Mutiny, which included riding from Agra to Delhi with dispatches, in Delhi and in Lucknow, and in operations in Bundelkhand, brought him to the attention of his superiors.

Stewart then served for nine years on the staff of the Bengal Army and commanded the Bengal Brigade during the Abyssinian War (1867–1868), being promoted to major general thereafter. He then served as superintendent of the Andaman Islands before commanding the Lahore Division (1875–1878).

When the Second Afghan War began in November 1878, three British columns invaded Afghanistan. Stewart, then a lieutenant general, commanded the 12,800-man Kandahar Field Force, which marched from Quetta in the south to Kandahar. His force reached Kandahar on 8 January 1879 to find that it had been evacuated by the Afghan garrison. Sher Ali Khan, Afghanistan's ruler, died on 21 February 1879 and was succeeded by his son, Yakub Khan. The Treaty of Gandamak was signed on 26 May 1879, ending, or so it was thought at the time, the Second Afghan War.

The Kandahar Field Force began returning to India on 1 September 1879, but after the 3 September massacre of the British Envoy in Kabul, Major Sir Pierre L. N. Cavagnari and other members of his staff and escort, the British struck swiftly. The order to withdraw was immediately canceled, and Stewart's Force remained in Kandahar and the surrounding area engaged in pacification operations.

In March 1880, having left the defense of Kandahar to troops from Bombay, Stewart's 7,000-man force marched to Kabul but found its way blocked by a strong tribal force at

Ahmad Khel on 19 April 1880. The enemy, about 15,000 strong, occupied an undulating ridge but advanced rapidly when it saw the British. The Afghans were soon within 400 yards of the British, whose artillery began firing case shot, then shrapnel, leaving heaps of dead and wounded Afghans before the guns. The Afghan cavalry attempted to turn Stewart's left flank, which was covered by the Bengal Lancers, but the momentum of the Afghan attack forced the Indians back to the main body of troops. Stewart's right flank had also been attacked by Afghan cavalry.

A gap appeared in the British front between one regiment and the guns, through which the determined Afghans poured, only to be met by point-blank fire. The Afghan cavalry attacks were finally blunted, and the British cavalry, no longer pressured in the rear, was able to attack the Afghans, forcing them to flee in what turned into a rout. This was a fierce, desperate battle, with the British losing 17 killed and 115 wounded, and the Afghans, about 1,000 killed and more than 2,000 wounded. The force then continued to Kabul.

Additional operations took place in Afghanistan, including the debacle at Maiwand (27 July 1880), and the war was basically over after the Battle of Kandahar (1 September 1880). Stewart was well rewarded for his Second Afghan War service, receiving a baronetcy, knighthood, and other honors.

Promoted to general in 1881, Stewart served as commander in chief, India, from 1881 to 1885. Afterward he was a member of the secretary of state for India's council. Stewart was promoted to field marshal in 1894, appointed governor of Chelsea Hospital the following year, and died on 26 March 1900.

See also Afghan War, Second (1878–1880); Afghanistan; Bengal Army; Cavagnari, Major Sir Pierre L.N.; India; Indian Army Operations; Maiwand, Battle of; North-West Frontier; Sher Ali Khan

References: Featherstone (1973); Heathcote (1974); Maxwell (1979); Roberts (1897)

Stewart, Major General Sir Herbert (1843–1885)

Major General Sir Herbert Stewart was a leading cavalry commander of his day. He was mortally wounded during the Gordon Relief Expedition.

Born on 30 June 1843 in Hampshire, Stewart was educated at Winchester and was commissioned in the army in 1863. He served in India with the 37th Regiment, and when he returned to England in 1873, Stewart exchanged into the 3rd Dragoon Guards. Stewart attended the Staff College in 1877 and in 1879 saw service in the Zulu War. Ostensibly disgusted with the slow rate of promotion and poor career opportunities, Stewart was considering retirement when General (later Field Marshal Viscount) Sir Garnet J. Wolseley arrived in July 1879 to assume command of the troops in South Africa and made him his military secretary.

After the conclusion of the Zulu War, Wolseley's Transvaal Field Force attacked the stronghold of Bapedi chief Sekukuni in a campaign that lasted two months. Stewart remained on Wolseley's staff, and when Wolseley returned to England in 1880 and was replaced as governor and commander in chief of Natal and the Transvaal by Major General Sir George Pomeroy-Colley, Stewart became Pomeroy-Colley's chief of staff.

When Wolseley was appointed commander of the British force sent to Egypt in 1882 to suppress the Arabi Rebellion, he selected many of the members of his "Ashanti Ring," plus Stewart and a few others, to accompany him. Stewart served as chief of staff of the cavalry division, and after the Battle of Tel el-Kebir (13 September 1882), he was responsible for the rapid pursuit of the vanquished enemy to Cairo and the surrender of Arabi.

Stewart, then a brigadier general, commanded the cavalry in the British force commanded by Major General (later Lieutenant General) Sir Gerald Graham, V.C., that arrived in Egypt in early 1884 to help fight the dervishes. He led rather impetuously the charge of two regiments at El Teb on 29 February 1884, and was knighted for his services in the Sudan.

In the fall of 1884, when Wolseley was commanding the expedition to relieve Major General Charles G. Gordon in Khartoum, Stewart returned to the Sudan. When Wolseley formed the River and Desert Columns in December 1884 to hasten the relief, Stewart was given command of the latter. Stewart's Desert Column fought a fierce battle at Abu Klea on 17 January 1885, and two days later, at Abu Kru, in another fight with the dervishes, Stewart was wounded. The wound turned out to be mortal, and Stewart died in the desert on 16 February 1885, shortly after he had been promoted to major general. Wolseley bemoaned Stewart's death: "I feel as if I had lost my right arm in this business & I cannot hope to see his like again" (Preston 1967, p. 149).

See also Abu Klea, Battle of; Arabi Rebellion; Ashanti Ring; Boer War, First (1880–1881); Dervishes; Egypt; Gordon Relief Expedition; Graham, Lieutenant General Sir Gerald, V.C.;

Pomeroy-Colley, Major General Sir George; Wolseley, Field Marshal Garnet J.; Zulu War

References: Barthorp (1984); Kochanski (1999); Lehmann (1964); Maxwell (1985); Preston (1967); Symons (1965)

Steyn, Marthinus T. (1857–1916)

Marthinus T. Steyn served as president of the Orange Free State in the years preceding the Second Boer War. He was considered a reasonable man and a moderating influence, and after the Second Boer War broke out, he campaigned in the field and was a determined nationalist.

Steyn was born in the Orange Free State on 2 October 1857 and studied law in London. He returned to the Orange Free State and began practicing law in 1882. In 1889, Steyn became state attorney and a judge, and was elected president in 1896. He arranged and hosted the unsuccessful Bloemfontein Conference (31 May–5 June 1899) between President S. J. Paulus Kruger of the South African Republic (Transvaal) and Sir (later Lord) Alfred Milner, British high commissioner for South Africa and governor of the Cape Colony.

After the outbreak of war on 11 October 1899, Steyn spent considerable time visiting the commandos in the field. The capital of the Orange Free State, Bloemfontein, was captured on 13 March 1900, and after the capture of Johannesburg and the Johannesburg armistice of 30 May 1900, Kruger seemed on the verge of surrendering. Steyn sent Kruger a telegram basically accusing the Transvaalers of cowardice, that it seemed they were then ready, "as the war reached their own borders, to conclude a selfish and disgraceful peace" (Pakenham 1979, p. 458). Steyn's spine-stiffening message "was the most important telegram of the war" (Pakenham 1979, p. 458).

After July 1900, the seat of the Orange Free State government was in the field, and for most of the rest of the war Steyn remained with Chief Commandant Christiaan R. De Wet's commando. Although relatively young, Steyn's health suffered considerably. He refused to surrender, however, and resisted all attempts by others to end the war. Steyn participated in the initial peace negotiations in May 1902, but, almost completely paralyzed, he resigned the presidency and departed for medical attention on 29 May 1902. As a result, he did not sign the Treaty of Vereeniging on 31 May 1902 that ended the war.

Steyn spent a number of years overseas seeking medical aid. After returning to the Orange Free State, Steyn supported the aspirations of his countrymen. He died on 28 November 1916.

See also Bitter-Ender; Boer War, Second (1899–1902); Boers; Commando System; De Wet, Chief Commandant Christiaan R.; Kruger, S. J. Paulus; Transvaal

References: Belfield (1975); Carver (1999); Pakenham (1979); Smuts (1952)

Stormberg, Battle of (10 December 1899)

The Battle of Stormberg was the first of three tremendous British defeats, followed by the Battles of Magersfontein (11 December) and of Colenso (15 December), during what came to be called Black Week during the Second Boer War (1899–1902).

Lieutenant General Sir William F. Gatacre arrived in South Africa in November 1899, nominally to command the 3rd Division. Except for one battalion, his entire division had been sent to Natal. By early December 1899, Gatacre received reinforcements, including three additional battalions, 300 regular mounted infantry, two artillery batteries, and 1,000 Cape volunteers. His mission was to guard the northeastern border of Cape Colony from Boer invasion.

On 26 November 1899, the Boers occupied Stormberg Junction in the northeastern Cape Colony, a vital rail junction on the line from the port of East London to Aliwal North, and where another line branched out to the west. While Gatacre had been told not to take any risks until he received more soldiers, he was an aggressive leader and determined to attack the Boers.

Gatacre's ad hoc force, numbering less than 3,000 men, was located at Sterkstroom, about 30 miles south of Stormberg. He moved his soldiers by train to Molteno, about 10 miles southeast of Stormberg, on 9 December 1899. His plan was to then march his force overnight and attack the Boers on the Kissieberg Heights, about 2.5 miles southwest of Stormberg, at dawn.

Gatacre had expected to receive reinforcements before his march, but, due to coordination problems, they did not materialize. Gatacre, called "Backacher" by his troops because he was in superb physical condition and marched his soldiers hard, expected to lead his force through the pass traversed by both the railroad and a road. The column departed Molteno at about 9:00 P.M. on 9 December 1899. At the last minute, Gatacre heard that Boers were defending the pass and he changed the route to the west, over rugged terrain that had not been reconnoitered. He did not use scouts, and his medical and supply elements were unable to reach him.

The British soldiers, inexperienced in night operations and weary from the aimless plodding, had unknowingly swung around and behind Boer positions. Boer rifle fire from the Boers on the Kissieberg to their east crashed incessantly into their packed ranks as they were caught in the open at first light on 10 December 1899. Gatacre tried to attack, and some British soldiers climbed the Boer-held Kissieberg, but outcroppings hindered their progress. Poorly aimed British artillery hit many British infantrymen, and the operation turned into a frantic retreat, with the force soon coming under Boer fire from the west.

During the course of this disaster, it seemed that Gatacre "forgot" about 600 of his soldiers near the Kissieberg, who later surrendered. British casualties in this ignominious defeat were 28 killed, 51 wounded, and 634 captured.

See also Boer War, Second (1899–1902); Boers; Gatacre, Lieutenant General Sir William F.
References: Barthorp (1987); Belfield (1975); Nasson (1999); Pakenham (1979)

Sudan

The Sudan, a generally poor and undeveloped region that was a center of the slave trade, underwent considerable turmoil under the occupation of various foreign regimes during this period.

Egypt, a part of the Ottoman Empire, controlled the province of Sudan by defeating the Mameluke dynasty and establishing a new government there in 1821. This began the Turkiya, or Turkish regime. The Egyptian occupation was initially harsh, but as it became more secure, severe rules were relaxed. Slavery increased and was a focus of Egyptian attention and profits. The Egyptians revised the legal system and attempted to modernize the administration and organization of the province. Part of the modernization included rebuilding the army on a European model without slave manpower, and in the 1860s attempts were made to suppress the slave trade.

British Army Colonel (later Major General) Charles G. Gordon served as governor of the Sudan's southern Equatoria Province in 1874–1876, and of the Sudan from 1877 to 1880. He made efforts to end the slave trade. Weak Egyptian leadership, foreign intervention, and heavy spending, coupled with increased taxation and a disruption of the Sudanese society and economy caused by attempts to end slavery, fomented religious fundamentalism.

The Mahdi appeared in 1881 in this unstable environment, and after seizing Khartoum and killing Gordon in 1885 ushered in a fundamentalist Islamic state called the Mahdiya. The British withdrew their forces. The Mahdi died later in 1885 and was succeeded by the Khalifa. The British began their reconquest of the Sudan in 1896, to avenge Gordon's death and ensure the Sudan remained within the British sphere of influence, which was completed in 1898. The Khalifa was in charge of the Sudan until killed by the British in battle in 1899.

An Anglo-Egyptian agreement in 1899 restored Egyptian rule in the Sudan as part of a joint authority, or condominium, shared by Great Britain and Egypt. Britain assumed the responsibility for governing the Sudan on behalf of the Egyptian khedive, and appointed a governor general. An executive council was formed in 1910 and retained legislative authority until 1948. Sudanese nationalism increased after World War I, and on 1 January 1956, the Sudan became an independent republic.

See also Dervishes; Egypt; Gordon, Major General Charles G.; Gordon Relief Expedition; Khalifa; Mahdi; Reconquest of the Sudan; Slavery
References: Chaille Long (1899); Ludwig (1937); Mansfield (1971); Metz (1991); Metz (1992); Moore-Harell (2001); Wingate (1892)

Suez Canal

The Suez Canal in Egypt extends slightly more than 100 miles from Port Said in the north to Port Tewfik (near Suez) in the south and connects the Mediterranean Sea with the Gulf of Suez and then the Red Sea.

British strategic interest focused on Egypt with the opening of the Suez Canal in 1869, which dramatically reduced the sailing distances and times from England to India and elsewhere. (For example, the sailing distance from Europe to the Far East was cut by about one-third, and to India by about half, with the opening of the Suez Canal.) The British were initially concerned that the Suez Canal was controlled by the Egyptian khedive (viceroy) Ismail and by the French, the latter influencing the Suez Canal Company. By 1875, the profligate khedive was in serious financial difficulties, and to pay his creditors, Ismail was forced to sell his shares in the

Suez Canal

Suez Canal Company. Realizing the strategic importance of the canal, and with four-fifths of all shipping through it sailing under the British flag, British Prime Minister Benjamin Disraeli was able to raise the money quickly and purchase the khedive's outstanding shares. For £4 million, the British acquired a controlling interest in the Suez Canal.

British control of the Suez Canal was important not only to maintain the imperial lifeline to India and the Far East but also to prevent France from expanding and perhaps contesting Britain's hegemony in the Persian Gulf. This was considered vital in order to maintain Persia as a buffer to Russian expansion toward India, especially after Russia's victory in the 1877–1878 Russo-Turkish War. Moreover, the British were concerned about Russian intentions in the Balkans and in the eastern Mediterranean.

Egyptian nationalist Colonel Ahmed Arabi began a rebellion in Egypt in 1881 that undermined the authority of the khedive. As the insurrection continued into 1882, public safety, the lives of about 90,000 Europeans living in Egypt, and free passageway on the Suez Canal were threatened. In sum, to bolster the Egyptian khedive's weakening authority, protect Europeans living in Egypt, and ensure the control of the Suez Canal, the British sent an expeditionary force to Egypt that soundly defeated the nationalists in a short, decisive campaign. This victory paved the way for the British occupation of Egypt and protection of the strategic Suez Canal, the latter continuing until 1956.

See also Arabi Pasha, Ahmed; Arabi Rebellion; Disraeli, Benjamin; Egypt; Great Game; Imperialism; India, British Army in

References: Barthorp (1984); Farwell (1972); Maurice (1887); Padfield (1981)

Taku Forts, Assault on (21 August 1860)

See China War, Second (1856–1860)

Tamai, Battle of (13 March 1884)

The British government had to take decisive action to restore stability to the Sudan after the dervish massacre of Major General William Hicks Pasha's Sudan Force at the Battle of Kashgil (3–5 November 1883) and the Mahdist rout of Lieutenant General Valentine Baker Pasha's Egyptian Gendarmerie at the Battle of El Teb (4 February 1884). Accordingly, the British sent a force under the command of Major General (later Lieutenant General) Sir Gerald Graham, V.C., to restore the situation.

Graham's force defeated Osman Digna's dervishes at El Teb on 29 February 1884. After Graham received additional reinforcements and assembled his force near Suakin, he decided to attack Osman's camp near the Tamai wells, about 15 miles to the west. Graham's force consisted of two infantry brigades, with the 10th and the 19th Hussars and artillery. The 1st Brigade (1st Battalion, Gordon Highlanders; 2nd Battalion, Royal Irish Fusiliers; and 3rd Battalion, 60th Rifles) was commanded by Brigadier General (later General) Sir Redvers H. Buller, V.C. Major General John Davis commanded the 2nd Brigade (1st Battalion, Black Watch; 1st Battalion, York and Lancasters; and Royal Marine Light Infantry, with a Gardner machine-gun detachment).

On 11 March 1884, Graham's 4,000-man force moved out from Suakin and advanced 11 miles before bivouacking for the night. The next day, the British were under constant enemy rifle fire while marching. On the morning of 13 March, cavalry scouts reported only a few dervishes to their front. The British force then advanced in two brigade-sized squares, with the 1st Brigade on the right and the 2nd Brigade about 500 yards to its left. As the force neared Tamai, the 2nd Brigade reached a ravine from which many hidden dervishes began the attack. In the confusion, it seemed that Graham, collocated with 2nd Brigade, ordered the Black Watch on the left front of the square to charge the dervishes. This created a gap in the brigade formation, and the rapidly assaulting dervishes were able to penetrate the square, which was "soon broken up into small groups of desperately fighting men, once again sword and spear against bayonet, the dervishes slashing first at the hands to disarm and then at the head and body to kill and maim" (Keown-Boyd 1986, p. 32). Immediately, British cavalry to the left of the 2nd Brigade dismounted and fired volleys into the dervishes, as did the artillery and Buller's 1st Brigade (which was also attacked on all sides) from the right, thus checking the Mahdist attack and permitting the 2nd Brigade to reform its square. The courage of the dervishes could not overcome British cold steel and accurate rifle and machine-gun fire.

Shortly after 10:00 A.M., the battle was over, and Graham's force crossed the ravine and occupied Tamai. In three hours of intense fighting, the British lost 109 all ranks killed and 112 wounded, and Osman Digna admitted losing 2,000 killed. The desert route from Suakin to Berber was open, from which Khartoum could have been reached via the Nile River. Rather than take a chance on a "dash" across the desert, Graham's force withdrew to Egypt.

See also Baker Pasha, Lieutenant General Valentine; Buller, General Sir Redvers H., V.C.; Dervishes; Egypt; Egyptian Army; El Teb, Battle of; Graham, Lieutenant General Sir Gerald, V.C.; Hicks Pasha, Major General William; Kashgil, Battle of; Machine Guns; Mahdi; Stephenson, General Sir Frederick C. A.; Sudan
References: Barthorp (1984); Caie (1987); Keown-Boyd (1986); Neillands (1996); Powell (1994); Robson (1993a); Robson (1995b)

Tantia Topi (c. 1819–1859)

Tantia Topi was a skillful, aggressive rebel leader during the Indian Mutiny, who was frequently handicapped by incompetent subordinate commanders.

Tantia Topi (*topi* meaning "captain" or "commander") was the pseudonym for Ramchandra Pandyranga. His origins were rather mysterious, and he was thought to have been born around 1819. Tantia Topi associated himself with Nana Sahib, a key Indian mutineer who assumed the leadership at Cawnpore, serving as an aide-de-camp, then in a position similar to chief of staff, and then as a recruiter of new troops before commanding his own troops.

Known for the able employment of their artillery, Tantia Topi's forces were defeated at Bithur on 16 August 1857. Tantia Topi's 25,000 soldiers, joined by Nana Sahib's followers, overwhelmed and defeated the British at Cawnpore on 28 November 1857, but were in turn defeated on 6 December 1857 by a force commanded by Lieutenant General (later Field Marshal Lord Clyde) Sir Colin Campbell.

After crossing the Ganges River, Tantia Topi's force seized Charkheri, capturing twenty-four guns and a large amount of cash. At the end of March 1858, Tantia Topi's force attempted to relieve the besieged insurgent garrison at Jhansi, but it was repulsed on 1 April 1858 at the Battle of Betwa River by a British force commanded by Major General (later Field Marshal Lord Strathnairn) Sir Hugh H. Rose. This was the decisive action of the Central Indian Campaign. Tantia Topi's force withdrew to Kunch and was driven out of it on 6 May 1858. It then withdrew into Rajputana, where a smaller, more disciplined rebel force eluded the British for over eight months.

Many of the rebels dispersed in early 1859. Tantia Topi was betrayed by another Indian who wanted favorable treatment from the British, and he was captured on 8 April 1859. He was tried by court-martial, found guilty of rebellion, and hanged on 15 April 1859. After the soldiers departed the execution site, "a great scramble was made by officers and others to get a lock of hair" (Hibbert 1978, p. 386). This officially ended the Indian Mutiny.

See also Campbell, Field Marshal Colin; Cawnpore, Siege and Relief of; India; Indian Mutiny; Nana Sahib; Rhani of Jhansi; Rose, Field Marshal Hugh H.
References: Edwardes (1963); Featherstone (1992b); Hibbert (1978); Mason (1974); Robson (1996); Ward (1996); Watson (1991)

Taranaki War (1860–1861)

Relations between the Maoris and colonizing British on New Zealand deteriorated during the late 1840s and 1850s. Protections and rights guaranteed the Maoris in the 1840 Treaty of Waitangi were gradually whittled away. The Taranaki War of 1860–1861 broke out because of this increasing friction and land sale disputes.

In 1859, local Maori chief Te Teira offered to sell to the Crown a 600-acre block of land at the mouth of the Waitara River in North Taranaki, on the west side of the North Island. Wiremu Kingi, recognized as the paramount Maori chief in the area, objected to the sale out of principle and tribal law and because about 2,000 Maoris lived on that land.

Around the same time the governor, Thomas Gore Browne, announced a new policy that the government would accept any land offer from any Maori who wished to sell it. No Maori, regardless of position, would be permitted to block the sale. This new policy was another British attempt to undermine the Maori tribal system and buy more land. Gore Browne saw this issue as the Crown versus the paramount Maori chief—and he would not permit the authority of the Crown to be questioned or compromised.

The Maoris were understandably upset and obstructed and then evicted surveyors who had come to measure the land plot. The governor considered this action tantamount to treason, and he ordered the Maoris to apologize and vacate the land. The Maoris then hastily built a *pa* (an earthwork stockade) inside a corner of the block of land.

The British governor apparently believed a quick, decisive victory over Kingi's Maoris would stop any objections to the land sale and deter other tribes from joining Kingi. The British force of about 500 soldiers from the 65th Foot, with artillery, under the command of Colonel C. E. Gold, attacked King's *pa* at Te Kohia on 17 March 1860. That night the Maoris, in typical fashion, evacuated the *pa*, which the

British found empty the following morning. This was the first action of the Taranaki War.

In the early months of this desultory conflict, the Maoris, fierce individual fighters in the dense forests, dominated the British. On 27 June 1860, the British attacked Kingi's *pa* at Pukatakauere, but the poorly coordinated assault was halted by the Maoris at the *pa* trenches and repulsed. This battle has been described as "one of the three most clear cut and disastrous defeats suffered by imperial troops in New Zealand" (Waitangi Tribunal 1996, chap. 4, p. 24).

British reinforcements were sent to New Zealand under the command of Major General Thomas Pratt, the general officer commanding Australia. Pratt ordered the British to dig saps to the ramparts of a *pa* before beginning an assault, a tactic used successfully in attacking the Mahoetahi *pa* on 6 November 1860. The 600-man British force conducted their final assault with fixed bayonets against the 150 Maoris. The Maoris suffered heavy casualties, with about one-third of their force killed and one-third wounded, while the British had 4 men killed and 16 wounded.

Pratt's new technique of capturing *pas* was successful, as the disconcerted Maoris frequently fled their defensive positions. The British then captured a number of *pas* with little fighting, and their advance culminated in the seizure of the *pa* and surrender of the Maoris at Te Arei on 19 March 1861. A cease-fire was formalized on 3 April 1861 and ended the Taranaki War. The terms included a promise by the governor to investigate the problems associated with disputed Maori land purchases.

See also Maori War, First (1843–1848); Maori War, Second (1863–1869), Maoris

References: Featherstone (1973); Haythornthwaite (1995); Knight (1996); Waitangi Tribunal (1996)

Telegraph
See Communications

Tel el-Kebir, Battle of (13 September 1882)

Tel el-Kebir (from the Arabic *El Tel el-Kebir,* or "The Great Hill") was the site of the main Egyptian Army encampment during the 1882 Arabi Rebellion. This heavily defended fortification was located on the Sweetwater Canal about 20 miles west of the Suez Canal and 40 miles northeast of Cairo, on the shortest overland route from the Suez Canal to Cairo.

The British expeditionary force sent to suppress the Arabi Rebellion was commanded by General (later Field Marshal Viscount) Sir Garnet J. Wolseley. The main force gathered at Ismailia, on the western side of the Suez Canal, on 1 September 1882. A week later the British force was on the outskirts of Tel el-Kebir. Ahmed Arabi Pasha was said to have over 26,000 regular and Bedouin troops, 2,500 cavalry, and about 60 guns defending this position, thought by Wolseley to be "a very hard nut to crack" (Williams 1967, p. 270).

Wolseley determined that the best course of action would be to assault the strong Egyptian position at dawn, when it was most vulnerable. In order to do so, the British would have to conduct an unusually large-scale night march. To enhance success, Wolseley had earlier directed the engineers to plant a line of telegraph poles, pointing directly toward the enemy fortifications, which would aid navigation at night.

At 3:00 P.M. on 12 September 1882, the soldiers were told they would move out that night and attack the Egyptian stronghold of Tel el-Kebir. To deceive any observing Egyptian spies, the British soldiers did not take their tents down until after sunset. They then marched silently to assembly areas. At 1:00 A.M. on 13 September, the British forces, numbering about 17,401 men and 61 guns, began their stealthy march across the trackless desert. Lieutenant General Sir Edward Hamley's 2nd Division was on the left, marching in half battalions in double company columns, with Lieutenant General G. H. S. Willis's 1st Division, advancing in half battalions in columns of companies, on the right.

The British force, assisted by a Royal Navy navigator, followed the stars to their assault positions. By doing so, however, they were slightly off course and had fortuitously missed an Egyptian outpost. Shortly before dawn, a single shot was fired from the Egyptian positions, and this alerted the defenders. Because of the angle of the attack, the 1st (Highland) Brigade of the 2nd Division was then nearest the enemy. Fixing bayonets, the Highlanders, followed by the rest of the force, assaulted Arabi's fortifications. The Cavalry Division, commanded by Major General D. C. Drury Lowe, swept around the crumbling enemy left flank, wreaking havoc in the Egyptian rear areas. Fighting was fierce, often hand to hand, with men hacked or stabbed to death, or blown apart by cannon. But the Egyptians, caught off guard by Wolseley's night march and surprise assault, were no match for the disciplined, well-led British soldiers. The battle was over in thirty-five minutes.

Tel el-Kebir was Wolseley's most decisive and overwhelming victory. The battle was won at a relatively low cost of 57 British dead, 382 wounded, and 30 men missing, as compared to about 2,000 Egyptian dead. A rapid pursuit of the vanquished enemy followed and Wolseley entered Cairo two days later. The war was over on 15 September 1882. Wolseley considered the Battle of Tel el-Kebir the decisive factor in "the tidiest little war ever fought by the British Army in its long history" (Lehmann 1964, p. 338). It probably was.

See also Arabi Pasha, Ahmed; Arabi Rebellion; Egypt; Egyptian Army; Hamley, Lieutenant General Sir Edward B.; Suez Canal; Wolseley, Field Marshal Garnet J.

References: Barthorp (1984); Farwell (1972); Jones (1993); Lehmann (1964); Maurice (1887); Raugh (2001b); Smith (1987); Williams (1967)

Temperance
See Army and Society; Sports and Recreation

Theodore, Emperor (c. 1818–1868)

Abyssinian Emperor Theodore II (Tewodros), an intelligent and natural leader, basically unified the feudal states of Abyssinia and was crowned emperor in 1855. After a perceived insult in 1864, Theodore imprisoned the British consul and other Europeans. In 1867, the British sent an expedition to free the hostages and punish Theodore for his brazen insolence. Theodore was a complex character, "a combination of robber-chieftain, idealist and madman" (Chandler 1967, p. 111).

Theodore, who was originally known as Lij Kassa, was born in about 1818. He was the son of a minor nobleman, but he claimed to be directly descended from the illegitimate offspring of King Solomon and the Queen of Sheba. His father died when he was young and he was educated by Coptic monks. Kassa succeeded his uncle as provincial governor but yearned for more power and authority. He became a brigand and an ambitious warlord who fought to unify the disparate kingdoms and provinces of Abyssinia. In 1855, he felt powerful enough to have himself crowned "Emperor Theodore II [Tewodros], King of Ethiopia, King of Kings, and the Chosen of God" (Chandler 1967, p. 111) by the Primate of the Coptic Church. Theodore began to consolidate and modernize the legal, administrative, and tax systems, reducing the autonomy of local rulers and antagonizing them in the process. He had two grandiose goals that he intended to accomplish: defeat and destroy his Muslim neighbors and then lead a crusade to liberate Jerusalem from the Ottoman yoke.

Revolts broke out as Theodore tried to modernize Abyssinia. In 1860, Walter Plowden, British consul since 1842 and a trusted adviser of Theodore, was murdered. Shortly thereafter, Theodore's wife died. It seemed the loss of these two key people in Theodore's life affected his reason.

Captain Charles D. Cameron arrived in Abyssinia in 1862 as Plowden's replacement. Cameron presented to Theodore a pair of engraved pistols as a personal gift from Queen Victoria. Theodore sent Queen Victoria a letter of thanks and also stated his intention of sending an Abyssinian delegation to London, probably for the purpose of attempting to muster British support in his war against the surrounding Muslim countries.

The British Foreign Office inadvertently failed to respond to Theodore's letter and he perceived this as an insult. At about the same time, Theodore and his forces had been defeated in battle by the Egyptians at Gedaril in the Sudan. In his state of paranoia, Theodore suspected Cameron, who had visited the Sudan to investigate the slave trade and the region's potential for growing cotton, of being sympathetic to the Muslim Egyptians. Consequently, Theodore imprisoned Cameron and a number of other Europeans in early 1864.

London eventually ascertained the situation in Abyssinia, and Queen Victoria sent a belated letter of 24 May 1864 to "our good friend, Theodore, King of Abyssinia" (Bates 1979, p. 59) to assuage Theodore's hurt feelings and help facilitate the release of Cameron and the other hostages. A special envoy was designated, and after tremendous trials and tribulations, Queen Victoria's letter was delivered to Theodore on 28 January 1866. By that time, Cameron and the others were imprisoned in the mountain fortress of Magdala.

Further communications ensued between Theodore and London, in which the emperor kept asking for additional material assistance. The British eventually realized that the cunning Theodore was blackmailing them, and on 13 August 1867 the British Cabinet authorized military intervention to free the prisoners.

Commanded by Lieutenant General (later Field Marshal Lord) Sir Robert C. Napier, the main body of the British expeditionary force landed at Zula on Annesley Bay, south of Massawa, in January 1868. The 14,214-man British force, with thousands of followers and transport animals, began the 400-mile march toward Magdala without Abyssinian interference. On 24 March 1868 the force entered Dildi, from which they could see Theodore's mountain fortress of Magdala. As Napier's advance guard neared Magdala, the Abyssinians attacked what appeared to be an unguarded supply train but were repulsed.

Theodore sued for peace but refused to surrender even as many of his loyal supporters vanished. When an armistice expired on 13 April 1868, Napier's artillery began its bombardment as troops stormed Magdala and released the hostages. Theodore, realizing the hopelessness of his situation, shot himself through the mouth with one of the pistols Queen Victoria had given to him as a gift.

See also Abyssinia; Abyssinian War; Magdala, Capture of; Napier, Field Marshal Robert C.
References: Bates (1979); Chandler (1967); Haythornthwaite (1995); Myatt (1970)

Tibet, Expedition to (1903–1904)

The Great Game, the competition between British India and Czarist Russia to exert influence and control over the vast, uncharted mountainous regions of Central Asia, focused on Tibet at the end of the nineteenth and early twentieth century.

The British remained committed to protecting India and were very concerned about Russian expansionism. Lord (later Marquess) George Curzon, viceroy of India, became alarmed when he learned of Tibetan missions to Russia in 1900 and 1901 and a rumored secret agreement between Russia and China pertaining to Tibet in 1902. The following year, Curzon sent the Tibet Frontier Commission, led by Major Francis E. Younghusband, to establish trade and other relations with Tibet and try to forestall any type of Russian political infiltration into Tibet. The commission entered Tibet in July, but the Chinese and Tibetans refused to negotiate with the British as long as they remained in Tibetan territory. As a result, the mission languished at Khamba Jong, about 20 miles north of the Sikkim-Tibetan border, for five months.

Excuses were sought to justify and explain the humiliation and failure of the Tibet Frontier Commission. Two low-grade Sikkimese spies for the British had failed to return to camp, and they were reportedly captured and tortured by the Tibetans. The ardent imperialist Curzon exaggerated this issue and reported that Tibetan troops had attacked Nepalese yak herders on the frontier and had stolen their yaks. Based on this information, the British authorized an expedition to obtain "satisfaction" and "reparation" from the Tibetan Government.

Younghusband, promoted to colonel to raise his prestige as a negotiator, was selected to be British commissioner and to command the Tibet Mission. The Tibet Mission Escort, commanded by Brigadier General J. R. L. Macdonald, consisted of about 1,150 soldiers from these units: one section (two 10-pounder screw guns), 7th Mountain Battery, Royal Garrison Artillery; two 7-pounder guns; 8th Gurkhas (six companies); 23rd Sikh Pioneers (eight companies); 2nd Sappers and Miners (half-company); Maxim gun detachment, 1st Norfolk Regiment; plus reserve and support elements. The expedition crossed the 14,390-foot Jelap La (pass) leading into Tibet on 11 December 1903, bound for Gyantse. In spite of the frigid cold and high altitude, Phari, at the northern end of the 60-mile-long Chumbi Valley, was occupied on 22 December. From mid-January to March 1904, the mission remained at Tuna pending negotiations.

The advance continued at the end of March. On 30 March 1904, about 10 miles from Tuna, at Guru, Tibetan soldiers blocked the British advance and demanded they return to India. Younghusband gave the Tibetans fifteen minutes to clear the path, and at the end of that time, directed Macdonald to order his force to advance and not fire until fired upon. While British detachments flanked the Tibetans, the main British line surged forward in silence toward the Tibetans behind their rock wall. The British reached the rock wall without a shot being fired, and Younghusband ordered that the Tibetans be disarmed. In the ensuing melee, a shot rang out, which heralded volley firing from the Gurkhas and Sikhs at a range of no more than 20 yards. Tibetans started to walk away and were mowed down by the hail of bullets as the two Maxim guns opened up. This engagement—considered by some a massacre—was over in minutes. Of the estimated 1,500–2,000 Tibetan soldiers involved, about 600–700 were killed and 168 wounded; the British had 12 wounded. The British were sickened and disgusted by this slaughter, but the advance continued.

The British reached Red Idol Gorge on 10 April 1904 and found the Tibetans on cliff-top positions prepared to defend it. Macdonald sent Gurkhas to climb the 3,000-foot cliffs, but a violent snowstorm hindered their movement and obstructed observation. When the storm cleared, the Gurkhas were on their objective but met no resistance. With artillery and Maxim support, the reserve 32nd Pioneers cleared the gorge and the Tibetans fled, leaving behind about 200 dead. The British had three soldiers wounded.

The mission reached Gyantse, its official destination, on 12 April and established itself at Chang Lo, a hamlet less than a mile from the Gyantse Fort. On 20 April, "Retiring Mac" Macdonald (as the troops called him) took half the force and returned to New Chumbi, 150 miles in the rear, reportedly to coordinate communications and resupply efforts. The senior escort officer at Chang Lo was Lieutenant Colonel Brander. With Younghusband's permission, he led a 380-man force on 3 May 1904 to destroy Tibetan positions built across a narrow defile at Karo La, 46 miles east of Gyantse on the road to Lhasa.

During Brander's absence, the Tibetans attacked Chang Lo on 5 May 1904 outside of the Gyantse fortress, but were repulsed easily. The following day, Brander's forces attacked and defeated the Tibetans at the 16,600-foot Karo La. With British soldiers fighting at an altitude of at least 18,500 feet, Karo La was reportedly the highest fought battle in British military history. Brander's force returned to Chang Lo the following morning.

May and June 1904 was a period of confusion, recriminations, ultimatums, and a siege of Chang Lo. Younghusband was made subordinate to and ordered to report to Macdonald at New Chumbi as a result of exceeding orders by permitting Brander to engage the enemy at Karo La. Younghusband arrived at New Chumbi on 10 June 1904 and left three days later with Macdonald and the reinforced escort. The escort moved in two columns: the first consisted of 125 mounted infantry, 8 guns, and 1,450 infantrymen, including followers and transport animals; the second contained the supply train, 500 infantrymen, and followers and animals. The reinforced escort reached the plain outside the Gyantse Fort on 26 June 1904.

Younghusband received word that the Tibetans would negotiate with him. However, negotiations in early July 1904 proved fruitless, and Younghusband sent an ultimatum demanding the evacuation of the Gyantse Fort on 4 July 1904, or face a British assault. The Tibetans ignored the demand, and the British stormed and captured the fort the following day. Lieutenant J. D. Grant of the Gurkhas earned the Victoria Cross that day for his gallantry and intrepidity in the assault on the Gyantse Fort.

With the capture of the Gyantse Fort, traditionally the key to Tibet, the road to Lhasa was open. The British force began the final 150-mile march to Lhasa on 14 July 1904, finally arriving in the Forbidden City on 3 August 1904. Lhasa was not the expected Shangri La, but an unimpressive area of filthy streets, scavenging dogs and pigs, and stagnant pools of water. No Russians were found, and the British Government later repudiated some of the concessions gained by Younghusband in the Lhasa Convention of 7 September 1904. Its mission complete, the Younghusband Expedition, as it came to be known, the first foreign mission to enter Tibet, returned to India on 25 October 1904.

See also Great Game; Imperialism; India; Indian Army Operations; Machine Guns; Victoria Cross; Younghusband, Colonel Sir Francis E.
References: Fleming (1961); French (1994); Wickham Legg and Williams (1959)

Tirah Field Force (1897–1898)

The North-West Frontier of India was ablaze in Pathan tribal hostilities in 1897. The British sent many punitive expeditions to suppress these tribal revolts. The Tochi Field Force was sent to quell the Isazais in the Tochi Valley, and the Mohmand Field Force was organized to suppress hostile Mohmands. The Malakand Field Force conducted operations against the Swatis, Utman Khel, Mamunds, and Salarzais, and the Buner Field Force punished the rebellious Bunerwhals.

The Afridis had been receiving a subsidy from the Indian Government for many years to safeguard the strategic Khyber Pass. On 23 August 1897, hostile Afridis and Orakzais attacked and seized the forts at the Khyber Pass. Four days later, Orakzais attacked in overwhelming strength the British posts on the Samana Ridge, about 30 miles south of the Khyber Pass and the southern boundary of the Tirah region, and close to Peshawar.

To punish the rebellious tribes and discourage any further hostilities to the south, especially in Waziristan, it was decided to form the Tirah Field Force and invade Tirah, the homeland of the Afridis and Orakzais. It was initially difficult to assemble a sufficient number of men due to other ongoing punitive operations. On 10 October 1897, however, under the command of General Sir William S. A. Lockhart, the Tirah Field Force was assembled at Kohat and prepared to advance. Numbering 34,506 British and Indian officers and troops, with 19,934 noncombatant followers and 71,800 transport animals, the Tirah Field Force was the largest British Army expedition to deploy to the field in India since the Indian Mutiny.

The Tirah Field Force consisted of two divisions, plus support and reserve elements. The 1st Division was commanded by Major General W. P. Symons, with its 1st Brigade commanded initially by Colonel (later General Sir) Ian S. M. Hamilton, then by Brigadier General R. Hart, V.C., and the 2nd Brigade commanded by Brigadier General A. Gaselee. Major General A. G. Yeatman-Biggs commanded the 2nd Division, which consisted of Brigadier General F. J. Kempster's 3rd Brigade and Brigadier General R. Westmacott's 4th Brigade. The lines of communication were commanded by Lieutenant General Sir A. P. Palmer, and the Rawalpindi Reserve Brigade by Brigadier General C. R. Macgregor. There were also two mobile columns (the Peshawar Column, commanded by Brigadier General A. G. Hammond, V.C., and the Kurram Movable Column, by Colonel W. Hill) to provide flank security and support. Support elements included 10 field and mountain artillery batteries, totaling 60 guns, and the first machine-gun detachment deployed to the North-West Frontier.

The Tirah Field Force strategy was to advance north, subjugate the Tirah region, then move farther northeast to recapture the Khyber Pass. The Tirah area, however, was basically unknown to the British, and the combined strength of the Afridis and the Orakzais was estimated at around 40,000–50,000.

The British advance began on 11 October 1897. Seven days later, routes over the Samana Ridge were reconnoitered, and fighting broke out almost immediately. The 5,000-foot-high Dargai Heights, key terrain dominating the area, were seized by the British on 18 October with casualties of 10 killed and 53 wounded. It was decided not to hold the Dargai Heights and the British evacuated the position.

After more units and supplies, including ammunition, had arrived, the Dargai Heights were again attacked on 20 October 1897. The Pathans had reinforced their positions on the Heights, and a British artillery barrage failed to dislodge the tribal warriors. Gurkhas led the attack, but were pinned down by accurate rifle fire. At about noon, the 1st Battalion, Gordon Highlanders—with bayonets fixed and the regimental bagpipes playing "Cock o' the North"—led a five-battalion assault. Before the British reached the summit, the tribesmen fled. The second capture of Dargai cost the British 36 killed and 159 wounded, and was the only set-piece battle of the campaign.

A pause in the hostilities ensued as the 1st Division and transport, traveling on bad roads, rejoined the leading 2nd Division. The advance continued on 28 October 1897, and the next objective was the 6,700-foot Sampagha Pass. The Tirah Valley was reached after little resistance on 1 November 1897. The following eight days were spent gathering supplies and reconnoitering the area. The Orakzais were showing signs of submission although there was constant harassment and sniping from the Zakha Khel, a powerful Afridi clan. Lockhart retaliated by launching a scorched earth campaign, leveling villages, destroying crops, and felling orchards. On 11 November, Orakzais tribal chiefs agreed with peace terms to return all captured weapons to the British, surrender 300 of their own breech-loading rifles, pay a 30,000 rupee (£10,000) fine, and forfeit all allowances and subsidies.

British units continued operating to eliminate resistance throughout November 1897, but the Zakha Khels engaged in frequent hit-and-run engagements, especially against vulnerable support and transport elements. The Afridis, as a tribe, had not submitted fully to the British, but with the approach of winter, the British began their 40-mile march through the Bara Valley to the Khyber Pass on 7 December 1897. Each division marched on a separate route. In snow and frigid temperatures, the British continued. The 2nd Division was harried the entire way and fought numerous rear-guard actions. The British march "looked more like a rout than the victorious withdrawal of a punitive force" (Miller 1977, p. 279). After having been separated, the Tirah Field Force's two divisions converged at the Indian frontier town of Barkai on 14 December.

Lockhart did not feel he had totally accomplished his mission. On 22 December 1897, the 1st Division marched to the Bazar Valley, the home of the Zakha Khel, and the Peshawar Column advanced to the Khyber Pass. (This latter operation is frequently called the Bazar Valley Expedition.) By 1 January 1898, three British brigades held the Khyber Pass, while two additional brigades blockaded the Afridi territory. The British fought a few engagements and destroyed Afridi villages and captured Afridi cattle and sheep. The last of the Afridi clans submitted to British demands in April 1898, signaling the end of the Great Pathan Revolt. From 12 October 1897 to April 1898, the British suffered 1,150 total casualties (287 killed, 853 wounded, and 10 missing).

See also Buner Field Force; Hamilton, General Sir Ian S. M.; India; Indian Army Operations; Lockhart, General Sir William S. A.; Malakand Field Force; Mohmand Field Force; North-West Frontier; Tochi Field Force

References: Barthorp (1982); Featherstone (1973); MacNeil (2001); Miller (1977); Nevill (1912)

Tochi Field Force (1897–1898)

A general uprising of the Pathan tribes on the North-West Frontier of India took place in 1897. There were many factors that caused the outbreak of widespread hostilities, including unrest fomented by those concerned with the spread of British authority and influence in the area caused by the formal demarcation with pillars of the border between Afghanistan and the North-West Frontier in 1893 (the Durand Line), and the potential loss of tribal independence. Muslim religious leaders, including Sadullah, the "mad fakir" from Swat, further inflamed fanaticism by calling for jihad (holy war) against all foreigners.

The first outbreak of violence took place on 10 July 1897 at the village of Maizar in the Tochi Valley. Mr. H. A. Gee, the political officer of Tochi, was visiting Maizar attempting to resolve a dispute involving a murder. The village headmen of the local Madda Khel (of the Isazais tribe) invited Gee and his entire military escort, commanded by Lieutenant Colonel A. C. Bunny, 1st Sikhs, to luncheon in the village. (The military escort commanded by Bunny consisted of 200 soldiers from the 1st Sikh Infantry, 100 from the 1st Punjab Infantry, 12 sabers from the 1st Punjab Cavalry, and 2 guns of the No. 6 Bombay Mountain Battery.) The British considered this an act of spontaneous hospitality and they were lulled into a false sense of security. During the meal, a man waving a sword was seen on a nearby tower, apparently signaling for an ambush to begin. The British, caught off guard, immediately returned fire. They had brought only 16 rounds of ammunition for each artillery piece, and after this was expended, the cannons fired blank rounds to deter the tribesmen. Bunny, mortally wounded in the stomach, ordered a withdrawal to a nearby ridge. Under steady fire from the enemy and maneuvering to prevent encirclement, the British force conducted a skillful withdrawal all afternoon until a defensible position on a nearby ridge was found. Reinforcements began to reach the British at about 6:15 P.M., causing the enemy to retire. A further withdrawal was conducted after dark, and the force returned to its camp at about midnight. Gee, Bunny, one other officer, and 21 other ranks were killed, and 28 wounded, in the "Maizar outrage." About 100 tribesmen were killed and many wounded.

The government of India subsequently decided to send a force as soon as possible to the Tochi Valley to "exact punishment from the treacherous tribesmen" (Nevill 1912, p. 218). Commanded by Major General G. Corrie Bird, the Tochi Field Force consisted of two brigades. The 1st Brigade, commanded by Brigadier General C. C. Egerton, consisted of 1 Squadron, 1st Punjab Cavalry; No. 3 Peshawar Mountain Battery; No. 2 Company, Bengal Sappers and Miners; 2nd Argyll and Sutherland Highlanders; 1st Sikh Infantry; 1st Punjab Infantry; and 33rd Bengal Infantry. Brigadier General W. P. Symons commanded the 2nd Brigade, which consisted of 1 Squadron, 1st Punjab Cavalry; No. 6 Bombay Mountain Battery (four guns); 3rd Rifle Brigade; 6th Jat Light Infantry; 14th Bengal Infantry; and 25th Bengal Infantry. There were many difficulties associated with assembling such a large force west of the Indus River in the summer, including the flooded waters of the Indus River itself, the intense heat, and the scarcity of potable water. These challenges were overcome, and the Tochi Field Force began operations on 28 June 1897.

The 1st Brigade's cavalry reached Maizar on 20 July 1897 and found the village deserted. The Field Force spent the next sixteen days destroying towers and hamlets in the area. The only fighting that took place was sporadic sniping by the tribesmen at night and small attacks on convoys during the day. The Madda Khel attempted unsuccessfully to enlist the assistance of other tribes, although news of further tribal unrest in the Swat Valley encouraged their resistance. The British systematically traversed, explored, and occupied the entire Tochi Valley and destroyed many villages. Finally, on 15 November 1897, the Madda Khel surrendered.

Its mission complete, the ad hoc Tochi Field Force was disbanded in January 1898. The force had 6 men killed and 8 wounded, although there was a high rate of sickness due to the terrible heat and lack of drinking water. "The record of the operations of the Tochi Field Force, under Major-General Corrie Bird," observed one officer, "is one of struggles against climate and Nature rather than a human enemy" (Nevill 1912, p. 222).

See also India; Indian Army Operations; North-West Frontier
References: Barthorp (1982); Featherstone (1973); Featherstone (1995); Haythornthwaite (1995); Nevill (1912)

Tofrek, Battle of (22 March 1885)

The Suakin Field Force, under the command of Lieutenant General Sir Gerald Graham, V.C., was organized after the fall of Khartoum in January 1885 to crush Osman Digna's dervish force in the Suakin area. When assembled, the Suakin Field Force consisted of two British infantry brigades, one Indian infantry brigade, a composite cavalry force, five artillery batteries, a Gardner machine-gun detachment, and later an Australian infantry battalion, totaling about 13,000 soldiers. Major General Sir John C. McNeill, V.C., commanded the 2nd Brigade, which included the 2nd Battalion, East Surrey Regiment; 1st Battalion, Berkshire Regiment; 1st Battalion, Shropshire Light Infantry; and Royal Marine Light Infantry.

About 1,200 dervish troops were thought to be located at Hashin, with the 7,000-man enemy main body near Tamai. The Suakin Field Force began its advance on 20 March 1885, and the 2nd Brigade captured the Hashin wells with little resistance the following day. The East Surreys were left as a temporary garrison at Hashin.

The Indian Brigade (17th Bengal Infantry, 28th Bombay Infantry, and 15th Sikhs) and a squadron of the 5th Lancers were then attached to the 2nd Brigade. On 22 March 1885, Graham ordered McNeill to march his force south in the direction of Tamai, hoping to find and fight the dervishes. The 2nd Brigade began its march that same day, plodded 5 miles through the heat and hard desert, and took a break at about 10:00 A.M.

McNeill's force began to build three zarebas (a stone and thorny mimosa bush enclosure) when a cavalry scout reported a large group of dervishes in the area. The largest zareba, to hold the stores and 1,500 transport animals, was in the center of the position. There were to be two smaller zarebas, one to the northeast (primarily for the Royal Marines) and one to southwest (for the Berkshires). The Indian brigade formed a perimeter facing northwest (28th Bombay Infantry), southwest (15th Sikhs), and southeast (17th Bengal Infantry) to protect the zarebas under construction. One half-battalion of the Berkshires in the northeast of the position was in reserve; the other half-battalion was building the southwest zareba. There were gaps in the perimeter, inadequate cavalry outposts, and soldiers building the positions had been forced to stack weapons.

McNeill intended to send the Indian Brigade back to Suakin at 3:00 P.M. As he was inspecting the redoubts at about 2:40 P.M., however, he received a message from the scouts that dervishes were assembling near their position. Within minutes, the dervishes assaulted the 17th Bengal Infantry and the weak southwest corner of the position. The 5th Lancers also galloped back though the 17th Bengal Infantry, which became disorganized. After firing one irregular volley, the 17th, except for two companies, broke and fled and left the central enclosure of the zareba exposed to the enemy. The Berkshires in reserve hastily formed a firing line and killed about 200 dervishes with their volleys. The Berkshires in the southwest zareba formed a small square, and eventually their firepower overwhelmed the attacking Muslims. In less than a half hour of fighting through clouds of dust and smoke, stampeding animals, and against fanatical dervishes, the battle was over.

Both Graham and General (later Field Marshal Viscount) Lord Garnet J. Wolseley, commanding the Gordon Relief Expedition, criticized McNeill for a lack of security and inadequate cavalry. McNeill never held another field command.

The Battle of Tofrek, or "McNeill's Zareba," was the most costly, in terms of British casualties, of those conducted in 1884 and 1885 in the eastern Sudan. The British lost 117 all ranks killed and 179 wounded or missing, with 176 followers casualties and the loss of 501 camels. At least 1,000 dervishes were killed. The results could have been much worse if the Berkshires, along with the Sikhs and Bombay infantry, had not gallantly and steadfastly defended their positions.

See also Dervishes; Gordon Relief Expedition; Graham, Lieutenant General Gerald, V.C.; Machine Guns; Mahdi; McNeill, General Sir John C., V.C.; Sudan; Wolseley, Field Marshal Garnet J.

References: Barthorp (1984); Caie (1985); De Cosson (1886); Keown-Boyd (1986); Neillands (1996); Robson (1993b)

Toski, Battle of (3 August 1889)

The Battle of Toski, fought almost entirely by troops of the Egyptian Army, was a notable success and halted the one serious dervish attempt to invade Egypt from the Sudan.

The dervish advance took place in 1889 under the Khalifa (the Mahdi had died in 1885). Fresh from victories in Abyssinia, they marched across the northern frontier of the Sudan. The 8,000-man dervish force was under the command of Emir Abdel Rahman Wad el Nejumi, who had led the final assault into Khartoum in 1885. Nejumi's force was small for such a major operation, due to either Nejumi's belief in the invincibility of his soldiers or the Khalifa's desire to dispose of a rival.

After leaving Dongola on 1 July 1889, Nejumi's plan was to march west into the desert, outflank British outposts, and attack on the Nile River near Aswan. British intelligence received early warning of this enemy advance, and the sirdar, Major General (later Field Marshal Lord) Sir Francis W. Grenfell, assumed personal command of this operation to intercept the dervishes.

Early on 3 August 1889, Egyptian cavalry (one squadron of the 20th Hussars, three squadrons of Egyptian cavalry, and one Camel Corps company), under the command of Colonel (later Field Marshal Earl) Horatio H. Kitchener, found the dervishes breaking camp west of the village of Toski, about 60 miles north of Wadi Halfa. Grenfell realized that the dervishes, numbering about 3,000, wanted to avoid fighting in the open desert where Egyptian firepower would play a key role in the battle and he could easily maneuver his units.

Grenfell's force consisted of the 1st Brigade (9th, 10th, and 13th Sudanese Infantry Battalions) and the 2nd Brigade (1st and 2nd Egyptian and 11th Sudanese Infantry Battalions), armed with Martini-Henry .450s, with two artillery batteries. Before waiting for reinforcement by a British brigade, Grenfell ordered Kitchener to prevent the dervishes from reaching a rocky area to the north and ordered his two brigades to advance from Toski. By 10:00 A.M., the two brigades were in position to block the dervish advance from reaching Toski and the Nile. Nejumi's men courageously charged the Egyptian Army units but were mowed down by accurate rifle fire, Maxim-Nordenfeldt guns, and artillery.

At about noon, Grenfell's force attacked and drove the dervishes to a small hill, which the latter defended bravely by repeated counterattacks. The Egyptian Army soldiers finally forced the survivors to retreat, but the pursuit was called off due to the ferocious heat.

While the dervish threat may have been exaggerated, the battle was a clear victory for the Egyptian Army. Nejumi was killed and less than a thousand dervishes survived, with one British officer referring to the battle as a "feast of blood" (Hunter 1996, p. 33). The dervishes never again threatened Egypt.

See also Dervishes; Egypt; Egyptian Army; Grenfell, Field Marshal Francis W.; Khalifa; Kitchener, Field Marshal Horatio H.; Machine Guns; Mahdi; Sirdar; Sudan
References: Barthorp (1984); Daly (1997); Hunter (1996); Neillands (1996); Keown-Boyd (1986)

Transvaal

The Transvaal was the territory north of the Vaal River first settled by Boers during the 1836–1846 Great Trek inland to establish their own independent nation away from the British and perpetuate slavery. The Vaal River separated the Orange Free State from what became the Transvaal.

Andries H. Potgeiter was the leader of the first large group of Boers to settle this area. They encountered opposition from the Matabele, who they defeated in a number of skirmishes and pushed further north.

The expansionist Boers caused friction with the local tribes whose lands they encroached. The British occasionally had to restore order in the area and annexed the Orange Free State on 3 February 1848. The Boers resented this action, and the British quelled their unrest at the Battle of Boomplaats (29 August 1848).

The Sand River Convention of 17 January 1852 recognized, with limitations, the independence of the Transvaal, and the independence of the Orange Free State was granted in 1854. The Transvaal was renamed the South African Republic (ZAR, or Zuid-Afrikaansche Republiek) in 1853, although it continued to be called the Transvaal in ordinary conversation. In 1864, the Transvaal was welded into one republic with one president.

Purportedly to prevent financial bankruptcy and potential anarchy, the British annexed the Transvaal in 1877 as a first step to federate South Africa. This was one factor leading to the First Boer War (1880–1881), in which the British were soundly defeated. In 1884, Transvaal independence was restored, with the British retaining a veto over external affairs.

Gold was discovered on the Witwatersrand in 1886. This caused an influx of foreigners *(uitlanders)* trying to make their fortune, but the Transvaal Government, in an attempt to maintain their Boer supremacy, refused to give viable political rights to these new immigrants. It was to help these immigrants receive political rights and to return the gold-rich Transvaal to the British Empire that Cecil J. Rhodes planned and Dr. Leander Starr Jameson led the ill-fated Jameson Raid to Johannesburg in 1895–1896. The resultant friction led to a treaty of mutual assistance between the Transvaal and the Orange Free State in 1897 and the outbreak of war with Britain in October 1899.

The Transvaal was reannexed by the British in 1900, but guerrilla warfare continued. The Treaty of Vereeniging, 31 May 1902, ended the Second Boer War and made the Transvaal (and the Orange Free State) a Crown colony of the British Empire. The Transvaal was granted self-government in 1907 and in 1910 was one of the four founding provinces of the Union of South Africa.

See also Boer War, First (1880–1881); Boer War, Second (1899–1902); Boers; Boomplaats, Battle of; Jameson Raid; Joubert, Commandant-General Petrus J.; Kruger, S. J. Paulus; Rhodes, Cecil J.

References: Barthorp (1987); Marix Evans (2000); Pakenham (1979); Wessels (2000);

Turkish Forces, Crimean War

The Turkish-led army of the Ottoman Empire was a very heterogeneous organization, including Muslim soldiers from its various provinces, such as Egypt, Serbia, the Danubian provinces, the Middle East, and North Africa. Numbering about 300,000 during the Crimean War, the Turkish Army consisted of conscripts who served for a period of twelve years, five on active duty and seven in the reserve.

Beginning in 1794, efforts were made to remodel the Turkish Army on a French and Russian model. The Janissaries, the elite, well-trained force of the Ottoman sultan, had become increasingly ineffective and politically unreliable and resisted these reforms. In 1826, the sultan ordered his artillery to bombard the Janissary barracks. Over 10,000 Janissaries were killed before they were disarmed and the force disbanded by ethnic Turks.

Since that time, the Turks created a modern military medical school and in 1834, a military academy. Foreign officers, many of them British, were brought to Turkey to assist in reforming, reorganizing, and training the Turkish Army. This was also a period of high fiscal inflation in Turkey, and the army did not receive the funding it needed.

The commander of Turkish forces during the Crimean War was Omar Pasha, a courageous officer. His original name was Michael Lattas, the son of a Croatian Army officer who converted to Islam and joined the Ottoman Army.

The Turkish Army was not fully equipped or adequately trained when Russia attacked in 1853. The Turkish infantry consisted of 38 regiments of poorly trained but loyal and fierce soldiers, armed with smoothbore muskets. There were 140 Turkish cavalry squadrons, each with an establishment of 143 horses, but these were also poorly equipped and ineffectively led. Turkish artillerymen and engineers did not have modern equipment or training at the beginning of the war, although they reportedly received British artillery during the conflict. The Turks had very few transportation assets and basically no commissariat, so they were forced to live off the land and suffered horribly during the harsh winter of 1854–1855.

The Turks also had a number of irregular forces, including frequently unreliable Bedouin cavalry units and Bashi-Bazouks. The latter (Turkish for "spoiled head") were very ill disciplined and undependable, little more than looters and bandits.

Many foreign, including British, officers volunteered to serve with Turkish Army units. They were generally junior officers, and the more senior Turkish commanders frequently delegated their authority to these better-trained and more audacious officers.

The British and French looked down on the Turks, and the Russians hated them. The allies generally restricted the Turks to minor roles in battles. Turkish casualties during the Crimean War probably numbered in the hundreds of thousands.

See also Crimean War; French Forces, Crimean War; Russian Forces, Crimean War; Sardinian Forces, Crimean War

References: Edgerton (1999); Judd (1975); Raugh (1988b); Royle (2000)

Ulundi, Battle of (4 July 1879)

The British soundly defeated the Zulu Army at the Battle of Ulundi, fought on 4 July 1879 near the royal homestead of Zulu King Cetshwayo kaMpande. This was the decisive battle of the 1879 Zulu War in which Zulu power was shattered.

After the disastrous Battle of Isandlwana (22 January 1879), additional troops were sent from England to augment the British forces in South Africa, commanded by Lieutenant General (later General) Frederick A. Thesiger, Second Baron Chelmsford. While most of these reinforcements arrived in March and April 1879, logistical and administrative preparations delayed the second British invasion of Zululand until 31 May 1879. This advance was marred by the death on 1 June 1879 of Louis Napoleon, the Prince Imperial of France.

In mid June 1879, as his force was about 50 miles from Ulundi, Chelmsford learned that he was to be replaced by General (later Field Marshal Viscount) Sir Garnet J. Wolseley. Chelmsford had no intention of permitting Wolseley to receive the rewards of his months of campaigning and preparations and pushed his force to advance more quickly. As Chelmsford's force neared Ulundi, halfhearted negotiations took place between the British and Cetshwayo.

The British reconnoitered the approach to Ulundi on 3 July 1879, and Chelmsford planned to attack the Zulus the following day. Early on 4 July, Chelmsford formed his 5,317-man force (of which 1,152 were Africans) into one large rectangular-shaped, "square" tactical formation, hoping to goad the Zulus into attacking. As the square advanced, the lead and rear faces were shorter than its right and left side. Five companies of the 80th Regiment, with two Gatling guns in the center and two artillery pieces on each flank, formed the front face of the square. The right side contained eight companies of 1st Battalion, 13th Light Infantry, and four companies of the 58th Regiment, with two guns in the center of the 13th and two guns between the battalions. On the opposite left flank were all eight companies of the 90th Light Infantry and four companies of the 94th Regiment, with two guns between battalions. The rear face of the square was covered by two companies of the 94th on the left and two companies of the 2nd Battalion, 21st Fusiliers on the right, with two guns in the right rear corner. Chelmsford and his staff, with engineer, ammunition, and hospital elements, were in the center of the square.

The square wheeled right at about 8:00 A.M., so that its longer sides faced north and south and the 80th Regiment's companies faced east toward Ulundi. As doubts arose about the Zulus attacking, the Frontier Light Horse appeared, and Zulu regiments waiting in the grass, one after another, sprang to their feet near the British square and soon encircled its northern, eastern, and southern sides. Elements of the King's Dragoon Guards and 17th Lancers that had been protecting the square's flanks fired into the attacking Zulus and then rode through a rear gap into the square.

The British artillery opened up on the Zulus at a range of 2,000 yards, which spurred on the attackers' advance. As the Zulus got closer, the Gatling guns also opened up, and this concentration of fire broke up the assault. The Zulu reserve attacked the southwest corner of the square, but the artillery and massed rifle fire halted this attack. Not a single Zulu reached the British bayonets.

Chelmsford recognized this decisive moment in the battle, and he directed the 17th Lancers and King's Dragoon Guards to depart the square. The cavalry formed in a line and charged the fleeing Zulus, "spearing them with their long lances as though they were pig-sticking" (Barthorp 1980, p. 163). Frontier Horse rode through a gap in the opposite end of the square and routed the remaining Zulus.

The battle was over in about half an hour. The British suffered 10 men killed and 87 wounded, some shot by Zulus with firearms. At least 1,000 Zulu dead were counted around the square, and many others were killed during the cavalry pursuit or later died of wounds. Even though Cetshwayo was not captured at the time, Chelmsford vindicated himself to a degree and deprived Wolseley of the opportunity to reap the laurels for successfully concluding the campaign. The Battle of Ulundi was the last large engagement of the Zulu War, which ended with the capture of Cetshwayo on 28 August 1879.

See also Cetshwayo kaMpande; Chelmsford, General Frederick A. Thesiger, Second Baron; Isandlwana, Battle of; Machine Guns; Wolseley, Field Marshal Garnet J.; Zulu War; Zululand
References: Barthorp (1980); Edgerton (1988); Knight (1990); Laband (1995); Morris (1965)

V

Vaal Krantz, Battle of (5–7 February 1900)

The Battle of Vaal Krantz was the third unsuccessful British attempt to relieve besieged Ladysmith.

After failure at the Battle of Spion Kop (23–24 January 1900) General Sir Redvers H. Buller, V.C., commanding the British troops in Natal, prepared another offensive operation to relieve Ladysmith. The Boer left flank was anchored on Vaal Krantz, a hill that dominated the eastern end of the Brakfontein Ridge and was about 4 miles east of Spion Kop. Buller's plan was to seize Vaal Krantz and, after supporting artillery was positioned on the hill to provide supporting fire, to send forward his cavalry to relieve Ladysmith.

The British attack began at 6:00 A.M. on 5 February 1900 with a feint from the British-held Maconochie Hills, north of the Tugela River, toward the Brakfontein Ridge. British guns on numerous hills supported the feint, while artillery on Swaartz Kop bombarded Vaal Krantz.

Determined to avoid the confusion that dominated the Spion Kop battle, Buller, who had about 20,000 men, did not commit the main attack until the feint was completed. This reduced the element of surprise and permitted the Boers to concentrate their forces in the area of the expected attack. A hesitant Buller allowed Major General (later General Sir) Neville G. Lyttelton's 4th Brigade to attack Vaal Krantz in late afternoon.

With two of Lyttelton's battalions across the Tugela, two battalions of Major General H. J. T. Hildyard's 2nd Brigade were prepared to cross the river and support the main attack by capturing Green Hill. The plan was that with both Vaal Krantz and Green Hill in British hands, the defile between the two hills would be secured, and British cavalry and infantry could advance to Ladysmith. Buller was seemingly concerned about being responsible for another failed attack and vacillated. He halted the advance of Hildyard's troops, which condemned the plan to failure, even if Lyttelton's force could have captured Vaal Krantz alone.

Lyttelton's troops continued the assault, and by 4:00 P.M., they had established weak positions on the southern and eastern sides of the hill. Buller ordered Lyttelton to withdraw, but he ignored the directive. Under intense pressure, Lyttelton moved his men to the western side of the hill to dig entrenchments and await reinforcements. Buller, however, refused to attack Green Hill or reinforce Lyttelton's men, deferring a decision to the next morning.

As Buller slept the night of 5–6 February 1900, the Boers reinforced their positions and moved artillery onto nearby hills and dominated Vaal Krantz. On the morning of 6 February, Buller gave a number of contradictory orders, then contacted his superior, Field Marshal Lord (later Earl) Frederick S. Roberts, V.C., ostensibly for guidance but more likely to receive an order to retire and be absolved of the responsibility for it. Roberts ordered Buller to continue the attack to relieve Ladysmith. Desultory artillery firing and skirmishes occupied the day, and some of Hildyard's troops replaced Lyttelton's on Vaal Krantz.

Buller held a council of war with many of his subordinate generals in the afternoon of 7 February 1900. After heated discussions, the generals unanimously agreed with Buller to withdraw. Buller had apparently underestimated the Boer tenacity and lost his resolve, and "his generalship was so singular that he had again managed to manoeuvre a British force much superior in numbers into a hopelessly untenable position" (Symons 1963, pp. 257–258). The British lost about 30 men killed and 350 wounded in this feeble attempt to relieve Ladysmith, while the Boers suffered about 30 men killed and about 50 wounded. Surprisingly, the British troops did not lose confidence in Buller, although officers behind his back called him "Sir Reverse Buller" and "the ferryman of the Tugela" (Powell 1994, p. 170).

See also Boer War, Second (1899–1902); Boers; Buller, General Sir Redvers H., V.C.; Ladysmith, Siege of; Roberts, Field Marshal Frederick S., V.C.; Spion Kop, Battle of

References: Belfield (1975); Carver (1999); Lyttelton (1924); Pakenham (1979); Powell (1994); Symons (1963)

Victoria Cross

The Victoria Cross, Great Britain's most highly coveted decoration for bravery and courage, was instituted on 29 January 1856 by Queen Victoria, reportedly at the request of Prince Albert. The Victoria Cross was unique in being the first British Army gallantry award to be awarded to deserving recipients, regardless of rank, who, "serving in the presence of the enemy, should have performed some signal act of valor or devotion to their country" (This England 1981, p. 6).

At the middle of the nineteenth century there were no tangible means of recognizing gallantry in the field, other than the occasional brevet promotion for the deserving captain, major, or lieutenant colonel, or a mention in dispatches, even though campaign medals for all participants, and later long service and good conduct and "meritorious service" medals, had been established. In the 1840s a number of senior officers recommended creating a military decoration that could be awarded to all ranks for gallantry in the field. In 1845, the *United Service Magazine*, a staunch advocate of military medals, predicted that an order for courage under fire would be named after Queen Victoria.

The unmitigated and well-publicized bravery of soldiers in the Crimean War reinforced the need for a medal recognizing combat gallantry. In December 1854, the Distinguished Conduct Medal was established to recognize sergeants and lower ranks who distinguished themselves in action. When the Victoria Cross (V.C.) was established in January 1856, its provisions were made retroactive to acts of heroism performed since the beginning of the Crimean War in March 1854. As Queen Victoria herself is said to have pointed out, the V.C. was not an order, offered no knighthood, bore no religious significance, and contained no ranks within itself. The Victoria Cross was intended solely as a decoration "to be highly prized and eagerly sought after by the officers and men of our naval and military services" (This England 1981, p. 6).

Queen Victoria herself chose the design for this decoration. It is in the form of a cross pattee on which is a lion guardant standing on the Royal Crown, with a scroll inscribed "For Valour" underneath. The reverse of the medallion contains the date of the action for which the decoration was awarded. The Victoria Cross was traditionally made from the bronze of cannons captured at Sevastopol during the Crimean War, although this supply was exhausted in March 1942. The original V.C. ribbon was blue for the navy and dark red (claret) for the army, the latter color adopted for all awards in 1920.

The first deed of valor to win the Victoria Cross took place on 21 June 1854, when twenty-year-old Mate Charles D. Lucas of H.M.S. *Hecla* distinguished himself during a naval attack on the fortress of Bomarsund in the Baltic. At a range of only 500 yards, a live shell with the fuse still burning landed on his ship's deck. Disregarding his own safety, Lucas picked up the shell with his bare hands and threw it overboard. The shell exploded as it hit the water, but Lucas's selfless bravery saved the crew and the ship from certain destruction or severe damage. Lucas was also promoted on the spot to lieutenant and eventually rose to the rank of rear admiral.

Further Royal Warrants over the years amended eligibility requirements for the Victoria Cross. In 1857 the European officers and men of the East India Company were declared eligible for the V.C., and the following year civilians who had distinguished themselves in the Indian Mutiny were also considered eligible (and was so granted in four cases). Officers and men of the colonial forces became eligible for the V.C. in 1867. In 1902 King Edward VII issued an order to award the Victoria Cross posthumously to deserving recipients, retroactive to the Crimean War. The award was further extended to native officers and men of the Indian Army by King George V in 1912. Pensions were granted to all awardees below commissioned rank. Moreover, anyone who had received the V.C. but was later convicted of treason, cowardice, felony, or "of any other infamous act," would be required to forfeit his medal and have his name erased from the list of V.C. recipients. Eight cases of forfeiture have taken place since the decoration was instituted in 1856, the last in 1908.

The first award of the Victoria Cross was announced in the *London Gazette* of 24 February 1857, and the first investiture was held in Hyde Park on 26 June 1857. Queen Victoria presented the new decoration that bore her name to sixty-two officers and men from the navy and from the army. All recipients, regardless of rank, stood shoulder to shoulder, the first time that officers and men had attended the same investiture or had been awarded the same decoration.

Holders of the Victoria Cross, Britain's preeminent gallantry award—of which 522 were awarded from institution to the eve of World War I—are entitled to use the initials "V.C." after their name.

See also Awards and Decorations; Campaign Medals
References: Dorling (1974); Farwell (1981); Gordon (1971); Raugh (1986); Strachan (1984); This England (1981)

Volunteers

The volunteers were one of the three main components, along with the militia and the yeomanry, of the auxiliary forces of the British Army in the nineteenth century.

Historically, the volunteers were supposedly self-sufficient forces raised during crises, notably during the 1650s, 1660s, 1715, 1745, and from 1778 to 1782. After the Napoleonic Wars, the volunteers were disbanded in 1816.

War scares after the revolutions in 1848 in Europe, and concern about the increasing powers and expansionist intentions of France, produced new enthusiasm for volunteering for part-time military service. Reestablished in 1859, elements of the Rifle Volunteer Corps (and some artillery and engineer units), consisting of middle-class volunteers, were raised in and funded by many towns in England. The British Government did not object to these units, since they consisted of middle-class recruits while most members of the militia were from the lower class. In 1860–1863, the Rifle Volunteer Corps units were organized into administrative battalions. In 1871, the War Office assumed administrative responsibility for the volunteer forces.

As a component of the linked battalion system completed in 1881, the Rifle Volunteer Corps units became volunteer battalions of regular infantry regiments. An example of this reorganization is the 1st Yorkshire East Riding Rifle Volunteer Corps which became the 1st Volunteer Battalion of the East Yorkshire Regiment.

In the 1880s and early 1890s, military debate frequently focused on home defense and the role of the volunteers. Many volunteers served on active service, however. The Post Office Volunteers and the Crewe Railway Volunteers served in the 1882 British expedition to Egypt. After the British defeat at Colenso (15 December 1899), some 6,000 volunteers joined the Imperial Yeomanry and manned blockhouses, among other duties, during the Second Boer War (1899–1902).

In 1908, the auxiliary forces were reorganized to provide a more effective and efficient system for reinforcing the regular army. The volunteers (infantry) and yeomanry (part-time cavalry) were merged as the Territorial Force, later to become the Territorial Army. This provided a reserve force of 14 infantry divisions and 14 cavalry brigades that in peacetime would serve in the United Kingdom only, but in wartime could volunteer for overseas service.

See also Boer War, Second (1899–1902); Haldane, Richard B.; Militia; Yeomanry
References: Bennett (1999); Brereton (1986); Mills (1996); Spiers (1992); Strachan (1984); Thomson (1986); Woodall (1900)

W

War of the Axe
See Cape Frontier Wars, Southern Africa

War Office

The War Office was the office of the civilian leadership of the British Army until 1870, when the formerly independent commander in chief and military component (the Horse Guards) became a part of it. Throughout this period the name did not change, although the composition of the War Office evolved with the development of the British Army.

In the 1790s, the secretary at war was the executive head of military administration. His department, the War Office, was in charge of controlling movements, establishments, and rates of pay. The secretary at war was also responsible to Parliament in the Army Estimates and over any issues in which civil and military interests were in conflict.

The position of secretary of state for war and the colonies was created in 1794. The first incumbent, Henry Dundas, also served as home secretary, treasurer of the navy, and president of the Indian Board of Control, and could spend only a fraction of his time and energy on military matters.

Throughout the nineteenth century there was continual friction between the War Office and the Horse Guards as the former tried to establish Parliamentary and civilian control over the latter, which the Horse Guards generally resisted as much as possible. There were also numerous reforms designed to ensure unity of command and control. At the end of the Napoleonic Wars, this unity was still lacking, as responsibility for the British Army was divided between the secretary at war, secretary of state for war and the colonies, treasury, commander in chief, and master-general of the ordnance.

The British success in the Napoleonic Wars, culminating with Field Marshal Arthur Wellesley, First Duke of Wellington's defeat of Napoleon at Waterloo in 1815, began a long period of military complacency, neglect, and decay. The death of the Duke of Wellington in 1852 removed a significant obstacle to reform. While reform on a limited basis began before the outbreak of the Crimean War in 1854, the lack of British preparedness for that conflict soon became scandalous and reinforced the urgent need for military reform.

Until the beginning of the Crimean War, the army was administered by about thirteen different departments. Even before the Crimean War began, radical reform was undertaken that established the primacy of civilian control over the military. In June 1854, the office of secretary of state for war was separated from that of the colonies, the first time Great Britain possessed a full-time secretary of state solely for military affairs. The post of secretary at war, which had been responsible for the Army Estimates and other financial matters, was eliminated and his responsibilities also consolidated under the secretary of state for war. All military departments came under the authority of the secretary of state for war. Most of the other Crimean War–era reforms helped consolidate the authority and responsibility of the secretary of state for war. The prevailing attitude that the army "belonged" to the sovereign and had to be weakened by external checks and a divided administration was abandoned. Parliamentary and civilian control of the military was unquestionably achieved for the first time.

Even though the commander in chief conceded that the secretary of state for war exercised supreme control of the army, he remained outside the consolidated War Office. There was a tremendous duplication of effort, with two separate headquarters (War Office and Horse Guards) and ill-defined and overlapping responsibilities. In 1869, the Northbrook Committee studied these issues, most of which were implemented in the War Office Act of 1870, one of the significant reforms of Secretary of State for War Edward T. Cardwell. The War Office Act of 1870 consolidated the War Office and the Horse Guards. It also delegated its responsibilities to three distinct executive officers: the "officer commanding in chief" (Field Marshal H.R.H. Prince George F., Second Duke of Cambridge), responsible for the strictly military aspects of the army; the surveyor-general of the ordnance, responsible for supply and equipment; and the financial secretary, responsible to the secretary of state for war for the Army Estimates and all military financial matters.

To further streamline the administrative efficiency of the War Office, Secretary of State for War Edward Stanhope enacted additional reforms in 1888. He abolished the position of surveyor-general of the ordnance and unified all the principal departments, with the exception of finance and military manufacturing, under the commander in chief. Supply and transport responsibilities were transferred to the quartermaster-general. The commander in chief, henceforth, became responsible for all personnel and matéeriel issues for the army and auxiliary forces, in addition to the collection of intelligence and the construction and maintenance of fortifications.

Controversy sprang up after invasion scares in 1888 with the commander in chief and key subordinates declaring that they could not be responsible for the efficiency of the army or for the defense of the country if they had no financial control over the military. The Hartington Commission was formed to look into this situation and found that the army and navy generally failed to coordinate any type of planning. It recommended the establishment of a defense committee in which army, navy, and cabinet ministers could coordinate their activities within imperial defense policies and service expenditures before the actual financial estimates were submitted to the Cabinet.

The Hartington Commission also recommended eliminating the office of commander in chief after the Duke of Cambridge's retirement and replacing it with a War Office Council. The council would consist of the secretary of state for war as president, the parliamentary and permanent undersecretaries, and the five senior military officers responsible to the secretary of state for the efficient operations of their respective departments. These five officers were the adjutant-general, the quartermaster-general, the director of artillery, the inspector-general of fortifications, and a chief of the staff. The chief of the staff would advise the secretary of state and coordinate intelligence collection and analysis and contingency and mobilization planning. A truncated War Office Council, without a chief of the staff, was in fact established, and in 1895 it was supplemented by an Army Board.

The Duke of Cambridge retired in 1895 and was replaced by Field Marshal Viscount Garnet J. Wolseley. Concurrently, changes were made in the duties of the commander in chief, who would also accept the responsibilities of a chief of staff. As such, he was still the principal adviser of the secretary of state on all military questions, would take direct control of the Intelligence and Mobilization Departments, and was charged with "general supervision" of the military departments of the War Office. The adjutant-general, quartermaster-general, inspector-general of fortifications, and inspector-general of the ordnance were made directly responsible to the secretary of state and, together with the commander in chief (serving as president), would compose the Army Board. The civilian financial secretary retained his authority in all financial matters. The military leadership, and especially the commander in chief, resented these changes, and the rift between the soldiers and the civilians in the War Office was widened even further.

The Second Boer War broke out in October 1899 and it soon became obvious that the British Army could have been much better prepared for the conflict. Wolseley, generally embittered, retired on 30 November 1900. Shortly thereafter, the Dawkins Committee of Inquiry was formed to look into the whole organization and operations of the War Office. The committee recommended a number of reforms that were enacted in November 1901, including the subordination (again) of the adjutant-general, military secretary, and director of mobilization and military intelligence to the commander in chief. The commander in chief was also made responsible for the discipline, training, mobilization, and staff planning of the forces under his command.

A Royal Commission on the War in South Africa, appointed in 1902 and named the Elgin Commission after its chairman, the Earl of Elgin, investigated administrative shortcomings that had been revealed by the Second Boer War, as did a subsequent committee, the War Office Reconstitution Committee. The latter was chaired by Lord Esher and became known as the Esher Committee. Its recommendations, made in 1904, also had a far-reaching impact on War Office and military reorganization.

Richard B. Haldane, secretary of state for war from 1905 to 1912, was also responsible for a number of reforms involving the War Office. He was responsible for consolidating the militia and volunteers and establishing the Territorial Force, and organizing the British Army into an expeditionary force in case of Continental deployment. Moreover, in 1906 he formally instituted and organized a general staff, and enumerated comprehensive duties and responsibilities for all general staff sections. Field Service Regulations provided common doctrine to be used throughout the army. Haldane's War Office and other reforms needed only minor adjustments prior to 1914, when Great Britain was plunged into World War I.

> **See also** Adjutant-General, British Army; Army Estimates; Boer War, Second (1899–1902); Cambridge, Field Marshal H.R.H. Prince George F., Second Duke of; Cardwell, Edward T.; Civil-Military Relations; Commander in Chief, British Army; Crimean War; Esher Committee; Haldane, Richard B.; Horse Guards; Master-General of the Ordnance, British Army; Quartermaster-General, British Army; Stanhope, Edward; Wellington, Field Marshal Arthur Wellesley, First Duke of; Wolseley, Field Marshal Garnet J.
>
> **References:** Barnett (1970); Bond (1972); Haldane (1929); Hamer (1970); Moyse-Bartlett (1974); Spiers (1980b); Spiers (1992); Strachan (1984); Strachan (1997)

War Office Act (1870)

See Cambridge, Field Marshal H.R.H. Prince George F., Second Duke of; Cardwell, Edward T.; Cardwell Reforms; Commander in Chief, British Army; War Office

Warren, General Sir Charles (1840–1927)

General Sir Charles Warren, a Royal Engineer officer, had a varied military career, most noteworthy for his archeological achievements and his command of British troops at the disastrous Battle of Spion Kop (23–24 January 1900) during the Second Boer War.

Warren was born in North Wales in 1840. His father was an Indian Army officer who later became a general, and the younger Warren was seemingly destined for a military career. Warren was educated at Cheltenham and commissioned into the Royal Engineers in 1857. He conducted surveys of Gibraltar from 1858 to 1865, when he became an instructor at the School of Military Engineering at Chatham. Between 1867 and 1870 he carried out explorations in Palestine of the topography of ancient Jerusalem and the archaeology of the Temple Mount/Haram al-Sherif area.

In 1876, Warren surveyed the border between the Orange Free State and Griqualand West, and was in South Africa when the Ninth Cape Frontier War broke out in 1877, in which he commanded the Diamond Field Horse. He returned to engineer instructor duty in England in 1878 but was selected for a special mission in 1882. His task was to find a Professor Palmer and his party who had disappeared while trying to rally the support of Sinai Bedouins in the British war against Egypt. Warren was able to ascertain that Palmer had been killed and brought the culprits to justice, receiving a knighthood for his performance.

Warren returned to Chatham in 1882 and in 1884 commanded the British expedition in Bechuanaland, which was established as a Crown Colony. He commanded the British garrison at Suakin, on the Red Sea, for a short time before becoming commissioner of the Metropolitan Police in London. His tenure was controversial, including the use of heavy-handed measures to suppress socialist meetings. The failure of the police to solve the Jack the Ripper murders in 1888 forced both the home secretary and Warren to resign their positions.

In 1889, Warren became commander of troops at Singapore, was promoted to major general in 1893, and returned to England in 1895 to become general officer commanding Thames and Medway District. He was promoted to lieutenant general in 1897. After the outbreak of the Second Boer War in October 1899, Warren was appointed to command the 5th Division in South Africa, under General Sir Redvers H. Buller, V.C., who was attempting to relieve Ladysmith.

Warren's selection was somewhat surprising, because of his age (fifty-nine), tactlessness, disagreeable temper, lack of recent troop experience, and previous disagreements with Buller. The relationship was made worse when Buller was informed that Warren held the "dormant commission," instructions to succeed Buller if he was killed or incapacitated.

Warren was put in charge of the January 1900 operation to relieve Ladysmith by outflanking the Boers to the west of Spion Kop. The ponderous advance began on 16 January, and initial efforts to seize Spion Kop were ineffectual. A night assault, 23–24 January, was successful, and by dawn on 24 January the British had taken the hill—and then realized their defensive trench was in the center of a large plateau sloping toward the enemy in the north. Boer artillery, virtually unopposed, pounded the British infantry, and Boer marksmen enfiladed the British trench. Command and control was a problem, both on Spion Kop and between British forces there and Warren, who had to rely on messengers. When Warren became aware of the critical nature of the battle, he failed to order a diversionary attack. Despite British reinforcements straggling in, the ebb and flow of battle and fierce hand-to-hand fighting continued for much of the day. When night fell, the British thought they were in an untenable position and withdrew from Spion Kop; the Boers, discouraged by their apparent failure to dislodge the British, were about to give up but reoccupied the summit and claimed victory. The British claimed their losses as 322 killed, 583 wounded, and 300 prisoners of war, but this may have been an underestimate. Buller placed the blame for the debacle on Warren, who was reassigned to Griqualand West and returned to England in August 1900.

Warren was promoted to general in 1904, retired the same year, and died in 1927.

See also Boer War, Second (1899–1902); Buller, General Sir Redvers H., V.C.; Cape Frontier Wars, Southern Africa; Spion Kop, Battle of
References: Pakenham (1979); Ransford (1969); Spiers (1992); Symons (1963)

Wauchope, Major General Andrew G. (1846–1899)

Major General Andrew G. Wauchope fought in many of the British military campaigns of the last quarter of the nineteenth century. He was killed leading the Highland Brigade at the disastrous Battle of Magersfontein (11 December 1899).

Wauchope was born on 5 July 1846 in Edinburgh, a scion of a wealthy family with a distinguished record of service to the Crown. Wauchope became a naval cadet in 1859 and a midshipman the following year. In 1862, he was discharged from the Royal Navy and became an ensign by purchase in the 42nd Highlanders (Black Watch). After routine training and garrison duty, Wauchope deployed with his battalion to serve in the Second Ashanti War (1873–1874) and was wounded severely on two separate occasions.

After recuperating, Wauchope rejoined his battalion and served on Malta (1875–1878) and Cyprus (1878–1880). He returned to the United Kingdom and was in the group of reinforcements sent to Natal in late 1880 during the First Boer War (1880–1881) but saw no action. In 1882, he served in the expedition sent to Egypt to suppress the Arabi Rebellion and fought at Tel el-Kebir (13 September 1882). Wauchope subsequently served on occupation duty in Egypt, participated in the Gordon Relief Expedition (1884–1885), and was wounded at the Battle of Kirbekan (10 February 1885).

Wauchope again served on Malta (1886–1889), then on Gibraltar (1889–1891). After returning to Scotland, he assumed command of the 2nd Battalion, Black Watch, in 1892. Wauchope and his battalion performed well in the military maneuvers in Sussex in the fall of 1897, and the following summer, when a British force was being assembled for the reconquest of the Sudan, Wauchope was designated the commander of the 1st Brigade, British Division. At the Battle of Omdurman (2 September 1898), Wauchope, "cool as a statue" (Baird 1907, p. 154), moved his brigade at a crucial moment to fill a gap in the British force threatened by enemy cavalry. For his superb leadership, Wauchope was promoted to major general.

Only days after the outbreak of the Second Boer War on 11 October 1899, Wauchope was appointed commander of the 3rd (Highland) Brigade. After arrival in South Africa and movement to the Modder River area, the Highland Brigade participated in operations designed to relieve Kimberley, protected by the Magersfontein and Spytfontein ridges. To capture the former, the British planned a night approach march and dawn bayonet attack, similar to the assault on Tel el-Kebir, led by the Highland Brigade.

Wauchope reportedly had misgivings about the plan but did not mention this to his superior, Lieutenant General (later Field Marshal) Lord Methuen, 1st Division commander. An artillery bombardment was conducted on the afternoon of 10 December 1899 but did little except alert the Boers to an imminent attack. After midnight, the 3,500-man Highland Brigade, in stormy weather and over rough terrain, began its approach march. Surprisingly, navigation was initially accurate, and the British were within 1,000 yards of the Magersfontein hill when dawn began to break. The staff officer navigating and two battalion commanders recommended to Wauchope that the brigade lines be extended, but Wauchope recklessly pressed on with the advance. When the lead elements were about 400 yards from the hidden Boer trenches, the Boers opened fire, and for about nine hours the British were pinned down. Even though British reinforcements were sent, the nerve of the Highland Brigade soldiers, during a period of confusion and terror, broke and they ran. Wauchope was killed, as were 201 other soldiers of the Highland Brigade, with 496 wounded. He was initially interred on the battlefield but was reburied a week later near Matjesfontein, 400 miles to the south.

See also Boer War, Second (1899–1902); Buller, General Sir Redvers H., V.C.; Cape Frontier Wars, Southern Africa; Spion Kop, Battle of

References: Baird (1907); Barthorp (1984); Barthorp (1987); Pakenham (1979)

Wellington, Field Marshal Arthur Wellesley, First Duke of (1769–1852)

Field Marshal Arthur Wellesley, First Duke of Wellington, was an aristocratic soldier-politician who was the most famous general of the first half of the nineteenth century. He defeated Napoleon Bonaparte at Waterloo in 1815 and became a national hero as the "Iron Duke." During his later service as prime minister and commander in chief, Wellington's conservative attitudes and reluctance to enact reform hindered the modernization of the British Army.

Wellington, the third son of the First Earl of Mornington, was born in Dublin, Ireland, on 1 May 1769. He was gazetted an ensign in the 73rd Highland Regiment in 1787. Family connections, patronage, and wealth permitted Wellington to advance rapidly in rank, and by 1796, he was a colonel. He arrived in India in 1797 and spent the following eight years there. These years were crucial to his development as a commander, and his successes at the Battles of Seringapatam (1799), Argaum (1803), and Assaye (1803) helped establish his reputation as a careful leader who tried to limit his casualties in battle.

After various military and political appointments, Wellington participated in the expedition to Copenhagen in 1807. The following year, he was promoted to lieutenant general and appointed to command the expeditionary force being sent to Portugal to fight against Napoleon. Wellington commanded forces and fought numerous battles in the Peninsular War on the Iberian Peninsula. He was promoted to field marshal after defeating the French at the Battle of Vitorio (21 June 1813). By early 1814, his forces had crossed the Pyrenees and entered France. Napoleon abdicated (for the first time) on 12 April 1814, after which Wellington was hailed as a conquering hero, elevated in the peerage to a dukedom, and appointed ambassador to France.

After Napoleon escaped from exile on Elba in February 1815, Wellington was appointed to command the British forces that, with allies, defeated Napoleon at Waterloo on 18 June 1815.

Wellington was appointed master-general of the ordnance in 1818, and he became commander in chief of the British Army in 1827, although he resigned the following year. In 1828, Wellington became prime minister and was known as an arch-conservative. As unemployment in Great Britain increased and economic prosperity decreased, a wave of riots took place in 1830. Political reform was considered a possible solution to the unrest, but Wellington dogmatically stuck to the Tory policy of no reform and no expansion of the franchise. As a result, his government lost a vote of no confidence on 15 November 1830 and he was replaced as prime minister.

General Viscount Rowland Hill, Wellington's peninsular colleague, served as commander in chief from 1828 to 1842. Wellington again became commander in chief in 1842 and served in that position until his death in 1852. Wellington's conservatism during his second term can be attributed to increasing age as well as his involvement in political affairs, and his "opposition to a host of proposals cannot be denied: introduction of the Minié rifled musket, improved staff training, army schoolmasters, abolition of purchase, [and] pensions to N.C.O.s under certain conditions" (Sweetman 1984, p. 19). It was also difficult for subordinates to question or criticize the great soldier's opinion.

Under Hill's and Wellington's "ancient and hallowed hands, the army remained preserved like a garment in a bottom drawer, sentimentally loved, but rotted and rendered quaint by the passage of time. Even its uniforms in 1854 were still essentially those of Waterloo" (Barnett 1970, p. 282). While Wellington alone did not prevent administrative and organizational reform of the British Army, his death in 1852 was expected to encourage reform. This tide of anticipated reform was accelerated by the British Army's inadequate preparations for and initial dismal performance in the Crimean War (1854–1856).

> **See also** Commander in Chief, British Army; Crimean War; Master-General of the Ordnance, British Army; Purchase System; War Office
> **References:** Anglesey (1961); Barnett (1970); Bryant (1971); Carver (1984); Fortescue (1925); Guedalla (1931); Hooper (1889); Longford (1969); Strachan (1984); Sweetman (1984)

White, Field Marshal Sir George S., V.C. (1835–1912)

Field Marshal Sir George S. White was a British Army officer with extensive experience and service in India, earning the Victoria Cross during the Second Afghan War. During the Second Boer War, White commanded Ladysmith during its 119-day siege, and as a result he and the garrison came to personify courage and determination.

White was born in Ireland on 6 July 1835. After attending Sandhurst, he was commissioned into the Inniskilling Fusiliers and fought during the Indian Mutiny. White was second in command of the Gordon Highlanders during the Second Afghan War (1878–1880). He led an attack at the Battle of Charasia (6 October 1879) and another later at Kandahar, gallant actions that earned him the Victoria Cross. White also served in the Gordon Relief Expedition (1884–1885).

As a brigadier general, White commanded the 2nd Brigade in the short Third Burma War (1885) and remained in Burma, pacifying the area. White received his first knighthood for his services in Burma. He commanded the punitive expedition to the Zhob Valley of the North-West Frontier in 1890, and three years later succeeded General (later Field Marshal Earl) Lord Frederick S. Roberts, V.C., as commander in chief, India. White advocated an aggressive forward policy in India.

In 1898, White returned to England and became quartermaster-general at the War Office. After the outbreak of the Second Boer War the following year, White was appointed second in command to General Sir Redvers H. Buller, V.C., and general officer commanding Natal. After arriving in Natal, White, who was seemingly ignorant of the realities of modern warfare, again began to think of a forward policy. After two small battles, White considered achieving what he thought would be the decisive victory of the war.

White devised a rigid, reckless plan to attack the Boers and attempted to execute the attack on 30 October 1899. This was arguably "the greatest strategic mistake of the entire war" (Pakenham 1979, p. 155), and the result—Mournful Monday—was Britain's worst military defeat since the Battle of Majuba during the First Boer War. White was on the verge of being relieved of command for incompetence when his force was besieged in Ladysmith on 2 November 1899. White's health deteriorated during the siege, and when it ended on 28 February 1900, he returned to England.

White then served as governor of Gibraltar (1901–1904) and was promoted to field marshal in 1903. In 1905, White became governor of Chelsea Hospital and died in 1912.

> **See also** Afghan War, Second (1878–1880); Boer War, Second (1899–1902); Buller, General Sir Redvers H., V.C.; Burma War, Third (1885); Charasia, Battle of; Ladysmith, Siege of; Quartermaster-General, British Army; Roberts, Field Marshal Frederick S., V.C.; Sandhurst, Royal Military College; Victoria Cross
> **References:** Bruce (1973); Griffith (1974); Lee (2000); Pakenham (1979); Roberts (1897); Sixsmith (1970)

White Sea Operations, Crimean War

The Royal Navy conducted minor blockade operations in the White Sea during the Crimean War.

In July 1854, a small British naval squadron of three ships—the 26-gun steamship *Eurydice*, the 16-gun screw corvette *Brisk*, and the *Miranda*—conducted an aggressive although necessarily partial blockade of the White Sea. After bombarding Kola in northern Lapland, this squadron sailed into the White Sea in August 1854 and then attacked Solovetski Island in the Gulf of Onega. While conducting their blockade operations in the White Sea in 1854, this squadron boldly boarded and examined over 300 merchant vessels, seizing any that could be legally claimed as war prizes.

> **See also** Baltic Sea Operations, Crimean War; Crimean War; Pacific Ocean Operations, Crimean War
> **References:** Judd (1975); Royle (2000)

Whitworth Rifled Breechloader
See Artillery, British Army—Weapons and Equipment

Willcocks, Colonel James
See Ashanti War

Williams, Major General Sir William Fenwick

See Kars, Siege of

Wilson, Brigadier General Sir Archdale

See Delhi, Siege and Storming of

Wilson, Major General Sir Charles W. (1836–1905)

Major General Sir Charles W. Wilson was a highly professional Royal Engineer officer who took part in numerous boundary, ordnance, and topographical surveys around the world. Even though his career culminated as director-general of military education, Wilson is probably best known for his role in the 1884–1885 Gordon Relief Expedition.

Wilson was born in Liverpool in 14 March 1836. Educated at Cheltenham College, he was commissioned a lieutenant in 1855 in the first open admission to the Royal Engineers. After military training and postings in England, Wilson was assigned in 1858 to the North American Boundary Commission in Canada. He returned to England in 1863, and from 1864 to 1869 conducted the Ordnance Surveys of Jerusalem (and other explorations in Palestine), Scotland, and the Sinai.

In 1869, Wilson became executive officer of the Topographical and Statistical (T&S) Department of the War Office. The following year the Ordnance Survey was separated from the T&S Department, and Wilson, only a captain, became director of the latter. He was instrumental in the reorganization of the department and establishment of the Intelligence Branch in 1873, of which he became assistant adjutant-general, serving in that position for three years. Wilson was in charge of the Irish Ordnance Survey (1876–1879), then served in sensitive political-military positions in Serbia, Anatolia, Rumelia, and (after being knighted in 1881) as official observer to the trial of Arabi Pasha in Egypt in 1882. He returned to Ireland in 1883.

Wilson was appointed deputy adjutant-general and chief of intelligence for the 1884–1885 Gordon Relief Expedition, commanded by Lieutenant General (later Field Marshal Viscount) Sir Garnet J. Wolseley. Wilson accompanied the Desert Column, commanded by Major General Sir Herbert Stewart, in their dash to relieve Gordon in Khartoum. At the fierce Battle of Abu Klea (17 January 1885), Lieutenant Colonel Frederick G. Burnaby, Stewart's second in command, was killed. Outside of Metemmeh, located on the Nile River, dervish forces attacked the Desert Column on 19 January 1885, and Stewart received an incapacitating wound. The command devolved on Wilson as the next senior officer.

Wilson was not sure what to do. A halfhearted attack on Metemmeh took place on 21 January 1885, when four steamers from Khartoum appeared on the Nile. Rather than use the steamers to immediately travel the 96 miles to Khartoum, Wilson spent 22 January reconnoitering the area. Finally, at about 8:00 A.M. on 24 January, Wilson took two of the steamers and headed for Khartoum, sighting the town at about 11:00 A.M. on 28 January. Khartoum had fallen and Gordon had been murdered two days earlier, on 26 January. While political procrastination and logistical difficulties had plagued the expedition from its beginning, it is difficult not to speculate on the outcome of the expedition if Wilson had steamed to Khartoum on 21 or early on 22 January. A scapegoat was needed for the failure. Wolseley recorded: "Sir Charles Wilson is clearly responsible for all those delays, but poor devil he had lost any nerve he ever possessed" (Preston 1967, p. 164).

Wilson returned to England in 1885, received a second knighthood, and immediately wrote his version of events in the Sudan, *From Korti to Khartoum: A Journal of the Desert March from Korti to Gubat, and of the Ascent of the Nile in General Gordon's Steamers*. He was in charge of the Ordnance Survey of Ireland for a short time before being appointed director-general of the Ordnance Survey of the United Kingdom in 1886. Promoted to major general in 1894, Wilson then served as director-general of military education from 1895 until retiring in 1898. He died in Kent on 25 October 1905.

See also Abu Klea, Battle of; Gordon Relief Expedition; Intelligence; Stewart, Major General Sir Herbert; Wolseley, Field Marshal Garnet J.
References: Barthorp (1984); Fergusson (1984); Mansfield (1971); Preston (1967); Symons (1965)

Wingate, General Sir (Francis) Reginald (1861–1953)

General Sir (Francis) Reginald Wingate devoted his life to service in Egypt and the Sudan. He was first assigned to Egypt as a lieutenant in 1883 and departed from the region for the last time in 1919. Despite his almost continuous and distinguished service in Egypt and the Sudan, Wingate's reputation has been eclipsed by those of Major General Charles G. Gordon, Field Marshal Earl Horatio H. Kitchener, and others.

Wingate was born on 25 June 1861 in Scotland. After graduating from Woolwich in 1880 he was commissioned a Royal Artillery lieutenant and posted to India the following year. Highly ambitious and having a skill for foreign languages, he was transferred in 1883 to Egypt and the Egyptian Army and participated in the Gordon Relief Expedition (1884–1885). In 1889, Wingate became chief of military intelligence of the Egyptian Army. A contemporary journalist observed that "whatever there was to know, Colonel Wingate surely knew it, for he makes it his business to know everything" (Steevens 1898, p. 64).

Wingate was active in the quest to avenge Gordon and defeat the French in the imperial scramble for the Sudan. Wingate was with Major General (later Field Marshal Earl) Sir Horatio H. Kitchener, the sirdar, at the Battles of Atbara (8 April 1898) and Omdurman (2 September 1898), and at Fashoda later that month. He was knighted for his services in the Sudan campaign. Wingate also commanded the forces at the Battle of Umm Diwaykarat (24 November 1899), where the Khalifa and many of his key subordinates were killed, thus ending the Mahdiya in the Sudan. In 1899, in succession to Kitchener, Wingate became sirdar (commander in chief) of the Egyptian Army and governor-general of the Sudan (1899–1916). Finally, Wingate served as high commissioner in Egypt (1916–1919). Wingate died at age ninety-one in 1953.

See also Atbara, Battle of; Egyptian Army; Fashoda Incident; Gordon, Major General Charles G.; Gordon Relief Expedition; Khalifa; Kitchener, Field Marshal Horatio H.; Omdurman, Battle of; Reconquest of the Sudan; Sirdar; Sudan; Woolwich, Royal Military Academy

References: Arthur (1920); Barthorp (1984b); Daly (1997); Neillands (1996); Steevens (1898); Wingate (1892); Wingate (1955)

Wolseley, Field Marshal Garnet J., First Viscount Wolseley of Cairo and Wolseley in the County of Stafford (1833–1913)

Field Marshal Viscount Garnet J. Wolseley dominated British military affairs to such a large extent during the second half of the nineteenth century that he was known as "our only General" (Lehmann 1964, p. 283). He epitomized unmitigated gallantry in battle and coolness under fire, was wounded on numerous occasions, and was a leading progressive and reformer with the goal of modernizing the British Army. His career culminated as British Army commander in chief (1895–1900).

Wolseley was born on 4 June 1833 in County Dublin, Ireland. His father, a retired army major, died when Wolseley was a child. After repeated applications to the Duke of Wellington, Wolseley received a commission without purchase on 21 July 1852. He was initially gazetted into the 12th Foot but immediately transferred to the 80th Foot (later the South Staffordshire Regiment), then on orders to active service in Burma.

Wolseley had a burning desire, an obsession, to excel in his military career and reach the pinnacle of his profession. He was brave almost to the point of being suicidal, and he was convinced "the best possible way to get ahead in the army was to try to get killed every time he had the chance" (Lehmann 1964, p. 13). He distinguished himself in action during the Second Burma War (1853); the Crimean War (1855–1856), when he was recommended for the Victoria Cross; the Indian Mutiny (1857–1859); and the Second China War (1860). At the age of twenty-seven, Wolseley was a lieutenant colonel—having earned each promotion without purchase—who had distinguished himself in four campaigns and had been mentioned in dispatches nine times.

In 1861, Wolseley was assigned as assistant quartermaster-general in Canada, where he spent the next decade and devoted himself to the study of the profession of arms and the testing of his theories of military organization and training. Wolseley visited the Confederate leadership during the American Civil War, and in June 1865 he was promoted to full colonel and assigned as deputy quartermaster-general. His collection of practical military information for the use of regimental officers and soldiers in the field, *Soldier's Pocket Book for Field Service,* was published in 1869. The blunt comments in this volume offended many traditionalists, but it brought him to the attention of the reform-minded secretary of state for war, Edward T. Cardwell.

In 1870, as the quartermaster-general in Canada, Wolseley was appointed to his first independent command—to lead an expedition to suppress a rebellion led by Louis Riel. The Red River Expedition (August–September 1870) was noted for its careful planning and logistical preparations, especially crucial considering the vast distances involved and lack of resupply capability.

This expedition was an unmitigated success at minimal cost, and Wolseley was knighted on his return to England.

Wolseley was gaining the reputation of a reformer and progressive thinker. He was summoned by Cardwell to the War Office in 1871 to serve as assistant adjutant-general and adviser to Cardwell on issues such as terms of service and the abolition of purchase. At the War Office, Wolseley was constantly at odds with the Field Marshal H.R.H. Prince George F., Second Duke of Cambridge, the commander in chief, over military reforms, and their adversarial relationship continued until Wolseley succeeded the Duke of Cambridge in 1895.

In 1873, the Second Ashanti War broke out and, based on his earlier successes and as a reward for his staunch support of and assistance to Cardwell, Wolseley was selected to command the expedition. He took with him a select group of officers, some of whom had served on the Red River Expedition and most of whom were to serve with him for the remainder of his career. This group, which became known as the Ashanti Ring (and later the Wolseley Ring or Wolseley Gang), was the target of much jealousy. Critics claimed Wolseley was "using the finest steel of our army to cut brushwood" (Lehmann 1964, p. 166), but in the absence of a general staff or permanent divisional structure, Wolseley was trying to be as effective and efficient as possible.

Wolseley reached Cape Coast Castle in October 1873, and his troops landed the following January. His plan was to keep his troops in the country for as short a time as possible, thereby diminishing the chances of casualties and disease contracted from the pestilent climate of the Gold Coast, known as the "white man's grave." On 21 January 1874, his troops defeated King Koffee at Amoaful, and four days later, the capital, Kumasi, was occupied. Again, this campaign epitomized flawless preparations. As a result of his relatively quick and inexpensive success in the Ashanti War, Wolseley was showered with honors on his return to England, including promotion to permanent major general and two knighthoods. Wolseley's recognition was probably also intended to subtly recognize and reinforce Cardwell's Reforms.

Wolseley became a popular hero in England. George Grossmith made himself up as Wolseley to sing "The Modern Major-General" in Gilbert and Sullivan's *The Pirates of Penzance* and caricatured his mannerisms and dress (Davis and Weavers 1927, p. 588). The press sang praises of Wolseley, whom Prime Minister Benjamin Disraeli gave the sobriquet of "our only General," and it became a national habit, in an emergency, to "send for Wolseley" (Morris 1973, p. 402). "All Sir Garnet" became the universal tonic for every national ailment, and "cough syrup and boot-polish manufacturers, as well as music-hall lyricists, who used his brand name to admonish the public, helped to perpetuate the legend of his enduring effectiveness" (Preston 1967a, p. xiii).

Wolseley continued to rise in his profession. He was assigned as governor of Natal in 1875. As a lieutenant general, Wolseley was selected in 1878 to be the high commissioner and commander in chief of the newly acquired island of Cyprus. After the British debacle at Isandlwana (22 January 1879) during the Zulu War, the government chose Wolseley to restore the situation. He replaced Lieutenant General (later General) Frederick A. Thesiger, Second Baron Chelmsford, as commander of Her Majesty's forces in South Africa, but Chelmsford won the Battle of Ulundi (4 July 1879) before Wolseley arrived in South Africa. After the capture of the Zulu chief Cetshwayo kaMpande and the suppression of the Sekukuni uprising, Wolseley returned to England in 1880. Wolseley then served as quartermaster-general before being selected as adjutant-general in 1882.

In January 1882, the Egyptian Army under Colonel Ahmed Arabi rebelled, threatening the khedive (viceroy) as well as British financial interests in and control of the Suez Canal. The British sent an expeditionary force under Wolseley's command to Egypt. This force eventually totaled 40,560 officers and men from England, and Mediterranean and Indian stations, and was one of the largest single expeditions ever dispatched by Britain to that time. Wolseley left England on 15 August 1882.

Through a feint at Alexandria and a plan that deceived some of his own generals, Wolseley captured the Egyptian garrison at Port Said and then secretly transferred his troops down the Suez Canal to Ismailia. A sharp action at Kassassin brought his force before Arabi's fortifications at Tel el-Kebir. Conducting a night march in battle formation—a maneuver almost unprecedented and seldom replicated—Wolseley seized the rebel stronghold at dawn on 13 September 1882, routed Arabi's forces, and promptly occupied Cairo. The secretary of state for war, Hugh Childers, called this "the most perfect military achievement England has seen for many a long year" (Barthorp 1984b, p. 73). As a result, Wolseley was promoted to full general and raised to the peerage as Baron Wolseley of Cairo, and Wolseley in the County of Stafford.

After his return to England, Wolseley resumed his position of adjutant-general. In January 1884, his friend, Major

Wolseley, Field Marshal Garnet J.

General Charles G. Gordon, accepted a special mission to go to the Sudan and investigate the possibility of evacuating the region after it was overrun by Muslim fanatics called dervishes. Gordon reached Khartoum early in February 1884, and on 12 March 1884 the dervish hordes descended on the Nile and laid siege to Khartoum. After considerable public and private debate and government procrastination, funding for an expedition to relieve Gordon was authorized in August 1884. Wolseley was appointed to command this expedition, and he arrived in Cairo on 9 September 1884. Finally, on 19 September, Wolseley received the order authorizing him to proceed to the rescue of Gordon, and on 8 October 1884 he received the final instructions that were to guide his mission.

The Gordon Relief Expedition, due to government procrastination and other factors, including Wolseley's route selection, was arguably a forlorn hope from the beginning. After tremendous efforts against the Nile River, deserts, and the dervishes, the expedition arrived near Khartoum on 28 January 1885, only to learn that the city had fallen and Gordon had been killed two days earlier, after holding out for 317 days.

Wolseley had believed totally in the cause of the expedition, telling his wife that "the campaign to save Gordon was on the highest level of chivalric enterprise," and that it was "the very first war in the Victorian era in which the object was entirely worthy" (McCourt 1967, p. 168). The murder of Gordon and military defeat shattered Wolseley mentally, physically, and professionally at a time when he was seemingly at the apex of his power. Though he received other honors, promotions, and selection to serve as commander in chief, Wolseley never recovered from this devastating blow and never received another command in the field.

Returning again to his assignment as adjutant-general, Wolseley continued to champion military reform, especially promotion based on merit, rather than seniority, and increased his military writing.

In April 1890, it was proposed that Wolseley replace General (later Field Marshal Earl) Sir Frederick S. Roberts, V.C.—his rival and "leader" of the opposing Roberts Ring—as commander in chief, India, a position Wolseley had coveted a decade earlier. But Wolseley had aged considerably in that ten-year period and preferred the less strenuous and less controversial position of commander in chief, Ireland. Eventually, Roberts was persuaded to remain in India, and Wolseley wanted to be close to home—and the War Office—in the event of an unexpected vacancy in the position of commander in chief.

Wolseley received his field marshal's baton in 1894, and when the aged Duke of Cambridge finally retired in 1895, Wolseley succeeded him as commander in chief. Wolseley found the long-sought position greatly reduced in power, importance, influence, and autonomy.

Wolseley's memory, unfortunately, faded quickly after he became commander in chief, and his effectiveness was reduced. Amid advances in preparedness and mobilization procedures, as well as the initial controversies of the Second Boer War (1899–1902), Wolseley, "the greatest soldier England produced since Wellington" (Lehmann 1964, p. 388), retired in November 1900. Wolseley was a prolific author and military commentator, and his autobiography, *The Story of a Soldier's Life*, an incomplete and sketchy document covering his life up to the Second Ashanti War, was published in 1903. Wolseley then faded away and died quietly near Mentone, France, on 26 March 1913. He was buried near Wellington's tomb in St. Paul's Cathedral.

There can be no question as to Wolseley's courage and indomitable spirit, his dynamic leadership attributes and organizational abilities, and his advocacy of reforms to modernize the British Army. Wolseley led a magnificent, adventurous life, but as one member of the Ashanti Ring commented, "The tragedy of Wolseley's life was that he never encountered a foe worthy of him" (Lehmann 1964, p. 391). In any event, Wolseley—heroic, ambitious, efficient, ruthless, outspoken, and generally progressive—was a dominant force in Queen Victoria's Army during the zenith of the British Empire.

See also Adjutant-General, British Army; Amoaful, Battle of; Arabi Pasha, Ahmed; Arabi Rebellion; Ashanti Ring; Ashanti War, Second (1873–1874); Boer War, Second (1899–1902); Burma War, Second (1852–1853); Cambridge, Field Marshal H.R.H. Prince George F., Second Duke of; Cardwell, Edward T.; Cardwell Reforms; Cetshwayo kaMpande; Chelmsford, General Frederick A. Thesiger, Second Baron; China War, Second (1856–1860); Commander in Chief, British Army; Crimean War; Dervishes; Disraeli, Benjamin; Gordon, Major General Charles G.; Gordon Relief Expedition; Indian Mutiny; Purchase System; Quartermaster-General, British Army; Red River Expedition; Roberts, Field Marshal Frederick S., V.C.; *Soldier's Pocket Book for Field Service;* Sudan; Tel el-Kebir, Battle of; Ulundi, Battle of; War Office; Wellington, Field Marshal Arthur Wellesley, First Duke of; Zulu War

References: Adye (1925); Barthorp (1984b); Beckett (1992); Biddulph (1939); Cavendish (1991); Davis and Weavers (1927); Holt (1958); Kochanski (1997); Kochanski (1999);

Lehmann (1964); Low (1883); Major (1913); Maurice and Arthur (1924); Maxwell (1985); McCourt (1967); Morris (1973); Pegram (1939); Preston (1967a); Preston (1971); Preston (1973); Raugh (1987b); Raugh (1988a); Raugh (1989); Raugh (2001b); Rawley (1964); Wolseley (1862); Wolseley (1903)

Women and the Army

The phrase "officers and their ladies; sergeants and their wives; soldiers and their women" (Neuberg 1989, p. 85) sums up army attitudes and values in regard to females during the nineteenth century. During this time, women did not officially serve as commissioned or enlisted members of the British Army, but they performed important functions that supported service members. In many respects, marriage was considered incompatible with soldiering during this period, although measures were eventually taken to improve the situation.

Armies have frequently attracted camp followers and others, especially women. Many of these women were wives of soldiers and were recognized by the army near the end of the seventeenth century. A small number of army wives accompanied their husbands on campaign during the Napoleonic Wars. Women were a normal feature of the British Army until late in the nineteenth century, as "sutlers trading in meat and drink, as wives, daughters, prostitutes, cooks, nurses, midwives, seamstresses and laundresses, women were an integral part of the military train and moved freely between these roles and others according to circumstances" (Trustram 1984, p. 11).

Soldiers' barracks were frequently unhealthy and unsanitary, and this situation was made worse when a small number of soldiers' families, beginning in about 1790, were permitted to live in the barracks. Generally wives and children would live in a screened-off corner of the barracks (called the corner system), or a number of families would be permitted to live together in a single room. In May 1857, for example, at seven army camps, there were 3,087 wives and 3,685 children. Generally, about 6 percent of the soldiers were allowed to marry and have their families live in the barracks. These authorized wives and children were considered "on the strength" of the soldier's regiment.

There were no regulations regarding officer marriages, although the informal rule, largely due to financial constraints, was that "subalterns may not marry, captains might marry, majors should marry, and lieutenant colonels must marry" (Farwell 1981, p. 233). About 25 percent of all officers were married in 1851 and 1861, a figure that increased to 34 percent in 1871.

When a regiment was ordered overseas during the first half of the nineteenth century, a lottery was held to determine which of the wives on the strength would be allowed to accompany their husbands. By regulation, 12 women for every 100 soldiers were allowed to accompany their husbands to India, with 6 women per 100 soldiers permitted to accompany their husbands to other overseas postings. Wives not permitted to accompany their husbands overseas were given a small monetary allowance to enable them to go to the place where they would live while their husband was overseas, and then claim parish and other relief. This frequently caused misery and destitution, and wives were known to engage in prostitution simply to survive. This situation was later improved by the introduction of separation allowances, methods the soldier could use to remit money to his family, and widows' and children's pensions.

The Crimean War (1854–1856) was the last major conflict in which wives were allowed to accompany their husbands on active service. Many suffered tremendous hardships, and when this news reached England, a relief fund for them was started. This also led to additional reforms and greater recognition of families by the military, as well as the construction of permanent quarters for married soldiers and their families.

The Crimean War also marked a watershed in services women were able to provide the British Army, especially in the medical field. Florence Nightingale read of the horrible conditions and soldiers suffering in the Crimea and volunteered to head a female nursing staff at the military hospital at Scutari. She initially recruited 38 female nurses to serve with her, and they contributed significantly to improving hospital conditions for the soldiers in the Crimea, especially over the first harsh winter of 1854–1855. Seven female nurses later accompanied the British force to South Africa in 1879, and 32 served in Egypt and the Sudan between 1882 and 1885. A modest expansion, from 60 female army nurses in 1890 to 72 in 1898, was made, and about 800 army nurses served in the Second Boer War (1899–1902).

British Army regulations in 1867 for the first time specified the number of soldiers who could be married in each regiment. These included all regimental staff sergeants, 60 percent of other sergeants, and 7 percent of the other ranks.

The other ranks were required to have served seven years in the army with demonstrated good conduct before they could request to get married. In 1885, for example, the 1st Battalion, Connaught Rangers, had 134 wives and 142 children on the strength.

Mid-Victorian efforts to regulate and accommodate the soldiers' families were also designed to help reduce soldier licentiousness and drunkenness, control prostitution, minimize venereal disease, and enhance the efficiency and effectiveness of the British Army. These measures were also taken to attempt to conform with and impose on the lower classes higher standards of morality, and to make military service more attractive to potential recruits.

Throughout the remainder of the Victorian era, improvements were made in the status of soldiers' wives and the living conditions of their families.

> **See also** Crimean War; Military Medicine, British Army—Medical Personnel; Military Medicine, British Army—Sanitation; Military Medicine, British Army—Venereal Disease; Nightingale, Florence
> **References:** Compton (1970); Edgerton (1999); Farwell (1981); Neuberg (1989); Skelley (1977); Summers (1988); Tisdall (1963); Trustram (1984)

Wood, Field Marshal Sir (Henry) Evelyn M., V.C. (1838–1919)

Field Marshal Sir (Henry) Evelyn M. Wood, a key member of the Ashanti Ring, was one of the most courageous and charismatic—and politically astute—senior British Army officers of the late Victorian era. He was also known as an innovative troop trainer.

Wood was born on 9 February 1838 at Cressing, Essex, England. He was educated at Marlborough College and entered the Royal Navy as a midshipman in 1852. He served in the Crimean War, first on a ship in the Black Sea then in a naval brigade ashore. Wounded in the arm, Wood was invalided to England, where he resigned from the Royal Navy and was gazetted a cornet in the 13th Light Dragoons. He returned to the Crimea in 1856 and at the end of the year returned to his regiment in Ireland. Wood was recommended for, but did not receive, the Victoria Cross for his gallantry in the Crimea.

When the Indian Mutiny broke out in 1857, Wood, eager to see action, exchanged into the 17th Lancers and participated in some of the final operations of the war. In December 1859, Wood led an attack that routed a group of eighty rebels at Sindhara, and was awarded the Victoria Cross for his gallant leadership in this successful mission.

After his return to England, Wood transferred to the 73rd Regiment in 1862 and completed the Staff College course two years later. He then served in a number of staff positions. Wood, largely as a result of his proven gallantry, was selected by Major General (later Field Marshal Viscount) Sir Garnet J. Wolseley to serve as a staff officer for the expedition deploying to Ashantiland. Wood commanded a regiment of native levies with distinction. Upon his return to England, he served on the staff at Aldershot before going with his regiment to South Africa in 1878.

Wood's timing was propitious. After participating in an expedition to suppress the Gaikas, the British invaded Zululand. Wood commanded the Left Flank Column during the Zulu War, and his force was routed at Hlobane (28 March 1879). At Khambula the following day, Wood's force was able to thwart and defeat Zulu attacks, and killed many Zulus in a ruthless pursuit. He participated in the capture of Ulundi (4 July 1879), at which the Zulu Army was basically destroyed. After returning to England, Wood was knighted for his Zulu War services and appointed to command the Chatham District. He became a favorite of Queen Victoria.

After the outbreak of the First Boer War in December 1880, Wood was sent to Natal with reinforcements and as second in command to Major General Sir George Pomeroy-Colley. After the Battle of Majuba Hill (27 February 1881), in which Pomeroy-Colley was killed, Wood signed a truce with the Boers on 6 March 1881. Wolseley and many others thought Wood should have resigned his commission instead of signing the "ignominious" treaty with the Boers.

Wood commanded a brigade under Wolseley during the British expedition to quell Arabi Pasha in Egypt in 1882 but saw little action. After the British occupied Egypt, Wood became the first sirdar (commander in chief) of the new Egyptian Army in early 1883, and held this position for two years. In 1885, Wood commanded the lines of communication during the Gordon Relief Expedition. During this period there was considerable friction between Wood and other members of the Ashanti Ring, many of whom held senior rank and were extremely ambitious, competitive, and jealous. While Wolseley praised him officially, he privately wrote that Wood was vain, self-seeking, and "puzzle-headed" (Preston 1967, p. 85).

Wood returned to England in June 1885 and commanded

the Eastern District until 1889, when he was given command of the army's main training center, Aldershot. Wood was instrumental in conducting innovative and realistic training, and improved many aspects of the soldiers' standard of living. He then served at the War Office for eight years, first as quartermaster-general (1893–1897), promoted to full general in 1895, and then as adjutant-general (1897–1901). Wood's last military assignment was as commander of the II Army Corps (later Southern Command) from 1901 to 1904. He was promoted to field marshal on 8 April 1903.

Wood remained concerned with soldiers' affairs and continued writing books on military history, including his own autobiography, *From Midshipman to Field Marshal,* in 1906. A plaque to memorialize Wood, who died in 1919, was erected in St. Paul's Cathedral. It read: "Intrepid in Action, Untiring in Duty[:] For Queen and Country" (Farwell 1985, p. 266).

See also Adjutant-General, British Army; Aldershot; Arabi Rebellion; Ashanti Ring; Ashanti War, Second (1873–1874); Boer War, First (1880–1881); Camberley, Staff College; Crimean War; Egypt; Egyptian Army; Gordon Relief Expedition; Indian Mutiny; Pomeroy-Colley, Major General Sir George; Quartermaster-General, British Army; Sirdar; Victoria Cross; Wolseley, Field Marshal Garnet J.; Zulu War
References: Farwell (1985); Knight (1990); Maxwell (1985); Preston (1967); Wood (1906); Wood (1908); Wood (1917)

Woodville, Richard Caton
See Artists, War

Woolwich, Royal Military Academy

The Royal Military Academy, Woolwich, was established in 1741, near the Royal Artillery Depot at Woolwich, with the objective, as stated in its first charter, of producing "good officers of Artillery and perfect Engineers" (Royal Military Academy 2001, p. 1). The Corps of Royal Engineers, originally an all-officer corps, remained a component of the Royal Regiment of Artillery until 1787. Both remained under the control of the Board of Ordnance and were collectively referred to as the Ordnance Corps until reforms were enacted in 1856.

The Royal Engineers and Royal Artillery were also referred to as the "scientific corps" because of the technical nature of their duties and the requirement to complete an examination prior to entry at Woolwich, complete the formal program of instruction there, and pass another comprehensive exam prior to commissioning. These were stringent requirements, considering that up to 1849, at least 90 percent of the new commissions in the guards, cavalry, and infantry in the British Army at home were either given to, or purchased by, men who had not undergone any formal admission or educational tests.

About 100 cadets entered Woolwich annually. Each spent two to four years in theory classes before passing into a final practical course, although the length of the entire program of instruction fluctuated with the demand for new officers. Seven hours per day were devoted to studying.

An incentive to study at Woolwich was the fact that upon commissioning, the new officers were placed on an order of merit list. This was significant because at the time promotion in the Ordnance Corps was by seniority, not purchase. (The system of purchasing officer commissions was abolished in 1871.) Moreover, when there were more candidates than vacancies in the Royal Engineers—which at one time offered better pay and had more assignment opportunities than the Royal Artillery—only those higher on the order of merit list became Royal Engineers.

The minimum admission age at Woolwich was initially fourteen years, but between 1855 and 1858, it was increased to seventeen years. Stiffer entrance examinations were required at Woolwich, and candidates were examined in eight subjects (Classics, mathematics, English, French or another modern language, history with geography, natural sciences, experimental sciences, and drawing). Admission to Woolwich also became partially competitive. Between 1855 and 1858, about 60 percent of those entering Woolwich were either university educated or public school educated. By 1890, about 90 percent of Woolwich entrants were public school educated.

In 1936, it was decided to amalgamate Woolwich and the Royal Military College, Sandhurst, a process completed in 1947 with the opening of the Royal Military Academy, Sandhurst.

Woolwich was also called the Shop, since its first building was a converted workshop at the Woolwich Arsenal.

See also Officers, British Army—Sources of Commissioning; Officers, British Army—Training and Education; Sandhurst, Royal Military College
References: Harries-Jenkins (1977); Otley (1973); Royal Military Academy (2001); Spiers (1992); Strachan (1984)

Y

Yeomanry

The yeomanry was British part-time volunteer cavalry. On 27 March 1794, at the beginning of the Napoleonic Wars when Britain feared possible invasion, a bill was introduced in Parliament to authorize the use of volunteers who did not want to serve with the standing forces or the militia. These forces were officially called the Gentlemen and Yeoman Cavalry, and they were called to duty in case of invasion and for "the suppression of riots and tumults" (Talbot 2001, p. 46). The name is derived from the Middle English "yeoman," roughly meaning a countryman of respectable standing. The nobility and gentry were commissioned as officers, and freeholders and others served in the ranks. Each man had to provide his own horse, while uniforms and saddlery were provided by the officers or by county subscription and the government provided weapons. Over time yeomanry units were combined into county regiments of about 500 men each.

On a number of occasions the yeomanry assisted the civil power, especially during the social and industrial unrest between 1816 and 1844. The last time the yeomanry served in this manner was in 1867, when a local magistrate called it out to "overawe" food rioters in Devon. The establishment of police forces also reduced the use of the yeomanry.

The home secretary was responsible for the yeomanry until 1871, when control was passed to the secretary of state for war. In 1888, yeomanry units became liable for service anywhere within the United Kingdom in case of invasion. After the British defeats of Black Week (December 1899) during the Second Boer War, it became obvious that the British Army had insufficient reserves. The yeomanry, which some considered "too largely a theatrical reminiscence of the Cavalry which fought in the Crimea and the Peninsular" (Pakenham 1979, p. 263), was renamed the "Imperial Yeomanry" and organized into regiments, with companies from each sent to South Africa. The performance of the Imperial Yeomanry, which totaled over 34,000 in South Africa, was considered mixed, and they sustained more casualties from disease than battle. After the capture of the 13th Battalion of the Imperial Yeomanry at Lindley on 31 May 1900, critics reputed that the "IY" on their hat badges stood for "I Yield."

On 17 April 1901, the yeomanry units in the United Kingdom were reorganized as Imperial Yeomanry in mounted infantry regiments of 596 all ranks, with four squadrons and a machine-gun section.

In 1908, the yeomanry was combined with volunteer infantry battalions to form the Territorial Force under War Office supervision.

See also Boer War, Second (1899–1902); Cardwell Reforms; Civil-Military Relations; Haldane, Richard B.; Home Defense; Militia; Volunteers; War Office

References: Bennett (1999); Farwell (1981); Mileham (1996); Mills (2001); Pakenham (1979); Spiers (1992); Strachan (1984); Talbot (2001)

Younghusband, Colonel Sir Francis E. (1863–1942)

Colonel Sir Francis E. Younghusband was a British Army officer, explorer, and avid participant in the Great Game who led the first foreign military expedition to Tibet, "the

Younghusband, Colonel Sir Francis E.

last, great, mysterious, unexplored country in the world" (French 1994, p. 66), in 1903–1904.

Younghusband was born on 31 May 1863 at Murree, India, where his father, a future major general, was serving in the Indian Army. Four of his uncles and two of his brothers also served in the Indian Army, and Younghusband's uncle, R. B. Shaw, was the first Englishman to cross the Himalayas to Yarkand and Kashgar. After graduation from the Royal Military College, Sandhurst, Younghusband was commissioned in 1882 in the King's Dragoon Guards, then posted in Meerut.

After two years of frustrating regimental soldiering, Younghusband was selected by his division commander to reconnoiter the Kohat frontier area. The Great Game was heating up again as Russia continued to expand in Central Asia toward India. This experience whet Younghusband's appetite for travel and adventure and he decided to become a "great explorer." After his first exploration, Younghusband was attached to the Intelligence Department of the Indian Army.

In 1886, Younghusband participated in an expedition to Manchuria, and on the return trip from Peking, he became the first European to cross the Gobi Desert by its direct route. Further expeditions in the Himalayas, where he explored various mountain passes, rivers, and so on—possible Russian invasion routes—followed. On one of his expeditions, he encountered Russian Army Captain Grombchevski, who was exploring possible routes into India from the north.

In 1889, Younghusband was appointed to the Foreign Department of the Indian Government and continued his explorations. He established a reputation as a Central Asian explorer "of the first rank." Younghusband became the first political officer in Hunza, and in 1893–1894 he was political agent in Chitral and met George Curzon (later Marquess of Kedleston), who became viceroy of India in 1899. In 1895, Younghusband accompanied the Chitral Relief Force. After a long leave, he returned to India and served in various locales.

Curzon became alarmed when he learned of Tibetan missions to Russia in 1900 and 1901 and of a rumored secret agreement between Russia and China pertaining to Tibet in 1902. Younghusband led the Tibet Frontier Commission in 1903 to establish trade and other relations with Tibet and try to forestall any type of Russian political infiltration into Tibet, but this mission was unsuccessful.

Later in 1903, the British authorized an expedition to Tibet to redress the humiliation of the earlier failed mission. Younghusband, promoted to colonel to raise his prestige as a negotiator, was selected to command the Tibet Mission. The mission, including its 1,150-man military escort, beginning in December 1903, traveled over unimaginably rugged terrain in inhospitable weather toward Gyantse. It fought a number of sharp engagements with Tibetan forces, defeating them each time, and finally arrived at the Forbidden City of Lhasa on 3 August 1904. After negotiations, the Treaty of Lhasa was signed on 7 September 1904, and contained ten articles, highlighting free trade between India and Tibet, free communications, rights of access, and so on. Its mission complete, the Younghusband Expedition, as it came to be known, returned to India on 25 October 1904. Younghusband was at the apex of his popularity, received a knighthood, and continued serving the Indian Government until 1909.

While Younghusband held no further official employment after 1909, he founded in 1915 a patriotic, short-lived movement, Fight for Right, and later a number of other philosophical, religious, and mystical organizations. In 1919, Younghusband became president of the Royal Geographic Society. He chaired the Mount Everest Committee, organizing the first four expeditions to the world's highest peak. Younghusband was astonishingly prolific, writing no fewer than twelve books between 1920 and 1930. He died on 31 July 1942.

See also Great Game; India; North-West Frontier; Penjdeh Incident; Sandhurst, Royal Military College; Tibet, Expedition to
References: Barthorp (1982); Fleming (1961); French (1994); Wickham Legg and Williams (1959)

Zulu War (1879)

The Zulu War was one of many colonial campaigns in which the British Army served as the instrument of British imperialism. The conflict, fought against an indigenous adversary the British initially underestimated, is remarkable for battles that included perhaps the most humiliating defeat in British military history—the Battle of Isandlwana (22 January 1879)—and one of its most heroic feats of martial arms—the defense of Rorke's Drift (22–23 January 1879).

In the 1870s, the British embarked on new imperialistic ventures to confederate South Africa and make the region economically self-sufficient. They were also concerned with forestalling the colonization of more territory by other European powers. The British annexed the neighboring Transvaal in 1877, determined to retain the diamond and gold deposits there. As a result, the British inherited the Boer border disputes with the Zulus. The British, who had previously supported the Zulus, reversed their policy and engineered a territorial dispute as a basis for a confrontation. Cetshwayo kaMpande, who had been Zulu king since 1872, was given an ultimatum on 11 December 1878 to dismantle his army and turn over to the British those guilty of recent border violations. He was bewildered by this turn of events.

The British assembled at Fort Pearson on the Tugela River and invaded Zululand on 11 January 1879 after their ultimatum expired. The British forces in South Africa, commanded by Lieutenant General (later General) Frederick A. Thesiger, Second Baron Chelmsford, totaled about 16,000 soldiers, which included about 9,000 native levies. Some 977 wagons, 56 carts, 10,023 oxen, 803 horse, and 398 mules, with 2,000 extra locals to drive them, were required to support this force.

The British force that invaded Zululand was divided into five columns. The center column (No. 3), which Chelmsford and his headquarters accompanied, was commanded by Colonel Richard Glyn. This 4,709-man column was to cross the Tugela River at Rorke's Drift and conduct the main attack directly at Cetshwayo's royal kraal (homestead) at Ulundi. The left column (No. 4) was commanded by Colonel (later Field Marshal Sir) (Henry) Evelyn M. Wood, V.C. Colonel Charles K. Pearson, commanding the right column (No. 1), was to initially establish an advanced base at Eshowe, then coordinate with Chelmsford so his column and Wood's column would converge with the center column at Ulundi. The No. 2 column, commanded by Lieutenant Colonel Anthony W. Durnford and consisting mainly of native troops, was broken up, although Durnford and the Natal Native Horse was subsequently ordered to join No. 3 column. Colonel H. Rowlands's No. 5 column guarded the Zululand frontier.

The center column reached Isandlwana, 10 miles from Rorke's Drift, on 20 January 1879. British forces reconnoitering the area found a number of Zulu soldiers the next day, but did not realize they were stragglers from the 23,000-man main Zulu Army. On 22 January, Chelmsford took about half the center column (mainly 2nd Battalion, 24th Regiment with four guns) to find and engage the Zulu Army. He left about 1,700 British and African soldiers (1st Battalion, 24th Regiment and two guns) to guard the base camp at Isandlwana. During Chelmsford's absence, the

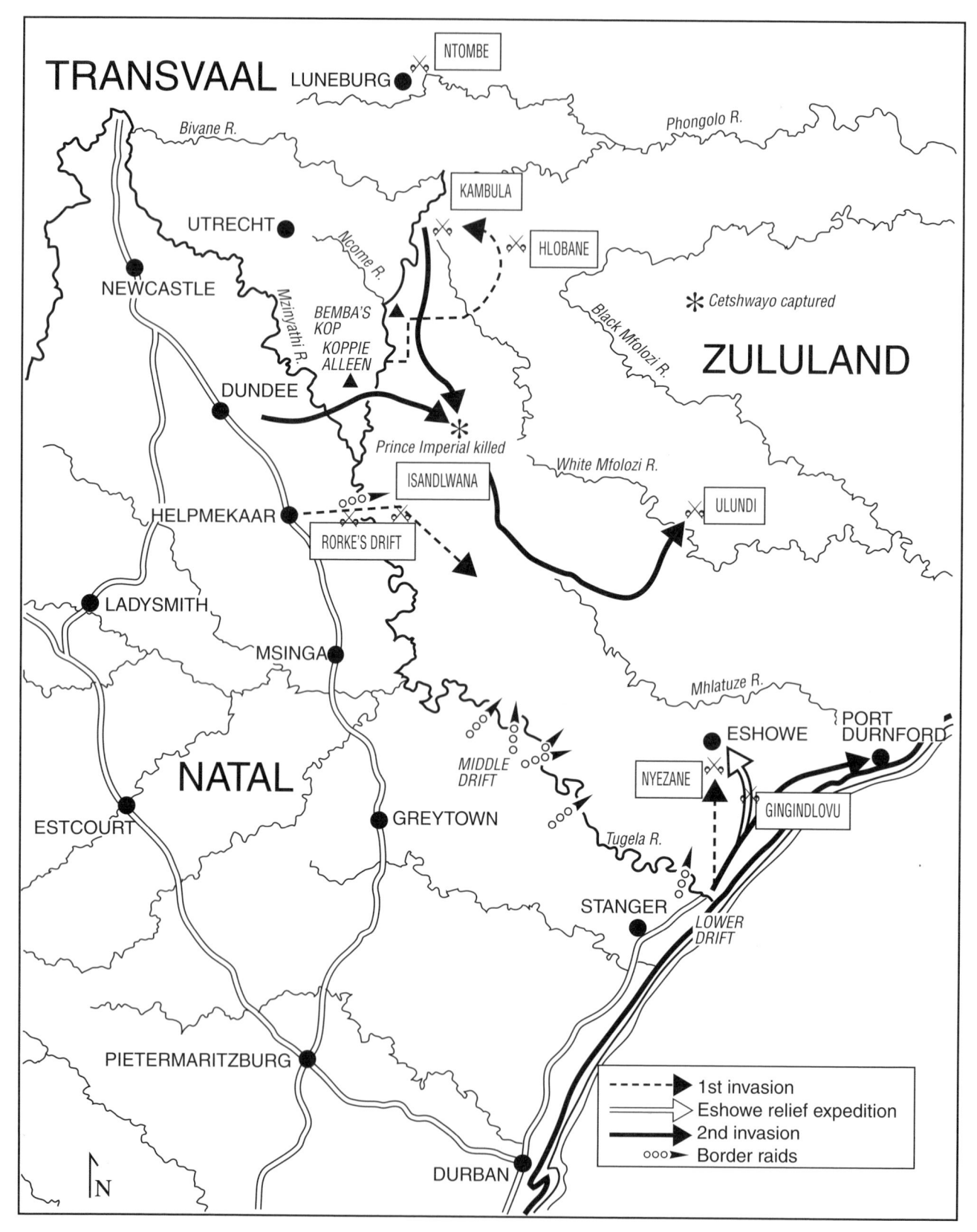

Zulu War, 1879: Area of Operations

Source: Ian Knight. *Brave Men's Blood: The Epic of the Zulu War, 1879.* London: Greenhill Books, 1990. p. 8.

main Zulu Army attacked and veritably wiped out the force at Isandlwana. At the Battle of Isandlwana, which was more of a slaughter than a battle, 1,329 of the white and African soldiers were barbarously killed in what was one of the most shameful defeats in British military history.

On the night of 22–23 January 1879, about 4,000 Zulus attacked the center column's small supply base and hospital at Rorke's Drift. The small force at Rorke's Drift (8 officers and 131 other ranks), the nucleus of which was Company B, 2nd Battalion, 24th Regiment, under the overall command of Lieutenant (later Colonel) John R. M. Chard, held off repeated Zulu onslaughts throughout the night. The gallant defense of Rorke's Drift was recognized by an unprecedented award of eleven Victoria Crosses.

Pearson's No. 1 column crossed the Tugela River into Zululand on 12 January 1879. His forces built Fort Tenedos, a mud fortification on the Zululand side of the Tugela across from Fort Pearson, and continued to advance. On 22 January, a 6,000-man Zulu force surprised Pearson's column near the Inyezane River. After a fierce skirmish, the British counterattacked and forced the Zulus to retreat, at a cost of 10 men killed and 16 wounded. The British reached the abandoned Norwegian Mission Station at Eshowe the following day. These soldiers began to establish a supply station by constructing a mud fort with entrenchment and timber ramparts called Fort Eshowe.

On 28 January 1879, Pearson learned of the Zulu victory at Isandlwana and decided to remain at Eshowe. After sending some mounted troops back to Fort Tenedos, Pearson had 1,700 soldiers with him at Fort Eshowe. This position was then besieged by Zulus.

After the disaster at Isandlwana, Chelmsford retreated and reassembled a 6,000-man force at Fort Pearson. This new force, including reinforcements from St. Helena, Ceylon, and the Naval Brigade, departed on 29 March 1879 from Fort Tenedos to relieve Fort Eshowe. On 1 April 1879, Chelmsford's relief column encamped 15 miles from Eshowe on the south bank of the Inyezane River near the kraal of Gingindlovu, which had been burned by Pearson's column ten weeks earlier.

Zulus were seen massing in the hills around Gingindlovu that evening. Two large enemy columns, totaling about 12,000 Zulus, attacked out of the thick mist the following morning, 2 April 1879. British Gatling guns opened up first on the attacking hordes, and well aimed rifle volley fire and rockets prevented the Zulus from coming within stabbing distance of the fortified British camp. As the Zulu attack wavered, Chelmsford ordered out his cavalry, which ruthlessly pursued and killed any fleeing Zulus. The entire battle was over in about ninty minutes and resulted in a total Zulu rout. About 500 Zulu dead were counted in front of the British positions, and another 600 were killed during their retreat. British casualties were 13 all ranks killed and 46 wounded. Eshowe was relieved on 3 April. After the Eshowe fortifications were destroyed, British forces returned to Natal.

Wood's No. 4 column had originally entered Zululand on 10 January 1879. It contained one Royal Garrison Artillery battery, two regular infantry battalions, two battalions of friendly Zulus, and six troops of Colonial Mounted Volunteers (four Frontier Light Horse troops, commanded by Lieutenant Colonel [later General Sir] Redvers Buller and two troops of Baker's Horse). Its mission was to distract a number of Zulu tribes in the northwest area of Zululand and prevent them from joining Cetshwayo's main army. There was a series of flat-topped mountains, named Zunguin, Hlobane, and Ityentika, in the area. After learning of Isandlwana, Wood moved his column to Kambula Hill from which his force could observe avenues of approach and the Zulus at Hlobane.

Wood's force received periodic reinforcements, some from Lydenburg in the Transvaal to the north. Heavy rains and flooded rivers occasionally impeded resupply and reinforcements. On 12 March 1879, Captain David Moriarty's Company H, 80th Regiment, which had been escorting convoys across the flooded Ntombe River, was surrounded and attacked at night by 800 Zulus. In the confusing melee that ensued, Moriarty, 62 soldiers, and 17 civilian drivers, out of 106 men, were killed.

Wood took advantage of his relative autonomy, and Buller's horse troops made numerous raids on the Zulus. Wood directed Buller to attack the Zulu camp at Hlobane on 28 March 1879, to drive off the cattle before Zulu reinforcements arrived, and to provoke them to attack Wood's well-fortified encampment at Kambula. Buller's force ascended the plateau in a thunderstorm, and in subsequent confusion, while rounding up the Zulu cattle, observed the main 26,000-man Zulu Army approaching. Many British casualties were sustained and much gallantry was shown, as Buller's force extricated itself and returned to Kambula. Buller and four others received the Victoria Cross for their gallantry at Hlobane, while 94 all ranks had been killed and 8 wounded.

The Zulu Army, as expected, attacked Kambula on 29 March 1879. Wood's 2,086-man, 6-gun force was defending the hilltop position. After midday, as Zulu troop deployments were observed, Buller's men rode out to fire on the Zulu right horn and provoke it into a premature attack. This tactic worked, and after about a thirty-five-minute fight, in which a few Zulus broke into the British position, the right horn withdrew. The Zulu center and left horn then attacked from the protection of a ravine, pressuring advanced British riflemen to withdraw to the main encampment. The right horn returned to action, and as the situation became precarious, Wood ordered two companies of the 90th Light Infantry to fix bayonets and charge the Zulu left. This well-timed counterattack drove the Zulus back into the ravine, where they came under intense British fire. The Zulus fearlessly and repeatedly charged the British, but well-aimed artillery and rifle fire broke up their assaults. The British shifted forces to make their fire more effective, and at about 5:00 P.M. the Zulus began to withdraw. Buller's cavalry pursued the Zulus for over 7 miles. Over 800 Zulus were killed near the British positions and hundreds more during the pursuit. British casualties were 18 all ranks killed and 65 wounded, of whom 11 later died. At the Battle of Kambula, which was clearly a British victory and the turning point of the war, the Zulus learned convincingly that their weapons were no match against those of the British.

Chelmsford had meanwhile been assembling reinforcements, and on 31 May 1879, he began his second invasion of Zululand. As his force plodded toward Ulundi, Chelmsford learned that he was to be replaced by General (later Field Marshal Viscount) Sir Garnet J. Wolseley. Chelmsford pushed his force to Ulundi, wanting to engage and defeat the Zulus before Wolseley arrived to supersede him. Finally, on 4 July 1879, Chelmsford's 5,317-man force formed into a large square and was attacked by the Zulus. With their spirit arguably broken at Kambula, the Zulus attacked the British, but they were never able to penetrate the wall of steel made by Gatling gun, artillery, and rifle fire. The Battle of Ulundi was the decisive and last large-scale battle of the war, which ended when Cetshwayo was captured on 28 August 1879.

The power of the Zulu kingdom was destroyed when it was divided into thirteen separate, independent chiefdoms, each with a British resident. Great Britain annexed Zululand in 1887.

See also Animals, Transport; Buller, General Sir Redvers H., V.C.; Cetshwayo kaMpande; Chelmsford, General Frederick A. Thesiger, Second Baron; Imperialism; Isandlwana, Battle of; Lines of Communication; Rorke's Drift, Defense of; Ulundi, Battle of; Victoria Cross; Wolseley, Field Marshal Garnet J.; Wood, Field Marshal Sir (Henry) Evelyn M., V.C.; Zululand

References: Bailes (1980); Barthorp (1980); Edgerton (1988); Emery (1982); Gillings (1978); Harford (1978); Knight (1990); Laband (1995); Laband and Knight (1996); Morris (1965); War Office (1881); Whitehouse (1880)

Zululand

Zululand, or kwaZulu, was established by the conquests of Shaka in about 1820. It consisted of about 11,500 square miles in South Africa, stretching from the Pongola River in the north to the Tugela River in the south, and from the Indian Ocean coast inland to the Blood River. Zululand rises steeply from the coast in a series of terraces through broken hill country to high, open prairies, all crisscrossed by rivers and valleys.

The Zulu Army that the British defeated in 1879 had its beginnings during the 1818–1828 reign of Shaka. He revolutionized Zulu warfare by introducing a short stabbing spear *(assegai)* to replace the throwing spear and by developing tactics based on double envelopment. The basic military unit was the *ibotho*, or regiment, consisting of men about the same age, a practice that helped reduce clan rivalry. When deploying for battle, the Zulu regiments were configured like the head or chest of a buffalo, with "horns" of soldiers protruding from each side that would envelop the enemy. The Zulus were courageous in conducting large-scale assaults and in close combat.

There was no fixed size for the *ibotho*, which ranged from 500 to 5,000 or more soldiers. Regiments formed a larger unit, similar to a brigade, of which there were 12 in the Zulu Army in 1879. The *ibotho* was subdivided into companies *(amaviyo)* of about 50 men each. Zulu soldiers married relatively late in life, and when permitted to marry, they returned to their villages but were subject to being recalled to their regiment.

Zulu soldiers were physically hardy and extremely mobile. Many could run barefoot for 50 or more miles a day for consecutive days, and then enter combat without resting. The Zulu warriors were formidable foes.

See also Cetshwayo kaMpande; Isandlwana, Battle of; Rorke's Drift, Defense of; Ulundi, Battle of; Zulu War

References: Bourquin (1978); Edgerton (1988); Knight (1995); Laband (1995); Morris (1965); Ritter (1955)

Appendix 1: Chronology of British Army Wars, Campaigns, and Other Operations (1815–1914)

1814–1816	Gurkha War in northern India and Nepal
1816	Anglo-Dutch fleet bombarded Algiers
1817–1818	Third Maratha (or Maratha and Pindari) War
1818–1819	Fifth Cape Frontier War, Southern Africa
1819	Operations of Hyderabad Contingent against Nowah
	Anglo-French naval demonstration on the Barbary Coast to discourage recurrent piracy
	British expedition against Jawasimi pirates in Persian Gulf
1821	British expedition against Beni Bu Ali pirates near Muscat
1822	British forces help native Manipur and Cachar rulers during Burmese invasion
1823–1824	Suppression of Demerara slave revolt in British Guiana
1823–1826	First Ashanti War
1824	British naval squadron bombards Algiers
1824–1825	Assam War
1824–1826	First Burma War
1824–1828	British occupation of Mombassa
1825–1826	Jat War: expedition to Bhurtpore, India
1827	Allied fleet, including British warships, destroys Turko-Egyptian fleet at Battle of Navarino, ensuring Greek independence
1827–1828	British intervention in Portuguese Oporto Revolution
1831–1832	Slave rebellion in Jamaica
1834	Operations in Coorg, India
	Skirmishes with Maoris, New Zealand
1834–1835	Sixth Cape Frontier War, Southern Africa
1835–1837	So-called Spanish Legion led by Sir George de Lacy Evans fights in Carlist War in Spain
1837	Insurrection in Canara, India
	Coorg rebellion, India
	Papineau's rebellion in Lower Canada
1837–1838	Mackenzie's rebellion in Lower Canada
	Second Goomsore campaign
1838	Nelson's rebellion in Canada
	Kurmool campaign

Chronology

	Jodhpur campaign
	Occupation of Kharak Island in the Persian Gulf
	Expedition against insurgents in Richelieu River area, Canada
1838–1839	Occupation of Durban
1839	Capture of Aden
1839–1840	Skirmishes in Aden
1839–1842	First Afghan War
	First China (or Opium) War
	Operations in Baluchistan
1840	Expedition into Kohistan
	Marri uprising in Sind
	British and Austrian naval force bombards and occupies Beirut and Acre in Second Turko-Egyptian War
1841	Expedition into Zurmatt
	Expedition against dacoits in Shahjehanpore district
1841–1842	Expedition against Walleng hill tribes on the Arakan frontier
1842	Expedition against Shinwaris
	Insurrection in Shorapore district, India
	Bundlecund campaign
	Military occupation of Natal
	Pirara expedition to expel Brazilian raiders from British Guiana
1842–1843	British-Boer conflict in Natal
	Operations to quell revolt in the Saugor and Nerbudda territories, India
1843	Operations in and conquest of Sind
	Gwalior campaign
	Disturbance in Malabar, India
1843–1844	Pirates of Borneo chastised
1843–1848	First Maori War
1844	Mutiny of two native regiments on Sind frontier
1844–1845	Campaign in southern Mahratta country
	Campaign against hill tribes on northern frontier of Sind
1845	British operations to support Griquas against Boers
	Suppression of pirates in Borneo
	Naval action against Argentines on Parana River
1845–1846	First Sikh War
1845–1849	Anglo-French occupation of parts of Uruguay and blockade of River Plate
1846	Kashmir campaign
	Anglo-French naval squadrons bombard Tamatave, Madagascar
	Aden besieged
	British naval force prevents insurrection by sailing into Brunei
1846–1847	Seventh Cape Frontier War, Southern Africa
1847	Operations against Baizais, North-West Frontier
	Cutchi Hill expedition in Sind
	Rebellion in Golcondah and Darcondah in the Golcondah Zemindary, India
	Capture of the Bogue forts, China
	Riots against Portuguese inhabitants of British Guiana
1847–1848	Expedition to Goomsore

1848	Sherbo expedition
	White Cloud expedition against the Braves
	Rebellion in Ceylon
	Expedition against King of Appolonia on Gold Coast
	Battle at Boomplaats against disaffected Boers
	Defeat of pirates in Borneo
1848–1849	Second Sikh War
	Indian raids from Yucatan into British Honduras
1849	Expedition against Baizais, North-West Frontier
1849–1850	Expedition against Afridis, North-West Frontier
1850	Mutiny of 66th Native Infantry, India
	Punitive expedition against Kohat Pass Afridis, North-West Frontier
	British naval blockade of Greece
1850–1853	Eighth Cape Frontier War, Southern Africa
1850–1863	Frontier incidents in Malaya
1851	Expedition against Miranzai, North-West Frontier
	Operations against Umarzai Waziris, North-West Frontier
	Occupation of Bahadoor Khail
	Siege of Dhasore
	Lagos seized
	Operations in Basutoland
1851–1852	Two expeditions against Mohmands, North-West Frontier
1852	Expedition against Umarzai Waziris, North-West Frontier
	Operations against Ranizais, North-West Frontier
	Expedition against Afridis, North-West Frontier
	Utman Khel expedition, North-West Frontier
	Operations against Basutos
1852–1853	Expedition to Black Mountains to punish Hassanzais, North-West Frontier
	Second Burma War
1853	Expedition against Kasranis and Shiranis, North-West Frontier
	Expedition against Hindustani Fanatics, North-West Frontier
	Operations against Bozdar tribe, North-West Frontier
	Punitive expedition against Jowaki Afridis of Bori Valley, North-West Frontier
1854	Operations against Rohillas, India
	Operations against rebels in Tondiman Rajah's area, India
	Rahim Dad expedition against Mohmands, North-West Frontier
	Rebellion of Burmese in Bassein district
	Relief of Christenborg on Gold Coast
	Battle of Muddy Flat, China
	Riots of Chinese in Singapore
	Eureka Stockade incident, Australia
1854–1855	Malageah expeditions
1854–1856	Crimean War
1854–1857	Anglo-French occupation of the Pireaus, Greece
1855	Expedition against Aka Khel Afridis, North-West Frontier
	Operations against Miranzai, North-West Frontier

Chronology

	Expedition against Orakzai tribe of Pathans, North-West Frontier
	Insurrection of Bedeers of Deodroog
	Storming of Sabbajee
1855–1856	Suppression of Santal rebellion, Bengal
1856	Miranzai expedition to disperse bandits, North-West Frontier
	Expedition against Turis, North-West Frontier
	Fights with hill Karens in Burma
1856–1857	Persian War
1856–1860	Second China ("Arrow") War
1857	Expedition to suppress disturbances at Shekh Jana, North-West Frontier
	Expedition to quell unrest at Naranji, North-West Frontier
	Punitive expedition against Boxdars, North-West Frontier
	Three minor expeditions against Hindustani Fanatics, North-West Frontier
	Expedition against villages on the Yusafzai border, North-West Frontier
	Expedition against Beydur Baluchis
	Expedition against hill tribes in Rajahmundry district
	Operations against Shans and Karens of the Younzareen district, Martaban Province
	Operations on Canton River, China
	Occupation of the island of Perim in the Strait of Bab-el-Mandeb, near Aden
1857–1859	Indian Mutiny
1858	Operations against Hindustani Fanatics around Sittana, North-West Frontier
	Expedition against the Crobboes
1858–1859	Expedition against Singhbhum rebels
1859	Expedition against Kabul Khel Waziris, North-West Frontier
	Great Scarcies River expedition
	Bundlesecund campaign
	Expedition against the Dounquah rebels
1859–1862	"Blue Mutiny" in Bengal
1860	Expedition against Mahsud Waziris, North-West Frontier
	Disturbances in Honduras
1860–1861	Taranaki War, New Zealand
	Sikkim expedition
	Baddiboo War on the Gambia
	Quiah War in Sierra Leone
1860–1862	Taiping rebellion, China
1861	Storming and capture of Rohea
	Attack on Madoukia
	Expedition against Porto Novo, Dahomey
	Bombardment and destruction of Massougha on Sierra Leone River
1861–1862	British expeditionary force to Canada
	Allied (British, Spanish, and French) occupation of Veracruz, Mexico
1862	Unrest in British Guiana
1862–1863	Cossiah rebellion
1863	Ambela campaign, North-West Frontier
	Action against Malay pirates
	British bombardment of Shimonoseki, Japan

	British naval punitive expedition against Kagoshima, Japan
1863–1864	Skirmishing between Mohmands and Shabkadr garrison, North-West Frontier
1863–1869	Second Maori War
1864	Allied bombardment and British and Dutch landing parties destroy stockades at Shimonoseki, Japan
1864–1866	British forces garrison Yokohama, Japan
	Bhutan War
1865	British, French, and Dutch fleets demonstrate western power, Japan
	Insurrection of freed slaves in Jamaica
	Bombardment of Cape Haitian in Haiti
1865–1866	Expedition into interior of Arabia from Aden
1866	Fenian raids from United States into Canada
1867	Expedition to Honduras
	Expedition to Little Andaman Island
1867–1868	Abyssinian War
1868	Expedition against the Bizoti Orakzais, North-West Frontier
	Expedition against Black Mountain tribes, North-West Frontier
	Basuto War
1869	Expedition against Bizoti Orakzais, North-West Frontier
1869–1870	First Riel rebellion and Red River expedition in Canada
1869–1872	Skirmishes with Maoris, New Zealand
1870	Fenian raids from United States into Canada
1871	Punitive expedition against bandits in Aden
	Fenian raid into Manitoba, Canada
1871–1872	Lushai campaign
1872	Expedition against Dawari Waziri tribe in Tochi Valley, North-West Frontier
	Operations against Santa Cruz Indians, British Honduras
1873	Skirmish against Hlubi clan of Zulus in Basutoland
	Operations in Selangor, Malay Peninsula
	Town of Omoa in Spanish Honduras bombarded
1873–1874	Second Ashanti War
1874–1875	Daffla expedition on North-West Frontier
1875	Naga Hills expedition
	Bombardment of villages on Congo River
	Rebellion in Griqualand
1875–1876	Rebellion of slavers against British-imposed antislavery laws in Mombasa and Kilwa
	Punitive expedition to Perak, Malay Peninsula
	Unrest in Barbados
1877	Rebellion in Darfur, Sudan
1877–1878	Expeditions against Jowaki Afridis, North-West Frontier
	Ninth Cape Frontier War, Southern Africa
	Expedition against Galeka and Gaika tribes, South Africa
1878	Expedition against Zakha Khel Afridis, North-West Frontier
	Punitive expeditions against Utman Khel, North-West Frontier
	Expedition against Ranizais, North-West Frontier
	British-Burmese border dispute
	British occupation of Cyprus

Chronology

	Unrest of slave traders in Kordofan, Sudan
	Southern Bechuanaland occupied by British
	Pirate strongholds in Borneo bombarded
1878–1879	Operations against revolting slave traders in Darfur, Sudan
	Campaign against Sekukuni, Transvaal
1878–1880	Second Afghan War
1879	Expedition against Zakha Khel Afridis, North-West Frontier
	Expedition against Suliman Khel Pawindahs and others, North-West Frontier
	Punitive expedition against Zaimukhts, North-West Frontier
	Expedition against Mohmands, North-West Frontier
	Zulu War
	Operations in Basutoland
1879–1880	Punitive expeditions to Naga Hills
1880	Operations against Marri Baluchis, North-West Frontier
	Expedition against Mohmands, North-West Frontier
	Expedition against Malikshahi Waziris, North-West Frontier
	Zhob expedition, North-West Frontier
	Expedition against Batanis, North-West Frontier
1880–1881	First Boer War
	Gun War against Basutos
1881	Expedition to Mahsud Waziris, North-West Frontier
1882	Arabi Rebellion, Egypt
1883	Bikaneer expedition, India
	Skirmishes with Shiranis at Takht-I-Suliman, North-West Frontier
	Rebel threat to Muscat dispersed by Royal Navy presence
1883–1884	Akha expedition, India
	Mahdist uprising in the Sudan
1884	Zhob Valley expedition, North-West Frontier
1884–1885	Gordon Relief Expedition
	Suakin Expedition, Eastern Sudan
	Expedition to Bechuanaland
1885	Operations against the Khalifa, successor of the Mahdi, Sudan
	Operations in Bechuanaland
	Third Burma War
	North-Western rebellion in Canada
1886	British and allied naval blockade of Greece
1887	Expedition against the Bunerwals, North-West Frontier
	Punitive expedition against Yonnie tribe, Sierra Leone
1887–1889	Emin Pasha relief expedition, Equatoria
1888	Black Mountain or Hazara expedition, North-West Frontier
	Sikkim expedition
	Operations against Mahdists around Suakin
	Zulu uprising
1888–1889	British navy assists in suppression of Coastal Arabs in German East Africa
1889	Lushai operations
	Tonhon expedition

	Expedition to Sierra Leone
	Khalifa's army routed at Toski
	Unrest in British Guiana
1889–1890	Chin Lushai expedition
1890	Malakand campaign, North-West Frontier
	Expedition to subdue Khiddarzai Shiranis in Zhob Valley, North-West Frontier
	Northern Lushai operations
	Mashonaland campaign
	Punitive expedition to Somaliland
	Expedition to Witu, coastal sultanate of British East Africa
	Expedition against Eeas Somel people in Aden
1890–1891	Operations in Uganda
1891	Hunza-Nagar campaign, North-West Frontier
	Hazara expedition to Black Mountains, North-West Frontier
	Two expeditions of Miranzai Field Force to Samana, North-West Frontier
	Manipur expedition
	Lushai operations
	Expedition against slavers in Mlanje area, British Central Africa
	Expedition against slavers in south Lake Nyasa area, British Central Africa
	Expedition against slaver chief Yao Kawinga, British Central Africa
1891–1892	Operations in Gambia
1892	Black Mountain expedition, North-West Frontier
	Eastern Lushai operations
	Isazai expedition
	Expedition against Jebu, Oil Rivers Protectorate (Niger)
	Punitive expedition to Tambi and Toniatabe, Sierra Leone
	Expedition against slaver chief Zafari, British Central Africa
1892–1893	Chin Hills expedition
	Kachin Hills expedition
1893	British and French shoot at each other by mistake in Sierra Leone
	Expedition against slaver chief Liwondi, British Central Africa
	Operations against slavers in Mlanje area, British Central Africa
	Expedition against slaver chief Chirandzulu, British Central Africa
	Expedition to quell unrest in British East Africa
	Operations to rescue captives at Juba River, British East Africa
	British-led Baganda army subdues rivals, Uganda
	Matabele-Mashona war
1893–1894	Abor Hills expedition, North-West Frontier
	Operations against Islamic raiders Sofas, Sierra Leone
	Operations against Ashantis
	Expedition against slaver Makanjira, British Central Africa
	Operations against Matabele
1894	Benin River punitive expedition, Niger
	Punitive expedition against slaver in Gambia
	British expedition to Sierra Leone
	Disturbances in Nicaragua

Chronology

1894–1895	Punitive expedition to Waziristan, North-West Frontier
	Nikki expedition
1895	Siege and relief of Chitral, North-West Frontier
	Kachin Hills expedition
	Brass River expedition, Niger
	Expedition against slaver chief Yao Kawinga, British Central Africa
	Final expedition against slaver Makanjira, British Central Africa
	Qatari fleet destroyed by Royal Navy near Bahrain
1895–1896	Jameson Raid
	Ashanti expedition
	Expedition to crush revolt of Arab clan in British East Africa
1896	Expedition against Angoni chief Tambola to end raiding, British Central Africa
	Operations against Angoni chief Odeti to cease raiding, British Central Africa
	Expedition against Angoni chief Chikusi to end raiding, British Central Africa
	Bombardment of Zanzibar
	Rebellion in Rhodesia
	Matabele uprising
1896–1897	Suppression of rebellion in Bechuanaland
	Mashona uprising
1896–1898	Reconquest of Sudan
	Minor expeditions on Gold Coast
1897	Operations in Bara Valley, India
	Operations of Mohmand Field Force, North-West Frontier
	Suppression of Afridi and Orakzai unrest in Kohat, North-West Frontier
	Punitive expedition to Benin, Niger
	Expedition against slave traders in Nupe, northern Niger
	Operations against Bida in West Africa
	Expedition against Angoni chief Serumba to stop raiding, British Central Africa
	Suppression of rebellion by Mwanga of Buganda, Uganda
	Operations in Bechuanaland
1897–1898	Malakand campaign, North-West Frontier
	Tirah campaign, North-West Frontier
	Punitive expedition into Tochi Valley, North-West Frontier
	Anglo-French dispute over Nigeria
	Punitive expeditions in Borneo
1897–1901	Mutiny of Sudanese units and unrest in Uganda
1898	Fashoda incident
	Defense of Dawkita, Gold Coast, against attacking slavers
	Expedition against Angoni chief Mpezeni to end raiding, British Central Africa
	Final expedition to stop Angoni raiding, British Central Africa
	Expedition against Ogaden Somalis in Jubaland
	Riots on Crete and bombardment of Candia
1898–1899	Operations in Sierra Leone
1898–1900	Final operations against dervish resistance in Sudan
1899	Bebejiya expedition, North-West Frontier
	Expedition to pacify Benin

Chronology

	Royal Navy action at Samoa
1899–1900	Tambunan expedition in Borneo
1899–1902	Second Boer War
1900	Ashanti War
	Punitive expedition to Jubaland
	Aden Field Force supports Haushabi tribe fight off Humar tribe from Yemen
1900–1901	Boxer Rebellion, China
1901	Punitive expedition in Gambia
1901–1902	Operations in Waziristan, North-West Frontier
1901–1904	Operations against Mad Mullah of Somaliland
1903	Unrest in Kordofan, Sudan
	British conquest of Kano and Sokoto, Northern Nigeria
1903–1904	Expedition to Tibet
1905	Expedition against Nandi people, British East Africa
	Riots in Georgetown, British Guiana
1906	Suppression of Sokoto rebellion, Northern Nigeria
	Operations against Nubas, Sudan
	Zulu uprising
1908	Operations against Zakha Khel and Mohmands on North-West Frontier
	Rebellion in Blue Nile Province, Sudan
1910	Expedition to South Kordofan, Sudan
1911–1912	Operations on North-West Frontier
1912	Operations in Sudan
1913	Defeat of Camel Corps by dervishes in Somaliland
1914	Operations against dervishes in Somaliland

References: Bond (1970); Callwell (1896); Dupuy and Dupuy (1986); Farwell (1972); Gooding (1994); Haythornthwaite (1995); Nevill (1912); Young and Calvert (1977)

Appendix 2: British Army Commanders in Chief, Chiefs of the General Staff, and Chiefs of the Imperial General Staff (1815–1914)

Commanders in Chief
1811–1827	Field Marshal H.R.H. Prince Frederick A., Duke of York and Albany
1827–1828	Field Marshal Arthur Wellesley, First Duke of Wellington
1828–1842	General Rowland Hill, First Viscount Hill of Almaraz
1842–1852	Field Marshal Arthur Wellesley, First Duke of Wellington
1852–1856	Field Marshal Henry Hardinge, First Viscount Hardinge of Lahore
1856–1895	Field Marshal H.R.H. Prince George F., Second Duke of Cambridge
1895–1900	Field Marshal Garnet J. Wolseley, First Viscount Wolseley of Cairo
1901–1904	Field Marshal Frederick S. Roberts, V.C., First Earl Roberts of Kandahar, Pretoria, and Waterford

Chiefs of the General Staff
1904–1908	General Sir Neville G. Lyttelton
1908–1909	Field Marshal William G. Nicholson, First Baron Nicholson of Roundhay

Chiefs of the Imperial General Staff
1909–1912	Field Marshal William G. Nicholson, First Baron Nicholson of Roundhay
1912–1914	Field Marshal John D. P. French, First Earl of Ypres
1914	General Sir Charles W. H. Douglas

Appendix 3: Indian Army Commanders in Chief (1815–1914)

1813–1823	General Francis R. Hastings, Earl of Moira and First Marquess of Hastings
1823–1825	General Sir Edward Paget
1825–1829	Field Marshal Stapleton Cotton, First Viscount Combermere
1830–1831	General George Ramsay, Ninth Earl of Dalhousie
1832–1833	Lieutenant General Sir Edward Barnes
1833–1835	General Lord William H. Cavendish-Bentinck
1835	General Sir James Watson (officiating)
1835–1839	General Sir Henry Fane
1839–1843	General Sir Jasper Nicolls
1843–1849	Field Marshal Hugh Gough, First Viscount Gough of Chinkiangfoo in China and of Maharajpore and the Sutlej in the East Indies
1849–1851	General Sir Charles J. Napier
1851–1856	Field Marshal Sir William M. Gomm
1856	General George Anson
1856–1857	Field Marshal Sir Patrick Grant (officiating)
1857–1861	Field Marshal Colin Campbell, First Baron Clyde of Clydesdale
1861–1865	Field Marshal Hugh H. Rose, First Baron Strathnairn of Strathnairn and Jhansi
1865–1870	General William R. Mansfield, First Baron Sandhurst
1870–1876	Field Marshal Robert C. Napier, First Baron Napier of Magdala and Carynton
1876–1881	Field Marshal Sir Frederick P. Haines
1881–1885	Field Marshal Sir Donald M. Stewart
1885–1893	Field Marshal Frederick S. Roberts, V.C., First Earl Roberts of Kandahar, Pretoria, and Waterford
1893–1898	Field Marshal Sir George S. White, V.C.
1898	General Sir Charles E. Nairne (officiating)
1898–1900	General Sir William S. A. Lockhart
1900–1902	General Sir Arthur P. Palmer
1902–1909	Field Marshal Horatio H. Kitchener, First Earl Kitchener of Khartoum and of Broome
1909–1914	General Sir Garret O'Moore Creagh, V.C.
1914–1916	General Sir Harry Beauchamp Duff

Appendix 4: A Note on Currency

The main British monetary unit during this period was the pound sterling (£). Twelve pence (or pennies, symbolized as *d*) made up one shilling *(s)*, and there were twenty shillings in one pound.

British money was written in the following order: pounds/shillings/pence, or £/s/d. An example would be £2 4s 6d, denoting two pounds, four shillings, and six pence. The values could be separated by a slash without the *s* and with or without the *d*, such as £2/4/6d or £2/4/6. Values of one shilling or more and less than one pound generally appeared as shillings/pence, such as 4/6d or 4/6. When the slash system was used, zero values were indicated by a dash, such as 3/–, which denoted three shillings exactly.

Throughout most of Queen Victoria's reign, £1 was equal to about U.S.$11.00.

Indian Army officers and soldiers were paid in rupees (Rs). In 1855, there were about ten rupees to the pound, so that each rupee equaled about two shillings. At the end of the nineteenth century, the exchange rate was stabilized so that there were fifteen rupees to the pound, with each rupee equal to one shilling and four pence.

Bibliography

Adye, John. 1860. *A Review of the Crimean War, to the Winter of 1854–5.* London: Hurst & Blackett; reprint, Wakefield, UK: EP Publishing, 1973.

———. 1867. *Sitana: A Mountain Campaign on the Borders of Afghanistan in 1863.* London: Richard Bentley; reprint, Milton Keynes, UK: Military Press, 2001.

———. 1895. *Recollections of a Military Life.* London: Smith, Elder.

———. 1925. *Soldiers and Others I Have Known.* London: Herbert Jenkins.

Airlie, Mabell, Countess of. 1933. *With the Guards We Shall Go: A Guardsman's Letters in the Crimea, 1854–1855.* London: Hodder & Stoughton.

Alexander, Michael. 1957. *The True Blue: The Life and Adventures of Colonel Fred Burnaby, 1842–85.* Reprint, New York: St. Martin's, 1958.

Allen, Charles. 2000. *Soldier Sahibs: The Daring Adventurers Who Tamed India's Northwest Frontier.* New York: Carroll & Graf.

Amin, A. H. 2000. "Chillianwala: The Forgotten British Reverse in India." *Defence Journal* 3 (July). www.defencejournal.com/july/chillianwala.htm (cited 12 November 2002).

———. 2002. "The Sepoy Rebellion of 1857–59: An Analysis." *Defence Journal* 5 (March): 110–119.

Anderson, Olive. 1967. "Early Experiences of Manpower Problems in an Industrial Society at War: Great Britain, 1854–56." *Political Science Quarterly* 82 (December): 526–545.

Anglesey, Marquess of. 1961. *One-Leg: The Life and Letters of Henry William Paget, First Marquess of Anglesey, K.G., 1768–1854.* New York: William Morrow.

Arthur, George. 1920. *Life of Lord Kitchener.* 3 vols. London: Macmillan.

———. 1942. *From Wellington to Wavell.* London: Hutchinson.

Arthur, George, ed. 1922. *The Letters of Lord and Lady Wolseley, 1870–1911.* New York: Doubleday, Page.

Baden-Powell, B. F. S. 1903. *War in Practice: Some Tactical and Other Lessons of the Campaign in South Africa, 1899–1902.* London: Isbister.

Bailes, Howard. 1980. "Technology and Imperialism: A Case Study of the Victorian Army in Africa." *Victorian Studies* 24 (Autumn): 83–104.

———. 1981. "Patterns of Thought in the Late Victorian Army." *Journal of Strategic Studies* 4 (March): 29–45.

Bailey, De Witt. 2002. *British Military Flintlock Rifles, 1740–1840.* Lincoln, RI: Andrew Mowbray.

Baird, William. 1907. *General Wauchope.* 5th ed. Edinburgh: Oliphant, Anderson & Ferrier.

Baker, Anne. 1996. *A Question of Honor: The Life of Lieutenant General Valentine Baker Pasha.* London: Leo Cooper.

Ballard, C. R. 1930. *Kitchener.* London: Faber & Faber.

Barber, Laurie, and Garry Clayton. 1989. "The Spider and the Web: Intelligence Networks of the 2nd New Zealand War." *Army Quarterly and Defence Journal* (October): 453–457.

Barclay, Glen St. J. 1976. *The Empire Is Marching: A Study of the Military Effort of the British Empire, 1800–1945.* London: Weidenfeld & Nicolson.

Barker, Tom. 1999. "Heliograph."

Bibliography

www.warlinks.com/oages/heliograph.html (cited 27 May 2002).

Barnard, C. J. 1970. "General Botha at the Battle of Colenso 15 December 1899." *Military History Journal* 1 (December). rapidttp.co.za/milhist/vol017cb.html (cited 13 December 2001).

———. 1971. "General Botha in the Spioenkop Campaign January 1900." *Military History Journal* 2 (June). rapidttp.co.za/milhist/vol021cb.html (cited 13 December 2001).

———. 1973. "Studies in the Generalship of the Boer Commanders." *Military History Journal* 2 (June). rapidttp.co.za/milhist/vol025cb.html (cited 13 December 2001).

Barnes, R. Money. 1968. *The British Army of 1914.* London: Seeley Services.

Barnett, Correlli. 1970. *Britain and Her Army, 1509–1970: A Military, Political, and Social Survey.* New York: William Morrow.

Barthorp, Michael. 1979. *To Face the Daring Maoris: Soldiers' Impressions of the First Maori War, 1845–47.* London: Hodder & Stoughton.

———. 1980. *The Zulu War: A Pictorial History.* Reprint, Poole, UK: Blandford, 1986.

———. 1982. *The North-West Frontier: British India and Afghanistan: A Pictorial History, 1839–1947.* Poole, UK: Blandford.

———. 1984a. "Valentine Baker of the 10th Royal Hussars: A Cautionary Tale for Gifted Officers." *British Army Review* 77 (August): 29–35.

———. 1984b. *War on the Nile: Britain, Egypt, and the Sudan, 1882–1898.* Poole, UK: Blandford.

———. 1987. *The Anglo-Boer Wars: The British and the Afrikaners, 1815–1902.* Poole, UK: Blandford.

———. 1993. "The Indian Mutiny: A Great or Small War?" *Soldiers of the Queen* 73 (June): 13–17.

———. 1995. "How Every Schoolboy Knew: The Work of G. A. Henty." *Soldiers of the Queen* 83 (December): 26–29.

———. 1999. "Guardsman and Intelligencer: Lord Edward Gleichen." *Soldiers of the Queen* 97 (June): 28–30.

Barthorp, Michael, ed. 1988. "An Account of Maiwand." *Soldiers of the Queen* 52 (March): 2–3.

Bates, Darrell. 1979. *The Abyssinian Difficulty: The Emperor Theodorus and the Magdala Campaign, 1867–68.* Oxford: Oxford University Press.

"The Battle of Rangiriri: The Application of Artillery in the New Zealand Land Wars." N.d. riv.co.nz/rnza/hist/index.htm (cited 13 April 2002).

Baumgart, Winfried. 1999. *The Crimean War, 1853–1856.* London: Edward Arnold.

Baylen, Joseph O., and Alan Conway, eds. 1968. *Soldier-Surgeon: The Crimean War Letters of Dr. Douglas A. Reid, 1855–1856.* Knoxville: University of Tennessee Press.

Baynes, John. 1995. *Far from a Donkey: The Life of General Sir Ivor Maxse, KCB, CVO, DSO.* London: Brassey's.

Beaumont, Roger. 1977. *Sword of the Raj: The British Army in India, 1747–1947.* Indianapolis: Bobbs-Merrill.

Beckett, Ian F. W. 1982. "Edward Stanhope at the War Office, 1887–1892." *Journal of Strategic Studies* 5 (June): 278–307.

———. 1984. "The Stanhope Memorandum of 1988: A Reinterpretation." *Bulletin of the Institute of Historical Research* 57 (November): 240–247.

———. 1992. "Wolseley and the Ring." *Soldiers of the Queen* 69 (June): 14–25.

———. 1994. "The Indian Expeditionary Force on Malta and Cyprus, 1878." *Soldiers of the Queen* 76 (March): 6–11.

Beckett, Ian F. W., ed. 1986. *The Army and the Curragh Incident, 1914.* Publications of the Army Records Society, vol. 2. London: Bodley Head for the Army Records Society.

Begbie, Harold. 1915. *Kitchener: Organizer of Victory.* Boston: Houghton Mifflin.

Belfield, Eversley. 1975. *The Boer War.* London: Leo Cooper.

Bell, George. 1956. *Soldier's Glory, Being 'Rough Notes of an Old Soldier.'* Ed. Brian Stuart. Reprint, Tunbridge Wells, UK: Spellmount, 1991.

Beloff, Max. 1996. "The British Empire." *History Today* 46 (February). www.findarticles.com/cf_0/m1373/n2_v46/17931243/print.jhtml (cited 7 May 2003).

Bennett, Ian. 1997. "The Conductors of Supplies, 1879–1892: Commissariat and Transport Department Commissariat and Transport Staff." *Soldiers of the Queen* 89 (June): 7–23.

———. 2001. *A Rain of Lead: The Siege and Surrender of the British at Potchefstroom, 1880–1881.* London: Greenhill.

Bennett, Will. 1999. *Absent-Minded Beggars: Yeomanry and Volunteers in the Boer War.* Barnsley, UK: Leo Cooper.

Berkeley, George F. H. 1899. "Sir Harry Smith: A Reminiscence of the Boer War in 1848." *Fortnightly Review*, 1 (December). www.researchpress.co.uk/bmh/smith1848.htm (cited 22 December 2001).

Best, Brian, and Adrian Greaves, eds. 2001. *The Curling Letters of the Zulu War: "There Was Awful Slaughter."* Barnsley, UK: Leo Cooper.

Biddulph, H., ed. 1939. "The American Civil War: Contemporary Letters from Lieutenant-Colonel G. J. Wolseley." *Journal of the Society for Army Historical Research* 18: 38–40.

Blake, Robert. 1966. *Disraeli.* Reprint, New York: St. Martin's, 1967.

Blanco, Richard L. 1965. "Reform and Wellington's Post-Waterloo Army, 1815–1854." *Military Affairs* 29 (Fall): 123–131.

———. 1967. "The Attempted Control of Venereal Disease in the Army of Mid-Victorian England." *Journal of the Society for Army Historical Research* 45: 234–241.

———. 1968a. "Army Recruiting Reforms, 1861–1867." *Journal of the Society for Army Historical Research* 46: 217–224.

———. 1968b. "Attempts to Abolish Branding and Flogging in the Army of Victorian England before 1881." *Journal of the Society for Army Historical Research* 46: 137–145.

Blumenson, Martin, and James L. Stokesbury. 1975. *Masters of the Art of Command.* Boston: Houghton Mifflin.

Bond, Brian. 1960. "Mr. Gladstone's Invasion of Egypt (1882): A Revelation of Military Weakness." *Army Quarterly and Defence Journal* 81: 87–92.

———. 1961. "The Late Victorian Army." *History Today* 11: 616–624.

———. 1962a. "Recruiting the Victorian Army, 1870–92." *Victorian Studies* 5 (June): 331–338.

———. 1962b. "Edward Cardwell's Army Reforms, 1868–74." *Army Quarterly and Defence Journal* 84: 108–117.

———. 1965. "Doctrine and Training in the British Cavalry, 1870–1914." In *The Theory and Practice of War.* Ed. Michael Howard. Reprint, Bloomington: Indiana University Press, 1975.

———. 1967. "The South African War, 1880–1." In *Victorian Military Campaigns,* ed. Brian Bond, 199–240. New York: Praeger.

———. 1970. "Colonial Wars and Punitive Expeditions, 1856–99." In *History of the British Army,* ed. Peter Young and J. P. Lawford, 172–181. London: Arthur Barker.

———. 1972. *The Victorian Army and the Staff College, 1854–1914.* London: Eyre Methuen.

Boon, J. B. 1985. "The Telegraph in the Firing Line." *Soldiers of the Queen* 41 (June): 2–3.

Bourquin, S. 1978. "The Zulu Military Organization and the Challenge of 1879." *Military History Journal* 4 (December). rapidttp.com/milhist/vol044sb.html (cited 26 May 2003).

———. 1985. "Col. A. W. Durnford." *Military History Journal* 6 (June). rapidttp.com/milhist/vol065sb.html (cited 26 May 2003).

Bowie, John. 1989. *The Empire at War.* London: Batsford.

Brackenbury, Henry. 1874. *The Ashanti War: A Narrative.* Edinburgh: Blackwood; reprint, London: Frank Cass, 1968.

———. 1885. *The River Column: A Narrative of the Advance of the River Column of the Nile Expeditionary Force, and Its Return down the Rapids.* Reprint, Nashville: Battery, 1993.

Brennan, Jim. 2000. "The Adventures of Fred Burnaby, Soldier, Writer, Politician and Balloonist." www.greystone2000.com/history/burnaby/fred_burnaby.htm (cited 28 May 2002).

Brereton, J. M. 1986. *The British Soldier: A Social History from 1661 to the Present Day.* London: Bodley Head.

Bridge, F. R., and Roger Bullen. 1980. *The Great Powers and the European States System, 1815–1914.* London: Longman.

Brighton, Terry. 1998. *The Last Charge: The 21st Lancers and the Battle of Omdurman, 2 September 1898.* Ramsbury, UK: Crowood.

"The British Army." 1855. *Putnam's Monthly Magazine.* www.researchpress/co/uk/bmh/britisharmy1855.htm (cited 5 January 2002).

"The British Soldier: At Home." 1859. *Chambers's Journal,* 14 May. www.researchpress.co.uk/bmh/athome.htm (cited 5 January 2002).

"The British Soldier: How and Why He Enlists." 1859. *Chambers's Journal,* 23 April. www.researchpress.co.uk/bmh/enlist.htm (cited 5 January 2002).

Brock, William. 1858. *A Biographical Sketch of Sir Henry Havelock, K.C.B.* 8th ed. London: James Nisbet.

Broehl, Wayne G., Jr. 1986. *Crisis of the Raj: The Revolt of*

Bibliography

1857 through British Lieutenants' Eyes. Hanover, NH: University Press of New England.

Brook-Shepherd, Gordon. 1972. *Between Two Flags: The Life of Baron Sir Rudolf von Slatin Pasha, GCVO, KCMG, CB.* London: Weidenfeld & Nicolson.

Brooke-Hunt, Violet. 1914. *Lord Roberts, A Biography.* 3rd ed. Reprint, London: James Nisbet, 1915.

Brown, Benjamin N. 2000. *Imperial Colours.* Millington, MD: Caltrop.

Brown, Ted. 1989. "Casting a Little More Light upon Isandlwana." *Soldiers of the Queen* 56–57 (June): 13–15.

Bruce, George. 1973. *The Burma Wars, 1824–1886.* London: Hart-Davis, MacGibbon.

Bryant, Arthur. 1971. *The Great Duke or The Invincible General.* Reprint, New York: William Morrow, 1972.

Bullock, Dave. 1980. "Kandahar at Bay." *Soldiers of the Queen* 21 (May): 25–30.

Buchan, John. 1934. *Gordon at Khartoum.* London: Peter Davies.

Burnham, Frederick Russell. 1926. *Scouting on Two Continents.* Garden City, NY: Doubleday, Page.

Burns, P. L., and C. D. Cowan, eds. 1975. *Sir Frank Swettenham's Malayan Journals, 1874–1876.* Kuala Lumpur: Oxford University Press.

Burroughs, Peter. 1980. "The Human Cost of Imperial Defence in the Early Victorian Age." *Victorian Studies* 24: 7–32.

———. 1982. "The Ordnance Department and Colonial Defence, 1821–1855." *Journal of Imperial and Commonwealth History* 10: 125–149.

———. 1986. "Imperial Defence and the Victorian Army." *Journal of Imperial and Commonwealth History* 15: 55–72.

———. 1994. "An Unreformed Army? 1815–1868." In *The Oxford Illustrated History of the British Army.* Ed. David Chandler and Ian Beckett. Oxford: Oxford University Press.

Butler, William F. 1907. *Charles George Gordon.* English Men of Action. London: Macmillan.

Buttery, David. 2001. "'A Signal and Decisive Blow': The Army of Retribution during the First Afghan War." *Soldiers of the Queen* 107 (December): 1–6.

Butzgy, Michael. 1999. "Americans in the Egyptian Army: Egypt Ho!" home.earthlink.net/~atomic_rom/egyptho.htm (cited 1 July 2002).

Caie, Richard. 1985. "The Gallant Berkshires: An Account of the Battle of Tofrek (McNeill's Zariba)." *Soldiers of the Queen* 40 (March): 19–22.

———. 1987. "The Role of M/1 Battery at the Battle of Tamai." *Soldiers of the Queen* 51 (December): 2–3.

———. 1998. "The Role of Lieutenant David Beatty, RN, and the Gunboat Flotilla in the Reconquest of the Sudan." *Soldiers of the Queen* 94 (September): 17–19.

Callwell, C. E. 1896. *Small Wars: Their Principles and Practice.* 3d ed. Lincoln: University of Nebraska Press, 1996.

———. 1927. *Field-Marshal Sir Henry Wilson, Bart., G.C.B., D.S.O.: His Life and Diaries.* 2 vols. London: Cassell.

Calthorpe, Somerset J. Gough. 1856. *Cadogan's Crimea.* Reprint, London: Book Club Associates, 1979.

Cannadine, David. 1990. *The Decline and Fall of the British Aristocracy.* New Haven, CT: Yale University Press.

Carleton, Neil. 2002. "The Lion's Teeth: The Artillery of the Maharaja Ranjit Singh." *Soldiers of the Queen* 109 (June): 3–7.

Carr, Caleb. 1992. *The Devil Soldier: The Story of Frederick Townsend Ward.* New York: Random House.

Carver, Field Marshal Lord. 1984. *The Seven Ages of the British Army.* New York: Beaufort.

———. 1999. *The National Army Museum Book of the Boer War.* London: Sidgwick & Jackson; reprint, London: Pan, 2000.

Cassidy, Martin. 2001. *The Inniskilling Diaries, 1899–1903: 1st Battalion, 27th Royal Inniskilling Fusiliers in South Africa.* Barnsley, UK: Leo Cooper.

Castle, Ian. 1995. "Majuba's 'Rorke's Drift'?" *Soldiers of the Queen* 83 (December): 19–25.

Cavendish, Anne, ed. 1991. *Cyprus, 1878: The Journal of Sir Garnet Wolseley.* Nicosia: Cyprus Popular Bank Cultural Centre.

Chadwick, G. A. 1978. "The Anglo-Zulu War of 1879: Isandlwana and Rorke's Drift." *Military History Journal* 4 (December). rapidttp.com/milhist/vol044gc.html (cited 26 May 2003).

Chaille Long, Charles. 1899. "England in Egypt and the Soudan." *North American Review* 168 (May): 570–581.

Chandler, D. G. 1967. "The Expedition to Abyssinia, 1867–8." In *Victorian Military Campaigns,* ed. Brian Bond, 105–159. New York: Praeger.

Child, Daphne, ed. 1978. *The Zulu War Journal of Colonel Henry Harford, C.B.* Pietermaritzburg: Shuter & Shooter.

Chisholm, Cecil. 1915. *Sir John French: An Authentic Biography.* London: Herbert Jenkins.

Chrastina, Paul. N.d. "Emperor of China Declares War on Drugs." *Old News.* www.oldnewspublishing.com/opium.htm (cited 2 January 2003).

Christenson, Maria. "The First Opium War." 1999. www.suite101.com/article.cfm/3760/19388 (cited 2 January 2003).

Churchill, Winston S. 1898. *The Story of the Malakand Field Force: An Episode of Frontier War.* London: Longmans, Green; reprint, New York: Norton, 1990.

———. 1900. *London to Ladysmith via Pretoria.* London: Longmans, Green; reprint, Durban: Griggs, 1982.

———. 1930. *My Early Life: A Roving Commission.* Reprint, London: Macmillan, 1944.

Clark, Peter. 1985. "The Fall of Khartoum." *Soldiers of the Queen* 40 (March): 5–15.

Clementson, John. 1985. "The Last of the Thin Red Line." *British Army Review* 81 (December): 64–71.

Clifford, Henry. 1956. *His Letters and Sketches from the Crimea.* London: Michael Joseph.

Clowes, William Laird. 1897–1903. *The Royal Navy: A History from the Earliest Times to the Death of Queen Victoria.* 7 vols. London: Sampson Low, Marston.

Coetzer, Owen. 1996. *The Anglo-Boer War: The Road to Infamy, 1899–1900.* London: Arms & Armour.

Collier, Richard. 1964. *The Great Indian Mutiny: A Dramatic Account of the Sepoy Mutiny.* New York: Dutton, 1964.

Compton, Piers. 1970. *Colonel's Lady and Camp-Follower: The Story of Women in the Crimean War.* New York: St. Martin's.

———. 1974. *The Last Days of General Gordon.* London: Hale.

Conan Doyle, Arthur. 1901. *The Great Boer War: A Two-Years' Record, 1899–1901.* London: Smith, Elder.

Cook, H. C. B. 1975. *The Sikh Wars: The British Army in the Punjab, 1845–1849.* 19th Century Military Campaigns. Ed. Brian Bond. London: Leo Cooper.

Cowan, C. D. 1961. *Nineteenth-Century Malaya: The Origins of British Political Control.* London: Oxford University Press.

Crawford, E. R. 1967. "The Sikh Wars, 1845–9." In *Victorian Military Campaigns,* ed. Brian Bond, 105–159. New York: Praeger.

Cromer, Earl of. 1908. *Modern Egypt.* 2 vols. New York: Macmillan.

Cross, J. P. 1986. *In Gurkha Company: The British Army Gurkhas, 1948 to the Present.* London: Arms & Armour.

Crouch, J. D. 1983a. "British Cavalry Regiments, 1899." *Soldiers of the Queen* 33 (July): 24–25.

———. 1983b. "British Infantry Training." *Soldiers of the Queen* 35 (December): 3–6.

Cunningham, John. 2001. "Assistant Surgeon Brydon's 'Melancholy Particulars' Describing the Retreat from Cabul in 1842." *Soldiers of the Queen* 106 (September): 2–8.

Cunningham, Mike. 2001. "'A' & 'Q' Services: Indian Army." *Durbar* 18 (Spring): 30–34.

D'Assonville, V. E., comp. N.d. "The First War of Independence." In *Battlefield: History.* www.battlefields.co.za/history/1st_war_of_independence/index.htm (cited 17 December 2001).

Daly, M. W. 1997. *The Sirdar: Sir Reginald Wingate and the British Empire in the Middle East.* Philadelphia: American Philosophical Society.

David, Saul. 1997. *The Homicidal Earl: The Life of Lord Cardigan.* London: Little, Brown.

Davis, H. W. C., and J. R. H. Weavers, eds. 1927. *The Dictionary of National Biography, 1912–1921.* London: Humphrey Milford.

Dean, Maurice. 1979. *The Royal Air Force and Two World Wars.* London: Cassell.

Denman, Terence. 1996. "'Ethnic Soldiers Pure and Simple'? The Irish in the Late Victorian Army." *War in History* 3 (November): 253–273.

De Beaumont, Marguerite. 1944. *The Wolf That Never Sleeps: A Story of Baden-Powell.* Reprint, London: Girl Guides Association, 1952.

De Cosson, E. A. 1886. *Fighting the Fuzzy-Wuzzy: Days and Nights of Service with Sir Gerald Graham's Field Force at Suakin.* London: John Murray; reprint, London: Greenhill, 1990.

De Santis, Edward. 2000. "Sapper James Campbell, Royal Engineers." members.aol.com/_ht_a/reubique/9093.htm?mtbrand=AOL_US (cited 28 September 2001).

De Villiers, J. C. 1983. "The Medical Aspect of the Anglo-Boer War, 1899–1902: Part I." *Military History Journal* 6 (December). www.rapidttp.co.za/milhist/vol062jc.html (cited 16 February 2002).

———. 1984. "The Medical Aspect of the Anglo-Boer War, 1899–1902, Part II." *Military History Journal* 6 (June). www.rapidttp.co.za/milhist/vol063jc.html (cited 16 February 2002).

Bibliography

De Watteville, H. 1938. *Lord Roberts.* London: Blackie & Son.

———. 1954. *The British Soldier: His Daily Life from Tudor to Modern Times.* New York: Putnam's.

Dietz, Peter. 1990. *The Last of the Regiments: Their Rise and Fall.* London: Brassey's.

Dinwiddy, J. R. 1982. "The Early Nineteenth Century Campaign against Flogging in the Army." *English Historical Review* 97: 308–331.

Dixon, Norman F. 1976. *On the Psychology of Military Incompetence.* Reprint, London: Jonathan Cape, 1984.

Dobrahner, Lesanna. 1998. "The Boxer Rebellion." www.farmington.k12.mn.us/intrview/ldboxreb.htm (cited 4 March 2003).

Dorling, H. Taprell. 1974. *Ribbons and Medals: The World's Military and Civil Awards.* Garden City, NY: Doubleday.

Dreilinger, Tamas F. N.d. "Menshikov at Inkerman: A Failure to Command." In *Studies in Battle Command.* Ed. Faculty, Combat Studies Institute, Ft. Leavenworth, KS: U.S. Army Command and General Staff College. www-cgsc.Army.mil/carl/resources/csi/battles/battles.asp (cited 19 May 2003).

Droogleever, R. W. F. 1991. "Prelude to Majuba: Ingogo Heights or Schuinshoogte (8 February 1881), Transvaal War of Independence." *Soldiers of the Queen* 67 (December): 7–11.

———. 1992. "Charles Fripp and 'The Battle of Isandhlwana.'" *Soldiers of the Queen* 70 (September): 5.

Dupuy, R. Ernest, and Trevor N. Dupuy. 1986. *The Encyclopedia of Military History from 3,500 B.C. to the Present.* 2d rev. ed. New York: Harper & Row.

Durrans, P. J. 1982. "A Two-Edged Sword: The Liberal Attack on Disraelian Imperialism." *Journal of Imperial and Commonwealth History* 10: 262–284.

Duxbury, G. R. 1968. "More about the Horse in War." *Military History Journal* 1 (December). rapidttp.com/milhist/vol013gd.html (cited 21 May 2002).

———. 1980a. "The Battle of Bronkhorstspruit 20 December 1880." *Military History Journal* 5 (December). rapidttp.com/milhist/vol052gd.html (cited 23 December 2001).

———. 1980b. "The Battle of Laingsnek, 28 January 1881." *Military History Journal* 5 (December). rapidttp.com/milhist/vol052gc.html (cited 23 December 2001).

Dyas, Eamon. 2002. "Winston Churchill, Soldier and Journalist." *Times,* 27 November. www.oldrufus.com/wiron/20021127chruchill.htm (cited 18 June 2003).

Edelman, Ian. 2001. "Development of 'The camp at Aldershott.'" www.hants.gov.uk/museum/aldshotm/faq/aldcamp.html (cited 29 October 2001).

Edgerton, Robert B. 1988. *Like Lions They Fought: The Zulu War and the Last Black Empire in South Africa.* New York: Free Press.

———. 1995. *The Fall of the Asante Empire: The Hundred-Year War for Africa's Gold Coast.* New York: Free Press.

———. 1999. *Death or Glory: The Legacy of the Crimean War.* Boulder: Westview.

Edwardes, Michael. 1963. *Battles of the Indian Mutiny.* New York: Macmillan.

———. 1973. *A Season in Hell: The Defence of the Lucknow Residency.* New York: Taplinger.

"Egypt." N.d. British Empire: The Map Room: Africa: Egypt. www.btinternet.com/~britishempire/empire/maproom/egypt.htm (cited 3 August 2001).

Ellis, John. 1978. *Cavalry: The History of Mounted Warfare.* Sydney: Books for Pleasure.

Elton, Lord. 1954. *The Life of General Charles G. Gordon.* London: Collins.

Elton, Lord, ed. 1961. *General Gordon's Khartoum Journal.* New York: Vanguard.

Emery, Frank. 1982. "The Anglo-Zulu War as Depicted in Soldiers' Letters." *Military History Journal* 5 (June). rapidttp.com/milhist/vol055fe.html (cited 26 May 2003).

———. 1986. *Marching over Africa: Letters from Victorian Soldiers.* London: Hodder & Stoughton.

England, Rai, and Andrew S. Gardiner. 1990. "In Defence of Colonel Durnford." *Soldiers of the Queen* 58–59 (January): 46–47.

England, Raimond M., and Andrew S. Gardiner. 1991. "Isandlwana, 22nd January 1879: Further Observations on Colonel Durnford's No. 2 Column." *Soldiers of the Queen* 65 (June): 24–27.

English, John A. 1981. *On Infantry.* New York: Praeger.

Erickson, Arvel B. 1959. "Abolition of Purchase in the British Army." *Military Affairs* 23 (Summer): 65–76.

Esher, Oliver, Viscount, ed. 1938. *The Captain and the Kings Depart: Journals and Letters of Reginald, Viscount Esher.* New York: Scribner's.

Fabb, John, and W. Y. Carmen. 1975. *The Victorian and Edwardian Army from Old Photographs.* London: Batsford.

Falls, Cyril. 1967. "The Reconquest of the Sudan, 1896–9."

In *Victorian Military Campaigns,* ed. Brian Bond, 199–240. New York: Praeger.

Farrar-Hockley, Anthony. 1975. *Goughie: The Life of General Sir Hubert Gough, GCB, GCMG, KCVO.* London: Hart-Davis, MacGibbon.

Farwell, Byron. 1972. *Queen Victoria's Little Wars.* New York: Harper & Row.

———. 1981. *Mr. Kipling's Army.* New York: Norton.

———. 1984. *The Gurkhas.* New York: Norton.

———. 1985. *Eminent Victorian Soldiers: Seekers of Glory.* New York: Norton.

———. 1989. *Armies of the Raj: From the Mutiny to Independence.* New York: Norton.

———. 2001. *The Encyclopedia of Nineteenth-Century Land Warfare: An Illustrated World View.* New York: Norton.

Featherstone, Donald. 1968. *At Them with the Bayonet! The First Sikh War.* London: Jarrolds.

———. 1973. *Colonial Small Wars, 1837–1901.* Newton Abbot, UK: David & Charles.

———. 1978. *Weapons and Equipment of the Victorian Soldier.* Reprint, London: Arms & Armour, 1996.

———. 1989. *Victoria's Enemies: An A–Z of British Colonial Warfare.* London: Blandford.

———. 1992a. *Victorian Colonial Warfare: Africa.* London: Cassell.

———. 1992b. *Victorian Colonial Warfare: India.* Reprint, London: Blandford, 1993.

———. 1995a. "General Sir Hugh Gough: Tipperary Tim?" *British Army Review* 111 (December): 29–33.

———. 1995b. *Khaki and Red: Soldiers of the Queen in India and Africa.* London: Arms & Armour.

Ferguson, Niall. 2003. "Why We Ruled the World," *Times Online,* 6 January. www.timesonline.co.uk/print Friendly/0,1-7-533679,00.html (cited 7 January 2003).

Fergusson, Thomas G. 1984. *British Military Intelligence, 1870–1914: The Development of a Modern Intelligence Organization.* London: Arms & Armour.

Fincastle, Viscount, and P. C. Eliott-Lockhart. 1898. *A Frontier Campaign: A Narrative of the Malakand and Buner Field Forces on the North West Frontier of India, 1897–1898.* London: Methuen; reprint, London: Leach, 1990.

"The First Afghan War: The Causes." N.d. www.geocities.com.Broadway/Alley/5443/afl.htm (cited 30 October 2002).

Fleming, Peter. 1959. *The Siege at Peking.* Reprint, New York: Dorset.

———. 1961. *Bayonets to Lhasa: The First Full Account of the British Invasion of Tibet in 1904.* London: Rupert Hart-Davis.

Forbes, Archibald. 1892. *The Afghan Wars, 1839–42 and 1878–80.* Reprint, London: Darf, 1987.

———. 1895. *Colin Campbell, Lord Clyde.* English Men of Action. London: Macmillan.

Fortescue, John. 1925. *Wellington.* London: Williams & Norgate.

Fraser, John, ed. 1994. "Field Surgeon at the Battle of Aliwal: The Letters of Dr. John Murray during the Sikh War." *Journal of the Society for Army Historical Research* 72 (Spring): 35–48.

Fredericks, Pierce G. 1971. *The Sepoy and the Cossack: The Anglo-Russian Confrontation in British India.* New York: New American Library.

Fremantle, Arthur J. L. 1863. *The Fremantle Diary, Being the Journal of Lieutenant Colonel Arthur James Lyons Fremantle, Coldstream Guards, on His Three Months in the Southern States.* Ed. Walter Lord. Reprint, Short Hills, NJ: Buford, 2001.

French, Gerald. 1931. *The Life of Field-Marshal Sir John French, First Earl of Ypres, K.P., G.C.B., O.M., G.C.V.O., K.C.M.G.* London: Cassell.

French, Patrick. 1994. *Younghusband: The Last Great Imperial Adventurer.* London: HarperCollins.

Furneaux, Rupert. 1958. *The Breakfast War.* New York: Crowell.

Gallagher, Thomas F. 1975a. "British Military Thinking and the Coming of the Franco-Prussian War." *Military Affairs* 39 (February): 19–22.

———. 1975b. "'Cardwellian Mysteries': The Fate of the British Army Regulation Bill, 1871." *Historical Journal* 18: 327–348.

Gardner, Brian. 1971. *The East India Company: A History.* Reprint, New York: Barnes & Noble, 1997.

Garrett, Richard. 1974. *General Gordon.* London: Arthur Barker.

"General Sir Archibald Alison, G.C.B." 1907. *Blackwood's* 181 (March): 442–444.

"Ghana: The Asante Wars." N.d. In *Ghana: A Country Study.* lcweb2.loc.gov/cgi-bin/query/r?frd/cstdy:@field (DOCID+gh0143) (cited 28 August 2001).

Gilbert, Martin. 1991. *Churchill: A Life.* New York: Henry Holt.

Bibliography

Gillings, Ken. 1978. "Inyezane, Gingindlovu and the Relief of Eshowe: The Forgotten Battlefields of the Zulu War, 1879." *Military History Journal* 4 (December). rapidttp.com/milhist/vol044kg.html (cited 26 May 2003).

Gleichen, Count. 1888. *With the Camel Corps up the Nile.* London: Chapman & Hall; reprint, Wakefield, UK: EP Publishing, 1975.

Glover, Michael. 1975. *Rorke's Drift: A Victorian Epic.* London: Leo Cooper.

Gooding, Norman, ed. 1994. *The Medals Year Book, 1995 Edition.* London: Naval and Military Press.

Gordon, Lawrence L. 1971. *Military Origins.* Ed. J. B. R. Nicholson. New York: Barnes.

Gordon-Duff, Lachlan. 1997. *With the Gordon Highlanders to the Boer War and Beyond: The Story of Captain Lachlan Gordon-Duff, 1880–1914.* Reprint, Staplehurst, UK: Spellmount.

Gosse, Edmund. 1900. "Sir Redvers Buller: A Character Study." *North American Review* 170 (January): 109–120.

Gough, Hubert. 1954. *Soldiering On.* London: Arthur Barker.

Greaves, Adrian, and Brian Best, eds. 2001. *The Curling Letters of the Zulu War: 'There Was Awful Slaughter.'* Barnsley, UK: Leo Cooper.

Greaves, George R. 1924. *Memoirs of General Sir George Richards Greaves.* London: John Murray.

Greaves, Rose L. N.d. "Mortimer Durand." www.afghan-politics.org/Reference/DurandLine/ . . ./Bio_Picture.mortimer_durand.htm (cited 31 July 2001).

Grenfell, Field Marshal Lord. 1925. *Memoirs of Field-Marshal Lord Grenfell, P.C., G.C.B., G.C.M.G.* London: Hodder & Stoughton.

Grey, Elizabeth. 1971. *The Noise of Drums and Trumpets: W. H. Russell Reports from the Crimea.* New York: Walck.

Grierson, James Moncrief. 1899. *Scarlet into Khaki: The British Army on the Eve of the Boer War.* Reprint, London: Greenhill, 1988.

Griffith, Kenneth. 1974. *Thank God We Kept the Flag Flying: The Siege and Relief of Ladysmith, 1899–1900.* London: Hutchinson.

Guedalla, Philip. 1931. *The Duke.* Reprint, London: Hodder & Stoughton.

Gupta, Partha Sarathi, and Anirudh Deshpande, eds. 2002. *The British Raj and Its Indian Armed Forces, 1857–1939.* New Delhi: Oxford University Press.

Gustafson, Kristian. 2002. "Impartial, Not Neutral; The *North China Herald* and the Making of 'Chinese Gordon.'" *Soldiers of the Queen* 108 (March): 1–4.

Haldane, Richard Burdon. 1929. *An Autobiography.* Garden City, NY: Doubleday, Doran.

Hall, Darrell D. 1971. "Guns in South Africa, 1899–1902." *Military History Journal* 2 (June). rapidttp.com/milhist/vol021dh.html (cited 21 May 2002).

———. 1972. "Field Artillery of the British Army, 1860–1960, Part I, 1860–1900." *Military History Journal* 2 (December). rapidttp.com/milhist/vol024dh.html (cited 21 May 2002).

———. 1973. "Field Artillery of the British Army, 1860–1960, Part II, 1900–1914." *Military History Journal* 2 (June). rapidttp.com/milhist/vol025dh.html (cited 21 May 2002).

Hallows, Ian S. 1991. *Regiments and Corps of the British Army.* London: Arms & Armour.

Hamer, W. S. 1970. *The British Army: Civil-Military Relations, 1885–1905.* Oxford: Clarendon.

Hamilton, Ian. 1905. *A Staff Officer's Scrap-Book during the Russo-Japanese War.* London: Edward Arnold.

———. 1944. *Listening for the Drums.* London: Faber & Faber.

———. 1957. *The Commander.* Ed. Anthony Farrar-Hockley. London: Hollis & Carter.

Hamilton, Ian B. M. 1966. *The Happy Warrior: A Life of General Sir Ian Hamilton, G.C.B., G.C.M.G., D.S.O.* London: Cassell.

Hamley, Edward. 1891. *The War in the Crimea.* London: Seeley.

Hannah, W. H. 1972. *Bobs, Kipling's General: The Life of Field-Marshal Earl Roberts of Kandahar, VC.* Hamden, CT: Archon.

Hanson, Lawrence, and Elisabeth. 1954. *Chinese Gordon: The Story of a Hero.* New York: Funk & Wagnalls.

Harcourt, Freda. 1980. "Disraeli's Imperialism, 1866–1868: A Question of Timing." *Historical Journal* 23: 87–109.

———. 1985. "Gladstone, Monarchism, and the 'New' Imperialism, 1868–74." *Journal of Imperial and Commonwealth History* 14: 20–51.

Harries-Jenkins, Gwyn. 1977. *The Army in Victorian Society.* London: Routledge & Kegan Paul.

Harrington, Peter, and Frederic A. Sharf, eds. 1998. *Omdurman, 1898: The Eye-Witnesses Speak.* London: Greenhill.

Harris, John. 1973. *The Gallant Six Hundred: A Tragedy of Obsessions.* Reprint, New York: Mason & Lipscomb, 1974.

Harris, Norman Dwight. 1914. *Intervention and Colonization in Africa.* Boston: Houghton Mifflin.

Harris, Roger S. 1999. "Congreve the Rocket-man: A Flawed Man or a Flawed Age?" *Soldiers of the Queen* 96 (March): 2–5.

Hart, David. 1999. "Study Guides on War Art: Lady Elizabeth Butler (1846–1933): Celebrating Victoria's 'Little Wars.'" www.arts.adelaide.edu.au/personal/DHart/ResponsesToWar/Art/ StudyGu . . ./Butler.htm (cited 3 October 2002).

Harvie, Ian. 1999. "'A Very Dangerous Man': A Profile of Henry Brackenbury." *Soldiers of the Queen* 96 (March): 12–17.

Hawkins, Richard. 1973. "An Army on Police Work, 1881–2: Ross of Bladensburg's Memorandum." *Irish Sword* 11: 75–117.

Haythornthwaite, Philip J. 1994. *The Armies of Wellington.* Reprint, London: Brockhampton, 1998.

———. 1995. *The Colonial Wars Source Book.* London: Arms & Armour.

Headrick, Daniel R. 1979. "The Tools of Imperialism: Technology and the Expansion of European Colonial Empires in the Nineteenth Century." *Journal of Modern History* 51 (June): 231–263.

Heathcote, T. A. 1974. *The Indian Army: The Garrison of British Imperial India, 1822–1922.* Historic Armies and Navies. Ed. Christopher Duffy. Newton Abbot, UK: David & Charles.

———. 1980. "England's Vietnam?" *Soldiers of the Queen* 21 (May): 2–7.

Hendrickson, Ken. 1996. "A Kinder, Gentler British Army: Mid-Victorian Experiments in the Management of Army Vice at Gibraltar and Aldershot." *War & Society* 14 (October): 21–33.

———. 1999. "Victorian Military Politics of Establishment and Religious Liberty: William H. Rule and the Introduction of Wesleyan Methodism into the British Army, 1856–1882." *War & Society* 17 (October): 1–23.

Hensman, Howard. 1900. *A History of Rhodesia, Compiled from Official Sources.* Edinburgh: Blackwood.

Herbert, E. J. 1983. "The Worst Army That Ever Marched to War: The Hicks Expedition, 1883." *Soldiers of the Queen* 34 (September): 10–21.

Hervey, Albert. 1988. *A Soldier of the Company: Life of an Indian Ensign, 1833–43.* Ed. Charles Allen. London: Michael Joseph/National Army Museum.

Hibbert, Christopher. 1961. *The Destruction of Lord Raglan: A Tragedy of the Crimean War, 1854–55.* Boston: Little, Brown.

———. 1970. *The Dragon Wakes: China and the West, 1793–1911.* New York: Harper & Row.

———. 1978. *The Great Mutiny: India, 1857.* New York: Viking.

Hibbs, Peter. 2002. "The South Coast Martello Towers." www.martello-towers.co.uk (cited 25 September 2002).

Hieronymussen, Paul. 1970. *Orders and Decorations of Europe.* New York: Macmillan.

Hilton, Richard. 1957. *The Indian Mutiny: A Centenary History.* London: Hollis & Carter.

"An Historical Sketch of the Purchase System, 'Official' Prices of Purchased Commissions, and General Pay Scale of the British Army, Circa 1854." 2002. www.cwreenactors.com/~crimean/purchsys.htm (cited 22 December 2002).

Hittle, J. D. 1944. *The Military Staff: Its History and Development.* Reprint, Harrisburg, PA: Stackpole, 1961.

Holmes, Richard. 1981. *The Little Field-Marshal: Sir John French.* London: Jonathan Cape.

Holt, Edgar. 1958. "Garnet Wolseley: Soldier of Empire." *History Today* 8: 706–713.

Hooper, George. 1889. *Wellington.* English Men of Action. London: Macmillan.

Horowitz, Richard S. 2002. "Beyond the Marble Boat: The Transformation of the Chinese Military." In *A Military History of China,* ed. David A. Graff and Robin Higham, 153–174. Boulder: Westview.

Howard, Michael. 1981. "Empire, Race and War in Pre-1914 Britain." *History Today* 31 (December): 4–11

Hulme, J. J. 1968. "Irregular Units of the 7th Kaffir War, 1846–7." *Military History Journal* 1 (December). rapidttp.co.za/milhist/vol013jh.html (cited 24 June 2003).

Hunter, Archie. 1996. *Kitchener's Sword-Arm: The Life and Campaigns of General Sir Archibald Hunter, G.C.B., G.C.V.O., D.S.O.* New York: Sarpedon.

Hurd, Douglas. 1967. *The Arrow War: An Anglo-Chinese Confusion, 1856–1860.* London: Collins.

Hussey, John. 1999. "The Armoured Train Disaster, and Winston Churchill's Escape from Prison, South Africa, 1899." *British Army Review* 123 (Winter): 84–103.

"Inkerman: The Opening Round." 1980. *Soldiers of the Queen* 23 (November): 14–17.

Bibliography

"Irish Troops Take Over Curragh." 1922. *Irish Independent,* 17 May. homepage.tinet.ie/~macker36/handover.htm (cited 27 January 2002).

Jablonksy, David. 1991. *Churchill, the Great Game, and Total War.* London: Frank Cass.

Jackson, Tabitha. 1999. *The Boer War.* London: Channel 4 Books.

Jalali, Ali A., and Lester W. Grau. 2001. "Expeditionary Forces: Superior Technology Defeated: The Battle of Maiwand." *Military Review* 81 (May–June): 71–82.

James, Harold, and Denis Sheil-Small. 1965. *The Gurkhas.* Reprint, Harrisburg, PA: Stackpole, 1966.

James, Lawrence. 1981. *Crimea, 1854–56: The War with Russia from Contemporary Photographs.* New York: Van Nostrand Reinhold.

———. 1985. *The Savage Wars: British Campaigns in Africa, 1870–1920.* New York: St. Martin's.

———. 1993. *Imperial Warrior: The Life and Times of Field-Marshal Viscount Allenby, 1861–1936.* London: Weidenfeld & Nicolson.

———. 1997. *Raj: The Making and Unmaking of British India.* Reprint, New York: St. Martin's, 1998.

———. 1999. *The Illustrated Rise and Fall of the British Empire.* New York: St. Martin's.

Jeal, Tim. 1989. *The Boy-Man: The Life of Lord Baden-Powell.* London: Century Hutchinson; reprint, New York: William Morrow, 1990.

Jeffery, Keith, ed. 1985. *The Military Correspondence of Field Marshal Sir Henry Wilson, 1918–1922.* Publications of the Army Records Society, vol. 1. London: Bodley Head for the Army Records Society.

Jerrold, Walter. 1901. *Lord Roberts of Kandahar, V.C.: The Life-Story of a Great Soldier.* London: Patridge.

Johnson, Doug. 1965. "The Myth of Ansar Firepower." *Savage and Soldier* 1. www.dnai.com/~songliu/SavageAndSoldier/su.../AnsarFirepower.htm (cited 30 June 2002).

———. 1972. "The Egyptian Army, 1880–1900." *Savage and Soldier* 8. www.dnai.com/~soongliu/SavageAndSoldier/sudan/Egyptian_Army.html (cited 3 June 2002).

———. 1977. "The Battle of Ginniss." *Soldiers of the Queen* 11. www.dnai.com/~soongliu/SavageAndSoldier/sudan/Ginnis.html (cited 30 June 2002).

Johnson, Douglas H. 1982. "The Death of Gordon: A Victorian Myth." *Journal of Imperial and Commonwealth History* 10: 285–310.

Johnson, R. A. 1998. "'Russians at the Gates of India': The Defence of India's Northern Flank." *Soldiers of the Queen* 95 (December): 6–10.

———. 1999. "'Russia and England Face to Face in Asia': The Penjdeh Incident of 1885." *Soldiers of the Queen* 98 (September): 9–13.

Jones, Jim. 1998. "African History Timeline: 19th Century Egypt and East Africa." In African History Since 1875. courses.weupa.edu/jones/his311/timeline/t-19egy.htm (cited 3 August 2001).

Jones, Maurig. 1996. "Blockhouses of the Boer War." *Colonial Conquest.* www.magweb.com/sample/scol/sccllblc.htm (cited 12 December 2001).

Jones, Meurig G. M. 1993. "The Highland Light Infantry at Tel-el-Kebir." *Soldiers of the Queen* 72 (March): 7–14.

Joslin, Edward C. 1974. *The Observer's Book of British Awards and Medals.* London: Frederick Warne.

Judd, Denis. 1973. *Someone Has Blundered: Calamities of the British Army in the Victorian Age.* Reprint, Gloucestershire, UK: Windrush, 1999.

———. 1975. *The Crimean War.* London: Hart-Davis, MacGibbon.

Karsten, Peter. 1983. "Irish Soldiers in the British Army, 1792–1922: Suborned or Subordinate?" *Journal of Social History* 17: 31–64.

Kaufman, Matthew H. 2001. *Surgeons at War: Medical Arrangements for the Treatment of the Sick and Wounded in the British Army during the Late 18th and 19th Centuries.* Westport, CT: Greenwood.

Kaul, Vivien Ashima. 2002. "Sepoys Links with Society: A Study of the Bengal Army, 1858–95." In *The British Raj and Its Indian Armed Forces, 1857–1939.* Ed. Partha Sarathi Gupta and Anirudh Deshpande. New Delhi: Oxford University Press.

Keegan, John. 1967. "The Ashanti Campaign, 1873–4." In *Victorian Military Campaigns,* ed. Brian Bond, 161–198. New York: Praeger.

Keeling, Brian, and John MacLellan. 1973. "Notes on the Pipes, Drums, and Military Bands to 1973." www.btinternet.com/~james.mckay/scotdivm.htm (cited 3 January 2002).

Kelsey, David. 2002. "The Destruction of Sir George Cathcart." In Crimean Texts. www.kelsey-family.demon.co.uk/topics/cathcart.html (cited 10 July 2002).

———. 2003. "Raglan Deluded on Sapoune: Yet Another Reason Why." *War Correspondent* 20 (January): 22–23.

Kempton, Chris. 1993. "The Persian War, 1856–57." *Soldiers of the Queen* 73 (June): 5–13.

Keown-Boyd, Henry. 1986. *A Good Dusting: A Centenary Review of the Sudan Campaigns, 1883–1899.* London: Guild.

———. 1991. *The Boxer Rebellion.* Reprint, New York: Dorset, 1996.

Kinsey, H. W. 1973. "The Sekukuni Wars." *Military History Journal* 2 (June). rapidttp.com/milhist/vol025hk.html (cited 26 May 2003).

———. 1987. "Churchill and Ladysmith." *Military History Journal* 7 (June). rapidttp.co.za/milhist/vol073hk.html (cited 24 June 2003).

Knight, Ian. 1990. *Brave Men's Blood: The Epic of the Zulu War, 1879.* London: Greenhill.

———. 1995. *The Anatomy of the Zulu Army, from Shaka to Cetshwayo, 1818–1879.* Reprint, London: Wrens Park, 1999.

———. 1996. *Go to Your God Like a Soldier: The British Soldier Fighting for Empire, 1837–1902.* London: Greenhill.

———. 1999a. *Great Zulu Commanders.* London: Arms & Armour.

Knight, Ian, ed. 1999b. *Marching to the Drums: From the Kabul Massacre to the Siege of Mafikeng.* London: Greenhill.

———. N.d. "The Battle of Isandlwana: 'Wet with Yesterday's Blood.'" In Battlefields: History: Anglo-Zulu War. www.battlefields.co.za/history/anglo-zulu_war/isandhlwana/isandlwana_ian%20knight . . . (cited 27 May 2003).

Knightley, Phillip. 1975. *The First Casualty: From the Crimea to Vietnam: The War Correspondent as Hero, Propagandist, and Myth Maker.* New York: Harcourt Brace Jovanovich.

Kochanski, H. M. 1997. "Field Marshal Viscount Wolseley as Commander-in-Chief, 1895–1900: A Reassessment." *Journal of Strategic Studies* 20 (June): 119–139.

Kochanski, Halik. 1999. *Sir Garnet Wolseley: Victorian Hero.* London: Hambledon Press.

Koss, Stephen E. 1969. *Lord Haldane: Scapegoat for Liberalism.* New York: Columbia University Press.

Laband, John. 1995. *The Rise and Fall of the Zulu Nation.* Reprint, London: Arms & Armour, 1997.

Laband, John, and Ian Knight. 1996. *The War Correspondents: The Anglo-Zulu War.* Stroud, UK: Sutton.

Lawrence, John. 1990. *Lawrence of Lucknow: A Biography.* Edited by Audrey Woodiwiss. London: Hodder & Stoughton.

Leadbetter, N. A. 1991. "A Training Scheme for British Officers, 1799–1858." *British Army Review* 98 (August): 60–63.

Leasor, James. 1956. *The Red Fort: The Story of the Indian Mutiny, 1857.* Reprint, New York: Reynal, 1957.

Lee, Emanoel. 1985. *To the Bitter End: A Photographic History of the Boer War, 1899–1902.* New York: Viking.

Lee, Harold. 2002. *Brothers in the Raj: The Lives of John and Henry Lawrence.* Oxford: Oxford University Press.

Lee, John. 2000. *A Soldier's Life: General Sir Ian Hamilton, 1853–1947.* London: Macmillan.

Lee, Sidney, ed. 1912. *The Dictionary of National Biography: Supplement, January 1901–December 1911.* Vol. 1, *Abbey-Eyre.* Reprint, Oxford: Oxford University Press, 1963.

Leggat, Robert. 1999. "A History of Photography: Photography of War." www.rleggat.com/photohistory/history/war.htm (cited 2 October 2002).

———. 2000. "A History of Photography: Fenton, Roger." www.rleggat.com/photohistory/history/fenton.htm (cited 2 October 2002).

Lehmann, Joseph H. 1964. *All Sir Garnet: A Life of Field-Marshal Lord Wolseley.* London: Jonathan Cape.

Lethbridge, Cliff. 2000. "History of Rocketry: 18th and 19th Centuries." www.spaceline.org/history/2.html (cited 8 January 2002).

"Lieutenant-Colonel John Carstairs McNeill, V.C." 1999. The Royal Sussex Regiment Victoria Crosses. www.eastbournemuseums.co.uk/redoubt/rsxvc.htm (cited 10 September 2002).

Lloyd, Alan. 1964. *The Drums of Kumasi: The Story of the Ashanti Wars.* London: Longmans.

Lock, Ron, and Peter Quantrill. 2002. *Zulu Victory: The Epic of Isandlwana and the Cover-up.* London: Greenhill.

Lococo, Paul, Jr. 2002. "The Qing Empire." In *A Military History of China,* ed. David A. Graff and Robin Higham, 115–134. Boulder: Westview.

Longford, Elizabeth. 1964. *Queen Victoria: Born to Succeed.* New York: Harper & Row.

———. 1969. *Wellington: The Years of the Sword.* New York: Harper & Row.

Low, Charles Rathbone. 1883. *General Lord Wolseley (of Cairo), G.C.B., G.C.M.G., D.C.L., L.L.D.: A Memoir.* 2nd ed. London: Richard Bentley.

Ludwig, Emil. 1937. *The Nile: The Life-Story of a River.*

Bibliography

Trans. Mary H. Lindsay. New York: Viking.

Lunt, James. 1969. *Bokhara Burnes.* London: Faber & Faber.

Luvaas, Jay. 1964. *The Education of an Army: British Military Thought, 1815–1940.* Chicago: University of Chicago Press.

———. 1965. "European Military Thought and Doctrine, 1870–1914." In *The Theory and Practice of War.* Ed. Michael Howard. Reprint, Bloomington: Indiana University Press, 1975.

Lyttelton, Neville. 1924. *Eighty Years: Soldiering, Politics, Games.* London: Hodder & Stoughton.

MacGregor-Hastie, Roy. 1985. *Never to Be Taken Alive: A Biography of General Gordon.* New York: St. Martin's.

MacLaren, Roy. 1978. *Canadians on the Nile, 1882–1898: Being the Adventures of the Voyageurs on the Khartoum Relief Expedition and Other Exploits.* Vancouver: University of British Columbia Press.

MacMunn, George. 1930. *Behind the Scenes in Many Wars.* London: John Murray.

MacNeil, Rod. 1997. "The Defence of Chakdara." *Soldiers of the Queen* 88 (March): 4–10.

———. 2001. "The 36th Sikhs and the Samana." *Soldiers of the Queen* 107 (December): 7–13.

Macrory, Patrick. 1966. *Signal Catastrophe: The Retreat from Kabul, 1842.* Reprint, London: History Book Club, 1967.

"Magersfontein." N.d. "The South African War, 1899–1902." www.rsi.co.za/boerwar/Magersfontein.htm (cited 25 July 2003).

Magnus, Philip. 1959. *Kitchener: Portrait of an Imperialist.* New York: Dutton.

Maitland, D. D. 1950. "The Care of the Soldier's Family." *Royal Army Medical Corps Journal,* 107–125.

Major, E. 1913. *Lord Wolseley.* London: James Nisbet.

Mangan, J. A. 1980. "Images of Empire in the Late Victorian Public School." *Journal of Educational Administration and History* 12 (January): 31–39.

Manore, J. I. 1987. "The Red River Expedition of 1870." *Army Quarterly and Defence Journal* 117 (July): 330–337.

Mansfield, H. O. 1973. *Charles Ashe Windham: A Norfolk Soldier (1810–1870).* Lavenham, UK: Dalton.

Mansfield, Peter. 1971. *The British in Egypt.* Reprint, New York: Holt, Rinehart & Winston, 1972.

Marix Evans, Martin. 2000. *Encyclopedia of the Boer War, 1899–1902.* Santa Barbara, CA: ABC–CLIO.

Masefield, Pamela, ed. 1995. *The Land of Green Tea: Letters and Adventures of Colonel C. L. Baker of the Madras Artillery, 1834–1850 (In India and the First Chinese Opium War).* London: Unicorn.

Mason, Philip. 1974. *A Matter of Honour: An Account of the Indian Army, Its Officers and Men.* New York: Holt, Rinehart & Winston.

———. 1985. *The Men Who Ruled India.* New York: Norton.

Maurice, F. 1872. *The Wellington Prize Essay: The System of Field Manoeuvres Best Adapted for Enabling Our Troops to Meet a Continental Army.* Edinburgh: Blackwood.

Maurice, F., and George Arthur. 1924. *The Life of Lord Wolseley.* Garden City, NY: Doubleday, Page.

Maurice, J. F. 1887. *Military History of the Campaign of 1882 in Egypt.* London: Her Majesty's Stationery Office; reprint, London: London Stamp Exchange, [c. 1987].

Mawson, Michael Hargreave, ed. 2001. *Eyewitness in the Crimea: The Crimean War Letters (1854–1856) of Lt. Col. George Frederick Dallas.* London: Greenhill.

Maxwell, Leigh. 1979. *My God: Maiwand! Operations of the South Afghanistan Field Force, 1878–80.* London: Leo Cooper.

———. 1985. *The Ashanti Ring: Sir Garnet Wolseley's Campaigns, 1870–1882.* London: Leo Cooper/Secker & Warburg.

May, R. K. 1984. "The Forgotten General: Lieutenant General Sir Alfred Keogh, GCB, GCVO, CH." *British Army Review* 76 (April): 51–59.

———. 1985. "'Keep Your Head Cool: And Your Feet Warm': India in the 1860s, A Sergeant Major's Story." *British Army Review* 79 (April): 24–28.

McCaig, A. D. 2000. "'The Soul of Artillery': Congreve's Rockets and Their Effectiveness in Warfare." *Journal of the Society for Army Historical Research* 78 (Winter): 252–263.

McCormick, Richard C., Jr. 1855. *A Visit to the Camp before Sevastopol.* New York: Appleton.

McCourt, Edward. 1967. *Remember Butler: The Story of Sir William Butler.* Toronto: McClelland & Stewart.

McEwen, Neal. 2002. "Victorian Era Visual Signalling Instruments." www.metronet.com/~ nmcewen/Black-Watch-Signal-Unit.html (cited 27 May 2002).

McLaughlin, Redmond. 1972. *The Royal Army Medical Corps.* London: Leo Cooper.

Melville, C. H. 1923. *Life of General the Right Hon. Sir Redvers Buller, V.C., G.C.B., G.C.M.G.* 2 vols. London: Edward Arnold.

Mercer, Patrick. 1998. *'Give Them a Volley and Charge!' The Battle of Inkermann, 1854.* Staplehurst, UK: Spellmount.

Meredith, John. 1998. *Omdurman Diaries, 1898: Eyewitness Accounts of the Legendary Campaign.* Barnsley, UK: Leo Cooper.

Metz, Helen Chapin, ed. 1989. *Iran: A Country Study.* 4th ed. Washington, D.C.: Federal Research Division, Library of Congress.

———. 1991. *Egypt: A Country Study.* 5th ed. Washington, D.C.: Federal Research Division, Library of Congress.

———. 1992. *Sudan: A Country Study.* 4th ed. Washington, D.C.: Federal Research Division, Library of Congress.

Mileham, Patrick, ed. 1996. *Clearly My Duty: The Letters of Sir John Gilmour from the Boer War, 1900–1901.* East Linton, Scotland: Tuckwell.

Miller, Charles. 1977. *Khyber, British India's North West Frontier: The Story of an Imperial Migraine.* New York: Macmillan.

Miller, Stephen. 1996. "Lord Methuen and the British Advance to the Modder River." *Military History Journal* 10 (December). rapidttp.co.za/milhist/vol104sm.html (cited 2 July 2002).

Mills, T. F. 1996. "British Militia, Territorials and Volunteers: An Introductory Overview." regiments.org/milhist/uk/targts/htm (cited 3 January 2002).

———. 2001. "Imperial Yeomanry." regiments.org/milhist/uk/yeo/ImpYeo.htm (cited 3 January 2002).

Minney, R. J. 1931. *Clive.* New York: Appleton.

Montgomery, John. 1963. *Toll for the Brave: The Tragedy of Major General Sir Hector Macdonald, K.C.B., D.S.O., A.D.C.* London: Parrish.

Moore-Harell, Alice. 2001. *Gordon and the Sudan: Prologue to the Mahdiyya, 1877–1880.* London: Frank Cass.

Moore-Morris, Ralph. 1998a. "The Sudan Military Railway." *Soldiers of the Queen* 94 (September): 8–10.

———. 1998b. "The Khalifa's Last Stand: Omdebreikat, 24th November 1899." *Soldiers of the Queen* 94 (September): 30–31.

Moritz, Garrett. 1998. "From the Jameson Raid to Bloemfontein: Debating the Origins of the Boer War." www.gtexts.com/college/papers/sl.html (cited 26 December 2001).

Morley, John. 1903. *The Life of William Ewart Gladstone.* 3 vols. London: Macmillan.

Morris, Donald R. 1965. *The Washing of the Spears: A History of the Rise of the Zulu Nation under Shaka and Its Fall in the Zulu War of 1879.* New York: Simon & Schuster.

Morris, James. 1973. *Heaven's Command: An Imperial Progress.* New York: Harcourt Brace Jovanich.

Mostert, Noel. 1992. *Frontiers: The Epic of South Africa's Creation and the Tragedy of the Xhosa People.* New York: Alfred A. Knopf.

Moyse-Bartlett, H. 1971. *Nolan of Balaclava: Louis Edward Nolan and His Influence on the British Cavalry.* London: Leo Cooper.

———. 1974. "The British Army in 1850." *Journal of the Society for Army Historical Research* 52: 221–237.

Murray, D. J. S. 1997. "Fashoda." *Soldiers of the Queen* 90 (September): 17–21.

Myatt, Frederick. 1970. *The March to Magdala: The Abyssinian War of 1868.* 19th Century Military Campaigns. Ed. Brian Bond. London: Leo Cooper.

———. 1983. *The British Infantry, 1660–1945: The Evolution of a Fighting Force.* Poole, UK: Blandford.

Nalson, David G. 1998. "The Lincolnshire Regiment at the Atbara." *Soldiers of the Queen* 94 (September): 12–14.

Napier, Priscilla. 1973. *Revolution and the Napier Brothers, 1820–1840.* London: Michael Joseph.

———. 1995. *Barbarian Eye: Lord Napier in China, 1834: The Prelude to Hong Kong.* London: Brassey's.

Napier, W. F. F. 1857. *The History of General Sir Charles Napier's Conquest of Scinde.* London: Charles Westerton; reprint, Oxford: Oxford University Press, 2001.

Nasson, Bill. 1999. *The South African War, 1899–1902.* London: Oxford University Press.

Nasson, W. R. 1983. "'Doing Down the Masters': Africans, Boers, and Treason in the Cape Colony during the South African War of 1899–1902." *Journal of Imperial and Commonwealth History* 12: 29–53.

Neillands, Robin. 1996. *The Dervish Wars: Gordon and Kitchener in the Sudan, 1880–1898.* London: John Murray.

Nevill, H. L. 1912. *Campaigns on the North-West Frontier.* Reprint, Nashville: Battery, 1999.

Neuberg, Victor. 1989. *Gone for a Soldier: A History of Life in the British Ranks from 1642.* London: Cassell.

Nijjar, Bakshish Singh. 1976. *Anglo-Sikh Wars, 1845–1849.* New Delhi: K.B. Publications.

O'Brien, Patrick. 1996. "Did Europe's Mercantilist Empires Pay?" *History Today* 46 (March). www.findarticles.com/cf_0/m1373/n3_v46/18099916/print.jhtml (cited 7 May 2003).

Bibliography

Otley, C. B. 1970. "The Social Origins of British Army Officers." *Sociological Review* 18: 213–239.

———. 1973. "The Educational Background of British Army Officers." *Sociology* 7: 191–209.

Owen, Edward. 1985. "March Across Afghanistan." *Army Quarterly and Defence Journal* 115 (July): 316–327.

Padfield, Peter. 1981. *Rule Britannia: The Victorian and Edwardian Navy.* London: Routledge & Kegan Paul.

Pakenham, Thomas. 1979. *The Boer War.* New York: Random House.

———. 1991. *The Scramble for Africa, 1876–1912.* New York: Random House.

Palmer, Alan. 1987. *The Crimean War.* Reprint, New York: Dorset, 1992.

Parkinson, C. Northcote. 1960. *British Intervention in Malaya, 1867–1877.* Singapore: University of Malaya Press.

Partridge, Michael Stephen. 1989. *Military Planning for the Defense of the United Kingdom, 1814–1870.* New York: Greenwood.

Pearson, Hesketh. 1951. *Dizzy: The Life and Personality of Benjamin Disraeli, Earl of Beaconsfield.* New York: Harper.

Peden, G. C. 1984. "The Burden of Imperial Defence and the Continental Commitment Reconsidered." *Historical Journal* 27: 405–423.

Pegram, Marjory. 1939. *The Wolseley Heritage: The Story of Frances, Viscountess Wolseley, and Her Parents.* London: John Murray.

Pemberton, W. Baring. 1962. *Battles of the Crimean War.* New York: Macmillan.

Pioneer Special War Correspondent. 1898. "The Mohmand Rising: The Raid on Shabkadr Fort." Reprint, *Soldiers of the Queen* 67 (December 1991): 17–22.

Pitman, Paul M., III, ed. 1988. *Turkey: A Country Study.* 4th ed. Washington, D.C.: Federal Research Division, Library of Congress.

Plaatje, Sol T. 2003. "The Siege of Mafeking: 11 October 1899–17 May 1900: The Experiences of Sol T. Plaatje." www.museumsnc.co.za/mcgregor/departments/history/blacksinwar/mafsiege/mafeking.htm (cited 22 July 2003).

Pollock, J. C. 1957. *Way to Glory: The Life of Havelock of Lucknow.* London: John Murray.

Pollock, John. 2001. *Kitchener: Architect of Victory, Artisan of Peace.* New York: Carroll & Graf.

Pottinger, George. 1983. *The Afghan Connection: The Extraordinary Adventures of Major Eldred Pottinger.* Edinburgh: Scottish Academic Press.

Powell, Geoffrey. 1994. *Buller: A Scapegoat? A Life of General Sir Redvers Buller, VC.* London: Leo Cooper.

Preston, Adrian W. 1964. "British Military Thought, 1856–90." *Army Quarterly and Defence Journal* 89 (October): 57–74.

———. 1967a. *In Relief of Gordon: Lord Wolseley's Campaign Journal of the Khartoum Relief Expedition, 1884–1885.* London: Hutchinson.

———. 1967b. "Sir Garnet Wolseley and the Cyprus Expedition, 1878." *Journal of the Society for Army Historical Research* 45: 4–16.

———. 1969. "Sir Charles MacGregor and the Defence of India." *Historical Journal* 12: 58–77.

———. 1971. *The South African Diaries of Sir Garnet Wolseley, 1875.* Cape Town: Balkema.

———. 1973. *The South African Journal of Sir Garnet Wolseley, 1879–1880.* Cape Town: Balkema.

———. 1978. "Wolseley, The Khartoum Relief Expedition and the Defence of India, 1885–1900." *Journal of Imperial and Commonwealth History* 6: 254–280.

Preston, Diana. 1999. *The Boxer Rebellion: The Dramatic Story of China's War That Shook the World in the Summer of 1900.* Reprint, New York: Walker, 2000.

Pretorius, Fransjohan. 1977. "For the Sake of Five Wagonloads of Flour: De Wet versus Broadwood." *Military History Journal* 4 (June). www.rapidttp.co.za/milhist/vol1041fp.html (cited 21 July 2003).

Raafat, Samir. 2001. "The Sirdaria." *Cairo Times,* 15 February. www.egy.com/landmarks/01-02-15.shtml (cited 12 October 2001).

Rainbird, Jonathan. 1999. "Public Opinion and the Art of Photography in War." www.cix.co.uk/~freedom/war/public_opinion_and_the_art_of.htm (cited 2 October 2002).

Ramsay, M. A. 2002. *Command and Cohesion: The Citizen Soldier and Minor Tactics in the British Army, 1870–1918.* Westport, CT: Praeger.

Ransford, Oliver. 1967. *The Battle of Majuba Hill: The First Boer War.* Reprint, London: John Murray, 1970.

———. 1969. *The Battle of Spion Kop.* Reprint, London: John Murray, 1971.

Raugh, Harold E., Jr. 1984. "The Keystone of Army Reform." *Soldiers of the Queen* 36 (March): 12–15.

———. 1985. "Tribes of Servants." *Soldiers of the Queen* 42 (September): 2–5.

———. 1986. "Generations of Gallantry and Glory." *Defence Force Journal* 60 (September–October): 56–59.

———. 1987a. "The British Army Gerontocracy in the Crimean War." *Soldiers of the Queen* 49 (June): 6–8.

———. 1987b. "Garnet Joseph Wolseley and the Gordon Relief Expedition." *Army Quarterly and Defence Journal* 117 (October): 441–451.

———. 1988a. "Garnet Joseph Wolseley and the Gordon Relief Expedition: Part Two." *Army Quarterly and Defence Journal* 118 (January): 65–73.

———. 1988b. "The Siege of Silistria, 1854: From the Journal of Captain James A. Butler, Ceylon Rifle Regiment." *Soldiers of the Queen* 53 (June): 4–12.

———. 1989. "Empire's Chief Defender." *Military History* 6 (August): 20–25.

———. 1992. "Wavell in the Great War: The Mud of Flanders and Mobility of Palestine." *Stand To!* 35 (Summer): 15–19.

———. 1993. *Wavell in the Middle East, 1939–1941: A Study in Generalship.* London: Brassey's.

———. 1994. "Training Ground for a Future Field Marshal: Wavell in the Boer War and Edwardian India, 1901–1908." *Journal of the Society for Army Historical Research* 72 (Spring): 8–18.

———. 2000. "Storming the Rebel Strongholds: The Perak War, 1875–76." *Soldiers of the Queen* 102 (September): 7–12.

———. 2001a. "Footslogging over the Veldt: A Subaltern's Boer War Odyssey." *Soldiers of the Queen* 105 (June 2001): 25–30.

———. 2001b. "British General Wolseley Steals a March by Making Intelligent Use of War Correspondents." *Military Heritage* 3 (October): 10, 12–14, 16.

Rawley, James A., ed. 1964. *The American Civil War: An English View: The Writings of Field Marshal Viscount Wolseley.* Reprint, Mechanicsburg, PA: Stackpole, 2002.

Razzell, P. E. 1963. "Social Origins of Officers in the Indian and British Home Army: 1758–1962." *British Journal of Sociology* 14: 248–260.

"The Red River Difficulty: Louis Riel." 1870. *Canadian Illustrated News,* 15 July. www.nlc-bnc.ca/cin/h1-205-e.html (cited 11 May 2003).

Reid, Brian A. 1996. *Our Little Army in the Field: The Canadians in South Africa, 1899–1902.* St. Catherines, Ont.: Vanwell.

Reynolds, E. E. 1942. *Baden-Powell: A Biography of Lord Baden-Powell of Gilwell, O.M., G.C.M.G., G.C.V.O., K.C.B.* Reprint, London: Oxford University Press, 1950.

Riall, Nicholas, comp. and ed. 2000. *Boer War: The Letters, Diaries and Photographs of Malcolm Riall from the War in South Africa, 1899–1902.* London: Brassey's.

Rice, Edward. 2002. "General Sir Charles Napier and the Conquest of Sind." The Victorian Web. 65.107.211.206/victorian/history/empire/napier.html (cited 13 July 2002).

Rizk, Yunen Labib. 2000. "The Bitter Harvest." *Al-Ahram Weekly* On-line, 12–18 October. www.ahram.org.eg/weekly/2000/503/chrncls.htm (cited 13 October 2001).

Ritter, E. A. 1955. *Shaka Zulu: The Rise of the Zulu Empire.* Reprint, London: Longmans Green, 1957.

Roberts, Field-Marshal Lord. 1897. *Forty-One Years in India, from Subaltern to Commander-in-Chief.* 2 vols. 19th ed. New York: Longmans, Green.

Roberts, Neil. 1995. "The Forgotten Mutiny." *Soldiers of the Queen* 82 (September): 16–19.

Robins, Colin. 1997. "Lucan, Cardigan and Raglan's Order." *Journal of the Society for Army Historical Research* 75 (Summer): 86–92.

Robins, Colin, ed. 2003. *Captain Dunscombe's Diary: The Real Crimean War That the British Infantry Knew.* Bowdon, Cheshire, UK: Withycut House.

Robson, Brian. 1993a. "Buller at Suakin in 1884." *Soldiers of the Queen* 75 (December): 2–7.

———. 1993b. *Fuzzy Wuzzy: The Campaigns in the Eastern Sudan, 1884–85.* Tunbridge Wells, UK: Spellmount.

———. 1995a. "The Reconstruction of the Bengal Army." *Soldiers of the Queen* 82 (September): 19–24.

———. 1995b. "The Evolution of the Bengal Army, 1862–95." *Soldiers of the Queen* 83 (December): 16–19.

———. 1996. "Tantia Topi: Traitor or Patriot?" *Soldiers of the Queen* 85 (June): 15–19.

———. 1997. "The Unknown General: A Reassessment of Sir Hugh Rose." *Journal of the Society for Army Historical Research* 302 (Summer): 93–105.

Rodgers, Nini. 1984. "The Abyssinian Expedition of 1867–1868: Disraeli's Imperialism or James Murray's War?" *Historical Journal* 27: 129–149.

Roy, Kaushik. 2002. "Logistics and the Construction of Loyalty: The Welfare Mechanism in the Indian Army, 1859–1913." In *The British Raj and Its Indian Armed Forces, 1857–1939.* Ed. Partha Sarathi Gupta and Anirudh

Bibliography

Deshpande. New Delhi: Oxford University Press.

"Royal Military Academy, 1741–1939." 2001. In Royal Military Academy, Sandhurst. www.atra.mod.uk/rmas/history/history3.htm (cited 16 August 2002).

Royle, Trevor. 1982. *Death before Dishonour: The True Story of Fighting Mac.* Edinburgh: Mainstream.

———. 2000. *Crimea: The Great Crimean War, 1854–1856.* New York: St. Martin's.

Rundle, Wilfred Charles. 1950. *The Baton: An Historical Study of the Marshalate.* London: Clowes.

Russell, William Howard. 1966. *Russell's Despatches from the Crimea, 1854–56.* Ed. Nicolas Bentley. Reprint, New York: Hill & Wang, 1967.

Ryan, Tim. 1986. "The Maori Warrior and Warfare." *Soldiers of the Queen* 47 (December): 16–18.

Rye, J. B., and Horace G. Groser. 1917. *Kitchener in His Own Words.* London: Fisher Unwin.

Sadka, Emily. 1968. *The Protected Malay States, 1874–1895.* Kuala Lumpur: University of Malaya Press.

Satre, Lowell J. 1976. "St. John Brodrick and Army Reform, 1901–1903." *Journal of British Studies* 15: 117–139.

"Scottish Regiments: The Black Watch: 1873–1881." Electric Scotland.com. www.electricscotland.com/history/scotreg/bwatch/bw27.htm (cited 28 September 2001).

Scudieri, James. 1988. "The Indian Army and the Scramble for Africa." *Soldiers of the Queen* 54 (September): 7–10.

Searight, Sarah. 1998. "Steaming through Africa." *History Today* 48 (July). www.findarticles.com/cf_0/m1373/n7_v48/20964198/print.jhtml (cited 7 May 2003).

Selby, John. 1967. "The Third China War, 1860." In *Victorian Military Campaigns,* ed. Brian Bond, 69–104. New York: Praeger.

———. 1968. *The Paper Dragon: An Account of the China Wars, 1840–1900.* New York: Praeger.

———. 1970. *Balaclava: Gentlemen's Battle.* New York: Atheneum.

Sewell, E. 1985. "The Burma Expeditionary Force." *Soldiers of the Queen* 43 (December): 1–3.

Seymour, William. 1991. *Great Sieges of History.* London: Brassey's.

Sheppard, E. W. 1952. *Red Coat: An Anthology of the British Soldier during the Last Three Hundred Years.* London: Batchworth.

Sherriff, R. C. 1968. "The English Public Schools in the War." In *Promise of Greatness.* Ed. George A. Panichas. London: Cassell.

Simkin, John. N.d. "Florence Nightingale." www.spartacus.schoolnet.co.uk/REnightingale.htm (cited 24 April 2002).

Simpson, Keith. 1985. "The Officers." In *A Nation in Arms.* Ed. Ian F. W. Beckett and Keith Simpson. Manchester: Manchester University Press.

Sixsmith, E. K. G. 1970. *British Generalship in the Twentieth Century.* London: Arms & Armour.

———. 1974. "Kitchener and the Guerrillas in the Boer War." *Army Quarterly and Defence Journal* 104: 203–214.

Skelley, Alan Ramsay. 1977. *The Victorian Army at Home: The Recruitment and Terms and Conditions of the British Regular, 1859–1899.* London: Croon Helm.

Slade, Andrew. 1985. "When Private Contractors Fed the Army." *Army Quarterly and Defence Journal* 115 (April): 160–166.

Slatin Pasha, R. 1896. *Fire and Sword in the Sudan: Fighting and Serving the Dervishes, 1879–1895.* London: Edward Arnold; reprint, London: Greenhill, 1990.

Smith, E. A. 1987. "Educating the Soldier in the Nineteenth Century." *Journal of the Society for Army Historical Research* 65 (Winter): 200–207.

———. 1988. "Educating the Soldier in the Nineteenth Century." *Journal of the Society for Army Historical Research* 66 (Spring): 35–45.

Smith, Harry. 1901. *The Autobiography of Lieutenant-General Sir Harry Smith, Baronet of Aliwal on the Sutlej, G.C.B.* Ed. G. C. Moore Smith. Reprint, London: John Murray, 1903.

Smith, Peter C. 1987. *Victoria's Victories.* New York: Hippocrene.

Smith, F. B. 1971. "Ethics and Disease in the Later Nineteenth Century: The Contagious Diseases Acts." *Historical Studies* 15 (October): 118–135.

Smithson, F. 1985. "Burmese Diary, 1886–87: Part I." *Soldiers of the Queen* 43 (December): 4–16.

Smuts, J. C. 1952. *Jan Christian Smuts.* London: Cassell.

Smythe, Graeme. N.d. "The Battle of Rorke's Drift, 22/23 January 1879." In Battlefields: History: Anglo-Zulu War. www.battlefields.co.za/history/anglo-zulu_war/rorkes_drift/rorkes_gs.htm (cited 27 May 2003).

Solomon, V. E. 1974. "The Hands-Uppers." *Military History Journal* 3 (June). http://rapidttp.co.za/milhist/vol031vs.html (cited 12 December 2001).

Somervell, D. C. 1926. *Disraeli and Gladstone: A Duo-Biographical Sketch.* New York: George H. Doran.

Spiers, Edward M. 1975. "The Use of the Dum Dum Bullet in Colonial Warfare." *Journal of Imperial and Commonwealth History* 4: 3–14.

———. 1979. "Rearming the Edwardian Artillery." *Journal of the Society for Army Historical Research* 57: 167–176.

———. 1980a. *The Army and Society, 1815–1914.* London: Longman.

———. 1980b. *Haldane: An Army Reformer.* Edinburgh: Edinburgh University Press.

———. 1981. "Reforming the Infantry of the Line, 1900–1914." *Journal of the Society for Army Historical Research* 59: 82–94.

———. 1983. *Radical General: Sir George de Lacy Evans, 1787–1870.* Manchester: Manchester University Press.

———. 1992. *The Late Victorian Army, 1868–1902.* Manchester: Manchester University Press.

St. Aubyn, Giles. 1963. *The Royal George, 1819–1904: The Life of H.R.H. Prince George, Duke of Cambridge.* Reprint, New York: Alfred A. Knopf, 1964.

Stanley, Peter. 1999. "'Being Dead Yet Speaketh': Berhampore, A Bengal Cantonment." *Soldiers of the Queen* 97 (June): 3–7.

Stearn, Roger T. 1990. "Archibald Forbes and the British Army." *Soldiers of the Queen* 61 (June): 6–9.

———. 1991. "Bennet Burleigh, Victorian War Correspondent." *Soldiers of the Queen* 65 (June): 5–10.

———. 1994. "Addiscombe: The East India Company's Military Seminary." *Soldiers of the Queen* 79 (December): 1–3.

———. 1996a. "Sir Henry Marion Durand, 1812–1871." *Soldiers of the Queen* 85 (June): 10–15.

———. 1996b. "'Congreve, the Rocket-man': Sir William Congreve, Second Baronet." *Soldiers of the Queen* 86 (September): 11–18.

———. 1999. "Richard Caton Woodville, 1856–1927." *Soldiers of the Queen* 97 (June): 14–27.

Steevens, G. W. 1898. *With Kitchener to Khartoum.* 4th ed. Edinburgh: Blackwood.

Stephen, Leslie, and Sidney Lee, eds. 1964–65. *The Dictionary of National Biography: From the Earliest Times to 1900.* Vol. 22, *Supplement.* Reprint, Oxford: Oxford University Press.

Stokesbury, James L. 1983. *Navy and Empire.* New York: William Morrow.

Stone, Jay, and Erwin A. Schmidl. 1988. *The Boer War and Military Reforms.* Lanham, MD: University Press of America.

Strachan, H. F. A. 1977. "The Origins of the 1855 Uniform Changes: An Example of Pre-Crimean Reform." *Journal of the Society for Army Historical Research* 55: 85–117, 165–174.

Strachan, Hew. 1978. "Soldiers, Strategy and Sebastopol." *Historical Journal* 21: 303–325.

———. 1980. "The Early Victorian Army and the Nineteenth-Century Revolution in Government." *English Historical Review* 95: 782–809.

———. 1984. *Wellington's Legacy: The Reform of the British Army, 1830–54.* Manchester: Manchester University Press.

———. 1985. *From Waterloo to Balaclava: Tactics, Technology, and the British Army, 1815–1854.* Cambridge: Cambridge University Press.

———. 1997. *The Politics of the British Army.* Oxford: Clarendon.

Strachey, Lytton. 1918. *Eminent Victorians.* Reprint, New York: Weidenfeld & Nicolson, 1988.

Strage, Mark. 1973. *Cape to Cairo: Rape of a Continent.* New York: Harcourt Brace Jovanovich.

Strawson, John. 1989. *Gentlemen in Khaki: The British Army, 1890–1990.* London: Secker & Warburg.

Stuart-Smith, James. 1969. "Military Law: Its History, Administration and Practice." *Law Review Quarterly* 85: 478–504.

Summers, Anne. 1988. *Angels and Citizens: British Women as Military Nurses, 1854–1914.* London: Routledge & Kegan Paul.

Sundaram, Chandar S. 2002. "Reviving a 'Dead Letter': Military Indianization and the Ideology of Anglo-India, 1885–91." In *The British Raj and Its Indian Armed Forces, 1857–1939.* Ed. Partha Sarathi Gupta and Anirudh Deshpande. New Delhi: Oxford University Press.

Sutcliffe, Victor. 1995. "The Causes of the Indian Mutiny." *Soldiers of the Queen* 82 (September): 13–16.

Sweet, William. 2000. "R.B. [Richard Burdon] Haldane (1856–1928)." www.stfx.ca/people/wsweet/Haldane.html (cited 31 March 2003).

Sweetman, John. 1973. "Military Transport in the Crimean War, 1854–1856." *English Historical Review* 88 (January): 81–91.

———. 1984. *War and Administration: The Significance of the Crimean War for the British Army.* Edinburgh: Scot-

Bibliography

tish Academic Press.

———. 1988a. "Public Attitudes towards the Army: Early Years, 1827–1852." *Army Quarterly and Defence Journal* 118 (January): 60–64.

———. 1988b. "'Ad Hoc' Support Services during the Crimean War, 1854–6: Temporary, Ill-Planned and Largely Unsuccessful." *Military Affairs* 52 (July): 135–140.

———. 1991. "The Battle of Inkerman, 1854." In *Great Battles of the British Army as Commemorated in the Sandhurst Companies.* Ed. David G. Chandler. Chapel Hill: University of North Carolina Press.

———. 1993. *Raglan: From the Peninsula to the Crimea.* London: Arms & Armour.

———. 2001. *Essential Histories: The Crimean War.* London: Osprey.

Sykes, Frank W. 1897. *With Plumer in Matabeleland.* Reprint, Bulawayo: Books of Rhodesia, 1972.

Symons, J. N. 1989. "Tipperary Tactics: The Failure of Command and Control at the Battle of Chillianwallah." *British Army Review* 93 (December): 25–27.

Symons, Julian. 1963. *Buller's Campaign.* London: Cresset.

———. 1965. *England's Pride: The Story of the Gordon Relief Expedition.* Reprint, London: White Lion, 1975.

Talbot, Philip. 2001. "The English Yeomanry in the Nineteenth Century and in the Great Boer War." *Journal of the Society for Army Historical Research* 79 (Spring): 45–62.

Tanner, Stephen. 2002. *Afghanistan: A Military History from Alexander the Great to the Fall of the Taliban.* New York: Da Capo.

Temple, Richard. 1889. *Lord Lawrence.* English Men of Action. Ed. John Morley. Reprint, London: Macmillan, 1890.

Teulie, Gilles. 1993. "The Key to Ladysmith." *Military History Journal* 9 (December). rapidttp.com/milhist/vol094gt.html (cited 23 July 2003).

———. 1995. "Tommy and the Press during the Anglo-Boer War." *Soldiers of the Queen* 81 (June): 22–28.

This England. 1981. *The Register of the Victoria Cross.* Cheltenham, UK: This England Books.

Thomas, Donald. 1974. *Cardigan.* Reprint, New York: Viking, 1975.

Thomson, J. T. 1986. "A Volunteer Artillery Group." *Soldiers of the Queen* 45 (June): 16–17.

Thornton, L. H., and Pamela Fraser. 1930. *The Congreves, Father and Son: General Sir Walter Norris Congreve, V.C. [and] Bt.-Major William La Touche Congreve, V.C.* London: John Murray.

Tisdall, E. E. P. 1963. *Mrs. Duberley's Campaigns: An Englishwoman's Experiences in the Crimean War and Indian Mutiny.* Chicago: Rand McNally.

Tomlinson, Richard. 1997. "Britain's Last Castles: Masonry Blockhouses of the South African War, 1899–1902." *Military History Journal* 10 (December). rapidttp.co.za/milhist/vol106rt.html (cited 12 December 2001).

Travers, T. H. E. 1978. "The Offensive and the Problem of Innovation in British Military Thought, 1870–1915." *Journal of Contemporary History* 13: 531–553.

———. 1979. "Technology, Tactics, and Morale: Jean de Bloch, the Boer War, and British Military Theory, 1900–1914." *Journal of Modern History* 51 (June): 264–286.

Travers, Tim. 1987. *The Killing Ground: The British Army, the Western Front and the Emergence of Modern Warfare, 1900–1918.* London: Allen & Unwin.

Trew, Peter. 1999. *The Boer War Generals.* Phoenix Mills, UK: Sutton.

Trustram, Myna. 1984. *Women of the Regiment: Marriage and the Victorian Army.* Cambridge: Cambridge University Press.

Tucker, Albert V. 1963. "Army and Society in England, 1870–1900: A Reassessment of the Cardwell Reforms." *Journal of British Studies* 2: 110–141.

Tylden, G. 1951. "The Sekukuni Campaign of November–December, 1879." *Journal of the Society for Army Historical Research* 29: 129–136.

———. 1968. "Ponies in Warfare with Especial Reference to South Africa." *Military History Journal* 1 (December). rapidttp.com/milhist/vol013gt.html (cited 21 May 2002).

Valiunas, Algis. 2002. *Churchill's Military Histories: A Rhetorical Study.* Lanham, MD: Rowman & Littlefield.

Waitangi Tribunal. 1996. *The Taranaki Report.* www.knowledge-basket.co.nz/waitangi/text/wai143/toc.html (cited 16 April 2002).

Waller, John H. 1988. *Gordon of Khartoum: The Saga of a Victorian Hero.* New York: Atheneum.

———. 1990. *Beyond the Khyber Pass: The Road to British Disaster in the First Afghan War.* New York: Random House.

War Office, Intelligence Branch. 1881. *Narrative of Field Operations Connected with the Zulu War of 1879.*

Bibliography

Reprint, London: Greenhill, 1989.

Ward, Andrew. 1996. *Our Bones Are Scattered: The Cawnpore Massacres and the Indian Mutiny of 1857.* New York: Henry Holt.

Warner, Philip. 1972. *The Crimean War: A Reappraisal.* Reprint, New York: Taplinger, 1973.

———. 1986. *Kitchener: The Man behind the Legend.* New York: Atheneum.

Warner, Philip, ed. 1977. *The Fields of War: A Young Cavalryman's Crimea Campaign.* London: John Murray.

Watson, Bruce. 1991. *The Great Indian Mutiny: Colin Campbell and the Campaign at Lucknow.* New York: Praeger.

Watt, S. A. 1992. "The Anglo-Boer War: The Medical Arrangements and Implications Thereof during the British Occupation of Bloemfontein, March-April 1900." *Military History Journal* (December). www.rapidttp.co.za/milhist/vol092sw.html (cited 16 February 2002).

Webster, Linden Bradfield. 1970. "Linden Bradfield Webster's Reminiscences of the Siege of Mafeking." *Military History Journal* 1 (December). rapidttp.com/milhist/vol017lb.html (cited 22 July 2003).

Weidhorn, Manfred. 1974. *Sword and Pen: A Survey of the Writings of Sir Winston Churchill.* Albuquerque: University of New Mexico Press.

Wessels, Andre, ed. 2000. *Lord Roberts and the War in South Africa, 1899–1902.* Publications of the Army Records Society, vol. 17. Phoenix Mills, UK: Sutton Publishing for the Army Records Society.

Wheeler, Owen. 1914. *The War Office, Past and Present.* London: Methuen.

Whitehouse, Howard, ed. 1880. *'A Widow-Making War': The Life and Death of a British Officer in Zululand, 1879.* Reprint, Nuneaton, UK: Paddy Griffith, 1995.

Wickham Legg, L. G., ed. 1949. *The Dictionary of National Biography: 1931–1940.* Reprint, London: Oxford University Press, 1950.

Wickham Legg, L. G., and E. T. Williams, eds. 1959. *The Dictionary of National Biography: 1941–1950.* Reprint, London: Oxford University Press, 1967.

Wilkinson-Latham, Christopher. 1977. *The Indian Mutiny.* Men-at-Arms Series. Ed. Martin Windrow. Reprint, Oxford: Osprey, 2002.

Williams, M. J. 1967. "The Egyptian Campaign of 1882." In *Victorian Military Campaigns,* ed. Brian Bond, 241–278. New York: Praeger.

Willmott, H. P. 1982. *Empires in the Balance: Japanese and Allied Pacific Strategies to April 1942.* Annapolis, MD: Naval Institute Press.

Wingate, Francis. 1892. *Ten Years' Captivity in the Mahdi's Camp, 1882–1892.* 15th ed. London: Sampson Low, Marston.

Wingate, Ronald. 1955. *Wingate of the Sudan.* Reprint, Westport, CT: Greenwood, 1975.

"With the Army Service Corps on the Red River Expedition of 1870." N.d. www.waggoners.co.uk/redriver.htm (cited 11 May 2003).

Wolseley, G. J. 1862. *Narrative of the War with China in 1860.* London: Longman, Green, Longman & Roberts; reprint, Wilmington, DE: Scholarly Resources, 1972.

———. 1873. *The Use of Railroads in War.* London: N.p.

———. 1878. "The Native Army of India." *North American Review* 127 (July–August): 132–157.

———. 1890. "The Standing Army of Great Britain." *Harper's New Monthly Magazine* 80 (February): 331–347.

———. 1894. *The Life of John Churchill, Duke of Marlborough, to the Accession of Queen Anne.* 2 vols. 4th ed. London: Bentley.

———. 1895. *The Decline and Fall of Napoleon.* London: Sampson Low, Marston.

———. 1903. *The Story of a Soldier's Life.* 2 vols. Westminster: Archibald Constable, 1903.

Wood, Evelyn. 1906. *From Midshipman to Field Marshal.* Reprint, London: Methuen, 1912.

———. 1908. *The Revolt in Hindustan, 1857–59.* London: Methuen.

———. 1917. *Winnowed Memories.* Reprint, London: Cassell, 1918.

Woodall, Robert. 1986. "Edward Cardwell at the War Office." *Army Quarterly and Defence Journal* 116 (January): 63–69.

———. 1990. "Come If You Dare: The Origins of the Volunteer Force of 1859–1908." *Army Quarterly and Defence Journal* 120 (April): 176–181.

Woodham-Smith, Cecil. 1953. *The Reason Why.* Reprint, New York: McGraw-Hill, 1954.

Woods, Frederick, ed. 1992. *Winston S. Churchill: War Correspondent, 1895–1900.* London: Brassey's.

Wright, Bill. 1980. "'Never Give In': The Defence of the British Residency at Kabul, 3rd September 1879." *Soldiers of the Queen* 23 (November): 6–12.

Bibliography

Wulfsohn, Lionel. 1991. "Hendsoppers of the Rustenburg Commando." *Military History Journal* 8 (December). rapidttp.co.za/milhist/vol0861w.html (cited 13 December 2001).

Yong, Tan Tai. 2002. "Sepoys and the Colonial State: Punjab and the Military Base of the Indian Army, 1849–1900." In *The British Raj and Its Indian Armed Forces, 1857–1939*. Ed. Partha Sarathi Gupta and Anirudh Deshpande. New Delhi: Oxford University Press.

Young, Peter, and J. P. Lawford, eds. 1970. *History of the British Army*. London: Arthur Barker.

Young, Peter, with Michael Calvert. 1977. *A Dictionary of Battles, 1816–1976*. Reprint, New York: Mayflower, 1978.

Younghusband, G. J. 1898. *Indian Frontier Warfare*. Reprint, Delhi, India: 1985.

Yu, Maichun. 2002. "The Taiping Rebellion: A Military Assessment of Revolution and Counterrevolution." In *A Military History of China,* ed. David A. Graff and Robin Higham, 135–152. Boulder: Westview.

Ziegler, Philip. 1974. *Omdurman*. New York: Alfred A. Knopf.

Zulfo, Ismat Hasan. 1980. *Karari: The Sudanese Account of the Battle of Omdurman*. Trans. Peter Clark. London: Frederick Warne.

Index

Page ranges set in **bold** type indicate main entries.

Abdullah, Khalifa, 120
Abdullahi ibn Mohammed, 200, 219, 220
Abdur Rahman Khan, 9, 10, 62, 124, 152, 220, 245, 261
Abu Hamed, Battle of, 201, 213, 280
Abu Klea, Battle of, **1–2,** 72, 148, 313, 341
Abu Kru, battle at, 313
Abyssinia, xv, **2–3,** 18, 320–321
Abyssinian War, **3–4,** 122, 172–173, 177, 217–218, 242, 243, 274, 287, 312, 320–321
Act for the Better Government of India (1858), 128, 129
Act for the Better Prevention of Contagious Diseases, 236
Act of Union (Canada, 1840), 78
Addiscombe Military Seminary, **5,** 255
Aden, expedition to, 177
Adjutant General, British Army, **5–6**
Adye, John M., **6–7,** 20
Afghan War, First **7–8,** 11, 152, 177, 179, 293, 303
Afghan War, Second, **9–10,** 11, 62, 84, 85, 90, 91, 122, 175, 177, 197–199, 220, 237, 261–262, 286, 297, 312–313
Afghanistan, **10–11,** 62, 123, 124, 152, 264, 296–297. *See also* Afghan War, First; Afghan War, Second
Africa
  imperialism in, xvi, 173
  See also Ashanti; Boer War, First; Boer War, Second; Boers; Egypt; South Africa; Sudan
Afridis, 247, 322, 323
Ahmad Shah, 304
Akazais, 163
Albert, Prince, 224, 332
Aldershot, **11–12,** 13, 224
Alexandria, Bombardment of, **12–13**
Ali wad Hilku, Khalifa, 120
Alison, Sir Archibald, **13,** 15, 16, 20, 36, 37, 189
Aliwal, Battle of, **13–14,** 300, 306
Allen, A. T., 305
Alma, Battle of the, **14–15,** 42, 61, 76, 84, 112, 137, 209, 244, 273, 295
Amanquatia, 34
Amar Singh, 156
Amherst, Lord Jeffrey, 105
Amoaful, Battle of, **15–16,** 37, 203, 343
Amritsar, Treaty of, 298, 302
Anglo-Egyptian Treaty (1936), 131, 304

Anglo-Russian Boundary Commission, 152
Anglo-Russian Convention, 152–153
Animals, Transport, **16–17**
Anson, A. E. H., 262, 263
Anson, George, 119, 367
Anstruther, Philip, 60
Arabi Pasha, Ahmed, 13, **17–18,** 19–20, 21, 130, 316, 343
Arabi Rebellion, 6–7, 12, 13, 17, **18–21,** 127, 130, 131, 150, 313, 319–320, 343
Ardagh, Sir John, 190
Armstrong, W. G., 27
Armstrong gun, 6, 27
Army Act (1881), 121
Army and Navy Pensioners and Time-Expired Men's Employment Society, 277
Army Board, 6, 106, 136, 336
Army Chaplain's Department, 90
Army Council, 5, 6, 136, 271
Army Enlistment Act (1870), 81, 82, 209, 275–276, 297, 298
Army Estimates, **22–23,** 102, 335
Army Hospital Corps, 234
Army Medical Corps, 234
Army Medical Staff, 289
Army Medical Staff Corps, 289
Army Nursing Service, 234, 235
"Army of the Indus," 7–8, 123, 177

391

Index

Army of Retribution, 8, 293
Army Regulation Bill (1871), 82, 83
Army Sanitary Commission, 235
Army Service Corps, **23–24**
Arrow, The, 100, 177
Artillery, British Army, 6, 15, **24–28,** 46, 105, 130, 133, 228, 229, 252, 347
Artists, War, **28**
The Ashantee War (Maurice), 110, 229
Ashanti, **28–30,** 203–204
Ashanti Expedition, **30–31**
Ashanti Ring, **31–32,** 35, 59, 72, 153, 229, 230, 266, 313, 343, 346
Ashanti War (1900), **32–33**
Ashanti War, First, 30, **33–34**
Ashanti War, Second, 13, 15, 30, 31, **34–37,** 59, 109, 110, 203–204, 266, 288, 343
Ashantiland, 29 (map), 32
Asquith, Herbert H., 115
Atbara, Battle of, **37–38,** 143, 168, 201, 213, 256, 280
Awards and decorations, xiii, **38–39,** 76–77, 332–333
Ayub Khan, 10, 198, 220, 221

Baden Powell, Sir Robert S. S., **41,** 216, 217
Bagyidaw (King of Burma), 67, 69
Bahadur Shah, 119
Baji Rao II, 88, 241
Baker, T. D., 91, 198
Baker Pasha, Valentine, **42,** 71, 132, 220, 317
Balaklava, Battle of, **42–43,** 76, 81, 84, 92, 112, 209, 270, 295
Balloons, **44**
Baltic Sea Operations, Crimean War, **44–45,** 124, 242
Baluchi tribes, 247
Baluchistan, 11
Baratieri, Oreste, 3
Baring, Evelyn, 82
Barnard, Sir Henry W., 119
Barnes, Sir Edward, 367

Barrett, Thomas Augustine, xvi
Barton, Maj. Gen. G., 104
Bashi-Bazouks, 327
Basutoland, 54
"The Battle of Dorking" (Chesney), 188
The Battle of Spicheren, August 6th (Henderson), 165
Becher, J. R., 305
Bechuanaland, 193–194, 216, 285, 337
Begbie lamps, 107
Belmont, battle at, 231
Bengal Army **45–46,** 55, 67, 69, 129, 130, 173, 175, 178, 179, 180, 210, 253, 254, 304, 312
Benson, G. E., 219
Bertie-Clay, Captain, 65
Betwa River, Battle of, 289
Bingham, George C. (Third Earl of Lucan) 14, 43, 81, 92–93, 112, **209–210,** 270
Birch, J. W. W., 262
Bird, G. Corrie, 324
Biscoe, Col., 238
Bithur, battle at, 163, 318
Bitter-Ender, **46–47**
Black Mountain expedition, 242
Black Sea Fleet (British), 211
Black Sea Fleet (Russian), 295
Black Watch, 15, 16, 37, 317
Black Week, 52, 63, 104, 143, 218, 314
Blackwell, Elizabeth, 244
Blockhouses, **47–48,** 275
Bloemfontein, capture of, 53, 287, 314
Bloemfontein Conference (1899), 307
Bloemfontein Convention (1854), 54
Blood, Sir Bindon, **48–49,** 65, 66, 223, 240
Blood River, Battle of, 54
Boer War, First, **49–50,** 54–55, 60–61, 113, 195–196, 206, 213, 221–222, 267, 326, 346
Boer War, Second, xii, xiii, 6, 17, 23, 24, 25, 26, 27, 41, 44, 46–47, **51–53,** 55, 56–57, 63–64, 72, 102, 104–105, 106, 107, 108, 113–114,
117–118, 134, 141, 143, 160, 166, 196, 202, 204, 205, 214, 216–217, 218, 228, 231, 234, 235, 237, 239, 259, 266, 275, 279, 282, 285, 286–287, 290, 306–307, 308–309, 314, 326, 331–332, 336, 337–339, 340, 345, 349
Boers, 46–47, **53–55,** 56–57, 80, 106, 108, 117–118, 193, 196, 204, 306–307, 314, 326. *See also* Boer War, First; Boer War, Second
Bombay Army, 10, 46, **55–56,** 129, 130, 173, 175, 177, 178, 243
Bombay-Burma Trading Company, 70
Boomplaats, Battle of, 54, **56,** 306, 326
Bosquet, Pierre, 93, 186, 187
Botha, Louis, **56–57,** 104, 108, 196, 309
Botswana, 194
Boxer Protocol, 58
Boxer Rebellion, **57–59,** 98, 177, 194
Brackenbury, Sir Henry, 31, 32, **59,** 188, 189–190, 238, 311
Brander, Lt. Col., 322
Brisk (ship), 240
British Army
 artillery, 6, 15, **24–28,** 46, 105, 130, 133, 228, 229, 252, 347
 cavalry, **85–86,** 349
 engineers, 15, 16, 26, 44, 105, **132–135,** 228, 229, 252, 341, 347
 in India, **175–176**
 infantry of, xiv, **181–185**
 officers, xiv, 159, **249–253**
 organization of, 24–25, 85–86, 133–134, 181–182
 strength of, xiv, 83–84, 176, 180, 181, 281
 supply and transport, 17, 23–24, 206–207
 tactics, 25–26, 86–87, 183–184
 training, 11–12, 26–27, 87, 134, 184–185, 252, 277–278
 weapons, 3, 6, 24–26, 27–28, 64–65, 87–88, 113, 134–135, 182–183, 184, 215, 266

Index

British Army of Occupation in Egypt, 144, 150, 311, 312
British Army Remount Department, 17
British Empire, size of, xvi, 172 (map)
British Expeditionary Force (BEF), 76, 141, 159, 181, 217, 273, 319, 343
British North America Act, 79
British School of Music, 236
British South Africa Company, 194
Bromhead, Gonville, **60,** 92, 288
Bronkhorstspruit, Battle of, 55, **60–61**
Brown, Sir George, 14, **61,** 112
Brown Bess, 64, 161, 180, 182
Browne, Sir Samuel J., 9, **61–62,** 85
Brownlow, C. C., 238
Bruce, A. McC., 238
Bruce, Henry W., 260
Brudenell, James, T. (Seventh Earl of Cardigan), 43, **80–81,** 84, 92, 93, 209, 269–270
Brunswick rifle, 64, 182
Brydon, William, 8
Buller, Sir Redvers H., 24, 31, 32, 51, **63–64,** 104, 105, 205, 224, 225, 231, 282, 308–309, 317, 331–332, 337–338, 340, 353–354
Bullets, **64–65**
Bundula, Maha, 67
Buner Field Force, 48–49, **65–66,** 322
Bunerwals, 65–66, 322
Bunny, A. C., 324
Burgoyne, John, Fox, 187
Burleigh, Bennet, 110
Burma, **66–67,** 68–71, 177
Burma War, First, 66, **67–69,** 177, 287
Burma War, Second, 66, 67, **69–70,** 177, 265
Burma War, Third, 67, **70–71,** 177, 340
Burmese Expeditionary Force, 67
Burnaby, Frederick G., 1, **71–72,** 132, 341
Burnes, Alexander "Bokhara," 152
Burrows, G. R. S., 10, 220

Bush Warfare (Heneker), 189
Butler, Lady Elizabeth, 28, 72–73
Butler, Sir William F., 28, 31, 32, **72–73,** 144, 147, 282

Callwell, Sir C. E., 189
Camberley, Staff College, **75,** 255, 293
Cambridge, Second Duke of (Prince George F.), 6, 14, 32, 63, 72, **76,** 83, 84, 103, 105, 106, 112, 153, 224, 336, 343, 365
Camel Corps, 17
Cameron, Charles D., 2, 320
Cameron, Sir Duncan, 226, 230
Cameroon, xvi
Campaign medals, xiii, **76–77**
The Campaigns of Hannibal, 214
Campbell, Sir Archibald, 67, 68
Campbell, Sir Colin, 13, 43, **77–78,** 80, 89, 96, 155, 210, 258, 318, 367
Campbell, Frederick, 13
Canada, 31, **78–79,** 230, 282–283, 342–343
Canada Act (1791), 78
Canning, Lord, 181
Cape Colony, 51, 54, 55, 56, 79–80, 84, 193, 204, 284–285, 306, 307
Cape Frontier Wars, 54, **79–80,** 306, 337
Cardigan, Seventh Earl of (James T. Brudenell), 43, **80–81,** 84, 92, 93, 209, 270
Cardwell, Edward T., 23, 31, 35, **81–82,** 83, 145, 189, 275, 298, 308, 336, 342, 343
Cardwell Reforms, 23, 76, 81, **82–83,** 113, 145, 167, 181, 188, 189, 237, 275–276, 336, 343
Cathcart, Sir George, 14, **84,** 112, 187
Cavagnari, Sir Pierre L. N., 9, **84–85,** 286, 312
Cavalry, British Army, 43, **85–88,** 349
Cavendish-Bentinck, William H., 367
Cavour, Count, 294
Cawnpore, siege and relief of, **88–89,** 163, 241, 318

Central Force for Home Defense, 160
Central India Field Force, 157, 284, 289
Central Indian Campaign, 157, 318
Cetshwayo kaMpande, **89–90,** 190, 329, 330, 343, 351, 354
Chamberlain, Joseph, 194
Chamberlain, Sir Neville, 85, **90**
Chang Lo, siege of, 322
Channer, Capt., 263
Channer, G. N., 163
Chaplains, **90–91**
Chapman, Sir Edward F., 190
Charasia, Battle of, **91**
Chard, John R. M., 60, **92,** 288, 353
Charge of the Light Brigade, 42, 80–81, 84, **92–93,** 112, 270, 274
Charge of the 21st Lancers, **93–94,** 102, 257, 281
Chartered Company, 193, 285
Chatham, School of Military Engineering, 134, 228, 252, 255
Cheape, Brig. Gen., 70
Chelmsford, Second Baron (Fredrick A Thesiger), 80, **94–95,** 190, 329, 330, 343, 351, 353, 354
Chenery, Thomas, 109, 265
Chernaya, Battle of, **95,** 113, 294, 296
Chesney, Charles C., **95–96,** 188
Chesney, Sir George, 188, 189
Cheunpi, Convention of, 99
Chief of the General Staff, 136, 365
Chief of the Imperial General Staff, 365
Childers, Hugh, 343
Chillianwalla, Battle of, 61, **96–97,** 150, 301
China, 57, **97–98,** 99–101, 149–150, 177, 194
China War, First, 97, **98–100,** 149–150, 177
China War, Second, 57, 97, 98, **100–101,** 177
Chitral Relief Force, 48, 143, 171
Chitralis, 247
Churchill, Winston L. S., 49, 93, **101–102,** 110, 223

393

Index

Chuttur Singh, 154, 300, 301
Civil-Military relations, **102–103**
Clarke, Andrew, 262
Clive, Robert, 128
Coastal Fortifications, **103–104**
Codrington, Sir William, 303
Colborne, Maj. Gen. F., 263
Colenso, Battle of, 26, 52, 57, **104–105**, 205, 314
Colley, George Pomeroy. *See* Pomeroy-Colley, Sir George
Collinson, John, 256
Commanders in chief
  British Army, **105–106**, 136, 167, 168, 229, 335, 336, 365
  Indian Army, 367
Commando system, **106**, 118
Commissariat and Transport Staff, 23, 24, 206
Commissariat Staff Corps, 23
Commissions, 250, 251, 253, 254–255, 269
Committee of Imperial Defense, 136
Communications, **107**, 208
Companion of the Most Honorable Order of the Bath, 39
Concentration camps, **108**, 166
Congo, xvi, 146
Congreve, William, 287
Congreve rocket, 287
Connaught and Strathearn, Duke of (Gen. H.R.H.), 224, 230
Conolly, Arthur, 151
Conspicuous Gallantry Medal, 39
Conspicuous Service Cross, 39
Contagious Diseases Acts, 236
Control Department, 23
Cook, James, 227
Coomassie and Magdala (Stanley), 110
Corn Laws, xv
Corps of Commissionares, 277
Corresondents, war, 101–102, **109–110**, 232
Cotton, Sir Sydney, 304–305
Cotton, Sir Willoughby, 7, 68

Cotton, Stapleton, 367
Council of Military Education, 75
Crewe Railway Volunteers, 333
Crimean War, xiii, 13, 14–15, 17, 23, 25, 28, 42–43, 44–45, 45 (map), 61, 76, 84, 92, 95, 109, **110–113**, 124, 136–137, 142, 181, 183, 186–187, 199, 206–207, 209, 211, 236, 237, 241–242, 244, 260, 265, 270, 273–274, 279, 281, 287, 289, 290–291, 294, 295–296, 302, 332, 340, 345
  medical reforms and, 233, 234, 235–236, 244–245, 345
  military reforms and, 187–188, 206–207, 233, 252, 310, 335
Cronje, Piet A., **113–114**, 118, 216, 218, 239, 259, 260
Cunynghame, Sir Arthur, 153
Cureton, C. R., 301
Curragh Camp, **114–115**
Curragh Incident (1914), 103, 114, **115–116**, 149
Curragh of Kildare Act (1868), 114
Curzon, George, 321, 350

Daguerre, Louis, 265
Daguerreotypes, 265
Dalhousie, Lord, 179
Dannenberg, P. A., 186, 187
Dartmouth, Lord, 228
Davis, John, 317
Dawkins Commission, 336
De la Rey, Jacobus, 51, 114, **117–118**, 218, 239, 307
De Wet, Christiaan R., 47, **118**, 259, 260, 314
Deane, Col., 206
The Defence of India (MacGregor), 189
Delhi Field Force, 119
Delhi, siege and storming of, **118–119**, 244
Denison, Lt., 228
Deolali, Staff College, 255
Derby, Lord, 122

Dervishes, 1, 37–38, 93–94, **119–120**, 122–123, 132, 144, 147, 151, 165–166, 199–200, 213, 219–220, 230, 256–257, 279–281, 317, 324–326
Desert Column, 1, 59, 72, 127, 147–148, 313, 341
Dick, Robert, 307
Directorate of Military Operations, 190
Directorate of Military Training, 239
Discipline and Justice, British Army, **120–122**
Disraeli, Benjamin, xv, 18, **122**, 172, 232, 316, 343
Distinguished Conduct Medal, 38, 39, 332
Distinguished Service Cross, 39
Distinguished Service Order, 39
Dongola, capture of, **122–123**, 213, 280
Dost Mohammed, 7, 11, **123**, 296, 298
Douglas, Sir Charles W. H., 365
Drury Lowe, D. C., 319
Duff, Harry Beachamp, 367
Dundas, Henry, 335
Dundas, Sir James W. D., 45, **124**, 211
Dundonald, Earl of, 104
Dunlop, Maj., 262
Durand, Sir Henry Marion, 124
Durand, Sir Henry Mortimer, **124–125**, 245
Durand Line, 11, 124, 125, 152, 245
D'Urban, Benjamin, 80
Durham, Lord, 78
Durnford, Anthony W., 351
Dutch East India Company, 54

Earle, William, 59, 72, **127**, 148
East India Company (British), 98, **127–128**, 130, 152
  Indian Mutiny and, 128, 156–158, 179–181
  military forces of, 5, 7–8, 55, **128–130**, 173, 175, 176, 177–178, 216, 253–255, 264, 332

394

Index

power transferred to British Crown, 5, 46, 174, 175
territory of, 11, 66, 128, 155, 171, 173, 174, 177, 262, 302, 303
Eastman, George, 265
Education, 252, 255–256, 277–278. *See also* Addisombe Military Seminary; Camberly; Chatham; Sandhurst; Staff College; Woolwich
Education Act (1870), 278
Edward VII, 135, 332
Egerton, C. C., 324
Egypt, xvi, **130–131,** 165, 305, 346
  Arabi Rebellion and, 6–7, 12, 13, 18–21, 127, 130, 132, 150, 313, 319–320, 343
  Battle of El Teb and, 42, 71, 132, 147, 151, 220, 312, 313, 317
  Battle of Tel el-Kebir and, 7, 13, 21, 131, 161–162, 319–320, 343
  Sudan and, 102, 120, 122–123, 131, 132, 144, 147, 199–200, 201–202, 219–220, 256–257, 279–281, 303, 305, 313, 315, 342–342
  Suez Canal and, xv, 12, 18, 20, 122, 130, 131, 173, 279, 303, 305, 315–316, 319, 341–342
Egyptian Army, 18, 38, 71, 93, 120, 122–123, **131–132,** 144, 147, 154, 165, 199, 201–202, 213, 220, 256, 280, 303–304, 319–320, 325–326, 341–342, 343, 346
El Obeid, massacre at, 165–166, 200, 220
El Teb, Battle of, 42, 71, **132,** 147, 151, 220, 312, 313, 317
Elandslaagte, Battle of, 141, 160, 205
Elgin, Earl of, 100, 135
Elgin Commission, 106, 135, 337
Ellenborough, Lord, 157, 162
Elles, E. R., 223, 240
Elliot, Charles, 99
Elliot, Commodore, 260
Elphinstone, William G. K., 7, 8
Enfield rifle, 64, 180, 182, 183, 305

Engineers, British Army, 15, 16, 25, 26, 44, 105, **132–135,** 228, 229, 252, 341, 347
England, Sir Richard, 14, 112
Enlistment
  length of, 209, 275–276, 282, 297–298,
  standards for, 232–233
Entente Cordiale (1904), 140
Esamen, battle at, 36
Esher, Reginald B. B., 106, **135,** 337
Esher Committee, 6, 106, **135–136,** 139, 239, 271, 337
Ethiopia. *See* Abyssinia
Eupatoria, Battle of, **136–137**
European Brigade, 15, 36
Eurydice (ship), 340
Evans, Sir George de Lacy, 14, 112, **137**

Fane, Henry, 367
Fashoda incident, xvi, **139–140,** 173, 202
Fawcett Commission, 166
Fenian Brotherhood, 79
Fenton, Roger, 265
Fergusson, Sir Charles, 115
Ferozeshah, Battle of, 13, **140–141,** 150, 162, 242, 299, 306
Festing, Lt. Col., 34
Field Artillery Drill, 25
Field Exercise, 183, 308
Field Exercises and Evolutions (1859), 184, 185
Field Exercise and Evolutions of the Army (1824), 184
Field Pocket Book for Auxilary Forces, 308
Field Service Pocket Book, 308
Field Service Regulations, 159, 337
Financial secretary, 23
Firket, Battle of, 168
1st Corps, 12
"Flagpole War," 225
Fomena, Treaty of (1874), 30, 203
Foord, H. H., 70
Forbes, Archibald, 109

Fortescue, Sir John, 14, 227, 306
Forward School, 152, 175
France, xvi, 70, 97
  Crimean War and, 14, 15, 44, 45, 95, 110–113, **142,** 186, 296, 302
  Egypt and, xv, 18, 19, 139, 173, 315
Franco-Prussian War, xvi, 82, 109, 238
Frederick, Duke of York, 5, 105, 167, 271, 365
Freemantle, Sir Arthur L., 188
French, John D. P., 115, 116, **141,** 365
Fripp, Charles E., 28
Frontier Brigade, 77
Frontier Field Force, 144
Frontier Light Horse, 329, 330

Galbraith, Brig. Gen., W., 163
Gandamak, Treaty of, 9, 85, 91, 124, 312
Gardner machine gun, 215
Gaselee, Brig. Gen., A., 323
Gaselee, Sir Alfred, 58
Gatacre, Sir William F., 38, 51, **143–144,** 256, 280, 314, 315
Gatling, Richard, 215
Gatling gun, 215, 329
Gee, H. A., 222, 324
General Service Enlistment Act, 180
General Staff, 5, 159, 160, 190, 365
Genouilly, Rigault de, 100
Gentlemen and Yeoman Cavalry, 349
George F., Prince (Second Duke of Cambridge), 6, 14, 32, 63, 72, **76,** 83, 84, 103, 105, 106, 112, 153, 224, 336, 343, 365
George V, 332
Germany, imperialism in Africa, xvi
Ghanzi, fortress of, 293
Ghulab Singh, 300
Gifford, Lt. Lord, 31, 32
Gilbert, Maj., Gen., 307
Gilbert, Sir Walter R., 96, 140, 155
Gilgitis, 247
Gillispie, Sir Rollo R., 155
Ginnis, Battle of, 72, 120, **144–145,** 154, 200, 312

395

Index

Girouard, Lt., Col., 275
Gladstone, William E., 6, 81, 83, 122, **145,** 147
Glover, John, 35, 36, 37
Glyn, Richard, 351
Godby, Brig. Gen., 14, 96
Godwin, Henry, 69
Gold, C. E., 318
Gold Coast, 28, 30, 32–36, 203, 343
"Golden Stool," 29, 32, 33
Gomm, Sir William M., 367
Gorchakov, P. D., 186
Gorchakov, Prince Michael, 95, 137, 290
Gordon, Charles G., 1, 59, 98, 127, **145–146,** 147–148, 150, 220, 279, 312, 315, 342, 344
Gordon, Sir J. J., 99
Gordon Relief Expedition, 1, 17, 28, 63, 72, 107, 144, **146–149,** 154, 177, 201, 220, 312, 313, 341, 342, 344, 346
Gore Browne, Thomas, 318
Gough, Sir Hubert de la P., 115–116, **149**
Gough, Hugh, 13, 96, 97, 99, 140, **149–150,** 154, 157–158, 162, 298–301, 306, 307–308, 367
Govind Singh, 302
Graham, Sir Gerald, 63, 132, 147, 148, **150–151,** 230, 312, 313, 317, 324–325
Grant, J. D., 322
Grant, Sir James Hope, 101, **151**
Grant, Sir Patrick, 367
Graspan, battle at, 231
Great Game, 7, 9, 11, 62, 124, **151–152,** 175, 261, 264, 321, 350
Great Pathan Revolt, 323
"Great Trek," 54
Greaves, Sir George R., 31, 32, **153**
Greer, H. H., 226
Grenfell, Francis W., 144, **153–154,** 201, 304, 326
Grey, John, 157, 158
Grombchevski, Capt., 350

Grossmith, George, 232, 343
Guards Brigade, 15
Gujerat, Battle of, 61, 97, 150, **154–155,** 242
Gurkha War, **155–156**
Gurkhas, 155, **156,** 321
Gwalior, Battle of, **156–157,** 181
Gwalior Campaign, **157–158,** 243
Gyantse Fort, 322

H.M.S. *Agamemnon,* 211
H.M.S. *Alexandra,* 12
H.M.S. *Hampshire,* 202
H.M.S. *Hecla,* 332
H.M.S. *Hyacinth,* 99
H.M.S. *Inflexible,* 12
H.M.S. *Invincible,* 12
H.M.S. *Perseus,* 195
H.M.S. *Volage,* 99
H.M.T. *Transit,* 311
Haines, Frederick P., 367
Haldane, Richard B., 135, **159–160,** 337
Hale rocket, 3, 287–288
Hamilton, Sir Ian S. M., **160–161,** 222, 323
Hamley, Sir Edward B., 20, 96, **161–162,** 188, 319
Hammond, A. G., 323
Hardinge, Henry, 11, 61, 76, 140, 150, **162,** 224, 298, 299, 308, 365
Harrington Commission, 106, 336
Hart, Brig. Gen., R., 323
Hart, Fitzroy, 104
Hashin, battle at, 151
Hassanzais, 163
Hastings, Francis R., 367
Hau Hau campaign, 227
Havelock, Sir Henry, 88, **163,** 210, 241, 258, 264
Hayden, Franz Joseph, 236
Hazara Field Force, **163–164**
Hearsay, Brig. Gen., 155
Heavy Brigade in Crimean War, 43, 81, 92
Heliograph, 107

Henderson, G. F. R., **164–165,** 188, 229
Heneker, W. C. G., 189
Henry, Prince (of Battenberg), 30
Henty, G. A., 109
Herbert, Sidney, 235
Hervey, Brig. Gen., 155
Hicks, Brig Gen., 14
Hicks Pasha, William, 132, 147, **165–166,** 199, 317
Highland Brigade, 13, 15, 186, 213, 214, 218, 219, 236, 259
Hildyard, H. J. T., 104, 331
Hill, Rowland, 339, 365
Hill, Col. W., 323
Hindustani Fanatics, 304, 305
Hinxman, Lt., 263
The History of General Sir Charles Napier's Conquest of Scinde (Napier), 243–244
History of the War in the Peninsula (Napier), 187
Hobhouse, Emily, 108, **166**
Hobson, William, 225
Hodgson, Sir Frederick, 32
Hoggan, Brig. Gen., 96, 155
Holy Boys, 283
Home Defense, **167**
Home Rule for Ireland, 115, 149
Hone Heke Pokai, 225–226
Hong Kong, 99
Hope, Sir James, 100
Horse artillery, 24, 25, 26
Horse Guards, 5, 6, 61, 76, 82, 83, 102, 103, 105, **167–168,** 335, 336
Hospitals, **233–234**
Htoon, Myat, 70
Hulme, William, 225
Hunter, Sir Archibald, 38, **168–169,** 256, 280
Huyshe, Brig. Gen., 144
Huyshe, Capt. G. L., 31, 32
Hyder Ally, 287

I Ho Chuan, 57
Ian Hamilton's March (Churchill), 102

Index

Imperial Conference (1907), 159
Imperial General Staff, 159, 365
Imperial Service Troops, **171**
Imperial Yeomanry, 349
Imperialism, xv, xvi, **171–173,** 231–232
Incorporated Soldiers and Sailors Help Society, 277
India, 155–156, 171, 172, **173–175**
  British Army in, **175–178**
  East India Company in, 127–128, 155, 171, 173, 174, 175–177, 179, 180
  North-West Frontier and, 48, 65, 90, 101–102, 124, 143, 208, 222–223, 237–238, 240, **245–248,** 304–305, 322–323, 324
  Russia and, 7, 9, 11, 62, 124, 151–152, 175, 261, 264, 321, 350
  See also Bengal Army; Bombay Army; Indian Army; Indian Mutiny; Madras Army; Sikh War, First; Sikh War, Second
India Act (1784), 128
India Act (1833), 5
Indian Army, 45–46, 55, 62, 175, **176–179,** 202, 208, 253–256, 268
  officers in, **253–256,** 285, 325, 367
Indian Distinguished Service Medal, 39
Indian Frontier Warfare (Younghusband), 189
Indian General Service Medal, 77
Indian Mutiny, xv, 13, 27, 46, 62, 78, 88–89, 90, 118–119, 128, 129–130, 156–157, 163, 172, 175, 177, 178, **179–181,** 183, 207, 210, 242–243, 244, 279, 284, 286, 287, 289, 303, 304, 318, 346
Indian National Congress, 175
Indian Order of Merit, 39
Infantry, xiv, **181–185**
Infantry Drill, 184, 185
Ingogo, Battle of, 50, 50 (map), 55, **185–186**
Inkerman, Battle of, 76, 84, 112, 137, **186–187,** 274, 295
Intellectuals, **187–189**
Intelligence, **189–190.** *See also* War Office: Intelligence Branch
Ireland, 22, 114–116, 149
Isandlwana, Battle of, 89, 94, **190,** 288, 351, 352, 353
Ismail (khedive of Egypt), 17, 18, 130, 131, 315

Jameson, Leander Starr, 51, 55, 114, **193,** 285, 326
Jameson Raid, **193–194,** 204, 326
Japan, **194,** 195
Jarry, Gen., 75
Jeffrey, P. D., 65, 223
Jervois, Sir William, 262, 263
Jhansi, siege of, 284, 289
Johannesburg armistice (1900), 314
Johannesburg, capture of, 53, 287, 314
Joint Anglo-French Note, 19
Joubert, Franz, 60
Joubert, Petrus J., 57, **195–196,** 204, 205, 206
Journalists, 101–102, 109–110, 232

Kabul, Afghanistan, 7, 11, 152, 293, 312
Kabul Field Force, 9–10, 91, 286, 297
Kabul to Kandahar March, **197–198**
Kabul-Kandahar Field Force, 198
Kaffir Wars, 80
Kalpi, battle at, 289
Kalunga, siege of, 155
Kambula, Battle of, 353, 354
Kandahar, Battle of, 10, **198–199,** 221
Kandahar Field Force, 9, 312
Kanjutis, 247
Karo La, battle at, 322
Kars Siege of, **199**
Kashgil, Battle of, **199–200,** 317
Kawati, 226
Keane, Sir John, 7
Kelly-Kenny, Sir Thomas, 259
Kempster, F. J., 323
Khalifa (Abdullahi ibn Mohammed), 119, 120, **200–201,** 219, 220, 256, 257, 279, 280, 281, 315, 325
Khalsa, 298, 300, 302, 307
Khartoum, fall of, 1, 147–148, 220, 279, 312, 313, 324, 341
Khrulev, Stephan A., 136
Kimberley, siege of, 51, 53, 114, 259
Kingi, Wiremu, 318, 319
King's Dragoon Guards, 329, 330
Kipling, Rudyard, 120, 232, 286
Kitchener, Lord Horatio H., 24, 37–38, 47, 52, 53, 93, 102, 122–123, 139, 154, 160, 168, 178, 200, **201–203,** 213, 215, 256–257, 259–260, 280, 281, 304, 326, 342, 367
Kofi Karikari, 15, 36, 37, **203–204,** 343
Komarov, Gen., 261
Kruger, S. J. Paulus, 195–196, **204,** 307, 314
Kumasi, 28
Kunch, battle at, 289
Kurram Field Force, 9, 286
Kwaka Dua III, 32
Kwaku Dua I (Ashanti King), 203

Ladysmith, siege of, 51, 52, 53, 57, 64, 104, 160, 196, **205–206,** 308–309, 331–332, 337, 338, 340
Lahore, Treaty of, 300
Laing's Nek, Battle of, 50, 50 (map), 55, 196, **206,** 221, 267
Lal Singh, 299
Lambert, Commodore, 69
Land Transport Corps, 23, **206–207**
Landsdowne, Marquess of, 124
Lattas, Michael, 327
Lawrence, John L. M., 207
Lawrence, Sir Henry M., **207,** 210
Le Marchant, John Gaspard, 75, 293
Lee-Enfield rifle, 65, 87, 183
Lee-Metford rifle, 65, 87, 183
Leopold II (king of Belgium), xvi, 146, 173
Lewis, D. F., 38, 256, 257
Lhasa Convention (1904), 322, 350

Index

Light Brigade, 43
   Charge of the, 42, 80–81, 84, **92–93,** 112, 209, 270, 274
Lime light lamps, 107
Lin Ze-xu, 99
Lines of communication, **208**
Liprandi, Pavel, 43
Littler, Sir John, 140
Localization Act (1872), 83, 167, 237
Localization Committee, 214
Lockhart, Sir William S. A., **208,** 238, 322, 323, 367
Lockwood, Brig. Gen., 155
London Convention (1884), 50, 55
London to Ladysmith via Pretoria (Churchill), 102
Long, C. J., 104, 105
Long service, **209,** 297–298
Longfield, Brig. Gen., 119
Low, Sir R. C., 48
Lucan, Third Earl of (George C. Bingham), 14, 43, 81, 92–93, 112, **209–210,** 270
Lucas, Charles D., 332
Lucknow, siege and relief of, 13, 163, 207, **210–211,** 243, 258
Lumsden, Harry, 268
Lumsden, Sir Peter, 261–262
Lyons, Sir Edmund, 124, **211**
Lyttelton, Sir Neville, 104, 256, 257, 309, 331, 365

Macbean, Col., 67
MacCosh, John, 265
MacDonald, Sir Claude, 57
Macdonald, Sir Hector A., 38, **213–214,** 222, 256, 257, 281
Macdonald, J. R. L., 321–322
MacDougall, Sir Patrick, 161, 188, 189, **214–215**
Macgregor, C. R., 240, 323
MacGregor, Sir Charles M., 188, 189, 198
Machine guns, **215**
Macnaghten, Sir William H., 8
Madda Khel, 324

Madras Army, 46, 55, 67, 69, 129, 130, 150, 173, 175, 177, 178, **216**
Mafeking, Siege of, 41, 51, 53, 114, **216–217**
Magdala, capture of, 4, **217–218**
Magersfontein, Battle of, 214, **218–219,** 314, 338–339
Maguire, Miller, 189
Maharajpore, Battle of, 150, 157–158, 306
Mahdi, 119, 120, 127, 132, 146, 147, 166, 199, 200, **219–220,** 315
Mahratta Army of Gwalior, 157–158
Maiwand, Battle of, **220–221,** 286
"Maizar outrage," 324
Majuba Hill, Battle of, 49, 50, 50 (map), 55, 114, 196, 205, 213, **221–222,** 267, 346
Malakand Field Force, 48, 49, 65, 102, **222–223,** 322
Malaysia, expedition to, 177
Malcolm, Maj. Gen. G., 4
Maneuvers, British Army, **223–225**
Mansfield, William R., 367
Maori War, First, **225–226,** 227
Maori War, Second, **226–227,** 230
Maoris, **227,** 318–319
Maps, **227–228**
Maqoma, Chief, 80
Maratha Confederacy, 128, 173
The March to Commassie (Henty), 110
Marchand, Jean-Baptiste, 139
Marines, 15, 43, 195
Markham, Brig. Gen., 155
Marmora, Alfonso de la, 294
Martello Towers, 103
Martin, R. M., 93, 94
Martini-Henry rifle, 65, 87, 183, 220, 326
Master-General of the Ordnance, **228–229**
Maurice, Frederick Denison, 229
Maurice, Sir (John) Frederick, 31, 32, 110, 165, 188, **229**
Maxim, Hiram, 215
Maxim gun, 215

Maxim-Nordenfeldt gun, 326
Maxwell, Sir John G., 38, 256, 257
Maxwell, William E., 30
McCalmont, Sir Hugh, 31, 32
McCarthy, Sir Charles, 33–34
McCreagh, Col., 67
McLeod, Brig. Gen., 155
McNeill, Sir John C., 31, 32, 153, **230,** 282, 325
McPherson, Herbert, 198
McQueen, J. W., 163
Medals, xiii, 38–39, 76–77, 332–333
Medical personnel, **234**
Medicine, Military, 109, 112, 234, 235, **232–236,** 244–245, 289–290, 310, 345
Mediterranean Expeditionary Force, 160–161
Mediterranean Fleet, 124, 211
Meiklejohn, W. H., 65, 66, 222, 223
Menelik (Emperor of Abyssinia), 279
Menelik I, 2
Menshikov, Prince Alexander Sergeevich, 14, 42, 112, 136, 137, 186, 290
Mercantilism, xv, 172
Meritorious Service Medal, 38
Methuen, Lord Paul S., 51, 52, 117, 218, **230–231,** 239, 338
Metis, 282
Meyer, Louis, 56
Miani, battle at, 243, 303
Michel, Sir John, 101
The Military History of the Campaign of 1882 (Maurice), 229
Military Train, 23, 207
Militia, 167, **237**
Militia Act (1852), 167, 237
Militia Acts (Canada), 78
Milner, Lord Alfred, 166, 204, 307, 314
Mindon (King of Burma), 70
Minié, Claude, 64, 182
Minié rifle, 64, 86, 113, 182, 183, 339
Miranda (ship), 340
Miranzai Field Force, 208, **237–238**
Mitchell, John, 187

Mobilization Planning, **238–239,** 311
Modder River, Battle of the, 117, 218, 228, 231, **239–240,** 259
Modderspruit, Battle of, 56
Modern Infantry Tactics (MacDougall), 188, 214–215
Modern Warfare as Influenced by Modern Artillery (MacDougall), 188, 214
Mohammed Ahmed ibn Abdullah, 219
Mohammed Ali, 17, 130, 131
Mohammed esh Sherif, Khalifa, 120
Mohmand Field Force, **240,** 322
Mohmands, 240, 247, 322
Mohumra, Battle of, 264
Montauban, Charles, 101
Moriarty, David, 353
Morse, S. F. B., 107
Mountain, Brig. Gen., 96, 155
Mountain Warfare (MacGregor), 189
Mournful Monday, 51, 205, 340
Mpande kaSenzangakhona, 89
Mudki, Battles of, 242, 306
Multan, siege of, 154, 242, 300
Muraviev, Michael, 199
Music, Military, **236–237**
Musket Wars, 227
Muslim League, 175
Mustapha Pasha, Zarif, 199
Myanmar, 66

Nairne, Sir Charles E., 367
Nana Sahib, 88, 163, **241**
Nanak, Guru, 301
Nanking, Treaty of, 100
Napier, Admiral Sir Charles, 44, 45, **241–242**
Napier, General Sir Charles J., 97, **243–244,** 258, 301, 303, 367
Napier, Maj. Charles F., 242
Napier, Sir Robert C., 2, 3, 4, 101, 217, 218, **242–243,** 320–321, 367
Napier, Sir William F. P., 187, 243
Napoleonic Wars, xiii, xiv, 335, 339
Natal, 51, 54, 55, 64, 141, 267

Natal Field Force, 49, 185, 205, 221, 267
Native Lands Act (New Zealand), 226
Navy, 12, 103–104, 195
 in China, 99, 100
 in Crimean War, 44–45, 124, 211, 241–242, 260, 340
'Ndondakusuka, Battle of, 89
Nejumi, Emir Adbel Rahman Wad el, 325, 326
Nelson, Robert, 78
Nemiao, Maha, 68
Nepal, 155, 156
Nesselrode, Karl, 151
New Zealand, 225–227, 230, 318–319
New Zealand Cross, 39
Nicholas I (Czar of Russia), 110–111
Nicholson, John, 61, 119, **244,** 304
Nicholson, William G., 365
Nicholson's Nek, Battle of, 118, 205
Nicolls, Sir Jasper, 367
Niepce, Joseph Nicephore, 265
Niger, xvi
Nightingale, Florence, 109, 112, 234, 235, **244–246,** 345
Nolan, Louis E., 93, 210
Nordenfeldt gun 215
Northbrook Committee, 83
North-West Frontier, 48, 65, 90, 101–102, 124, 143, 177, 208, 222–223, 237–238, 240, **245–248,** 304–305, 322–323, 324
Nott, Sir William, 8
Nurses, 234, 235, 244–245, 345

Ochterlony, David, 155, 156
Office of Civilian Commissary-General, 24
Officers
 British Army, xiv, 159, **249–252**
 Indian Army, **253–256**
Officers Training Corps, 159
Oltenitza, Battle of, 111
Omar Pasha, 111, 136, 199, 327
Omdurman, Battle of, 93–94, 102, 120, 131, 139, 143, 168, 200, 201–202, 213, 215, **256–258,** 280, 281, 290, 338
O'Moore Creagh, Garret, 367
The Operations of War (Hamley), 161, 188
Opium War, 97, 98, 149–150, 177
Orakzai tribe, 237, 238, 247, 322, 323
Orange Free State, 54, 55, 56, 106, 118, 193, 314, 326
Order of Merit, 39
Ordnance Board, 227–228, 266, 347
Ordnance Corps, 228, 347
Ordnance Department, 133, 228–229
Ordnance Survey, 341
Osman Azrak, 257
Osman Digna, 132, 151, 257, 317, 324
Ottoman Empire, 44, 110–113, 130, 295, 315, 327. *See also* Turkey
Oudh, 179, 180, 207, 210, 258
Outram, Sir James, 163, 210, 243, **258,** 264

Paardeberg, Battle of, **259–260**
Pacific Ocean Operations, Crimean War, **260**
Pagan Min (King of Burma), 69, 70
Paget, Sir Arthur, 115, 116
Paget, Sir Edward, 367
Palmer, Prof., 337
Palmer, Sir Arthur P., 323, 367
Papineau, Louis Joseph, 78
Paris Peace Conference (1856), 45, 113, 294
Pathan tribes, 222, 237, 240, 245, 304, 322–323, 324
Paul (Czar of Russia), 151
Pavlov, P. I., 186, 187
Pax Britannica, xiii, xiv
Pay, 249, 253, 269, 276
Pearson, Charles K., 351, 353
Peiwar Kotal, Battle of, **260–261,** 286
Peking, Peace Protocol of, 58
Peking, Treaty of, 101
Penjdeh Incident, 124, 152, **261–262**
Penny, Brig. Gen., 96, 155
Pennycuick, Brig. Gen., 96

Index

Pensions, 250, 253, 276–277
Perak, punitive expedition to, **262**
Perry, Matthew, 194
Persia, 7, **263–264,** 265
Persian War, 177, 263, **264–265**
Peshawar, 7, 123
Peshawar Movable Column, 240
Peshawar, Treaty of, 264
Peshawar Valley Field Force, 9
Phayre, Col., 217
Photographers, war, 3, **265–266**
Piedmont-Sardinia, 294
The Pirates of Penzance (Gilbert and Sullivan), 232, 343
Pistols, **266**
Plassey, Battle of, 128
Plowden, Walter, 320
Pollock, Sir George, 8
Pomeroy-Colley, Sir George, 31, 32, 49, 50, 55, 82, 185, 206, 221–222, **266–267,** 313, 346
Popular Culture, Military, **231–232**
Post Office Volunteers, 333
Potgeiter, Andries H., 326
Pottinger, Eldered, 152
Pratt, Thomas, 319
Prempeh (Kwaka Dua III), 30
Prendergast, Harry, 70, 71
Pretoria, capture of, 53, 287
Pretoria, Convention of, 50, 55
Pretorius, Andries, 56
Pretorius, Marthinus, 195, 204
Price, David, 260
Primrose, J. M., 10, 198
Prinsloo, Marthinus, 47
Prior, Melton, 28
Promotions, 250, 254, 268, 269
Punialis, 247
Punishment, 120–121
Punjab, 11, 90, 152, 155, 162, 163, 173, 177, 178, 245, 247, 268, 298, 300, 302
Punjab Frontier Force, 77, 90, 178, **268**
Punjab Moveable, Column, 90, 244
Purchase system, xiv, 22, 76, 82, 83, 113, 137, 250, 251, 252, 253, **268–270,** 339
Purdon, Lt. Col., 34

Quartermaster-General, British Army, **271**
Queen Alexandra's Imperial Military Nursing Service, 235
Queen's Regulations, 308
Quetta Division, 168
Quetta, Staff College, 255

Raglan, First Baron (Fitzroy J. H. Somerset), 14, 15, 42, 61, 81, 84, 92–93, 111, 112, 124, 187, **273–274,** 295, 302
Railways, 256, **274–275,** 280
Ramsay, George, 367
Ranjit Singh, 11, 152, 298, 302
Rank and file, xiv, **276–279**
Read, N. A., 95
Reade, W. Winwood, 109, 110
Recollections of a Military Life (Ayde), 7
Recruiting, **281–282**
Red River Expedition, 31, 63, 64, 79, 230, **282–283,** 342–343
Reed, Maj. Gen., 119
Reforms, British Army
  medical, 109, 112, 233–234, 235–236, 244–245, 290, 310, 345
  military and administrative, xiv, 22–23, 76, 81–83, 102, 105–106, 113, 135–136, 137, 145, 159–160, 167, 168, 181, 187–188, 189, 224–225, 234, 237, 335–337, 339, 343
Regulating Act (1773), 128
Reid, Al J., 223
Reid, Charles, 119
Religion, **283–284,** 310
Renny, Lt. Col. H., 305
Retirement, 250, 253–254, 276–277
Rhani of Jhansi, **284,** 289
Rhodes, Cecil, 51, 55, 193, 194, **284–285,** 326
Rhodes, Herbert, 285

Rice, S. R., 47
A Ride to Khiva (Burnaby), 71
Riel, Louis, 79, 282–283, 342
Riel Rebellion, 79, 282–283, 342
Rietfontein, engagement at, 205
Rifle Brigade, 15, 16
Rifle Volunteer Corps, 167, 333
River Column, 59, 72, 127, 148, 313
The River Column (Brackenbury), 59
The River War (Churchill), 102
Roberts, Sir Abraham, 285–286
Roberts, Frederick (son), 105
Roberts, Sir Frederick S. (father), 9–10, 24, 32, 52, 64, 91, 105, 109, 115, 124, 144, 153, 160, 197–198, 202, 232, 259–260, 261, 275, **285–287,** 297, 331, 340, 344, 365, 367
Roberts Ring, 32, 286, 344
Robertson, James, 265
Rockets, 3, **287–288**
Rorke's Drift, 92, **288,** 351, 353
Rose, Sir Hugh H., 156–157, 243, 284, **289,** 318, 367
Ross, Brig. Gen. J., 198, 263
Rowland, Col. H., 351
Royal Army Medical Corps (RAMC), 235, **289–290**
Royal Artillery, 6, 15, **24–28,** 46, 105, 130, 133, 228, 229, 252, 347
Royal Canadian Rifle Regiment, 78
Royal Commission on the War in South Africa, 135
Royal Engineers, Corps of, 15, 16, 25, 26, 44, 105, **132–135,** 228, 229, 252, 341, 347
Royal Horse Artillery, 24, 25, 27
Royal Marines, 15, 43, 195
Royal Military Artificers, Corps, 133
Royal Military Colleges. *See* Camberley; Chatham; Sandhurst; Woolwich
Royal Navy, 12, 103–104, 195
  in China, 99, 100
  in Crimean War, 44–45, 124, 211, 241–242, 260, 340

400

Royal Red Cross, 39
Royal Sappers and Miners, Corps, 133, 228
Royal Titles Act, 175
Runjoor Singh, 14
Russell, Sir Baker, 15, 16, 31, 32, 37
Russell, William Howard, 43, 109, 265, 274
Russia
   Afghanistan and, 7, 9, 11, 123, 124, 151–153, 261, 264, 297
   Crimean War and, 14, 15, 42–43, 44, 45, 95, 110–113, 136, 186–187, 199, **290–291**, 295–296
   See also Great Game
Russo-Japanese War, 152, 160, 194
Russo-Turkish War, 9, 18, 42, 316

Sabertash, Orlando, 187
Sadullah, 324
Saint-Arnaud, Jacques Leroy de, 14, 42, 142
Sale, Sir Robert, 7, 8, 68, **293**
Sand River Convention (1852), 54, 326
Sandhurst, Royal Military College, 5, 75, 251, 254, 255, **293–294**, 347
Sanitation, **235**, 236
Sanitation, School of, 235
Sannaspos, Battle of, 53
Sardinian forces in Crimean War, 95, 110, 113, **294–295**
Scarlett, Sir James Y., 43, 209
Scotland, 22
Scott, Sir Francis, 30
Secretary at war, 23, 102, 335
Secretary of state for the colonies, 23, 105, 168
Secretary of state for war, 23, 102, 105, 168, 229, 335, 336
Seely, J. E. B., 115, 116
Segauli, Treaty of, 156
Sekukuni (Bapedi chief), 54, 313
Sekukuni uprising, 54, 313, 343
The Senior Department of the Royal Military College (MacDougall), 214
Service
   length of, 209, 250, 275–276, 282, 297–298
   long, **209**, 297–298
   short, 275–276, 282, **297–298**
Sevastopol, siege of, 43, 95, 112, 113, 186, 211, 273, 274, 291, **295–296**, 302
Seven Weeks War, 82
17th Lancers, 329, 330
Seymour, Sir Beauchamp, 12, 20
Seymour, Sir Edward H., 57, 58
Seymour, Sir Michael, 100
Shaka, 354
Sher Ali Khan, Amir, 9, 10, 62, 85, 152, **296–297**, 312
Shere Singh, 154, 300
Sherpur, Battle of, **297**
Short Service, 275–276, 282, **297–298**
Shujah, Shah, 7, 11, 123, 152
Sikh War, First, 13–14, 128, 140–141, 150, 162, 242, 268, **298–300**, 302, 306, 307
Sikh War, Second, 11, 61, 96–97, 128, 150, 152, 154–155, 173, 242, 245, 265, **300–301**
Sikhs, 7, 11, **301–303**, 321. *See also* Sikh War, First; Sikh War, Second
Simpson, Sir James M., **302–303**
Sind, 11, 128, 173, 243, 298, **303**
Sino-Japanese War (1894), 194
Sirdar, **303–304**
Sirpura, battle at, 62
Sittana Field Force, **304–305**
Slavery, **305**, 315
Small Wars (Callwell), 189
Smith, Sir Harry G. W., 13, 14, 54, 56, 80, 140, 300, **306**, 307
Smith, Hope, 34
Smuts, Jan Christian, **306–307**
Smyth, Sir Henry, 41
Snider, Jacob, 183
Snider carbines, 87
Snider-Enfield rifle, 3, 65, 183, 217
Snyman, J. P., 216
Sobraon, Battle of, 150, 242, 306, **307–308**
Social background
   of officers, xiv, 250–251, 254, 268–269
   of rank and file, xiv, 277
Social Darwinism, xv, 171, 173, 232
Society, Army and, **21–22**
Society of the Righteous and Harmonious Fists, 57, 98
Soimonov, F. I., 186–187
Soldiers Homes, 284, 310
"The Soldiers of the Queen" (song), xvi
Soldier's Pocket Book for Field Service (Wolseley), **308**, 342
Somerset, Fitzroy J. H. *See* Raglan, First Baron
South Africa, xvi, 284–285, 286–287
   Boers in, 46–47, **53–55**, 56–57, 80, 106, 108, 117–118, 193, 196, 204, 306–307, 314, 326
   Cape Colony in, 51, 54, 55, 56, 79–80, 84, 193, 284–285, 306, 307
   Cape Frontier Wars in, 54, **79–80**, 306, 337
   Orange Free State and, 54, 55, 56, 106, 118, 193, 314, 326
   Transvaal and, xvi, 49, 50, 51, 54, 55, 57, 60, 106, 193, 194, 195, 204, 221, 267, 285, 307, **326–327**, 351
   Union of, 55, 57, 117, 118, 193, 326
   Zulus and, 54, 63, 89, 92, 94, 122, 190, 267, 288, 329–330, 346, 351–354
   See also Boer War, First; Boer War, Second
South African Field Force, 63, 104
South African Republic. *See* Transvaal
South African Women and Children Distress Fund, 108, 166
South-West Africa, xvi
Special Reserve, 159, 237
Spinks, Sir Charlton W., 304
Spion Kop, Battle of, 57, 205, **308–309**, 331, 338

Index

Sports and recreation, **309–310**
St. Petersburg Declaration (1868), 65
Stack, Sir Lee O. F., 304
Staff College, 75, 161, 188, 252, 255
A Staff Officer's Scrap-Book (Hamilton), 160
Staff Tour, 224
Stalker, Foster, 264
Stanhope, Edward, 105, 167, 238, **310–311,** 336
Stanhope Memorandum, 238, **311**
"Stanhope Storehouses," 167
Stanley, Henry M., 109–110
Staveley, Sir Charles, 4
Stedman, Brig. Gen, 14
Steel, Gen., 70
Steevens, G. W., 110
Stephenson, Sir Frederick C. A., 144, 154, **311–312**
Stewart, Sir Donald M., 9, 10, 148, 197–198, **312–313,** 367
Stewart, Sir Herbert, 1, 72, 127, **313–314,** 341
Steyn, Marthinus T., 47, 118, **314**
Stirling, Adm., 260
Stone, Charles P., 131
Stormberg, Battle of, 52, **314–315**
The Story of a Soldier's Life (Roberts), 344
The Story of the Ashantee Campaign (Reade), 110
The Story of the Malakand Field Force (Churchill), 49, 102, 223
Strategy and Tactics in Moungain Ranges (Maguire), 189
Stuart, Leslie, xvi
Suakin Field Force, 148, 151, 230, 324–325
Sudan 119–120, 130 (map), 132, 143, 144, 165, 168, 199–200, 219–220, 303, 305, **315,** 317, 325
 Arabi Rebellion and, 6–7, 12, 13, 18–21, 127, 130, 131, 150, 313, 319–320, 343
 Gordon Relief Expedition and, 1, 17, 28, 63, 72, 107, 144, 146–149, 154, 177, 201, 220, 312, 313, 341, 342, 344
 reconquest of, xii, 102, 122–123, 131, 139–140, 173, 200, 201–202, 256–257, 274–275, **279–281**
Sudan Military Railway, 256, 275, 280
Suez Canal, xv, 12, 18, 20, 122, 130,131, 173, 279, **315–316,** 319
Sveaborg, bombardment of, 45
Sym, Col., 238
Symons, W. P., 323

The Tactics of the Three Arms (Brackenbury), 59
Taiping Rebellion, 98
Talbot, William Henry Fox, 265
Tamai, Battle of, 120, 151, **317–318**
Tamanieb, battle at, 220
Tamati Waka Nene, 225
Tantia Topi, 89, 284, 289, **318**
Taranaki War, 227, **318–319**
Te Kooti Rikirangi Te Turuki, 227
Te Teira, 318
Tej Singh, 140, 299
Tel el-Kebir, Battle of, 7, 13, 21, 131, 161–162, **319–320,** 343
Telegraph, xiii, 3, 107, 109, 113
Telegraph Battalion, 107
Tennyson, Alfred, Lord., xiv
Territorial and Reserve Forces Bill, 159
Territorial Army, 160, 167, 333
Territorial Force, 159, 167, 237, 333, 337, 349
Tewfik (khedive of Egypt), 17, 18–19, 130
Thackwell, Sir Joseph, 96
Theodore II (emperor of Abyssinia), 2, 3, 4, 217, 218, 243, **320–321**
The Theory of War (MacDougall), 188, 214
Thesiger, Frederick A. (Second Baron Chelmsford), 80, **94–95,** 190, 329, 330, 343, 351, 353, 354
Thibaw (King of Burma), 70
"Thin red line," 43, 81

Thompson, Elizabeth (Lady Elizabeth Butler), 28, 72–73
Thorneycroft, Alec, 309
Tibet, Expedition to, **321–322,** 350
Tibet Frontier Commission, 321, 350
Tibet Mission, 321, 350
Tientsin, Treaty of, 100, 101
Tipperary Flying Column, 230
Tippoo Sultun, 287
Tirah Field Force, 177, 208, **322–323**
Tochi Field Force, 65, 222, 322, **324,**
Tofrek, Battle of, 148, **324–325**
Togoland, xvi
Toldeben, Franz E. I., 295
Topographical and Statistical Department, 341
Toski, Battle of, 120, 154, 200, **325–326**
Training
 British Army, 11–12, 26–27, 87, 134, 184–185, 252, 277–278
 Indian Army, 255
Transvaal, xvi, 49, 50, 51, 54, 55, 57, 60, 106, 193, 194, 195, 204, 221, 267, 285, 307, **326–327,** 351
Transvaal Field Force, 313
Tsu His (Empress Dowager of China), 57
Tunisia, xvi
Turkey, 14, 44, 110–113, 124, 136, 199, **327.** *See also* Ottoman Empire
Turner, A. H., 238
21st Lancers, 93–94, 102, 257, 281

Ulster Volunteer Force (UVF), 115
Ulundi, battle at, 288, **329–330,** 343, 346, 351, 354
Umm Diwaykarat, Battle of, 120, 200, 281, 342
Uniforms and equipment, 252–253, 255–256, 278–279

Vaal Kraantz, battle at, 205, **331–332**
Vaughan, J. L., 304
Venereal disease, **235–236**
Vereeniging, Treaty of (1902), 46, 57,

Index

117, 118, 202, 307, 314, 326
Victoria, Queen, 28, 83, 84, 89, 94, 122, 175, 206, 216, 236, 270, 320, 332–333, 346
Victorian Cross, 39, **332–333**
Volunteer Act (1863), 167
Volunteers, 167, 237, 275–276, 281, **333**, 349
Von Straubenzee, Charles, 100

Waitangi, Treaty of, 318
Waldersee, Albrecht von Graf, 58
Walker, Edward, 277
"War of the Axe," 80, 306
War Office, 333, **335–337**
  consolidation with Horse Guards, 76, 82, 83, 102–103, 105, 168, 335, 336
  Intelligence Branch, 59, 189, 190, 214, 239, 336, 341
  Mobilization Department, 190, 239, 336
  reforms in, 105–106, 135–136, 159, 167, 168, 189, 335–337
War Office Act (1870), 23, 76, 82, 83, 102–103, 105, 168, 336
War Office Council, 5, 136, 336
War Office Reconstitution (Esher) Committee, 6, 106, 135–136, 239, 271, 337
Ward, Frederick Townsend, 98
Warden, Henry, 56
Warren, Sir Charles, 308, 309, **337–338**
Waterloo Medal, 77
Watson, Sir James, 367
Wauchope, Andrew G., 218, 256, 257, **338–339**
Waziris, 247
Weapons, 3, 6, 24–26, 27–28, 64–65, 87–88, 113, 134–135, 182–183, 184, 215, 266

Wellesley, Arthur. *See* Wellington, First Duke of
Wellington, First Duke of (Arthur Wellesley), xiii, xiv, 5, 14, 21, 102, 111, 150, 187, 224, 232, 273, 275, 335, **339–340**, 365
West India Regiments, 15, 37
Westmacott, Brig. Gen., R., 240, 323
Wheeler, Brig. Gen., 14
Wheeler, Sir Hugh M., 88
Whish, William S., 154, 300, 301
White, Brig. Gen., 96, 155
White, Sir George S., 70, 91, 160, 168, 205, **340**, 367
White Mutiny, 46
White Sea Operations, Crimean War, **340**
Whitworth rifle breechloader, 27
Willcocks, James, 33
Williams, Sir William Fenwick, 199
Willis, G. H. S., 319
Wilson, Archdale, 119, 244
Wilson, Brig. Gen., 14
Wilson, Sir Charles W., 147–148, 189, **341**
Wilson, Sir Henry, 115
Wingate, Sir (Francis) Reginald, 304, **341–342**
Wodehouse, J. H., 223
Wolseley, Garnet J., xiii, 18, 70, 72, 92, 97, 101, 109, 110, 130, 150, 153, 154, 161, 188, 229, 267, 269, 274, 308, 311, 342–345
  Arabi Rebellion and, 6–7, 18–21, 127, 130, 319–320, 343
  as commander in chief, 6, 53, 103, 106, 225, 336, 365
  Gordon Relief Expedition and, 1, 71, 72, 146, 147, 148, 220, 312, 325, 341, 344
  military reforms and, 76, 82, 225, 336, 343

  Red River Expedition and, 31, 63, 72, 78, 230, 282, 283, 342
  Second Ashanti War and, 13, 15, 31–32, 35–37, 59, 153, 203, 231, 232, 266, 343, 346
  in South Africa, 94, 313, 329, 330, 343, 354
Wolseley Ring, 31–32, 343. *See also* Ashanti Ring
Women and the army, 234, 236, 244–245, **345–346**
Wood, Sir (Henry) Evelyn M., 15, 31, 32, 36, 37, 50, 63, 131, 154, 221, 303–304, 312, **346–347**, 351, 353
Woodgate, E. R. P., 309
Woodville, Richard Caton, 28
Woolwich, Royal Military Academy, 5, 26, 134, 228, 251, 255, **347**
Woon, Col, 240
World War I, 22

Yaa Asantewaa, 32, 33
Yakub Khan, 9, 10, 62, 85, 312
Yandabo, Treaty of, 69
Yasinis, 247
Yeatman-Biggs, A. G., 323
Yeomanry, 167, 237, **349**
York, Duke of (H.R.H. Frederick), 5, 105, 167, 271, 365
Younghusband, Francis E., 152, 321, 322, **349–350**
Younghusband, G. J., 189
Younghusband Expedition, 322, 350
Yusafzais, 247

Zulu War, 54, 63, 89, 92, 94, 122, 267, 288, 329–330, 343, 346, **351–354**
Zululand, 89, 351, **354**
Zulus, 54, 89, 190, 351–354
Zwartkopjes, engagement at, 56

About the Author

Harold E. Raugh, Jr., is the command historian, Defense Language Institute Foreign Language Center and Presidio of Monterey, Monterey, California. He retired from the U.S. Army in 1998 as a lieutenant colonel after twenty years of service as an infantry officer. Dr. Raugh served on active duty in the United States and in West Berlin, South Korea, the Persian Gulf, with the United Nations in Egypt and Jordan, in Saudi Arabia, and as a NATO detachment commander in the former Yugoslavia. He also served as an assistant professor of history at the United States Military Academy, West Point, as well as at the Pentagon and at the National Security Agency. Dr. Raugh, who received his Ph.D. in History from the University of California, Los Angeles (UCLA), became an adjunct professor of military history, American Military University, Manassas Park, Virginia, in 2000. Dr. Raugh is the author of the highly acclaimed *Wavell in the Middle East, 1939–1941: A Study in Generalship* (1993), *Fort Ord* (2004), and *Presidio of Monterey* (2004). He has also written over 400 articles and book reviews published in prominent international military and historical journals, and is the book review editor of the *Journal of America's Military Past, Military Heritage,* and the *Defence Journal* of Pakistan. Dr. Raugh was elected a fellow of the Royal Historical Society in the United Kingdom in 2001.